J. KREIFELDT

MENTAL WORKLOAD
Its Theory and Measurement

NATO CONFERENCE SERIES

I   Ecology
II   Systems Science
III   Human Factors
IV   Marine Sciences
V   Air–Sea Interactions
VI   Materials Science

III HUMAN FACTORS

Volume 1   Monitoring Behavior and Supervisory Control
Edited by Thomas B. Sheridan and Gunnar Johannsen

Volume 2   Biofeedback and Behavior
Edited by Jackson Beatty and Heiner Legewie

Volume 3   Vigilance: Theory, Operational Performance, and Physiological Correlates
Edited by Robert R. Mackie

Volume 4a   Recent Advances in the Psychology of Language: Language Development and Mother–Child Interaction
Edited by Robin N. Campbell and Philip T. Smith

Volume 4b   Recent Advances in the Psychology of Language: Formal and Experimental Approaches
Edited by Robin N. Campbell and Philip T. Smith

Volume 5   Cognitive Psychology and Instruction
Edited by Alan M. Lesgold, James W. Pellegrino, Sipke D. Fokkema, and Robert Glaser

Volume 6   Language Interpretation and Communication
Edited by David Gerver and H. Wallace Sinaiko

Volume 7   Alcoholism: New Directions in Behavioral Research and Treatment
Edited by Peter E. Nathan, G. Alan Marlatt, and Tor Løberg

Volume 8   Mental Workload: Its Theory and Measurement
Edited by Neville Moray

MENTAL WORKLOAD
Its Theory and Measurement

Edited by
Neville Moray
University of Stirling
Stirling, Scotland

Published in coordination with NATO Scientific Affairs Division
PLENUM PRESS · NEW YORK AND LONDON

Library of Congress Cataloging in Publication Data

Nato Symposium on Theory and Measurement of Mental Workload, Mátion, Greece, 1977.
Mental workload.

(NATO conference series: III, Human factors; v. 8)
Proceedings of the symposium sponsored by the NATO Special Program Panel on Human Factors.
Includes index.
1. Psychology, Industrial — Congresses. 2. Work — Psychological aspects — Congresses. I. Moray, Neville. II. Nato Special Program Panel on Human Factors. III. Title. IV. Series. [DNLM: 1. Work — Congresses. 2. Task performance and analysis — Congresses. 3. Stress, Psychological — Physiology — Congresses. 4. Psychophysiology — Congresses. W3 N138 v. 8 1977/BF481 N11m 1977]
HF5548.8.N18 1977   158.7   78-26922
ISBN 0-306-40144-4

Proceedings of the NATO Symposium on Theory and Measurement of Mental Workload, held at Mati, Greece, August 30—September 6, 1977, sponsored by the NATO Special Program Panel on Human Factors

©1979 Plenum Press, New York
A Division of Plenum Publishing Corporation
227 West 17th Street, New York, N.Y. 10011

All rights reserved

No part of this book may be reproduced, stored in a retrieval system, or transmitted, in any form or by any means, electronic, mechanical, photocopying, microfilming, recording, or otherwise, without written permission from the Publisher

Printed in the United States of America

PREFACE

Early in 1976 a conference sponsored by the NATO Human Factors Special Panel was held at Berchtesgarden on the topic of "Monitoring Behaviour and Supervisory Control". It attracted a large number of participants: Psychologists and engineers, both theoretical and applied. Topics which were addressed included vehicular control, vigilance, process control, monitoring of plant, instrumentation and optimisation of man-machine interfaces, attention, and ergonomics. Repeatedly the authors of papers and discussants made reference to "mental workload" and problems associated both with too heavy and too light a load. Furthermore, in workshop discussions the same topic appeared. It became evident that almost everyone needed the concept. In particular the designers of man-machine systems badly wanted a measure which would allow them to predict whether a new system would be satisfactory for human operators who would have to use it.

In one of the discussions someone remarked that we have an enormous amount of knowledge about workload, and many models for it: surely it would now be possible to synthesize that knowledge into a coherent summary which would be both theoretically sound and practically useful. Perhaps what was needed was not a conference on workload, but some kind of intensive workshop at which such a synthesis could be attempted, gaps in our knowledge identified, research planned, and areas where our knowledge was adequate defined. This book is the outcome of that suggestion.

In 1977 the NATO Special Panel on Human Factors sponsored a small workshop. A few experts from each of several disciplines were invited, chosen largely in the light of discussions at Berchtesgarten. It was clear that research into Mental Workload was being done by engineers - particularly control engineers - by physiological psychologists, and by experimental psychologists. In addition, since measurement theory and problems of probability, prediction and time series analysis might be expected to be prominent, some people working on mathematical models of human behaviour were invited. Finally, a group of non-academic human factors specialists, all active in the application of workload concepts to

the solution of problems of systems design in the real world were
added to prevent the discussions becoming theoretically elegant
but of little practical value.

Each participant was asked to submit a "position paper"
summarizing his views about mental workload. He was asked to
define the concept, to say how he found it useful, how he measured
it, what he would like to know about it, and the boundary conditions
within which he considered it applicable. The papers – which appear
in this volume – were circulated to participants in advance of the
opening of the symposium.

At the symposium, the first day was spent in disciplinary
discussions. The psychologists discussed their own position papers
with each other, as did the engineers with the engineers, etc.
On the basis of these discussions each discipline presented a
summary of their (more-or-less) agreed joint position, and then
the discipline groups, for two days, met in pairs. The physiological psychologists met first with the mathematicians, then with the
experimental psychologists: the engineers met the applied group,
then the psychologists, then the physiologists; and so on. New
groups were then formed, each containing one member from each
discipline, and discussion continued for a day. Finally, the
original single-discipline groups met again as on the first day,
and wrote a single position paper putting forward the agreed, common opinion of the group, together with suggestions for future
research. This final paper was edited in each case by the chairman
of the group and appears in this volume as the "Final Report" of
each discipline.

What has been gained by this procedure? There is a certain
amount of redundancy in the initial position papers. For example
the physiological psychologists all tend to discuss the same
measures, and several of the experimental psychologists deal at
length with "secondary tasks". Such redundancy however reflects
the degree of interest in such topics and measures among leading
research workers, and there are important qualifications and
nuances of emphasis which only become apparent when several such
papers can be compared. Indeed, it is both surprising and somewhat worrying to see how many people can discuss a single methodology without exhausting the topic. What is perhaps more surprising is the extent of consensus across disciplines. The accepted
wisdom of approaches and concerns is emphasised when workers with
interests as diverse as control engineering, academic psychology,
and physiology of the metabolic effects of them all agree on the
value (or lack of it) of particular approaches.

Secondly, at least for those who were present at the conference, there was a real rapprochement between disciplines. Technical terms which are commonplace within a discipline may be

PREFACE

extremely difficult for workers with a different background to understand. Intensive interaction in pursuit of an agreed set of definitions and rules for translation from one discipline to another "concentrates the mind wonderfully", and the participants undoubtedly left the conference with a greatly improved understanding of the value and difficulties of alternative approaches.

These proceedings are possibly unique in the extent to which multidisciplinary approaches to a single topic are not merely available, but stated with sufficient clarity and interrelationship for one really to grasp the relation between the techniques used by the different disciplines.

The very ambitious aims of the symposium are summarised by Johannsen's remarks in the first paper.

"In this workshop, we should therefore try to -

(1) find a consensus among all attendees of a strong definition of workload;

(2) form an application-oriented theory or procedure of workload assessment which integrates all known aspects; and

(3) find relationships between measurement techniques or applicable combinations of them corresponding to the theoretical concepts."

How far the participants fell short of those aims is perhaps equally well summarised by some remarks of Hopkin in the final paper.

"As of this point in time, theory has not produced an umbrella technique to partition, predict or measure the multitude of variables in an operational field problem. It is difficult to distinguish ... concepts, and no single individual can hope to have the breadth and depth of knowledge to accomplish the interdisciplinary integration of information that appears to offer significant advancements for applied settings".

Hopkin's point is underlined by the enormous list of "problems for future research" produced by the different groups. However, three things stand out. The first is that regardless of the groups to which participants belonged, they left the conference with a firm conviction that interdisciplinary co-operation is absolutely mandatory for progress. More: that in _any single investigation or project_ the simultaneous application of methods from several disciplines will be mandatory. The other side of the coin is, however, that there is a remarkable degree of consensus among the final reports. Regardless of discipline or approach, participants came to very similar conclusions about the validity, usefulness, and promise (or lack of each) for a wide variety of methods for approaching the assessment of workload in the human operator. The careful reader will find a rather clear picture at least of the pitfalls involved in many techniques which are often assumed to be "standard". On the other hand, he will equally well notice that in certain specific areas, and for problems of certain kinds, substantial success is even now possible. Thirdly, it is of interest that since the conference, several interdisciplinary projects, and indeed international projects, have resulted from co-operation between participants.

As editor and convenor of the symposium, it remains for me to make the acknowledgments to those who made the symposium possible. Thanks are first due to the Special Advisory Panel on Human Factors of the NATO Science Committee for supporting the Symposium. Secondly, I must thank H. Ursin and H. Stassen for their help in organising the conference, and all the Group chairmen for preparing the Final Reports of their Groups. Particular thanks are due to Dr. Mary Vakali of the Department of Psychology of the University of Thessaloniki for her untiring work as liaison officer in Greece; and to N. Durham and his staff at Condor Travel, Athens and T. Shakalis of Grecian Holidays, London who dealt with considerable problems caused by an air traffic controllers' strike at the time of arrival and departure of participants. The preparation of the typescript gave an added burden to our secretaries, Gill Johnston and Ina Mack, which they bore with their usual fortitude, and Donald McLeod proof read with skill and ingenuity. Finally, I would like to thank all the participants for the exceptionally hard work they put in both before and during the conference. Several of the position papers deserve to become classical references of the state-of-the-art in 1977, and in the light of the discussions give one hope that a significant break through in applied psychology may be possible: one moreover which may significantly contribute to what Norbert Weiner called "the human use of human beings".

N. Moray
Stirling 1978.

CONTENTS

PART I: EXPERIMENTAL PSYCHOLOGY AND MENTAL WORKLOAD

Workload and Workload Measurement   3
   G. Johannsen

Models and Measures of Mental Workload   13
   N. Moray

Secondary Tasks and Workload Measurement   23
   R. W. Pew

Reflection on the Concept of
      Operator Workload   29
   J. Rasmussen

Some Remarks on Mental Load   41
   A. F. Sanders

Measures of Workload, Stress
      and Secondary Tasks   79
   C. D. Wickens

Final Report of Experimental Psychology Group 101

PART II: CONTROL ENGINEERING AND WORKLOAD MEASUREMENT

Mental Load in Monitoring Tasks 117
   R. E. Curry

Defining and Measuring Perceptual-Motor
      Workload in Manual Control Tasks 125
   H. R. Jex and W. F. Clement

A Proposed Set of Standardised Sub-Critical Tasks
      for Tracking Workload Calibration 179
   H. R. Jex

A Model for Mental Workload in Tasks
        Requiring Continuous Information
        Processing   189
    W. H. Levison

Definitions, Models and Measures
        of Human Workload   219
    T. Sheridan and H. Stassen

Final Report of Control Engineering Group   235

PART III: MATHEMATICAL MODELS AND MENTAL WORKLOAD

Approaches to Mental Workload   255
    W. B. Rouse

Axiomatic Models of Workload   263
    J. W. Senders

Final Report of Mathematical Modelling Group   269

PART IV: PHYSIOLOGICAL PSYCHOLOGY AND MENTAL WORKLOAD

Process Entropy and Cognitive Control:
        Mental Load in Internalised
        Thought Processes   289
    P. Hamilton

Mental Load, Mental Effort and Attention   299
    G. Mulder

Sinusarrythmia and Mental Workload   327
    G. Mulder

Measurement of Mental Workload   345
    H. Strasser

Physiological Indicators of Mental Workload   349
    H. Ursin and R. Ursin

Final Report of Physiological Psychology Group   367

PART V: APPLIED PSYCHOLOGY AND MENTAL WORKLOAD

Mental Workload Measurement in
        Air Traffic Control   381
    V. D. Hopkin

CONTENTS

Current Workload Methods and Emerging
        Challenges   387
   D. L. Parks

Measurement of Pilot Workload   417
   A. Rault

Determination of Stress and Strain at
        Real Work Places: Methods and
        Results of Field Studies with Air
        Traffic Control Officers   423
   W. Rohmert

Mental Load and Reduced Mental Capacity:
        Some Considerations Concerning
        Laboratory and Field Investigations   445
   M. Soede

Final Report of Applications Group   469

Participants   497

Index   501

PART I:

EXPERIMENTAL PSYCHOLOGY AND MENTAL WORKLOAD

WORKLOAD AND WORKLOAD MEASUREMENT

Gunnar Johannsen

Forschungsinstitut für Anthropotechnik (FAT)

5309 Meckenheim, F. R. Germany

I.   INTRODUCTION

It has been stated for many years that workload is an important problem area for man-machine-systems research and development. In order to evaluate alternative solutions in systems design, it is often deemed necessary to measure not only system performance, but also human operator workload. However, there exist too many conflicting ideas about the definition and measurement of workload (see, e.g. (1), (2), (3), (4)). The term workload frequently is used even without any definition of what it is.

In this workshop, we should therefore try to:

1) find a consensus among all attendees of a strong definition of workload,

2) form an application-oriented theory or procedure of workload assessment which integrates all known aspects, and

3) find relationships between measurement techniques or applicable combinations of them corresponding to the theoretical concepts.

In the following, some contributions to these points will be given.

II.   DEFINITION OF WORKLOAD

A most useful concept for the assessment of workload has been proposed by Jahns (5). He divides the broad area of human operator workload into three functionally relatable attributes: input load, operator effort, and performance or work result (Fig.1). Similar concepts have been proposed, e.g., by Rohmert et al. (6), (7), (8) and Rolfe, Lindsay (9). Input load concerns factors or events external to the human operator while operator effort is internal to the human operator. Performance is traditionally defined as purposeful data outputs generated by the human operator which serve as inputs to other components of the man-machine-environment system and may provide feedback on effort adequacy. Some measures of performance are listed in Fig.1.

Major sources of input load may be separated into three classes: environmental, design-induced or situational, and procedural (See Fig.1). Environmental variables are noise, vibration, temperature etc. Design variables are, e.g. characteristics of displays and control devices, crew station layout, and vehicle dynamics. Procedural variables are, e.g. briefing and instructions, task sequencing, and mission/task duration.

Operator effort depends on a number of factors including the input load and the performance requirements of a given task. It can be characterized by the following functional relationship:

Effort = f(Load, Operator-State, Internal Performance Criteria)

The operator state depends on many factors; relatively stable ones such as psychophysical characteristics, general background, personality; and fluctuating ones such as experience, motivation, attentiveness (5). Internal performance criteria are maintained by the human operator and influence his tolerated error level.

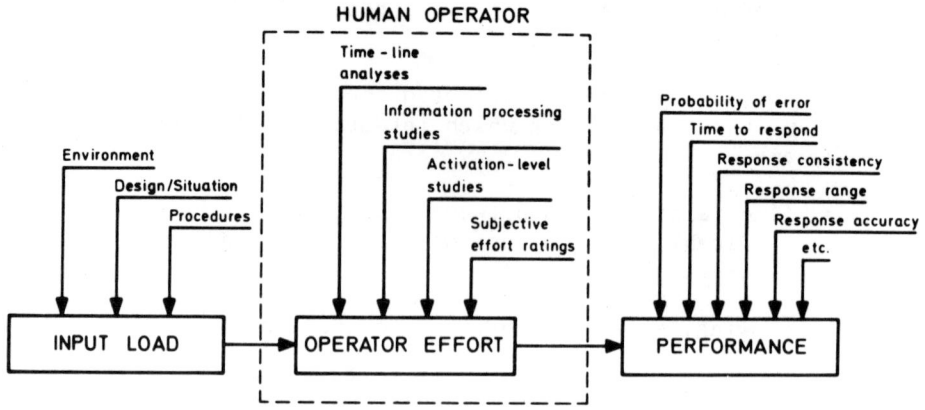

Fig.1: Attributes of operator workload (after (5), (10)).

They depend on factors of the operator state (e.g., motivation), performance requirements, and instructions. Not all these functional relationships are clearly defined or measurable in mental workload situations as opposed to physical workload.

Sometimes, the terms stress and strain instead of load and effort are used with the same or nearly the same meaning (see, e.g. (6), (11)). However, it is more common to use the term stress for peak load.

As the human operator is able to show the same performance in alternatively designed systems which may represent different loading situations, it is absolutely necessary to assess the effort exerted in order to evaluate the difference between alternative system designs. Both performance and effort usually have to be assessed in man-machine systems evaluation, whereas input load is mainly a predetermined factor. Workload is only an umbrella concept which includes input load and operator effort.

III. CLASSIFICATION OF WORKLOAD MEASURES

Workload measures have to be differentiated as between measures of input load and measures of operator effort associated with the definition of workload.

Measures of input load include descriptions of environmental, procedural, and design or situational variables. They are predetermined or given in a particular situation and depend on the immediate environmental situation, overall man-machine system design features, and current operation policy of the systems users. Loading variables may be time-variant as, e.g., the number of planes controlled by an ATC controller.

Measures of operator effort are of great concern. They are often regarded as workload measures as such. All techniques usable for the evaluation and measurement of operator effort can be classified into four groups (see Fig.1):

      (1) time-line analyses,

      (2) information processing studies,

      (3) operator activation-level studies, and

      (4) subjective effort ratings.

In time-line analyses, the execution times of all particular task elements of a certain task are assessed as well as the total task time needed. Available time margins or expected time pressures correlate with different degrees of effort expended by the human operator (see, e.g. (12)).

In information processing studies, the human operator is often regarded as an information processing element with a fixed, limited channel capacity. Secondary or loading tasks have been used to measure the spare mental capacity of the operator. Other approaches apply control or information theory.

Performance in a secondary task is taken as a measure of the operator's spare mental capacity. The relative performance decrement in the secondary task may show how much additional effort would have to be spent by the human operator in the main task as opposed to the secondary task alone. Examples of secondary tasks are arithmetic tasks, tapping tasks, choice reaction tasks, critical tracking tasks, and cross-adaptive loading tasks (see, e.g. (13), (14), (15)).

Control theoretic measures of operator effort are based on time history and frequency domain measures or on human controller models. Amplitude distributions and power spectral density functions of the human operator outputs may be regarded as indications of effort expended. Another quantity is the lead which has to be generated by the human operator in order to compensate for controlled element dynamics in accordance with the crossover model (16). A measure which is based on the optimal control model is defined as the minimal fraction of information processing capacity or attention of the human operator necessary to meet a predetermined performance criterion level (17), (18), (19). This effort index is calculated as the ratio P_o/P where P_o and P are the reciprocal signal-to-noise ratios of the observation noise, P_o for full capacity of the human operator and P for the actual level of attention. The effort index allows the calculation of attention allocation between different information sources.

Operator activation-level studies are based on the hypothesis that the level of physiological activity of the human operator depends on his effort (see, e.g., (10), (20), (21)). The sinus arrhythmia of heart rate is considered by some investigators as a measure of mental effort (see, e.g., (22), (23)). Another measure is the pupillary dilation (see, e.g., (24), (25)).

Subjective rating of effort is an additional useful assessment technique (see, e.g. (14), (26)). As usual in rating techniques, only overall measures can be obtained. The instructions have to explain very carefully what is to be rated, i.e. the meaning of the effort. A number of operator biases may degrade the accuracy of subjective ratings.

IV. APPLICATION-ORIENTED PROCEDURE OF WORKLOAD ASSESSMENT AND RELATIONSHIPS BETWEEN MEASUREMENT TECHNIQUES

The four classes of measurement techniques of effort differ to the extent that they assess different aspects of effort. Time-line analyses are load-oriented; information processing studies are performance-oriented; operator activation-level studies are operator-state-oriented; and subjective effort ratings assess only conscious aspects of effort. It follows that only a small portion of the multi-facetted area of human operator workload can be assessed by a single measure. So far, all measures have this same shortcoming.

When real operational man-machine systems are considered, multi-task situations for the human operator dominate. In these cases, the relationship between operator performance and input load is hypothesized to be that shown in Fig.2. Three regions of load are distinguished according to time considerations. For these three regions, some traditional areas of research are listed in Fig.2. Again, it can be seen that workload is a multi-facetted area, a generalized construct. It can gain its justification only from an application in real multi-task procedures where overall measures are needed. Research with single workload measures has its value mainly in testing these single measures against such criteria as reliability, validity, and freedom from interference (see also (15)). It should be mentioned that meeting these criteria is a main problem in work-load research.

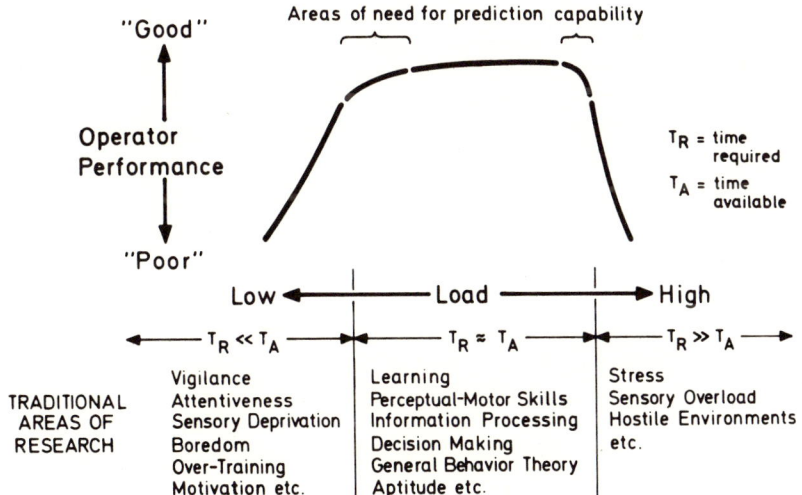

Fig.2. Hypothetical relationship between operator performance and input load on multi-task procedures (after 27).

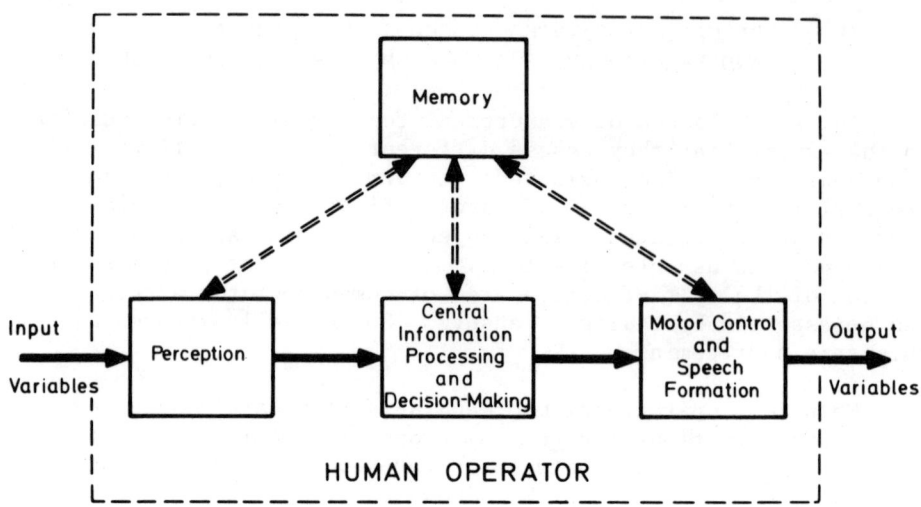

Fig.3. Functions of information processes in human operator

In order to assess the relative value of different workload measures, one has to distinguish between different loading factors and between different types of effort expenditure. This would be the basis for a selected combination of single workload measures in application-oriented problems. In Fig.3, a simple sketch of human information processes is shown. Dependent on a specific combination of loading factors in a given multi-task situation, different types of operator effort may occur which are related to the different functions of human information processes illustrated in Fig.3. Some examples are: scanning effort, perception effort, central processing effort, decision effort, memory recall effort, motor effort, and communication effort. In addition, emotional factors sometimes are considered which occur as a function of the operator state, e.g. in unforeseen peak load situations.

Different measures are especially suitable for different types of effort, e.g., eye-movement recording for scanning effort, attention allocation index for perception effort, lead time-constant for central processing effort, and talking duration for communication effort.

An approach which permits integration of most of these effort measures is given by the time-line analyses which calculate percent workloading for different channels of the human operator (5), (27). An integration of the above mentioned measures into this framework might be possible by transforming all measures into fractions of channel occupation.

In addition to a time-line type integrative workload analysis, operator activation-level measures should be taken in order to assess peak load (especially momentary) situations, emotional factors, and conflicting situations in which task-dependent priority control of information channels is necessary. Subjective effort ratings should be used in any case, as it is often the least unreliable overall measure.

V. REFERENCES

(1) Nicholson, A.N. (Ed.): Simulation and Study of High Workload Operations. AGARD-CP-146, 1974.

(2) Sheridan, T.B., Johannsen, G. (Eds.): Monitoring Behavior and Supervisory Control. New York: Plenum Press, 1976.

(3) Methods to Assess Workload. AGARD-CPP-216, 1977.

(4) Studies on Pilot Workload. AGARD-CPP-217, 1977.

(5) Jahns, D.W.: A Concept of Operator Workload in Manual Vehicle Operations. Forschungsinstitut Anthropotechnik, Meckenheim, Bericht Nr. 14, 1973.

(6) Rohmert, W.: An International Symposium on Objective Assessment of Work Load in Air Traffic Control Tasks - Introduction. Ergonomics, Vol.14 (1971), pp. 545-547.

(7) Rohmert, W., Laurig, W.: Zusammenhang zwischen Belastungs- und Beanspruchungsparametern bei Fluglotsen in der Flugverkehrskontrolle. Arbeitsmedizin, Sozialmedizin, Arbeitshygiene 7 (1972), S. 252-257.

(8) Rohmert, W.: Psycho-physische Belastung und Beanspruchung von Fluglotsen. Berlin: Beuth-Vertrieb, 1973.

(9) Rolfe, J.M., Lindsay, S.J.E.: Flight Deck Environment and Pilot Workload: Biological Measures of Workload. Applied Ergonomics, Vol. 4 (1973), pp. 199-206.

(10) Johannsen, G.: Preview of Man-Vehicle Control Session. In Sheridan, T.B., Johannsen, G. (Eds.): Monitoring Behavior and Supervisory Control. New York: Plenum Press, 1976, pp. 3-12.

(11) Meye-Delius, J., Liebl, L.: Evaluation of Vigilance Related to Visual Perception. In Sheridan, T.B., Johannsen, G. (Eds.): Monitoring Behavior and Supervisory Control. New York: Plenum Press, 1976, pp. 97-106.

(12) Siegel, A.J., Wolf, J.J.: Man-Machine Simulation Models.
New York: Wiley, 1969.

(13) Johannsen, G.: Nebenaufgaben als Beanspruchungsmessverfahren in Fahrzeugführungsaufgaben. Z. Arbeitswiss. 30 (2 NF) 1976/1, S 45-50.

(14) Johannsen, G., Pfendler, C., Stein, W.: Human Performance and Workload in Simulated Landing-Approaches with Autopilot-Failures. In Sheridan, T.B., Johannsen, G. (Eds.): Monitoring Behavior and Supervisory Control. New York: Plenum Press, 1976, pp. 83-95.

(15) Rolfe, J.M.: The Measurement of Human Response in Man-Vehicle Control Situations. In Sheridan, T.B., Johannsen, G. (Eds.): Monitoring Behavior and Supervisory Control. New York: Plenum Press, 1976, pp. 125-137.

(16) McRuer, D.T., Krendel, E.S.: Mathematical Models of Human Pilot Behavior. Advisory Group Aerospace Research Development, Neuilly sur Seine, France, AGARDograph No. 188, 1974.

(17) Levison, W.H., Elkind, J.I., Ward, J.L.: Studies of Multivariable Manual Control Systems: A Model for Task Interference. NASA CR-1746, 1971.

(18) Baron, S., Levison, W.H.: An Optimal Control Methodology for Analyzing the Effects of Display Parameters on Performance and Workload in Manual Flight Control. IEEE Trans. Syst. Man Cybern., Vol. SMC-5 (1975), pp. 423-430.

(19) Wewerinke, P.H., Smit, J.: A Simulator Study to Investigate Human Operator Workload. In Nicholson, A.N. (Ed.): Simulation and Study of High Workload Operations. AGARD-CP-146, 1974, pp. A2/1-A2/6.

(20) Mulder, G.: Man as a Processor of Information. In Kraiss, K.-F., Moraal, J. (Eds.): Introduction to Human Engineering. Koln: Verlag TUV Rheinland, 1976, pp. 27-60.

(21) Sanders, A.F.: Experimental Methods in Human Engineering. In Kraiss, K.-F., Moraal, J. (Eds.): Introduction to Human Engineering. Koln: Verlag TUV Rheinland, 1976, pp. 351-383.

(22) Kalsbeek, J.W.H.: Sinus Arrhythmia and the Dual Task Method in Measuring Mental Load. In Singleton, W.T., Fox, J.F., Whitfield, D. (Eds.): Measurement of Man at Work. London: Taylor and Francis, 1971, pp. 101-113.

(23) Stasser, H.: Physiological Measures of Workload-Correlations between Physiological Parameters and Operational Performance. In Methods to Assess Workload. AGARD-CPP-216, 1977, pp. A8/1-A8/7.

(24) Klix, F.: Information und Verhalten. Bern: Huber, 1971.

(25) Beatty, J.: Pupillometric Measurement of Cognitive Workload. Proc. 12th Annual Conf. on Manual Control, NASA TM X-73, 170, 1976, pp. 135-143.

(26) Pasmooij, C.K., Opmeer, C.H.J.M., Hyndman, B.W.: Workload in Air Traffic Control. In Sheridan, T.B., Johannsen, G. (Eds.): Monitoring Behavior and Supervisory Control. New York: Plenum Press, 1976, pp. 107-118.

(27) Linton, P.M., Jahns, D.W., Chatelier, P.R.: Operator Workload Assessment Model: An Evaluation of a VF/VA-V/STOL System. In Methods to Assess Workload. AGARD-CPP-216, 1977, pp. A12/1-A12/11.

MODELS AND MEASURES OF MENTAL WORKLOAD

Neville Moray

Department of Psychology

University of Stirling, Stirling, Scotland

At the meeting on Monitoring Behaviour and Supervisory Control held in Berchtesgarten in 1976, someone made the point that we possess a very large body of knowledge about human performance and how to measure it, and yet we are still unable to put it to efficient use in designing man-machine systems. Surely, he said, it should be possible to find a unifying theory which would tie it all together in a useful way.

On the other hand, when one looks at the papers for this Conference one recurring theme is striking. It is that perhaps there is no value which can be assigned as a measure of the load imposed on a man. The extent to which a man is loaded is a function not merely of the man, but of the task-specific situation in which he finds himself. The implication would be that there are as many measures as there are types of task, and the hope for a unified theory of load is a false hope.

What does one have in mind when talking of "mental load"? As Rasmussen points out, there is an overtone of physical effort in the phrase. A load is something which imposes a burden on a structure, or makes it approach the limit of its performance on some dimension. Go far enough along that dimension and the system will fail in some way. In the case of mental workload, the central concept is the rate at which information is processed by the human operator, and basically the rate at which decisions are made and the difficulty of making the decisions.

Put that way, the most obvious metrics would be information theory and signal detection theory. The first of these fell out of favour with psychologists after a brief but striking popularity in the early 1950s. But the extent of its current unpopularity is somewhat surprising. It is true that many experiments have shown that information theory is not a "true" model of the human operator. Even when we know the bit rate of the source we cannot completely predict human performance. The well known experiments of Mowbray & Rhoades, (1959); Davis, Moray and Treisman, (1961), and Leonard (1959) in which apparently infinite transmission rates were obtained are enough to show that. Since no system can have an unlimited channel capacity, the theory's performance is not as good as that of man. But the fact remains that for many situations, in particular when the human operator knows the objective probabilities of the signals well, the number of alternatives is up to about 16; the stimulus response compatibility is not unusually great, and the observer is not excessively practised, the classical relation between response latency, accuracy and information content is readily obtained for whatever reason; and the metric is therefore <u>useful</u> (even if not true) over such ranges of application.

At the other extreme lie some of the new models such as the theory of optimal adaptive control using Kalman filtering, as developed by Jex & Allen (1970), Gai & Curry (1976) and others. Although not well known to psychologists, these models are strikingly successful, and are beginning to flourish with a vigour comparable to information theory and TSD in earlier years. Here, it seems to me the problem is the opposite. Applied to low band-width monitoring tasks, performance is rather too good. While adaptive control models can readily simulate the human as a high frequency controller there is no reason why they should show vigilance decrements. But this in its turn does not seem to be a reason for rejecting these models in appropriate applied settings nor for doubting that they might be modifiable in the directions necessary to serve more adequately as models of the human operator.

In the case of all the theories, we can, by searching the literature, find quite a bit about the <u>boundary conditions</u> within which the theories are good predictors. That, it seems to me, is where we should concentrate our efforts.

Among theoretical models, I would suggest the following to be the most important:

1. Random walk and accumulator models for response latency.
2. Shannon Information Theory.
3. Theory of Signal Detection (TSD).
4. Sheridan's Supervisor Theory.
5. Linear Control Theory (LCT).
6. Optimal Adaptive Control Theory (OACT).
7. Single Channel Queueing Theory.

All of them can be used as normative theories. That is, they provide a number which represents the most efficient possible performance, in the same way as Quantum Theory can provide an absolute measure of the efficiency of the retina as a photodetector. Thus TSD and Information Theory define performance in terms of $\underline{d'}$ and the bit rate of the source respectively. Control Theory defines the necessary equalization function and phase-gain relations to achieve stability. Optimal control theory measures performance against the criterion of minimum squared error, or some other specified value.

Several of them provide means of making explicit the observer's payoff structure, notably Supervisor Theory and TSD. Others could be modified to do so. For example, the maximum information transmission rate defined by discrete information theory is only achieved if the observer adopts an optimal decision criterion in the TSD sense (Moray & Fitter, 1973). Presumably OACT could be modified to incorporate subjective payoffs in the choice of criterion, or in biases to the Kalman filter weighting function.

All the above theories imply another fact to which we shall return. Optimal performance by the human operator requires him to construct an internal model of the statistical properties of the task.

Accumulator theory requires the observer to learn how long he can continue to gain information. Supervisor Theory requires knowledge of the bandwidth, mean and variance of the signals. Information Theory requires knowledge of the probabilities of signals, as does TSD. LCT requires a model of the describing function of the controlled element. OACT makes this most directly explicit, since the Kalman filter is the embodiment of a dynamic model, sensitive to changes in the environment. Perhaps the neatest summary of what is required is given by Young (1969) (See Figure 1.).

There would seem to be two empirical starting points to the measurement of load. One might regard error and latency scores as indices of workload. If errors rise or latency increases, the task is more difficult for the operator. In some respects this would be expected from "a priori" theories. Both information theory and signal detection theory, for example, would lead one to expect such a relation. Empirically the picture becomes more complicated due to the human operator's ability to choose a speed-accuracy tradeoff point in the light of his understanding of the situation, that is to say how he imagines causality to be directed, what he sees as the payoff structure, and so on. But at least in situations where errors and latency are positively correlated, one can be sure that the operator's load is increasing. The payoff structure might be regarded as part of the boundary conditions referred to earlier, and in order accurately to predict performance it must somehow be stabilised.

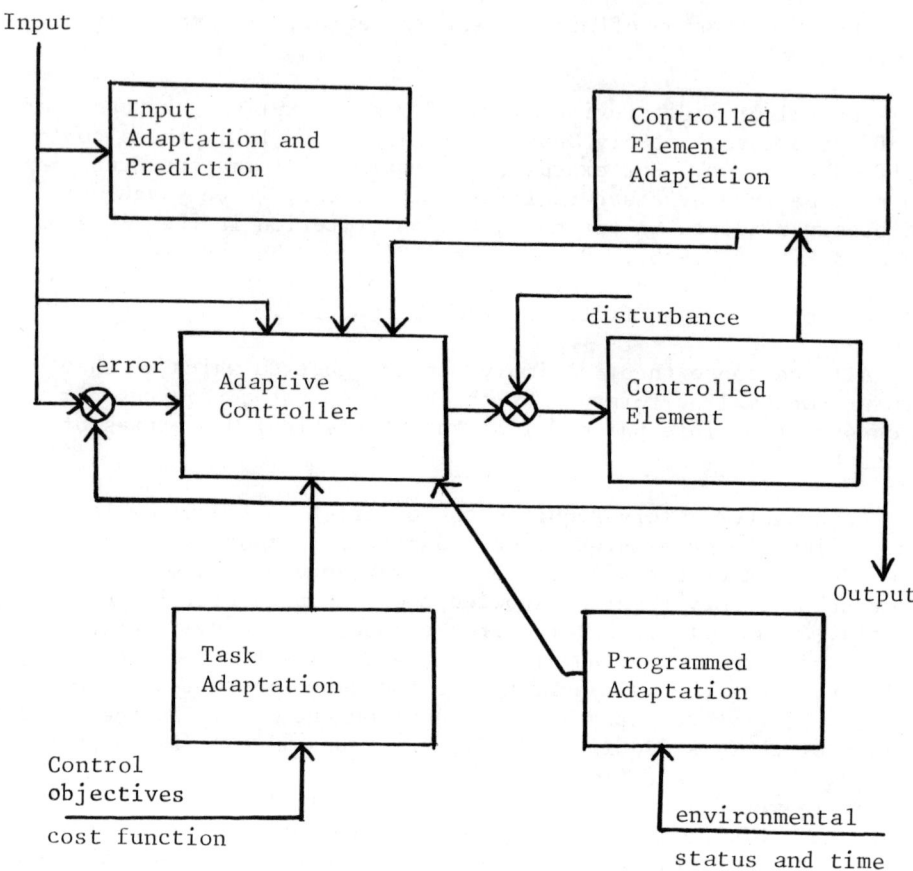

Figure 1. Major adaptive functions in manual control.

The second starting point might be to take seriously the
concept of "effort". This has recently been popularised by
Kahneman (1973) but it is difficult to see how to use it on the
basis of his writing. In one sense it seems to mean almost the
same as "capacity" in the classical sense, especially if one can
extend that concept to processing capacity rather than channel
capacity (Moray, 1967). On the other hand, it can also refer to
the subjective feelings of stress and strain experienced by the
operator, and would then be related to such instruments as the
Cooper Scale. To be useful on a moment to moment basis, however,
one needs some way to measure the feeling of effort experienced
by an operator. The most obvious candidate would seem to be
physiological measures of state. (I am not certain how the concept
of subjective effort would fit into low-load vigilance tasks. Such
tasks in the laboratory do feel effortful - but the effort is one
of concentrating , not of performing the task itself. I am not
so sure, based on a limited experience of working in a factory, that
in real life tasks low load monitoring tasks do feel stressful,
unless they are associated with danger, as is the case with sonar
and radar monitoring. The point made by Crossman some years ago
may clarify this, that monitoring tasks consist of low bandwidth
tasks for long periods interspersed with monitoring high bandwidth
interruptions. It is in this area that the work of people like
Bainbridge (1976) on operator protocols is likely to prove very
important). But one question which needs to be answered is the
direction of causality between physiological state, effort, and
performance. Using physiological measures - if any reliable ones
exist - as indicators of effort would imply that the state of
effort , or the extent to which the operator is loaded,results
in measurable physiological changes, such as heart rate, muscle
tension, etc. Thus if we measure the latter we obtain an estimate
of the load imposed on the operator, providing once again that any
boundary conditions are stated. On the other hand, the Yerkes-
Dodson law (or any other law relating physiological state to
performance) seems to imply that by getting himself into a particular state an operator could alter his efficiency, and hence the
effort required. Does load change the state, or can the state
alter the load? If there is an optimum level of arousal, what
exactly does that mean? Is the net average information transmission rate hoop shaped with respect to arousal? Or is it merely
the _feeling_ of effort which is hoop-shaped? If a man changes
his position on the arousal continuum, does he _feel_ more or less
stress, _feel_ more or less efficient, or is he _in fact_, more or
less efficient? (There may also be problems here to do with
individual differences of personal style between those who like
working near their limit and those who do not. Are the former
less loaded than the latter for a given objective load? And are
they in fact more efficient?). There are also good grounds to
believe that it is mainly at those moments when conscious control
is exercised that a task feels effortful. Probably such moments

correspond to a failure by the internal model to operate open-loop and a consequent return to closed-loop servo-control.

The development of theories of information processing and mental load by psychologists has, on the whole, concentrated on discrete tasks. Thus information theory and TSD have been applied to discrimination, attention, languages and reaction times. The mathematical models developed by psychologists have likewise been mainly of discrete tasks such as reaction times (Audley, (1973); Lamming (1968)) and others. By contrast, engineers and engineering psychologists have concentrated on continuous tasks, especially those involving manual control, and only recently have begun extending their theory into other fields (Levison, 1971); Gai & Curry (1976); Sheridan, (1970). But similar remarks could have equally well been made about the work on continuous tasks. The a priori measures now become bandwidth, amplitude, order of control, etc. and the empirical measures estimates of the human operator's bandwidth, gain, time-delay, remnant, rms error and position on a stability plane such as a Nyquist diagram. Table I is an attempt to list the a priori, empirical, and physiological measures. It should be compared with the excellent review by Rolfe (1976) and the table by Jex in the present volume. What we need to know is the relation between them, the range over which they can be used, ("boundary conditions" again) and finally, the population statistics on individual differences.

Table 1

Normative Measures (LOAD)	Empirical Measures (PERFORMANCE)	Physiological Measures (EFFORT)
Random walk theory	Latency (R.T.)	EEG
Accumulator theory	Error-absolute	Heart rate
Information theory (discrete)	RMS	Ventilation
Information theory (continuous)	Bit rate	Blood Pressure
Supervisor theory	d' and β	Catecholamines
Queueing theory	Bandwidth	Muscle tension
Theory of Signal Detection	gain	Pupil dilation
Linear Control Theory	equalization function	G.S.R.
Optimal Control Theory	phase and gain spectrum	
Adaptive Control Theory		

The table should be read column by column. Items in a given row do not correspond to each other. For example, RMS is not the empirical measure associated with discrete Information Theory.

Can some of these be equated? In certain cases the answer is plainly that they can. Latency should be proportional to bit rate. Information can be mapped onto d'. Continuous information maps onto bandwidth, amplitude and permissible error. But in other cases the problem is not straightforward. If the input is even stochastically predictable then the load is reduced if the observer constructs an appropriate model. "Automation" of skill may plausibly be related to the construction of such models, with the aid of which the observer goes open loop and begins to generate, rather than transmit, information. Kelley (1968) has written in a stimulating and provocative way about predictive models in the human operator. Again, it is frequently very difficult to show any evidence of task interference in zero order or first order dual axis control tasks. But interference is found, with a loss of information transmission, when higher orders of control are required, or when heterogeneous dynamics are present (Levison 1971 Wempe & Baty, (1968)). Can a formal relation in the "normative" column be found between information and equalization? Does equalization correspond to a fixed rate of recoding? Can we, in short, quantify the load by operations performed on data - equalization, delay, translation (in linguistic tasks) etc.?

Finally, I would like to draw attention to some problems of methodology and measurement. On the one hand, in discrete tasks, there is always an inter-stimulus interval which the observer may use for covert processing. In continuous tasks, on the other hand, the human operator's effective bandwidth is far lower than his perceptual bandwidth, and what looks like continuous loading need not be so treated by the human operator. Moreover, the most powerful analytic methods such as autocorrelation, Fourier analysis, Bode Plots, and Laplace operator representation of human operators all suffer from a major drawback. They represent long term time averages of performance. If mental overload is transitory it may never be detected by classical methods of analysis. In laboratory tasks where we can detect it, the tasks are so far removed from real tasks that they become unusable for another reason. The physiological measures frequently are unstable or have very long latencies. We recently simulated some tracking data and found that if the "observer" held his response at a constant D.C. voltage for up to 20% of the time it was virtually undetectable by conventional measures. It may be that some of the new techniques such as the critical task of Jex and Allen (1970) will get over this problem, but a problem it remains, as is the question of how long the human takes to detect that the statistics of a process have changed. Optimal adaptive control theory may be particularly well suited to examine the latter point.

In summary, my hope lies in a systematic and careful study of the formal relation between normative measures, and a corresponding empirical analysis of the interrelation of the scores of the differant empirical measures (including physiological ones). Just as each normative model gives an "ideal" score, so should they provide normative intercorrelations. And finally, I think that a practical

SECONDARY TASKS AND WORKLOAD MEASUREMENT

Richard W. Pew

Bolt, Beranek and Newman, Inc.

50 Moulton Street, Cambridge, Massachusetts

1.0 DEFINITIONS AND SCOPE OF INTEREST

The need for a theory and measurement strategy for workload arises from the growing number of activities in which a human operator is assigned jobs of monitoring, supervisory control, clerical activities and problem solving as opposed to activities involving physical effort. As systems become more automated the question of function allocation and allocation of personnel to jobs requires answers to questions, such as "How much can a person do?" or "How demanding is this job?"

The term workload is a construct that can only be inferred from measurements of performance and most efforts to define theory or measurement strategies derive from the conception of the human as a limited-capacity single-channel information processing system. The limited-capacity assertion is well accepted but elusive because we have only poor indices of the amount of effort applied to any particular task, and we have no universal metric with which to compare task demands across the range of tasks that are of interest. Researchers are moving beyond the single-channel assertion as a general principle and we have begun to analyze the nature and extent of mutual structural interference among tasks or task components that compete for processing resources. These are issues that are discussed in the literature under the rubric of human time-sharing performance. It is concerned with the extent to which two or more tasks can be carried out concurrently as a function of the nature of the tasks and the conditions under which they are undertaken. This empirical work is the background out of which will come theories of workload and more useful measurement tools.

The theoretical developments of Kahneman (1973) and of Norman and Bobrow (1975) represent the beginnings of more sophisticated theory, but only the beginnings. I hope that this conference is able to bring together individuals from different theoretical backgrounds to define a more realistic model of human resource allocation, which can then be validated and used as a source of measurement tools for the assessment of workload in practical situations. From my perspective, the ultimate purpose of workload research is the measurement and prediction of operator mental workload in situations where it is of substantial practical importance. We can assess the demands of shoveling coal or sweeping the floor, and can set sensible standards, but we have only the crudest of tools for accomplishing the same goals in clerical tasks, in process control supervision and monitoring, or in intellectual or problem-solving activities. It seems unlikely that a single measure will ever serve such a variety of purposes, but these are the domains for which appopriate measures and models should be sought. Although prediction is important, the development of measures that would permit monitoring of workload without disrupting on-going activities would also be a very desirable tool. Finally, as we look toward a point in the future when it might be possible to set standards for acceptable mental workload in a variety of practical jobs, we also need to be thinking about ways to set criteria for acceptable loads analogous to time standards for industrial work or noise level standards for working environments.

In the meantime ergonomists and human factors specialists have been setting out to predict and measure workload on the basis of the limited tools now available. They attempt predictions on the basis of moment by moment time lines of activities required of a task or job, and some attempts have been made to extend this approach to produce computer simulation models of human performance in systems, such as Siegel and Wolf (1969) and HOS (Analytics, 1975) with workload prediction as one of the goals.

With respect to measurement, the primary tool that has been applied is the use of the secondary task methodology to make inferences concerning spare mental capacity and it is the practical application of this methodology that I wish to discuss in more detail.

2.0 MEASURING WORKLOAD WITH A SECONDARY TASK

Secondary task methodology derives directly from the limited-capacity single-channel hypothesis. It is argued that to the extent that a second task can be successfully performed concurrently, spare capacity is available over and above that required for performance of the primary task. The secondary task may be such that a scale of performance quality is available to use as an index of "how much" of it is performed. Alternatively performance of the secondary task may be so demanding that nothing else can be done concurrently and the measure of spare capacity is the percentage of time the subject can spend on this task and still maintain performance on the primary task. Or finally, versions of the secondary task may vary in difficulty or level of demand and we determine the level that can just be maintained without degrading the primary task.

To make this discussion more specific, consider the ideal case. We wish to determine the percentage of full load contributed by a particular primary task, Task A. To accomplish this measurement, we introduce the requirement to perform a secondary task, Task B, concurrently. In our ideal case Task B is calibrated in units of workload so that performance of none of it (or performance none of the time) contributes no workload and performance of all of it contributes "full" workload. When no change in the quality or quantity of performance of Task A occurs under the loaded conditions, then we may estimate the percentage of full load of Task A by the formula:

$$\% \text{ Workload} = 1 - \frac{\text{Quantity of Task B concurrently with Task A}}{\text{Quantity of Task B performed \underline{alone}}}$$

As the reader will surely recognize, this ideal has never been achieved in practice. Let us now examine a few of the myriad of reasons why:

1. As was mentioned in the introduction, workload is a construct whose properties cannot be directly observed, they can only be inferred indirectly through performance. Many variables produce changes in performance on Task B that we might not want to attribute to the workload of Task A. Practice, fatigue, and boredom immediately come to mind.

2. It is difficult, if not impossible to ensure that concurrent performance on Task A will be maintained at single task levels. Several factors are operating here. The subject develops subjective criteria of relative task importance, and while the introduction of specific payoff schemes that reward performance contingent on maintaining Task A at single task levels will help, they will never completely solve the problem. Kahneman (1973) introduces the concepts of Demand_1 to mean that a task <u>requires</u> attention and Demand_2 to imply that the task <u>captures</u> attention to emphasize the point that some tasks are intrinsically attention compelling (Demand_2) while for others the subject is

more free to vary workload allocation according to task requirements ($Demand_1$). For example, it is frequently found that performance decrements are observed in the easier of two concurrent tasks, presumably because the more difficult one is more attention compelling, ($Demand_2$).

3. The introduction of Task B may change in a qualitative way the performance of Task A so that even if performance in terms of measured output variables does not change, the performance strategy may change and produce different workload levels. The attempt to perform two rhythmic tasks having non-commensurate periods together may provide an extreme but illustrative case in point.

4. It has been shown experimentally that even the expectation that a secondary task will be required can change the performance of the primary task. To interpret such changes as having an impact on the workload ascribed to Task A is, at best, misleading.

5. As Kahneman (1973) has suggested, the effort supplied to a task depends in a non-linear way on the effort demanded ($Demand_1$). Each additional increment in demand produces a smaller increment in the effort supplied until finally an asymptote is reached. When the requirement to perform Task B is added to the requirements of Task A, the subject is shifted to a new operating point on the effort-required dimension and because of this nonlinear function the effort supplied to the two tasks is not additive, even in the range of performance where spare capacity is available. One would hope the function is at least monotonically increasing, permitting ordinal comparisons of spare capacity with different primary tasks.

6. Workload inferences will depend in substantive ways on the choice of Task B. If we take the view that human information processing takes place in a set of stages, different tasks can be expected to interfere differentially with different stages, hence the nature of specific structural interference will produce different apparent spare capacity inferences depending not only on the general workload demands but also on the specifics of the tasks in question. The extreme example is the case of a secondary task with a heavy motor output demand compared with one requiring little output, but a heavy memory load.

We have yet to identify the universal secondary task.

7. There are problems concerning the scales of measurement of performance on Task B. The ideal task has a dynamic measurement range that is perfectly correlated with workload from zero performance with no workload to full performance with full workload. But this is very difficult to achieve in practice, partly because of the characteristics of the demand vs. supply curve described above and partly because it is not clear that calibration of the full performance values in a single task control condition is the proper normalization.

8. In any particular realization of Task B, practice tends to improve performance, and we must either pick tasks for which practice has little effect or we must practise Task B to asymptote prior to its use as a secondary task. A further problem results from the fact that practice also improves the subject's ability to perform two tasks concurrently, even when both are practised to asymptotic values individually.

3.0 GENERAL DISCUSSION

Three methods of developing measurement scales for Task B were mentioned; (1) scales based on quality of Task B performance, (2) scales based on percentage of time Task B is performed, and (3) using several versions of Task B that vary in demand for a given quality level. If method (2) is used, the measurement scale becomes direct and many of the problems described above are reduced or eliminated.

This suggestion is consistent with Senders' position. Some years ago he argued that secondary task selection for the scientist interested in time sharing of mental activities should be based on different criteria from task selection for the practical assessment of workload (personal communication, 1967). In the former case one seeks to localize the source so that specific inferences concerning structural interferences can be made. If one is interested in the latter, then tasks should be used that interfere in an all-or-none fashion with performance of the task under study.

For the second case of practical workload assessment, if Task A is a monitoring task for which the predominant activity is information intake, then a simple procedure which temporarily eliminates the opportunity for intake, such as Senders' opaque visor that periodically or aperiodically interrupts vision may be thought of as the limiting case of method 2. While it requires no performance on the part of the subject it produces a direct index of the percentage of time vision may be obscured without degrading Task A performance. If Task A is predominantly motor, then a secondary task that requires use of the same response member may be a good choice. The difficult case is one that involves internal processing or thinking and little input or output. A self-paced serial reaction time task may be a good candidate in this case.

So long as we have no better theories or models to predict workload on the basis of a priori task characteristics nor even have a clear identification of the dimensions of mental activities that contribute to workload, the best we can do is to adopt a measurement strategy that forces the subject to allocate his resources in an all-or-none manner, that is, to study only conditions for which the single-channel theory can be adopted for all practical purposes. In the meantime the main work of this conference should be to advance the state of theory development so that this crude model can be replaced by one that is more predictive and useful for measurement.

REFERENCES

Analytics, Inc., The Human Operator Simulator, Vol.I, Introduction and Overview. Analytics Technical Report 1117-1, August 1975.

Kahneman, D., Attention and Effort. Englewood Cliffs, N.J., Prentice Hall, 1973.

Norman, D.A., Bobrow, D.G., "On Data-Limited and Resource. Limited Processes", Cognitive Psychology, 7, 1975, 44-64.

Siegel, A.I., and Wolf, J.J., Man-Machine Simulation Models, New York, J. Wiley and Sons, 1969.

REFLECTIONS ON THE CONCEPT OF OPERATOR WORKLOAD

Jens Rasmussen

Risø National Laboratory

Denmark.

In the context of our research at Risø on the data processing functions of human operators in automated, modern process plants, the concept of operator work load seems to be a rather qualitative, ambiguous characteristic of a work situation rather than a measure of the amount of work implied in a task.

Also, recent reviews of problems in the context of "Measurement of Man at Work" (Singleton, ed., 1971) suggest an increase in the diversity of measures and ambiguity of concepts following from a shift of emphasis from manual skill to data processing and decision making as the result of automation and computerization of technical systems.

This shows that the time has come to break away from the present analogies to physical work and to develop new descriptions of man's functions in automated systems; i.e., "we need to develop a philosophy of man-machine systems" (Singleton, 1971, p.58) to serve as an explicit frame of reference for meaningful measures of work performance.

There is a tendency to extrapolate from analytical, quantitative models developed for manual skills and sensory-motor responses in vehicle control into the field of supervisory control independently of a simultaneous development of models of human data processing within the fields of artificial intelligence, robotics, and linguistic research. A new philosophy of man-machine systems should be a frame of reference which allows research to draw upon the results from all these different approaches which place emphasis on different human abilities.

MENTAL LOAD

The different meanings of "mental work load" in our context are very well formulated by the "Webster" interpretations of the word "load".

From "load" as "an item .... carried"; "a .... weight supported by something", Webster associates to "something that weighs down the mind or spirit", a very precise formulation of the emotional quality of work which directly influences the amount of effort that an operator can or is willing to spend.

"External resistance overcome by machine or prime mover" leads to "the amount of work that a person carries or is expected to carry" which are quantitative statements referring to the demands placed on man by the environment. These interpretations are appropriate as long as the capacity problem is related to the human motor system, i.e. his physical power. The introduction of communication systems, such as railways and telephone exchanges creates the same problem for Webster as our human data processor does for us, and the solution is: load is "the demand upon the operating resources of a system".

However, even this definition is useful only as a measure of work load in one-dimensional demand/resource systems. In general, a demand/resource relation is multidimensional and the different measures must be used to characterize the global "load". The different aspects of human resources in a complex mental task are not independent; the actual capacities of different mental resources are interconnected and the overall "load" cannot be evaluated unless a description or model of the operator's mental processes in available.

STRESS AND STRAIN

Stress and strain are supposed to indicate the <u>effects</u> of work load upon man, and again there seems to be a <u>simple</u> transfer from the loading of physical structures through manual work and physiology to mental activities. As with the term "load", however, the concepts become ambiguous in this context. Mental work load does change man's mental 'shape' in terms of the resources he makes available. The relation, however, is complex and the source of much debate. It is not even monotone; if load increases the resources we call the effect "motivation"; if the opposite is the case we talk about "stress". Physiological variables change with mental activity, but the different measures tend to be divergent and the calibration of measures is typically not stable with time (Wisner, 1971). Physiological measures seem to be suited mostly as indicators of changes in mental work demand.

To conclude, in the context of monitoring and supervisory tasks of the operator in automated plants, the concept of work load is mainly useful as a measure of the degree to which work demands "weigh down the mind or spirits" of the operator; i.e. of the subjective quality of work situations, and stress as an indication of the resulting emotional state of the operator. The question of the fit between amount and context of work demand and operator resources must be evaluated within a much more refined framework.

DEMANDS AND RESOURCES; MEASURES AND MODELS

The work situation of a human supervisor in automated plants has several characteristic features.

He has a large variety of tasks related to a system which he comes to know very intimately. What he learns from one task will be used in others and his performance in different tasks cannot be described in isolation. Furthermore, the operator will use several mental mechanisms which have basically different limiting properties and which are most adequately described by different types of models. A "morphology of models" is therefore needed to interrelate the different measures derived from different types of models and to define the limitations of use of the models.

Another characteristic of the operator's situation as a supervisor are the demands arising from unfamiliar, infrequent situations - he is a diagnostician and a decision maker. Models as well as measures must therefore cover not only the average performance in frequent tasks but also his response in special, infrequent tasks, which very likely can be related to events implying high risks.

The system we are considering is shown in Fig. 1. A man supervises an automated system. He monitors the information from the system to see if he recognizes the situation as normal or acceptable. This may very well be a one dimensional demand problem and the fractional time spent on reading instruments will then indicate how near he is to the limits of his resources (Senders, 1970). However, if he detects a need to intervene with the system, he has to identify the actual state of the system, decide on the proper corrective task and to perform the manual actions. Now, in this case, the man has a complex data processing task, and it is as inappropriate to discuss his mental load without referring to his mental equipment and strategies as it is meaningless to discuss physical load in a manual task without referring to the power tools used.

In general, a data processing system will be a multi-

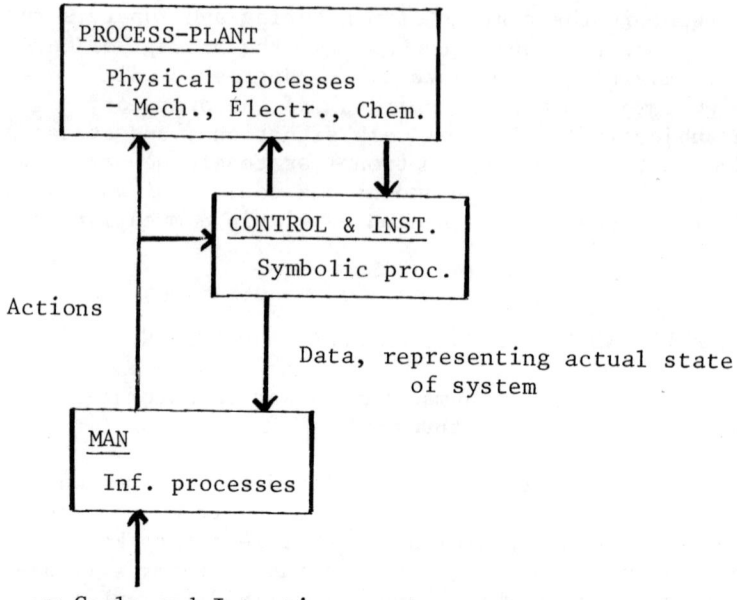

- Goals and Intentions
- Model, representing system properties
- Strategies, rules to control data processes
- Performance criteria, to select from repertoire
  of data processes.

Figure 1

dimensional demand/resource system. The flexibility of such a system very often makes it possible to solve a demand/resource conflict along one of the dimensions by a change in strategy or type of process (Bruner et al., 1956, Rasmussen and Jensen, 1974).

Some dimensions of the human resource system in data processing typically are:

- the time allowed for the task, when paced by the system;
- the amount of input information available or the cost of observations;
- the a priori information on system structure and function or useful analogies (mental models);
- the capacity of short term memory;
- the capacity of the mental processes used (sensory motor or cognitive);
- the code, level of abstraction, used in processing;
- the repertoire of ready-made-solutions - i.e. experience and skill;
- the risk, the cost of mistakes.

CONCEPT OF OPERATOR WORKLOAD

Demand/resource conflicts in one dimension can be solved by spare capacity in another: lack of input information can be compensated by use of a more complex mental model; capacity problems by recoding and "chunking" information to a higher level of abstraction, etc.

It is general practice as a last resort to let the operator take over pacing from the system. In crowded air traffic, controllers may "stack" aircraft in waiting positions; in process control, "set back" to safe operating condition is used.

Taken as a global measure of the extent to which a given task loads the operating resources of a human operator, work load turns out to be a measure characterizing a specific man-machine encounter, a situation, not the task itself.

The data processing task can be considered as a recoding of input information into a problem space and a search guided by a representation (mental model) of the properties of the environment. A major problem in the present context is the great flexibility of human data processors which is due to the availability of different categories of mental models and consequently different sets of limiting properties of the related data processes.

Such categories are illustrated by Fig.2, and discussed elsewhere in more detail. The point in the present context is that, depending upon model category, the strategies will be tightly connected to specific task or system properties. This means that the adaptation to changes in system conditions or task which is a typical aspect of a monitoring and supervisory task, can imply a switch-over to another category of models and strategies. A key question in any case is: How sensitive is the demand/resource relation along the different axes to changes in task or system? And which transformation is needed to map changes in the environment onto changes in the characteristics of the problem space and strategies? How is this relationship described? We are now in the complex situation of Fig.3, with an observer having several levels for representing the operator's representation of his environment. And we have to face this complexity in order to discuss preferences for a priori or empirical measures versus systems and models for prediction of man-machine system performance.

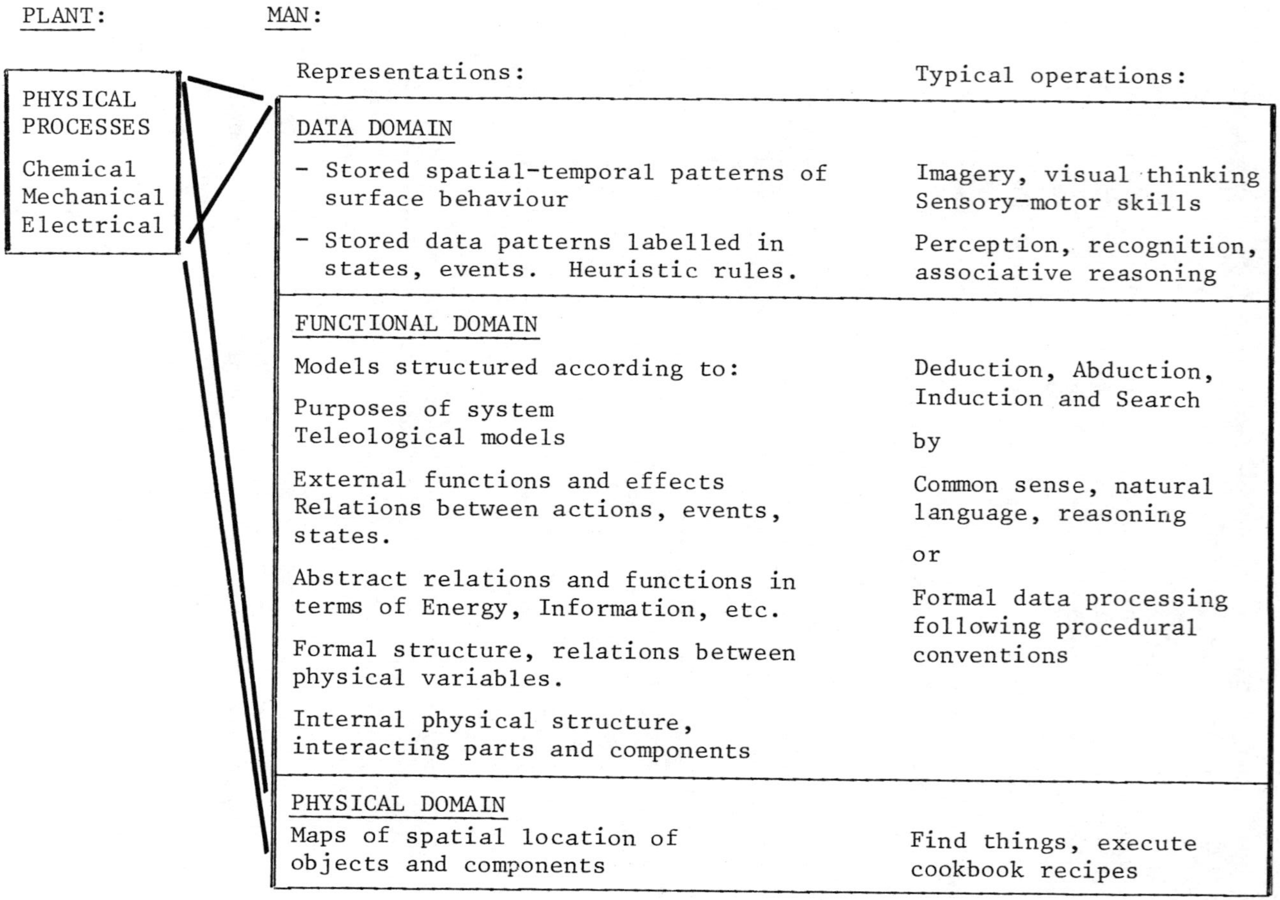

PLANT:

PHYSICAL PROCESSES
Chemical
Mechanical
Electrical

MAN:

Representations: | Typical operations:

DATA DOMAIN
- Stored spatial-temporal patterns of surface behaviour — Imagery, visual thinking Sensory-motor skills
- Stored data patterns labelled in states, events. Heuristic rules. — Perception, recognition, associative reasoning

FUNCTIONAL DOMAIN
Models structured according to:

Purposes of system
Teleological models

External functions and effects
Relations between actions, events, states.

Abstract relations and functions in terms of Energy, Information, etc.

Formal structure, relations between physical variables.

Internal physical structure, interacting parts and components

— Deduction, Abduction, Induction and Search

by

Common sense, natural language, reasoning

or

Formal data processing following procedural conventions

PHYSICAL DOMAIN
Maps of spatial location of objects and components — Find things, execute cookbook recipes

Figure 2

CONCEPT OF OPERATOR WORKLOAD

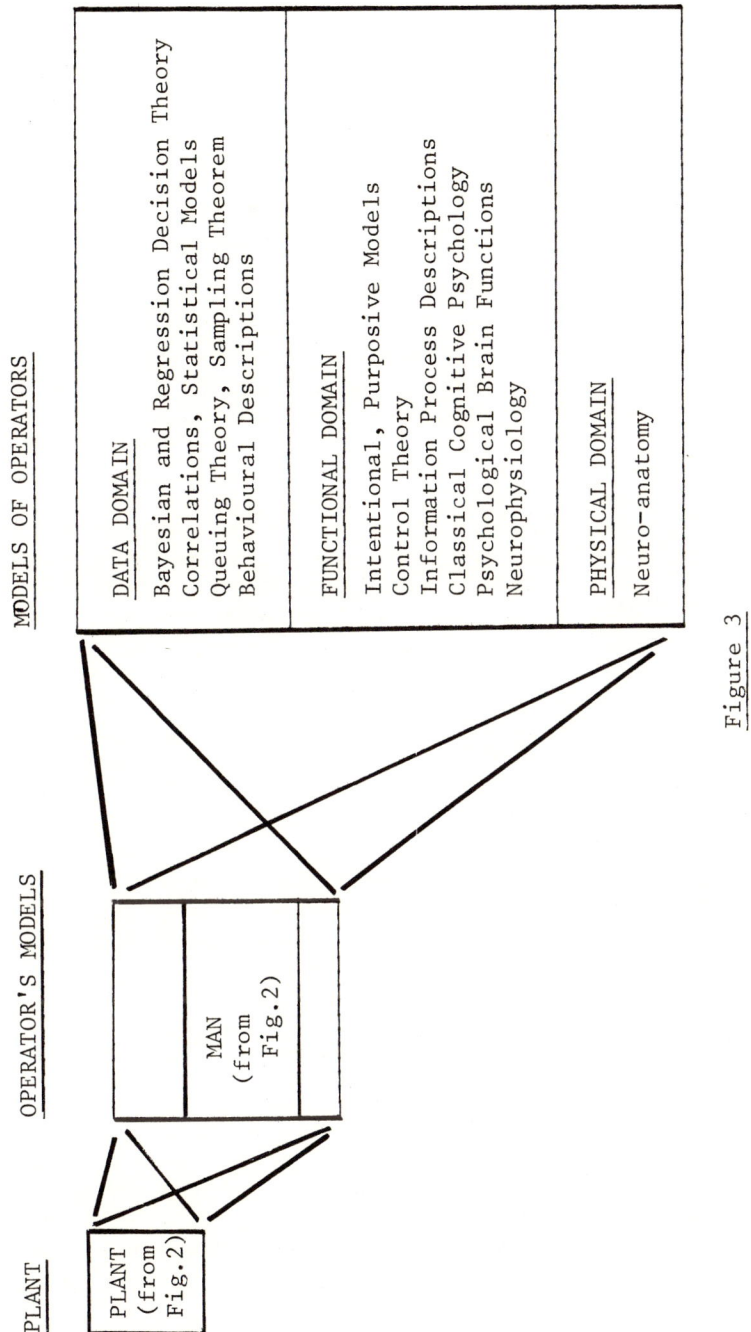

Figure 3

PREDICTION OF HUMAN PERFORMANCE IN MAN-MACHINE SYSTEMS

In supervisory control of automated process plants, man acts as an adaptive, selforganizing and goal oriented data processor and therefore attempts to predict his performance lead to several problems resulting from his great flexibility. At present we find the major problem that of establishing the necessary <u>categories</u> of models, of defining their interrelation and their relation to basic human mechanism with their various limiting properties rather than to find <u>quantitative measures</u> of human performance.

The effectiveness of the human data processor is due to the availability of a large repertoire of data subroutines. They are of basically different categories with respect to process type and limiting properties, and are conveniently modelled within different frameworks. Very frequent and repetitive functions are served by a kind of high capacity parallel processing which is holistic, i.e. not decomposable into separable subfunctions. This is the case for manual skill where attention, perception and complex movements are controlled by an internal, dynamic world model, etc. This category of functions is typically modelled within the framework of control theory and information theory (Curry, Moray, Senders, Sheridan, in: Sheridan and Johannsen, 1976).

In less familiar situations the data processes have the character of associative chaining of events, states, actions, i.e. processes which are typically described by decision theory (Slovic et al., 1973), fuzzy set theory (Zadeh et al., 1975), semantic networks (Rieger, 1976, Schank, 1975).

In unique, new situations, the processes turn into genuine problem solving based on formal operations such as deduction and a search in problem space. Such processes have been modelled in detail within artificial intelligence (Newell and Simon, 1972).

The problem in modelling real life situations is that all of these process types are involved and they cannot be studied in isolation. We need to know how the basic human mental mechanisms and their limiting properties are reflected in the different process models and how the models are interrelated. For instance, is there any connection through a basic human mechanism between the features of the temporal-spatial internal model behind attention and manual skill and the systematic bias due to "representativeness" in intuitive judgements found by Tversky and Kahnemann (1974)?

Can the concepts of models, data and strategies be formalized in a stringent way and used to interrelate the different categories of process descriptions? In practice, we do

not need to predict the data processes of an operator in detail
As far as we can predict the type of model, data and strategy he
will use in a specific task, we will be able to support him by
proper design of interface.

Being an adaptive data processor, the complexity of man's
behaviour "will reflect characteristics largely of the outer
environment" (Simon, 1969, p.25). This means that a model of
supervisory man cannot be developed by adding together models of
different subroutines found separately from selective experiments.
A model of supervisory man must be determined from analysis of
real life performance. At present we see no other method than a
structure and process analysis of verbal protocols and
conversations. This is, however, a time consuming task and
good protocols are difficult to obtain. Hopefully, a more
stringent frame of reference for the different categories of human
data processes and mental mechanisms and a clever use of the
recording facilities in modern interactive computer control
systems will make this research more efficient.

Simon continues ".... in the light of the current goal".
This is obvious, but far from trivial. First of all, research on
real life strategies must be based on an intimate knowledge of the
functional properties of the system supervised and its demands
upon the operator. The initial goal of finding the cause of an
event can develop into locating a change in the data domain (for
immediate association to counteraction); in the functional domain
(to plan a compensating action) or in the physical domain (to
repair or readjust the initial cause). Even when the system's
actual demand is well specified, there will be great freedom for
a subjective formulation of the "current goal" and of the
performance criteria used for trade-offs among the demand/resource
dimensions. This makes the individual task sequence vary
depending upon person- and situation-related details. It also makes
higher level analysis in terms of formal strategies - based on
consistent sets of models, data and process rules - and heuristic
rules for leaps between them attractive.

One thing still remains to be considered, the emotional
aspect. How much effort can or is the operator willing to spend
upon a specific task? This relates to the short-term emotional
load from a work situation like motivation and stress, but also
to the long term aspect such as attitudes, acceptance and beliefs
which becomes more and more important as systems are designed for
complex interactive data processing or man-computer cooperation
(Halpin, et al., 1973). Research in this field is extremely
important, but again in supervisory tasks we do not find the key
problem to be one of measures and quantification, but rather to
be related to definition and identification of categories: which

are the characteristics of work situations resulting in positive attitudes?

CONCLUSION

These general characteristics set the stage for the concluding remarks:

In future complex systems, man will typically be allocated functions as a monitor and supervisor. Models of his performance must not only be able to predict his average response in frequent situations, but also his response in unique, infrequent tasks.

He is a highly adaptive and goal-oriented information processor. Models of his performance in well adapted situations are mainly models of his environment. Models of his performance must also reflect the limiting properties of his internal mechanisms.

The overall quality of human performance in a monitoring and supervisory task is typically measured by his reliability - i.e. the probability that a change or fault in the system is met by an appropriate action - or by the time it will take him to restore normal operation. The effect of random human errors can only be predicted from statistical models based on empirical fault data (Swain, 1976). The effect of system properties must be considered in at least three independent ways:

- The efficiency with which the interface activates the appropriate intention or goal within the operator. Which information is used to update his internal model, to direct his attention and activate his value system?

- The freedom given the operator to develop and use a repertoire of data processing which allows efficient trade-offs in resource/demand conflicts. This freedom strongly depends upon the selection, precondition, coding and formatting of the information presented to him. This must not be judged from the viewpoint of rational, formal choices, but from the performance criteria in actual use, e.g. like the "law of least resistance".

- The extent to which the operator will be willing to or can use his normal resources and the resources offered by the system without his performance being impaired by negative attitudes, stress or distrust.

In general, these qualities cannot be quantified or measured; the attributes of an optimal system design cannot even be defined qualitatively. Question: Will today's research add up to an integrated view of the process operator or are we using shot-guns?

We cannot predict operator performance in general in the complex systems we design. However, we may be forced to design systems in which we can predict the performance of operators, at least in safety related tasks. Question: Which are the attributes of a task for which we today are able to predict the performance quantitatively?

REFERENCES

Bruner, J.S., Goodnow, J.J. and Austin, G.A. "A Study of Thinking", Wiley, New York, 1956.

Halpin, S.M., Johnson, E.M. and Thornberry, J.A. "Cognitive Reliability in Manned Systems". IEEE Transactions on Reliability. Vol. R-22, No.3, August 1973.

Newell, A. and Simon, H.A. "Human Problem Solving", Prentice-Hall, 1972.

Rasmussen, J. and Jensen, A. "Mental Procedures in Real Life Tasks": A Case Study of Electronic Trouble Shooting", Ergonomics, 17, No.3, p. 293-307, 1974.

Rieger, C. "An Organization of Knowledge for Problem Solving and Language Comprehension". Artificial Intelligence 7 (1976), p. 89-127.

Schank, R.C. "Conceptual Information Processing", North-Holland Publishing Company, Amsterdam, Oxford, 1975.

Senders, J.W. "The Estimation of Operator Workload in Complex Systems", in Systems Psychology, K.B. DeGreene (Ed.), McGraw-Hill, 1970.

Sheridan, T.B. and Johannsen, G. (Ed.) "Monitoring Behaviour and Supervisory Control", Plenum Press, New York and London, 1976.

Simon, H.A. "The Sciences of the Artificial", M.I.T. Press, 1969.

Singleton, W.T. (Ed.) "Measurement of Man at Work", Taylor and Francis Ltd., London, 1971.

Slovic, P. and Lichtenstein, S. "Comparison of Bayesian and Regression Approaches to the Study of Information Processing in Judgement", in L. Rappoport and D.A. Summers (Eds.): Human Judgement and Social Interaction, 1973, Holt,

Rinehart and Winston.

Swain, A.D. "Sandia Human Factors Program for Weapon Development", Sandia Laboratories SAND 76-0327, June 1976.

Tversky, A. and Kahneman, D. "Judgement under Uncertainty: Heuristics and Biases", Science, 185, 1124-1131, 1974.

Wisner, A. "Electrophysiological Measures for Tasks of Low Energy Expenditure". in "Measurement of Man at Work", Singleton (Ed.), Taylor and Francis, London, 1971.

Zadeh, L.A. et al. (Eds.) "Fuzzy Sets and Their Applications to Cognitive and Decision Processes". Academic Press, New York, 1975.

SOME REMARKS ON MENTAL LOAD

A.F. Sanders

Institute for Perception TNO

Soesterberg, The Netherlands

Abstract

This paper aims to present an analysis of the concept of mental load from the point of view of human performance theory. In the first section the theoretical status of the concept of mental load is considered. It is concluded that it is based upon common sense, which cannot be supposed to be empirically founded in a simple way. Then an outline is given of the main procedures of measurement. The next section describes a number of theoretical bases which are all related to some kind of limited capacity notion. It is concluded that the original idea of channel capacity in terms of information theory fails to provide a sound theoretical framework. Other capacity concepts in terms of limited capacity processors and in terms of effort are described. Three types of processors are distinguished, which have different consequences for the measurement of mental load.

The fourth section describes some experimental trends. It is concluded that a multichannel type of processor, composed of a network of internal mechanisms is most favoured by the data. This has the consequence that mental load cannot be conceived of as a single dimension. The question is which mechanisms are involved in a task and to what extent. Performance failures occur if a single mechanism is overloaded, but that does not imply that other mechanisms are also overloaded. Ultimately a task may be described therefore in terms of a pattern of mental load. Some consequences for applied work are discussed.

I. THE STATUS OF THE CONCEPT

In discussing what "we know" about mental load in general and about methods of measurement and assessment in particular it should be clear from the very start that we are dealing with a concept which is defined in common sense terms. Intuitively, mental load is related to the extent one is "mentally occupied" and to the effects of this occupation on the human organism. Thus, one can be overloaded, underloaded or reasonably loaded, and this is fairly self-evident. It will be argued in the course of this paper that various models of human performance underlie this simple formulation, each of which directs the concept - and in particular its empirical analysis - in different directions. The matter is not as simple as it may seem.

When it was introduced, theoretical considerations about mental load did not dominate. For example in the Netherlands mental load appeared on the scene as a mere analogy to physical load. Following successful research on the measurement of physical load in terms of oxygen consumption and following the introduction of the bicycle ergometer test as a standard task for assessing physical loadability, load was defined in terms of changes in the organism due to the task and its environment (Burger, 1964). Subsequently psychologists were invited to develop analogous measures and devices for the evaluation of mental load and loadability. Thus from the beginning, emphasis was on measurement rather than on theoretical and empirical foundation.

There are at least two basic problems with this procedure. The first is that when speaking about mental load - or any intuitively defined concept - different researchers have different things in mind. Two major types of conceptualisation may be distinguished. In the first, mental load is only related to demands in perceptual-motor tasks. The question is limited to what extent a human operator is "too busy or too bored" (Mackworth, 1957). Within this conceptualisation opinions also diverge. At the one extreme mental load refers to a state of the organism and becomes almost equivalent to the notion of mental effort (e.g. Jahns, 1973). At the other extreme it is merely a label for a task variable. One may be reminded of Conrad's "sensory-motor load" variable which merely indicated the number of independent signal sources in a visual reaction task (Conrad, 1951, 1954).

The second conceptualisation of mental load is much wider in that the task environment with its physical components (environmental stressors) and in particular its social and emotional components (leadership, management relations, personal relations) are also included. Emotions, tensions and frustrations all add to mental load. Thus, there can be mental load in the absence of formal task performance. The concept, then, becomes almost equivalent to something as general as stress or strain.

It is clear then that the attempts towards measurement of mental load will depend on its conceptualisation. In the present paper the discussion will be limited to perceptual-motor load. This does not mean that the social and emotional components are irrelevant. The problem is one of scope. One may say that the more limited concept of load in perceptual motor tasks encompasses at least the whole domain of human performance theory, while the wider notion involves almost all of Psychology.

The second problem in relation to intuitive definitions is perhaps even more basic. It concerns the question to what extent a postulated notion can be expected to correspond to a homogeneous set of operational anchors. This question is relevant with respect to measurement: Do we measure what we want to measure with the usual measures of mental load? This is more than an academic question. It may be illustrated with measures of the "legibility of lettertype". It is intuitively evident that some lettertypes may be more legible than others and that their legibility should be measurable. This seems to be a fairly limited problem, certainly in comparison with that of mental load. Indeed, there exists a diversity of measures, some of which have been listed by Chapanis (1971). In itself this would not be worrying if the various measures would ultimately render the same results. In other words if the measures, however different, were still measuring "legibility" as a single dimension and, consequently, if they would lead to the same recommendation about the lettertype to be used. However, the problem is that the correlations between the various measures are rather low, which implies that the "measures" are related to different matters. Consequently, legibility, albeit intuitively clear, has no sound operational anchors.

In particular psychology seems to be teased by intuitive concepts that lack a sound theoretical basis as well as an empirical foundation. It may seem a commonplace that, before thinking about measurement, at least some kind of predictive model and an integrated set of operational anchors should underlie the hypothetical construct. One can say that experimental tasks and behavioral concepts are separated by a dividing line (see Table 1) and that going from right to left is usually only permitted when predictions of specific models are tested. Conversely, one should never arbitrarily choose a task or measure standing for some hypothetical attribute. Instead, the analysis of tasks, and in particular of task variables, should result in <u>inferring</u> the existence of internal mechanisms. Hence the predominant movement should be from left to right of the dividing line. As long as no

Table 1

Tasks, task variables and internal mechanisms. Tasks and task variables are under reasonable experimental control. Concepts are inferred or are postulated in a priori models.

Tasks	task variables	internal mechanisms
a choice reaction test	S-R compatibility	response selection
long term driving	duration	fatigue
working under loud noise	intensity of the noise	state of arousal
an inspection task	signal discriminability	stimulus encoding
a recall test	retention interval	memory

(Dividing line between task variables and internal mechanisms.)

sufficient evidence is available, a description in terms of task variables is preferable. Task variables do not lead to misunderstanding about what is meant; obviously they do not ask for measures, since they do not pretend to correspond to a unique internal mechanism. Yet, they represent a first abstraction beyond the individual task level. The statement that a certain stressor has an effect on task X is a good deal less informative than that it has an effect on task variable X. Information of the latter type specifies where the effect of the stressor is located, while this remains unknown in the former case.

According to most definitions, mental load is on the right of the dividing line. It remains to be seen whether it can be based upon sufficient evidence on the left of the dividing line. It should be noted that mental load enjoys a considerable popularity which might be due to the fact that the concept has found its way into the common language, in particular of those who are faced with applied problems. It is relevant to note that interest in the measurement of mental load primarily came from those who are faced with applied problems. Thus it is striking that mental load, or some related concept, does not appear in the subject index of the Psychological Abstracts. Most of the work has been reported in applied journals, in proceedings of applied meetings and in unpublished communications.

The applied nature of the interest is hardly surprising in view of the issues that are at stake. Comparative assessment of mental load would have consequences for a score of issues, ranging from pay scales to the question whether an operator can be reasonably expected to do well. If, in addition, it were possible to determine individual "loadability", a tool for selection would be available and questions about, say, ageing and performance would be open to systematic recommendations.

The relevance of these problems should make us reluctant to reject the concept of mental load too hastily. Moreover, even if the scientific community would reject "mental load" as a fruitful concept, one would have a hard time to alter common language! Thus, if the concept should seem unpromising, an alternative should be searched for.

The composition of this paper is as follows. In the next section methods of measuring mental load will be briefly described. Then, some models underlying the concept will be discussed and the consequences for the proposed measures will be outlined. The next section summarizes some main experimental trends with regard to the models. A final paragraph is devoted to conclusions and prospects.

II. SOME PROPOSED MEASURES

The proposals for measuring mental load may be subdivided into three main groups, reflecting the major empirical tools of experimental psychology: measures of behavior, of psychophysiology and of subjective judgment (Sanders, 1977).

1. Behavioral measures

In this group, human performance is either estimated or measured with reference to some theoretical maximum performance, which is set equal to maximum load. The general underlying idea is that, when exceeding the limits of maximum load, performance will break down. Workload indices are formulated as a proportion of the maximum.

a) <u>Measures of time and motion study</u>: Here the question is whether a subject can satisfactorily accomplish all activities allocated to him within the timeframe available (e.g. Siegel and Wolf, 1961, 1969). There is a maximum load if one is occupied all the time. The method requires a detailed function analysis in which all activities are fractionated in measurable parts. This is most possible in tasks with predominant manual components (e.g., Hopkin, 1971) and there the method has found rather wide application. Yet it has also been applied to more "perceptual" tasks, like the operability of flightdecks (Zipoy et al., 1970).

b) <u>Measures of optimal control theory</u>: Here one is mainly interested in the extent of <u>error correction</u> as found in manual tracking or supervisory control (e.g. Levison, 1969). Workload is defined as the ratio between P_o - i.e. the observation noise ratio corresponding to the subjects' "full capacity" - and P_c - i.e. the maximum observation noise ratio that allows the subject to achieve the required performance level. P_c can be varied by varying the admissable error level (criterion level), the input level, etc.

c) <u>Testing the limits of performance:</u> In simulated tasks one may increase the input load to a level where errors or missed signals are unavoidable. The degree to which the usually observed input load may be increased before reaching this breaking point provides an estimate of the mental load in that particular task. Obviously it is a rough estimate since the relation between "experienced" mental load and input load below the maximum is unknown. The same is true of course for measures of time and motion study and optimal control theory. A measure of a hypothetical attribute can at best assume a monotonic relation between performance and the attribute and, consequently, the rankorder level of measurement is not exceeded.

d) <u>Subsidiary task performance</u>: This method, originally introduced by Bornemann (1942) attempts to measure "spare capacity" by the extent a second task can be carried out together with the main task. Usually primary task load (W_1) is defined as:

$$W_1 = 100 - (W_2 + W_t)$$

where W_2 refers to subsidiary task performance in terms of the percentage of reactions when the subsidiary task is carried out together with the primary task, as compared to the case where only the subsidiary task is performed. W_t refers to a constant, reflecting the time needed to shift between tasks (e.g. eyeshifts) (Knowles, 1963).

A variety of subsidiary tasks has been investigated during the last three decades with an emphasis on laboratory studies (Rolfe, 1971). Examples are solving arithmetic problems (Bornemann, 1942), choice reaction time (e.g., Bertelson et al., 1966), generating a random sequence (Baddeley, 1962) and regularity of tapping (Michon, 1966).

It has been realised that not every task is suitable as a subsidiary task and that some basic requirements should be met: the task should require little learning (to avoid practice effects), it should be self-paced (to avoid interference with or disruption of primary task performance, and the method of scoring should deliver comparable results for different situations (Knowles, 1963). The synergistic character of dual task performance (Jahns, 1973) may still cause a decrease of primary task performance, mostly without the experimenter's knowledge. A special method to avoid negative effects on the primary task is provided by "cross adaptive subsidiary tasks" where the level of difficulty is regulated by the performance level on the main task (Kelly and Wargo, 1967).

2. Psychophysiological measures

These start from the minimal assumption that task demands "lead to activation of the organism" (Haider, 1972). Hence it might be possible to measure mental load indirectly by measures of physiological activation. Regularity of heart rate or sinusarrythmia, (Kalsbeek, 1967), pupil dilatation, and increase of skin conductance (Kahneman and Beatty, 1966; Kahneman, 1973) belong to the most popular proposals.

3. Subjective judgments

Here mental load is evaluated by subjective estimates in the sense of ratings or rankordering of tasks with the aim of arriving at some subjective scale. For example Bartenwerfer (1970) has tried to scale the general central activity level in degrees of mental tension. Table 2 lists some of his results for various types of activities.

Table 2

Subjective estimates of mental load (Bartenwerfer, 1970)

Listening to a student translating a latin text	23
Listening to the discussion of homework mathematics	25
Listening to the explanation of new problems in physics	30
Writing a mathematical test	34
Second melter at a blast furnace	30
Driving a car	32
Control machinist on a train	34
Stripper crane operator in a foundry	36

Some recent applications have served more limited aims as, for example, comparing workload in flying various types of military aircraft (Goerres, 1977) or determining acceptability of cockpit layouts (Steininger, 1977). As Weyer and Hadapp (1975) state,"The subject is urged to be introspective. This is very well in agreement with scientific work. It is accomplished by asking man more or less direct questions concerning his subjective experience of strain or workload".

The theoretical and empirical foundations of the behavioral and psychophysiological approaches will be discussed in the remaining sections of this paper. At this point a few remarks will be made about subjective assessment. Inherently methods of subjective judgment can be considered as highly valuable tools for many issues in psychology. Hence it is agreed that there is nothing unscientific in collecting this type of data. The main serious consideration seems to be what kind of questions a subject can be expected to answer with some reasonable confidence. Can one reasonably expect someone to compare the inner tension experienced in operating a train with writing a mathematics test?

At least three types of problems are involved. First, the degree of expertise in any of these activities. It is virtually impossible to appeal to introspection about situations one does not know. To ask a subject "how he views the work of others" means asking for his prejudices rather than for his experiences. It is highly unlikely that one is measuring what one wants to measure - i.e. mental load.

Secondly, even if one has general expertise, comparing car driving and a mathematics test, or the job of a helicopter and a jet pilot seems asking for the impossible. It is never a task as such which is intuitively loading but rather certain elements of the task or certain conditions under which the task is carried out: driving in city traffic, under conditions of fog or rain, on a motorway; flying during take off and landing, etc. A general judgment about the task as such seems an impossible request. Unfortunately subjects yield to the psychologist's questions almost unanimously and produce ratings or comparative judgments, whatever they are asked to do.

Thirdly, it is clear that subjective judgments of mental load do not pretend to make any contribution to the theoretical foundation of the concept. Mental load can be interpreted in various ways and, thus, when asked to rate mental load one rater may use considerations which are dissimilar to those of another rater.

A general conclusion may be that the prospects of measuring mental load by subjective judgments are not high. Perhaps the method is applicable to limited sets of task conditions. Indeed a bus driver may rate his experiences about the effect of various environmental conditions on his "inner tension", experienced task difficulty, etc. There are methods of determining the internal consistency of sets of questions. In turn, such measures are most important as external criteria to validate behavioral and physiological measures. In several instances the results of the latter types of measures have been correlated with subjective judgments of task difficulty. The limited applicability should be always kept in mind, however.

III. CONCEPTS UNDERLYING MENTAL LOAD

When the concept of mental load appeared on the scene in the fifties, <u>the</u> underlying concept was that of channel capacity. Despite considerable changes in the meaning of this concept during later years it remained the main basis. Thus, maximal load means that one is operating at the limits of one's capacity. Overloading means making errors or missing signals. In case of underload there is considerable spare capacity. What does the term "channel capacity" really mean?

1. The constant capacity communication channel

Originally then, human channel capacity was based upon the idea that the human operator could be conceptualised as a communication channel with limited capacity (or limited bandwidth) or perhaps that the human operator is comparable to a system of interrelated channels each with its own limitations (e.g. Attneave, 1959; Garner, 1962; v.d. Geer, 1963). The capacity of communication channels was usually expressed in bits (or in bits/sec), and numerous attempts have been made to determine human capacity limits.

The issue is clearly that a <u>constant</u> channel capacity, irrespective of the type of processing involved, would define the upper limit of mental load in bits. Overload would occur if a signal (or if the signal rate) contained more bits than can be transmitted. Below the upper limit the number of bits and of bits/sec would be at least monotonically related to mental load.

This approach failed however and the general feeling in the sixties is well expressed by the following rhyme:

Shannon, Wiener and I
Have found it confusing to try
To measure sagacity
and channel capacity
By $\Sigma p_i \log p_i$

(Behavioral Sciences, 1962, Volume 7, p.395)

The problems encountered concerned in particular the constancy of channel capacity expressed in bits or bits/sec.

a) <u>Processing rate:</u> If a subject is presented with a paced series of signals to be responded to, one may vary information load by either increasing the rate of presentation or by changing the amount of information contained in each signal. In such tests transmission in bits increases to a certain level after which there is a decline. The peak value represents an estimate of channel capacity. Figure 1 shows some peak values obtained in a simple continuous reaction test with highly practised subjects. The problem is obviously that these values are not upper limits in any absolute sense. In the example, the subjects appear to make about 2 reactions per second irrespective of the amount of information contained in the signal. This would even suggest that channel capacity is unlimited!

It may be objected, of course, that results as displayed in Figure 1 only occur in cases of extreme compatibility between signals and responses. As S-R compatibility is less RT is found to increase more as a function of $\log_2 n$, and usually linear relations are obtained (Hick, 1952; Brainard et al., 1962, Simon and Wolf, 1963; see Figure 2).

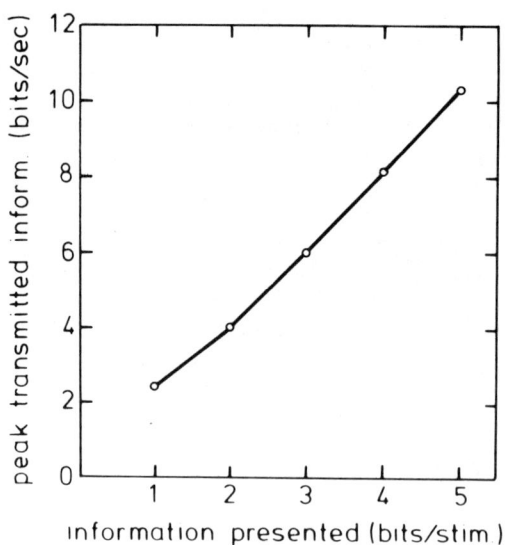

Figure 1

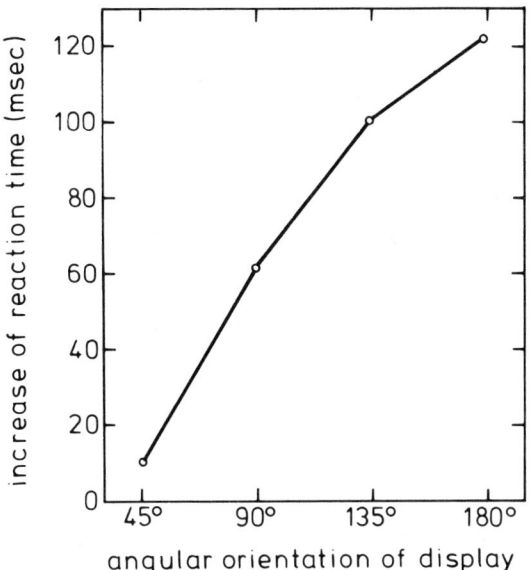

Figure 2

However, if the peak values depend on S-R compatibility, this emphasises that the rate of information processing does not depend on channel capacity in bits but on the complexity of internal processes translating a signal into a response. Moreover, a time-consuming process such as response execution is insensitive to event uncertainty as well as to S-R compatibility (Fitts, 1954; Frowein and Sanders, 1978). It rather depends on properties of the target and size of the movement to be made.

What remains is the observed linear relation between RT and stimulus information at a constant level of S-R compatibility (Hick's law). Even this has been under attack since the size of the set of alternatives is confounded with the probability of repetitions of the same signal in successive trials, unless special precautions are taken. Kornblum (1969) found considerable differences between RT's to signals containing equal signal information but a different conditional probability of repetition. The conclusion is that stimulus information is neither necessary nor sufficient to account for choice reaction time data.

b) <u>The problem of absolute judgment</u>: Next to processing rate there is the absolute momentary limit to channel capacity, which has been found to amount to the well known 2 to 3 bits in studies of absolute judgment of stimuli on perceptual dimensions like pitch and loudness. Allowing a longer response time does not increase performance in such situations. It seems a matter of acute overloading in the sense of failures in finding the correct response if the set of alternatives exceeds about 7 items.

Again, S-R compatibility or the complexity of internal translation processes seems to be a basic background of these phenomena. In the experiments, subjects are usually required to assign a number to the stimulus, which constitutes a highly incompatible S-R relationship. Presumably one would do much better when one were allowed to sing or whistle in response to pitch or loudness! It has been suggested that man is more tuned to logon content than to metron content (Mackay, 1952), but this may very much depend on the extent that the response mode fits the way of encoding the signal. In other words, the question is whether a subject can employ some set of learned relations. If not, he must go through a tedious process of comparing the internal code of the presented signal to the remaining alternatives in order to arrive at the correct response. In fact, these comparisons may be subject to short-term memory limitations in that a subject cannot "recall" the alternatives-to-be-compared if the set grows too large. In the case of well learned relations, such as identifying words, the "capacity" is virtually unlimited again.

Thus, a constant capacity for information in the sense of direct input-output relations is an unrealistic assumption. This is not to deny that the size of the set of alternatives and in particular the connected probabilities of occurrence are relevant. The point is, however, that the ways these factors influence performance are more complex than assumed in a simple communication channel. Much depends on the internal processing programmes available to translate the information into responses. Information theory did not take account of programmes and therefore it failed. Consequently a measure of mental load in terms of information transmission in bits is not feasible.

Despite this failure, the idea of a limited channel capacity has survived, even in the absence of a unit of measurement. As earlier suggested, the observations of performance failures - both in the sense of failures to find the correct response in discrete trials and of failures to respond (or to make a correct response) at high rates of signal presentation - make a notion of limited channel capacity highly attractive. Thus new capacity concepts emerged.

2. Limited capacity processors

According to a group of formulations channel capacity is described in terms of a limited capacity processor. In theory these models still assume a constant capacity but in practice the efficiency of information processing is highly variable, depending on the complexity of the programmes for certain activities. A complex programme requires allocation of much capacity, hence processing time is relatively long and the programme may even fail altogether. In the course of learning, simpler programmes may develop with considerable savings in capacity.

With regard to mental load this general formulation emphasises that practice reduces load - as was the main message of the previous section. This is well taken into account as is clear for example from the requirement that a subsidiary task should require little learning. Yet the formulation does not immediately suggest direct measures of mental load since there is no actual measure of processor capacity. However, the general frame can be further specified in various directions. They will be briefly outlined.

Processor type A: This model assumes that capacity constitutes a kind of common pool to be allocated rather freely to various internal processes and concurrent activities. The amount devoted to each process is determined by the needs of the moment. In the case of shared capacity processing - for example discrimination of two simultaneously presented signals-special programming is required to monitor the sharing procedure, which uses itself a certain proportion of the capacity. More generally, each programme consumes capacity (Moray, 1967).

It is relevant to note that in this formulation it makes sense to speak about available capacity at a distinct moment in time - perhaps in the form of short duration time samples (e.g. Kristofferson, 1967). As long as total capacity limits are not exceeded, capacity may be divided at any time among concurrent activities. In other words, parallel processing is possible within capacity limits. One ongoing activity may have considerable spare capacity, in particular if it is a well practised activity.

This model has consequences for measures of mental load. Thus, time and motion study does not seem suitable since it only refers to occupied time and not to occupied capacity during the time. Error measures are acceptable, when it is assumed that one spends as much capacity as needed to avoid errors. The subsidiary task is a doubtful approach. Dual task performance needs extra programming to integrate the two activities and it is unknown how much capacity this requires. Moreover, sharing capacity between some tasks may be easier than between other tasks, hence the estimate of spare capacity may be severely biased. The only possibility to save the subsidiary task is to ignore extra programming requirements and to assume that it is the capacity, used by each task separately, which counts. Possibly a constant, like Knowles' (1963) shifting constant, might be assumed.

Processor type B:. Here the capacity concept makes sense over longer time segments only. The capacity needed for a particular activity is expressed in the time taken by that activity, a more complex activity taking more time. Spare capacity during an activity does not exist, since, if it were available, it would reduce processing time. Thus, spare capacity only refers to empty segments of time. Allocation of capacity refers to the priorities in allocating time. Parallel processing is not possible.

In fact this type of processor represents a very strict single channel theory, the basic assumption of which is that the human operator is performing as an intermittent correction servo (Craik, 1947; Welford, 1967). While occupied with processing a signal - or possibly a group of signals - any other incoming signals are supposed to be blocked. They may be temporarily stored, which enables their processing after the previous process is completed (Broadbent, 1958).

Incidentally, the storage assumption already suggests that the whole process is not supposed to be single channel. In particular at the input stages there would be some space for parallel processing. Yet for all practical purposes, the relation between capacity and time might be maintained.

It is clear that the single channel theory solves a lot of problems with regard to mental load, since it suggests that one has merely to consider signal frequency, their spacing in time and their processing times to calculate the amount of occupied capacity. "Decisions take time and if this is more than the time available, responses will be delayed or omitted" (Welford, 1967, p. 12). Mental load, then, equals input load, which can be largely defined in terms of task variables and can be directly measured by the times taken by the activities. This provides a basis for time and motion study, as well as for subsidiary tasks. In fact the single channel assumption is often made in the latter. In a recently developed human operator simulator, the estimation of spare capacity using a simulated subsidiary task is through completely blocking the simulator for any processing during fixed samples of time (Lane al., 1977). Finally, errors have two possible bases. Either the allocated processing time may not have been sufficiently long or, when the correct response cannot be found, time requirements are infinite. In both cases one can speak about overload.

Processor type C: In both previous processors, capacity remained largely a general reservoir, from which activities may draw, either in time (Processor B) or both in time and internal space (Processor A). Activities are predominantly treated as unitary events. Conversely, there is considerable evidence for the presence of internal mechanisms intervening between the signal and the response. For example, application of Sternberg's additive factor method to traditional choice reaction times has shown evidence for at least three processing stages: Stimulus encoding, response choice and motor preparation (Sternberg, 1969; Sanders, 1977). It is very likely, however, that there are many more mechanisms, that do not play a role in choice reaction times. The point is that each mechanism may well have its own capacity which is not exchangeable with that of another mechanism. The main relevance of this idea is that a considerable amount of capacity may remain unused in a single reaction, because only a limited number of mechanisms may be involved in that reaction. The capacity of unemployed mechanisms cannot be used to speed up the reaction process. The more complex the task, the more mechanisms are involved, and, consequently, more 'capacity' is used.

Hence, spare capacity at a distinct moment refers at least to the capacity of the unemployed mechanisms. Besides, one may wonder whether the capacity of the employed mechanisms is exhausted by one activity. In fact this may be the case for some and not for others. In some cases all capacity may be used, an easier task being completed faster than a more complex one. In other cases there may be opportunities for parallel processing, hence the processing time of a single activity may not use all capacity of that mechanism.

A main implication of processor C is that a human subject may act more as a single channel processor as two simultaneous activities are more similar, i.e., as they use many common mechanisms and in particular to the extent that these mechanisms operate as single channels. It is obvious that Processor C suggests dim prospects for behavioral measures of mental load to the extent that a general measure of capacity consumption is searched for. As in processor A the time taken by the activities is not representative of capacity consumption. Subsidiary tasks suffer from the problem of similarity vs. dissimilarity with the primary task. Error measures may at best suggest overloading of a subset of mechanisms but do not say anything about spare capacity. In fact an "easy" task may overload one or two mechanisms and hence show failures of performance or time delays, while a "difficult" task may be well completed, if no single mechanism is overloaded. Basically, processor C suggests a complete reconsideration of the capacity concept, as well as a redefinition of what is meant by mental load.

3. Effort

It is commonly agreed upon that next to structural mechanisms, like encoding and response choice, functional or energetical mechanisms, like arousal, play an important role in processing information. Arousal is usually considered to affect the efficiency of the information flow to a large extent. In the study of human performance its effect is usually investigated in situations involving abnormal conditions - e.g. sleep loss or environmental stressors (e.g. Poulton, 1970) - where sizeable effects have been observed, in particular when the activation level is low. It suggests that structural mechanisms, as assumed in the limited capacity processors are only a part of the story.

This is the background of a functional aspecific capacity concept, which is synonymous with "effort" or "attention" (Kahneman, 1973). The general idea is that man's limited ability to carry out multiple activities at the same time, can be explained by the fact that the total amount of effort which can be deployed at any time is limited. This limited capacity can be allocated with considerable freedom among concurrent activities, as in processor A. The existence of structural bottlenecks is not denied by Kahneman but plays a subordinate role. The main question is how much effort - or attention - a certain mental activity requires from the common pool. As long as a mental activity or a combination of mental activities can be completed, there is always spare capacity. This is used for continuous monitoring of the surroundings. As the effort invested in the primary task increases, attention is withdrawn from perceptual monitoring and concentrated on the main task (Kahneman, 1973).

Kahneman's theory has two further main characteristics. The first is that, although total effort is limited, it is not a constant. In fact, available capacity increases with the task

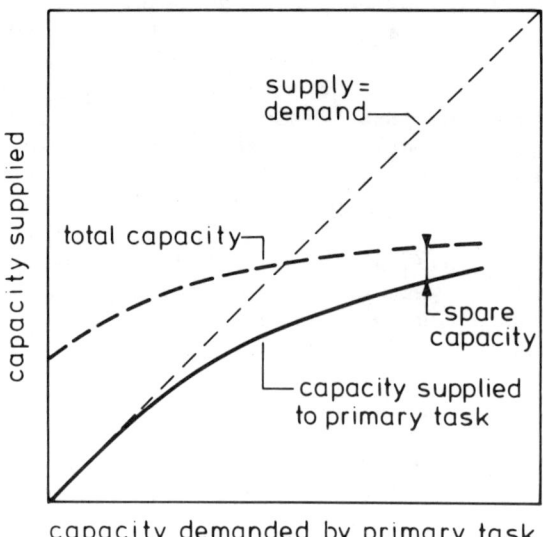

Figure 3

demands as illustrated in Fig. 3. The second is that the amount of effort needed is largely determined by the task. "Doing better by trying harder" is almost not possible. However, one may do less well than possible, but there is an ongoing evaluation of the performance level, hence a decrement below an acceptable minimum results in extra effort allocation. Knowledge of results is of course important for the functioning of this evaluation.

At first sight it seems that Kahneman regards effort and activation as synonyms. However, activation has a wider meaning and includes, besides effort, also miscellaneous determinants, which are related to the state of the subject: time of the day, effects of stressors and drugs and in general "what happens to the subject". To the extent that these determinants lower or raise the level of activation, they affect, however, the total capacity and in particular the evaluation mechanism. For example loss of sleep has no clear effect on "interesting" tasks, which presumably are sufficiently activating. Conversely, it has an effect on monotonous tasks. However, this is effectively counteracted by knowledge of results, which, again, is activating and informs about performance level (e.g. Wilkinson, 1969). This close relation between activation and effort makes an operational distinction between these two mechanisms rather arduous.

The relevance of this type of model is that, unlike processor models, it suggests the measurement of mental load through psychophysiological variables, since it is a largely functional model. Mental load equals the effort needed, to transform the actual input into an adequate work result, and "the" ultimate objective of workload research should be "the development of techniques for reliable prediction of effort" (Jahns, 1973, p.14). Measures of input load are distrusted in view of possible differences in expenditure of effort, which may make performance relatively invariant with changes in task difficulty. According to Fig. 3, a subsidiary task is also suspect; it increases the task demands and, hence, the total capacity. Therefore, it can never provide a reliable estimate of effort supplied to the primary task. Error scores may be used, since they reflect a discrepancy between supply and demand of effort. Conversely it does not provide a measure of spare capacity (Fig. 3).

Hence according to effort theory psychophysiological measures offer the best solution for measuring mental load and research should be directed towards finding a good measure of invested effort.

4. EXPERIMENTAL TRENDS

The experimental evaluation of the theoretical positions outlined in the previous paragraph must be necessarily sketchy and limited in the context of this paper. Only some main trends will be discussed and subjective biases will be unavoidable. I think, then, that it is fair to state that a processor B type of model has been the subject of most research. This may not surprise since it is the only model with rather precise predictions. Conversely, the assumption of a common pool of capacity, either structural (Processor A) or functional (Effort), runs the risk of accommodating almost any result with an appeal to the flexibility of allocating capacity. Thus, to come to grips with any general capacity model would at least require a measure of capacity consumption and the formulation of rules about allocating capacity. A processor C model has more internal constraints but is teased by the requirement of specifying the intervening mechanisms and which mechanisms are involved in completing an activity. Moreover there remains the issue whether or where the subcapacities behave according to processor A or B.

1. <u>Single channel theory</u>: Hence, single channel theory is by far the most simple and straightforward. Tests of this model come from a number of paradigms, the most popular of which are speeded responses to simultaneous or immediate successive signals,(psychological refractory period, performance in paced and self-paced continuous reaction tasks), tests of selective attention and performance in multiple tasks.

a) Psychological refractory period (PRP): It is generally observed that, when two signals are presented in rapid succession, reaction time to the second signal (RT_2) is delayed in comparison with its proper control. Usually this has been considered as support for a single channel theory. However, there are some inconsistencies which have led several authors to interpret the results in terms of a common pool of capacity in the sense of a processor A (e.g. Triggs, 1968; Kahneman, 1973). Yet, I feel that the general trend of these studies provides support for at least some single channel bottlenecks and that Bertelson's (1966) conclusions still largely hold. In view of its relevance to discriminating between processor A and B, a more detailed discussion is justified.

There seem to be two major sources of confusion. The first is that subjects do not necessarily complete the first response prior to processing the second. In many experiments, the reaction to the first signals is also delayed in comparison with the control. Subjects appear to prefer collecting perceptual information about both signals before emitting a response, in particular when the signals are simultaneously presented or in very close succession. The last strategy (grouping) appears to be more efficient than handling the reactions successively (Sanders, 1964). This has been considered as evidence favouring a processor A model, one allocation strategy being more efficient than the other (e.g. Triggs, 1968). However, the greater efficiency of grouping seems to be mainly determined by the possibility of initiating one integrated response,

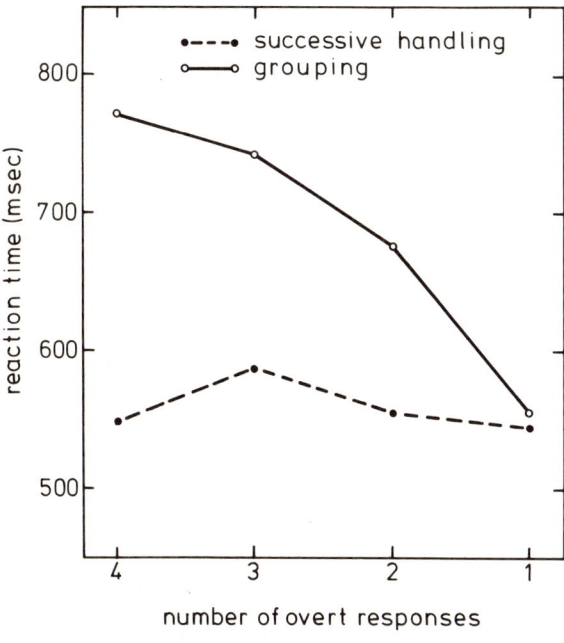

Figure 4

either simultaneously or in rapid succession. Fig. 4 shows that the advantage of grouping in a PRP study with four simultaneous or immediately successive signals depends on the number of overt responses. (Each signal required either an overt or a covert response). With only one overt response (to the last signal), RT did not differ between conditions in which "grouping" and "successive handling" was instructed, suggesting that no basically different processes were involved. At the same time these results suggest quite pronounced single channelness during response execution, since overt responding delayed the responses to the next signals. One integrated set of responses to several signals does not seem to consume extra time.

The fact that subjects can interrupt processing a signal at some convenient stage in order to process the next signal, does not contradict single channel theory as long as the processes involved are sequential rather than parallel. The only assumption, which is disproved, is that a reaction process is a completely unitary process that cannot be interrupted. Grouping a larger number of signals followed by emitting an integrated succession of responses is a typical procedure in high speed skills like typing. A beginner in typing reads a word or a group of words and, then, searches for responses in a strictly sequential manner. A skilled typist has developed motor programmes enabling a large number of closely spaced responses. It is a matter of the size of the stimulus and the size of the response rather than an argument against single channel theory.

Yet, interrupting the processing of signal 1 in a PRP study poses obvious problems of interpreting the course of RT_2 - or the interresponse interval - as a function of interstimulus interval, which are the most common procedures of analysis of the PRP. As usually observed RT_2 is less delayed than predicted when grouping effects are not taken into account.

There is a second source of confusion with regard to the finding that RT_2 is often also delayed if S_2 is presented after completion of S_1^2. Although various explanations have been offered for this phenomenon, the most acceptable one seems to be that a prepared response is possible to S_1 but not to S_2. Preparation for two separate responses at the same time seems to be hard and this is in line with Processor B. Also, during completion of R_1 a subject appears unable to prepare for R_2, which probably causes an extra delay to RT_2. This result complicates a simple prediction about the size of the delay. If a preparatory set delays RT_2 when S_2 is presented after the completion of RT_1, single channel theory must assume that the same source of delay does also exist when S_2 is presented during completion of RT_1. Hence a strict Processor B model would predict that the size of the delay would be maximally a full reaction time plus the time of the preparatory component. This is never found and hence, as suggested earlier, not the whole reaction process is single channel. Yet PRP studies suggest pronounced single channel bottlenecks: response selection, response execution and preparatory set.

b) <u>Continuous reaction tests</u>: Usually single channel processing is also favoured by this type of study. One example will be treated in some detail. It concerns experiments on relative performance in self-paced and paced tests (Wagenaar and Stakenburg, 1975; Frowein, 1978). In a self-paced test, a subject cannot process the next signal prior to completion of the previous reaction. In a paced test, processes might overlap if the next signal arrived prior to completion of the previous one. Thus, if the pacing tempo is set equal to the 70th percentile of the distribution of self-paced reaction times - individually for each subject - a processor A model and an effort model would expect that paced performance is superior to self-paced performance for several reasons. First, the average time available for a reaction is longer. Second, the proportion of cases where the next signal arrives prior to completion of the previous reaction should not offer problems. Extra capacity allocation and the possibilities for shared capacity processing would make up arrears. In particular the effort model would suggest a stronger effort in the paced test, since there is more time pressure than in the self-paced test.

Conversely, single channel theory predicts considerable problems with paced performance, since the long RT's will cause delays leading to complete failures to respond. Superior paced performance is only expected at the lower deciles of the distribution: a certain proportion of the responses will be sufficiently short to provide a response-signal interval in which the next response can be prepared.

Some typical results are in Fig. 5. They largely confirm the prediction from single channel theory. On the average, 8 percent of the signals are not responded to at all; paced RT is only shorter than self-paced RT at the low deciles and becomes increasingly longer at the high dectiles. At a slow pacing rate, paced performance is superior throughout the distribution due to the fact that the ample response-signal intervals allow prepared responses all the time.

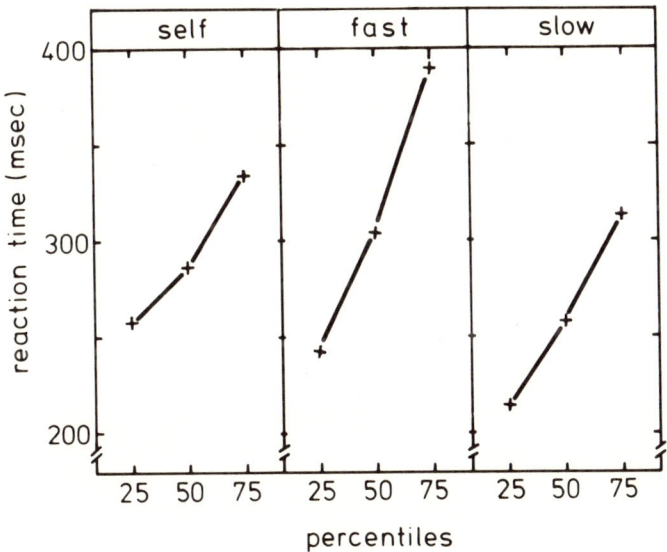

Figure 5

c) <u>Selective attention and dual tasks</u>: Other evidence favouring
the single channel hypothesis for at least a proportion of an
activity stems from experiments on dual task performance, shadowing
and selective listening. The dual task studies (Noble et al., 1967;
Trumbo et al., 1967; Noble and Trumbo, 1970; Kerr, 1975) suggest
a single channel bottleneck during response selection. In shadowing
it has been a common finding that, when shadowing an auditory
message presented to one ear, the contents of another auditory
message, presented to the other ear, are virtually blocked for
analysis, although there are exceptions in the case of a strong
response set (Broadbent, 1971). Even when only searching for
targets from any of two messages - i.e. without shadowing - a
considerable proportion of targets is missed when two targets
happen to arrive simultaneously. In that case only one target
is usually detected (Moray, 1975). Thus if one stimulus requires
further activity, including a response, processing of the other
one is hampered. Allocating extra capacity does not seem to help.

The main exceptions to single channel processing in these
types of tasks are found at the level of signal detection. Detecting the presence or the absence of a near threshold target out of
a simultaneously presented set from different modalities is not
inferior to detecting a single target (Shiffrin, 1975). There
seems to be fair opportunities for parallel or automatic processing
at this level. A similar suggestion follows from the "probe RT
paradigm", developed by Posner and co-workers. In a visual same/
different letter matching task, where the letters are successively
presented, an auditory signal is presented at the various stages of
the process: before, and during presentation of the first letter,
during the interval between the letters and during the matching
process. RT for the auditory signal does not increase during
presentation of the first letter, but it does during the interval
between the letter and is even more pronounced during the matching
(Posner and Klein, 1973).

In conclusion, then, there seems considerable support for the
type B processor, in particular during response selection and
execution. If this were the whole story, one could measure mental
load for all practical purposes by measuring the time spent on all
activities during a task, and conceive of spare capacity as the
empty time.

Most of these results do not favour a type A processor with
free allocation of capacity at any distinct moment of time. The
common capacity pool would be of a negligible size if even simple
activities as described above, cannot be shared. This is not to
say that there are no strategies of capacity allocation but, as
Processor B suggests, it is a matter of distribution in time and of
integration of activities rather than a matter of space at any
distinct moment.

It should be noted that the effort model cannot be simply discarded by these data since the observed interference might be considered as structural interference. Kahneman has argued that effort allocation is related to the difficulty of simultaneous tasks and that the concept is meant to explain interference that cannot be accounted for by structural interference. Hence the effort model requires a separate discussion.

2. <u>Evidence for multichannel processors (type C)</u>: All experiments discussed so far have in common that the competing activities are highly similar: manual responses to highly similar signals and vocally shadowing one out of two similar simultaneous messages. In terms of processor C such tasks need about the same mechanisms. Consequently, they are not very suitable to distinguish between processor B and C.

Indeed, several publications have appeared in recent years suggesting that several tasks can be well combined if the activities are sufficiently different or if subjects are sufficiently skilled. Thus if a visual and an auditory information flow are simultaneously monitored for targets, interference occurs in the case of simultaneously arriving targets (e.g. Shiffrin, 1975), but the performance level is considerably better than with dichotic presentation where both information streams are auditory (Treisman and Davies, 1973). It seems that in the case of a positive response on one channel, the information of the other channel remains available if this other channel is of a different sense modality. Moreover, the superiority of bimodal presentation is also found if the auditory information flow is shadowed and a recognition test for visual items is carried out afterwards. Visually presented words are reasonably recognised but especially pictures appear to be well retained (Allport et al. 1972). As Treisman and Davies have proposed, the perceptual system may consist of a number of **independent sets of analysers** and the question is to what extent various sets are used.

The evidence for multichannel processing is not limited to stimulus encoding, where, as argued before, there is already fair evidence for parallel processing. Thus, Allport et al. (1972) found that experienced piano players are capable of simultaneously playing and shadowing an auditory message with little evidence of interference. Similarly Shaffer's (1975) highly skilled typist combined shadowing with typing out a visually presented text. McLeod (1976) had subjects perform a continuous visual manual tracking task simultaneously with a 2-choice auditory reaction task. He found considerable interference when the reaction to the tones was also manual - i.e. with the hand not involved in the tracking task - but very little interference when vocal responses were made. McLeod (1977) also found no interference between Posner's visual same/different letter match task and auditory probe reaction time if the reaction to the auditory signal was vocal. Were there an absolute central demand of the letter match task, which could be measured by a probe technique, this should appear irrespective of the form of the probe.

Again, Kalsbeek (1967) found heavy interference between an auditory binary choice task - paced at a maximal speed - and various perceptual motor tasks, including handwriting and maze learning. However, Ruyssenaars (personal communication) found little interference between the binary choice task and the Raven matrices - a visual pattern perception test - in conditions where the motor element was largely removed.

Such results strongly suggest a type C processor, which allows for better multi-task performance as less common stages are involved. The examples show effects of employing both different in- and outputs. In the case of simultaneous decisions the question is to what degree actions call on a central decision mechanism. From studies on the reaction process (e.g. Sanders, 1977) it is known that the response selection mechanism is hardly used when S-R relations are highly compatible. The same is probably valid for any automatized action structure, where "automatized" refers to the absence of central search for adequate responses and to the absence of central control on the results of the action structure (e.g. Shiffrin and Schneider, 1977). It has been argued that, as practice increases, movements are more characterized by an open loop process (Keele, 1973).

If the response selection mechanism is not involved it may be open for use by another activity. It is interesting to note in this respect that, in contrast to McLeod's results, Green and Flux (1977) found heavy interference between a visual tracking and an auditory communication task, but the auditory tasks used by McLeod and Green and Flux differed in S-R compatibility. McLeod's task was a compatible binary choice reaction, while Green and Flux presented digits and asked subjects to add three on to the digit he heard and then report the result. Presumably the last task requires the response selection mechanism to a large extent, while McLeod's task may have hardly needed this mechanism.

As said earlier, a processor C model meets the problem of specifying the internal mechanisms involved in a task. Concepts like encoding, response-selection, motor-programming etc. cannot be loosely introduced since they are at the right of the dividing line (see table 1). One approach that was briefly mentioned at the introduction to Processor C (page 55) is Sternberg's additive factor method for the analysis of reaction processes. This method assumes that, if two task variables have additive effects on RT, they affect different processing mechanisms, while, if they interact, they affect at least one common mechanism. Thus one may infer mechanisms (right of the dividing line) from effects of task variables (left of the dividing line).

Although Sternberg's assumptions have been critized (Taylor, 1976), the analysis of reaction process according to the additive factor method has delivered a fairly consistent picture (Sanders, 1977, see Figure 6) of processing stages. Therefore it may be a promising start towards specifying internal mechanisms. Incidentally, it may be noted that the results of Figure 6 are incompatible with a processor A model. Free allocation of capacity would imply that, say, in the case of difficult stimulus discriminability, more capacity can be allocated to stimulus encoding when S-R compatibility is high than when it is low. In the last case the more complex programme for response selection would draw more capacity from the common pool at the cost of capacity allocated to discriminating the signal. Hence low S-R compatibility should have the effect of increasing the effect of stimulus discrimination, hence an interaction between these variables is predicted. As shown in Fig. 6, additive effects are found (Sternberg, 1969; Frowein and Sanders, 1978) which contradicts the free allocation hypothesis. As suggested by processor C exchange of capacity may only occur within mechanisms and not between mechanisms.

In summary, from the three processor types described, processor C appears to be most in line with the experimental trends. Type B seems to account only for certain task combinations. The main problem with type A is that there really is not much evidence for the free allocation hypothesis.

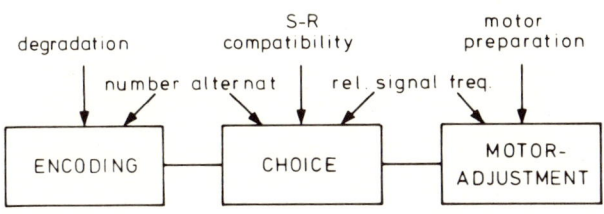

Figure 6

3. <u>Effort</u>: There remains the question about an aspecific functional pool of effort. What is the role of energetic factors on the efficiency of human performance? Two issues might be clearly distinguished.

a) The role of energetic factors is obvious in unusual situations, like long continuing workspells, administration of depressant drugs, lack of sleep and abnormal environmental conditions. Negative effects under such conditions may well be attributed to a lack of effort. Restoration of performance level by motivational stimuli fits this picture, as well as the relevance of evaluation of the performance level in allocating effort.

b) It is another matter whether next to structural interference between concurrent tasks there is a need for interference due to effort limits in otherwise normal conditions. As mentioned, Kahneman suggests that effort may cover those situations where <u>task difficulty</u> rather than <u>task similarity</u> is the major determinant of interference. A more difficult task requires more effort, hence two difficult tasks will exceed capacity limits to a larger extent than two easy tasks. Yet it should be realised that task difficulty is a very vague concept. Kahneman's examples of easier and more difficult activities (e.g. recalling four verbal items in a memory span test versus making three multiplications by heart) suggest that the more difficult tasks are characterised by longer chains of computations, by occupying longer periods of time and by the involvement of more mechanisms. Does the latter task merely consume more structural (computational) capacity, both in time and in number of mechanisms involved or does it require more aspecific energetical effort? Or perhaps both? Does an error in a three by three multiplication reflect insufficient effort allocation or failures in some computational process? Or both?

Perhaps one possibility to answer this type of question is in the study of the relation between structural and functional aspects of performance. Under abnormal conditions, where total capacity, or at least allocated effort, is supposed to be less, there should be more pronounced effects on more difficult tasks. One instance where this was studied concerns some experiments by Moraal (1975) on signal detection during dynamic and static inspection of noisy visual fields. Considerably lower d' was obtained with dynamic presentation, suggesting greater difficulty of the last task. Yet, the condition of static presentation proved to be more sensitive to the effect of one night sleep deprivation (Fig. 7). This result suggests that certain mechanisms involved in static presentation - presumably related to preparation - are more sensitive to lack of sleep. It does not confirm the hypothesis that a more difficult task is more sensitive to lack of sleep.

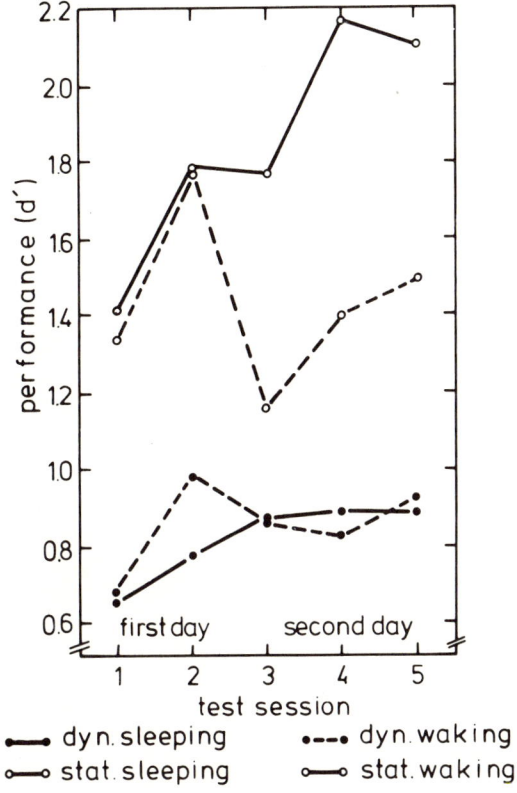

Figure 7

Again the results of Truijens, Trumbo and Wagenaar (1976) do not easily fit the effort theory. Visual tracking and generation of random numbers were performed singly and in combination. In the dual task situation there was evidence for some interference and, since these tasks seem fairly different, one might say that supplied effort did not meet the demands. Administration of barbital affected performance of both tasks in the single condition, suggesting some decline of supplied capacity. Hence in the dual task one would predict more serious effects of barbital than in the single tests. Yet, the results showed complete additive effects of the drug and dual task variable. One may suggest that the effects of the drug express decreased effort while dual task performance reflects structural interference, but this raises the problem that despite the dissimilarity between the tasks, their interference is not explained by failures of effort allocation.

Thus, the preliminary conclusion may be that the value of the effort concept is as yet hard to assess. There are certainly instances where it is indispensable but, probably, we should not rely too soon on effort as an explanatory concept. In particular not since task difficulty has not yet proven to be a manageable notion. Next to the objections that were mentioned earlier, it should be realised that it is not task difficulty as such which is supposed to affect effort allocation, but the subjective evaluation of task difficulty. If a subject or an operator feels that he has difficulties in maintaining a satisfactory performance level, he experiences his task as difficult. Alternatively, there are various tasks, for example in quality control, where many errors are made, while the operator still feels he does a good job. The reason is clearly that the errors remain unnoticed. In my opinion such a task is mentally overloading since encoding of correct and incorrect items is deficient. Yet variations in discriminability between corrects and errors do probably not change the subjectively experienced task difficulty and, hence, will not affect effort allocation.

Nevertheless, an independent psychophysiological measure of effort would be of great help in studying the limits of the concept. Kahneman has argued that pupil dilatation is sensitive to effort allocation, and in particular to short term changes in effort demands (e.g. Kahneman and Beatty, 1966; Kahneman, 1973). Continuation of this research is extremely relevant. Yet effort, in normal performance at least, could prove to be effect rather than cause. In other words, effort could be a process accompanying the extent of structural capacity rather than a process controlling structural capacity consumption. Whatever may be the case, a generalised psychophysiological measure of effort would mean an important step ahead.

V. MENTAL LOAD: CONCLUSIONS AND PROSPECTS

A general conclusion from this discussion seems to be that presently a type C processor, with perhaps some additional effort elements, tends to be favoured. As said, such a processor does require a reconsideration of what is meant by mental load. Do we mean capacity consumption in the sense of the number of mechanisms that are operating at the same time? Or, do we mean "being busy" in the sense of a threat of performance failures which may already occur when a single mechanism is overloaded? Only in the last case can measures of time and motion study and optimal control theory be properly used, but it should be realised that, even when approaching maximal load, some other highly dissimilar activity may well be combined with the primary task. Hence, "too busy" becomes a very relative notion! Again, as said before, mental load is detached from task difficulty in the sense that a variety of mechanisms is operating at the same time.

Whatever definition one may prefer, a subsidiary task is always suspect, since performance on the subsidiary task is largely determined by the extent that mechanisms common to the main task are involved. This was already indicated by Brown (1968) who observed that a tapping measure was most sensitive in discriminating between tasks involving a fair amount of motor activity, while the generation of a random series was especially sensitive to tasks of a predominantly perceptual nature. As said earlier Ruyssenaars made a similar observation with respect to Kalsbeek's binary choice reaction task. Even Bornemann (1942) in his original paper, has considered this possibility, since he observed that the "percentages" of subsidiary task A and B, when carried out together with some primary task did not deliver a sound prediction for the mutual effects of A on B and vice versa.

Which definition may be preferred? I am tempted to say that in the long run we should think in terms of <u>patterns of mental load</u>, qualitatively different, based upon which mechanisms are involved and to what extent. It is clearly a composite concept reflecting an end result of various contributing factors, relating to the task, as well as to internal human dispositions and to the state of practice. It is already common usage in the literature to speak about "perceptual load", "memory load", "motor load" and "decision load", reflecting an attempt to fractionate the general concept into specific elements. The extent to which a subject is mentally loaded would depend on the pattern as a whole.

Any mechanism, exceeding its capacity limits, would cause overload, but, clearly, a load-reducing measure with regard to that mechanism has a different impact for mental load if other mechanisms are close to being overloaded than if they are far from being overloaded or not loaded at all. This is the main reason that I feel that a mental load concept in terms of performance failures will finally fail to lead to a satisfactory solution.

There is of course the problem that the patterns of mental load are not yet easy to state. Besides requiring a much more developed performance theory it asks for a satisfactory task taxonomy, translating tasks into behavioral requirements. So far, attempts towards a task taxonomy, either in terms of behaviour (Gagne, 1963) or of task categories (Fitts, 1964) have not led to a commonly accepted scheme (Christensen, 1968). From the present point of view, fractionating a task into task variables seems preferable but is certainly not easy, in particular when the tasks differ from simple piecework. Yet, even if it would concern only a limited range, attempts towards an inventory of task variables would be useful. There are some inventories, meant as ergonomic checklists (e.g. Klinkhamer, 1965) that deserve closer scrutiny.

This short discussion illustrates that the discovery of the mental load pattern is at best a long term endeavour, if ever feasible. This does not mean that the idea should be abandoned altogether and also not that human performance theory has nothing to say about loading elements. It belongs to the every-day practice of applied experimental psychology to recommend load reducing measures in real world tasks. These activities are not directed however to the original aim of developing a mental load scale of measurement on which various tasks might be compared.

It is useful to note that the idea of qualitatively different patterns of mental load do not suggest such a scale. Rather the idea is that the pattern is highly multidimensional and that various tasks may be loading in qualitatively very different ways.

The only theoretical possibility of a general scale would be through psychophysiological measurement, if a measure reflecting overall capacity consumption could be found. It is outside the scope of this paper to discuss the results on psychophysiological measures but I am very interested to learn about the opinions of the psychophysiologists during this workshop. Here are just two remarks. First a quotation from Michon (1966), namely: "the crucial question with respect to physiological methods is whether we should in fact expect macroenergetic disturbances of a sufficiently high level to show during information transmission" (p. 402). Second, the relation between a psychophysiological measure and capacity consumptions will be very hard to prove. A simple relation between the physiological measure and a task variable is clearly not enough to qualify the measure as one for mental load in the sense of processor C.

In conclusion mental load as a single quantity probably does not exist. The concept just does not seem to work. But how then do we respond when we are asked about mental load in applied work? I think it depends on how the question is stated . If we are asked whether one task is more loading than another one, I feel that no answer is possible except when the tasks are highly similar and differ only on some limited task element. We should be very clear that attempts towards a mental load scale are probably based upon false premises. If the question is whether <u>this</u> particular task is loading, the question should be translated into something like "to what extent can the demands of this task be increased before unacceptable performance failures occur?" That question can be answered: sometimes by time and motion study - if the proper task analysis can be carried out - sometimes by control theoretical measures - if a minimal observation noise ratio is present - and sometimes by testing the task to its limit.

A few final words may be devoted to this last method, since, as far as I know, it has not been seriously considered. It is a weak method in that it does not lead to a common scale. It even does not lead to a measure in the strict sense of the word. But, on the basis of the argument these restrictions are not worrying. It is also dependent on the availability of a simulator. Given that these constraints are accepted it also has possibilities: it tells how much more information can be presented before performance of a system breaks down and in that sense it is an estimate of the weak points of the mental load pattern of a specific task. I may conclude this paper by giving an example where this method worked. In air-traffic control - usually considered as a highly loading task - the controller monitors a certain number of aircraft per unit time (say half an hour). How loading is a certain number of aircraft? This varies according to the total flight pattern, and the corresponding occurrence of conflicts. Therefore the load is not constant. Yet, there is presumably a <u>correlation</u> between load and number of aircraft per half hour. On this assumption, simulated flight patterns were constructed with the number of aircraft as a variable. It turned out that, at least in that system, simulated patterns of 30 aircraft per half hour were beyond the possibilities of an experienced controller, in the sense that he violated the rules about mutual distances between aircraft and about airspace limits. On occasion, 25 aircraft per half hour were judged to be very difficult but not impossible. These results are important in that they suggest that more than 20 airplanes per half hour is within the danger zone. Less than 20 airplanes should not be particularly loading for an experienced controller. In principle the method permits comparison of total system performance between various systems of air-traffic control. It can estimate effects of improvements. Usually one also finds suggestions about which features of the task are most vulnerable. It is also possible to study individual differences of performance of, say, different age groups. For the present I consider this method as one of the best solutions in the short-term. In the long-term I still have my hopes for a mental load pattern. But there is a long way to go.

REFERENCES

Allport, D.A., Antonis, B. and Reynolds, P. (1972) On the division of attention: A disproof of the single channel hypothesis. Quart. Journ. of Experimental Psychology, 24, 225-235.

Attneave, F. (1959) Applications of information theory to Psychology. Henry Holt, New York.

Baddeley, A.D. (1962) Some factors influencing the generation of random letter sequences. M.R.C. Applied Psych. Unit report 122..

Bartenwerfer, H. (1970) Psychische Beanspruchung und Ermüdung. In: Handbuch der Psychologie, Volume 9, Gottingen.

Bertelson, P, (1966) Central intermittency twenty years later. Quart. J. Ex. Psychol., 18, 153-163.

Bertelson, P., Renkin, A., Lamye, D. and Taverne, G. (1966): L'évaluation de la capacité résiduelle par la methode de la tâche ajoutée. Report of the Free University of Brussels.

Bornemann, E. (1942) Untersuchungen über den Grad der geistigen Beanspruchung. Arbeitspsychologie, 12, 142-191.

Brainard, R.W., Irby, T.S., Fitts, P.M. and Alluisi, E.A. (1962) Some variables influencing the rate of gain of information. Journ. Exp. Psychol. 63, 105-110.

Broadbent, D.E. (1958) Perception and Communication, Pergamon Press London.

Broadbent, D.E. (1971) Decision and Stress, Academic Press London.

Brown, I.D. (1968) Criticisms of time-sharing techniques for the measurement of perceptual-motor difficulty. Proceedings XVI Inter.Congr. Appl. Psych., Amsterdam Swets and Zeitlinger 322-328.

Burger, G.C.E. (1964) Permissible load and optimal adaptation. Ergonomics, 7, 397-417.

Chapanis, A. (1971) The search for relevance in applied research. In: measurement of man at work, Singleton, W.T., Fox, J.G. and Whitfield, D. (Eds.) 1-14.

Christensen, J.M. (1958) Trends in human factors. Human Factors. 2, 2-7.

REFERENCES (contd.)

Conrad, R. (1951) Speed and load stress in a sensori-motor skill. British Journal of industr. Medicine, 8, 1-7.

Conrad, R. (1954) Missed signals in a sensory-motor skill. Journal of exp. Psychol., 48, 1-9.

Craik, K.J.W. (1947) Theory of the human operator in control systems: I the operator as an engineering system. Brit. J. Psychol., 38, 56-61.

Fitts, P.M. (1954) The information capacity of the human motor system in controlling the amplitude of movement. Journ. of exper. Psychol. 47, 381-391.

Fitts, P.M. (1964) Human motor learning. In: Categories of human learning. A.W. Melton Editor, Academic Press, New York.

Frowein, H.W. (1978) Effects of amphetamine and barbiturate in a serial RT-task under paced and selfpaced conditions. Submitted for publication.

Frowein, H.W. and Sanders, A.F. (1978) Effects of stimulus degradation, SR-compatibility and foreperiod duration on choice reaction time and movement time. Submitted for publication.

Gagne, R.M. (Ed) (1962) Psychological principles in system development. Holt, New York.

Garner, W.R. (1962) Uncertainty and structure as psychological concepts. Wiley, New York.

Geer, J.P. v.d. (1963) Data Presentation. In: Communication Processes. Geldard, F.A. (Ed), Pergamon London, 21-43.

Goerres, H.P. (1977) Subjective stress assessment as a criterion for measuring the psychophysical workload on pilots. Agard Conference preprint 217, B12.

Green, R. and Flux, R. (1977) Auditory communication and workload. Agard Conference preprint 216, A4.

Haider, M. (1971) Comparison of objective and subjective methods of the measurement of mental workload. In: Displays and Controls, R.K. Bernotat and K-P Gartner Eds. 17-27. Amsterdam, Swets and Zeitlinger.

Hick, W.E. (1952) On the rate of gain of information. Journal of exp. Psychol., 4, 11-26.

REFERENCES (contd.)

Hopkin, V.D. (1972) Measures in manual workload. In: Displays and controls. Bernotat, R.K. and Gärtner, K-P (Eds) 175-192. Amsterdam, Swets and Zeitlinger.

Jahns, D.W. (1973) A concept of operator workload in manual vehicle operations. Forschungsinstitut für Anthropotechnik, Report No. 14.

Kahneman, D. (1973) Attention and effort, Prentice Hall, N.J.

Kahneman, D. and Beatty, J. (1966) Pupil diameter and load on memory. Science, 154, 1583-1585.

Kalsbeek, J.W.H. (1967) Mentale belasting; Assen, van Gorkum.

Keele, S.W. (1973) Attention and Human Performance, Pacific Palisades, California.

Kelly, C.R. and Wargo, M.J. (1967) Cross adaptive operator loading tasks, Human Factors, 9, 395-404.

Kerr, B. (1975) Processing demands during movement. Journal of motor behavior, 7, 15-27.

Klinkhamer, H.A.W. (1965) Ergonomische controlelijst. Ned. Instituut voor preventieve Geneeskunde.

Knowles, W.B. (1963) Operator loading tasks. Human Factors, 5, 155-161.

Kornblum, S. (1969) Sequential determinants of information processing in serial and discrete choice reaction time. Psychological Review, 76, 113-132.

Kristofferson, A.B. (1967) Attention and psychophysical time. Acta Psychologica, 27, 93-100.

Lane, N.E., Wherry, R.J. and Streib, M. (1977): The Human Operator Simulator: Estimation of workload reserve using a simulated secondary task. Agard Conference preprint 216, A11.

Levison, W.H. (1969) A model for task interference. IEEE Conference Record No. 69C 58 - MMS. Vol.3.

Mackay, D.M. (1952) The nomenclature of information theory. In: Cybernetics, von Foerster, M. (Ed), New York.

REFERENCES (contd.)

Mackworth, N.H. (1957) Too busy or too bored. Proceedings of the 15th international congress of Psychology, North Holland, Amsterdam.

McLeod, P. (1977) A dual task response modality effect: support for multiprocessor models of attention.

McLeod, P. (1977) Does probe RT measure central processing demand? Paper to the experimental Psychology society, Sheffield, March, 1977.

Michon, J.A. (1966) Tapping regularity as a measure of perceptual motor load. Ergonomics, 9, 401-412.

Moraal, J. (1975) The analysis of an inspection task in the steel industry. In: Human Reliability in quality control, Drury, C.G. and Fox, J.G. (Eds), Taylor and Francis, London, 217-230.

Moray, N. (1967) Where is capacity limited? A survey and a model. Acta Psychologica, 27, 84-92.

Moray, N. (1975) A data base for theories of selective listening. In: Attention and Performance, V, Rabbitt, P.M.A. and Dornic, S. (Eds) Academic Press London, 119-134.

Noble, M. Trumbo, D.A. and Fowler, F.(1967) Further evidence of secondary task interference in tracking. Journal exper. Psychol. 73, 146-149.

Posner, M.I. and Klein, R.M. (1973) On the functions of consciousness. Attention and Performance IV, Kornblum, S. (Ed), Academic Press, New York, 21-37.

Poulton, E.C. (1970) Environment and human efficiency. Thomas, Springfield.

Rolfe, J.M. (1971) The secondary task as a measure of mental load. In: Measurement of man at work, Singleton, W.T., Fox, J.G. and Whitfield, D. (Eds) Taylor and Francis 135-148.

Ruyssenaars, N.J.M.G. (1977) Personal communication.

Sanders, A.F. (1977) Structural and functional aspects of the reaction process. In: Attention and Performance VI, Dornic, S (Ed). Erlbaum, 3-25.

REFERENCES (contd.)

Sanders, A.F. (1977) Experimental methods in human engineering. In: Introduction to human engineering, Kraiss, K-F and Moraal, J. Rheinland, Köln, 351-383.

Sanders, A.F. and Keuss, P.J.G. (1969) Grouping and refractoriness in multiple selective responses. Acta Psychologica, 30, 177-194.

Schneider, W. and Shiffrin, R.M. (1977): Controlled and automatic human information processing in detection, search and attention. Psychol. Review, 84, 1-66.

Shaffer, L.H. (1975) Multiple attention in continuous verbal tasks. In: Attention and Performance V; Rabbitt, P.M.A. and Dornic, S. (Eds). Academic Press London, 157-166.

Shiffrin, R.M. (1975) The locus and role of attention in memory systems. In: Attention and Performance V; Rabbitt, P.M.A. and Dornic, S. (Eds). Academic Press, London.

Siegel, A.I. and Wolf, J.J. (1961) A technique for evaluating man-machine system design. Human Factors, 1961, 2, 18-27.

Siegel, A.I. and Wolf, J.J. (1969) Man-Machine simulation models. Wiley New York.

Simon, J.R. and Wolf, J.D. (1963) Choice reaction time as a function of angular stimulus-response correspondence and age. Ergonomics, 6, 99-107.

Steininger, K. (1977) Subjective ratings of flying qualities and pilot workload in the operation of a short haul jet transport aircraft. Agard Conference preprint 217, B11.

Sternberg, S. (1969) The discovery of processing stages: Extensions of Donders' method. Acta Psychologica 30, 276-315.

Taylor, D.A. (1976) Stage analysis of reaction time. Psycholog. Bulletin, 83, 161-191.

Treisman, A.M. and Davies, A. (1973) Divided attention to ear and eye. In: Attention and Performance IV, Kornblum, S. (Ed). Academic Press, New York 101-118.

Triggs, T.J. (1968) Capacity sharing and speeded reactions to successive signals. Human Performance center report No. 9. Ann Arbor, Mich. USA.

REFERENCES (contd.)

Trumbo, D.A. and Noble, M.E. (1970) Secondary task effects on serial verbal learning. Journal of Exper. Psychol. 85, 418-424.

Trumbo, D.A. Noble, M.E. and Swink, J. (1967). Secondary Task interference in the performance of tracking tasks. Journ. of exp. Psychol. 73, 232-240.

Truijens, C.L., Trumbo, D.A. and Wagenaar, W.A. (1976) Amphetamine and barbiturate effects on two tasks performed singly and in combination. Acta Psychologica, 40, 233-244.

Wagenaar, W.A. and Stakenburg, H. (1975). Paced and selfpaced continuous reaction time. Quart. J. exp. Psychol. 27, 559-563.

Welford, A.T. (1967) Single channel operation in the brain. Acta Psychologica, 27, 5-22.

Weyer, G. and Hodapp, Y. (1975): Entwicklung von Fragebogenskalen zur Erfassung der subjektiven Belastung. Arch. Psychol., 3/4, 161-188.

Wilkinson, R.T. (1969) Some factors influencing the effect of environmental stressors upon performance. Psychological Bulletin, 72, 260-273.

Zipoy, D.R., Premselaar, S.J., Gargett, R.E., Balyea, I.L. and Hall, J.J. (1970) Integrated information presentation and control system study. Volume 1. System development concepts. Technical Report AFFDL-TR-70-79. Wright Patterson AFB.

MEASURES OF WORKLOAD, STRESS AND SECONDARY TASKS

Christopher D. Wickens

Department of Psychology, University of Illinois

Champaign-Urbana, Illinois, U.S.A.

1. HUMAN OPERATOR WORKLOAD AND STRESS

Workload

In the context of my approach, the concept of operator workload is defined in terms of the human's limited processing resources. Operator workload scales monotonically with the extent to which the tasks performed by the operator utilize these limited resources. Since workload is defined in terms of the hypothetical construct of "processing resources", some operational definition must be provided of the latter term. This definition is provided in terms of secondary task performance.

It is asserted that: (1) processing resources are demanded by a task to the extent that the performance of a second, independent task performed concurrently deteriorates from its single task level; (2) changes in the objective characteristics of a task will vary the processing resources demanded by its performance at a constant level, to the extent that secondary task performance varies concomitantly. In either instance therefore, the manipulation of adding the primary task or of changing its characteristics will be described as increasing operator workload to the extent that secondary task performance deteriorates.

The general schema proposed above is associated with the concept of undifferentiated capacity (Moray, 1967; Kahneman, 1973; Norman & Bobrow, 1975). That is, the concept of a general pool of processing resources available to all tasks and allocated to each according to its difficulty and demanded level of performance.

As the objective difficulty of one task is increased, requiring allocation of more processing resources to maintain constant performance, fewer resources are available to process any secondary task and therefore its performance will invariably deteriorate.

There are, however, clearly instances in which manipulation of the objective characteristics of a primary task will produce changes in the performance of one secondary task, but not of another, even as primary task performance is held constant across all difficulty levels of both secondary tasks. These instances are normally those in which the manipulation of difficulty is associated with a particular processing structure or stage of information processing, different from that which is heavily utilized in the processing of the secondary task. Examples of this "difficulty insensitivity" phenomenon are provided by the research of North (1977), who found that varying the complexity of a discrete digit processing task failed to change the extent of interference with a concurrent analog tracking task. Wickens and Kessel (1977) observed that increasing the difficulty of a critical instability tracking task (Jex, 1977) did not affect the performance of subjects in detecting system failures on a separate time-shared tracking task. Wickens, Israel and Donchin (1977) found that increasing tracking task complexity (from 1 to 2 dimensions) failed to attenuate the amplitude of evoked cortical potentials elicited by a concurrent auditory information processing task. In all of these studies, the manipulation of task difficulty had previously been validated as one that produced differing levels of interference with other secondary tasks.

A second phenomenon, difficult for undifferentiated capacity theories to account for, are the numerous instances in which a simple change in processing structure (e.g. modality of input, or response mechanism) may dramatically alter the degree of task interference, despite the approximate equivalence, before and after the change, of the information processing demands (task difficulty) of the single task components (Triesman & Davies, 1972; Brooks, 1968; Knight & Kantowitz, 1976).

These two phenomena, difficulty insensitivity and structural change, seemingly require that the concept of processing resources be elaborated to account for what will be referred to as structure specific resources - a concept closely associated to the ideas of Kantowitz & Knight (1976). Under this conception, resources that are associated with a particular processing structure or mode of processing (e.g., perceptual, response, memory, analog, semantic), are available in restricted quantity to tasks sharing those particular structures, but not (or to a lesser extent) to tasks requiring exclusively different structures.

This implies that any given secondary task performance measure will not be universally sensitive to all objective manipulations of primary task difficulty. Certain secondary tasks (or task performance measures), those dependent upon perceptual resources for example, will reflect manipulations of perceptual loading in the primary task, but not of response loading, while other secondary tasks might show the converse relation.

A critical challenge presented to the researchers in the area of workload measurement is to identify the meaningful distinctions between different structures. Instead of initiating what appears to be a fruitless search for a single ubiquitous secondary task or workload measure sensitive to all dimensions of primary task workload, the goal of workload research should be instead to identify the minimum set of processing structures within which the concept of structure-specific resources is meaningful. An associated challenge is to identify and catalog the particular tasks or measures maximally sensitive to each structural resource. Thus a given task configuration may be accurately categorized, for example according to its perceptual load, memory load, and response load as indexed by perceptual, memory and response sensitive secondary tasks.

The rationale behind this non-parsimonious (and some might argue unwarranted) complexification is twofold. First, there does appear to be evidence that structural factors play a very strong role in predicting interference between tasks, and therefore that a pure undifferentiated capacity viewpoint is inadequate (Kantowitz & Knight, 1976; Roedinger, Knight & Kantowitz, 1977; North, 1977; Wickens, 1976). Additionally, and perhaps more directly to the point, is the assertion that an important reason for collecting data (either on-line or off-line) regarding structure-specific task loading is to enable a prediction of the operator's ability to perform other tasks concurrently that also have structural specificity. It is potentially valuable to know for example that at a particular instant in time, an operator's task demands are heavily response loaded. Therefore he may be unable to initiate an additional manual action, but at the same time his perceptual demands may be relatively minimal, so that it is realistic to expect him to continue to perform in a monitoring function. The information provided by a general undifferentiated capacity measure of workload would be unsatisfactory for this purpose.

In summary, the concept of task workload - in the context of my research - is ultimately provided meaning in terms of the ability to perform <u>concurrent</u> tasks that are either required, or might potentially be required. Therefore the ability to perform such concurrent tasks must be predicted. These concurrent tasks may be characterised and in fact defined in terms of their processing demands within processing structures.

Stress

Whereas considerations of workload here are associated with secondary task performance, the concept of stress on the other hand is not intrinsically related to the multiple task environment. In relation to dual task performance, stress will normally increase with the imposition of additional tasks, and with increases in their workload. Objective changes in task difficulty, however, need not reduce performance, even as they may produce higher levels of stress. The absence of effect can result from the well known ability of the operator to compensate for increased demand by increased mobilization of resources in order to maintain constant performance (Kahneman, 1973). Presumably however a penalty is ultimately paid for this compensatory mobilization. This is measurable in terms of physiological changes, either immediate or long term, or long term performance changes (e.g., Poulton, 1965). In such cases the penalty provides the operational definition of stress induced by the high workload situation. This relation is depicted in Figure 1.

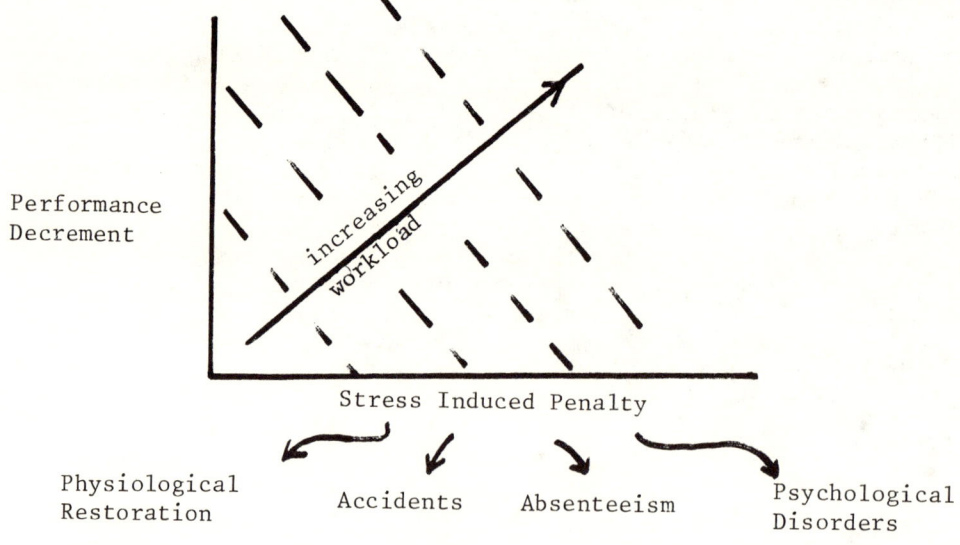

Figure 1

2. PURPOSE OF WORKLOAD MEASURES

Information concerning task workload is viewed as equally important in two quite different contexts: that of off-line measurement, of use to the system designer, and that of on-line assessment for use in adaptive computer aided man-machine systems. The procedures and requirements of the workload measure in the two contexts however are quite different. For the system designer, concerned that the choice of a particular system component is dictated by the criterion of minimizing the workload imposed by its use, knowledge of structure specific workload may be utilized to construct a task environment that does not simultaneously overload the limits of particular processing structures.

The on-line use of workload measures in many respects presents a considerably greater challenge to the engineering psychologist because of the unique constraints that it imposes upon whatever measure is deployed. In the on-line adaptive context, it may be asserted that an intelligent computer-based adaptive system, in order to optimally deploy the resources of human and computer, should be provided with a real-time, updatable estimate or model of the state (availability and allocation) of the operator's attentional resources, so that adaptive procedures may be initiated. The characteristics of this state estimate and their potential use to the adaptive decision maker are as follows.

(1) The available resources must be sufficient to meet the demands imposed by all tasks which challenge the operator at any time: the characteristic of task workload or reserve capacity. If the momentary workload demands become sufficiently great, adaptive aiding procedures can be implemented to temporarily unburden the human operator. These may take the form of initiating alternate strategies of computer processing or information display, implementing automatic control systems, or of calling for extra manual assistance where such is available.

(2) Even if the resources are adequate, the attention must be allocated _properly_ to the critical tasks, displays or sources of information, so that important sources are not ignored: the characteristic of attention allocation. The distinction between workload and allocation is crucial. It is self-evident that adequate capacity inadequately deployed may lead to non-optimal performance. Thus if resources are allocated incorrectly along channels of incoming information, or if critical sources of information are being ignored, warning or cueing signals might be provided to redirect the proper distribution of attention as determined by some preset establishment of priorities. Alternatively, system characteristics might be altered using derived knowledge of the distribution of operator attention. For

example, computer resources might be allocated to monitor for, or process signals along information channels that are inferred to be non-attended.

There is an additional potential benefit of an on-line estimate of the status of the operator's processing resources that is present in complex man-machine systems in which two or more operators, not in visual proximity to each other are required to coordinate their actions. Weiner (1977) has graphically depicted such a relationship inherent in the Air Traffic Controller-Pilot-Aircraft system. The reader of Weiner's article may easily envisage instances in which an action that might have prevented a fatal accident was withheld because the ground controller did not have an objective estimate of momentary pilot workload and of the deployment of the pilot's attentional resources - that is to which aspects of the display/warning/ control configuration he was attending and to which he was not.

The utilization of workload measures in an on-line context imposes two unique constraints upon whatever measure is deployed that are not shared by its off-line employment. These constraints relate to the obtrusiveness of the workload assessment tool itself, and to the frequency response of the measure, to variation in operator processing resources.

Obtrusiveness of Assessment Task

When employing traditional secondary tasks as workload measures, performance of the secondary task is assumed by its very nature to "absorb" any spare capacity or residual attention, even when it does not disrupt performance of the primary task. For an off-line evaluation or comparison of system workload demands, this may be desirable. However, for use in an on-line adaptive loop, such a characteristic is unacceptable. The operator cannot afford to have the attention assessment tool saturate the very resources that it was incorporated ultimately to ensure; that is, to absorb the margin of reserve capacity presumed essential for safe performance. Thus a criterion of the measure is that it should be relatively "unobtrusive", requiring the operator to invest only minimal processing resources in order to extract reliable information.

Frequency Response of Measure

Assuming that the moment to moment fluctuations in operator resources are real, and are to be detected by an on-line workload measure, an effective measure must be sensitive to these fluctuations to the extent that it can provide estimates of resources available at a relatively high signal to noise ratio. This requirement is imposed because the limited time available to obtain a workload estimate, dictated by the need for relatively high frequency resolution in effective adaptive systems, prohibits the normal off-line procedure of aggregating sufficient data over time so that random noise sources will cancel.

In summary, the constraints imposed by an on-line workload measure for adaptive environments are that such a measure should be: (1) informative in the sense of providing structure specific information, (2) relatively non-obtrusive, (3) one whose reliability following short time estimates is either high, or rapidly increasing.

3. OPTIMAL MEASURES: WHAT AND WHY

The criteria of an effective on-line measure outlined in the preceding section appear to preclude many traditional secondary task workload measures as effective tools for generating data to update a model of the attentional state. The starting point argued here will not be the identification of a single workload measure, but rather a consideration of the multiple sources of information that can most effectively update such a model. The limitation imposed by the frequency response criterion argues that rather than integrating or averaging a single measure over time, multiple measures should be combined at a single instant in time. This approach exploits the fact that the workload-sensitive "signals" in these measures will be perturbed by partially uncorrelated noise sources. The random error in the combined workload signal of all sources will therefore converge to zero as their number increases.

The limitation imposed by the non-obtrusiveness criterion reduces the effectiveness of many tasks that are normally employed to index residual attention as an inverse measure of workload (e.g., Michon's (1965) Tapping measure or the "Critical" tracking task (Jex, 1967)). Although relatively unobtrusive measures of physiological indices are available, and will be discussed below, it is proposed here that considerable information can also be gained by assessing not only the amount of resources not deployed (residual attention), but also where resources are deployed along relevant channels. For example in a complex cockpit environment it may be possible to establish the extent of resource allocation to axes of control from open loop gain measures (Wickens and Gopher, 1977) to establish the allocation of resources to discrete signals in the environment from response latencies or evoked potentials to those signals.

From the perspective of this goal, the following measures appear to meet the criteria imposed:

1. <u>Time Estimation</u>. Subjective estimates of the passage of time during performance of different tasks have been found to correlate with the workload demands of these tasks (Hart, 1976; Hicks, 1976). This measure is clearly unobtrusive since no stimuli are processed nor responses required during performance. However, the extent and direction of the workload relation has not been clearly established, and because the estimate is not made until after a duration of task performance, the measure is not entirely "on-line".

2. <u>Probe Reaction Time to Unexpected Stimuli</u>. Depending upon the frequency of delivery of the probes, this measure may, or may not be obtrusive on primary task performance. However its validity as a workload measure is clearly established in heavy demand situations (see the work of Posner, Keele and their colleagues). A potential drawback of this measure is that it appears to draw heavily upon response-structural resources and thus may be less sensitive to other structural loadings. Its reliability of course is directly related to the frequency of probes which in turn, directly affects the obtrusiveness of the measure.

3. <u>Physiological Indices</u>. All physiological indices appear to meet the criterion of non-obtrusiveness, since overt responses are not generally required. However, the frequency response, validity and structural specificity of some of these measures may potentially be called into question. In one experimental context or another, all of the following measures have shown some correlation with task workload:

(1) EKG (beats per minute)(Sem-Jacobsen, 1977)

(2) Sinus arrhythmia suppression (Kalsbeek & Sykes, 1967)

(3) Pupil diameter (Beatty, 1976)

(4) Evoked cortical potentials (Lafayelle, Dinand & Gentil, 1971; Wickens, Isreal, McCarthy, Donchin & Gopher, 1976)

In the Cognitive Psychology Laboratory at the University of Illinois, we have been engaged in a research program to validate the Evoked Cortical Potential (a transient voltage response to discrete environmental events recorded by scalp electrodes) as a workload measurement index.[1] In brief our technique is to "probe" the operator periodically with discrete auditory or visual stimuli, requiring at most a covert response to those stimuli (e.g., counting them). Workload inferences are then based upon the amplitude of the elicited EP response (Wickens et al., 1976, 1977). The Evoked Potential has 3 distinct advantages over other physiological measures. (1) It represents the direct reflection of the information processing activities of the subject, rather than an index of autonomic activity which may often be influenced by factors other than workload. (2) It is a multivariate measure, characterized by different latency peaks, and different responses across scalp location, and therefore provides a greater amount of potential information per a single observation. (3) Because it is elicited by discrete events in the environment, a greater specificity of information can be obtained. For example, to the extent that visual and auditory modalities represent different structural resource pools, information can potentially be gained concerning visual vs. auditory workload by observing the attenuation of the EP elicited by visual vs. auditory probes respectively. On a more general level, to the extent that EP amplitude is determined by resources at the perceptual and decision making stages of processing, the EP may represent a workload measure that is relatively less contaminated by response structural factors (Wickens et al. 1977). This is a characteristic that is clearly not shared by secondary task measures which, by their nature entail the performance of overt responses.

4. <u>Allocation of Resources</u>. In an environment in which the operator must make overt responses to different sources of relevant stimulus information, the allocation of attention to these sources may be inferred by measures of response latency or accuracy if the responses are discrete, or by tracking parameters such as open loop gain or remnant (Wickens & Gopher 1977) if the responses are analog or continuous in nature. The only constraint imposed in this situation is that the workload measurement computation system must have available precise information concerning the spatial-temporal properties of the stimuli themselves, so that the relation between these stimuli and the response measures can be determined.

In a passive monitoring environment, when overt responses are not required, measurement of the allocation of attention becomes more difficult. Eye fixation assessment represents one possible solution, but this becomes difficult in environments in which the operator has considerable freedom to move about. A potential solution to allocation measurement in the passive environment is provided by exploiting a unique property of the evoked potential. It is precisely time-locked to discrete events in the environment, enabling the eliciting event to be unambiguously associated with the recorded EP. One aspect of our research at the University of Illinois has investigated the extent to which the EPs elicited by events in a multi-element visual display can be employed to make inferences concerning the particular items of the display that are or are not attended. The display used simulates an air traffic controller's terminal in which symbols traverse across on linear paths, occasionally undergoing changes in course. Results suggest that, as long as the eliciting events are designated a priori as relevant to the observer, analysis of the EP waveforms can produce a highly successful classification of those EPs elicited by events that were attended, and those that were not. (Heffley, Wickens and Donchin, 1977).

5. <u>Shortcomings</u>. Many of the shortcomings of the measures have been indicated in the preceding section. However, they will be briefly reiterated here:

<u>Secondary task measures</u>: (1) obtrusiveness, (2) primary sensitivity to response loading.

<u>Time-estimation</u>: (1) uncertain validity, (2) not truly an on-line measure, (3) only one data point per estimated time interval.

<u>Probe reaction time</u>: potential obtrusiveness with increasing probe frequency.

<u>EKG, Sinus Arythmia</u>: (1) influenced by non-workload variables, questionable reliability, (2) not structure specific.

<u>Pupil diameter</u>: (1) difficult measurement problem for operator in mobile environment (2) also sensitive to other sources, (3) not structure specific.

<u>Evoked potentials</u>: (1) low signal to noise ratio of single trial EP's requires fairly extensive filtering and application of discriminant analysis to obtain reliable single trial estimates (computer power), (2) may be contaminated by motor artifacts, (3) current research still indicates that reliable estimates require subject to covertly count stimuli. This is slightly obtrusive.

6. <u>Measures and Models</u>.

(i) <u>a priori measures</u>. A priori measures such as the Information metric can provide a valuable service by quantifying objective or experimenter-defined levels of task workload as when one creates 1 bit, 2 bit and 3 bit levels of a decision making task (e.g. Briggs, Peters & Fisher, 1972). There is a danger however in believing too strongly in the effectiveness of an a priori manipulation of primary task loading, without a careful consideration of its effect on primary task performance. As a specific example consider an investigation of the effects of tracking load - as defined a priori by forcing function bandwidth - upon secondary task performance. Such a measure has a high a priori validity as a workload manipulating variable: higher bandwidths generate a greater rate of stimulus information. However, if increasing primary task error is obtained with increasing bandwidth, caution must be exercised in generalizing to the effects on secondary task measures. Secondary task performance should not be evaluated only as a function of the a priori difficulty level, but rather as a joint function of this variable and of primary task performance. In the example cited above, a continuous information transmission rate (Baty, 1972) would be appropriate. However, other manipulations of task load are not quite as tractable for combining the difficulty-performance tradeoff into a single metric (e.g. stimulus-response coding rules, stimulus intensity, tracking system stability).

(ii) <u>empirical measures</u>   These represent the core of workload assessment research, as it is only through them that meaningful assertions can be made concerning the efficacy of a priori measures.

(iii) <u>systems and models</u>   Models of performance, particularly normative models such as signal detection theory, optimal control, or Bayesian decision making, play a critical role in workload measurement by specifying precise dimensions of performance, and thereby dimensions along which performance under workload may depart from a model-defined optimal level. These models then provide a higher powered microscope for examining performance change under workload and, accordingly for implementing appropriate counteractive measures to compensate for such changes (Wickens & Gopher, 1977). Thus for example a computer aided decision system, provided with knowledge that the operator's decision criterion becomes increasingly conservative under workload could implement a compensatory counterbias. Similarly compensatory gain changes might be implemented to compensate for workload related gain attenuation in manual control tasks; or procedures initiated to insure a return to an optimal sampling strategy if this is abandoned under task workload in a display scanning task.

In short, knowledge that "performance deteriorates" with increasing workload is not necessarily sufficient to initiate adaptive or corrective procedures. The understanding of <u>how</u> it deteriorates, gained by placing this performance in the context of a normative model, demonstrates greater promise towards fulfilling this requirement.

7. <u>Boundary Conditions</u>. Boundary conditions of a workload measure are here defined in terms of: (a) the range of processing workload (concurrent mental activity) and, (b) the range of

physical activities, over which it continues to be a reliable index.

Range of workload. When phrased in terms of Norman & Bobrow's (1975) distinction between data limited and resource limited processes, the first boundary condition may be reformulated by asking over what range of concurrent task demands a particular measure is resource limited, such that the measure varies monotonically with the resources allocated ot it.

With regard to the evoked potential measure, precise determination of this boundary condition awaits empirical validation. A study by Lafayelle, Dinand and Gentil (1971), in which EP amplitude was used to assess the workload demands of a concurrent cognitive reasoning task suggests that the measure only differentiated between the control condition (no concurrent task) and the easiest reasoning task, while failing to reflect changes at higher levels.

The research in our laboratory has also indicated that the EP elicited by counted auditory probe stimuli are most sensitive to workload differences at lower levels (here operationally defined in a one dimensional visual tracking task as variation of the band-limited forcing function cutoff between 0 and 0.4 Hz). Sensitivity appears to be somewhat reduced, but still present, at the higher workload levels between one and two dimensional tracking. Although the measure appears to be most sensitive at the lower levels of our experimental manipulations, it should be noted that the highest levels employed (2 dimensional tracking of independent Gaussian noise inputs with a 0.4 Hz cutoff using second order undamped dynamics) produce a level of demand far exceeding that which normally typifies the control task of the airplane pilot. Furthermore, recent research indicates that when visual probes are employed, the EP may be relatively less sensitive at low levels and more sensitive at high levels of the visual tracking task.

Concerning our assessments of attention allocation in a visual display, we have found that the EP continues to provide reliable estimates at what can be considered as high levels of display load: monitoring for events on any of 5 channels of a 10 element display. One further point should be noted in conclusion. To the extent that the EP measure is employed to predict an operator's ability to process additional external signals, the range of usefulness of the measure should accurately reflect the range of this ability. This is true because the EP itself is generated by the same signal processing that it is designed to predict.

Range of Physical Activity. As noted above, a potential source of difficulty with the E.P. lies in its contamination by other scalp-localized electrical artifacts. Prominent among these are muscular artifacts, particularly those from the eyes, articulatory mechanisms and neck. Efforts are presently under way to overcome these artifacts by developing appropriate filtering and subtractive techniques, to produce an uncontaminated estimate of the true cortical generated "signal". A second limitation is obviously imposed by the presence of the scalp electrodes and the restrictions of the physical links from these electrodes to the analyzing computer. Because the amplitudes of the E.P. signals themselves are small, unless pre-amplifiers are employed the communications link between electrode and computer should be relatively short and noise-free. This constraint partially limits the operator's freedom to "move around" in the recording environment.

These physical limitations suggest that the E.P. measure is optimal in an environment in which the operator is seated in front of a display-control unit, and in which his primary communication is with the machine interface, rather than vocally with other operators. It is, nevertheless, important to bear in mind that many of these physical limitations are not inherent in the measure itself, but rather in the measurement technique - and thereby await technological developments to be overcome. While the problems in these developments cannot be underestimated, their feasibility is greatly increased by the rapid developments in micro-computer technology.

8. Questions to be Answered: The following pages present a very ambitious request!

a) Theoretical/Empirical Questions

i. Structure-specific resources. What is the utility of the distinction drawn between undifferentiated capacity and structure-specific resources, in section 1 of this paper? Is the distinction meaningful in terms of experimental data on time-sharing abilities? If it is, are the consequences of the presence of structure-specific resources sufficiently important, in terms of their implications for workload measurement, that an attempt should be undertaken to define these structure-specific resources and to identify tasks that are maximally sensitive to these resources.

ii. Macro and Micro tradeoffs in resource allocation. Pachella (1974) has distinguished between macro and micro speed accuracy tradeoffs in reaction time. The macro tradeoff refers to the tendency for S's to respond less accurately in conditions of speed stress, and more slowly in conditions of accuracy stress. Thus the macro tradeoff between conditions appears almost universally to be a negative correlation between speed and accuracy. The micro tradeoff refers to variations in accuracy and speed <u>within</u> an experimental condition: the extent to which error responses are faster, or slower than correct responses. Here the correlation is <u>not</u> invariably a negative one, but may vary from negative to zero to positive depending upon the nature of the task.

An analogous representation can be made of data in a dual task framework. When the workload demand of (or resources allocated to) a primary task is varied between sessions, performance on that task almost invariably shows a negative correlation with secondary task performance - a negative macro tradeoff (Wickens & Gopher, 1977; Norman & Bobrow, 1975). Such between-session variation may be conceptualized as reflecting a subject's "set" for allocation of processing resources to one task vs. the other. However, as the resource demands of (or resources supplied to) a primary task fluctuate <u>within</u> the ongoing stream of performance, it is not as clear that the correlation between primary and secondary task performance will be a negative one. For example, momentary fluctuations in overall arousal, or an ability to integrate performance of the two tasks into a single processing strategy might result in a positive correlation, or at least in the absence of a negative one (Wickens, 1974).

The implication of positive vs. negative micro tradeoffs is important for on-line measures of task workload. It is necessary to consider for example whether a drop in secondary task performance, which in the macro tradeoff indicates either improved primary task performance or more difficult primary task demands, in fact has the same interpretation in an on-line context, or whether it might instead indicate deteriorating performance on <u>both</u> tasks. Similarly, careful consideration should be made of whether the indices of performance that most accurately reflect macro tradeoffs are also those that reflect micro tradeoffs. In manual tracking, for example, Wickens & Gopher (1977) citing their own data and data of Enstrom and Rouse (1976) argue that tracking gain might be an equally sensitive index of resource allocation in both a macro and micro tradeoff, but that tracking error is only a valid index in the former condition.

iii. The dimensions of performance. Considerations of task workload and attention are inexorably linked with those of performance measurement. It is therefore essential to consider how the dimensions of performance may be identified using normative models (see Section 7) and how these vary with workload. Secondly, it is important to determine the implications of dimensional scaling upon workload measurement. Questions such as the following should be addressed: Is the scale underlying a particular performance measure an interval scale or a ratio scale? Is a 1 unit change in secondary task performance at a high level characteristic of low primary task workloads, psychologically equivalent to a 1 unit change at a low level, when primary task load is great? To what extent should performance measures be those that have a "natural" physical basis (e.g. time)? How robust are conclusions drawn from workload comparison across different secondary tasks, or across different levels of a given task, to changes in the underlying scale (i.e. ratio vs. interval scales, linear vs. log transforms)? Should single and dual task performances be compared by proportion or difference measures? Should performance be scaled by individual variability units following Fechnerian psychophysical assumptions? (ie. that equal units of performance variability correspond to equal subjective units of effort, Wickens & Gopher, 1977). Consideration of these issues clearly opens a Pandora's Box of problems and complexities - many of which are potentially beyond the scope of the current workshop. An appropriate goal therefore should probably not be for resolution of these issues, but rather for identification of those that are of greatest importance in influencing the conclusions drawn concerning workload assessment.

iv. Practice and learning. The traditional employment of secondary task techniques implicitly assumes a relative stability of the performance-resource function over time (following an initial period of skill acquisition). However, Neisser (1977) emphasizing points made previously by Moray (1974, 1976) and by Norman and Bobrow (1975) argues vehemently that time-sharing is a "skill" and therefore that dual task performance is subject to the same laws and trends of skill learning as single task performance, with automation as an eventual endpoint. While the thrust of this argument is not held in question, my view is that it is nevertheless reasonable to consider capacity as limited - within a given "slice", or range of practice. An important question to be answered concerns the "width" of this slice, or the duration of practice during which secondary task measures continue to provide a constant estimate of available resources. Although beyond the domain of the conference, the issue of training and transfer of time-sharing skills (Damos & Wickens, 1977) is one that has many important implications.

v. <u>Individual differences</u>. Evidence is emerging that a substantial component of between-subject variance in dual task performance cannot be attributed to single task proficiency. (Gopher & Kahneman, 1971; North & Gopher, 1976). There are in other words relatively large differences between subjects in time-sharing abilities. Whether these represent differences in the amount of available capacity, the ability to switch or re-allocate resources between tasks, or in the level of development of a time sharing skill is far from clear. Nevertheless, the implications of these individual differences is that particular workload measures might have to be "calibrated" for different operators, particularly as applied in an on-line context where group data cannot be pooled. At the same time these individual differences might actually be exploited to enhance system performance by employing them to provide guidelines for assigning operators to specific systems, or by modifying systems to the limitations and strengths of individual operators (Pew, 1970).

b) Methodological Questions

i. <u>Evaluation of workload measures</u>. What criteria should be used to evaluate workload measures and to separate good ones from bad ones? If a particular workload measurement tool is insensitive to a manipulation of primary task difficulty, how does one determine which of the following factors are responsible: (a) the manipulation was a poor one and/or primary task performance was not controlled; (b) the workload measure was faulty or was data-limited in the range of manipulations employed; (c) there was a mis-match between processing structures involved in the primary task manipulation and those involved in the assessment tool.

This issue is in many respects closely related to that described in item a) iii. above (dimensions of performance), since the meaningfulness of performance changes in a workload measure should be provided with some converging validity by correlating these changes with any or all of the following: a priori measures of primary task workload, subjective estimates of primary task difficulty, or similar variations in other secondary tasks whose validity is established.

ii. Closing an adaptive feedback loop. This methodological issue relates exclusively to workload assessment techniques in closed loop systems. The specific question to be answered is: for a given system, provided that one has a reliable estimate of the state of the operator's processing resources, what adaptive decisions can be made, or actions taken on the basis of this knowledge. At a more general level, however, other issues are raised in considering adaptive systems. For example, the fact that this system now contains a closed loop demands a careful consideration of the implications of the feedback loop on system performance. What is the likelihood that instability of operator performance will result from "overapplying" any adaptive changes thereby creating a high gain system? What are the implications of the time-delay inherent in extracting a reliable workload measure? What are the implications of the fact that the workload "signal" communicated to the computer is stochastic rather than deterministic and how sensitive are the feedback properties of the closed loop system to the reliability of the estimate? What kinds of non-linearities - thresholds and limiters - should be built into the adaptive algorithm to ensure stable performance in light of time delays and stochastic data? Finally what represents an appropriate control, non-adaptive system against which to compare adaptive system performance? Should this control be one that functions with maximum aiding or minimum, or an intermediate level? Should it perform under best-case or worse-case environments? The latter refer to those conditions that are not typical of real world operations, occurring only very infrequently, but with potentially disastrous consequences? What performance index should be used to evaluate and compare such systems?

As a specific hypothetical example, consider the following: An adaptive multi-loop control system is developed which will shift an axis to automatic autopilot control, when concurrent task workload is inferred to excede some criterion. A tracking performance index of this system can clearly be measured. However, against what should it be compared? The performance of a maximum-aiding (all auto-pilot) system - to which it will almost inevitably be inferior, or to that of a minimum-aiding (all manual) system to which it will probably be superior. To complicate matters, this superiority relationship might be reversed, by introducing "worse-case" environments: e.g. levels of disturbance which the autopilot is incapable of handling, or autopilot or system failures which, it has been argued, are less easily detected under autopilot than in-the-loop situations (Young, 1969). Under these circumstances, what arbitrary costs should be assigned to latencies in failure detection, as opposed to errors in tracking performance, when deriving an ultimate performance index? These again, are questions whose answers may lie beyond the scope of the conference, but which inevitably arise when adaptive uses of workload measures are considered.

Footnote

[1] The research concerning the evoked potential at the Cognitive Psychobiology Laboratory has been carried out in conjunction with Professor Emanuel Donchin, Professor Danny Gopher, Jack Isreal, Greg McCarth, Greg Chesney and a number of other graduate students in the Department of Psychology. The ideas and analytic techniques contained in this paper represent the output of this team research effort, and reflect the valuable contributions of all concerned.

REFERENCES

Baty, D.L. Human transinformation rates during one-to-four axis tracking. Proceedings 7th Annual Conference on Manual Control. NASA, SP-281. Washington, D.C.: U.S. Government Printing Office, 1972.

Beatty, J. Pupilometric measurement of cognitive workload in complex man/machine systems. Proceedings 12th Annual Conference on Manual Control. Urbana, Illinois, May 1976.

Briggs, G., Peters, G., and Fisher, R.P. On the laws of the divided attention effects. Perception and Psychophysics, 1972, 11, 315-320.

Damos, D. and Wickens, C.D. A quasi-linear control theory analysis of time-sharing skills. Proceedings 13th Annual NASA Conference on Manual Control. M.I.T. Cambridge, Mass., 1977.

Enstrom, K.D. and Rouse, W.B. Telling a computer how a human has allocated his attention between control and monitoring tasks. Proceedings 12th Annual Conference on Manual Control. Urbana, Illinois, May 1976.

Gopher, D. and Kahneman, D. Individual differences in attention and the prediction of flight criteria. Perceptual and Motor Skills, 1971, 33, 1335-1342.

Hart, Sondra. Time estimation as a secondary task to measure workload. Proceedings 11th Annual Conference on Manual Control, NASA TMX 62, 464, Moffett Field, California, 1975.

Heffley, E., Wickens, C. & Donchin, E. Intra modality selective attention and the P-300 - a reexamination in a visual monitoring task. Paper presented at Society for Psycho-Physiological Research, Philadelphia, Nov. 1977.

Hicks, R.H. Attention and prospective judgments of temporal duration. Paper presented at 17th Annual Meeting, The Psychonomics Society, St. Louis, 1976.

Jex, H. Two applications of a critical-instability task to secondary workload research. IEEE Transactions on Human Factors in Electronics, 1967, HFE-8, 279-282.

Kahneman, D. Attention and Effort. New York: Prentice-Hall, 1973.

Kalsbeek, J.W. and Sykes, R.N. Objective measurements of mental load. In Sanders (Ed.), Attention and Performance I. Amsterdam: North Holland Publishing Co., 1967.

Kantowitz, B.H. and Knight, J.L. Testing tapping time sharing: II. Auditory Secondary Task. Acta Psychologica, 1976, 40, 343-362.

Kantowitz, B.H. and Knight, J. On experimenter limited processes. Psychological Review, 1976, 83, 502-507.

LaFayelle, Dinand, and Gentil. Average evoked potentials in relation to attitude, mental load, and intelligence. In W.T. Singleton, R.S. Easterby, and D.E. Whitfield (Eds.), Measurement of Man at Work. London: Taylor and Francis, 1971.

Michon, J.A. Tapping regularity as a measure of perceptual motor load. Ergonomics, 9, 401-412.

Moray, N. Where is capacity limited? A survey and a model. Acta Psychologica, 1967, 27, 84-92.

Moray, N. and Fitter, M. A theory and measurement of attention. In Kornblum, S. (Ed.), <u>Attention and Performance IV</u>. New York: Academic Press, 1974.

Moray, N. Attention, control and sampling behavior. In Sheridan and Johanssen (Eds.), <u>Monitoring and Supervisory Control</u>. New York: Plenum Press, 1976.

Neisser, U. <u>Cognition and Reality</u>. San Francisco: Freeman, 1977.

Norman, D. and Bobrow, D. On data-limited and resource limited processes. <u>Cognitive Psychology</u>, 1975, 7, 44-64.

North, R. Task Functional Demands as Factors in Dual Task Performance. <u>Proceedings, 21st Annual Meeting, Human Factors Society</u>. San Francisco, October 1977.

North, R. and Gopher, D. Measures of attention as predictors of flight performance. <u>Human Factors</u>, 1976, <u>18</u>, 1-14.

Pachella, R. The interpretation of reaction time in information processing research. In Kantowitz, B.H. (Ed.), <u>Human Information Processing</u>. Hillsdale, N.J.: Lawrence Erlbaum, 1974.

Pew, R.W. Comments on "Promotion of Man": Challenges in Sociotechnical systems: Design for the individual operator. <u>Global Systems Dynamics Intl. Symposium</u>. Charlottesville, N.C., 1969, pp.59-65.

Poulton, E.C. On increasing the sensitivity of measures of performance. <u>Ergonomics</u>, 1965, <u>8</u>, 69-76.

Roediger, H., Knight, J. and Kantowitz, B. Inferring decay in short-term memory: The issue of capacity. <u>Memory and Cognition</u>, 1977, <u>5</u>, 167-176.

Sem-Jacobsen, C.W. EKG monitoring of heart failure and pilot load/overload by the Vesla seatpad. <u>Aviation, Space and Environmental Medicine</u>, 1977, in press.

Wickens, C.D. The effect of time-sharing on the performance of information processing tasks. (Technical Report No. 51) Ann Arbor: <u>University of Michigan Human Performance Center</u>, August 1974.

Wickens, C.D. The effects of divided attention on information processing in manual tracking. <u>Journal of Experimental Psychology; Human Perception and Performance</u>. 1976, <u>2</u>, pp. 1-17.

Wickens, C.D. and Gopher, D. Control theory measures of tracking as indices of attention allocation strategies. *Human Factors*, 1977, *19*, 349-365.

Wickens, C., Israel, J., McCarthy, G., Gopher, D., and Donchin, E. The use of event related potentials in the enhancement of man-machine system performance. *Proceedings 12th Annual Conference on Manual Control*. Urbana, Illinois, May 1976.

Wickens, C.D., Israel, J., & Donchin, E. The event-related cortical potential as an index of task workload in adaptive man-machine systems. *Proceedings Meeting of the Human Factors Society*, San Francisco, October, 1977.

Wickens, C.D. & Kessel, C. The effect of participatory mode and task workload on the detection of dynamic system failures. *Proceedings of the 13th Annual Conference on Manual Control*. U.S. Government Printing Office,

Wiener, E.L. Controlled flight into terrain accidents: System-induced errors. *Human Factors*, 1977, *19*, 171-182.

Young, C.R. On adaptive manual control. *IEEE Trans. on Man-Machine Systems*, 1969, MMS-10, 292-351.

FINAL REPORT OF EXPERIMENTAL PSYCHOLOGY GROUP

G. Johanssen, N. Moray (Chairman), R. Pew, J. Rasmussen,

A. Sanders, C. Wickens

The origin of the concept of "mental workload" is in the ordinary everyday experience of human beings who perform tasks which are not necessarily physically demanding but which are experienced nonetheless as exhausting and stressful. The concept reflects a genuine dimension or dimensions of human experience in daily work, including - perhaps especially - modern automatic and semi-automatic man-machine systems. As such it is a concept absolutely required for the adequate analysis and description of such tasks and for predicting, at the design stage, the future performance of such systems, and also to allow for the needs and properties of the human operator.

On the other hand the concept is at present very ill-defined with several probably distinct meanings. Some of them will be outlined below. There is at present no satisfactory theory of "mental workload". Indeed, a case can be made for dropping the term "mental" in contrast to "physical", and substituting some neutral term such as "human operator workload". This is because even a simple "physical" task like digging a ditch requires that information be processed, decisions be made, and control be exercised; while even simple mental arithmetic uses energy and may induce muscle tension. The <u>proportion</u> of physical to mental load may vary from task to task, but all tasks have some of each component in their total contribution to the human operator workload. Hereafter, for brevity we will refer to the <u>H</u>uman <u>O</u>perator <u>W</u>ork <u>L</u>oad by the acronym HOWL, which draws attention to its subjectively experienced nature!

A complete and adequate theory of HOWL will be one of two things, we believe: the end product of a total theory of human performance, or alternatively merely a description of how people _feel_ when doing a task. In the discussion which follows we begin by discussing absolute measures of HOWL, and later develop the idea that at present only relative and task specific measures may be possible.

We believe that HOWL is multidimensional. This is important, for it is common in applied psychology to be asked to estimate _the_ mental load imposed by a task, and the answer is expected to be a single number. Often the aim is to assign such a number to each of two or more tasks so that the single numbers represent the rank order of difficulty. The reasons for the request may be many, but often one reason is to allow tasks to be ordered in discussions of pay, conditions of work, etc. We believe that in general no such single number exists for the measurement of HOWL. It is appropriately measured as a vector, not a scalar variable. There may be special occasions on which a scalar can be used but each such use requires explicit and specific justification. (It is interesting to contrast this with, for example, the claim in the Theory of Signal Detection that signals which vary on several dimensions can nonetheless be scaled onto the liklihood axis, and a scalar measure of discriminability found. We do not believe that such is the case with HOWL). Although we have some ideas about the identity of some of the dimensions we are not confident that we know them all, let alone the appropriate metrics on each dimension, the limiting values which the variables may take, or the correlation - if any - between measures on different dimensions.

The most we can expect to do at present is to specify a vector which describes the HOWL for a particular task. The measure will, in general, be _task specific_. That is, once we have specified the variables in the vector for a particular task we can say whether or not the HOWL is increased for that task as a result of manipulating some independent variable. If the structure of two or more task situations are precisely known, one might reasonably expect that the more similar they are the more likely it is that their HOWL vectors will be comparable and the measures on the tasks be capable of being compared. But we cannot, without careful justification, say that the value of the vector for one task is greater than that of the HOWL vector for a different task. Between two tasks some variables in the vector may be deleted or added, the values of some variables in the vector increased and others decreased, and we have no method at present of measuring the "resultant length" of the vector.

If the concept of HOWL is indeed multidimensional it may be because the human's ability to process information is itself multidimensional. Several approaches taken in the position papers written before this conference converge on such an idea. Thus Johanssen suggests that the different dimensions of HOWL may relate to properties of the different "black boxes" in the human operator, such as input limitation, decision limitation, memory limitation, response limitation, etc. Sanders has suggested a "Processor Model C" which again distributes limitations among distinct but parallel processors, and Wickens speaks of "structure specific" capacity. We are agreed that these ideas are helpful both to generate ideas about the nature of HOWL and to account for the origin of the multidimensionality of the measures. (Note, however, that none of them relates explicitly to the subjective feelings of the operator engaged on the task, nor to physiological measures of stress and strain). We also would suggest that even were the structure of the information processing system accurately known not all problems of measuring HOWL would be solved, for the load experienced will also depend on the strategy adopted by the operator, who may choose different combinations of processing units depending on how he sees the task and how he thinks it may best be tackled, and not all choices will be optimal or equally efficient.

It is at least certain that man is not a "single channel" system, and when sufficiently well practised may not even be of "limited capacity". But on occasions and in certain tasks he may behave like either, and hence we should stop asking the question, "Is man single channel?" and ask instead, "When does man appear to be single channel and when does he not appear to be single channel?". The way in which human limits on information processing is manifested is task specific. If we could identify tasks in which he does behave like a single channel then we could safely apply single channel models and measures to those tasks, even though they cannot be used as a general measure. For example, when information is presented by means of several dials each of which requires visual fixation to be accurately read, the redirection of fixation means that information is absorbed in a way which approximates to a single channel system. Under such conditions Queueing Theory or Information Theory would be appropriate ways to measure load providing they are modified to account for the relative values of the sources. This can be done, for example, using Sheridan's Supervisory Theory, (Sheridan, 1970). If exactly the same information were presented using an integrated display in which eye movements were not required, the single channel measures might be quite inappropriate.

We have spoken thus far as if "workload" were at least a single concept, but we have already hinted that it must contain behavioural, performance, physiological, and subjective components, each of which needs appropriate measures. (We find the distinction between behaviour and performance useful: the first is the output of the human operator in a man-machine system, the latter the output of the entire system). As we shall see below, the subjective component of load is probably related to the concept of "Effort" which has recently been popular in writings on information processing (Kahneman, 1973: Jahns, 1973). If workload, capacity and effort are such complex concepts, what kind of quantitative measures and models can we use to describe them? A beginning might be the following list.

1. <u>Formal Models</u>. There are certain cases where the use of such models can be justified. This is particularly the case where man is an element in a closed loop, where classical and optimal control theory are appropriate and extremely powerful. It is necessary that the human operator be well practised, and that the system as a whole is in a (relatively) steady state. It is <u>certain</u> that higher order control, which requires the human operator to generate "lead" (e.g. acceleration control) is <u>always</u> effortful in all senses. "Lead" and load are highly correlated, and requiring "lead" will usually produce a "limited capacity" style of behaviour. Again, where single channel behaviour is known to be probable time line analysis and Queueing Theory, or Supervisory Theory, will be applicable. In dealing with the load produced by very rare events (such as power station failures, or reactor failures) Queueing Theory may be the only way to estimate unacceptable load, given the impossibility of collecting empirical data.

2. <u>Time Line Analysis</u>. This is a strong candidate for a priori prediction of load, and for real time load assessment at the design stage. Such a claim emphasises our belief that time stress is very important indeed in producing HOWL. High levels of practice can reduce time stress in certain kinds of task.

3. <u>The Theory of Signal Detection</u>. The concepts embodied in the theory are of great importance even if the laboratory experimental paradigms are not. The distinction between sensitivity and response bias is of great importance. Human operators commonly adopt a speed-accuracy tradeoff by means of criterion shifts, and this can be assumed to happen in such a way as to minimise the feelings of load, unless steps are taken to prevent it. TSD concepts may turn out to be useful in understanding what it means to ask someone to "try harder": can he respond by changing his "sensitivity" or only by changing his criterion: by increasing only hits, or necessarily false alarms as well?

4. <u>Computer Theory Analogies</u>. It may be that for cognitive processing in particular, theories such as semantic networks, fuzzy set theory, multiprocessor computer architecture, and even grammar theory will be appropriate. Little has been done in this area.

5. __Physiological Measures__. It would be highly desirable to have an unobtrusive physiological measure of HOWL, but we remain highly sceptical of those at present on offer. There are problems of technology, problems of baseline calibration, and problems of sensitivity. Correlation and significance are not enough. We need measures with a sufficient range of change to follow the whole continuity of load and effort from very light to very heavy. This is particularly true where load may be building up but no observable changes in behaviour and performance have yet appeared, since the breakdown level is being approached from below. We would also like such a measure for predicting long term effects of HOWL in jobs where the human operator may perform the task for many years.

6. __Subjective Estimates__. Despite all the well-known difficulties of the use of rating scales we feel that these must be regarded as central to any investigation. If the person __feels__ loaded and effortful, he __is__ loaded and effortful whatever the behavioural and performance measures may show. As with physiological measures, investigations are needed of the validity and sensitivity of such measures, and of their correlation with performance and behaviour measures. The problem of making comparisons across tasks rather than within tasks is extremely difficult. A generalised "Cooper-Harper" scale would be very useful.

7. __Protocol Analysis__. This is useful both as a source of data and as a way of gaining valuable insights into the cognitive operations used by the human operator, and hence for new models. Protocol analysis should always be used if possible during the task analysis of existing systems. (For an example, see Bainbridge, L.

8. __Secondary Tasks.__ There are far greater difficulties in the use of these methods than is generally acknowledged. There is no "universal" secondary task, and one must not be chosen arbitrarily for convenience. Selection of appropriate secondary tasks should be task specific and the particular choice justified. A secondary task should not show structural interference with the primary task. It should be a task which goes "naturally" with the primary task (for example, acceleration with steering in vehicle control, rather than counting backward by three). Jex's Adaptive Critical Task is very powerful but its exact implementation should be given careful thought in each case. (See Jex's paper in this volume).

9. __Task Demands.__ Measurements of task demand tend to scale well with subjective estimates of workload and effort. Among things which may be measured are the physical parameters of the task and work setting, the performance criteria (accept-

able level of error) adopted explicitly or implicitly by the human operator, the payoffs and cost benefit structure of the task as perceived by the operator. Task demands are not merely the outcome of a task analysis but amount to a model of the task.

10. <u>Workload Checklist</u>. As mentioned earlier it would be useful to have a "workload checklist" for use at the design stage of a man-machine system. The beginnings of such a checklist are given at the end of this paper. It should act as a reminder to the designer of the ways in which the operator may become over (or under) loaded. In addition compendia such as the Human Engineering Guide to Equipment Design (Van Cott and Kinkade, 1973. Washington) and the Bioastronautics Data Book (1973, NASA) should always be consulted.

What is really required is a measure or measures which are <u>not task specific</u>. Although we doubt whether this is in fact possible two lines of enquiry seem worth following up. The first is the notion of "difficulty margin". This we define as the difference between the maximum possible and required <u>performance</u>. (It may be that it should be the difference between the maximum possible and required <u>behaviour</u>, but we shall see when we consider the effects of practice that there are great difficulties in using the latter definition). At first sight this seems attractive. But a good case can be made for using not the maximum attainable momentary performance, but the maximum performance which can be sustained over "a considerable period of time", the tonic, not the phasic maximum. The second candidate is the "generalised Cooper-Harper scale". The original scale, based on subjective judgements of experienced pilots is very successful in assessing the handling characteristics of aircraft, and measures on the scale correlate well with order of control, Critical Task stability margins, and other objective measures. It would be good to develop a more general scale with which a wide variety of tasks could be rated. Just as systems rated poorly by the Cooper-Harper Scale are difficult or impossible to fly, so we might hope that a system rated poorly on our new scale would be too effortful, too demanding, for adequate control by a human operator. Even a (small) <u>set</u> of such scales each applicable within a limited but well-defined task description would be well worth having.

Out of such measures, and those outlined earlier, should come the set of variables needed for the HOWL vector. Whatever measures are used it seems likely that the vector will need to include, in some way or another, task specifications (including physical parameters of the input load, criteria, and payoffs), system performance requirements, physiological measures, subjective feelings, and behavioural measures. (Bear in mind the earlier distinction we make between performance and behaviour. What is of interest to the customer is <u>performance:</u> what is of interest to the operator is his <u>behaviour</u> and <u>feelings.</u> This contrast brings up a further set of contrasts, and the various pairings may be instructive when considering how to measure the (usually nonlinear) combination of man and machine. The contrasts include:

        Performance vs. Behaviour

        Behaviour vs. Feelings

        Feelings vs. Physiological measures

        Performance vs. Feelings

                    and so on.

Some comparisons should be polyadic rather than dyadic, and some may in fact already be well known in the literature under other names. For example, where is the distinction drawn by Norman and Bobrow (1973) between resource-limited and data-limited systems? Perhaps the idea of voluntary effort is only applicable to resource limited tasks. Do physiological changes correlate with the closeness of the resource limits or with the strain imposed by data limits?

    Moreover, where do the well known concepts of "capacity" and "effort" fit in, and with what measures do they scale? Whatever "capacity" may be, it is obvious that "work load" is to do with the extent that capacity is absorbed by the task, and with the way in which the human operator mobilises his capacity, and the feelings which accompany the use of capacity -in other words with the feelings of "effort". The latter term has become very popular since its introduction by Kahneman (1973) and Jahns (1973). There are, however, considerable difficulties in using it since it is no more precisely defined than is capacity, and is probably even more complex a concept.

    One sense of "effort" is certainly the <u>feelings</u> which accompany load, when the human is under stress. We are inclined to think that, as Wundt suggested long ago, most of the subjective feelings are due to muscular tension and changes in physiological variables such as blood pressure and heart rate. A person may <u>feel</u> that he is loaded and is putting out a lot of effort even when there is no change in his behaviour and performance. Indeed, as a task increases in difficulty there will be a period just before behaviour and performance falter when he must be working much harder precisely in order that no detectable changes shall be present. It is for this reason that performance or behavioural measures by themselves are inadequate as a measure of HOWL.

Another sense of effort is expended effort, that is, what the operator mobilises to deal with the task. It seems plausible that effort allocation in this sense can be altered by altering the operator's subjective criterion or response bias. Probably this sense of effort is relevant only to voluntary, conscious cognitive activity and has no place in the discussion of highly practised automatic behaviour.

A third sense of effort is whatever is measured physiologically when a person comes progressively under more and more load. It is related to physiological activation and whatever is being measured by GSR, heart rate, sinus arrythmia, respiration rate, etc. In this sense, then, it is a physiological variable.

Finally, we feel there may be a sense in which effort is the variable best described as "whatever it is that causes changes in behaviour and performance without a change in task demands or plant characteristics, but excluding practice".

A problem is that there is no compelling reason to think that measures on these four dimensions are perfectly, or even positively, correlated. One can conceive of a person feeling that he is putting out more effort when none of the other measures change. One can imagine a change in performance and activation without the human operator feeling any different, and so on. It may be that changes in task demands occur without time for the physiological mechanisms to respond; or, as Ursin points out, that a stressor which acts on a human operator for a few minutes has detectable effects for many hours, long after the person would claim any effortful involvement with the task.

What, indeed, are we asking when we ask someone to "try harder"? He might, in the language of the Theory of Signal Detection, think that we want more "hits", or fewer "misses", or some combination. He might interpret it to mean a more rapid response, or to reduce tracking lag, or r.m.s. error. Conceivably he could improve his performance by relaxing and adopting a less stringent criterion, thus reducing his feelings of effort and muscle tremor. Or he might respond by adopting a different overall strategy towards the entire task. We know that it is possible experimentally to decouple felt effort and performance, as is seen in Figure 7 of Sanders' paper, where sleep deprived dynamic performance feels much harder, but is actually better than static task performance in the alert operator.

One generalisation which can safely be made is that with practice performance improves and effort declines. This seems to be linked to the fact that prolonged practice in highly motivated human subjects makes the single channel limited capacity model of the human operator less and less appropriate. High levels of practice lead to "automatic" behaviour in which no conscious control is exercised. Simultaneously with the development of automaticity it seems as though the decision stages of information processing which are so evident early in practice disappear, and little or no effort is felt to be expended; and no effort is experienced as a feeling of stress. Behaviour and performance flow smoothly to their goal, and only if there is an emergency, a sudden change in system properties requiring a change in strategy by the operator, does a significant work load reappear.

What happens during practice to reduce HOWL, abolish effort, and apparently make considerations of capacity inapplicable? As yet rather little is known about the course of practice. Moreover, research into practice on tasks which bear directly on our understanding of practical, daily skills will be rather dissimilar from conventional research. Laboratory research is usually reductionist. It sets the human operator very simple and well ordered tasks with a minimum and fixed number of degrees of freedom which he can use to cope with the task. Real tasks, such as process control, vehicular control, or the control of nuclear power plants are quite different. In almost all cases there are at least several behaviour patterns which can produce acceptable performance. The sequence of actions can be altered, the timing of component subtasks altered, and so on. The human operator develops hypotheses about the causal structure of the task and system, he invents flexible strategies in the light of those hypotheses, and he adopts subjective personal criteria in addition to, or in place of, those suggested by the initiator of the task. He may find ways of increasing or decreasing his degrees of freedom, and thus alter the load. He becomes better at adapting to plant characteristics and at compensating for changes in them.

It seems likely that a key to understanding how skill acquisition proceeds is the idea of an Internal Model. By an Internal Model we mean that the increasing knowledge which a human operator has of the system and the task become embodied in the brain as a model of the system which allows him to predict future states from present evidence, and hence allows him to become at least partly independent of the need to know the current moment to moment input. Early in practice information is received, processed cognitively and consciously to the point where a decision about the appropriate response can be made, and this process is "limited". As the model develops the need for conscious cognitive decision making becomes less and less, and the Internal Model is the way in which processes become automatised. If this is so, then to account for behaviour early in practice we need both a model of the task environment and also a model of the cognitive decision processes of the human operator. Late in practice we do not require a model of the operator's decision processes. These become transparent, and we require only a model of the task environment filtered by the man-machine system. It should be noted that where analytic models such as Control Theory have had their greatest success has always been where human operators have had a great deal of practice; that is, where they have had time to acquire a good model of the system characteristics.

As practice proceeds and the operator acquires his predictive model of the environment the fluctuations in performance due to capacity allocation and effort expenditure tend to disappear, and the human operator, now embodying a progressively more accurate representation of the task can use it automatically to handle the task requirements. This, as long as the model remains appropriate, produces nearly loadless and effortless behaviour. Early in practice a man may process information using models of other tasks which he has performed, and which he judges to be similar to the task with which he is currently confronted. Late in practice he processes information in a way which he has discovered to be particularly well suited to the present task demands, and the reduction in uncertainty associated with this discovery reduces the load, and effort. Almost certainly however, load is never reduced to zero, since at least some monitoring is required to make sure that the model is still apposite, and if the operator chooses a non-optimal strategy in the light of the model there is still room for a load reduction. It should be noted that some of the difficulties associated with low load tasks such as monitoring slow process control systems may on this view arise because of the difficulty for humans of building up an adequate model on the basis of information presented very slowly over a long period of time. There may be implications for training here.

The above considerations suggest the need for experiments rather unlike conventional laboratory experiments. They should be of long duration, and include very complex, behaviourally rich tasks. Usually if a subject in an experiment "takes control" of the situation by performing in an unorthodox way at variance with the experimenter's instructions we regard him as a "poor" subject even if his performance is adequate. In real life situations the ability to develop idiosyncratic strategies may be of enormous importance, and we need to invent experimental paradigms to investigate this.

There are important questions of the level of analysis which is appropriate for such research. Traditionally cognitive psychologists have looked for the properties of component processes, memory, attention, perception, etc., and have hoped to combine these components to account for molar behaviour. But it may be that such an analysis is misdirected. Consider how one might understand what computations a computer is carrying out. Knowing the properties of ferrite cores or diodes or logic circuits will not tell you what computation is being performed. For that one needs to know the programming language, and perhaps something about the architecture of the computer. The analogy may be valid for

understanding human behaviour in complex tasks. If so, then rather
than reaction times and TSD parameters we may need conceptual tools
such as associative networks, fuzzy set theory, and the like when
discussing early practice.

It is perhaps worth looking at the differences between
laboratory work and so called "real life" more closely. Laboratory
tasks tend to have a well-defined goal or target. Payoff matrices
are artificial and have low values. The subject is controlled by
the task. Task instructions are specific. Task requirements
are stable. Subjects are relatively untrained. By contrast in
"real" tasks only a (sometimes vague) overall performance criterion
is given and the detailed goal structure must be inferred by the
operator. Task instructions are inferred by the human operator
from rather general commands about how to perform the task. The
task may vary as the demands of the system vary in real time.
Operating conditions and the system itself are liable to change.
Costs and benefits may have enormous values. There is a hierarchy
of performance goals. The operator is usually highly trained, and
largely controls the task, being allowed to use what strategies he
will. Risk is incurred in ways which can never be simulated in
the laboratory.

Again and again one comes back to the multidimensionality of the HOWL concept. "Workload", "Capacity", "Effort" are all
multidimensional, and no simple metrics such as Information Theory
will be adequate except in extremely specific, very limited cases.
We do not know how to combine measures on the different dimensions
and hence end up with an appropriate vector rather than a set of
scalars. Do the terms "capacity" and "effort", which constantly
turn up in discussions of HOWL, actually clarify anything? Or have
they become too general now, even if, as with "capacity", they once
had a very precise meaning? The following phrases give something
of the flavour of our discussions in trying to define them.
Capacity "is a context sensitive index of the maximum performance
available"; "multidimensional"; "should be normalised with respect
to performance which can be sustained for very long periods"; "should
be normalised with respect to the maximum possible performance".
Spare capacity "with reference to a specific task or situation is
indexed by the difference (or ratio) between maximal performance
and actually measured performance"; "is measured by the difference
between typical and breakdown levels of task demand". "Prediction
of workload will come from the ability to assess the extent of the
use of component processes in any particular task".

Topics requiring investigation

1. Calibration and comparison of secondary tasks.
2. Correlation of physiological and behavioural measures, and
   an examination of the causal factors behind the physiological
   measures.

3. When is it appropriate to regard man as a single channel and when otherwise? What are the boundary conditions?
4. Develop an approach to measurement using multiple measures.
5. Careful delineation of the limits of application of the various formal models.
6. Definition and testing of concepts associated with "effort".
7. Attempts should be made to develop models empirically using a data base derived from real life tasks, rather than using a priori analytic models.
8. A systematic exploration of the relation between Kahneman's "$Effort_1$", "$Effort_2$", Performance measures and Task Demands.
9. The development of new measures of behaviour and performance with particular application to situations of low load and underload, and a study of the relation between vigilance tasks, monitoring behaviour, and process control.
10. The development of task taxonomies and a designer's "checklist" for practical application.
11. Validation of any and <u>all</u> measures involved in mental workload research and applications.

These are very vague concepts and do not preclude the use of traditional (or new) scalar quantitative measures in specific situations where that use can be justified. But such justification should be explicit, which would at least have the added virtue of making details of the task situation more apparent to other investigators and improving the chance of replication and successful applications of findings.

In conclusion, while all these concepts remain somewhat vague at present a considerable degree of consensus can nonetheless be reached. The most appropriate conclusion may be the following statement made by Sanders during one of the conference discussions.

"None of these methods and theories can, by itself, provide us with an acceptable assessment of workload, either before the design or after the fact. But the perspective of all of them is useful to the expert who is called upon to make workload evaluation".

FIRST STEPS TOWARDS A DESIGNER'S MENTAL WORKLOAD CHECKLIST

In designing a man-machine system, the following points should be borne in mind so that the human operator will suffer neither from underload or overload.

1. <u>The Structure and Quality of input information</u>

1.1 <u>Information Rate or Bandwidth</u>: Above some level performance will fall, and the task will seem harder. But the level is not absolute, and varies between individuals, and with the level of practice, the strategies adopted by the human operator, and personality characteristics such as the extent to which he enjoys "challenge". Some human operators prefer heavy load situations, others light loads.

1.2 Number of Independent Sources: Providing enough sources are present to provide adequate information for the task to be done, an increase in the number of independent sources lowers performance and raises the experienced load.

1.3 Predictability and Preview: Always improves performance and decreases experienced load, except when novel (unexpected) events occur.

1.4 Gestalt Formation: Where the human operator can learn to see the information sources as a unified pattern ("gestalt") in space and time, performance is increased and the experienced load decreased. A danger is that details of the display may be ignored, and strong response sets developed, and unusual events be ignored.

1.5 Correlated Sources: Performance is increased and experienced load decreased.

2. Memory Load: If the human operator has to handle a "running memory" load, performance will be decreased and the experienced load increased.

3. Computation and Transforms of Information

3.1 If the human operator is required to perform computations on the input, or to transform or translate it, performance will be lowered and experienced load increased.

3.2 Lead Generation: If the operator must generate "lead" in a control theory sense to compensate for higher order control in a man-machine system, performance will be decreased, and experienced load increased.

3.3 Heterogeneous Plant Characteristics: If a human operator must control more than one loop, and the plant characteristics of the loops have different transfer functions, performance will be decreased and experienced load increased.

3.4 Loop delays in closed loop tasks: Any delay in the control loop will lower performance and increase experienced load.

4. Practice

Practice improves performance except in dealing with unforeseen events, providing knowledge of results is given. Experienced load is reduced. Late stages of practice may induce boredom which will offset beneficial effects, which otherwise may continue for hundreds of hours.

5. System Stability

5.1 Reduced stability lowers performance and increases experienced load.

5.2 The degree of interaction between stability and the accuracy of error perception is important. If error is too accurately perceived the operator may amplify his own random error.

6. Error Perception

6.1 Prominent error display always leads to improved performance except for handling irrecoverable mistakes.

6.2 Subjectively experienced load may either increase or decrease with perceived error.

Etc. etc.

(Note: "Performance" is a measure of man-machine system output. "Experienced Load" is whether the task feels difficult to the human operator).

References

Bainbridge, L. 1974 in Lee F. and Edwards, E. The Human Operator in Process Control. Taylor and Francis. London.

Jahns, D. 1973. A concept of Operator Workload in Manual Vehicle Operations. Forschungsinstitut, Anthropotechnik, Meckenheim. Bericht, Nr. 14.

Kahneman, D. 1973. Attention and Effort. Prentice Hall N.Y.

Norman, D. & Bobraw, D. 1975. On data-limited-resource limited processes. Cognitive Psychology, 7, 44-64.

Sheridan, T. 1970. On how often the Supervisor should sample. IEEE, SCC-6, 140-145.

PART II:

CONTROL ENGINEERING AND WORKLOAD MEASUREMENT

(For readers unfamiliar with control theory the following readings may be consulted:

Milsum, J.H. Biological Control Systems Analysis, McGraw-Hill, N.Y. 1966.
Toates, F. Control Theory in Biology and Experimental Psychology. Hutchison, London. 1975.
Van Colt, H., and Kinkade, R. Human Engineering Guide to Equipment Design. Chapter 6. U.S. Government Publications. Washington D.C. 1972.
Gelb, A. Applied Optimal Estimation, M.I.T. Cambridge. 1974.
Human Factors journal, volume 19 Numbers 4 and 5, 1977. (Special tutorial edition on applications of control theory to psychology).

MENTAL LOAD IN MONITORING TASKS

Renwick E. Curry

NASA Ames Research Center

Moffett Field, CA 94035 USA

ORGANIZATIONAL BACKGROUND

In this paragraph I will briefly give the background of the Aviation Safety Research Office at NASA Ames to provide the viewpoint from which I will make the comments that follow. The ASRO has been set up to define operating problems in today's aviation system and to suggest solutions that can be implemented in a relatively short time; a typical time horizon is of the order of 2-5 years. Part of our organization administers the Aviation Safety Reporting System which solicits incident reports from users (controllers, pilots, etc.). This program is set up to identify situations requiring immediate action, e.g., a new operating quirk of a particular aircraft or class of aircraft; and to identify other problems through the accumulation of incident data, for example, the prevalence of altitude excursions. These data cannot be used to test hypotheses, but they may be used to formulate hypotheses which in turn may be examined by experimental programs. The research section of the ASRO consists of separately identified groups concerned with operational problems (crew procedures, communications, etc.), statistics, and, for want of a better name, behavioral research. The responsibilities of this latter group are to support research in the operational problems area with basic studies leading to models which can be used to predict behavior in the more complex setting. Current topics of interest are

Allocation of control between man and automatic systems. Analyzing the effects of different crew procedures on system performance and system reliability.

Crew coordination and crew resource utilization.
The influence of flight director commands on crosschecking of situation displays.
Pilot decision making identifying attributes of good judgement.

WORKLOAD AND STRESS

In examining the type of tasks confronted by pilots and other crew members, we find the definitions of workload (or categorization of workload) given by Gartner and Murphy (1976) to be particularly valuable, especially when trying to classify the various contexts in which the term workload is used. Gartner and Murphy use the following classifications based on their literature survey:

Task Demands. This version of workload is defined in terms of what the human must accomplish and the operating constraints during the time of task completion. Stress is manifested in this interpretation of workload by environmental and task constraints such as time available to complete the task, physiological factors, possible embarrassment, etc.

Effort. This interpretation of workload depends on how hard the operator is "working". It is based on the idea that the operator may feel he is "working hard", "working at a leisurely pace", etc. In many ways this is perhaps the most basic definition. Is it the original source of the term? By itself, however, it gives an incomplete picture because of the lack of specification of what the operator is actually accomplishing.

Accomplishments and Performance. This interpretation is based on the actual accomplishments of the operator, not what is required (task demands), or how hard he is "working" to achieve these accomplishments. As with the effort version, it is of little use by itself, but the combination of effort and performance is an intuitively appealing and useful construct.

GOAL OF MEASUREMENT

In the study of aviation human factors problems, primarily pilot problems, the major factors revolve around the following:

Peak, instantaneous task demands exceeding capabilities.
Masking or interference.
Errors, apparently random.

Effects of motivation, arousal and expectancy.

Our overall goal is to use measures to predict (via models) the effort and performance tradeoff curves from the task demand and environmental specifications.

MEASURES CURRENTLY USED

Subjective Reports. We have used subjective reports on workload with good results. The advantages of this technique (primarily magnitude estimation) are that it is very close to that which is reported by the ultimate user (although we have not done validation studies on that question). Moreover, it is readily accepted by professional pilot-subjects as a means of communicating their perceptions of effort. The disadvantages are that unless the scale is well anchored, there is likely to be some intersubject variability. Also, we have found that pilots are not always correct in reporting what the real source of difficulty may be (e.g., they may confuse clutter effects on performance with controlled-element instability). Multidimensional scaling techniques may alleviate this problem somewhat, and we are currently experimenting with these.

The major boundary conditions for the use of magnitude estimate scales are that they must be done after a trial run has been completed, and that the scales must be well defined, even to the point of using a decision tree structure as in the Cooper-Harper scale.

Reserve Capacity. We have also used a nonloading side task to measure reserve capacity; this has been, for the most part, a visual detection of 1 of 2 lights appearing at random times in the subject's peripheral vision. We have used the linear combination of percent missed and response latency as prescribed by Spyker, et al. (1971) to arrive at a workload index.

The advantages and disadvantages of this technique are well known. However, we have found it to be an index that varies in the manner expected in spite of the lack of specificity of the visual side task. It has been sensitive to additional auditory input loading during tracking tasks in our simulator studies. Professional pilots are somewhat reluctant to use the side task and sometimes forget to perform it. However, it is more readily accepted than a loading type of side task.

The primary boundary conditions we observe in the use of this measure are that the subjects must be practised in the use of the side task, and that the performance in the primary task should be checked without any side task, to measure possible loading effects of the side task on primary task performance. Moreover, we find that more sensitive results are obtained by normalizing each subject's scores.

Communications. To obtain a measure of communication workload among members of a group, or among airplanes and the ATC controller, some easily measurable statistics of the communications (number of messages, percent time channel used, number of words per message) have been collected. These correlate as expected with subjective reports, but no real patterns have yet emerged.

Model Measures. Components of models which describe the tracking workload have been developed through the efforts of manual control investigators. Information theory, which was reasonably good in describing some experiments, never was able to express the multi-modal aspects of control and monitoring (Wempe and Baty, 1968). It would be very beneficial, of course, to have a common measure for the many and varied tasks we all ultimately wish to describe. Senders' information theoretic model for display sampling has been used in conjunction with display design procedures and provides a good measure of visual scanning workload. This is adequate for many applications and has been used widely.

A more recent development in this line has been the idea of Levison (1970) who proposed a parameter in the Optimal Control Model of the human operator. Levison's idea is phrased in terms of the "attention" the operator places on a display element, but does not make specific predictions of what instrument will be the object of the eye scan. The fact that good pilots use peripheral vision to accumulate information makes the eye movement data difficult to interpret anyway, especially in integrated displays. The attention parameter, however, gives a relative "importance" of a display element for the control task. The attention parameter enters into the perceptual or observation noise covariance of the Kalman Filter portion of the model so that the covariance varies from the full-attention value to the no-attention value (infinity). Levison has compared this parameter with subjective assessments of effort with gratifying results, although it appears to be better at predicting relative rather than absolute values of effort. Wewerinke (1974) has used the structure of the Optimal Control Model to derive an even more valid correspondence between the attention parameter and subjective ratings. An important addition is the inclusion of the slope of the performance vs. attention or effort curve, since a steep slope suggests a high performance sensitivity to momentary lapses in attention toward the control task.

While the above discussion is related to tracking workload, another very important problem is the modeling of performance and effort for the monitoring task and/or simultaneous monitoring and controlling. Levison (1971) has developed a model for decision making with respect to the excursion of a signal beyond certain bounds. This model used the optimal estimator (Kalman Filter) portion of the control model and assumes normative estimation within the human constraints. Another approach to the problem of monitoring is described in Gai and Curry (1976). This paper proposed a model for a failure detection task, in particular, detecting changes in the mean of the observed random process. The concept of the attention on multiple displays used in models of the human controller has been extended to predict failure detection performance while observing multiple, correlated displays (Gai and Curry, 1977). Further work (Curry and Govindaraj, 1977) deals with failures (changes of bandwidth and variance)of the random process. The attention concepts appear to carry forward from Levison's earlier work in these studies, but modifications were made to the attention on display position and display rate as usually used in the control model.

To make the monitoring models useful, they must provide estimates of the performance vs. effort relation. Kleinman and Curry (1977) discuss this problem in the context of control-theoretic models and the more conventional monitoring models (e.g. Senders), but a very difficult problem presents itself: what is monitoring, i.e., what are the objectives of the monitoring task? Even, if as suggested by Curry and Gai (1976), monitoring can be described as:

(a) Assessment of performance occurring at the present time;

(b) Assessment of performance which will occur at some time in the future;

(c) Detection of failure or change;

determining the actual objective of human monitors will be extremely difficult in complex systems where many possible objectives exist. Laboratory experimentation is currently underway to explore some of the more basic considerations: for example, is there an interaction between simultaneously monitoring for limit exceedance (present performance assessment) and changes in bandwidth (failure detection)?

In summary, the model measures of "attention" seem to predict control performance and effort (especially when accounting for the sensitivity of performance). Success has been achieved in the use of this parameter for the limited experiments in monitoring as well, but virtually no knowledge about monitoring goals or interference of other tasks is available at the present.

RELATIVE VALUE OF DIFFERENT MEASURES

The different measures under consideration are limited to a priori (here I use the term to mean something more like task demands, rather than theories), empirical measures, and models. The three usual functions to be performed are:

<u>Prediction</u> - The only way to make any prediction about workload is through the use of models (almost by definition). Even statements such as "the operator will commit more errors when simultaneously tracking and communicating" is an elementary form of a model.

<u>Model Development</u> - The models described above must be derived from a judicious blend of empirical measures, fundamentals, and experimental data. A model is a method of summarizing data relationships, in this case relating the effects of task demands and environment on the empirical measures, effort, and performance. Submodels would be helpful to estimate the subjective workload or effort from the physiological measures, to allow experimentation without a constant reporting of perceived workload by the operator.

<u>System Evaluation</u> - Empirical measures, both physiological and performance-related can be fruitfully used to evaluate current systems in the laboratory or work situation.

QUESTIONS FOR THE CONFERENCE

This conference offers a unique opportunity to consolidate the many and varied results from the literature. A very useful product would be a summary of the "state-of-the-art", and suggestions for further experiments within an agreed-upon overall framework. This may be difficult, but nonetheless is worth the effort involved.

1. Can we arrive at a consensus on the different meanings of workload as usually used (e.g. task demands, effort, and accomplishments)?

2. Is it possible to define the major dimensions or attributes for each type of workload and, for several important conditions, specify the relative importance of each dimension?

3. Can we arrive at a functional model for human activity (e.g. block diagram with important elements such as short term memory) and show where the previously identified dimensions have a point of influence?

4. Aside from the functional model in 3, is there a descriptive model which summarizes the important relationships? I am thinking here of an analogy to the Theory of Signal Detection as applied to psychology: the description can be made in terms of decision ability (d') and criterion (beta). Many factors are known to influence these parameters, but the summary of the effects shows up primarily in these two parameters.

5. Can we suggest important research questions for the near future, and can these questions be phrased in terms of the functional or descriptive models mentioned above?

REFERENCES

Curry, R.E. and Gai, E.G., Detection of random process failures by human monitors, In Monitoring Behaviour and Supervisory Control (Sheridan and Johannsen, Ed.) Plenum Press, 1976.

Curry, R.E., and Govindaraj, T., The human as a detector of changes in bandwidth and variance, Proc. 13th Annual Conf. on Manual Control, June 1977.

Gai, E.G. and Curry, R.E., A model of the human observer in failure detection tasks, IEEE Trans. Systems, Man and Cybernetics, February, 1976.

Gai, E.G. and Curry, R.E., Failure detection by pilots during automatic landing: models and experiments, AIAA Journ. of Aircraft, February, 1977.

Gartner, W., and Murphy, M., Pilot workload and fatigue; a critical survey of concepts and assessment techniques, NASA TN D-8365, November, 1976.

Kleinman, D.L., and Curry, R.E., Some control theoretic models of human operator display monitoring, IEEE Trans. Systems, Man and Cybernetics (in press).

Levison, W.H., A model for task interference, Proc. Sixth Annual Conf. on Manual Control, 1971.

Levison, W.H., A control-theory model for human decision-making, Proceedings of the Seventh Annual Conf. on Manual Control, NASA SP-281, 1971.

Sypker, D., Stackhouse, S., Khalafalla, A., and McLane, R. Development of techniques for measuring pilot workload, NASA CR-1888, 1971.

Wempe, T., and Baty, D., Human information processing rates during certain multiaxis tracking tasks with a concurrent auditory task, IEEE Trans. Man Machine Systems, Dec. 1968.

Wewerinke, P.H., Effort involved in single and two axis control systems, National Aerospace Laboratory NLR, Report NLR TR 75060 U, 1974.

DEFINING AND MEASURING PERCEPTUAL-MOTOR WORKLOAD

IN MANUAL CONTROL TASKS

       Henry R. Jex and Warren F. Clement

       Systems Technology, Inc.
       Hawthorne, California 90250

INTRODUCTION

1. <u>The Problem</u>

   "Everyone knows" when he is subjected to a high mental workload or stress in a complex manual control task such as driving a car, steering a ship, or flying an airplane. Nevertheless, there is, as yet, no accepted definition of operator workload. This is mainly due to the incommensurate dimensions of various loading tasks and the lack of any comprehensive theory or validated models.

   For example, even for well-practiced (stable) conditions, no single measure exists for representing the perceptual-motor load due to perception of sensory inputs from different modalities (vestibular and/or visual) or for representing cognitive mental loads versus pure sensorimotor loads (failure management versus multi-axis control). For non-stationary conditions, where the adaptation and improving skill of the operator has a profound effect on the additional workload he can handle, workload measures are even more elusive.

   This paper offers our present understanding of answers to the following related questions:

   a) How can one define, manipulate, and measure, <u>in a useful way</u>, perceptual-motor workload in manual control tasks?

b) What are the parameters most relevant to an index of perceptual-motor loading (PML)?

c) What are some efficient techniques that have been developed to measure these PML parameters and indices?

d) What are the advantages and shortcomings of such techniques and measures?

e) What is needed in terms of future research?

The situations in which we wish to measure and optimize workload versus task performance are quite complex when viewed as a stream of sequential and parallel events; i.e., flying three axes of a V/STOL fighter while tracking a landing beam, coping with unseen gust disturbances, and communicating with the ground controller. Dozens of parameters must be known to describe such situations properly. It is not too surprising that there has not been evolved a comprehensive and validated theory which can encompass all the variations and interactions observed in these real-world cases. After all, only in the last decade (late 60's, early 70's) has a fairly comprehensive theory of human behavior in many control tasks arrived at a practical stage of development (e.g., Refs. 1-5). It has creatively used new disciplines as they emerged; sophisiticated "classical" and "modern" control theories, frequency- and time-domain signal-processing technology, perceptual and neuromuscular physiological properties, multivariate statistical analyses, and ever-more-potent analog, digital, and hybrid computers. We suspect that the major catalyst for evolving a comprehensive theory of perceptual motor workload may be a technology of efficient-time-shared-processes which has now been developed for the burgeoning field of time-shared central computers and multiprocessors. The time is ripe for real progress.

2. Approach

Despite the lack of a theory to guide definitions, set structure, provide parameters, and yield predictions for testing, there is still a sizeable body of relevant data and empirical observations about pilot workload. The underlying theme in much of these data is that: <u>the more unexpected items that must be handled per unit time the higher the "mental workload"</u>, up to some point where no further workload can be handled. Our basic interpretation of these observations about pilot workload may be summarized in the following working hypotheses:

a) Operational manual control systems are typically designed and developed to require far less than the operator's ordinary limiting capabilities; therefore performance degradation due to environmental stress or workload is

a) (contd.)

   seldom observed except in emergencies.

b) Intrinsic ability (skill, workload) limits can be
   measured only under high-stress conditions; but the
   operator's capabilities improve with habituation to such
   conditions.

c) Workload or skill decrements due to exogenous stresses
   are most apparent when the operator is near his limiting
   performance.

d) Specialized control tasks or surrogates for control
   tasks can be designed to emphasize particular skill or
   workload factors.

The remainder of this paper is intended to offer support for these assertions. Our general point-of-view fits remarkably well (and vice versa) with that of Jahns in Ref. 4, in which an excellent and modern overview of the workload problems is presented.

3. Synopsis

First, various terms such as stress, strain, PML workload etc., are defined and illustrated. After discussing the interacting conflicts an operator must resolve in a high workload manual control situation, we reintroduce (after Sheridan, Ref. 15) the concept of a "metacontrol system" which governs operation of the human's multiprocessor, time-shared subroutines. It is in the metacontrol system that meaningful definitions and measures of PML workload may be made. Next comes a series of subsections on controlling and measuring PML workload in the context just established. Numerous examples are given, and summaries of some of the more useful ones are included in tabular form. Some of our relevant work (Cross-Coupled Instability Task and psychophysiological measures) is discussed in more detail. We end with some needs and suggested directions for future research.

DEFINITIONS AND CONCEPTS

1. Definitions

It is pertinent to establish an introductory context by providing some working definitions and a practical illustration. First, the definitions:*

*Based on American Heritage Dictionary.

Sensory input - An exogenous stimulus received and possibly operated upon by the human operator, but not necessarily consciously.

Neuromuscular activity - Autogenous commands to execute skeletal muscular actions and the ensuing response. The physical response need not occur for the neuromuscular system to be "involved", however.

Perceptual-motor task - Perceptual-motor tasks are regarded as a conscious awareness of a sensed stimulus and action thereon, involving neuromuscular system activity. The perceptual-motor activity may be continuous or discrete, but must involve the higher centers (i.e., cerebral cortex) as a direct link in the stimulus response chain to be classified as "perceptual". (e.g. Sleepwalking is not considered a perceptual-motor task, although it involves sensorimotor activity).

Perceptual-motor load (PML) - The perceptual-motor load is the intensity of perceptual-motor task activity in an appropriately specified context, to be discussed later herein.

Cognitive task - A task in which knowledge is gained about something through perception, reasoning, or intuitive mental processes. As used in man-machine situations, cognitive tasks are usually distinct mental tasks of short duration and may or may not affect the controlled element directly, and the neuromotor aspects are minimal (examples: recognition, judgment, adaptation, computation, and communication).

Stress, (Workload-, Environmental-, Motivational-) - A measure (in a state vector sense) of the applied (exogenous) condition which causes increased operator attentional demands. Perceptual-motor-load one type of stress vector; others may be vibration, hypoxia and fatigue, for examples. Internal (endogenous) states (e.g. concern for consequences of failure) can also cause operator stress

Strain - A measure (in a state-vector sense) of the effects of operator stress. These may include measures of: somatic system response (e.g. systemic muscle tension, scanning parameters), autonomic system response (e.g. heart rate, breathing frequency) endocrine system response (e.g. catecholamine excretion rates); or subjective responses (e.g. ratings).

We make a plea, herewith, for the use of these definitions of operator "stress" and "strain", which are consistent with those used originally in the engineering and science fields, rather than the malapropos usage of "stress" as the syndrome-of-effects from "stressors", as promulgated by Hans Selye and others (e.g. Ref. 7).

As the practical illustration of the intended use of such perceptual-motor loadings and criteria, we can use the exemplary study by Benson, Huddleston, and Rolfe (Ref. 6) on the advantages of digital "counter" versus "counter-pointer" altimeters under test conditions with and without secondary task loadings, and using both pilots and nonpilots as subjects. A battery of psychophysiological measurements was used (e.g. Electroencephalograph {EEG}, Galvanic Skin Resistance {GSR}, Electromyograph {EMG}, breath rate, tidal volume). The main task was similar to flying an airplane to various command altitudes. With secondary task loading, the counter pointer proved distinctly better, with respect to not only the error performance but also most of the psychophysiological variables as well. Finally, the pilot's subjective ratings ranked the counter-pointer better in regard to subjective workload.

This study illustrated the common fallacy of using simple performance evaluations of displays or controls; i.e. under no-load conditions the error performance was about the same with either of the alternative displays - only under the loaded conditions did the detrimental effects of the pure digital display show up. It also showed the advantage of multiple measures in workload assessments; there was enough change in a combination of autonomic, somatic, and subjective measures to perceive clear indications within a relatively efficient experiment.

With the context set by this illustration we can proceed to detailed discussions of perceptual-motor loading, its measurement, and control.

2. Basic Concepts

a) Interactive Nature of PML Adjustment. Here, we are concerned primarily with PML of operators controlling vehicles as an ongoing activity. In such situations, there are a number of competing objectives that must be achieved by the operator:

- Stable operation is of prime importance (e.g. the direction of travel must be under some control)

- Performance results must satisfy the operator's goals and mission criteria (e.g. stay within safe landing parameters, provide accurate weapon delivery)

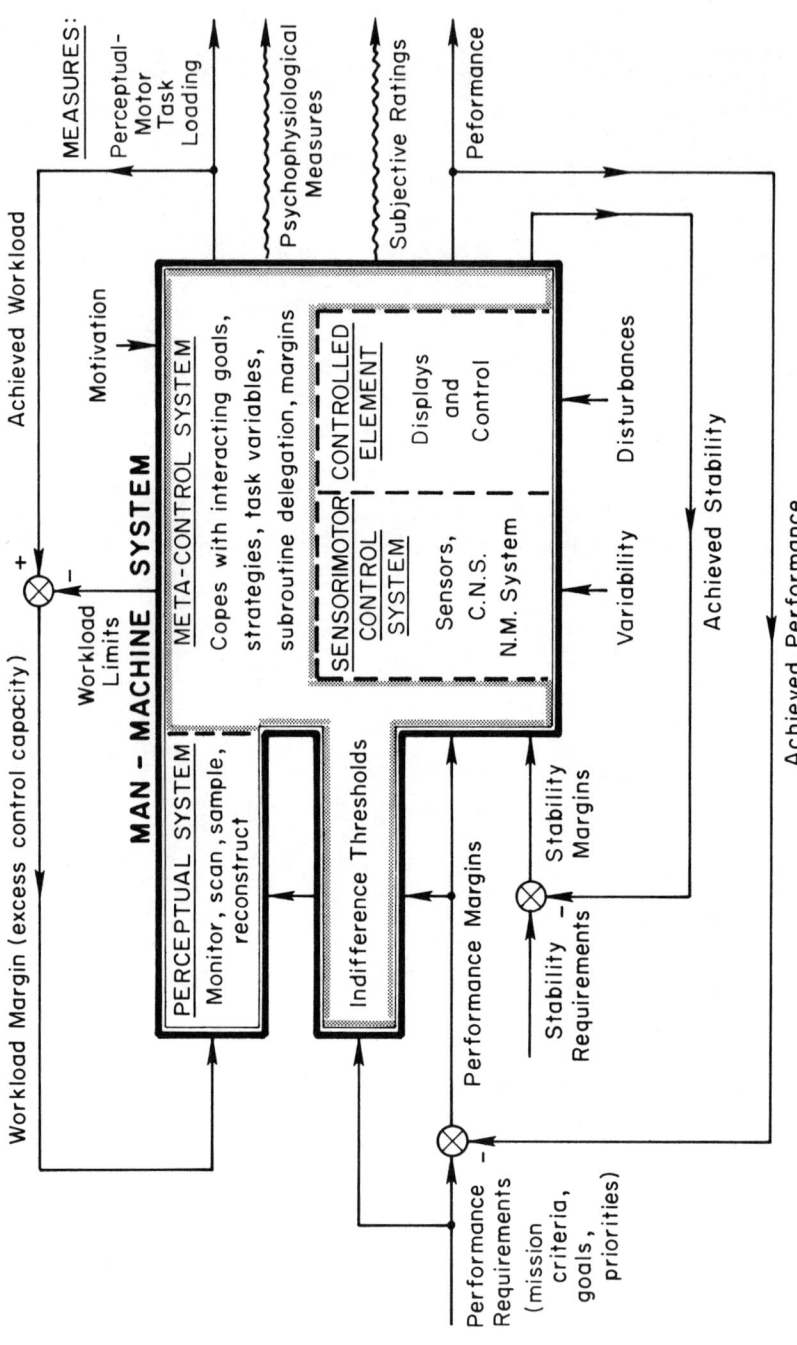

Figure 1. Block diagram showing interactions among man-machine stability, performance, and workload. (The abbreviation C.N.S. refers to the central nervous system and N.M., the neuromuscular system).

• ○ The achieved <u>perceptual-motor workload</u> must lie within the operator's current limits, as set by intrinsic abilities, practice, and as influenced by motivation.

Figure 1 is a block diagram illustrating the strong interactions involved as an operator seeks an acceptable compromise or optimum among these often conflicting criteria. The inherent feedback nature of the ongoing tradeoffs is designated by the comparison operations $\left(\begin{array}{c} + \to \otimes \to \\ -\uparrow \end{array} \right)$. Other influences, such as the degree of environmental disturbance (e.g. road bumps, gusts) and operator stochastic variability can indirectly affect the adopted strategies for monitoring, scanning, selecting control variables, and signal sampling-and-reconstruction.

Perceptual sampling operations are heavily involved in multi-axis vehicular control, where the operator must achieve a balance among a variety of options. These range from frequent sampling with zero- or first-order extrapolation between samples, to infrequent sampling with more elaborate mental extrapolation of the signal based on his internal model of the system response. The theory and much data on these aspects of perceptual operations are given in Refs. 8-10 and Section F, herein. The evolving "modern-control theory" approaches to manual control use a Kalman estimator in the perceptual subsystem to perform optimal estimation of useful information from observed states (e.g. Ref. 2). One of the prime roles of practice is to let the operator learn the response properties of his vehicle so that he may less frequently sample the displays (actual or proprioceptive), thereby reducing his perceptual loading.

Another important point noted on Fig. 1 is that performance tolerances - are more properly called "indifference thresholds" - are adjusted by the operator depending on both the required performance as well as the margins achieved. Usually, relaxing of performance tolerances has a powerful effect in reducing the perceptual-motor workload. Thus, <u>control over allowable tolerances must be exerted</u>, or known, <u>if meaningful workload measures are to be made.</u>

The basic difficulty in measuring, modelling, and predicting PML is that the operations in Fig. 1 are highly coupled and interdependent; thus changes in any of the inputs or blocks shown may alter each of the achieved results or margins. We will get to the "metacontrol system" which controls these factors, and measures of its activity, after a digression to discuss the concept of skill development and its role in perceptual-motor workload.

b) <u>Role of Skill Development</u> Perceptual-motor load has been carefully defined herein to involve only <u>conscious</u> perceptions and actions. As has been noted, sleepwalking would not be classed as a perceptual-motor load, nor would the mere execution of a highly complex (but well-learned) discrete aircraft manoeuvre. However, the activity involved in deciding which manoeuvre to make and when to make it does constitute a perceptual-motor load in our definition. It is handling the non-routine, unpredictable subtasks which taxes the operator's workload capacity.

One of the most commonly observed characteristics of psychomotor skill development is the progression from an instant-by-instant conscious perceptual-motor action, to a rapidly executed subroutine to a single command. The Successive Organization Of Perception (SOP) theory of manual control skill development was derived by Krendel and McRuer to model this situation (Refs. 1,11). Let us compare the three stages of SOP on a perceptual-motor load basis:

(1) Initial stage ("Compensatory" or error correcting control). The early phases of learning predominantly involve continuous, conscious activity. We would, therefore, expect a high PML during compensatory control.

(2) Intermediate stage ("Pursuit" or goal-pursuing control). A considerable portion of the controller's output results from execution of learned responses to discrete cues in the input (e.g. axis crossings for sine wave tracking). Compensatory control activity, although present, experimentally shows a regression in emphasis. This implies a lower sensorimotor activity level. Therefore, we would expect the pursuit of operation to have a lower PML than the compensatory stage, and it does (Ref. 12).

(3) Final stage ("Precognitive" or programmed control). At this level of skill, most of the operator's output consists of execution of learned and stored commands, and his conscious perceptual activity is mainly concerned with decision-making activity. This should result in a lower PML for a given control task, which it does (Ref. 13).

This progression in skill can be observed on a single complex task (e.g. tracking a quasi-predictable narrowband input with a K/s^2 controlled element), and results in an order-of-magnitude reduction in PML as practice and skill develop. Again we emphasize the need to allow for skill amd practice in measuring and predicting perceptual-motor load. More workload investigations have been rendered worthless by ignoring the role of skill development than by any other factor.

(c) The Metacontrol System. The perceptual-motor load is thus seen to relate mostly to the organizing, adaptive, and decision-making aspects of tracking rather than to the properties of the tracking signals themselves. Recognition of this important distinction should help to reconcile the fact that pilots rate a pursuit display as requiring less subjective workload than a compensatory display (Ref. 12). Our interpretation is that the perceptual-motor load is not correctly indicated by the displayed signal transinformation rate*, but rather by the traffic through that portion of perceptual-motor system required to organize and maintain the appropriate internal structure (e.g. compensatory, pursuit, precognitive).

Such a concept of perceptual-motor loading thus involves the "supervisory" control system of the human operator. Appropriately, this has been termed the metacontrol system** by Sheridan (Ref. 15). It is the channel capacity limitation of the metacontrol system which sets the pilot workload margin. Therefore, measures such as PML transinformation rate should be applied to the metacontrol system activity rather than to the tracking signals per se. Think of a large central telephone exchange. The measure of activity and workload is not the enormous number of information bits-per-second handled, nor the number of channels in use (they wax and wane); but it is the size of the operating work force and its excess capacity for new calls that is the true measure of system workload and workload margin. Even more relevant is a centralized, time-shared computing system, where each of several on-line customer's (buffered) demands are: scanned, allocated expected computing times based on stored averages from previous demands, and deferred if the system's excess data handling capacity drops below a certain margin. We believe that the roots of a serious PML workload theory will lie in this evolving technology of time-shared multiprocessor systems (e.g. Ref. 16).

---

* Metacontrol = The human's activity-supervising control, transcending the various directly-involved systems such as the perceptual, central, and neuromuscular systems. (from Greek: "meta" - "involved with changes").

** Transinformation rate = $W_{eff} \log_2 \left[\dfrac{1}{1 - r^2} \right]$ (from Ref. 14)

where r is the correlation between input and output amplitudes at each sample point and W_{eff} is the effective bandwidth of the input signal as defined in Ref. 31.

The importance of skill development in assessing PML is naturally contained in the metacontroller concept. As skill develops in a given sensorimotor task the metacontroller's involvement, and hence the PML, becomes less. It is known that many tasks involve an extremely lengthy learning period to achieve the "precognitive" skill level which is so desirable. Yet it is not appropriate to measure the operational perceptual-motor loading of such a task until the desired skill level has been reached. Although task performance measures such as mean-square-error may reach acceptable levels and remain there, the metacontroller's degree of involvement, and hence the PML, may change more slowly (e.g. driving a car). Many past experiments which have attempted to measure PML may have been seriously confounded by the relatively slow improvement in supervisory abilities relative to the sensorimotor skill per se (e.g. Refs. 17, 18).

By the same line of reasoning, a well-learned auxiliary task should show lower perceptual-motor loading than in its initial stages. Therefore, <u>any index of PML should be normalized with respect to the present ability of that subject in that task.</u> Practically speaking, this means referencing workload or performance margins to the achievable performance level in that task alone. Some authors, notably Broadbent (Ref. 19) and Knowles (Ref. 20), feel that PML tests should not be well practised so as to preserve their unexpected value. In our terms this means restricting the loading tasks to the "compensatory" level of metacontrol skill (i.e. of SOP).

The metacontroller model for perceptual-motor loading is not without problems, however. For one thing, the metacontroller system is not a distinct physiological unit and one cannot easily measure inputs to it and outputs from it. At best, external symptoms of attentional activity must be measured; e.g. successive eye fixations in a pattern recognition or a scanned display situation, or EEG changes. Furthermore, there is no a priori to believe that the metacontroller acts as a single-channel information handler. We know that sensorimotor activity can proceed in a multi-channel manner (e.g. driving our own car on a familiar route while conversing with a passenger). Unfortunately, we are still limited to verbal hypotheses for modeling the metacontroller system, whereas we need a quantitative index for PML.

In practice, then, we cannot directly measure the metacontroller system parameters for defining a pilot workload index but must focus our attention on the external symptoms of attentional activity. In the spirit of offering a more practical definition of workload which can be measured and predicted, we suggest that a suitable definition of <u>workload margin is the ability (or capacity) to accomplish additional tasks.</u> How to accomplish this will be discussed next.

PERCEPTUAL-MOTOR WORKLOAD IN MANUAL CONTROL TASKS

TECHNIQUES FOR CONTROLLING AND MEASURING PERCEPTUAL-MOTOR LOAD

In the absence of a comprehensive model like a metacontroller, a wide variety of techniques have been evolved to produce a controllable perceptual-motor load and to measure its effect on pilot workload and performance. We have divided these into seven basic techniques:

1. Subjective Ratings (e.g. Questionnaires, Cooper-Harper type rating scales).

2. Auxiliary Task Techniques.

    (i) Auxiliary Workload <u>Margin</u> at a <u>Constant</u> Main Task

    (ii) Main Task <u>Decrement</u> at Prescribed Auxiliary Task <u>Loads</u>

    (iii) Varying Difficulty Main Task

3. Scanning and Eye Traffic.

4. Psychophysiological Measurements.

5. Operator's Dynamic Behavior (e.g. Describing Function and Remnant Parameters).

6. Time-Line Analyses.

A summary of the more relevant workload identification techniques is given in Tables Ia, b, c in approximate order of increasing difficulty of measurement. A brief review and critique of each technique and reference has been given in Chapter VI Ref. 21, and an updated annotated bibliography, arranged in the order of Table I, is available as Ref. 53.

THE CROSS-COUPLED INSTABILITY TASK

1. Background

The basic objective in developing the STI Cross-Coupled-Instability Task (CCIT) was to provide a secondary control-type task which could load a pilot in a manner similar to the secondary control axes in a multi-degree-of-freedom task (e.g. while making a landing approach using ailerons and elevator as primary controls the pilot must also control speed with his throttle). In this context the CCIT is a surrogate for axes of control other than the

Table Ia

SCHEME	CRITERIA	COMMENTS	INVESTIGATORS
1. SUBJECTIVE PILOT RATINGS			
A. Pilot Rating Scales for aircraft, displays, controls	Low numerical rankings imply low workload	Highly developed and useful; requires experiments	(See References for Table I, pp. 46-51)
	Levels		
1) Cooper-Harper	Mission-related handling qualities H1-H10	Three-stage evaluation	Cooper, Harper, Ashkenas, McDonnell
2) Attentional Demand	Demands on subjects D1-D5	Continuum with verbal definitions	Clement, Hess
3) Controllability	Ease of control C1-C5	Two-stage evaluation	
4) Status Utility	Usability of information S1-S5	Continuum; verbal definitions	
5) Clutter	Clutter of display K1-K5	Continuum; verbal definitions	
B. Detailed pilot comments of "profile" evaluations	Key workload factors in profile	Complex, useful, tedious, hard to quantify	Harper, McDonnell
2.1. AUXILIARY WORKLOAD MARGINS AT GIVEN MAIN TASK LEVEL			
A. Discrete motor-task loads:			
1) Visual discrimination with bi-stable motor reaction, two-plate tapping, warning light response, etc.	Reduction in auxiliary response rate is measure of main task PML.	Number of similar tasks developed, easy to quantify as bits/sec. Relevance not always clear.	Bahrick, Knowles, Adams, Spyker, et al. Crossman; Benson
2) Foot-tapping irregularity, Interval Production Task (IPT)	Variation in interval of successive taps is measure of main task PML. Latency and errors or misses increase with PML of main task.	Easy to learn, but wide inter-subject variations imply progressive improvement. Easy to learn, well developed, hard to score and interpret. Gradual improvement.	Michon
3) Auditory shadowing; subject reverbalizes each seen or heard alphanumeric character group, as quickly as possible, under primary load and under no primary load.	$W = 1 - (A/B)$; where A = Rate of correct responses under load, B = Highest rate correct with no primary load. $W \equiv$ Workload fraction.	Takes numerous no-load runs to learn and set maximum no-load rate, B.	Price
B. Variable-difficulty auxiliary tracking tasks:			
1) Cross-adaptive inputs (CAI): auxiliary task input level is function of main task (error criterion).	$\sigma_{i_2} \sim \sqrt{(|e_1| - e_c)}$; σ_{i_2} is inversely related to main task workload.	On-line adaptation, easy to use. Task load increases required auxiliary-control work and main loop "tightness."*	Kelly
2) Cross-coupled instability (CCI): auxiliary task dynamics made more unstable as function of main task (error criterion).	$Y_{c_2} = K/[s - \lambda_2(t)]$; $\lambda_2 \sim \sqrt{(|e_1| - e_c)}$ λ_2 is inversely related to main task workload.	On-line; easy to use; relevant to multiloop control. Increasing λ_2 increases attentional demand of auxiliary task. Well validated in nonadaptive version. Adaptive λ_2 correlates well with Cooper ratings.	McDonnell, Jex

*Loads operator's control of auxiliary input amplitude or frequency without necessarily modulating mental workload.

Table Ib

SCHEME	CRITERIA	COMMENTS	INVESTIGATORS
2.1. AUXILIARY WORKLOAD MARGINS AT GIVEN MAIN TASK (Continued)			(See References for Table I, pp. 46-51)
C. Elapsed time interval estimation (ETI). "Concurrent": subject estimates end of a set interval (e.g., 10 sec). "Retrospective": subject estimate duration of a signaled interval.	Measures of central tendency, variability, skewness and kurtosis of distributions of elapsed time estimates provide measures of the cognitive, perceptual and motor loads imposed by concurrent primary tasks.	Concurrent or retrospective time estimation is a relevant, unobtrusive and minimally loading task for many flight scenarios. Easy to learn, but requires individual baseline calibration and considerable repetition to establish statistically significant changes in moments of distribution.	Hart, McPherson, Rosch
D. Item recognition using a variable memory set size, visual or auditory. Subject given "memory sets" of N items (e.g., 1-8 letters). A displayed letter has to be identified as in or out of each set; letters are presented as soon as previous one is responded to; Latency ≡ RT(N).	Increases in the slope of the Sternberg function [RT(N) vs. N] are a measure of higher cognitive loads imposed by concurrent primary tasks. Increases in the intercept of the Sternberg function are a measure of higher perceptual motor loads imposed by concurrent primary tasks.	Definite loading of primary task occurs, but may be independent of differential memory loads. Relatively easy to learn, but may not be motivating to subjects in some flight scenarios if mean interstimulus interval is too long. Requires individual baseline calibration and considerable repetition to establish statistically significant Sternberg function.	Sternberg; Swanson, Johnsen, Briggs; O'Donnell; Peters Barbato; Chase, Calfee
2.2. MAIN TASK DECREMENTS AT PRESCRIBED AUXILIARY TASK LOADS			
A. Discrete-response auxiliary task. Auditory discrimination task (ADT); subject responds to random binary-tone choice; auxiliary task load ~ rate of presentation.	"Perfect response to tones required, gives main task decrement which is related to its workload.	Well-developed and correlated with psychophysiological measures. Applicable to complex simulations. Relevance not always clear. Progressive learning.	Kalsbeek; Walker
B. Forced scanning task: Changes in scanning forced by "subcritical" instability auxiliary task.	Unstable Y_{c2} requires controllable attention. Main task sensitivity is measure of its workload.	Good relevance to certain aircraft situations, if substituted as one of multitask loops. Hard to learn, but has fairly stable asymptote.	Allen, Clement, Jex
2.3. VARYING DIFFICULTY MAIN TASK			
A. Sudden change in task dynamics; usually adverse (like damper failure)	Time to re-adapt. Percent lost. Latency for reacquiring control.	Relevance to workload is not always good. Low workload may increase percent loss. High relevance to failure-management load.	Elkind, Miller; Weir, Phatak
B. Critical Instability Task: $Y_c = K/s^n[s - \lambda(t)]$; n = 0, 1, 2. Instability λ increased gradually to loss of control.	"Critical instability" ↑ λ_c. Decrement in λ_c results from increased workload.	Mainly applicable to PML changes due to displays, controls, or auxiliary loadings.	Jex, et al., McDonnell

Table Ic

SCHEME	CRITERIA	COMMENTS	INVESTIGATORS
3. SCANNING AND EYE TRAFFIC			(See References for Table I, pp. 46-51)
A. Dwell fractions (probabilities of fixation) and look fractions	Should be largest on centrally located displays.	Useful only as relative measure of fractional scanning workload because of "Parkinson's Law" for the eye.	Fitts, et al.; Senders, et al.; Allen, Jex, Clement; Weir, Klein
B. One and two-way link values	Should be largest on shortest transition paths with respect to centrally located displays.	Hard to measure in field. May reveal "stare mode" or "tunnel vision" on integrated displays by absence of scanning traffic.	Same as above
4. PSYCHOPHYSIOLOGICAL MEASUREMENTS			
A. Cardiovascular parameters (heart rate, respiratory rates and flux, etc.).	Increased levels or rates imply heavier system demands.	Respiratory amplitudes and rates mostly highly correlated with auxiliary task measures of workload, but connections not yet clear; some measurements redundant; homeostatic dynamics interact.	Kalsbeek; Benson, et al.; Roman, Lewis; Sayers; Spyker, et al.
B. Electroencephalograph (EEG) (α waves); pupil diameter; galvanic skin resistance (GSR).	Changes imply more arousal or emotional involvement.	Hard to measure (except GSR) in field; connections not yet clear.	Anderson, Pietrzak (pupil diameter) Spyker, et al.; Beatty (pupil diameter)
C. EEG (evoked response)	Average power and latencies of peak amplitudes.	Connections not yet clear. Latency decreases with workload, but inter-subject variance is large.	Spyker, et al. Wickens, et al.
D. Electromyograph (EMG)	Average neuromuscular tension, grip pressure and tremor frequency.	Average tension inversely correlated with effective time delay.	McRuer; Spyker, et al.
E. Voice Tone Voice-print analyzer measures harmonic spacing of key words.	Increasing average tone indicates more systemic "Tension" or involvement.	Voice pitch is sensitive to both arousal state and to emotional state, perhaps mostly the latter. Highly developed by Russians, on Space Program	Luk'yanov, Frolov
5. OPERATOR'S DYNAMIC BEHAVIOR			
A. Describing functions and model parameters (gain, lead, lag, τ_{eff}, remnant, stability margins)	K_P vs. K_{Popt}; T_L relative to 1.0 sec, τ_e vs. τ_{eo}, σ_{nne}/σ_e^2, K_M, ϕ_M	Low and high regions established for single loop and some multiloop cases.	McRuer, Ashkenas, Stapleford, Ringland Craig, Weir
B. Control and error spectra resonance peaks	"Peaks imply difficulty" (low ζ_{CL}).	Still embryonic, flight tests in progress.	Schweizer
6. TIME LINE ANALYSES			
A. Checklists, truth tables	Time to perform tasks, probability of error.	Very gross and subjective. Unreasonably complex and costly for their utility; relevance to workload is not always good.	Pickrel, McDonald Cole, Shoquist
B. Simulation models	Time to perform tasks, probability of error, operator overload and underload.	Require such extensive calibration based on similar existing systems that only relative judgments can be made.	Siegel and Wolf Senders, Carbonell Pritsker, Dickey, Linton, Wherry

primary task under investigation. Because much of the material is not in easily available form, in this section we will summarize first the background of Critical Tasks and scanning research that underlies the CCIT.

(a) Critical Task - (Single Axis). Our earlier Critical-Task Test (CTT) has been developed to measure the operator's limits of control in a fully-demanding single-axis task. We (and others) were able to demonstrate close control over the operator's compensatory control behavior so that selected model parametrs could be correlated with the critical-instability score (Ref. 22 through 25). In short, CTT uses an unstable controlled element having an adjustable first-order divergence:

$$Y_c(s) = \frac{K}{-T_\lambda s + 1} = \frac{K}{\frac{-s}{\lambda} + 1} = \frac{-K\lambda}{s - \lambda} \quad (1)$$

Where: K = DC gain

T_λ = Divergence time - constant (sec)

λ = $1/T_\lambda$ the level of instability (break frequency, rad/sec.)

The level of instability is increased by a special "autopacer", rapidly at first and then gradually, until the subject just loses control. This defines the "Critical Instability" λ_c (rad/sec), which has been found by numerous investigators to be a very stable parameter for a given combination of display, control, and operator. An operator can track continuously at some "sub-critical" level of λ, less than his critical level for the given control display combination, and his describing function parameters can be modelled and measured quite precisely. The input can be quite small (sufficient for identification) because the operator's own remnant excites the system.

By means of theory and describing function measurements, λ_c has been shown to be primarily dependent on the net effective operator perceptual-motor delay τ_e (sec) (e.g., Refs. 26 and 27). An empirical function found to be valid with correlation coeffecient of R = 0.86 over two orders of critical task and several different experiments (all with CRT displays and pressure controls) is:

$$\lambda_c \doteq \frac{\tau_e^{-1} + 0.04}{1.52} \quad (2)$$

It is the CTT, with its extensive theoretical and empirical background that forms the foundation for the cross-coupled instability task.

(b) <u>Interference Between Two Subcritical Tasks.</u> Consider an operator controlling simultaneously two unstable tasks, one with his left hand and one with his right with separate but nearly identical displays. One task (call it the secondary task) has constant λ at different subcritical levels, the other (call it primary) is autopaced to the critical limited. The subject must timeshare these tasks rapidly because looking away for even one second would result in loss of control. We have found that the critical instability score depends strongly on the presence and degree of instability of the subcritical task (See Fig. 2, taken from Ref. 28).

The key observation is that: for both subjects the presence of the secondary task causes an initial decrement in λ_c, after which the achievable score decreases at an accelerating rate (shown by dashed fairings, based on other data). More importantly, reflection will show that running λ_1 to its (autopaced) limit λ_{c1} also results in λ_2 being at its (constant) limit. However, there does <u>not</u> appear to be a simple arithmetic relationship among λ_{c1}, λ_2, and λ_{c0} in Fig. 2 (e.g. $\lambda_{c1} + \lambda_2 \neq \lambda_{c0}$) such as might be suggested by the inverse proportionality between λ_c and τ_e in Eq. 2 (e.g. $\tau_{e1}^{-1} + \tau_{e2}^{-1} \neq \tau_{e0}^{-1}$, either).

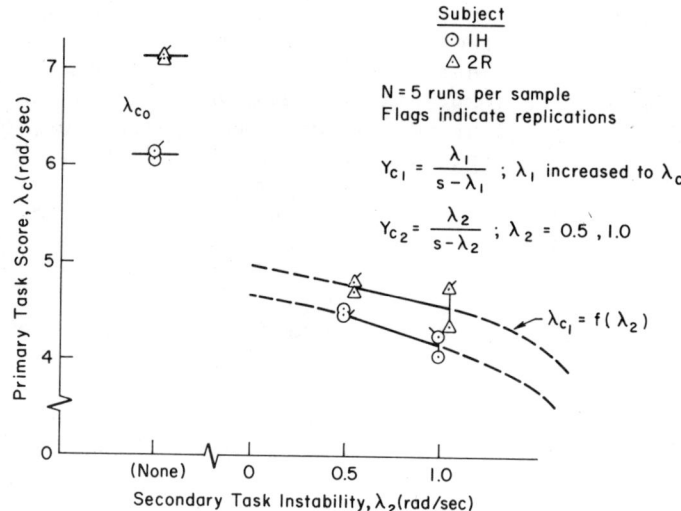

Figure 2. Effect of Secondary Task Instability on the Primary Task Critical Instability (Revised from Jex, Ref. 28).

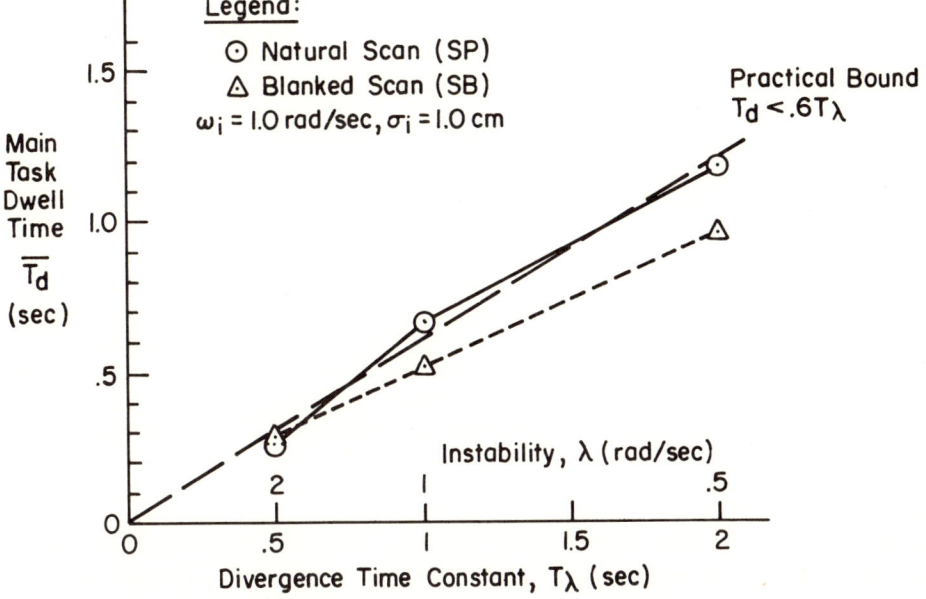

Figure 3. Main Task Dwell-Time as Limited by the Side Task Divergence Time Constant (from Allen, et al, Ref. 9).

Clearly more subcritical tasks can be handled simultaneously than would be implied by alternating attention based on a single-channel theory with an upper bound on displayed signal transinformation rate. This finding has been corroborated in Ref. 38 with up to four simultaneous tasks, where it has been discovered that the transinformation rate increases relatively more with the number of simultaneous tasks than with the bandwidth of the tracking signal. Therefore, by any simple theory, the interference effects do not appear to be arithmetically additive in terms of λ. We have not yet mapped out the complete range of λ_{c1} versus λ_2 (from 0 to λ_{c0}); which, with concurrent eye scanning and psychophysiological measurements, would make an excellent undergraduate thesis! Nevertheless, we shall see that this concept of using a subcritical task to control the workload of a primary task in a natural manner is a most useful tool.

(c) <u>Effect of Secondary Task Instability on Scanning</u>. The success of the previous experiment led us to use a subcritical instability to control the scanning behavior in a series of experiments designed to validate certain models of display scanning (eye-point-of-regard), sampling (perception), and signal reconstruction (state estimation and control). The experiments involved simultaneous compensatory tracking with separated controls and with displays separated by 10, 20 and 30 degrees visual angle, measurements of performance, describing functions, and eye-point-of-regard, and (in some cases) "blanking" the non-fixated display to preclude parafoveal perception of it. References 8-10 (especially Ref. 9), 29, and 30 can be consulted for the voluminous details, and only some key results relevant to the control of and measurement of perceptual workload will be summarized here.

The most useful discovery was that the level of subcritical instability of the secondary task λ_2 could be used to control eye scanning in a way quite natural to the pilots used as subjects. With no input other than the pilot's remnant, the secondary display would diverge off scale in a time proportional to $T_\lambda = 1/\lambda_2$. Theoretically, the pilot can afford to look away from the subcritical task only for a period less than T_λ or he will lose control. Figure 3 verifies this hypothesis: for natural scans of 30 degrees (where some parafoveal detection of the secondary task error is possible), the primary task dwell time T_d (i.e. time away from the subcritical task) was about 60 per cent of T_λ; for the case with the non-fixated display blanked the time away from the subcritical task was about 50 per cent of T_λ. A simple rule of thumb for cases where parafoveal viewing is minimal is that: the time away from an isolated subcritical task display is limited to about: $T_d \leq 0.5\, T_\lambda$, or $T_d \leq 0.5/\lambda$.

Considering that the minimum dwell time on the primary display was found to be about 0.4 seconds, it can be shown that these two findings imply that:

Main Task Dwell Fraction: $\eta = \dfrac{T_d}{T_s}\bigg|_{max} \leq \dfrac{1}{1 + 0.67\,\lambda}$ (3)

Where: T_d = dwell time (sec)

T_s = total scan intervals (sec)

λ = secondary task instability (rad/sec)

This result closely matches the data as shown on Figure 4a.

Figure 4 also illustrates that in the naturally scanned case, the primary task error was only mildly affected by this relatively demanding secondary tracking task, although it increased substantially when parafoveal monitoring (hence optimal scan allocation) was precluded. Incidentally, close visual analysis of time traces with scan patterns superimposed showed no evidence for signal reconstruction between samples in the main task (where the input masks error trends) but some evidence for it in the form of zero-order-holds of the stick on the secondary task, which had no input (see Ref. 9).

From a theoretical point of view, these data offer solid clues to the activity of the "metacontrol system" of the CNS in Fig. 1 which monitors and allocates attentional scanning to keep within the constraints of: stability, acceptable performance, and perceptual motor workload. From a practical point of view the subcritical secondary task offers a reliable and simple way to

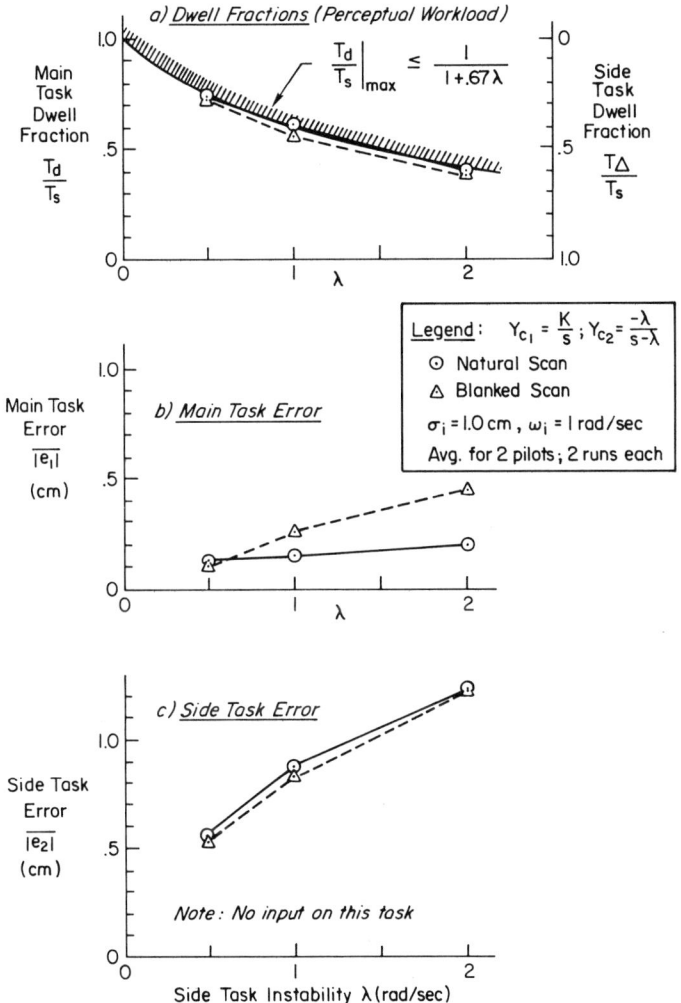

Figure 4. Effects of Side-Task Instability on Performance and Perceptual Workload in a Scanned-Display Task (From Ref. 9).

control its attentional demand, and to permit calibration of various other types of workload strain measures against an easily defined and meaningful workload stressor. A suggested set of standard tasks is included in Ref. 54.

2. Cross-Coupling the Subcritical Task

(a) Description. Building on the previously described findings that a subcritical secondary task could act as a surrogate for other control axes and attentional demands without seriously changing the primary task strategy or behavior, we carefully developed formalized structure and algorithms to use this effect for precise measurement of excess control capacity in a multiaxis control situation. Figure 5 shows the main elements and their functions, with each block representing more or less complex operations. For those who wish to use this task, a detailed mechanization and description from Ref. 32 will be given in the Appendix of the formal paper.

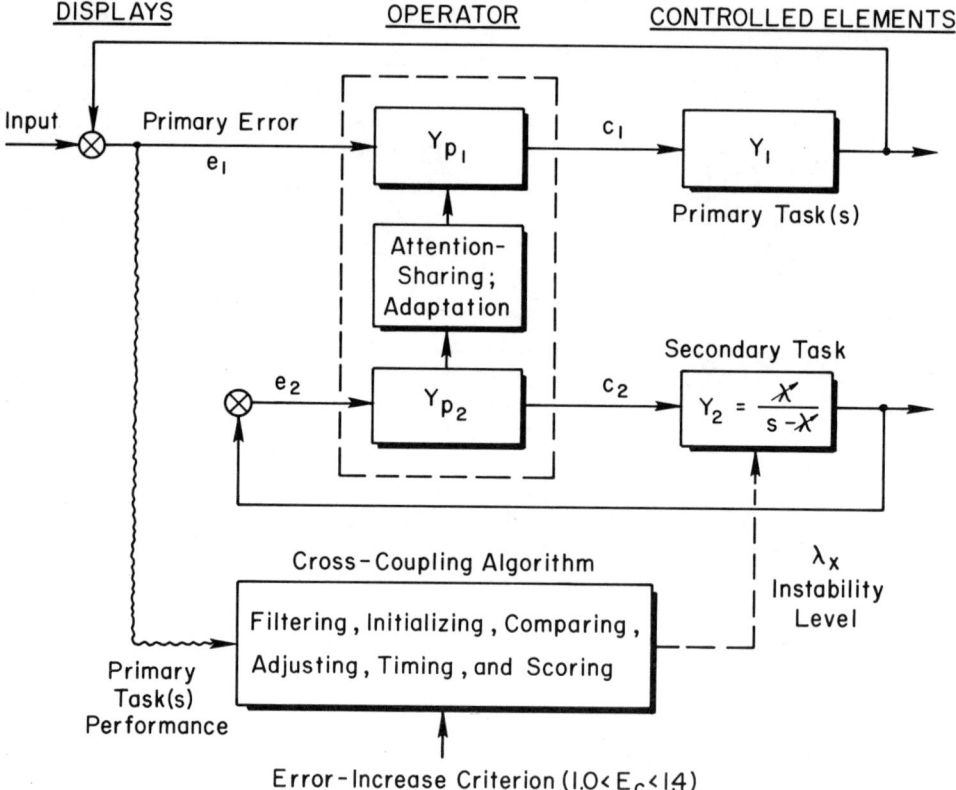

Figure 5. Elements of the Cross-Coupled Instability Task (CCIT) (From Jex, Ref. 32).

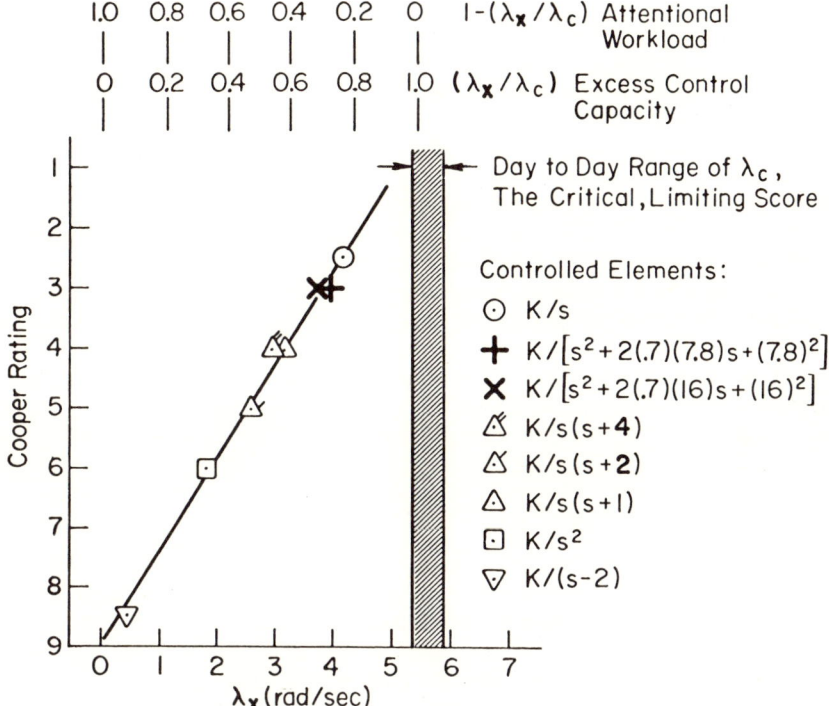

Figure 6. Cross Adaptive Measure of Excess Control Capacity For Several Examples of Primary Controlled Elements (From McDonnell, Ref. 33).

.. Increasing controlled-element-difficulty (more lead equilization required) clearly increases the workload relatively more than the error.

.. Increasing quantization also increases workload relatively more than error in most cases, except for K/s^2.

.. For K/s^2, quantization actually helps the perceptual system to generate lead equalization (derived rate), without escalating workload but at the expense of more errors.

Referring to Fig. 5, notice that a given primary task or ensemble (e.g. longitudinal and/or lateral aircraft control) is monitored for performance, which is not allowed to grow more than 10 to 30 per cent over the unloaded performance, measured at the beginning of each run to normalize effects of skill, learning, and individual variations from session to session. Special filtering and trend circuits detect when the unloaded primary task performance is stable, at which point the performance (accuracy = $1/\sigma_e$) is logged for later use, and the cross-coupling activated. A plausible secondary task, in the primary task context (e.g. speed control by throttle), is simulated with a first-order-instability whose level is slowly increased as long as the smoothed primary task error is less than the "error-increase criterion" (E = loaded/unloaded performance, where $1.1 < E < 1.3$). As the primary performance increase approaches E, the cross-coupled instability becomes asymptotic and its average is scored as the cross-coupled-limit, λ_x. The "Excess Control Capacity," EC (an index of workload margin), is found by dividing λ_x by λ_c, the subjects' critical instability score for the same session, using the secondary task control and display with no primary task:

$$EC = \lambda_x/\lambda_c \mid \text{same Ss, session, task} \qquad (4)$$

As previously established, λ_x is an inverse measure of the fraction of time the operator can spend away from the primary task; thus it is a direct measure of excess control capacity. Normalizing by the individual concurrent level of λ_c makes the EC score truly representative of workload margin and not just skill in secondary task tracking. Reference 32 describes the development of this task, the detailed operation, and a series of experiments which validate the assumption that the primary task behavior is not changed in form and by only a small and controlled degree.

Individual measurements of excess control capacity for each of two or more primary tasks can be combined by a multiplication process (Ref. 5) to estimate the combined value of EC which would be measured if all of the given "primary" tasks were performed in concert. The combined value of EC is given by the product of the individual values of EC:

$$(EC)_n = \prod^n (EC)_i$$

This empirical "product rule" has been validated with more extensive multiaxis Cooper-Harper rating data in Ref. 51. In effect, the product rule results in the physically satisfying vector addition of individual and combined fractional values of EC, regardless of the number of "primary" tasks.

For an overall figure of performance, we sometimes calculate a Performance Penalty index, P, which combines the input-normalized error with the inverse of excess control capacity (call it workload index = λ_c/λ_x)

$$P = \frac{\sigma_e}{\sigma_i} + \frac{\lambda_c}{\lambda_x} \quad (6)$$

where P = Performance Penalty

σ_e = rms <u>unloaded</u> error

σ_i = rms input

λ_c = critical instability with no primary task

λ_x = cross-coupled instability

Note that limiting $\sigma_{e\ loaded}/\sigma_{e\ unloaded}$ to $\leq$ E during each run, still allows a better tracker to achieve a lower penalty score.

(b) <u>Application.</u> An early form of cross coupled instability, obtained by manually increasing λ while observing smoothed error, was used by McDonnell (Ref. 33) to correlate excess control capacity versus the type of controlled element in the primary task. A subjective estimate of difficulty was the Cooper-Harper handling qualities rating, made by each pilot. With each controlled element at its "best gain" setting, the correlation of λ_x with Cooper-Harper rating was excellent, as shown in Fig. 6.

In another successful application Hess and Teichgraber (Ref. 34) measured the λ_x and performance for a series of three increasingly difficult controlled elements, and within each element tested the effects of increasingly coarse quantization of the error display. Results adapted from their work are displayed in Fig. 7, where the components of Performance Penalty index, P, (Eq. 6) are shown by the components of each bar. (The data presented in Ref. 34 required the use of an ensemble λ_c for this subject). The P index and components in Fig. 7 show the following:

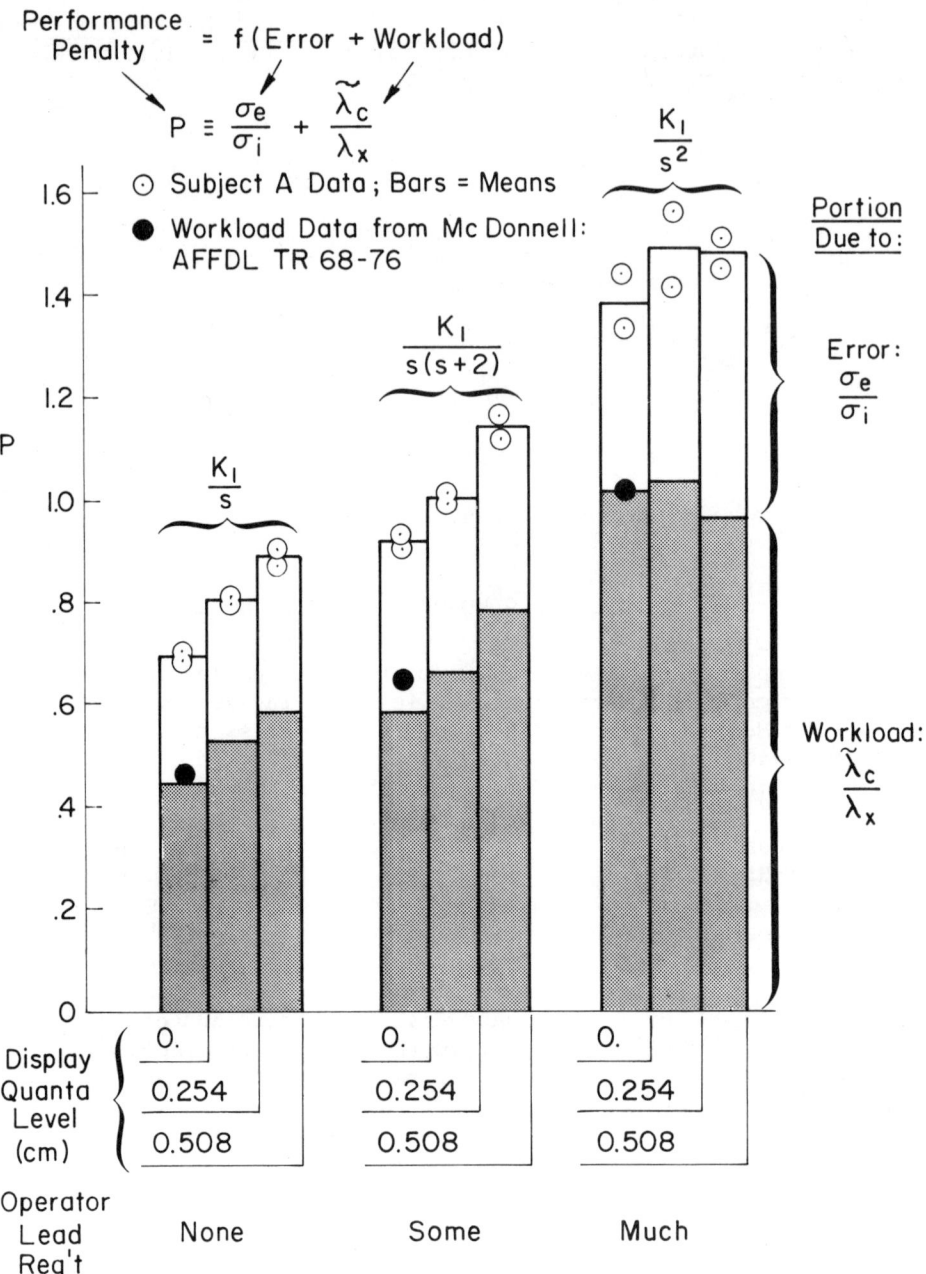

Figure 7. Typical Application of Adaptive-Workload Testing (From Hess and Teichgraber, Ref. 34).

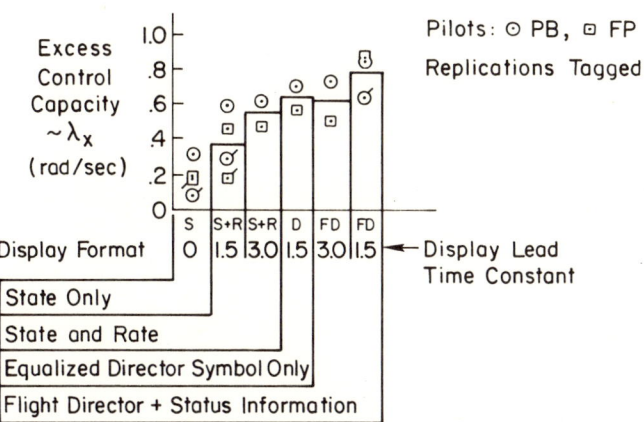

Figure 8. λ_x as a measure of excess control capacity for various VTOL integrated displays (from Clement et al., Ref. 35).

.. (Not shown) The subjective difficulty correlated with the P index.

.. Independent data on the workload index portion of P (i.e., λ_c/λ_x) is available from McDonnell's work (Ref. 33) and correlates very well with Ref. 34.

Such combined measures of error and workload can help to untangle the often anomalous trends in pure performance measures.

A third application of the CCIT in complex display research is given in Ref. 10 and 35, in which various flight director laws and integrated displays were tested with varying lead equalization time constants. The primary task was pitch and speed control during a simulated helicopter landing approach, while the cross-coupled secondary task was simulated roll control, but with an unstable element in lieu of the actual dynamics. Some results are shown in Fig. 8. Due to task complexity the achieved values of λ_x are low but they still distinguish among the displays in a manner consistent with concurrently sampled subjective evaluations of display workload.

Very recently, the CCIT has been employed to compare several pilots' use of a moving-map display with their use of a horizontal situation indicator (HSI) in a STOL airport-approach navigation task (Ref. 36). Here the average λ_x/λ_c was evaluated over several segments of the complex approach path shown in Fig. 9 which presents an example of results by one pilot using the HSI. The cross-coupled scheme was digitally mechanized on the NASA

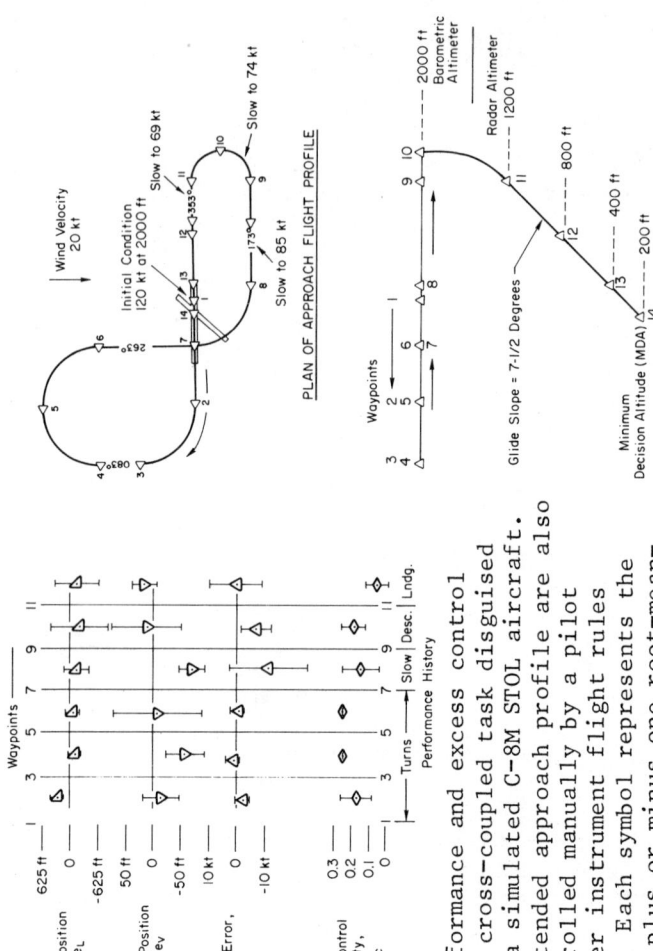

Figure 9. Sampled error performance and excess control capacity statistics with the cross-coupled task disguised as the spiral divergence of a simulated C-8M STOL aircraft. The plan elevation of the intended approach profile are also shown. The aircraft was controlled manually by a pilot using raw situation data under instrument flight rules without any flight director. Each symbol represents the time-averaged mean value and plus or minus one root-mean-square value between the numbered waypoints on the approach profile. The adaptive spiral divergence was cross-coupled to a weighted linear combination of the three error performance measures shown, and the weighted error reference was ten per cent greater than the pilot's own baseline error performance without the cross-coupled adaptive loading task. The maximum possible value of the excess control capacity measurement was limited at 0.25. This maximum value was reached between waypoints 3 and 7. (From Clement, ref. 36).

STOLAND* simulator using a weighted linear combination of the three error performance measures examples of which are also represented in Fig. 9. The caption for the figure describes the application. The average trends in λ_x/λ_c were supported by the pilots' subjective impressions and by measurements from another secondary caution-light-cancelling task. The excess control capacity provided by the moving map display was superior to that provided by the HSI in missed approaches and holding patterns, where maintaining geographic orientation involved more attentional demands when using the HSI.

Finally, the CCIT has been used by Merhav and Ben Ya'avoc with a digital primary task to evaluate some novel control-feel devices used in the cross-coupled task (Ref. 37). The error measure was the latency in responding to digital voltmeter readings, and the Performance Penalty index P (Eq. 6) was the figure of merit. The novel control feel used showed great improvements over conventional spring sticks in terms of λ_x and P.

Thus, we believe that the cross coupled instability task has a well validated basis, considerable successful experience in use, and it deserves to be one standard tool, among others, in the workload measurement arsenal.

WORKLOAD IN DISCRETE TASKS AND MONITORING TASKS

The measures of workload which we have discussed for simultaneous control tasks are often difficult to use for discrete primary tasks and monitoring tasks, either because such tasks have no continuously measurable performance, or because they are so absorbing of short-term attention that other control tasks are impossible in a continuous control sense. The interval between stimulus and action may be exceptionally long and variable in such cases, making any on-line measure of workload almost meaningless.

Normally, the excess control capacity of the pilot or other crew member is, by design, sufficient to handle discrete and monitoring tasks. When a lengthy discrete task, an intrusion, distraction, or failure replaces prior attentional demands which occupy the excess control capacity, the normal full-time attentional equilibrium is upset. Often the pilot must postpone attention to some of his discrete and monitoring tasks or compromise his tracking performance. It is appropriate to seek models and measures for such situations from unsteady queueing theory (renewal theory).

---

* STOLAND is a versatile digital navigation, guidance, and control system developed by Ames Research Center for conducting experiments with advanced STOL aircraft.

1. Average Duty Cycle

Before we consider renewal theory, however, it is worthwhile to mention another "steady-state equivalent" analytical technique which is especially useful for incorporating the average time required to perform discrete tasks. If we identify the total average time allowed for a short segment of the flight profile at $\bar{T}$ and the total average time used for discrete tasks as $\bar{T}_u$, we can define the average or "steady-state equivalent" discrete task duty cycle, $\bar{T}_u/\bar{T}$. This discrete task measure is commensurate with (but not equal to) excess control capacity, λ_x/λ_c. If $\bar{T}_u/\bar{T} < \lambda_x/\lambda_c$ for the pilot, presumably he is, in an average sense, less than fully occupied (i.e. unsaturated) with both steady-state tracking and discrete tasks over the segment of the flight profile in question. But what about his potential for dealing with unexpected intrusions or emergencies in such a case?

2. Oversaturated Demands.

Senders (Ref. 39) has suggested that the attentional overloading process is analogous to the load on an oversaturated queueing process. This is called a "renewal" type of load. Each source of information for each discrete task is a focal point of attention which, in turn, "loads" a channel in one modality at intervals which obey some probability distribution. The combined stream of attentional demands formed by pooling the demands from the many sources has some sort of special distribution of inter-arrival times. It can be shown that in such cases the statistical form of the distribution of several pooled demands is approximately random over periods shorter than the mean inter-arrival interval from any one source (see Fig. 10).

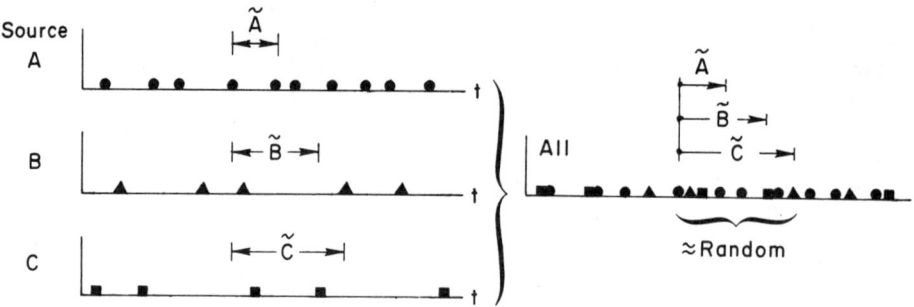

Figure 10. Sketch illustrating Randomness of Pooled Parallel Demands.

There is no problem as long as the duration of attention to each demand is sufficiently short so that none interferes with another. However, when the ensemble demand intervals are shorter than their attention time, others must wait and a queue develops. As the average demand duty cycle approaches 100 per cent, the process becomes oversaturated. Since an oversaturated queueing process is not in equilibrium, and since time-dependent analytical solutions to queueing problems are either unobtainable or unmanageable, we shall subsequently adopt some results from renewal theory for a more practical model of average overloading.

Lee (Ref. 40) has analyzed the human errors of a departure traffic controller in air terminal ground operations. The relative frequency of controller errors was directly proportional to the volume of short-term work backlog in times of oversaturation. Since the short-term backlog was supposed to occupy (by definition) the controller's mind, the results may be applicable to the pilot's transient cockpit workload buildup in oversaturated conditions.

Cox and Smith (Ref. 41) offer an approximate analytical method based on renewal theory which can be adopted for predicting the mean and variance of the volume of attentional "backlog" when the attentional loading becomes oversaturated. The average number of unattended "demands" during the oversaturated period, t, can be estimated from the following sum:

$$\bar{N}_t \doteq \bar{N}_o + \left(\bar{f}_d - \frac{1}{\bar{T}_d}\right) \cdot t \qquad (7)$$

where $\bar{N}_t$ is the average backlog of unattended "demands" in an oversaturated interval, t, since onset of the "emergency"

$\bar{N}_o$ is the initial backlog associated with the emergency

$\bar{f}_d$ is the average demand frequency associated with the emergency

$\bar{T}_d$ is the average demand interval required by the pilot in performing the task

For a given situation the demand frequency of "emergencies" $\bar{f}_d$ must be given or estimated. The particular instant of occurrence in time is unknown and, indeed, is not even required. Only an incremental demand interval $\bar{T}_d$ which is characteristic of an emergency need be established. For example, in case of control failure, this time interval may be taken as the sum of one or more of the three phases of failure management given in Ref. 42:

"retention of prior strategy","nonlinear control reacquisition," and "readjustment of control". Then the conditional probability of human error in coping with the backlog of demands can be estimated in direct proportion to $\bar{N}_t$ by Eq. 7.

So far we have considered only the build-up of oversaturation. If the frequency of demand slacks off, such that $\bar{f}_d < 1/\bar{T}_d$, the average recovery time, T_r, is given by the following equation:

$$\bar{T}_r \doteq \frac{\bar{N}_{t_{max}} - \bar{N}_r}{\frac{1}{\bar{T}_d} - \bar{f}_{d_r}} \qquad (8)$$

where $\bar{N}_{t_{max}}$ is the maximum value of N_t associated with the incident

$\bar{N}_r$ is the average number of distinct "fixations" associated with the post failure steady-state

$\bar{f}_{d_r}$ is now the average fixation frequency demand associated with the recovery steady-state and $\bar{f}_{d_r} < 1/\bar{T}_d$

The longer the recovery interval, the greater may be the likelihood of compounding the probability of human error, for example through fatigue.

We believe that some of these simple concepts from queueing theory can be useful in modelling and measuring perceptual motor workload in cases where discrete tasks are predominant, or where they impinge on already highly loaded control situations (e.g. landing certain V/STOL aircraft which do not have good stability augmentation systems). In the next article, a theoretical development which may help to tie these two types of situation together will be presented.

SAMPLING NOISE

1. Finite-Dwell Random Sampling Theory

The theory for modelling the increased control "remnant" (that portion of a signal not linearly correlated with the input) for cases where the display is scanned intermittently also turns out to be applicable to other task interferences with monitoring or control process. This theory will be summarized here, because it gives great insight and may be applicable in problems beyond those for which it was derived. (See Refs. 8-10).

Consider a human operator randomly scanning and sampling one or more displays with an average intersample period T_s (sec), and some variability denoted by the standard deviation σ_{T_s}. (Scanning interval distributions can be represented by a Pearson Type III {modified gamma function} distribution having lower bound T_o such that $T_s - T_o$ approximates σ_{T_s}.) Each signal is perceived for a finite dwell time T_d, for an average dwell-time fraction of $\eta = T_d/T_s$. The perceived signal thus consists of the actual signal $x(t)$ over T_d and zero over $T_s - T_d$, as sketched for one sinusoid in Fig. 11. Now, subtract that portion linearly correlated with the actual signal (and given by its "describing function" - shown by an interrupted line). The shaded difference represents the scanning and sampling noise, or "remnant". From the early work of Bergen, followed by the finite dwell model (Ref. 9), it can be shown that, when sampling is <u>not</u> periodic (has rms variations σ_{T_s}), this remnant becomes wideband noise and is demodulated to frequencies well below the average scanning and sampling frequency. The noise can be characterized at these lower frequencies by a first-order power-spectral density in terms of circular frequency ($\omega = 2\pi f$) π

$$\Phi_{nn_s}(\omega)\Big|_{\omega \ll \omega_s} \doteq \frac{\overline{x^2}(1-\eta)\sigma_{T_s}}{\pi\{1+(\omega T_d/2)^2\}} \quad ; \quad \frac{(\text{signal units})^2}{\text{rad/sec}} \tag{9}$$

where T_s = Mean sampling time; T_d = Mean dwell time;

$\eta \doteq T_d/T_s$ $(0 > \eta < 1)$ σ_{T_s} = rms sampling variation

Thus, the low-frequency scanning remnant level is increased by both lower dwell time (via $1 - \eta$) and by increased scanning variability (via σ_{T_s}). The term $(1 - \eta)$ is that fraction of the average sampling period in which the sampled display is <u>not</u> perceived, i.e. the "undwell fraction".

Notice that the sampling remnant level scales with $\overline{x^2}$, the mean square of the signal being sampled. Thus the low frequency level of root-mean square (rms) noise is proportional to the rms signal. This means that random scanning creates <u>multiplicative</u> noise(i.e. it has a noise/signal ratio which behaves like Weber's law). This has important consequences for performance and workload, as shown next. Similar expressions result from parallel channel noise theory (Ref. 2).

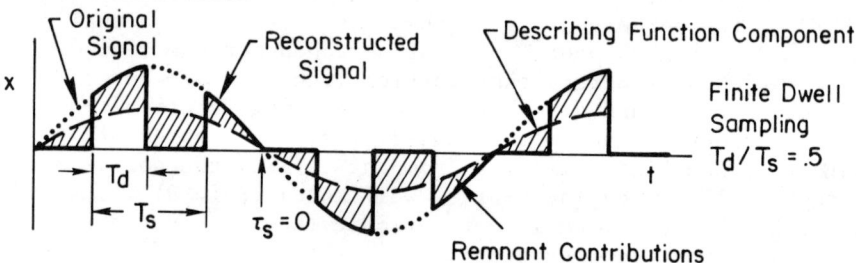

Figure 11. Effects of Finite Dwell Sampling on the reconstructed Signal's Describing Function and Remnant.

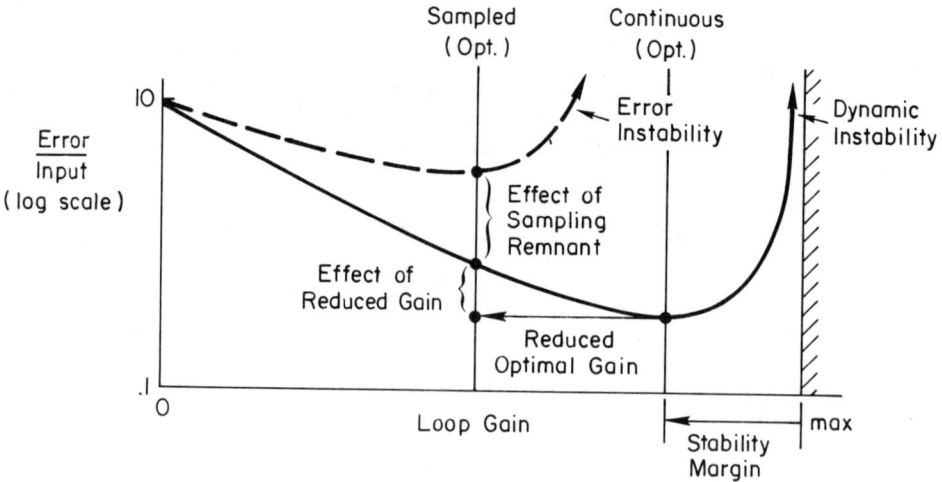

Figure 12. Sketch of Scanning Implications on Loop Closure and Performance.

2. Effects on Control Performance

We have applied finite dwell random sampling theory to model scanned tracking displays in Refs. 8-10. The details are too complex to give here, but the key results for closed-loop tracking tasks are as follows (and have been verified empirically, especially in Refs. 9 and 10):

- Finite-dwell quasi-random scanning and sampling reduces the loop gain, but adds little to the effective loop delay. The optimum gain is less, too.

- Because the scanning and sampling noise is multiplicative, lightly damped modes are greatly excited by sampling noise, and the closed loop errors can blow up as gain is increased, before the loop becomes dynamically unstable. (This is termed error instability in the mean-square sense).

- Various types of signal "reconstruction" during the undwell period (e.g. state- and/or rate-extrapolation) can reduce the sampling noise, but at the expense of increased mental workload and signal processing delays which, in turn, destabilize the man-machine loop, thereby making it hard to overcome the detrimental effects of scanning in some situations.

The sketch in Fig. 12 shows the three-way effects of sampling on manual control loop closure and performance. The scanning experiments reported in Refs. 9 and 10 have validated these theoretical implications.

3. Discrete Task Interference

Although it was derived for display scanning, this model and these results have a far wider application. Any task sharing which requires the operator to divert attention more-or-less periodically will produce similar effects - and this includes: internal sharing of attention among various control axes, concurrent discrete tasks (e.g. communications, configuration, or navigation procedures), cognitive tasks, and workload measurement tasks. The type and degree of interference could be estimated by this approach, if a better data base were available.

Among the more interesting implications of this theory in the discrete task situation are:

- Task interference will be proportional to the average discrete demand duty-cycle (via $1 - \eta$) and to the randomness of demand (via σ_{T_s}).

- The quality of the ongoing control task loop closure must always suffer, albeit not very much if the closure is near optimum, and the sampling remnant is small.

- Paradoxically, dynamic stability margins (gain and phase-margins) will increase with sampling (see Fig. 12) although error instability may be incipient. Experiments (e.g. Ref. 9) bear out this implication.

- Discrete task interference can be reduced by proper mental signal reconstruction (extrapolation) during the diversion of attention, but only at the expense of additional mental workload and possibly additional loop delays, if the human operator be restricted to the compensatory level in the successive organization of perception (SOP). If, instead, the pursuit or pre-cognitive levels of SOP can be adopted, discrete task interference may well be reduced without as great a cost in additional workload, as discussed previously.

We think this approach has much for workload research, and would like to hear of any experimental or theoretical work along these lines by other investigators. Again, this sort of research requires only basic theory and equipment, yet produces dramatic results, thereby lending itself to thesis work.

PSYCHOPHYSIOLOGICAL MEASURES OF WORKLOAD

The desire to avoid changing the operator's task variables while measuring mental workload, coupled with a belief that there must be some measurable manifestation of the mental loading if only one could find it; has resulted in much research in psychophysiological (PP) correlates of mental workload such as: heart-rate and its variations, breathing rate, neuromuscular tension, palmar skin response, pupillometry and endocrine-gland excretions (e.g. Refs. 6, 43-45). The Russians have been especially diligent in this area. (See the books translated as Refs. 46 and 47). So far, (except for subjective ratings!) the search for the "mental-workload-signal" has found only _ignes fatui_*in the form of most of the easily

---

* Ignis fatuus - phospherescent light that flits over swampy areas; hence, something that misleads or deludes one into a morass
(Ed.)

PERCEPTUAL-MOTOR WORKLOAD IN MANUAL CONTROL TASKS

measured external symptoms. We would like to discuss a few facets of this approach, based on our work of several years ago.

1. <u>PP Correlates of Difficult Tracking Tasks</u>

During the development of a battery of difficult tracking tasks for the NASA Ames Research Center, (Ref. 48) measured several psychophysiological variables during compensatory tracking with first-, second-, and third-order unstable (subcritical) tasks. These were subjectively rated, respectively, as: "mildly difficult", "very difficult", and "almost impossible". Concurrent measures were made of: finger-stick grip-pressure (normal to the direction of applied force), bipolar sternum electrocardiogram (EKG). heart-rate (via on-line cardiotachometer), breath flow (via a lag-compensated nasal thermistor, mouth closed), electromyograms (EMG; rectified and filtered) at several active- and passive-limb sites, and palmar akin resistance (at constant current). See Ref. 48 for details.

Figure 13 gives some of the typical results for four subjects showing: heart rate, passive arm EMG, breathing frequency, and palmar skin resistance, for a series of 100-second alternating rests and tracking runs with the first-, second-, and third-order tasks in succession. These data are like many results obtained by us and others, and they illustrate some of the key points we wish to make with regard to each measure:

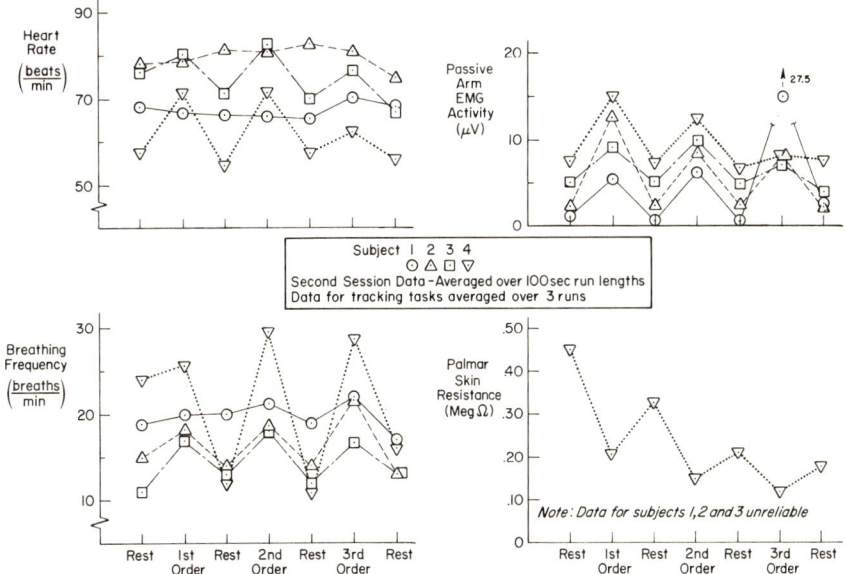

Figure 13. Psychophysiological measurements during rest periods and tracking runs.

(a) <u>Neuromuscular (NM) tension</u> (Passive EMG) consistent increases during tracking versus resting, but not of a magnitude correlated with subjective perceptual motor load (worst task had least increase). In general increased NM tension is a natural consequence of alarm or arousal, and should have some relevance to PML. However, it is difficult to measure and to calibrate surface-electrode EMG on an absolute scale (note the wide ranges on Fig. 13). Measurements at several sites are required to get a meaningful average NM tension. We think that the measurement of average NM tension is still a worthwhile goal.

(b) <u>Palmar-Skin Resistance</u> (PSR, similar to GSR) follows anomalous trends on an across-the-run average. Detailed inspection shows that "interesting events" in the data (e.g. large errors or startles) result in sudden drops in PSR, but rapid restoration follows. We have concluded, from these and other data, (e.g. in Ref. 46) that PSR or GSR are not well suited to workload measurement.

(c) <u>Average Heart Rate</u> (HR) shows the typical idiosyncracies among subjects, with a tendency to rise somewhat for some subjects during tracking (and to show less variability - see later herein). The problem is that heart rate per se seems to correlate more with physical work and apprehension about an activity than with perceptual motor load itself (e.g. also found by Roman, Ref. 45). Heart rate is of some medical interest and is relatively easy to measure if a cardiotachometer is available for easy on-line processing . Again the average heart rates did not correlate with subjective workload.

(d) <u>Heart-Rate Variations</u> (not shown) were less during tracking, as experienced by others (e.g. Ref 44), and were very well correlated with breathing frequency (pure sinus arrhythmia - see later). The key problem lies in validly scoring heart rate variations. Kalsbeek's weighting schemes seem like fairly arbitrary rules, and without some theoretical basis we are uncertain as to how to interpret such variations properly.

(e) <u>Breathing Frequency</u> (BF) or Respiratory Rate seems to be a much more stable and consistent correlate of PML. All subjects show increases in BF (and shallower breaths) under tracking and the resting-to-tracking differences roughly correlate with subjective PML. Breathing frequency is easy to measure with a variable resistance chest strap or nasal thermistor. As will be shown, almost all of the heart-rate variations we observed were highly correlated with variations in BF, so why not use the simpler instrumentation and measure BF in the first place? The only serious difficulty is that variations in physical workload (as well as heart rate) will change the breathing frequency so that those physical effects will be confounded with PML.

PERCEPTUAL-MOTOR WORKLOAD IN MANUAL CONTROL TASKS

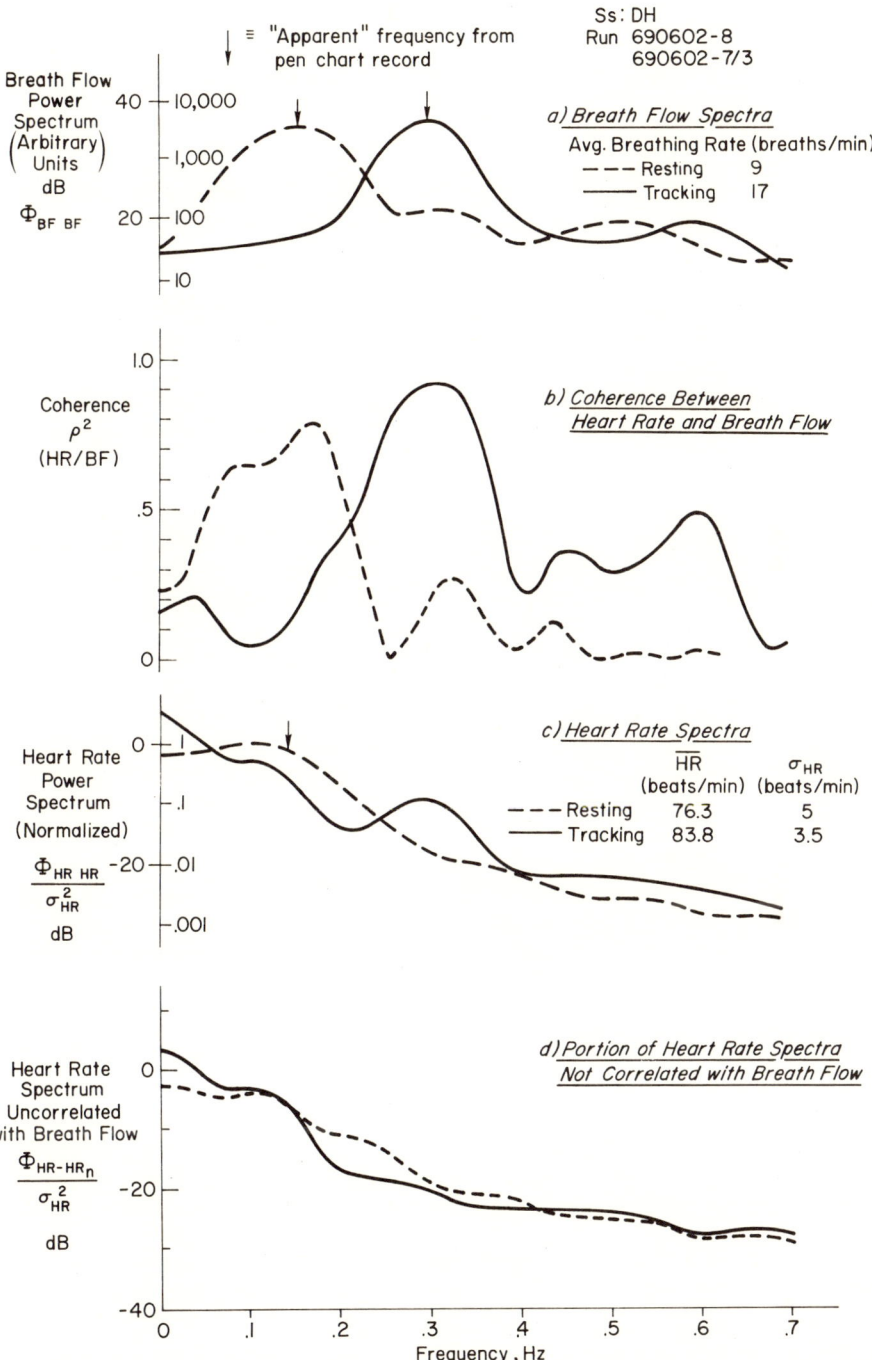

Figure 14. Breath Flow-Heart Rate Cross-Spectral Analysis Data.

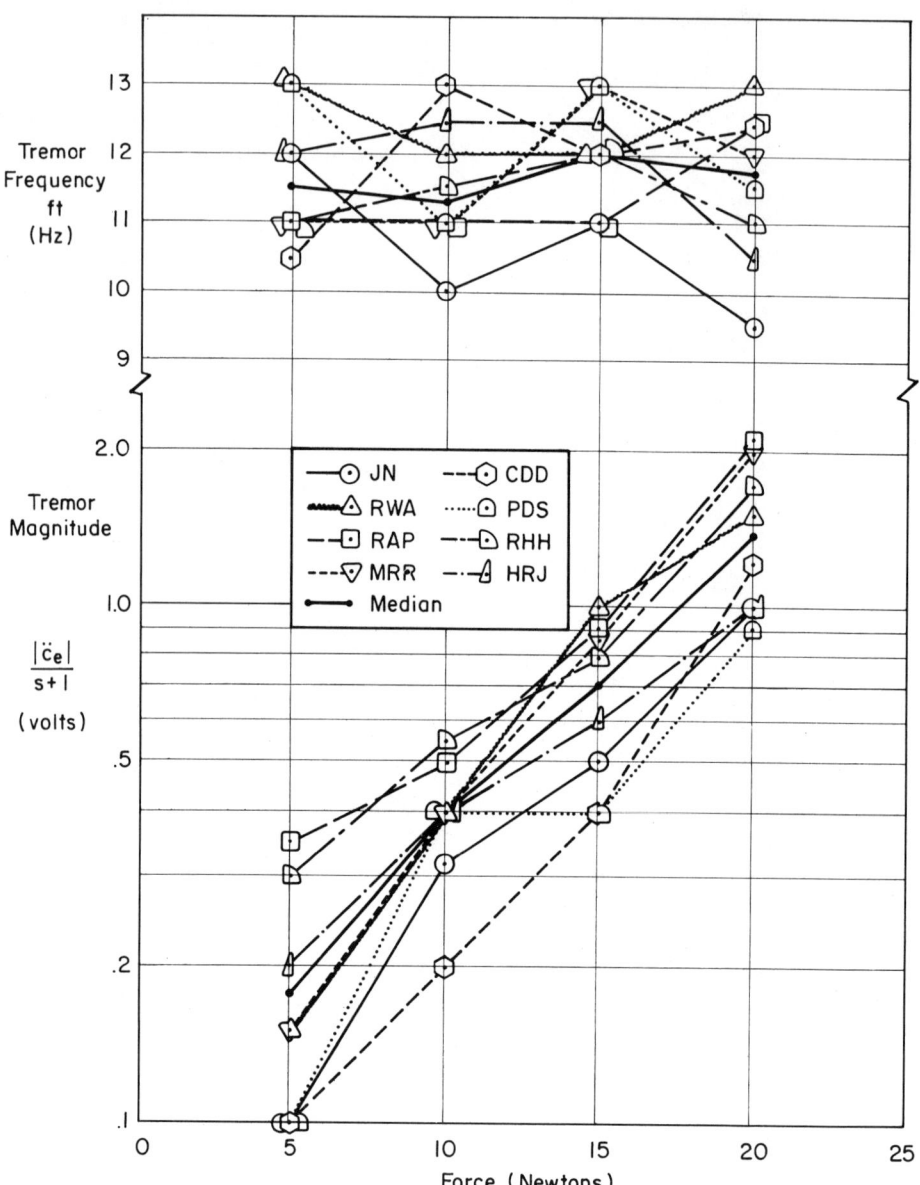

Figure 15. Tremor Intensity as a Function of Applied Force.

2. Sinus Arrhythmia

We have made some careful cross spectral analysis between breath-flow-rate (signal from a nasal thermistor, compensated for thermal lag) and instantaneous heart-rate (HR, measured by an on-line cardiotachometer). Typical results are shown in Fig. 14. Also noted thereon by arrows are the "apparent" breath and heart rate frequencies from visual inspection of time traces. Key findings were:

- Power spectra of HR and BF show sinus arrhythmia peaks at the apparent respective breathing frequencies, which are highly correlated (coherency = 0.8 resting, 0.95 tracking). The first and second harmonics of breathing frequency are also apparent (e.g. see Fig. 14b).

- Subtracting the breath-flow-correlated portions of the HR spectra leaves wideband, low pass spectra, which show little difference between resting and tracking.

- During tracking, one measure of HR variability ($\sigma_{HR}/\overline{HR}$ went from $5/76.3 = 0.066$ to $3.5/83 = 0.0422$.

We conclude that most of the heart rate variations due to PML are attributable to sinus arrhythmia, in accord with the models of M. Clynes (Ref. 49; also used, without referencing, in Ref. 47). The real question should be: why is sinus arrhythmia correlated with PML? We believe that the answer lies in the general systemic neuromuscular tension which develops as PML increases. This tension manifests itself to both the pulmonary and cardiovascular systems by increased resistance to blood flow and a slightly higher energy consumption. The BF and HR variations we see are homeostatic responses to this increased systemic tension. Much more careful research is required to trace the complex interactions involved. An exemplary summary of past work and start in this direction is given in the recent work of B. Sayers at the Imperial College of London, e.g. Ref. 52.

An interesting observation (shown in Ref. 48) is that the envelope of the EKG R-wave peaks seemed to correlate with the breath flow signal quite precisely. Whether or not this is an artifact of EKG lead locations on the heaving sternum relative to the heart, or another sinus arrhythmia effect is uncertain. It does offer a retrospective means to correlate heart rate with apparent breathing frequency, when no breathing data were recorded - simply identify the breathing frequency from the R-wave peak envelope of the EKG!

3. Future Needs

(a) *Standardized PML Tasks.* We believe that the search for a PML monitor or probe is worthwhile, but it will be fraught with difficulties, frustrations, and *ignes fatui*. We recommend that a set of standardized PML workloads be agreed on, which would have clearly defined criteria, tasks, mechanizations, and subjective workload ratings, against which to test such measures.

As detailed in Ref. 54, we suggest that a compensatory subcritical task be employed, with a vertical moving error line on a RT display of 5 cm diameter, placed about 50 cm from the eye, with an isometric finger-operated pencil controller having a stiff force gradient and "optimum" gain (about 1.0 to 1.4 Newtons force for 1 cm motion of the CRT line). Use a first-order subcritical element with dynamics $Y_c = -\lambda/(s-\lambda)$ where λ can range from 1.0 to 10. Let λ_c be the critical limit for the subject, with that control and display. Define Excess control-capacity, as earlier herein, as $EC \equiv \lambda/\lambda_c$. Measure λ_c at the beginning and end of each session, and interpolate it between, if it varies. With λ/λ_c at 0.2, 0.4, 0.6, 0.8 of the limit, measure the psychophysiological correlates and plot various indices versus $\lambda/\lambda_c \equiv EC$.

(b) *Simple Measures of NM Tension.* Because it is our contention that increased general neuromuscular tension underlies many of the other PP correlates of PML, a second need is for some simple way of measuring NM tension. A battery of surface electrodes is clumsy, expensive, and unreliable. There must be some other correlate of NM tension that can be measured more easily; our suggesions include: the lag between EKG R-wave peak and arrival of pulse-pressure at a distal passive limb (the pressure wave is slowed by intervening muscle tension), neck muscle tone (if some way can be found to separate head motion effects), bite-pressure on an inter-dental pressure cell, and eyelid-blink intervals (which we have noticed always decrease when tracking). Voice tone is sensitive to systemic tension but is strongly influenced by emotional state, as thoroughly explored by Frolov, et al., in Russia (Ref. 47).

Limb tremor amplitude increases under tension and operator fatigue. We have made some careful measurements of finger tremor while pulling precise loads with one finger (Ref. 50), and typical results are shown in Fig. 15. Notice that among 8 subjects the tremor frequency is relatively invariant while the magnitude varies widely with tension. Perhaps this effect could be exploited in an NM tension measuring system.

(c) *Measures of "Motivation" and "Effort".* One of the most confounding and frustrating factors in measuring PML ability is the role of individual "motivation" and mental effort. Engineering psychologists should have come up with a workable definition, measurements, and experimental controls for motivations long ago, but that is not the case. We and others still artfully control this variable by using test pilots (with professional motivations), by posting spurious "best-scores-to-date" and by offering financial incentives. Workload results are particularly vulnerable to uneven motivation, so creative research in this area is urgently needed.

CONCLUSIONS

This long review of some of our findings and positions with respect to defining and measuring perceptual-motor workload (PML) leads to the following concluding points:

- PML measurement will continue to be an art for some time to come, because: there is no comprehensive theory to unify and guide the research or procedures, the psycho-physiological processes are extremely complex and inaccessible to direct measurements, and the applications are so diverse (e.g. short-term tracking and decision-making, longer term vigilance, daily or weekly fatigue, overall health, and work-quality).

- There seems to be a consensus that the workload of a vaguely defined supervisory mental activity (involving the "metacontrol system") should be measured for a basic PML index. Until more valid and precise measures are developed, a properly structured subjective rating is about the most reliable index of PML, in our opinion.

- Several carefully researched control tasks are now available to help in regulating and/or measuring PML (e.g. critical-instability tasks and their cross-coupled offspring).

- The theory of finite-dwell-sampling of displays may have a wider application to model the interference effects from concurrent discrete or cognitive tasks.

- Better measures of systemic neuromuscular tension need to be developed because it is believed to underlie several of the conventional psychophysiological variables.

- Usable definitions of "motivation" and better means for measuring and controlling it are urgently needed.

REFERENCES

1. McRuer, D.T., and E.S. Krendel, <u>Mathematical Models of Human Pilot Behavior,</u> AGARDograph No. 188, Jan. 1974.

2. Baron, S., and W.H. Levison, "An Optimal Control Methodology for Analyzing the Effects of Display Parameters on Performance and Workload in Manual Flight Control," <u>IEEE Trans.,</u> Vol. SMC-5, No. 4, 1975, pp. 423-430.

3. Sheridan, Thomas B., and William R. Ferrell, <u>Man-Machine Systems: Information, Control and Decision Models of Human Performance,</u> The MIT Press, Cambridge, MA, 1974.

4. Jahns, Dieter, W., "Operator Workload: What is it and How Should It Be Measured?", <u>Management and Technology in the Crew System Design Process Conference</u>, Los Angeles, CA, Sept. 1972.

5a. Klein, Richard H., and Warren F. Clement, <u>Application of Manual Control Display Theory to the Development of Flight Director Systems for STOL Aircraft</u>, AFFDL-TR-72-152, Jan. 1973.

5b. Clement, Warren F., Lee Gregor Hofmann, and Richard E. Blodgett, <u>Application of Manual Control Display Theory to the Development of Flight Director Systems for STOL Aircraft. Part II: Multi-Axis Sampling, Pilot Workload, and Display Integration,</u> Systems Technology, Inc., TR-1011-2, Jan. 1974.

6. Benson, Alan J., J.H.F. Huddleston, and John M. Rolfe, "A Psychophysiological Study of Compensatory Tracking on a Digital Display". <u>Human Factors,</u> Vol. 7, No. 5, Oct. 1965, pp. 457-472.

7. Selye, Hans, "The Evolution of the Stress Concept - Stress and Cardiovascular Disease," in the L. Levi, ed., <u>Society, Stress and Disease,</u> Oxford Univ. Press, 1971, pp. 299-311.

8. McRuer, Duane, Henry R. Jex, Warren F. Clement, and Dunstan Graham, <u>A Systems Analysis Theory for Displays in Manual Control,</u> Technology, Inc., TR-163-1, Oct. 1967 (rev. June 1968).

9. Allen, R.W., W.F. Clement, and H.R. Jex, <u>Research on Display Scanning, Sampling, and Reconstruction Using Separate Main and Secondary Tracking Tasks,</u> NASA CR-1569, July 1970.

10. Clement, W.F., R.W. Allen, and D. Graham, Pilot Experiments for a Theory of Integrated Display Format, JANAIR Rept. No. 711107, Oct. 1971.

11. Krendel, E.S., and D.T. McRuer, "A Servomechanisms Approach to Skill Development", J.Franklin Inst., Vol. 269, No. 1, Jan. 1960, pp. 24-42.

12. Allen, R.W., and H.R. Jex, An Experimental Investigation of Compensatory and Pursuit Tracking Displays with Rate and Acceleration Control Dynamics and a Disturbance Input, NASA CR-1082, June 1968.

13. Magdaleno, R.E., H.R. Jex, and W.A. Johnson, "Tracking Quasi-Predictable Displays," 5th Annual NASA University Conference on Manual Control, NASA SP-215, 1970, pp.391-428.

14. Wempe, T.E., and D.L. Baty, "Human Information Processing Rates during Certain Multiaxis Tracking Tasks with a Concurrent Auditory Task", 4th Annual NASA University Conference on Manual Control, NASA SP-192, 1969.

15. Sheridan, T.B., "The Human Operator in Control Instrumentation", Progress in Control Enginering, Vol. 1, R.H. Macmillan, et al., eds., Academic Press, N.Y., 1962 pp. 141-187.

16. McGreachie, J.S. "Multiple Terminals Under User Control in a Time-Sharing Environment", CACM, Vol. 16, 1973, pp. 587-590.

17. Michon, J.A., "Tapping Regularity as a Measure of Perceptual Motor Load", Ergonomics, Vol. 9, No. 5, Sept. 1966, pp. 401-412.

18. Jex, Henry R., Richard J. DiMarco, and Warren F. Clement, Effects of Simulated Surface Effect Ship Motions on Crew Habitability - Phase II. Vol. 3: Visual-Motor Tasks and Subjective Evaluations, Systems Technology, Inc., TR-1070-3, Jan. 1977.

19. Broadbent, D.E., "The Concept of Capacity and the Theory of Behavior", Information Theory: Proceedings of Third London Symposium, E.C. Cherry, ed., Butterworth, London. 1956.

20. Knowles, W.B., "Operator Loading Tasks", Human Factors, Vol. 5, 1963, pp. 163-168.

21. Duning, Kenneth E., Craig, W. Hickock, Kenneth C. Emerson, and Warren F. Clement, Control Display Testing Requirements Study, AFFDL-TR-72-122, Dec. 1972.

22. Jex, H.R., J.D. McDonnell, and A.V. Phatak, "A 'Critical' Tracking Task for Manual Control Research", IEEE Trans., Vol. HFE-7, No. 4, Dec. 1966, pp. 138-145.

23. Jex, H.R., J.D. McDonnell, and A.V. Phatak, A "Critical" Tracking Task for Man-Machine Research Related to the Operator's Effective Delay Time: Part I. Theory and Experiments with a First-Order Divergent Controlled Element, NASA CR-616, Oct. 1966.

24. McDonnell, J.D., and H.R. Jex, A "Critical" Tracking Task for Man-Machine Research Related to the Operator's Effective Delay Time: Part II. Experimental Effects of System Input Spectra, Control Stick Stiffness, and Controlled Element Order, NASA CR-674, Jan. 1967.

25. Stassen, H.G., P.L. Brinkman, et al., "Chapter III: Application of Describing Function Methods," Progress Report, January 1970 until January 1973 of the Man-Machine Systems Group, Delft Univ. of Technology, Rept. No. WTHD-55, Nov. 1973, pp. 45-92.

26. Allen, R. Wade, and Henry R. Jex, "Visual-Motor Response of Crewmen During a Simulated 90-Day Space Mission as Measured by the Critical Task Battery", 7th Annual Conference on Manual Control, NASA SP-281, 1972, pp. 239-246.

27. Jex, H.R., and R.W. Allen, "Research on a New Human Dynamic Response Test Battery, Part II: Test Development and Validation", 6th Annual Conference on Manual Control, AFIT, Wright-Patterson AFB, OH, Aprl. 1970.

28. Jex, H.R., "Two Applications of the Critical Instability Task to Secondary Work Load Research", IEEE Trans., Vol. HFE-8, No. 4, Dec. 1967, pp. 279-282.

29. Jex, H.R., R. Wade Allen, and Raymond E. Magdaleno, Display Format Effects on Precision Tracking Performance, Describing Functions, and Remnant, AMRL-TR-71-63, Aug. 1971.

30. McRuer, D.T. and H.R. Jex, "A Systems Analysis Theory of Manual Control Displays", 3rd Annual NASA-University Conference on Manual Control, NASA SP-144, 1967, pp.9-28.

31. Blackman, R.B., and J.W. Tukey, The Measurement of Power Spectra, Dover Publications, Inc., N.Y., 1958.

32. Jex, H.R., W.F. Jewell, and R.W. Allen, "Development of the Dyal-Axis and Cross-Coupled Critical Tasks", 8th Annual Conference on Manual Control, AFFDL-TR-72-92, Jan. 1973, pp. 529-552.

33. McDonnell, J.D., Pilot Rating Techniques for the Estimation and Evaluation of Handling Qualities, AFFDL-TR-68-76, Dec. 1968.

34. Hess, Ronald A., and Walter M. Teichgraber, "Error Quantization Effects in Compensatory Tracking Tasks", IEEE Trans., Vol. SMC-4, No. 5, July 1974, pp. 343-349.

35. Clement, W.F., D.R. McRuer, and R.H. Klein, "Systematic Manual Control Display Design", Guidance and Control Displays, AGARD CP-96, Feb. 1972, pp. 6-1- 6-10.

36. Clement, Warren F., Investigation of the Use of an Electronic Multifunction Display and an Electromechanical Horizontal Situation Indicator for Guidance and Control of Powered-Lift Short-Haul Aircraft, NASA CR-137922, Aug. 1976.

37. Merhav, S.J. and Orna Ben Ya'acov, "Control Augmentation and Work Load Reduction by Kinesthetic Information from the Manipulator", IEEE Trans., Vol. SMC-6, No. 12, Dec. 1976, pp. 825-835.

38. Etchberger, K., "Performance and Control Behavior of Humans Tracking Stochastic Signals", Bio-Cybernetics, Vol. 17, No. 2, 1975.

39. Senders, J.W., J.I. Elkind, M.C. Grignetti, and R.D. Smallwood, An Investigation of the Visual Sampling Behavior of Human Observers, NASA CR-434, Apr. 1966.

40. Lee, A.M., Applied Queueing Theory, Macmillan, London, 1966.

41. Cox, D.R., and W.L. Smith, Queues, Methuen, London, 1961.

42. Weir, D.H., and W.A. Johnson, <u>Pilot Dynamic Response to Sudden Flight Control System Failures and Implications for Design</u>, NASA CR-1087, June 1968.

43. Spyker, D.A., S.P. Stackhouse, A.S. Khalafalla, and R.C. McLane, <u>Development of Techniques for Measuring Pilot Workload</u>, NASA CR-1888, Nov. 1971.

44. Kalsbeek, J.W.H., and J.H. Ettema, "Physiological and Psychological Evaluation of Distraction Stress", <u>Proc. of 2nd International Congress on Ergonomics</u>, Taylor and Francis, Ltd., London, 1964, pp. 443-447.

45. Roman, James, "Long-Range Program to Develop Medical Monitoring in Flight - The Flight Research Program - I", <u>Aero. Med.</u>, Vol. 36, No. 6, June 1965, pp. 514-518, et seq.

46. Kutayev-Smyk, L.A., I.P. Neumyvakin, and V.A. Ponomarenko, "Contribution to the Question of the Methods of Evaluating the Psychophysiological State of a Pilot in an Emergency Situation During Flight". <u>Problems of Engineering Psychology</u>, NASA TT F-312, May 1965.

47. Luk'yanov, A.N., and M.V. Frolov, <u>Signals of Human Operator State</u>, NASA TT F-609, June 1970.

48. Jex, H.R., and R.W. Allen, "Research on a New Human Dynamic Response Test Battery. Part II: Psychophysiological Correlates", presented at the 6th Annual Conf. on Manual Control, AFIT, Wright-Patterson Air Force Base, Ohio, 1970.

49. Clynes, Manfred. "Respiratory Control of Heart Rate: Laws Derived from Analog Computer Simulation", <u>IRE Trans.</u>, Vol. ME-7, No. 1, Jan. 1960, pp. 2-14.

50. Magdaleno, R.E., H.R. Jex, and R.W. Allen, "Modelling and Measuring Limb Fine-Motor Unsteadiness", <u>Proc. of the 9th Annual Conf. on Manual Control</u>, NASA CR-142295, 1973, pp. 335-349.

51. Ashkenas, I.L., <u>Requirements for Airplane Normal and Failure States</u>, Systems Technology, Inc., WP-1017-2, Aug. 1972.

52. Sayers, B., "Analysis of Heart Rate Variability", <u>Ergonomics</u>, Vol. 16, pp. 17-32, 1973.

53. Clement,W.F., "Annotated Bibliography of Procedures Which Assess Primary Task Performance in Some Manner as the Basic Element of a Workload Measurement Procedure", STI TR-1104-2, January 1978.

54. Jex, H.R., "A Proposed Set of Standardized Sub-Critical Tasks for Tracking Workload Calibration", Appendix to Control-Theory Group Report at the AGARD Mental Workload Conference, Mati, Greece, October, 1977.

REFERENCES FOR TABLE I

1. <u>Subjective Pilot Ratings</u>

   Cooper, G.E., "Understanding and Interpreting Pilot Opinion", <u>Aeron. Eng. Rev.</u>, Vol. 16, No. 3, Mar. 1957, pp. 47-52.

   Harper, R.P., Jr., and George E. Cooper, <u>A Revised Pilot Rating Scale for the Evaluation of Handling Qualities</u>, Cornell Aero. Labs., Rept. 153, Sept. 1966.

   Ashkenas, I.L., and D.T. McRuer, "A Theory of Handling Qualities Derived from Pilot-Vehicle System Considerations", <u>Aero. Eng.</u>, Vol. 21, No. 2, Feb. 1962, pp. 60, 83-102.

   McDonnell, John D., <u>Pilot Rating Techniques for the Estimation and Evaluation of Handling Qualities</u>, AFFDL-TR-68-76, Dec. 1968.

   Clement, Warren F., R. Wade Allen, and Dunstan Graham, <u>Pilot Experiments for a Theory of Integrated Display Format (Final Report)</u>, JANAIR Report 711107, Oct. 1971.

   Hess, R.A. "Nonadjectival Rating Scales in Human Response Experiments", <u>Human Factors,</u> Vol. 15, No. 3, June 1973, pp. 275-280.

2.1. <u>Auxiliary Workload Margins at Given Main Task Level</u>

   Bahrick, H.P., M. Noble, and P.M. Fitts, "Extra-Task Performance as a Measure of Learning a Primary Task", <u>J. Experimental Psychology</u>, Vol. 48, No. 4, Aug. 1954, pp. 298-302.

Knowles, W.B., "Operator Loading Tasks", Human Factors, Vol. 5, 1963, pp. 163-168.

Adams, J.A., H.H. Stenson, and J.M. Humes, "Monitoring of Complex Visual Displays - II. Effects of Visual Load and Response Complexity on Human Vigilance", Human Factors, Vol. 3, No. 4, June 1961. pp. 213-221.

Spyker, D.A., et al., Development of Techniques for Measuring Pilot Workload, NASA CR-1888, Nov. 1971.

Crossman, E.R.F.W., "The Information-Capacity of the Human Motor-System in Pursuit Tracking", Quart. J. Experimental Psychology, Vol. XII, Part I, Feb. 1960.

Benson, A.J., J.H.H. Huddleston, and J.M. Rolfe, "A Psychophysiological Study of Compensatory Tracking on a Digital Display", Human Factors, Vol. 7, No. 5, Oct. 1965, pp. 457-472.

Michon, J.A. "Tapping Regularity as a Measure of Perceptual Motor Load", Ergonomics, Vol. 9, No. 5, Sept. 1966, pp. 401-412.

Mowbray, G.H., "Some Human Perceptual Limits", APL Technical Digest, Vol. 1, No. 3, Jan-Feb. 1962, pp.21-24.

Price, D.L., "The Effects of Certain Gimbal Orders on Target Acquisition and Workload", Human Factors, Vol. 17, No. 6, Dec. 1975. pp. 571-576.

Kelly, C.R., and M.T. Wargo, "Cross-Adaptive Operator Loading Tasks", Human Factors, Vol. 9, No. 5, 1967, pp.395-404.

McDonnell, J.D., and H.R. Jex, A "Critical" Tracking Task for Man-Machine Research Related to the Operator's Effective Delay Time: Part II. Experimental Effects of System Input Spectra, Control Stick Stiffness, and Controlled Element Order, NASA CR-674, Jan. 1967.

Hart, S.G., "Time Estimation as a Secondary Task to Measure Workload", 11th Annual Conference on Manual Control, NASA TM X-62, 464, May 1975, pp. 64-77.

Hart, S., D. McPherson, and C.A. Simpson, "Airline Pilot Time Estimation During Concurrent Activity Including Simulated Flight", presented at the 47th Annual Meeting of Aerospace Medical Association, Bal Harbour, Florida, May 1976.

Rosche, E., and T. Wempe, <u>Secondary Task for Full Flight Simulation Incorporating Tasks That Commonly Cause Pilot Error:</u> Time estimation, NASA TM X-74153, 1 Nov. 1974.

Sternberg, S., "Memory-scanning: Mental Processes Revealed by Reaction-time Experiments", <u>American Scientist,</u> 57, 1969, pp. 421-457.

Sternberg, S., "The Discovery of Processing Stages: Extension of Donder's Method," in W.G. Koster (Ed.), <u>Attention and Performance II,</u> Amsterdam, North Holland, 1969.

Sternberg, S., <u>Quart. J. Exp. Psychol.,</u> 27, 1975, pp. 1-32.

Swanson, J.M., A.M. Johnsen and G.E. Briggs, "Recoding in a Memory Search Task", <u>J. of Exp. Psychophysics</u>, 93, 1972, pp. 1-9.

O'Donnell, R.D., "Secondary Task Assessment of Cognitive Workload in Alternative Cockpit Configurations", <u>Higher Mental Functioning in Operational Environments,</u> AGARD-CP-181, Apr. 1976, pp. C-10-1 to C-10-5.

Peters, G.L., and G.J. Barbato, <u>Information Processing of DOT Matrix Displays,</u> AFFDL-TR-76-82, Oct. 1976.

Peters, G.L., "Coding Processing in Active and Inactive Memory", <u>J. Experimental Psychology,</u> Vol. 102, 1974, pp.423-430.

Chase, W.G., and R.C. Calfee, "Modality and Similarity Effects in Short-Term Recognition Memory", <u>J. Experimental Psychology,</u> Vol. 21, 1969, pp. 189-191.

2.2. Main Task Decrements at Prescribed Auxiliary Task Loads

Kalsbeek, J.W.H., "On the Measurement of Deterioration in Performance Caused by Distraction Stress", <u>Ergonomics,</u> Vol. 7, No. 2, 1964, pp. 187-195.

Walker, N.K., E. DeSocio, H. Mowbray, and L. Durr, <u>The Effect of a Particular Stress on One Man's Performance of Various Tracking Tasks,</u> USAMEDS Contract No. DA-49-193-MD-2369, Oct. 1964.

Walker, N.K., and J.F. Burkhardt, "The Development of Tracking Tasks as Indicators of Stress", <u>Proceedings of a Contractors Conference on Behavior Science,</u> Edgewood Arsenal, Oct. 1965.

Allen, R.W., W.F. Clement, and H.R. Jex, Research on Display Scanning, Sampling, and Reconstruction Using Separate Main and Secondary Tracking Tasks, NASA CR-1569, July 1970.

2.3. Varying Difficulty Main Task

Elkind, J.I., and D.C. Miller, Adaptive Characteristics of the Human Controller of Time-Varying Systems, AFFDL-TR-66-60, Dec. 1967.

Miller, D.C., and J.J. Elkind, "The Adaptive Response of the Human Controller to Sudden Changes in Controlled Process Dynamics", IEEE Trans., HFE Vol. 8, No. 3, 1967, pp. 218-223.

Weir, D.H. and A.V. Phatak, A Model of Human Operator Response to Step Transitions in Controlled Element Dynamics, NASA CR-671, Jan. 1967.

Jex, H.R., J.D. McDonnell, and A.V. Phatak, A "Critical" Tracking Task for Man-Machine Research Related to the Operator's Effective Delay Time: Part I. Theory and Experiments with a First-Order Divergent Controlled Element, NASA CR-616, Oct. 1966.

McDonnell, J.D., and H.R. Jex, A "Critical" Tracking Task for Man-Machine Research Related to the Operator's Effective Delay Time: Part II. Experimental Effects of System Input Spectra, Control Stick Stiffness, and Controlled Element Order, NASA CR-674, Jan. 1967.

3. Scanning and Eye Traffic

Fitts, P.M., R.E. Jones, and J.L. Milton, "Eye Movements of Aircraft Pilots During Instrument-Landing Approaches", Aeron Eng. Rev., Vol. 9, No. 2, Feb. 1950, pp. 24-29.

Senders, J.W., J.I. Elkind, M.C. Grignetti, and R.D. Smallwood, An Investigation of the Visual Sampling Behavior of Human Observers, NASA CR-434, Apr. 1966.

Senders, J.W., J.R. Carbonell, and J.L. Ward, Human Visual Sampling Processes: A Simulation Validation Study, NASA CR-1258, Jan. 1969.

Allen, R.W., W.F. Clement, and H.R. Jex, Research on Display Scanning, Sampling, and Reconstruction Using Separate Main and Secondary Tracking Tasks, NASA CR-1569, July 1970.

Weir, D.H., and R.H. Klein, The Measurement and Analysis of Pilot Scanning and Control Behavior During Simulated Instrument Approaches, NASA CR-1535, June 1970.

4. Psychophysiological Measurements

Kalsbeek, J.W.H., and J.H. Ettema, "Physiological and Psychological Evaluation of Distraction Stress", Proceedings of 2nd International Congress on Ergonomics, Taylor and Francis, Ltd. London, 1964, pp. 443-447.

Benson, Alan, J.H.F. Huddleston, and John M. Rolfe, "A Psychophysiological Study of Compensatory Tracking on a Digital Display", Human Factors, Vol. 7, No. 5, Oct. 1965, pp. 457-472.

Roman, James, "Long-Range Program to Develop Medical Monitoring in Flight - The Flight Research Program - I", Aero. Med., Vol. 36, No.6, June 1965, pp. 514-518, et seq.

Lewis, C.E., Jr. et al., "Aeromedical Monitoring of Naval Aviators During Aircraft Carrier Combat Operation", Aerospace Medicine, Vol. 38, No. 6, June 1967, pp.593-596.

Sayers, B., "Analysis of Heart Rate Variability", Ergonomics, Vol. 16, 1973, pp. 17-32.

Spyker, D.A., et al, Development of Techniques for Measuring Pilot Workload, NASA CR-1888, Nov. 1971.

Anderson, R.O., and P.E. Pietrzak, "Pupil Dilation as a Measure of Workload", Third Annual NASA-University Conference on Manual Control, NASA SP-144, 1967, pp. 305-308.

Beatty, Jackson, "Pupillometric Measurement of Cognitive Workload" 12th Annual Conference on Manual Control, NASA TM X-73, 170, May 1976, pp. 135-143.

Wickens, Christopher, Jack Israel, Gregory McCarthy, Daniel Gopher, and Emanuel Donchin, "The Use of Event-Related-Potentials in the Enhancement of System Performance" 12th Annual Conference on Manual Control, NASA TM X-73, 170, May 1976, pp. 124-134.

McRuer, D.T., et al., New Approaches to Human-Pilot/Vehicle Dynamic Analysis, AFFDL-TR-67-150, Sec. VI, Feb. 1968.

Luk'yanov, A.N., and M.V. Frolov, Signals of Human Operator State, NASA TT F-609, June 1970.

5. Operator's Dynamic Behavior

McRuer, D.T., and E.S. Krendel, Mathematical Models of Human Pilot Behavior, AGARDograph No. 188, Jan. 1974.

Ashkenas, I.L., and D.T. McRuer, "A Theory of Handling Qualities Derived from Pilot-Vehicle System Considerations", Aerospace Engineering, Vol. 21, No. 2, Feb. 1962, pp. 60, 61, 83-102.

Stapleford, R.L., R.A. Peters, and F.R. Alex, Experiments and a Model for Pilot Dynamics with Visual and Motion Inputs, NASA CR-1325, May 1969.

Stapleford, R.L. Pilot Describing Function Measurements in a Multiloop Task, NASA CR-542, Aug. 1966.

Ringland, R.F., R.L. Stapleford, and R.E. Magdaleno, Motion Effects on an IFR Hovering Task - Analytical Predictions and Experimental Results, NASA CR-1933, Nov. 1971.

Craig, S.J., R.L. Stapleford, and J.A. Tennant, Measurement of Pilot Describing Functions in Single-Controller Multiloop Tasks, NASA CR-1238, Jan. 1969.

Weir, D.H., and D.T. McRuer, Pilot Dynamics for Instrument Approach Tasks: Full Panel Multiloop and Flight Director Operations, NASA CR-2019, Nov. 1971.

Schweizer, G., Contributions to the Theory of Linear Models for the Human Operator Under Stationary Tasks, Dornier Werke Paper 22, undated.

6. Time Line Analyses

Pickrel, E.W., and T.A. McDonald, "Quantification of Human Performance in Large Complex Systems", Human Factors, Vol. 6, 1964, pp. 647-662.

Cole, G., et al., Study of Pilot-Controller Integration for Emergency Conditions, AF RTD-TDR-63-4092, Jan. 1964.

Shoquist, R.R., Reliability Analysis Technique for Man-Machine Systems, Honeywell, Inc., Paper No. T-228, undated.

Siegel, A.I., and J.J. Wolf, "A Technique for Evaluating Man-Machine System Designs", Human Factors, Vol. 3, No. 1, 1961, pp. 18-28.

Senders, J.W., J.R. Carbonell, and J.L. Ward, Human Visual Sampling Processes: A Simulation Validation Study, BBN Rept. 1681, NASA CR-1258, Jan. 1969.

SIMTAK, Evaluation of Mission Success Based Upon Man-Machine Task Delays and Failures Due to Man's Stress Characteristics, Honeywell, Inc., Doc. No. 5D-H-509-1, Dec. 1965.

Pritsker, A.A.B., D.B. Wortman, C.S. Seum, G.P. Chubb, and D.J. Seifert, SAINT: Volume I. Systems Analysis of Integrated Network Tasks, AMRL-TR-73-126, Apr. 1974.

Dickey, L.R., Flight Deck Certification Computer Programs: Cockpit Crew Workload, Boeing Aerospace Co., Report No. D6-29906-3, 1969.

Linton, P., D.W. Jahns, and P. Chatelier, Operator Workload Assessment Model: An Evaluation of a VF/VA-V/STOL System, presented at the NATO/AGARD Aerospace Medical Panel Specialists Meeting, Koln, FRG, 18-22 Apr. 1977.

Wherry, R.J., Jr., "The Human Operator Simulator: HOS", in T. Sheridan and G. Johannsen (Eds.), Monitoring Behavior and Supervisory Control, Plenum Press, N.Y., 1971, pp. 283-293.

ACKNOWLEDGEMENT

The work reported herein was performed over the 1967-1977 time period under a variety of sponsors, notably: NASA Ames Research Center (M. Sadoff); U.S. Air Force 6750 Aerospace Medical Research Laboratory (P. Kulwicki); U.S. Navy Office of Naval Research (D. Siegel); and U.S. Army Air Mobility Research and Development Lab (R. Dunn).

A PROPOSED SET OF STANDARDIZED SUB-CRITICAL TASKS FOR TRACKING WORKLOAD CALIBRATION

Henry R. Jex

Systems Technology Inc. Hawthorne, California

INTRODUCTION

The following set of "sub-critical" tracking tasks are proposed as one portion of a future standardized battery of different types of task, each having graded levels of mental workload, against which various investigators could calibrate and validate their measures of workload against those made previously by other workers. This Appendix provides the recommended task description, mechanization (including controlled element, displays and controls), (optional) inputs, operating procedures and evaluation criteria so that measurements made in different locations can be validly compared.

We recommend "Sub-critical" Tracking Tasks as the first set in the standardized test battery for several reasons:

- Since its introduction in 1966, this task has been thoroughly researched and cross-validated (in terms of operator behavior) in a number of independent laboratories around the world (e.g., USA: Refs. A-1, A-2, and A-3; Netherlands: Ref. A-4 Germany: Ref. A-5).

- The task is highly motivating because the displayed error quickly diverges off scale if the operator ignores it, and the typical operator behavior is well understood and universally achieved (see the above references).

.. A number of workload-index measurements have already been made for these tasks, which have indicated good gradation of effort and have shown some mutual agreement among each other (e.g. Refs. A-6 to A-9).

Task Description

This is a "compensatory" (error correcting) tracking task, in which the operator views an analog display of the error between the command input and plant output, and corrects these with opposite pressure on a control stick. The plant dynamics are those of a first-order unstable system (one pole in the right-half plane).

In Laplace operator form:

$$Y_c(s) = \frac{m}{F} = \frac{K_c}{(s/\lambda) - 1} = \frac{K_c \lambda}{s - \lambda} \qquad (1a, 1b)$$

In state-variable form:

$$\dot{m} = \lambda m + K_c \lambda F \qquad (2)$$

The degree of instability, λ (the unstable-root value, also the "break-frequency" on a Bode plot of frequency response), sets the task difficulty and attentional demand.

It has been shown that as λ is increased from low values of about 0.1 rad/sec towards typical limits of control at 4-8 rad/sec, the subjectively evaluated attentional demand increases from "low" to "completely demanding" (Ref. A-10).

At levels approaching full-attention, there is a sharply defined "critical-instability limit", λ_c, beyond which control is lost. For any individual, the level of λ_c increases towards a well-practised asymptote over several dozen tests distributed evenly over several days, following a typical learning curve. The objective parameter for adjusting the control task's attentional workload (mental effort) is the ratio of given λ to that level of λ which demands maximum attention (i.e., λ_c). Let us define this ratio: $\lambda/\lambda_c = L$ the task -loading parameter. Workload measures are calibrated vs. L.

Determining the critical instability is an important step in calibrating a person's control capacity. It is possible, under primitive circumstances, to determine λ_c by letting the experimenter manually increase λ, rapidly at first, then slowly as the limit is approached, and stop as soon as control is lost. However, an automated method for determining the critical-instability limit is very desirable, and has been carefully developed and proven in over one decade of applications - this is the Autopaced Critical-Task;

it is described in detail in Ref. A-1, and the mechanization is also given later herein.

Summarizing this overall description: each subject is given sufficient practice on the (autospaced) Critical Task to reach a reasonably stable asymptote. At each subsequent workload test session the 5-trial-mean critical instability, $\bar{\lambda}_c$, is measured at the start of the session, then levels of sub-critical instability are set to desired fractions of this maximum: i.e., at $\bar{L} = \lambda/\lambda_c = 0.2, 0.4, 0.6, \ldots$ etc., tracking runs of 100 sec are given at these levels. The method(s) being used to measure "workload" (e.g. subjective ratings, psychophysiological measures, or auxiliary tasks, etc.[1]) are concurrently applied, and a crossplot of those measures vs. $\bar{L}$ provides the desired workload calibration.

If more than one workload measure is made under a given level of L, then a correlation matrix may be established among the different types of workload measures.

MECHANISATION

Controlled Element

An analog computer block diagram for the critical-instability task is given in Fig. A-1 taken from Ref. A-1.[2] The following considerations must be observed in mechanising the task:

- The circuits for the unstable controlled element must be very accurate, (within 1 percent).

- An accurately calibrated means for setting and reading λ must be provided.

- The autopacer functions can be much less precise (within 10-20 percent) as long as λ is accurately known.

If the task is mechanised on a digital computer, other precautions must be taken, such as: adequate resolution through all the interfaces (at least 10-bit A/D and D/A resolution), minimal computing and interface delays (from stick force to display motion, the cumulative delay should be less than 0.020 sec) and means must be provided for preventing "hang-up" at zero control input and rate (whereby the display could remain centered, hands-off).

For running at continuous subcritical levels, the Switch A is moved to the SET λ position and a precision 10-turn potentiometer is used to set the desired level of λ. It may be difficult to start tracking at levels of λ/λ_c above about 1/3, so a gradual increase from $\lambda = 1$ to the desired level is recommended.

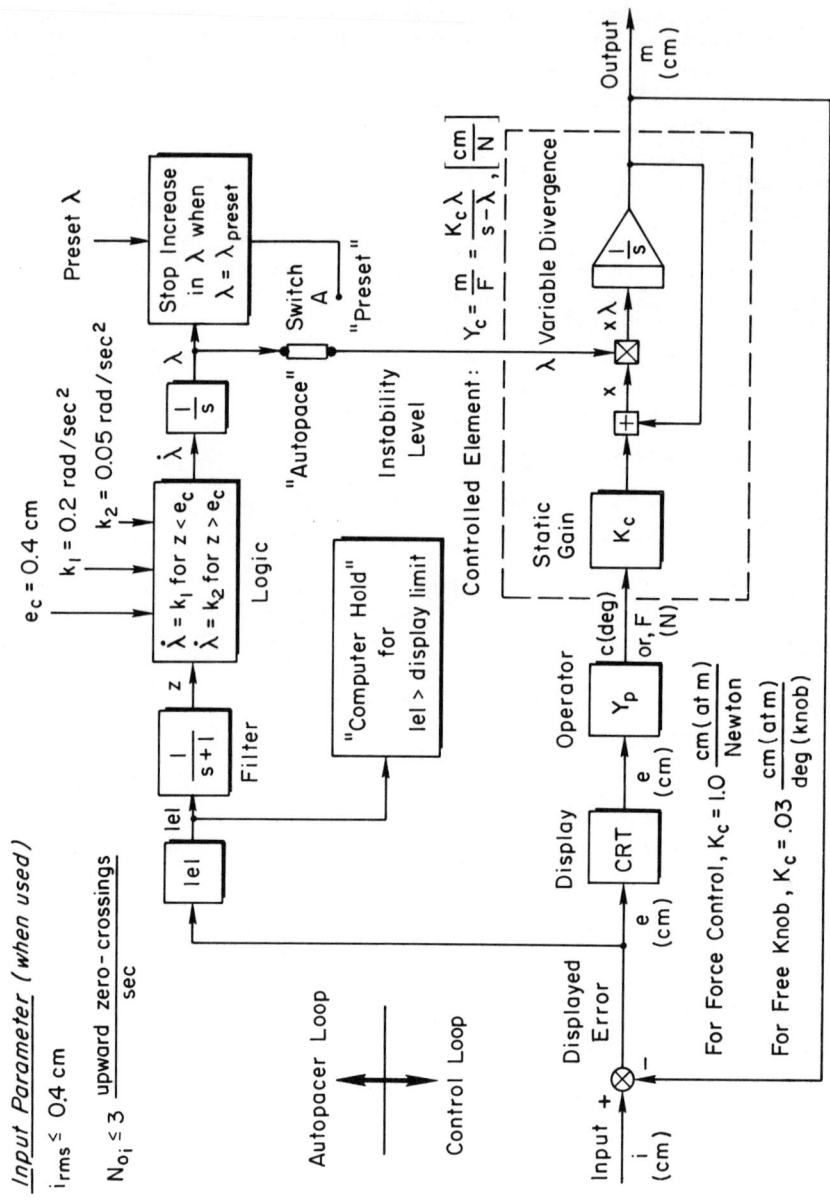

Figure A-1. Mechanisation of Autopaced and Preset Critical Task.

STANDARDISED SUB-CRITICAL TASKS

Display

The ideal display (for highest λ_c scores) is a large moving line on a CRT display, having a total visual angle of at least 5-10 deg. Generally, meter movements are either too slow or too underdamped to give comparable scores as a CRT. (A special meter/amplifier system has been developed by STI for its commercial critical-task testers which has a lag less than 0.05 sec and gives scores comparable to a CRT). For correlations among various workload measures, a more sluggish display may be used, but the absolute calibration may not match those taken with a CRT display. Ideally, the control should be a nearly isometric (pressure sensitive) stick, with a range of ±10 newtons, and a resolution of better than 1/2 percent of full scale, because a wide range of control forces is used in performing these tasks. As noted in Fig. A-1 the overall display/control gain should be 1.0 cm (at CRT)/newton on stick (at a viewing distance of 30-60 cm). For particular studies it is permissible to use almost any control device, provided that it has: excellent resolution (i.e., negligible friction, deadband, quantization or detents), a wide dynamic range, and comfortable operating forces or motions. Of course, some decrement in score must be expected as the control device properties deviate from the optimum values listed above.

The experimenter may sometimes desire to "imbed" these workload calibration tasks in a larger "scenario", i.e., as one axis of a multiaxis vehicular control task (e.g., see Ref. A-6). In those cases, it is advisable to use the actual display and control for the scenario task (e.g., for an automobile speed control task, use an actual speedometer and accelerator pedal). If the critical instability is carefully trained for and measured on these actual displays and controls then to a first approximation the normalized loading ($L = \lambda/\lambda_c$) should be valid for values of actual λ_c not too far from the maximum with ideal controls and displays (i.e., within 30 percent). However, this assumption has not been carefully tested or validated (mainly due to a lack of any means for accurately measuring the "true" workload!)

Input

Because this task is unstable, the operator's own "noise" or remnant is sufficient to continuously excite the subcritical and critical tasks, so no forcing function (command input or disturbance) is necessary. Should an input be needed to verify the operator's control behavior, it must be quite small and have a carefully shaped spectrum. A discussion of these considerations is beyond the scope of this note, but is covered in some detail in Ref. A-12. It was shown that a quasi-random command input having an rms level about 10 percent of the display screen caused a decrement in critical instability of about 10 percent. Again, if the same input is used for both λ and λ_c runs, then the normalised workload should be similar to the no-input case. (This assumption, too, needs validation).

PROCEDURES

From much experience in training and administering the Critical Task, the following procedures are tentatively recommended for workload calibration:

1. Explain and demonstrate to the subject how the display diverges if no control is used, and recommend a rapid and roughly proportional correction by the stick as the best strategy.

2. Use the Critical-Task (increasing λ to the unstable limit) for training. Give the subject his scores after each trial, and pause for one minute after each run of 5 trials to rest the subject, compute the median score, and tell the subject of his score and trend. The median scores should increase rapidly for the first several runs, then level off. No more than 20-30 trials should be given in any one session, as eye or hand fatigue will set in due to the intense concentration required.

3. About 2-3 days of distributed practice (20-30 trials in morning and afternoon) should yield adequately trained subjects and fairly stable critical task scores. We often provide a tangible incentive (in cash or spirits) for the achievement of $\lambda_c = 4.0$ or 5.0 r/s, awarded after the session, of course! Once a reasonably stable asymptote has been reached, continued intensive practice should be discouraged to prevent continued improvement to untypically high ("Olympic-level") performance. We emphasise here the importance of near-asymptotic training, because many workload experiments have had inadequate practice and been confounded by simultaneous learning and fatigue effects.

4. For the actual workload calibration runs select levels of λ as fractions of the subject's 3- or 5-trial-median critical task score at the start of that session, λ_c^s, i.e. if $\lambda_c^s = 5.0$ then the loadings would be as follows:

Normalized Workload: L =   0.1, 0.2, 0.3, 0.4, 0.5, 0.6
λ (for $\lambda_c^s = 5.0$) =   0.5, 1.0, 1.5, 2.0, 2.5, 3.0 (r/s)
Divergence Time Constant, T = 2.0, 1.0, 0.67, 0.5, 0.4, 0.3 (sec)

We suggest loads of L = 0.1, 0.3, 0.5 as a minimal set for
workload calibration, ranging from "fairly easy" to
"difficult" and with three points to better define any non-
linear trends. (Note: some workload measures may be related
more linearly to the time constant T_λ (see above) than to
λ per se).

5. Each subcritical loading should be given for at least a
   100 sec trial (after reaching λ), in order to allow the
   autonomic system adaptive mechanisms to reach a fairly
   steady state. Allow two minutes rest between trials.

6. The various levels of L should be given in a random order
   (different each sitting), then reversed, so that each is
   given twice (from opposite directions of difficulty), and
   trials should be balanced around the mid-session to minimise
   fatigue or learning effects. (For example, give: L = 0.3,
   0.5, 0.1, rest, 0.1, 0.5, 0.3 in one half-hour session).

7. During each 100 sec trial, measure simultaneously the desired
   psychophysiological variables of interest, stopping their
   measurement <u>before</u> the subject is told the trial is over (to
   avoid end-spurt effects). Where possible, make on-line time
   records of the variables, because the variability of such
   measures is often as useful as the variable itself (e.g.,
   heart-rate variability, per the work of Kalsbeek in Ref.
   A-13 or Sayers in Ref. A-14).

8. At the end of each session, again measure the end-of-session
   critical instability λ_c^E (3-trial median). If it differs by
   more than ±1.0 r/s from the start-of-session λ_c^S, the values
   of L may have to be corrected for learning or fatigue by a
   factor inversely proportional to the assumed (or measured)
   trend in λ_c over the span of the calibration runs. (A
   mid-session λ_c run (3 trials) may be desirable to show such
   trends.

9. Because there are likely to be as yet unknown diurnal effects
   on the subject's tracking workload capabilities, these should
   be controlled for by doing the tests at the same time of day,
   if possible, and reporting the values of λ_c and the time
   they were measured.

10. Asymptotic $\tilde{\lambda}_c$ scores vary significantly among subjects
    ranging from 4-7+ r/s. Therefore, subjects should be used
    as their own controls in the experimental design and stat-
    istical analysis of the data. (This is why L is based on
    the individual subject's $\tilde{\lambda}_c$ for that session). There are
    some clues that the individual $\tilde{\lambda}_c$ levels may correlate with
    body somatotype (Ref. A.15), so data on each subject's

somatotype should accompany all basic research data bases. (This is another area needing research).

CONCLUDING REMARKS

The foregoing recommendations, although based on many years of critical task development and application, must be considered tentative. A few assumptions, noted above, still need to be validated, and optimum training and calibration procedures need to be developed. The author would like to hear from anyone working with these tasks and will be happy to help in any way with obtaining valid data and in exchanging information. Please address correspondence to:

> Henry R. Jex
> Systems Technology, Inc.
> 13766 South Hawthorne Boulevard
> Hawthorne, CA 90250 USA

1. It should be mentioned that one of the candidate methods for measuring the workload of a primary task is via the "Cross-Coupled-Instability Task"(Ref. A-6) . This is an adaptive, auxiliary task in which the secondary task is a sub-critical task with $\lambda(t)$ adaptively increased to the level λ_x, where the primary task performance (error) shows a just-noticeable worsening. It has been used to calibrate the "Excess-control-Capacity" (EC = λ_x/λ_c) of a number of complex control situations as mentioned in Ref.A-11.

2. Commercial applications are subject to patents owned by Systems Technology, Inc.

REFERENCES

A-1. Jex, Henry R., J.D. McDonnell, and A.V. Phatak, "A 'Critical' Tracking Task for Manual Control Research," IEEE Trans., Vol. HFE-7, No. 4, Dec. 1966, pp.138-145.

A-2. Jex, Henry R., and R. Wade Allen, "Research on a New Human Dynamic Response Test Battery. Part II: Test Development and Validation", 6th Annual Conference on Manual Control, AFIT, Wright-Patterson AFB, OH, April. 1970.

A-3. Allen, R. Wade, and Henry R. Jex, "Visual-Motor Response of Crewmen During a Simulated 90-day Space Mission as Measured by the Critical Task Battery", 7th Annual Conference on Manual Control, NASA SP-281, 1972, pp. 239-246.

A-4. Stassen, H.G., P.L. Brinkman, et al. "Chapter III: Application of Describing Function Methods," Progress Report, January 1970 until January 1973 of the Man-Machine Systems Group, Delft Univ. of Technology, Rept. No. WTHD-55, Nov. 1973, pp. 45-92.

A-5. Stein, Willi, and E. Pioch, On the Application of Tracking Tasks in Ergonomics Research, Forschung Institut fur Anthropotechnic, Meckenheim, Germany, Rept. 23, Oct. 1975.

A-6. Jex, Henry R., W.F. Jewell, and R. Wade Allen, "Development of the Dual-Axis and Cross-Coupled Critical Tasks", 8th Annual Conference on Manual Control, AFFDL-TR-72-92, Jan. 1973, pp. 529-552.

A-7. Hess, Ronald A., and Walter M. Teichgraber, "Error Quantization Effects in Compensatory Tracking Tasks", IEEE Trans., Vol. SMC-4, No. 5, July 1974, pp. 343-349.

A-8. Stassen, H.G., (Ed.) "Application of Describing Function Methods", Chapter III of Progress Report January 1970 Until January 1973 of Man-Machine Systems Group, Delft Univ. of Technology, Rept. 55, Dec. 1973, pp. 45-92.

A-9 Merhav, S.J., and Orna Ben Ya'acov, "Control Augmentation and Work Load Reduction by Kinesthetic Information from the Manipulator", IEEE Trans., Vol. SMC-6, No.12, Dec. 1976, pp. 825-835.

A-10. McDonnell, J.D., Pilot Rating Techniques for the Estimation and Evaluation of Handling Qualities, AFFDL-TR-76, Dec. 1968.

A-11.   Jex, Henry R., and Warren F. Clement, "Defining and Measuring Perceptual-Motor Workload in Manual Control Tasks", presented at AGARD Conference on Mental Workload, Mati, Greece, Sept. 1977.

A-12   McDonnell, J.D. and Henry R. Jex, A "Critical" Tracking Task for Man-Machine Research Related to the Operator's Effective Delay Time. Part II. Experimental Effects of System Input Spectra, Control Stick Stiffness, and Controlled Element Order, NASA CR-674, Jan. 1967.

A-13.   Kalsbeek, J.W.H. and J.H. Ettema, "Physiological and Psychological Evaluation of Distraction Stress", Proc. of 2nd International Congress on Ergonomics, Taylor and Francis, Ltd. London, 1964, pp. 443-447.

A-14   Sayers, R., "Analysis of Heart Rate Variability", Ergonomics, Vol. 16, No. 1, Jan. 1973, pp. 17-32.

A-15.   van Wulfften Palthe, P.M., "Somatotyping", in Anthropometry and Human Engineering, AGARDograph No. 5, 1955, pp. 104-112 (also see pp. 31-35).

A MODEL FOR MENTAL WORKLOAD IN TASKS REQUIRING CONTINUOUS INFORMATION PROCESSING

William H. Levison

Bolt Beranek and Newman Inc., 50 Moulton Street

Cambridge, Massachusetts 02138

INTRODUCTION

The object of this paper is to define and justify a model for mental workload that is appropriate to tasks in which a human operator is required to process sensory information in a continuous fashion. The primary application of this model has been to continuous manual tracking tasks, although certain non-tracking tasks are also candidates for application. The model appears to be most useful as a design and evaluation tool for predicting the relationship between performance and workload; measurements of workload using concepts suggested by the model can be obtained only under highly constrained situations.

In this paper we define workload not in physiological terms but in terms of a performance characteristic of the human operator. Specifically, workload is related to the relative amount of randomness in the human operator's information processing activity, where decreasing randomness is associated with increasing mental effort. Since operator randomness can be associated with a parameter of an existing model for human operator behavior, analytic predictions of performance/workload tradeoffs can be obtained.

The terms "attention" and "workload" are both used in this treatment. It is perhaps natural to consider "attention" as a level of mental effort voluntarily committed to a task, and "workload" as a level of mental effort required by the task. For purposes of model development, the terms are used inter-changeably (i.e. the degree of voluntarism is irrelevant to the mathematics of the problem).

The primary intent of this paper is not to present original research results, but to provide a unified treatment of theory, validation, and application of the model for workload and attention proposed and reported by this author and his colleagues (1,2). The section on theoretical development presents the basic assumptions underlying the proposed workload model, shows the equivalence of time-sharing and capacity-sharing notions of attention, presents the basic model of workload, and reviews a human operator model that allows one to predict the relationship between performance and workload. The reader is then directed to the literature for results that validate the basic human operator model as well as the specific model for mental workload, and some pilot-opinion results are cited to support the argument that response randomness can be related to workload and attentional demand. The third major section of the paper discusses predictive and diagnostic applications of the workload model. Finally, some thoughts are offered relating the concepts and techniques discussed in this paper to the goals of the workload symposium to which this paper is submitted.

THEORETICAL DEVELOPMENT

Basic Assumptions

The proposed model for workload is based on the following key assumptions:

1. The mental effort involved in performing a task requiring continuous information processing may, for purposes of mathematical treatment, be attributed to perceptual processing. For example, the workload associated with a single-variable tracking task is equivalent to the attentional demand of the tracking display.

2. The workload imposed by a task requiring processing of multiple sensory inputs is equal to the attentional demands of the various inputs, independent of the degree of linear correlation between these inputs. That is, total workload is computed in the same manner whether the sensory variables relate to a single task or to independent tasks performed concurrently.

3. Each perceptual variable used by the human operator may be considered to be corrupted by a gaussian "white noise" process that is linearly uncorrelated with the sensory input and with other similar noise processes. This "observation noise" process is intended as a mathematical representation of the combined effects of

various sources of randomness in the human operator's sensory, central-processing, and response mechanisms. The perceptual information available to the operator from sensory variable "y" is therefore

$$y_p(t) = y(t) + v_y(t) \tag{1}$$

where $y_p(t)$ is the perceived variable, $y(t)$ the variable presented by the display, and $v_y(t)$ a white noise process having an autocorrelation function

$$\phi_{vv}(\tau) = V_y \delta(\tau) \tag{2}$$

or, equivalently, a uniform power spectral density function of $V/2\pi$ over all frequencies.[1] We shall refer to the quantity V as the "covariance" of the noise process.

Although not physically realizeable, the notion of a white noise disturbance is a useful mathematical fiction that we adopt because it provides a representation of human operator randomness that is readily handled within the framework of modern control and estimation theory, and because it allows us to model human control behavior with considerable accuracy. In effect, we are assuming that the bandwidth of the observation noise process is substantially greater than the response bandwidth of the man-machine system.

Equivalence of Time-Sharing and Parallel Processing

The model for attention-sharing and workload presented in this paper has been formulated in the past around the assumption that the human operator processes various sources of information in parallel but with interference between processes (1, 2). That is, the human has a certain amount of "capacity" that must be shared among processes; the workload attributed to a particular process is then related to the fraction of capacity used by that process. Most of the psychological literature that deals with attention-sharing, however, assumes that tasks are processed sequentially; workload and attention are then related to the fraction of time devoted to a particular task.

Fortunately, for control situations in which sampling among

display variables is rapid with respect to the time fluctuations of these variables, time-sharing and capacity-sharing have the same mathematical implications. A simplified mathematical treatment is provided below to demonstrate this equivalence; a more rigorous treatment in modern control theory format has been presented by Kleinman and Curry (3).

Let us assume that the human operator time-shares his attention between the perceived display variable $y_p(t)$ described in Equation (1) and other information sources. The signal $y(t)$ as perceived by the operator now becomes

$$y_p(t) = [y(t) + v_y(t)] \cdot s(t) \quad (3)$$

where $s(t)$ has value 1 when the signal $y(t)$ is attended to and value 0 otherwise.

Assume that the scan rate is arbitrarily fast, that the scan is aperiodic, and that "f" is the fraction of time that the signal "y" is attended to. The autocorrelation function of the scan process is then

$$\phi_{ss}(\tau) \equiv E\{s(t) \cdot s(t+\tau)\} = \begin{cases} f^2 & \tau \neq 0 \\ f & \tau = 0 \end{cases} \quad (4)$$

That is, the state of the scanner at time $t+\tau$ is independent of the state at time "t" (except for $\tau=0$), and the autocorrelation is simply the square of the probability of the scanner being "on". For $\tau=0$, the expected value is the probability "f" that the scanner is on.

Assume that the signals $y(t)$, $v(t)$, and $s(t)$ are linearly independent. The autocorrelation of the perceived signal $y_p(t)$ may thus be written as

$$\phi_{y_p y_p}(\tau) = \overbrace{\phi_{yy}(\tau) \cdot \phi_{ss}(\tau)}^{\phi_1} + \overbrace{\phi_{vv}(\tau) \cdot \phi_{ss}(\tau)}^{\phi_2} \quad (5)$$

The "signal" portion of this autocorrelation function is thus

$$\phi_1(\tau) = f^2 \phi_{yy}(\tau) + (f-f^2) \phi_{yy}(\tau)\bigg|_{\tau=0} \quad (6)$$

That is, the autocorrelation of the original signal $y(t)$ has been scaled by the square of the fractional allocation of attention, with the addition of a term at zero time shift.

Since the noise has non-zero correlation only for zero time shift, the "noise" portion of the perceived autocorrelation function is

$$\phi_2(\tau) = f\, V\delta(\tau) \qquad (7)$$

The total autocorrelation function for the signal $y_p(t)$ may be written as

$$\phi_{y_p y_p}(\tau) \simeq f^2\left[\phi_{yy}(\tau) + \frac{V}{f}\delta(\tau)\right] \qquad (8)$$

We have neglected the second term of Equation (6), as it represents a vanishingly small white noise process that is overshadowed by human operator noise.

Two major consequences of time-sharing are seen: the signal is scaled overall by the factor f^2, and the noise power, relative to signal power, increases inversely with attention. In terms of the ability of the operator to use the perceived signal, the scale factor f^2 is unimportant, since the human operator can (theoretically) compensate by adjusting his response gain. The change in signal/noise property, on the other hand, may be of considerable importance. As attention decreases toward zero, the noise power becomes so large relative to signal power that the operator is unable to extract useful information about $y(t)$.

The parallel-processing model proceeds as follows. Assume that the operator has a total of N "channels" available for continuous information processing. Assume that each channel is corrupted by a white noise process $v_i(t)$ with autocorrelation $V\delta(t)$ where the v_i are assumed linearly independent of one another and of the signal $y(t)$. Let some fraction "f" of these channels be applied in parallel to process the signal $y(t)$, and let the perceived variable be defined as the sum of the outputs of these channels.

The perceived signal $y_p(t)$ is thus

$$y_p(t) = \sum_{i=1}^{fN} y_i(t) + v_i(t) \qquad (9)$$

where fN is the number of channels devoted to signal "y". Since the signal $y_i(t)$ is the same for all channels, the above expression reduces to

$$y_p(t) = fN\, y(t) + \sum_{i=1}^{fN} v_i(t) \tag{10}$$

The "signal" portion of the autocorrelation of $y_p(t)$ is simply the autocorrelation of the displayed variable $y(t)$ scaled by the constant $(fN)^2$. Since the noise terms are assumed linearly independent, the autocorrelation of the sum is equal to the sum of the autocorrelations. Thus, we obtain

$$\phi_{y_p y_p}(\tau) = f^2 N^2 \left[\phi_{yy}(\tau) + \frac{V}{fN}\delta(\tau)\right] \tag{11}$$

As is the case with time-sharing, the notion of capacity-sharing leads to the conclusion that noise power, relative to signal power, scales inversely with the fraction of attention devoted to processing the display variable. Note that total capacity influences noise/signal properties in the same manner; for a fixed fractional allocation of attention to variable "y," noise power relative to signal power decreases inversely with increasing total capacity.

Thus, the question as to whether increased workload reflects more time on a task or more "capacity" is irrelevant to the model developed in this paper (provided time-sharing is rapid compared to the correlation times of the system variables); both assumptions lead to the same consequences in terms of the ability of the human operator to use information for continuous processing. Accordingly, we shall avoid inferences with regard to the physiological mechanisms for attention-sharing in the remainder of this paper; instead, we shall relate attention and workload to signal/noise characteristics of human operator response-characteristics that are well defined in terms of the human operator model (to be discussed later) and, to some extent, are measurable quantities as well.

Basic Model for Workload

From Equations (8) and (11) we conclude that the effects of attention can be represented by considering the covariance of the white observation noise to vary inversely with attention. In developing this model, we shall make use of the empirically observed phenomenon that the observation noise covariance scales with the variance of the displayed quantity for certain idealized display conditions (i.e. when sensory-related threshold and saturation effects are negligible). In this situation, the observation noise covariance may be written as

$$V_y = \sigma_y^2 \, P_y \tag{12}$$

where P_y is referred to as the "observation noise/signal ratio".

For many laboratory tracking tasks, we have found the ratio P_y to be remarkably consistent across experimental conditions, across subjects, and across observational variables (i.e. displacement and rate) (4). We have therefore associated the noise/signal ratio with a basic limitation on the human's central-processing capabilities.

Let us define $P_y = P_o$ for single-variable sensory processing. In this situation, the observation noise is given as

$$V_y = \sigma_y^2 P_o \qquad (13)$$

In the case of multiple-display processing, the noise covariance associated with the ith display variable is, from Equations (8) and (12)

$$V_{y_i} = \sigma_{y_i}^2 P_{y_i} = \sigma_{y_i}^2 \frac{P_o}{f_i} \qquad (14)$$

This leads to the following basic model relating attention to observation noise:

$$P_{y_i} = \frac{P_o}{f_i} \qquad (15)$$

which may also be written as

$$f_i = \frac{P_o}{P_{y_i}} \qquad (16)$$

Equation (15) emphasizes the predictive aspect of the attention/workload model: given a reference value for P_o and the relative attention devoted to each display variable, one can predict the noise/signal ratio associated with each display variable and, using the pilot model described below, one can then predict system performance.

Equation (16) emphasizes the diagnostic aspect of the model: given values for the P_{y_i} derived from experimental measurements, one can compute overall task workload.

$$\text{Workload} \quad \sum_i f_i = \sum_i \frac{P_o}{P_{y_i}} \qquad (17)$$

It must be emphasized that Equations (15) through (17) are models of <u>relative</u> workload, since we have yet to determine the value for P_o that corresponds to "full attention". Predictive applications of this concept have tended to use a value of 0.01π (or -20 dB) for P_o, because this value appears to reflect human operator noise characteristics in a variety of standard laboratory tracking tasks (4). This value can be considered only a convenient reference point, however, because tasks can be designed that will force a lower value for the noise/signal ratio (2, 5).

In order to use this model for workload, either in a predictive or diagnostic application, it must be incorporated in a larger model that allows one to predict the relationship between system performance, pilot response behavior, and attention. The state-variable, (or "optimal-control") model for pilot/vehicle systems has a structure that is compatible with the workload model and has been applied extensively to predict performance/workload tradeoffs. A very brief description of the basic features of this model is given below; the reader is referred to the literature for details relating to theoretical development validation and application of the model (2, 6-12).

A Model Relating Performance and Attention

This model is based on the assumption that the well-motivated, well-trained human operator behaves in a near optimal manner subject to his inherent constraints and limitations. A block diagram of the pilot-vehicle model is given in Figure 1. The portion of the model which pertains specifically to the operator is shown within the dashed line. Principal model elements are:

(a) A linearized description of the vehicle dynamics given by the following state equation:

$$\underline{\dot{x}}(t) = \underline{A}\,\underline{x}(t) + \underline{B}\,\underline{u}(t) + \underline{w}(t) \qquad (18)$$

where $\underline{x}(t)$ is the vector which describes the state of the vehicle, $\underline{u}(t)$ the pilot's control output, and $\underline{w}(t)$ a vector of white driving noise processes. (If the external forcing functions are rational noise spectra of first order or higher, the resulting "input states" are incorporated into the state vector $\underline{x}(t)$.)

(b) A "display vector" which, in general, consists of a linear transformation of the state variables and is given as

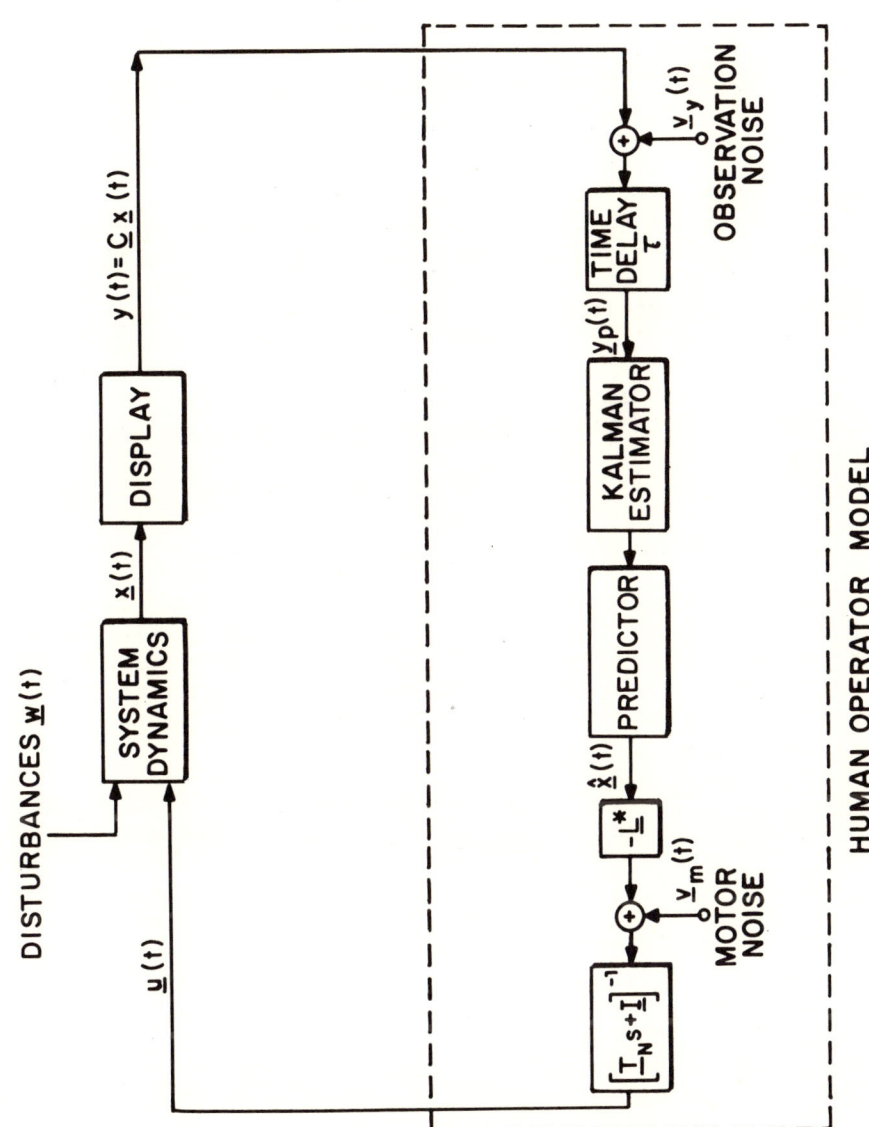

Figure 1. Structure of the Optimal Control Model.

$$\underline{y}(t) = \underline{C}\,\underline{x}(t) \tag{19}$$

This vector contains the set of sensory variables used by the pilot. Since both displacement and rate information will be available from a single display element, and non-visual (e.g. motion) sensory inputs may be used as well, the number of elements in the $\underline{v}_y$ vector may exceed the number of physical display elements used in a specific flight-control task.

(c) A representation of the pilot's limitations by means of an equivalent perceptual time delay τ and an equivalent observation noise vector $\underline{v}_y(t)$ to account for the stochastic portion of the human operator's response (referred to as "pilot remnant" in the jargon of manual control research.)

(d) A least mean-squared predictor to compensate partially for the inherent time delay.

(e) A set of optimal gains acting on the best estimate of the state vector, the output of which is the commanded control signal $\underline{u}_c(t)$.

The primary output variable of the optimal-control model is the pilot's control signal, $\overline{u}(t)$. Once the characteristics of this signal have been determined, it is a relatively straightforward procedure to calculate pilot response characteristics (e.g. describing functions and remnant spectra) and various measures of overall system performance.

The optimal predictor, optimal estimator, and optimal gain matrix represent the set of "adjustable parameters" by which the pilot tries to optimize his behavior. The general expressions for these model elements depend on system dynamics, according to well-defined mathematical rules that are described in the literature (6,7). The controller is assumed to adopt a response strategy to minimize the following weighted sum of averaged display and control variances:

$$J(t) = \sum_{i=1}^{N} q_i\, \sigma_i^2 + \sum_{i=1}^{N_u} (r_i\, \sigma_{u_i}^2 + g_i\, \sigma_{\dot{u}_i}^2) \tag{20}$$

For all of the single-variable control situations we have explored, good approximations to experimental measurements have been obtained with a cost functional consisting simply of a weighted sum of system error variance plus control-rate variance (6,7). The cost on control rate represents, in part, a subjective penalty imposed by the controller on making rapid control motions. In addition, this term may account indirectly for physiological limitations on the pilot's bandwidth. The inclusion of such a term results in a lag matrix $\underline{T}_n$ -- often associated with the neuromuscular system -- which is generated in the optimal controller.

The time delay, observation noise, and, to some extent, cost functional parameters of the model represent inherent human limitations. Numerical values for these parameters (or rules for obtaining such numerical values) must be decided prior to the analysis or adjusted in an iterative scheme to match pilot response characteristics in a particular situation.

The time delay required to match pilot response behavior usually lies with the range of 0.15 to 0.22 seconds, for predictive applications of the model, a time delay of 0.2 seconds is a reasonable choice. For single-variable laboratory tracking tasks, experimental data are often well matched if the relative cost coefficient on control-rate is adjusted to yield a lag T_n of 0.1 seconds. For more complex, "real world" tracking tasks, reasonable values for both control-related and display-related cost coefficients can be obtained from consideration of maximum attainable (or allowable) values for these system variables (10).

Each component of the set of observation noise covariances $\underline{V}_y$ is determined according to Equation (14)[2], which, for convenience, is repeated below:

$$V_{y_i} = \sigma^2_{y_i} \cdot \frac{P_i}{f_i} \qquad (21)$$

Thus, once we have selected the f_i, along with other pilot-related parameters, we can run the pilot/vehicle model in an iterative fashion until the relationship specified by Equation (21) are satisfied. (Note that the variances $\sigma^2_{y_i}$ are model outputs and can be determined only by obtaining a model solution.)

While the workload model has been applied mainly to prediction of performance/workload characteristics of continuous control tasks, it should be noted that the model diagrammed in Figure 1 is a model for <u>estimation</u> as well as for <u>control</u>. Specifically, the Kalman filter and predictor provide an estimate of the state $\hat{x}(t)$, and the covariance of the estimation error is predicted to provide a measure of the reliability of the state estimate. Given a suitably defined metric for monitoring performance, the model of Figure 1 (minus elements relating to generation of control response) can be used to predict the tradeoff between attention and monitoring performance (13).

If the control-generation elements of the model of Figure 1 are replaced by a Bayesian decision algorithm, one has a model for predicting decision behavior. Such a model is appropriate for decision tasks where the human operator has to decide whether or not the system is within some acceptable region (e.g. whether or not an airplane is within the "approach window").

The decision algorithm is developed as follows. Let $h_0(t)$ and $h_1(t)$ represent the mutually exclusive events that the system is within (without) the desired region of state space, and let $H_0(t)$ and $H_1(t)$ be the operator's decision as to whether or not the system is within the desired region. Assume that the operator bases his decision to maximize the expected "utility" (or minimize the "cost") associated with the various combinations of decision and fact. The decision rule is then given as

$$H(t) = H_1 \quad \text{if} \quad \frac{P(h_1(t)/y_p(s), s \leq t)}{P(h_0(t)/y_p(s), s \leq t)} > \frac{U_{00} - U_{10}}{U_{11} = Y_{01}} \quad (22)$$

$$H(t) = H_0 \quad \text{otherwise}$$

where U_{ij} is the utility of deciding H_i when the true event is h_j, and $P(h_i(t)/y_p(s), s \leq t$ is the probability that h_i is true, given the past history of the sensory data $y_p(s)$, $s \leq t$. As shown by Levison and Tanner (14), this probability is derived in part from the state estimate and estimation error statistics, which, in turn, are influenced by the operator's observation noise. Thus, the workload model can be included in the modified human operator model to allow predictions of the relationship between decision performance and attention.

MODEL VALIDATION

Considerations of length preclude extensive validation of the various concepts offered above. We shall therefore present only a few key illustrative examples, and we shall direct the reader to the literature for additional validation.

The Basic Human Operator Model

Central to the theme of this paper is the notion that we have a valid model for predicting monitoring and control performance, that this model accounts for the stochastic component of operator response, and that response randomness can be largely

represented as a set of linearly independent gaussian white
observation noise processes.

This model has been validated for a variety of control
situations -- mostly single-variable laboratory tracking tasks
(2,7,9,15), but some complex tasks as well (8,11,16). The
reader is especially directed to Kleinman, Baron, and Levison (7),
where it is shown that detailed pilot response behavior (as
well as mean-squared error scores) can be reproduced by the model
using values for pilot parameters (time delay, motor lag, and
observation noise/signal ratio) that are nearly invariant across
control tasks. The tasks considered in that reference span a
range of operator response characteristics, indicating that the
so-called "pilot parameters" reflect primarily limitations of
human-operator information processing that are relatively
independent of the control task parameters. In particular, the
notion of treating response randomness (mathematically) as an
observation noise process is supported by the ability of the model
to reproduce the spectrum of the stochastic portion of the
operator's response ("remnant") across a set of tasks in which
this spectrum varies substantially. (A graphical example of data-
matching capability is presented later in this discussion.)

Attention-Sharing and Interference

The notion that total-task workload is the sum of the
workload imposed by each source of sensory information can be
tested in a number of ways. If the operator can be trained to
devote a fixed amount of attention to an information source,
independent of the number of sources used, overall task workload
should increase as the number of subtasks increases. Conversely,
if the operator can be persuaded to work at a fixed level of
total-task workload, independent of the number of subtasks,
subtask performance should degrade as the number of subtasks is
increased. In this case, the model for workload implies
"interference" among concurrent tasks.

A set of experiments were performed by Levison, Elkind,
and Ward (2) to test the notion of task interference. Subjects
were provided with two 2-axis controls and four separated
displays and were required to perform up to four concurrent
linearly independent rate-control tracking tasks. The tasks were
performed singly and in combination. When performing multiple
tasks, fixation was maintained on a single display and the
remaining three displays were tracked using peripheral vision
(i.e. scanning was not allowed).

The subjects were instructed to minimize the sum of the
mean-squared errors of the component tasks. They were urged to
work as hard on a single-variable task as on the combined task;

that is, an attempt was made to keep total workload constant.

The single-variable tasks were used as "calibration" experiments to define numerical values for pilot-related parameters (including a "residual noise" term that was added to the expression for observation noise to account for peripheral viewing). Using the constraint that the subtask workload must sum to unity (i.e. the assumption that total-task workload was kept constant), both attentional allocation and system performance were predicted for the four-axis tracking task.

There was considerable interference among tasks; that is, subtask and total-task scores were greater when the tasks were performed concurrently than when performed singly. Model predictions for the multiple-task case were in good agreement with the data, especially for the total-task score (which is the quantity the subjects were instructed to minimize). Agreement with some of the subtask scores was less good, apparently because total-task performance was relatively insensitive to allocation of attention among the component tasks.

Figure 2 shows the effect of attention-sharing on the normalized observation noise (a linear transformation of the pilot's remnant spectrum) and on the pilot's describing function (i.e. control strategy). Results are presented for the foveally-fixated display. Model results agree quite well with the data and show that the effects of multiple-task requirements were to increase the observation noise spectrum (as predicted by the model for attention-sharing) and to decrease the amplitude ratio and increase high-frequency phase lag of the describing function (an adaptive response by the pilot to filter out some of the effects of increased observation noise).

In a companion experiment, Levison, Elkind and Ward showed that the model for attention-sharing could be applied to multiple displays within a single axis of control. In this experiment, subjects were required to perform a difficult single-axis task with a simple display of system error as the baseline condition. They were then provided with an additional display element (on the same display screen) that provided some derivative information. The model correctly predicted that addition of this display element would reduce mean-squared system error, but that this improvement would be limited by the increased operator noise associated with attention-sharing.

The model relating attention to performance has also been validated for decision tasks and, to some extent, for combined decision and control tasks. Levison and Tanner (14) showed that the model for attention-sharing provided excellent agreement with the observed decrement in performance between a single decision

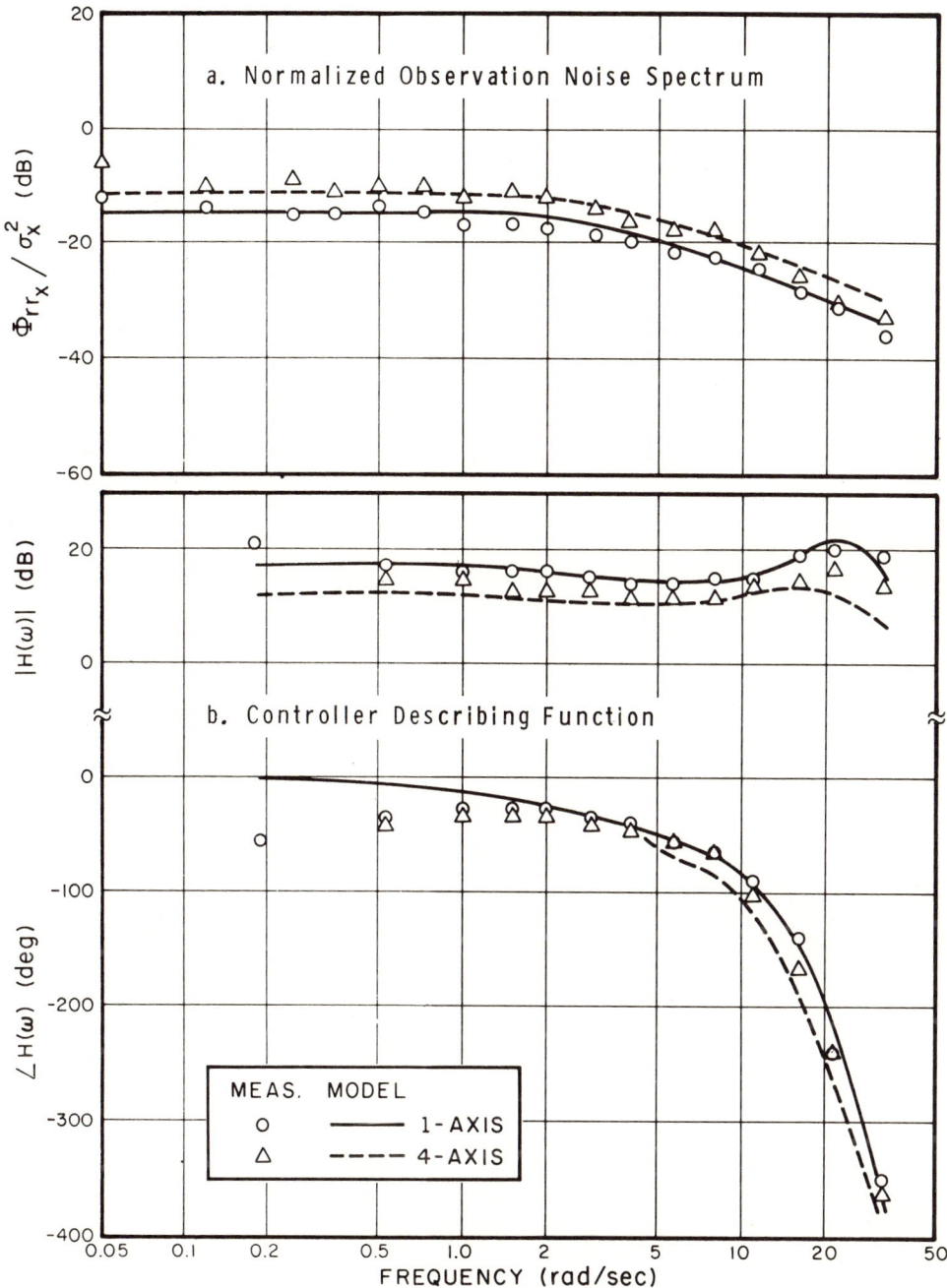

Figure 2. Effect of Number of Axes Tracked on Frequency-Domain Measures: Foveal Viewing.
Average of 4 subjects, 2 trials/subject

task and two concurrent tasks. Predictions were less accurate for concurrent decision and control tasks; combined-task performance suggested that some interference was present, but to a lesser degree than predicted by the constraint of fixed total-task workload.

Wewerinke also tested the model relating decision performance to attention in a series of experiments involving multiple decision tasks as well as combined decision and control (17). In general, good agreement was obtained between measured and predicted performance decrements between single-task and multiple-task performance.

Task-Induced Workload

We have thus far discussed experimental situations in which subjects have been encouraged to maintain a constant total-task workload. In general, however, one would not expect workload to remain constant across tasks. Where adequate performance could be achieved at low-to-moderate workload levels (or if performance were insensitive to attention), the operator would be unlikely to expend a great deal of mental effort in minimizing performance scores. On the other hand, if the control task were such that high attention was required to maintain vehicle control, one would hope that the operator would respond accordingly!

Some especially demanding control taks have been found that encourage the human operator to reduce his noise/signal ratio well below the nominal -20 dB found in "standard" laboratory tracking situations. Levison, Elkind, and Ward identified an observation noise/signal ratio of -26 dB from the response behavior of subjects who tracked unstable vehicle dynamics of the form $K/s(s-1)$. The divergence time constant of 1 second made these dynamics particularly difficult to control. These results were consistent with those reported earlier by Jex and Magdaleno (5), who found that the remnant spectrum, when normalized appropriately, shifted downward as the divergence time constant was decreased. One explanation for these results is that tracking errors obtained with unstable controlled-element dynamics are especially sensitive to operator "remnant" and, therefore, the operator is motivated to reduce his response randomness.

Model analysis was performed to compare the sensitivity of mean-squared error to noise/signal ratio for the unstable dynamics explored by Levison et al. with the corresponding sensitivity for stable dynamics of the type explored in earlier studies (2). Figure 3 shows, for example, that a reduction of noise/signal ratio from -20 dB to -26 dB reduced the predicted error score by about 6.5 dB for the unstable dynamics. The same

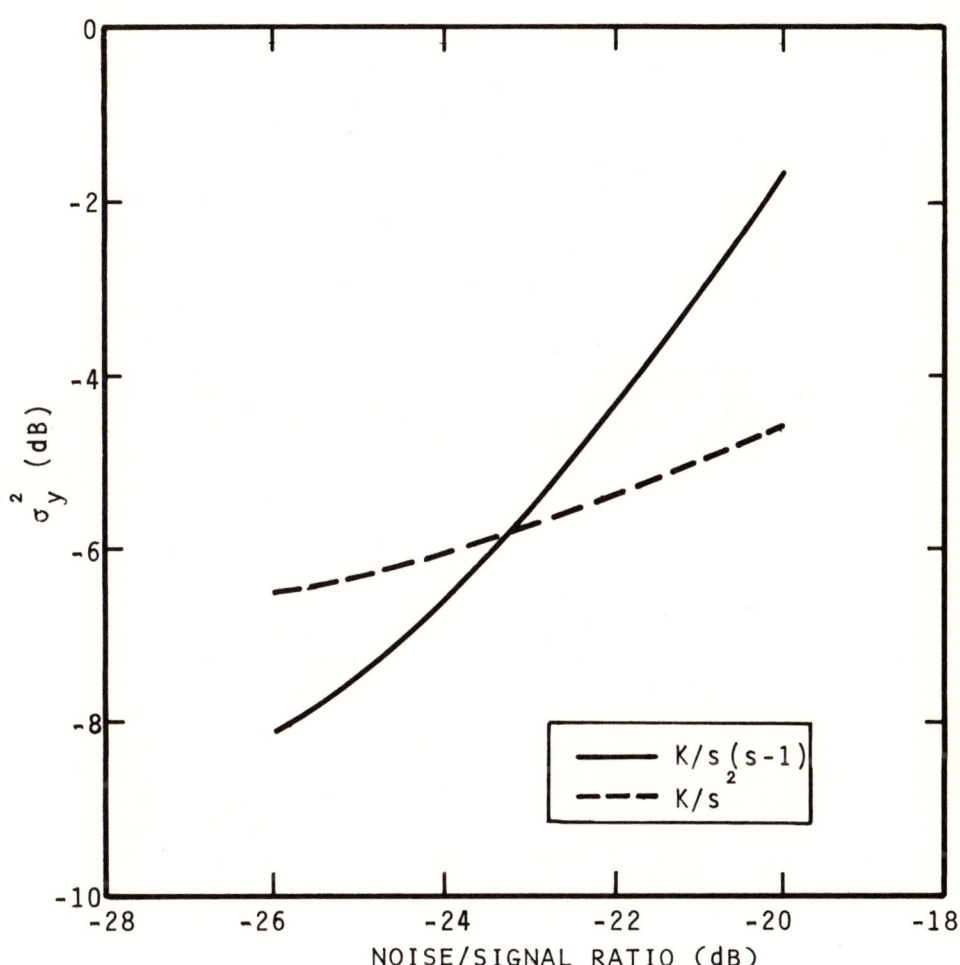

Figure 3. Effect of Noise/Signal Ratio on Predicted Error Variance.

decrement in noise/signal ratio led to a predicted reduction of about 2 dB in error score for the stable acceleration-control dynamics (K/s^2). Hence, the subjects apparently found it worth the extra effort to reduce observation noise in the unstable tracking task because of the large payoff.

Correlation with Subjective Opinion

We have attempted to show that the operator's signal/noise ratio behaves in a manner consistent with the notions of workload and attention adopted in this paper. That is, in situations in which an attempt has been made to maintain a fixed level of total-task workload, multiple-task requirements have caused readjustments of noise/signal ratios (and consequent changes in other response measures) consistent with the model for attention-sharing. Similarly, tasks which might expect to require exceptional mental effort have lead to lower-than-usual levels of measured operator noise/signal ratios. To further validate the argument that noise/signal ratios are related to operator workload, we shall compare the trends implied by the workload model with trends of subjective opinion data reported in the literature.

Wewerinke has reported a set of experiments that were especially well designed for testing the implications of the workload model presented in this paper (18). The primary experimental variable was controlled-element dynamics, which ranged from simple proportional control to a second-order instability of the form $K/s(s-1)$. Among the measurements Wewerinke obtained were subjective ratings of "demands on the pilot" and operator noise/signal ratios (inferred from matching response behavior with the optimal-control pilot/vehicle model), and he computed a "workload index" based on a modified model for operator workload.

Subjective opinion correlated with vehicle dynamics in the manner suggested earlier in the paper; that is, the pilot's reported impression of task demand increased with increasing vehicle instability. Wewerinke also reported excellent correlation between subjective rating and his "workload index", which was defined to be $w = S/P$

$$\text{where} \quad S = \frac{\partial \sigma^2_x}{\sigma^2_x} \Big/ \frac{\partial P}{P} \tag{23}$$

and P the noise/signal ratio. That is, workload was based not only on the noise/signal ratio achieved by the pilot, but also on the sensitivity of fractional changes in mean-squared error to fractional changes in noise/signal ratio. Wewerinke hypothesized that subjects would tend to operate at the "knee" of the performance/workload tradeoff curve; that is, that they would reduce their noise/signal ratios until the payoff for doing so became insufficient. This contention was largely confirmed by Wewerinke's results and is consistent with the results reported by Levison, Elkind and Ward for unstable controlled-element dynamics.

The trend of the noise/signal ratio was not entirely as expected and was not totally consistent with the trend of the subjective opinion data. Although the ratios obtained for the three sets of unstable dynamics were, on the average, lower than those obtained for the three sets of stable dynamics, the rank ordering of dynamics by signal/noise ratio was not identical to the ordering by opinion. That is, noise/signal ratio did not decrease monotonically with increasing vehicle instability.

Because some of the reported noise/signal ratios were at variance with earlier results, this author suspects that these measures were less reliable than the subjective opinions. For example, ratios measured for simple proportional control were about the same as found with one of the unstable dynamics and were considerably lower than reported by Kleinman, Baron and Levison (7). One suspects there may have been some difficulty in uniquely determining observation noise/signal ratios from the data, which, as discussed in the following section, is one of the problems encountered when trying to apply the workload model in a diagnostic (rather than predictive) mode.

APPLICATION OF THE MODEL FOR WORKLOAD

Two modes of application of the workload model are discussed: (1) the predictive mode, in which the model is included in a more general analysis procedure to predict performance/workload characteristics, and (2) the diagnostic mode, in which one attempts to infer levels of operator workload from experimental measures of operator response behavior.

Predictions of Performance/Workload Characteristics

As stated at the outset, the primary application of the model for workload presented in this paper is to predict performance/workload tradeoffs in tasks (mainly, manual control) in which the operator is required to process sensory information in a near-continuous manner. To demonstrate application of the workload model, let us therefore review the procedure for predicting performance as a function of workload for a flight-control task in which the pilot must process a number of displayed variables.

In a problem of this sort it is often useful to consider various levels of attention-sharing. For example, let us assume that the pilot must share attention between control and non-control tasks; that attention must be divided among major components of the control task (e.g. longitudinal-axis and lateral-axis control); and that attention must be further allocated among the sensory variables relating to a given axis of control. The noise/signal ratio corresponding to the ith display variable is then computed as

$$P_i = \frac{P_o}{f_T \cdot f_S \cdot f_i} \qquad (24)$$

where f_T is the (relative) level of attention devoted to the flight-control task, f_S the fraction of this attention devoted to subtask S, and f_i the allocation among individual displays.

The following constraints are implied by this treatment:

$$\sum_i f_i = 1 \qquad (25)$$

$$\sum_S f_S = 1 \qquad (26)$$

There are some exceptions to the constraint imposed by Equation (25). In the case of an integrated display (as might be realized by a well-designed pictorial format), we would assume no attention-sharing among perceptual variables obtained from such a display, and these variables would obey the constraint

$$f_i = 1 \qquad (27)$$

(This constraint serves as a working definition of an integrated display.)

If overt scanning were required (with scan intervals assumed small with respect to correlation times of displayed variables), the constraint of Equation (25) would be modified as follows:

$$\sum_i f_i = 1 - f_o \qquad (28)$$

where f_o is the fraction of "dead time" associated with the loss of useful perceptual input during large eye movements (19). In order to determine the appropriate value for f_o in a given control situation, one would have to estimate the time lost per scan (of the order of 200 milliseconds) as well as the average scanning rate.

We must first select numerical values for the f_i as well as for other pilot parameters in order to obtain model predictions of system performance and pilot response. Typically, the total-task attentional variable f_T is taken as an independent variable of the analysis. To be consistent with the notion of optimality, the remaining attentional variables should be selected -- subject to appropriate constraints -- to provide the lowest overall performance "cost". That is, both the attentional and control strategies are optimized.

To minimize the computational burden of optimizing among a large number of display variables, one may relax the constraint of optimality by determining the set of display variables actually required for flight control, and by assuming equal allocation of attentions to these variables within an axis of control. Attention is then optimized between control subtasks. Because performance is usually not strongly dependent upon attentional strategy (given that all required variables -- and only those variables -- are attended to) this suboptimal procedure may be adequate (12). However, if it is suspected that performance is especially sensitive to attentional allocation, or if predictions of attentional allocation are of interest, the full optimization procedure should be adopted.

In a recent application, the models described here were employed to determine the effects of control augmentation and display design on approach-to-landing performance of a simulated 737-100 (20). Two display configurations were explored: a "baseline" display in which display quantities required for flight control were presented electronically in symbolic format, and an "advanced" display in which these variables were presented in pictorial format. Two control configurations were also considered: a form of attitude hold ("attitude control wheel steering") and a form of flight-path-angle hold ("velocity control wheel steering").

Steady-state analysis was performed to explore performance-workload relationships for the four task configurations. Analysis was performed for zero-mean turbulence appropriate to the 100-foot decision height. Performance criteria (i.e. weighting coefficients for the quadratic cost functional) were selected on the basis of the "category II" approach requirements as well as on physical limitations of aircraft response.

To obtain the curves of path error versus relative attention shown in Figure 4, attention was assumed to be divided equally between lateral and longitudinal control. For the baseline (symbolic) display, attention was assumed to be divided equally

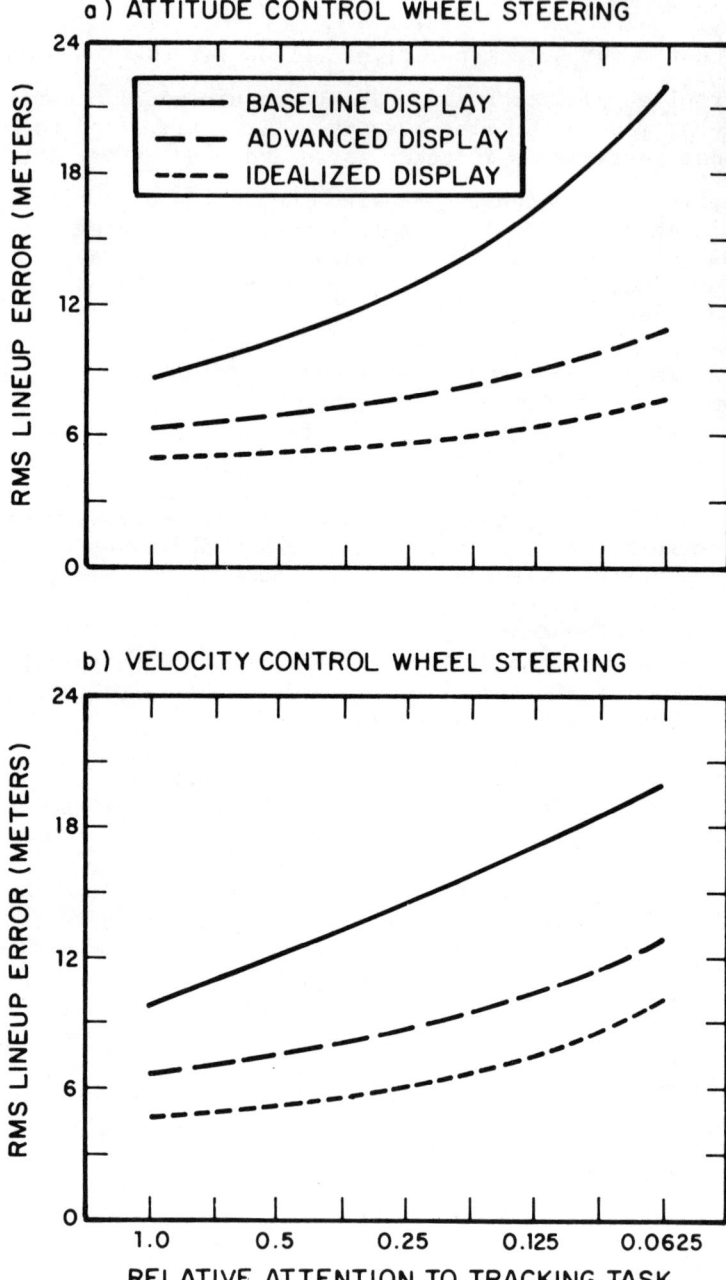

Figure 4. Effect of Display on Lineup Error/Workload Tradeoff.

between path error, path angle error, and attitude variables. (Since speed was controlled automatically, the pilot did not need to monitor his airspeed continuously.) Since overt scanning was required, the constraint of Equation (28) was adopted, with the fraction of "lost" time f_o estimated to be 30%. The workload associated with the task as a whole, f_T, served as the independent parameter of the analysis (the abscissa of Figure 4).

When analyzing the advanced (pictorial) display, we assumed that flight-control information was integrated, and the constraint of Equation (27) was adopted. Threshold-related display effects were considered for both displays.[3]

Figure 4 shows that the advanced display can be expected to provide substantial improvement over the baseline display with regard to both performance and workload. That is, for either of the control configurations, the pilot should be able to achieve superior performance at considerably reduced workload when provided with the advanced display.

As reported by Levison and Baron (20), experimental studies of approach-to-landing in the simulator tended to confirm the conclusions with regard to performance. Lineup errors were significantly less for the advanced display, whereas there was no significant effect of control augmentation (as indicated from a comparison of the curves in Figure 4a and 4b). Contrary to expectations, no changes in workload were found experimentally. The workload measure used in this case was related to stick activity (rather than, say, attention to a secondary task) and may not have been sufficiently sensitive to changes in mental workload. Clearly, here is a situation in which a reliable independent measure of workload would have been invaluable in testing the workload model!

Hoffman et al. have suggested a similar procedure to predict both control and monitoring requirements for VTOL aircraft (13). They assume that attention must be shared between the control and monitoring tasks, even though the tasks relate to the same flight control problem. They postulate a given performance requirement, and the model of Figure 1 (incorporating the concept of attention and workload described in this paper) is used to determine the control task workload. The difference between an assumed maximum level of attention and the control workload yields the amount of attention available for monitoring. Monitoring performance is then predicted according to one or more specific performance criteria.

MEASUREMENT OF WORKLOAD

Measurements of workload are usually desired either to determine operator workload in a realistic task environment (often to determine whether or not the operator is being unduly stressed), or to validate models for workload. Measurements are obtained either directly from measures related to performance of the task of interest, or indirectly from measures related to performance of a concurrent secondary task. As we shall show, the workload concepts presented in this paper do not readily lend themselves to direct assessment of workload in realistically complex tasks, with some difficulty, workload can be determined for highly-constrained tasks which may be used as primary tasks for model validation or as secondary tasks for indirect workload assessment.

Direct Measurement of Workload

Equation (16) suggests a method for measuring relative workload; specifically, we compute workload as

$$\frac{P_o}{P} \qquad (29)$$

where P is the observation noise/signal ratio measured in the task situation of interest and P_o is the ratio measured in a baseline tracking task. Experimental determination of P, however, is complicated by the following factors:

1. Although we desire to measure observation noise/signal ratios, we can only measure overt operator response. Thus, we are basically limited to continuous tracking tasks.

2. The stochastic portion of the operator's response may be properly interpreted as inherent information-processing randomness only if the operator is responding with an essentially fixed strategy. In order to meet this constraint, the task should be steady-state (i.e. disturbance signal have time-stationary statistics), and the operator should be highly trained and highly motivated to perform well.

3. Since noise/signal ratios are inferred by model-matching procedures, a tracking task is desired in which operator response can be modelled with as few independent parameters as possible to facilitate

unique identification of model parameters.

4. Performance should be at least moderately sensitive to human operator randomness to facilitate model identification of operator noise characteristics and to minimize subject-to-subject variability in attentional effort.

Because of these constraints, direct measurement of operator workload in terms of the concepts presented here are confined to a rather restricted set of laboratory-type tracking tasks. As noted above, such tasks can be employed for validating the workload model or as secondary tasks for determining workload requirements of more realistic tasks.

Techniques for identifying operator noise/signal ratios have not yet reached their full state of development. The most reliable technique applied so far appears to be a search technique which, at present, involves a trial-and-error procedure by the analyst. More work is needed to precisely define and automate a search procedure.

Indirect Measurement

Given that one has a laboratory-type tracking task that yields reliable measures of operator noise/signal ratios (i.e. workload as defined herein), such a task may be used in one of two ways as a secondary task to measure primary-task workload. One may obtain the full set of measures to compute noise/signal ratios from the secondary task, or one may obtain a reduced set of measures and compare secondary-task performance with that obtained in a preliminary "calibration" experiment.

Jex, McDonnell and Phatak (21) have developed a tracking task for which performance appears to correlate well with workload. In one implementation of the task, the degree of instability of an unstable plant varies, and the maximum instability that can be controlled by the operator is taken as a measure of workload (i.e. the greater the instability, the greater the attention to the unstable tracking task, and the lower the primary-task workload). Alternatively, one may fix the instability and relate workload to performance obtained on this task. It would be interesting to explore the relationship between maximum controllable instability and operator noise/signal ratios. (Model analysis indicates that maximum instability will decrease as noise/signal ratio increases because of the destabilizing effects of operator randomness.)

PERSPECTIVE

Let us now consider the contributions of this paper in light of the goals of the symposium on mental workload. Ideally, we would like to achieve the following objectives:

1. Develop a theory of mental workload that allows one to predict workload requirements for a wide range of tasks involving human operators.

2. Develop techniques for measuring the level of the operator's mental effort without interfering significantly with performance of the primary task of interest.

The focus of this paper has been directed toward the goal of model development, with the desired level of generality not yet achieved. The theory as presented here has been limited to the prediction of the relationship between performance and workload for tasks involving continuous processing of information. The workload model has been validated and applied primarily with respect to continuous manual control tasks, with some applications to monitoring and decision tasks.

In order to build upon this work to achieve the above-stated goals, the following avenues of research are suggested:

Absolute Prediction of Workload

The reader may have noticed that the workload model has been applied almost exclusively toward predicting the relationship between performance and attention. We have not directly addressed the problem of predicting the absolute level of workload imposed by a particular task. Because of the functional relationship between performance and workload, we would have to predict how the operator would trade performance for workload; that is, how hard is he willing to work to attain what level of performance?

As noted earlier, Wewerinke (18) has suggested that the operator will operate at the "knee" of the sensitivity curve relating performance to workload. A somewhat similar approach would be to expand the "cost functional" of Equation (20) to include a workload metric along with the quadratic performance metric. Further research is needed to determine a reliable means for predicting how the operator will trade workload for performance in a specific situation.

Treat a Wider Range of Tasks

The theoretical framework presented in this paper should be expanded to include a wider range of relevant human operator tasks. The restriction of continuous-information processing can be relaxed somewhat; that is, the basic model structure should be applicable as well to tasks in which sensory inputs are sampled. The boundary of applicability might properly be restated as tasks that require the human operator to reconstruct the "state" of systems having linear dynamical response characteristics. To the extent that other kinds of tasks (e.g signal detection, failure detection and identification) can be put in this framework, the applicability of the workload model can be expanded.

Treat "Slow" Attention Switching

The workload model presented in this paper has been based on the assumption that switching of attention among sensory variables (or tasks) is rapid with respect to the time constants of relevant system variables. This assumption greatly simplifies the model structure, for it allows us to treat observation noise as a stationary statistical process, with the (presumably time-invariant) noise covariance inversely proportional to attention. Not all tasks conform to this assumption, however, and model applicability would be greatly enhanced if multiple-task situations could be treated in which the switching of attention is not necessarily rapid with respect to signal fluctuations.

There has been some effort to provide a more general treatment of attention-sharing within the framework of the optimal-control model (6). Basically, for slow scanning rates, the observation noise covariance is treated as a time-varying process: one level of noise is associated with central viewing when a display is attended, a much larger noise level is associated with peripheral viewing. Further refinement and validation of this aspect of the model are desired if the model is to be applied extensively to task situations of this sort.

Determine a Physiological Basis for the Workload Model

A physiological basis for the workload model would be helpful in allowing predictions of the effects of certain kinds of environmental stress on human operator performance. For example, if we could determine the relationship between randomness of neural firing rates and oxygen transport to the brain, we might be able to predict the effective loss of attention due to stressors such as hypoxia and high sustained acceleration.

Develop Techniques for Measuring Workload

As noted earlier, various factors mitigate against development of techniques to measure observation noise/signal ratios in most "real world" human operator tasks. A more promising approach would be to develop a secondary task (such as a tracking task using unstable dynamics) which would allow identification of noise/signal ratios and, therefore, an indication of operator workload.

FOOTNOTES

[1] The variable $\delta(\tau)$ is a "unit impulse" function, located at $\tau=0$, that has zero width, infinite value, and an integral over τ of unity.

[2] This expression is modified to account for situations where threshold-related display limitations are important (12); for simplicity of exposition, however, we shall ignore such effects in this treatment.

[3] A third display -- the "idealized display" -- was analyzed to indicate the maximum benefit that could be derived from an optimally-designed flight director. In this case, threshold effects were ignored, and display integration was assumed.

REFERENCES

1. Levison, W.H., "A Model for Task Interference", Proc. of the Sixth Annual Conference on Manual Control, Wright-Patterson Air Force Base, Ohio, April 1970.

2. Levison, W.H., J.I. Elkind and J.L. Ward. "Studies of Multi-Variable Manual Control Systems: A Model for Task Interference", NASA CR-1746, May 1971.

3. Kleinman, D.L. and R.E. Curry, "An Equivalence Between Two Representations for Human Attention Sharing", IEEE Trans. on Systems, Man, and Cybernetics, Vol. SMC-6, No. 9, Sept. 1976.

4. Levison, W.H., S. Baron and D.L. Kleinman, "A Model for Human Controller Remnant", IEEE Trans. on Man-Machine Systems, Vol. MMS-10, No.4, Dec. 1969.

5. Jex, H.R. and R.E. Magdaleno, "Corroborative Data on Normalization of Human Operator Remnant", IEEE Trans. on Man-Machine Systems, Vol. MMS-10, No.4, Dec. 1969.

6. Baron, S. and D.L. Kleinman, "The Human as an Optimal Controller and Information Processor", *IEEE Trans. on Man-Machine Systems*, Vol. MMS-10, No.1, March 1969.

7. Kleinman, D.L., S. Baron and W.H. Levison, "An Optimal Control Model of Human Response, Part 1: Theory and Validation", *Automatica*, Vol. 6, 1970.

8. Kleinman, D.L. and S. Baron, "Analytic Evaluation of Display Requirements for Approach to Landing", NASA CR-1952, Nov.1971.

9. Kleinman, D.L., S. Baron and W.H. Levison. "A Control Theoretic Approach to Manned-Vehicle Systems Analysis", *IEEE Trans. on Auto. Control*,, Vol.AC-16, No.6, Dec. 1971.

10. Baron, S. and W.H. Levison, "A Manned Control Theory Analysis of Vertical Situation Displays for STOL Aircraft", NASA CR-114620, April 1973.

11. Kleinman, D.L. and W.R. Killingsworth, "A Predictive Pilot Model for STOL Aircraft Landing," NASA CR-2374, March 1974.

12. Baron, S. and W.H. Levison, "An Optimal Control Methodology for Analyzing the Effects of Display Parameters on Performance and Workload in Manual Flight Control," *IEEE Trans. on Systems, Man, and Cybernetics*, Vol. SMC-5, No.4, July 1975.

13. Hoffman, W.C. et al., "Display/Control Requirements for VTOL Aircraft", ASI-TR-26, Aerospace Systems, Inv., Burlington, Mass., August 1975.

14. Levison, W.H. and R.B. Tanner, "A Control-Theory Model for Human Decision Making", NASA CR-1953, Dec. 1971.

15. Levison, W.H., "The Effects of Display Gain and Signal Bandwidth on Human Controller Remnant", Wright-Patterson Air Force Base, Ohio, AMRL-TR-70-93, March 1971.

16. Baron, S. and D.L. Kleinman, et al., "An Optimal Control Model of Human Response - Part II: Prediction of Human Performance in a Complex Task," *Automatica*, Vol. 6, Pergamon Press, London, England, May 1970.

17. Wewerinke, P.H. "A Theoretical Study of the Pilot as a System Monitor", *Eleventh Annual Conference on Manual Control*, NASA TM X-62, 464, May 1975.

18. Wewerinke, P.H. "Human Operator Workload for Various Control Situations", *Tenth Annual Conference on Manual Control*, Wright-Patterson Air Force Base, Ohio, 1974.

19. Volkmann, F.C., A.M.L. Schick, and L.A. Riggs, "Time Course of Visual Inhibition During Voluntary Saccades," Jl. Opt. Soc. Am., Vol. 58, 1968.

20. Levison, W.H. and S. Baron, "Analytic and Experimental Evaluation of Display and Control Concepts for a Terminal Configured Vehicle," BBN Report No. 3270, Bolt Beranek and Newman Inc., Cambridge, Mass., July 1976.

21. Jex, H.R., J.D. McDonnell and A.V. Phatak, "A "Critical" Tracking Task for Manual Control Research," IEEE Trans. on Human Factors in Electronics, Vol. HFE-7, No.4, Dec. 1966.

DEFINITIONS, MODELS AND MEASURES OF HUMAN WORKLOAD

T.B. Sheridan, Department of Mechanical Engineering

M.I.T., U.S.A.

H.G. Stassen, Technische Hogeschool, Delft, Netherlands

1. INTRODUCTION

In the study of man-machine systems, whether we deal with manual or supervisory control/decision situations, there exists a great need to model human behavior quantitatively, since in order to describe the overall behavior of a man-machine system, we must know the behavior of the individual sub-systems man, and machine. Most of the research is focussed on performance studies. Well known are the performance models based on the control theory, such as the cross-over model (McRuer (4)) and the optimal control model (Kleinman and Baron (3)), and on decision and detection theory (Green and Swets (2); Sheridan and Ferrell (5)). These models have been shown to be of great help in the design of man-machine systems. Relatively little has been done in the field of "work load". Some measurement techniques are available, and are used, for lack of something better, in practical situations, but the results thus far are rather poor. Since in the design of man-machine systems workload appears to play such an essential role, development of better analytical models and measurement techniques are certainly of high priority.

"Workload" has been defined, in various contexts, to mean different things: (D1) what physical task is assigned, including both endogenous system elements and exogenous inputs or disturbances and including the "secondary task" if used (see below); (D2) what criterion is to be followed (ideally) in performing that task, including relative decision-risks and temporal-attentional demands; (D3) information processing which the human operator actually performs; (D4) energy actually expended by the human operator; (D5) what emotional stress he experiences; and (D6) the overall system performance which finally results. There is a real question whether performance on the assigned task (D6) is properly called workload; we assert that it is not workload. Note that the first two are assigned a priori and therefore (with an exception noted below) are independent of the person performing the task; the next three are a function of the actual behavior of persons; the last is dependent upon both. These alternative definitions of workload are illustrated by the labels D1 through D6 in a control system paradigm of Figure 1. D3 and D5 taken together are sometimes called "mental load".

Empirical measurements of workload corresponding to the above definitions are shown in Figure 1 by labels M1 through M3. M4, analysis of primary task behavior, is used by some experimenters to study mental load. Empirical measurement of D1 and D2 is not necessary (with exception noted below) since these functions are prespecified, though if workload is conceived as a scalar quantity and D1 and D2 are inherently multi-parameter operations, some scaling transformation is necessary. Since D3 is cognitive and inside the operator, it must be inferred either by M1, subjective judgement or by M3, the score on a secondary task which the operator is asked to perform as he has "spare capacity" available. A better score on the secondary task supposedly indicates more capacity available and therefore less workload on the primary task. Some physiological measures may correlate with D3; the evidence is unclear. D4 can be measured more directly by various physiological indices such as respiration, heart rate, and calorimetry. D5 is of course a very complex factor; it is commonly measured by subjective judgement (of the human operator himself or an outside human observer) or by physiological indices such as galvanic skin response or biochemical analysis of urine or blood. In regard to D6, while performance measurements are sometimes used as an index of workload (we think incorrectly), other "analyses" of behavior may be properly utilized to indicate mental load (see later discussion of "moments of conscious control").

The exceptions noted above to the independence of D1 and D2 from the human operator are that, even though assigned to tasks and criteria for their performance, people mostly set their own tasks and criteria. That is, the actual task and criterion workloads, D1 and D2, are actually some compromise between externally-imposed and self-imposed task and criterion assignments.

2. TRADE-OFFS BETWEEN WORKLOAD FACTORS

It is worth considering the relations between variables defined in Figure 1.

DEFINITIONS, MODELS AND MEASURES OF WORKLOAD

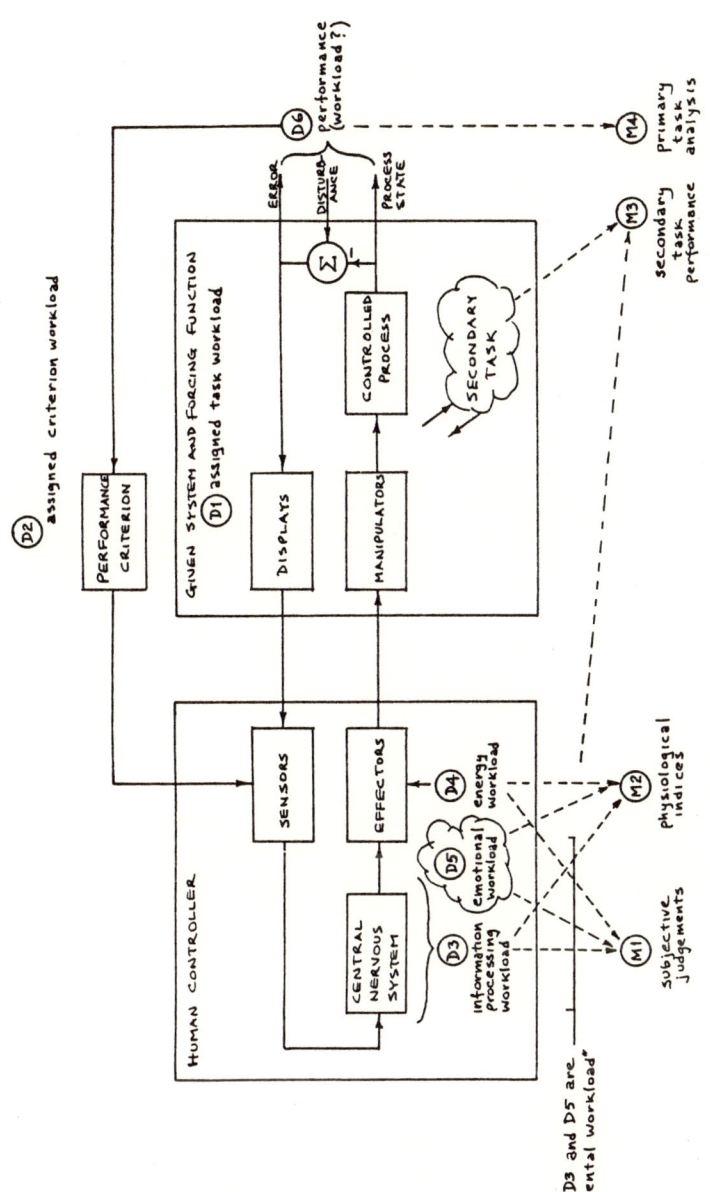

Figure 1: Alternative Definitions of Workload and Performance Illustrated in a Control Paradigm

Performance vs. Mental and Energy Workload

First consider the trade between D6, performance, D2, criterion, and D3-5, the three workload components of the human operator himself. For performance to be perfect, an infinite control effort and, with any disturbance, infinite information processing rate is required. Better performance tends to correlate with higher workload. Thus, by some arbitrary subjective decision, the operator must compromise on "trade-off" error, and the concommitant workload factors of cost and anxiety, against the workload of processing information and expending energy (Stassen and Soede).

Servolevel vs. Management Level of Control

Another kind of trade-off occurs between different levels of task hierarchy at which a human operator functions. For example, at one assigned workload level, a pilot controls the aircraft in a more or less continuous servo-mechanical fashion, with concommitant mental load and energy load. At a higher level he "manages" or "supervises" his course, his fuel and avionics sub-systems, etc., and this function has its workload cost. The coordination of his efforts at both levels poses additional mental load, and, we suspect, is the major contributor to the emotional workload component.

Functional vs. Social

Still another kind of trade-off similar to that described above, is between purely functional activities and social activities. In any real-world behavior the human operator is devoting some of his mental and physical capacities to communication with other people and to doing favors for them which are not part of his nominally assigned tasks.

3. DISCUSSION OF MEASUREMENTS, ESPECIALLY AS THEY RELATE TO MENTAL LOAD

A number of different measurement techniques will now be discussed, especially those relating to mental load; all have been experimentally tested and applied in practical situations. However, none of them really seems to be a particularly promising answer in the application to real-world problems. It therefore seems worthwhile to review the methods in order to understand better their possibilities and restrictions.

One way to judge the methods is on the basis of how well they meet the general specifications of sensors: (1) whether the measure is selective to the variable to be measured, hence not sensitive to disturbances; (2) whether there is any influence of the sensor on the process to be measured; (3) whether the statics and the dynamics of the sensor are known in the right bandwidth, (4) whether the method is accurate and reproducible, and finally, (5) some remarks with reference to the use of the method (Table 1).

Physiological Variables

The most commonly used indices are the heart rate variability, respiration rate, galvanic reflex, blood circulation, calorimetry, pupillary diameter, biochemical changes in blood and urine components, EMG or muscle tension and EEG. The use of all these variables is based on the laboratory-determined correlation with work load defined by other measures. In general a causal relation is not proven, the dynamics of the mechanism are not understood; and the variables are highly sensitive to disturbances, as indicated in Table 2.

Dual-task (or Secondary Task) Methods

The dual tasks methods, such as the binary choice task, the sub-critical instability task, and the tapping task, are based on the "one-channel" concept; they imply superposition of tasks for the human operator. The principle problem with this method is the possible interaction between primary and secondary task.

Primary Task Measures Based on Information Theory and Task Analysis

These methods require that a task can be split into subtasks, and joint probabilities of various events can be determined. Work load is measured in terms of choice uncertainty and time uncertainty. The subtasks should be tasks which can be performed as automatic reflexes; where no uncertainty is involved within each subtask. Well-defined criteria for specifying the end of one subtask and the start of the next (sometimes called moments of conscious control) are necessary to the theory, but are presently not available in practice. The method promises to be directly applicable in real-world problems, but the definition of criteria for the division into subtasks is very difficult.

Attention Allocation

Many authors claim that measurement of the attention

Table 1: Judgement of Mental Load Indices on the Basically Required Properties of a Sensor.

Properties / Methods	Sensitivity to Disturbances	Influence on Variables to be measured	Statics and Dynamics Sensor	Accuracy Reproducibility	Remarks in Use
Physiological Variables (M2)	very	none	unknown	poor	easy to use
Dual or Secondary Task Methods (M3)	not likely	may be, difficult to measure	known	reasonable	easy to use
Information Measures, Task Analyses (M4)	none	none	known	unknown	very difficult
Attention Allocation (M4)	none	very little	unknown	unknown	easy to use
Subjective Measures (M1)	unknown	very little	unknown	reasonable	easy to use

Table 2: Some Physiological Variables as a Function of Mental and Energy Load.

Load / Physiological Variables	Mental Load		Energy Load
	Information Processing	Emotional	
Heart Rate Variability	decrease	decrease	decrease
Heart Rate	constant	increase	increase
Respiration Rate	increase	constant	increase

allocation, often done by recording eye movements, is related to mental load. The problem is that one gets information as to which instruments the human operator is looking at, but that does not say that he really uses or needs to get that information.

Subjective Measurements

The easiest way to estimate the mental work load of a person who performs a certain task, is to ask him what he subjectively feels about the mental load of his task. Sometimes a list of key words or definitions describing different levels of load will be given; the subject then has to rate his load referring to these levels. More sophisticated subjective scaling techniques include multi-attribute utility, multi-dimensional scaling, Thurstonian scaling, policy capturing, semantic differentials and verbal protocols (interviews).

4. METAPHORICAL DESCRIPTIONS OF WORK LOAD

There are various metaphors used to characterize the various component concepts of work load.

Stress and Strain

One such metaphor relates to the simple mechanics of "stress" and "strain". "Stress" is the task performance required; "strain" is the distortion of the person ("effort" or mental load) who is involved in responding to the "stress". His (or the system's) skill or strategy then becomes a "stiffness" or "compliance" characteristic.

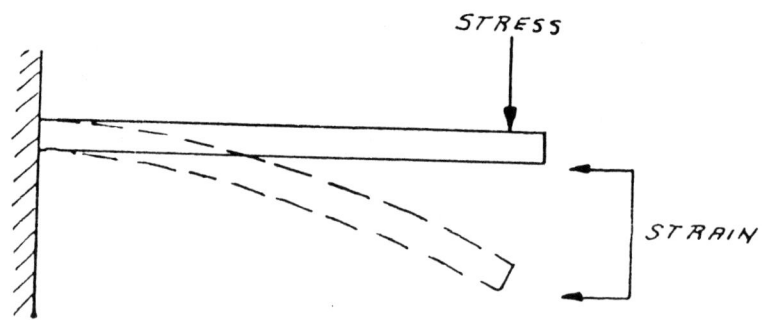

Figure 2: <u>Stress and Strain</u>

When considering system performance, stress is the appropriate concept. When considering operator effort or mental load strain is the appropriate concept.

This particular metaphor can be played out in some interesting ways. There should be a maximum load beyond which failure occurs. It might be very expensive to make a system with high stiffness (resulting in very little strain).

Different systems will fail in different ways. A very "stiff" system is likely to have catastrophic failures; it would be difficult to detect increased strain. A "softer" system would bend to accommodate loads, and these might decrease with deflection (e.g., the requirement is reduced if not achieved – "elastic" demand).

Capacity

Mental load can be explained on the basis of capacity. The assigned task and criterion work loads might exceed the capacity, but the mental load cannot exceed capacity. Mental load is expressed as fraction of capacity. What is left is the spare capacity.

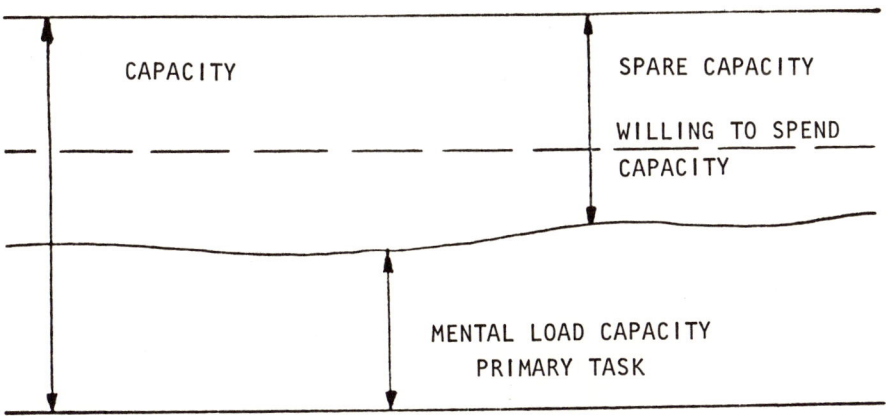

Figure 3: The One Channel Capacity Model

The use of easily quantified secondary tasks as measures of mental load relies on this concept. The secondary task, on top of the primary task, fills up or loads the operator to capacity. (Usually the tasks must be done so that "error" is zero, in order that the amount of number of subtasks per unit time gives the score.) A poorer score on the secondary task is taken as an indication that the primary task requires more effort.

The concept of capacity also appears when the human operator is modelled as a communication channel having a fixed "channel capacity", such that when more bits of information are put into the channel (greater speed), more errors are made and thus information rate is constant.

Attention Allocation

An even simpler notion than capacity is that of allocating the time available to do different tasks. Here, performance is considered to be a function of the task attended to and the amount of time devoted to that task.

One method of applying this concept to mental load is to assume a minimum time necessary to accomplish (each of) the component task(s). The actual time used is then assumed equal to the time required (minimum necessary) plus the "rest time" or spare capacity. The minimum necessary over the total used is the percent mental load. This is similar to the approach in industrial practice of "predetermined time" systems (e.g. "methods-time-measurement"). It requires extensive calibration and pretesting of all the component tasks and makes assumptions about their independence and interdependence when combined.

The time-allocation metaphor has been used in the application of the optimal-control-model to multiple tasks. The noise added to each variable observed is taken as function of the fraction of

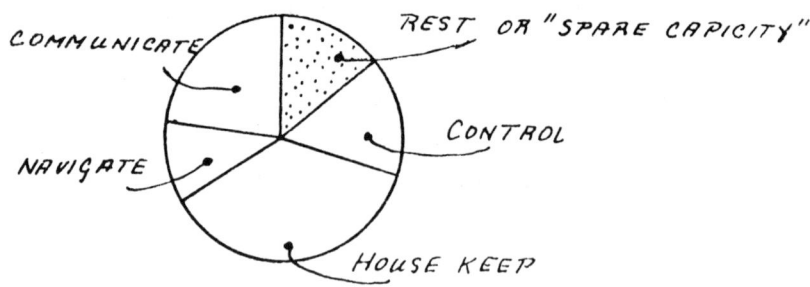

Figure 4: <u>Attention Allocation Metaphor for Airplane Piloting</u>

attention devoted to observing that particular variable. The fractions of attention sum to one.

5. FORMAL MODELS WITH LINKS TO MENTAL LOAD

Four models, originally derived to describe human performance should be mentioned, mainly because they provide a link to mental load.

The Optimal Control Model

The development of the optimal control model originally proposed for continuous manual control, may be extended to model supervisory control and the associated mental load. The basic structure of the model, that is, the division into an observer (which makes a best estimate of system state) plus an optimal controller or decision maker is extremely useful here. It may provide a direct way to relate mental load and performance. As suggested in recent literature, mental load may be associated with observation time-allocation, which determines the observation noise, which in turn relates to the overall performance of the model.

The observer (or Kalman state estimator) includes an internal model of the system under control. Control signals fed to the actual system are also fed to this model, and any discrepancy between the two outputs (called an "innovations process") are used to tune the internal model.

Where the human operator is characterized as such an optimal state estimator plus an optimal controller (optimal for the given controlled process by the given criterion) operating on the assumed valid state variable, the magnitude of the innovations process is a direct index of the degree to which the human's internal model does not match the external reality. This innovations process has been employed among others by Curry and his colleagues to model pilot failure detection. It also may appear to be an indicator of mental load, assuming that improving the apparently inadequate internal model is tantamount to conscious mental effort, whereas routine control based on a good internal model is either open-loop, or, at worst, a routine or low-level closed-loop control -- with less intensive sensory observation and less corruption by observation noise. This idea needs further research in order to verify the relation between observation noise properties, attention allocation and mental load; and to verify the relation between the internal model; that is, state estimation and performance, and innovations process and mental load, respectively.

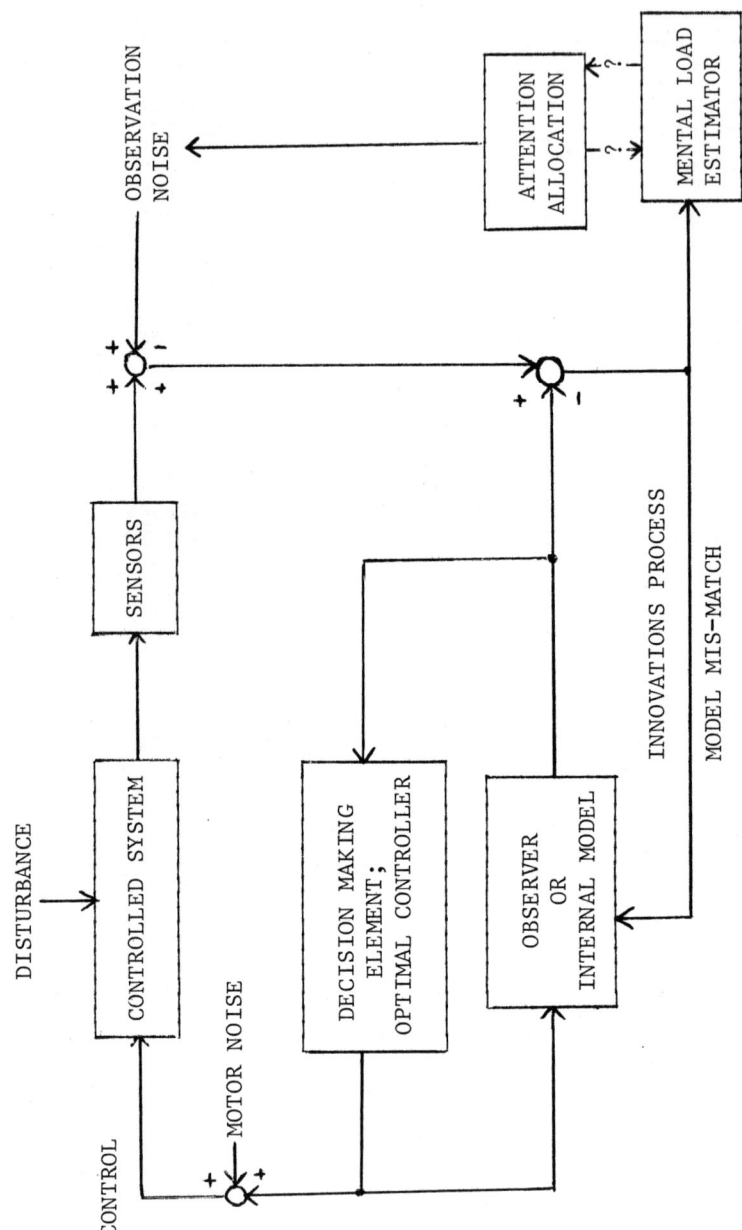

Figure 5: The Optimal Control Model

DEFINITIONS, MODELS AND MEASURES OF WORKLOAD

Decision Models

Various decision system models have been put forward having to do with the operator's scheduling of tasks, and his sampling behavior (for both observing multiple displays and making multiple adjustments in controls).

One type of model which seems particularly relevant for dynamic decisions assumes that the human operator can actively focus his mental effort to do only one thing at a time, though he may be scanning the cockpit (or scanning his memory or internal model of the situation) continuously. Discrete, well-defined tasks appear in his view at random times (or he may have expectation or forewarning) as represented by the blocks in the figure below. When they appear it is evident how important they

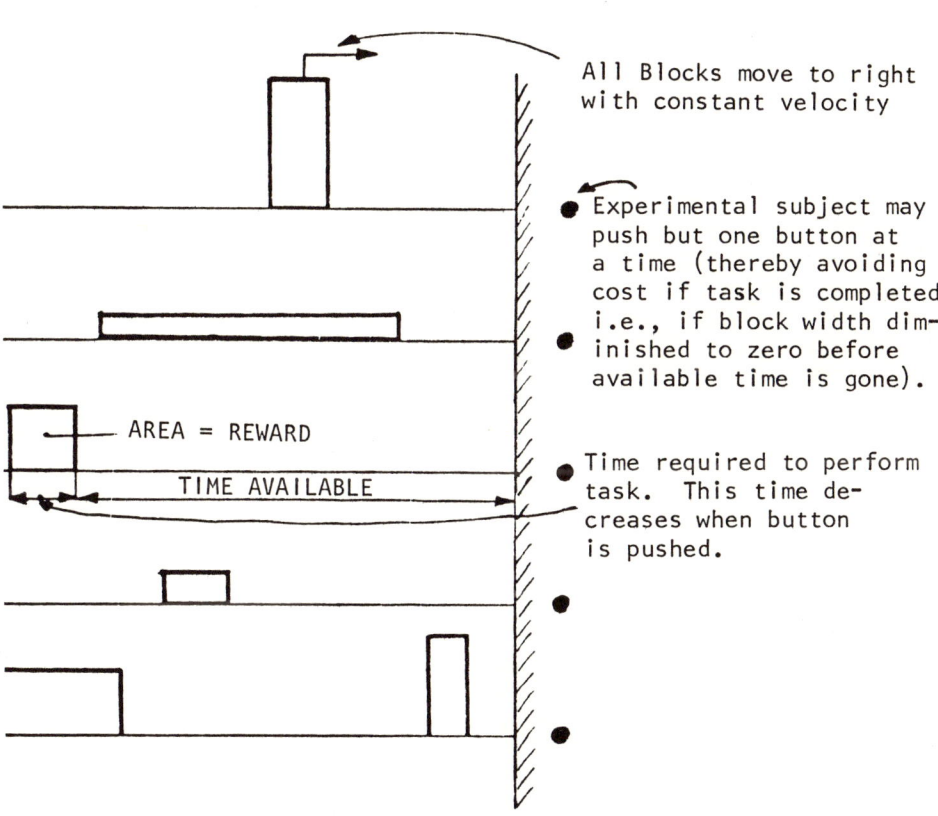

Figure 6: <u>Experimental Setup for a Supervisory Task</u>

are from their area, and how much time remains to "do" them by their velocity toward the deadline. The operator may service tasks one at a time by moving his cursor alongside the appropriate task, and the block will then diminish in width at a fixed rate, earning him a score in proportion to the diminished area. Because tasks of varying importance appear simultaneously, and because the operator pays a time penalty in changing queues, he experiences uncertainty in deciding where to attend at any instant (where to put his cursor). An optimal decision/control model has been developed which employs dynamic programming and a Bayesian estimator of future tasks on each queue. The model decides on an optimal future trajectory, where future gains are discounted by an exponential function, and takes the first step of this trajectory before iterating the calculation and including new inputs. Experimental data fitted to this model indicate that the operator does indeed discount the future, at the same time anticipating where important tasks may appear on a probabilistic basis (Tulga and Sheridan).

Information Channel Models

Information theory has been used by Senders, Carbonell and others in characterizing an aspect of pilot's mental load. In particular, pilot eye movements have been measured to determine how their sampling behavior corresponds to the frequency and importance characteristics of display signals as predicated by the Shannon sampling theorem. In simple laboratory experiments involving independent instruments with stationary signals, it is clear that eye movements follow the theoretical norm, but in real world problems, such as car driving, landing an airplane, eye movements apparently follow a more complex pattern due to the nonstationary characteristics of the situation.

It is not clear that in real world problems the signals adapt to the sampling theory model in the simplest form. Information transmission models may also be useful, and are applied in the next section.

Activation/Uncertainty Models

Work load measures should predict the ability to respond to abrupt transitions in task demand (emergencies) and the stability of long-term performance. One method of explicitly accounting for the latter two effects of mental load is through appeal to the concept of "activation". The doing of the task itself can have a facilitating effect on performance, especially at low mental loads levels. What has been proposed is an inverted-U shaped relationship between activation and performance. At low levels of activation, performance may deteriorate with time because of boredom or lack of activation (like the vigilance decrement). At high levels of activation in sustained, long-term tasks, performance may deteriorate because of fatigue.

A suitable operational definition of activation might be some averaging of the complexity or uncertainties in the task. In continuous control tasks there are several sources of uncertainty including the external disturbance and internal uncertainties such as observation noise and motor noise. One summary statistic for combining uncertainties is information transmission rate. Thus, an operational question might be: What is the relationship between information transmission rate (including internal as well as external sources), long-term performance, and mental load?

6. REFERENCES

1. Curry, R.E. and Gai, E. Failure Detection by Pilots During Automatic Landing: Models and Experiments. NASA Annual Meeting on Manual Control (1975).

2. Green, D.M., and Swets, J.A. Signal Detection Theory and Psychophysics, Wiley (1966).

3. Kleinman, D., Baron, S., and Levison, W. A Control Theoretic Approach to Manned-Vehicle System Analysis. IEEE/AC (1971).

4. McRuer, D.T. and Krendel, E.S. Mathematical Models of Human Pilot Behavior. NATO AGARDograph No. 188 (1974).

5. Sheridan, T.B. and Ferrell, W.R. Man-Machine Systems: Information, Control and Decision Models of Human Performance. M.I.T. (1974).

6. Stassen, H.G., van Dieten, J.S.M.J. and Soede, M. On the Mental Load in Relation to the Acceptance of Arm Prosthesis. IFAC (1975).

7. Tulga, M.K. and Sheridan, T.B. Supervisory Dynamic Decision-Making in Multi-Task Monitoring and Control. NASA Annual Meeting on Manual Control (1977).

FINAL REPORT OF CONTROL ENGINEERING GROUP

Renwick Curry, Henry Jex, William Levison,

Henk Stassen (Chairman)

1.   INTRODUCTION

Workload and performance are critical factors in the evaluation of man-machine systems. Systems are designed with certain performance requirements in mind, and the attempt to meet these requirements imposes a certain workload on the human operator. Although a precise definition of mental workload has proven elusive, we must nevertheless deal with this concept because we feel intuitively that such a phenomenon exists, and is an important limitation to both system performance and operator acceptance.

This position paper is organised around the following topics (i) definitions, (ii) measurement techniques, (iii) state of the art of workload models, and (iv) recommendations for future research. Our point of view is that of practical control engineers, experienced in experimenting, modelling and designing of complex systems under manual control.

2.   DEFINITIONS

After considerable debate and reflection, we have adopted the following definitions to guide our discussions of mental workload.

> .. <u>Task demands</u> are the entire set of task variables determining the task environment, such as system dynamics, external disturbances and system performance requirements.

- System performance is determined by objective measures of system output variables relative to the desired characteristics of these variables.

- Operator behavior is defined as the human's operations in performing the required task. Thus, we consider BEHAVIOR a human-centered attribute, in contrast to PERFORMANCE which is an attribute of the total man-machine system. Task demands and overall system evaluation may include criteria for both system performance and operator behavior.

- Workload is defined as the mental effort that the human operator devotes to control and/or supervision relative to his capacity to expend mental effort. By this definition, workload is never greater than unity; like behavior, workload is a human-centered variable.

Our definition of workload includes the concepts of mental effort and capacity which are difficult to define and to measure, but which nevertheless are critical determinants of operator behavior. We consider mental effort to have the following attribtes:

- Mental effort is that portion of the total human effort involved in performing a perceptual-motor task that is not accounted for by well-defined descriptors of physical effort (e.g. control force, oxygen consumption, etc.).

- A direct relationship exists between mental effort and performance. For all psychomotor tasks, an increase in mental effort will, up to some point, result in improved system performance. Consequently diminished mental effort will generally degrade system performance.

- The mental effort associated with performing a multiplicity of concurrent tasks is the accumulation of the efforts associated with the individual tasks.

- A limiting value, or "capacity" is associated with mental effort. That is, there is a level of effort beyond which a human being is unable to operate. In this context we can also define a "willingness to spend effort" to reflect the level of mental effort at which the human prefers to operate in a specific task situation. This is especially appropriate for sustained tasks, as it is unlikely that the human operator will want to operate near his actual (instantaneous) capacity for a (very) long duration. For purposes of this discussion, however, we define workload in terms of instantaneous or short term capacity.

Although a useful concept, the phenomenon of capacity is difficult to deal with operationally. First of all, we have no theoretical or empirical basis for quantifying an upper limit to the human's capacity to expend mental effort. Secondly, capacity is a function of the human's psycho-social state as well as his intrinsic capabilities. For example, the operator's perceived workload may be less in a task he likes than in a task he does not enjoy at all, even though the two tasks require the same amount of mental effort. In effect, the operator may have a greater capacity for the enjoyable task because he is more willing to concentrate on it.

In order to circumvent the need to specify capacity one may reference mental effort to the effort associated with the behavior of a "typical" well-trained operator in a well-defined, standardized, task. This reference level would be determined empirically from studies of many subjects and should reflect what is generally agreed to be "high" workload. Thus, we define a relative workload measure which only for unusually difficult tasks could be greater than unity. This use of the workload concept is often adopted for model analysis. Related concepts that have been prominent in the discussion of mental workload are those of stress and strain. We will define STRESS as the set of task demands applied to the human operator, and STRAIN as the human's response to these demands. For example, the task demands as defined above may be considered as stress, and the resulting workload perceived by the human operator as a form of strain.

Models relating task demands, workload, and performance are derived both for predictive and diagnostic purposes. With a predictive model we can explore:

.. How performance changes with workload for a given task.

.. How workload changes with one or more aspects of the task if performance is to be held constant.

.. How performance changes with task demands, if the human being operates at fixed workload.

Such models can offer insight into human behavior through identification of relevant model parameters from experimental data. We consider two broad classes of models. The UNSTRUCTURED model attempts to interrelate problem variables through correlational analysis of empirical data. Such a model contains no physical structure reflecting cause and effect relationship, and should be applied only to situations within the range of those already studied experimentally. A STRUCTURED model contains elements that attempt to quantify the dominant cause and effect relationship between input and output variables. The basic structure is determined from theoretical analysis of the system. Quantitative values for independent model parameters are determined either theoretically or empirically. A model of this sort may be applied beyond the set of tasks for which data exist, provided the theory can be reasonably presumed to apply to the new situations. If the theoretical model contains parameters that can be identified with human information processing limitations, it gains in validity and can be used for extrapolation as well, i.e. situations not previously tested.

Figure 1 shows the hypothetical relationship between performance and relative workload for two tasks. As drawn, increasing distance from the origin represents either improving performance or increasing workload. The curve shown for Task A may be identified with, say, the performance/workload trade-off of a task requiring control of an unstable vehicle. In this hypothetical situation, considerable workload is required to achieve reasonable performance levels. The curve shown for Task B could represent the performance

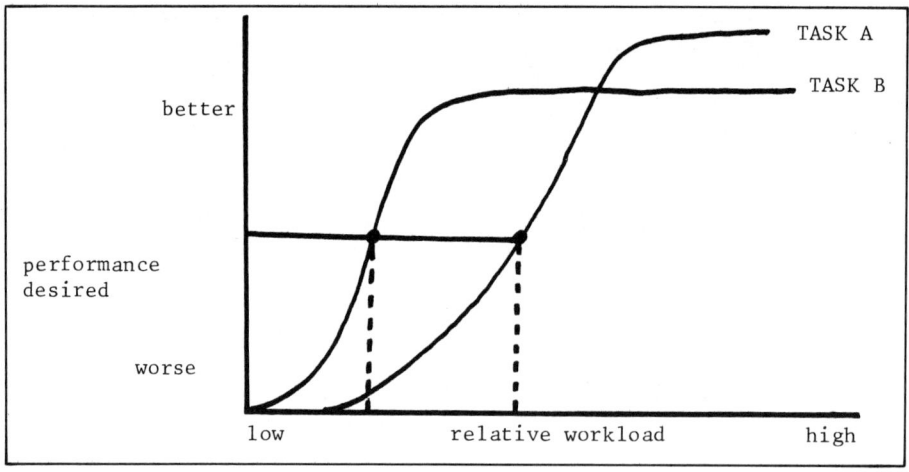

Figure 1: Hypothetical performance/workload relationship

workload trade-off that results if the vehicle used in Task A is provided with automatic stabilization. Maximum performance is less, but workload requirements to approach this performance level are also less. If performance capabilities are satisfactory, the human operator will greatly prefer Task B to Task A because of reduced workload requirements to meet the desired performance level.

3.   MEASUREMENT OF WORKLOAD

As noted above, a comprehensive model of the man-machine system and its behavior is one of the main interests of control or system engineers, since such a model describes in terms of costs and benefits the overall performance of a man-machine system. The control engineer's approach to handling these problems is to try to MODEL the relations among task demands, a measure of workload and a measure of performance, in order to be able to understand, analyse, and/or predict mental workload and performance in a variety of situations, i.e. new designs or past experiments.

3.1. Workload Measurement as a Transducer Problem

Before one can model workload, there must be good measurements of workload in some context, and this requires adequate methods for measuring workload. We, therefore, have attempted to judge the existing measurement methods against the basic REQUIREMENTS for a good transducer, i.e. that which transforms a variable into a measurable (recordable) quantity (Table A).

We have surveyed the various papers at this conference and find a consensus as to six basic categories into which most mental workload measurement schemes seem to fall:

1. Subjective evaluations or structured questionnaires
2. Auxiliary or dual task methods
3. Eye scanning movements
4. Psychophysiological variables
5. Time-line and transinformation-rate measures on control outputs
6. Model parameters derived from operator's output signals

An evaluation was made (within the limited scope of our collective experience in doing all these types of measurement) of such methods against the desired transducer properties from Table A; these are summarized in Table B. The first five columns relate to the desired properties (Requirement 1: Sensitivity to Workload is assumed a priori), while the sixth contains certain remarks on their use.

Table A: Transducer requirements for workload measures

Requirements for good transducers	Requirements for good measures of workload
Sensitivity to primary variable	Monotonic variation with some defined context of workload (usually assumed a priori, often calibrated versus subjective ratings of workload).
Minimal interference with quantity being measured	Behavior on basic (primary) task is not affected by workload measurement.
Insensitivity to other variables, with known interactions	Insensitivity (or small and known interactions) to other variables such as states of training, motivation, etc.
Known (and suitable) bandwidth and dynamics of transducer system	Proven cause-effect connections between workload and measured or inferred index with measured lags and other relevant dynamics (e.g. on-line, post-run, longtime averages, etc.).
Repeatability and reliability	Repeatability of run-to-run measures on a given individual. Consistency of measures and variations among subjects.

Table B: Evaluation of workload measurement methods against good transducer requirements

Methods \ Desired properties	Immunity to other variables	Interference with variables to be measured	Cause-effect relationship	Run-to-run repeatability	Consistency among subjects	Remarks on use
Subjective measurement	fair	very little	direct	reasonable	reasonable	fairly easy to use, requires training
Auxiliary Task methods	mostly	intrinsic	partly known	reasonable	fairly good	easy to use, must be in context
Eye scanning movements	fair	very little	partly known	fair	moderate	easy to use
Physiological variables	low	very little	unknown	poor	poor	most are easy to use in laboratory
Information measures, task analyses on control output	fair	none	partly known	not yet known	poor	very difficult discrete tasks only
Derived parameters from behavioral signals	poor	none	partly known or assumed	good	good	requires a model

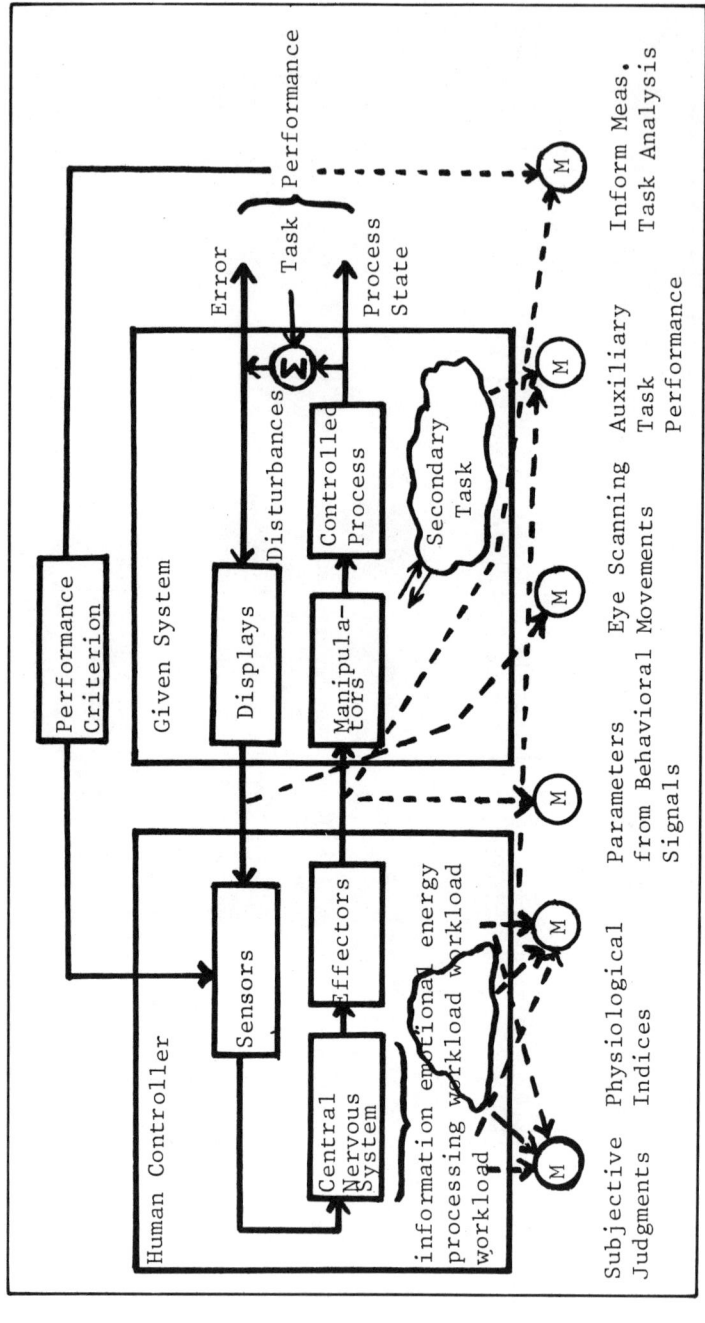

Figure 2: Workload and performance measures illustrated in a control paradigm.

The different measurements for mental workload (and performance) can be elucidated by Figure 2, in which the different methods are illustrated in a control paradigm; in the diagram three forms of workload are distinguished: information processing workload, emotional workload and energy workload.

3.2. Modelling of Workload, Performance and Behavior

Mathematical modelling of the relationship betweek task demands, workload and performance should be achieved for three reasons:

- .. Explaining the underlying phenomena in order to most efficiently and validly encode the empirical laws among them.

- .. Reducing and interpolating measured data.

- .. Predicting likely results for new situations.

In general one tries to base the model on the minimal number of independent variables, so as to obtain a model with the simplest physical structure and the lowest number of parameters. This structure and/or the parameters will then be a function of task demands, workload and performance indices. In section 3 we will discuss the status of various comprehensive man-machine system models of this type, but here we shall comment on modelling of workload measures per se. First we note in Table B that the basic cause-effect relationships between the measurements and implied mental workload are mostly unknown. One should not expect simple (few parameter) models for workload measures and their interdependance on performance and behavior, since such interactions involve inherently complex psycho-physiological feedback mechanisms. Furthermore, the psychophysiological processes which underlie the measured correlates of workload (e.g. heart rate, EEG, P_{300} component, etc.) have very complicated dynamics. Even the measurement process (e.g. rectification, smoothing, etc.) may introduce distortions and lags which complicate data interpretation. Consequently, we urge researchers to carefully measure and report the dynamics of their measurement systems, and to show at least one TYPICAL set of simultaneous time-histories of the task and workload variables where possible (we know it will be the best one!) Even if the original researcher does not understand the detailed workload measure dynamics, later theoreticians can use such traces to guide or validate their models.

As engineers with some experience in the measurement of complex, time varying and adaptive control systems, we must caution against the interpretation of CORRELATED signals as causally related. Just because breath flow and heart rate covary with high coherency does not mean that one effect (that with the lowest phase lags) CAUSES the other; they may originate from a more-or-less common source. The simultaneous operation, in many of the psycho-physiological variables, of homeostatic mechanisms having long time constants greatly complicate their interpretation and use as ongoing measures of workload. Much more laboratory research, using a battery of tasks with KNOWN, i.e. previously established, workload levels, should be done to establish the measurement dynamics and statistical properties, so that valid statistical tests may be applied to the data. (Such investigations make excellent thesis topics - educational, simple equipment, modern techniques - and we especially recommend it to our academic colleagues).

As a second main point about modelling workload, we note that many at this conference think that it is the activity of those functional parts of the CNS which SUPERVISE the perceptual motor system: i.e. select priorities and strategies, direct attention, order the use of previously-learned (stored) sensorimotor subroutines - the human's META-CONTROLLER of Sheridan and Jex (See paper by Jex in this volume) that should be modelled and measured with respect to workload processes. There is a remarkable parallel to these processes in large, modern, time-shared-central-computer facilities, for which a sophisticated technology is developing. Such facilities include: monitoring incoming demands and outgoing replies, evaluation of the priority and likely duration of each request (frequently based on gradually learned expected-values), assignment of priorities and reserve capacity margins, buffers for matching inputs and outputs to CPU intermittent activities, and an EXECUTIVE ROUTINE (metacontroller?) which supervises these activities and logs the use of various central and peripheral equipments for purposes of cost billing. The parallels in human operator time-shared activities are obvious. Although mathematical models of such systems are not widely published (for competitive proprietary reasons apparently) they are being developed by sophisticated computer technologists, and we ought to look in that direction for some new approaches to modelling mental workload. (Ref. 2).

4. STATE OF THE ART OF WORKLOAD AND PERFORMANCE MODELS

In analysing the state of art of workload and performance models, we will start with characterising the human operator tasks by three main aspects:

      .. Task complexity
      .. Task dynamics
      .. Number of subtasks

The task complexity has to do with the difficulty of performing the task; simple tasks can be completed almost at a reflex

FINAL REPORT OF CONTROL ENGINEERING GROUP   245

level, i.e. as a learned skill, whereas highly complicated tasks will be performed at a more cognitive level. We will distinguish three main levels.

- LEVEL I: Simple manual control or ancillary servofunctions

- LEVEL II: More complex supervisory functions where functions like monitoring and interpreting the data displayed, intervention and failure detection, set-point control and/or teaching, and strategy planning are involved.

- LEVEL III: The diagnostics, management and optimization functions, where almost entirely cognitive processing of data must be achieved.

The task dynamics take into account the spectra of the commands and disturbances acting on the system to be supervised, and the dynamics of the plant and internal noise characteristics. The dynamics will be represented by the dominating time constants of the system and/or bandwidth of human input and output.

The number of subtasks is the entire set of tasks as they have to be performed by the human operator, such as the number of loops which have to be closed, monitoring tasks and supervisory tasks, communication with other supervisors, etc.

On the basis of these three aspects, complexity, dynamics and number of subtasks, we can imagine a three dimensional space, in which the existing models or tasks/applications can be placed.

The first level mainly covers the continuous manual control tasks and the discrete manipulation tasks. Examples are simple tracking, multidimensional tracking, vehicle control, control of arm prosthesis and manipulators, etc. These tasks with sensory inputs and control outputs which are more or less continuous, have been extensively modelled and validated in the last 20 years. The resulting models are focussed mainly on the aspect of performance description; seldom has workload _per se_ been modelled. In general many more investigations have been reported in the field of the control of rapidly responding systems than in that of the slowly responding ones. In particular scanning behavior has received much attention in such tasks as the landing of aircraft using separated or integrated displays, and hovering of helicopters. The models which have been proven to be applicable, and thus have been validated, are the frequency domain models (McRuer, Ref. 3) the optimal control model (Baron, Kleinman and Levison) and the great variety of non-linear models.

The second level deals with those tasks where not skills, but cognitive processing of data plays an important role. We now shift from manual control to supervisory control, in which case monitoring tasks, failure detection, teaching of the system under supervision, and planning of strategies are the most important tasks. Some models to describe performance are reported and validated, such as the decision model (Elkind and Miller), failure detection models (Gai and Curry), and a human supervisor model based on the philosophy of the optimal control model (Kok and Van Wijk). NONE of these models include workload explicitly; only the models based on the queueing theory can be regarded as workload models (Senders). In general we might say that this area is a new interest, where only some isolated models have been developed. We expect that a more general solution can be obtained in the near future from the philosophy of the optimal control model (i.e. the recognition of an observer part)including the internal representation and the controller part and/or decision making element, combined with workload models as presented by Levison). We also expect that queueing theory may contribute in terms of models in understanding performance and workload problems. Finally, the emerging technology of large, central, time-shared computer facilities should be ideal for modelling these problems.

Finally, we will discuss those man-machine problems where all data processing appears to be cognitive. Tasks belonging to this highest level of task complexity are the diagnostic procedures to detect and understand failures, management problems and for instance the daily operation of large production plants or government operation. In general only very, very few control models, describing only the performance (Crossman; Krendel) can be mentioned; these do not contain workload explicitly, but such a measure could be constructed from the activity of the controller or decision maker. As we become more and more concerned with problems of this kind, e.g. the progress in process automation, consideration becomes increasingly necessary. A major factor here is that we now probably deal with the problem of frequent underloading and occasional but potentially catastrophic overloading, whereas at the levels I and II the problem of frequent overloading is of primary concern. Table C summarises the state of the art at the different task complexity levels.

5. RECOMMENDATIONS FOR FUTURE RESEARCH

The recommendations that follow are made from the perspective of control and estimation theory applications to man-machine system

Task Complexity	Level	Models available	
		Performance	Workload
Manual Control	I	Frequency domain models Optimal Control model Non-linear models	Frequency domain models. Optimal control model.
Supervisory Control	II	Optimal control model Queueing theory models Qualitative descriptions	None
Diagnostic Management etc.	III	None	None

Table C: Summary of existing workload and performance models at different levels of task complexity

problems. As such, they are primarily concerned with the prediction of overall system performance and operator workload. It should also be noted, however, that these recommendations have benefitted enormously from our group interaction with other attendees at the conference. Interestingly enough, and already mentioned in subsection 3, our review of control theory models discovered only two cases where workload on effort was clearly identified with a parameter of the model: the perceptual noise/signal ratio in the optimal control model of the human operator (Levison) or monitor (Gai and Curry), and the scanning dwell-fraction in the frequency domain approach to multi-axis tasks (Elkind, Ref. 6; Clement et al. Ref. 3).

There are two underlying themes to the topics proposed below: First, increased automation is placing the human increasingly in the role of a monitor of slowly varying signals. Second, our colleagues from other disciplines have pointed out the features, and the limitations of various measurement techniques. It is hoped that some of these restrictions or limitations can be removed.

CONTINUOUS AND DISCRETE TASKS: At present the modelling approach for continuous tracking is fairly well validated even to the point of accounting for attention sharing among several concommitant tasks. To our knowledge, the incorporation of discrete tasks into these models has not been extensively explored and remains a topic of high priority. While Monte Carlo techniques (Siegel and Wolf, HOSAINT) may offer a solution to this problem, they appear to require extensive analytic and computer resources to account for continuous tracking concepts and possible interactions.

INTERNAL REPRESENTATION AND TRAINING: One of the most important concepts from the control theory point of view is that of the internal representation or internal model of task, disturbances and system dynamics. Further exploration of this seems warranted even though (complex) internal models may not be completely identifiable from input/output data. Of particular interest are changes in the internal model throughout the skill acquisition phase and the determination of workload reduction during training. These measures may ultimately be more sensitive than the traditional measurement of performance in this regard. Another aspect of this internal model is the appropriate representation for complex, long time-constant systems. Progress in this direction may be the key to describing performance and workload for this class of systems. Does a more accurate internal model lead to a lower workload meeting a certain performance level, or will it lead to a better performance if the workload is kept at a level which the operator is willing to expend, i.e. what is the trade-off between performance and workload as a function of the internal model accuracy? And what is the influence of deviate internal models on performance and workload? Such questions need to be answered.

SLOWLY VARYING SIGNALS: There has been an increase in interest in the human's role in monitoring and supervisory control, especially in the fields of process control, conventional and nuclear power plants, and large vehicles, (e.g. supertankers). While it might appear that the models of higher bandwidth control would apply in a straight forward manner, there is ample evidence that perceptual limitations (e.g. rate sensing) and strategy selection play a very important role and will certainly affect workload and performance. Thus we feel that specific attention to this facet of control is necessary in order to understand this important class of human operator tasks.

MONITORING: The monitoring of automated systems represents a particularly difficult methodological problem, since overt responses are rare as, indeed, are the unusual events for which monitoring is being performed. Nevertheless, workload/performance models are required, since this is becoming one of man's more important functions in system operation. We only mention here the important topics of inattention, boredom, and familiarity with a system which is under automatic control except in critical phases or times.

UNDERLOADING: One of the outcomes of increased automation is that the operator will have less to do. The Yerkes-Dodson Law suggests that overall performance will decrease with task underloading, but there are few if any studies which substantiate this in the concept of control. In practical terms, however, a performance decrement may occur because the operator is not performing the low-workload task e.g. monitoring. Such considerations are intuitively related to the longer-term aspects of motivation, job-satisfaction, ability to cope with failures and other anomalies, etc. For short term research, we feel the conditions leading to performance decrement in underload situations should be identified, and in the long term prescriptive means should be developed to insure efficient system operation through appropriate personnel selection, training, level of workload etc.

SUBJECTIVE RATINGS OF WORKLOAD: In our opinion, one of the most direct (and common) methods of measuring mental workload is by subjective evaluation. In fact, a sophisticated rating technique has been developed for predicting and/or measuring handling qualities in aircraft development. It is also evident that severe biases such as familiarity and job/employer satisfaction may have influenced these responses. Thus we propose a concentrated effort on developing subjective rating techniques, so that investigators and system designers may more fruitfully utilize these methods, especially to "calibrate" more objective measures.

CORRELATION OF WORKLOAD MEASURES AND MODEL PARAMETERS: Predictions of workload and performance can be made by developing relationships between empirical workload measures and task descriptions or model parameters. Realistically, correlations between workload measures and model parameters are likely to be more fruitful since the (assumed) model structure will account for many of the interrelationships in human response behavior.

We urge investigations to incorporate as many as possible of the psycho-physiological measures because of the many interrelationships involved. It is important that a detailed account of the measuring and data processing procedures be provided, so that subsequent investigators may properly interpret the results in light of later scientific developments.

Lastly, we propose that a battery of simple and sensitive tasks be developed for calibration of workload measures among various investigators. The appendix contains our proposal for such a standard battery of tasks. This set employs graded

SUBCRITICAL tracking tasks, which have been extensively studied and modelled, and on which several workload measures have been made. Detailed consideration should be given to the design of the calibration task techniques to insure it will produce reliable gradations in the many psycho-physiological measures currently being collected.

PHYSIOLOGICAL MODELS: Physiological measures constitute a major class of workload-related indices. As shown in Table B of measure assessments, however, there are many unknown factors with regard to the cause/effect relationships between the changes in the task and the subsequent changes in physiological variables. For the short term, we propose continued efforts in data processing methods to improve the sensitivity of these measures; whereas the long term needs call for a more basic understanding of the fundamental causal relationships to further improve the specificity and accuracy of the physiological measurements.

In Table D we summarise the areas of future research recommendations by the short-term and long-term elements.

Table D. Summary of research areas that need further investigations: Short term and long term projects

Research area	Short term projects	Long term projects
Continuous and discrete tasks	Tracking and well-defined discrete task elements	Complex systems
Internal representation and training	Workload and internal models during learning	Complex, slow, nonlinear, systems
Slowly varying systems	Perceptual limits	Strategies
Monitoring	Determine workload and performance measures of monitors	Monitoring of long time constant systems and rare events
Underloading	Determine conditions of performance decrement	Prevention of degraded system efficiency
Subjective ratings	Develop techniques which are insensitive to biases	Calibration of ratings using standard tasks in different labs.
Correlation of workload measures with model parameters	Urge use of battery of tests. Accurate reporting of methods. Universal test/calibration.	
Physiological modelling	Data processing to remove variabilities	Develop dynamic cause/effect relationships to prove specificity of measurements.

REFERENCES

Baron, S., and W.H. Levison "An Optimal Control Methodology for Analysing the Effects of Display Parameters on Performance and Workload in Manual Flight Control" IEEE Trans. Vol. SMC-5, No. 4, 1975. pp. 423-430.

Gai, E.G. and Curry, R.E. "A model of the human observer in failure detection tasks". IEEE Trans. on Systems, Man, and Cybernetics, February, 1976.

Jex, Henry R. and W.F. Clement: "On Defining and Measuring Perceptual Motor Workload in Manual Control Tasks". Systems Technology Inc. Working Paper WP. 1104-1 July 1977 (included in this Proceedings).

McCreachie, J.S. "Multiple Terminals Under User Control in a Time-Sharing Environment", CACM. Vol. 16, 1965. pp. 587-590.

McRuer, D.T. and E.S. Krendel. Mathematical Models of Human Pilot Behavior. AGARDograph, No. 188, 1974.

McRuer, D.T. and H.R. Jex, W.F. Clement, E.D. Graham, "A Systems Analysis Theory for Displays in Manual Control", Systems Technology Inc. TR. 163-1. June 1968.

Pritsken, A., Wortman, D., Seum, C. Chubb, G. and Seifert, D. "SAINT: Systems Analysis of an integrated network of tasks". AMRL-TR-73-126, Wright Patterson AFB, Ohio, April 1974.

Siegel, A.I., and Wolf, J.J. Man-machine simulation models, New York: Wiley, 1969.

PART III:

MATHEMATICAL MODELS AND MENTAL WORKLOAD

APPROACHES TO MENTAL WORKLOAD

William B. Rouse

University of Illinois

Urbana, Illinois 61801

INTRODUCTION

There appear to be two main reasons for being interested in human workload. The first reason concerns the impact of workload on human performance. This concern reflects the system design point of view where human performance is an important factor in system performance. The second motivation for being interested in human workload concerns task design and job satisfaction. This consideration emphasizes the fact that humans have interests beyond optimization of traditional indices of system performance.

Thus, system design should perhaps include consideration of both system goals (e.g. minimal downtime) and individual goals (e.g. personal development). Intuitively at least, it would seem that human workload affects both system and individual goals. Within this paper, alternative approaches for pursuing this notion will be discussed.

However, before considering specific alternatives, it is important to discuss the range of system design problems to which one would like to apply these ideas. Much research has been motivated by tasks where humans control multi-degree-of-freedom dynamic systems in real time. Yet, the role of the human operator appears to be evolving away from in-the-loop real time control. It may soon be appropriate to use the term "manager" instead of "operator". Further, it seems unnecessary to limit design goals to managers of aircraft and industrial processes. Instead, the domain of discussion can be expanded to include, for example, users of on-line management information systems. Perhaps the main difference among managers of aircraft, industrial processes, banks, insurance companies, etc. is the time horizon within which they plan. Thus, it seems reasonable to discuss workload in a fairly robust context.

DEFINITIONS

There are a variety of ways to define workload (Jahns, 1973; Gartner and Murphy, 1976). Frequently, definitions involve consideration of the fraction of attention demanded by a task or set of tasks. Thus, a task that requires 90% of one's attention imposes a higher workload than a task requiring 10% of one's attention.

Applying this definition simplistically, one might say that a task that requires devotion of 90% of one's time to vacationing imposes a higher workload than a task that requires devotion of 10% of one's time to performing brain surgery. Clearly, the fraction of attention definition is only appropriate for comparing alternative ways of performing the same task. Thus, one might say that display A imposes less workload than display B in, for example, a particular air traffic control situation.

However, even if two displays require the same fraction of attention, the workload associated with each display may be different because the intensity of effort required with each display may differ. For example, one display may be very easy to use while the other display may require awkward mental transformations of the displayed information. But would not one expect the fraction of attention required to be greater for the display where the intensity of effort required was greater? To respond affirmatively, one must assume that humans always work to their capacity and thus, higher intensity of effort requires greater fractions of attention. Not only does it seem unreasonable to accept this assumption, but also it seems unreasonable to design tasks that would require humans to work to their capacity over extended periods of time.

While fraction of attention and intensity of effort may be sufficient to describe workload, performance (e.g. reaction time or RMS error) is definitely easier to measure. Thus, performance measures are often discussed as indices of workload. Nevertheless, while performance may be affected by workload, it is not workload itself. The topic of measures of workload will be pursued in the next section of this paper.

Fraction of attention and intensity of effort appear to be the components of workload. The product of these components (i.e. fraction of attention x intensity of effort) may be a reasonable

composite definition of workload. This definition has the
desirable property of simplifying to the traditional fraction of
attention definition if one assumes that the human always works
to capacity. On the other hand, this composite definition presents
difficulties in terms of measuring intensity of effort. This
difficulty will be considered in more detail later.

Based on the literature (Jahns, 1973; Gartner and Murphy,
1976) and the arguments presented here, it seems reasonable to
choose fraction of attention and intensity of effort as components
of workload. Now, models and measures appropriate to these definitions will be considered.

MODELS AND MEASURES

To pursue this discussion, one must first discriminate between models and measures. A model of mental workload is some
procedure for predicting workload based on a priori conditions.
On the other hand, a measure of mental workload is some physically
measurable quantity that allows one to determine the presence of
some specific level of workload.

From a system design perspective, a model is used to predict
how (usually physically non-existent) alternative designs will
perform while measures are used to evaluate designs once they have
resulted in a particular system being produced. Thus, a measure
of mental workload would be useful to validate the predictive
ability of a model of mental workload.

Information Theory Models

The model of Senders (1964) is based on information theory
concepts and the assumption that the human operates at his capacity.
Thus, fraction of attention is the workload metric. For instrument
scanning tasks where the displayed information can be modeled as
band-limited white noise, this model seems reasonable. However,
it is difficult to apply this model to more robust situations.

The problem lies with the information theory approach which
is much too structured to apply to many realistic tasks. Information
theory measures rely on conditional probabilities that are highly
context and individual dependent. In all but very simple tasks,
it is virtually impossible to assess these a priori conditional
probabilities. For example, when a pilot observes an integrated
flight director, how can one determine the conditional probabilities
of interesting events without knowledge of the specific flight
scenario and the training of the particular pilot?

On the other hand, one of the advantages of the information theory model is that it yields fractions of attention in a fairly direct manner. This cannot be said of all models, especially those based on control theory.

Control Theory Models

Several control theory approaches to modeling workload have been developed (Levison, 1970; Kleinman and Curry, 1976). As with the information theory approach, these models assume that the human operates at capacity and thus, that fraction of attention is a sufficient definition of workload. For tracking tasks involving linear dynamic systems, these models incorporate the fractions of attention required by each displayed signal and produce predictions of the expected task performance in terms of RMS error.

The control theory models seem adequate for tasks that can be modeled as the tracking of outputs of linear dynamic systems. However, it must be admitted that this is a small subset of the set of all tasks for which workload predictions are of interest. For example, it is difficult to model the tasks of assembly line workers as controlling linear dynamic systems subject to quadratic criteria functions.

Another difficulty with the control theory models is that they, in effect, employ the fractions of attention as free parameters which are used to match RMS error measures of model and data. Thus, the workload measure becomes obscured within the rather strong structural assumptions of the model. In essence, the workload measure is only a means to a system design end. Nevertheless, control theory models may be quite appropriate for the fairly small set of tasks for which the assumptions can be justified.

Queueing Theory Models

Queueing theory allows one to model a more robust set of tasks than possible with information theory or control theory. This is accomplished by ignoring the structure of the task and concentrating on the time involved in performing the task. Thus, it is implicitly assumed that the task is performed appropriately and performance measures such as RMS error are no longer relevant.

Queueing theory models are particularly appropriate for situations where task demands randomly occur and the performance measure of interest is the time that a task waits to be performed. Within these constraints, a queueing formulation will allow representation of tasks ranging from control of dynamic systems to management decision making (Rouse, 1977).

Models based on queueing inherently produce predictions of fractions of attention. In other words, fractions of attention are not free parameters as they are with the control theory models. In addition, queueing models allow prediction of the fractions of attention as functions of time and not just as averages. This type of prediction is not obtained with the models based on information theory or control theory.

The main disadvantage of queueing models is that they disregard task performance other than as reflected by task completion time. While at least one investigator (Carbonell, 1966) has avoided this difficulty by combining some aspects of control theory with queueing theory, the situation to which this solution applies is somewhat limited. Succinctly, the disadvantage of queueing models noted here is only a problem if the task is structured enough to allow development of a fairly detailed model of task performance. Thus, analysis of tracking tasks might benefit from the type of detail possible with control models while more robust tasks like system management are more amenable to queueing formulations.

Performance Measures

As noted earlier, one probably cannot measure workload. This is particularly true if one includes intensity of effort as a component of workload. Thus, workload has to be inferred from other measures. Performance measures such as reaction time, RMS error, and time-on-target are familiar choices. Often the performance measures on a secondary task are used as measures of workload in a primary task.

Even if the problem of inferring intensity of effort is solved, short-term performance does not necessarily reflect workload. For example, in a particular control and monitoring task, it has been shown experimentally that short-term performance on the control task (i.e. RMS error) does not correlate with attention allocation (Enstrom and Rouse, 1977).

On the other hand, long-term performance measures may allow inference of relative workload, although this would seem to provide at best an ordinal scale of workload. Further, unless one is willing to assume that humans always operate to capacity and that all humans have the same capacity, the workload scale developed would only reflect the particular individuals for which the data were collected. In other words, inter-human comparisons might not be valid.

Physiological Measures

Physiological measures such as sinus arrhythmia are frequently used as measures of workload. It would seem that such measures

are better indices of physiological workload than of psychological
workload. Perhaps brain activity might be related to mental workload. However, viewing this author's background, this comment
must be viewed merely as a conjecture.

Physiological measures have the same scaling problems as
psychological measures. It would seem that these problems are
only potentially resolvable for within task (and perhaps within
individual) comparisons.

Subjective Measures

Subjective measures involve direct or indirect queries of
the individual for his opinion of the workload involved in a task.
A good example of such measures are those developed for pilot
ratings and handling qualities. (See Hess (1977) for a brief
review of such measures).

Subjective measures might be generalized as utility functions
for which a variety of assessment techniques have been developed.
Despite the difficulties of inter-scale comparisons, it seems to
this author that some form of subjective measurement is inevitable
if mental workload is to be assessed.

A SYNTHESIS

Based on the above discussion of definitions, models, and
measures, this section will present a synthesis of a possible
composite approach to mental workload. It should be emphasized
that this approach is only what the author feels is reasonable
and that no direct empirical support of these ideas is available.

An instantaneous measure of workload $w(t)$ might be given by

$$w(t) = f(t) \times i(t), \quad 0 \leq t \leq T,$$

where $f(t)$ is the fraction of attention and $i(t)$ is the intensity
of effort at time t and $(0,T)$ is the time interval of interest.

The fraction of effort $f(t)$ might be predicted using a
queueing model while the intensity of effort $i(t)$ might be
measured physiologically or perhaps assessed via subjective measures. If one is willing to assume that humans always operate to
capacity, then $i(t)$ can be eliminated.

The interval of interest is included because the workload
associated with a task might very well depend on how long it must
be performed. Further, one might be interested in short-term

workload (e.g. T equals one hour) or in long-term workload (e.g. T equals ten years).

Instantaneous workload might be transformed to an overall workload measure W by a subjective transformation of $w(t)$. This might include consideration of particular characteristics of $w(t)$ (e.g. the frequency components) as well as the particular task in question. Thus, the mapping of $w(t)$ into W will depend on the particular individual and the particular task. This mapping might be accomplished using the individual's choices among alternative workload scenarios and discriminant analysis (Tatsuoka, 1971; Afifi and Azen, 1972).

For example, consider the task of writing this paper. This author's preference is for a $w(t)$ without high frequency components. More specifically, the presence of frequency components with periods of less than two hours results in a substantial loss in utility (i.e. increase in W). On the other hand, the task of jogging (i.e. running) is such that high frequency (short period) values of large $w(t)$ superimposed on low frequency (long period) values of small $w(t)$ are preferred.

Characteristics of $w(t)$ other than frequency are probably also important and the specific procedure for mapping $w(t)$ into W needs considerable thought. Further, measurement of $i(t)$ will present a great deal of difficulty. Thus, the approach to mental workload presented here needs refinement and, of course, substantial empirical work is also necessary.

CONCLUSIONS

This paper has addressed the issues involved in defining, predicting, and measuring mental workload. It has been argued that fraction of attention and intensity of effort are the essential components of mental workload. An approach utilizing queueing models and utility functions has been suggested.

The difficult issues considered include measurement of intensity of effort as well as inter-task and inter-individual comparisons. Also, it was noted that development of other than an ordinal scale of mental workload may prove difficult.

The main benefit of the approach discussed in this paper is that it is not limited to highly structured tasks such as instrument scanning and tracking. It has the potential of being applicable to situations as robust as management decision making. Nevertheless, the ideas presented here are, as yet, only conjectures.

REFERENCES

Afifi, A.A. and Azen, S.P. 1972. *Statistical Analysis.* New York: Academic Press, 1972.

Carbonell, J.R. 1966. "A Queueing Model of Many-Instrument Visual Sampling". *IEEE Transactions on Human Factors in Electronics,* Vol. HFE-7, No. 4, pp. 157-164, December 1966.

Enstrom, K.D. and Rouse, W.B. 1977. "Real Time Determination of How a Human Has Allocated His Attention Between Control and Monitoring Tasks". *IEEE Transactions on Systems, Man and Cybernetics,* Vol. SMC-7, No. 3, pp. 153-161, March 1977.

Gartner, W.B. and Murphy, M.R. 1976. *Pilot Workload and Fatigue: A Critical Survey of Concepts and Assessment Techniques.* Moffett Field, CA: NASA Ames Research Center, NASA Technical Note TN D-8365, November 1976.

Hess, R.A. 1977. "Prediction of Pilot Opinion Ratings Using An Optimal Pilot Model". *Human Factors,* in press.

Jahns, D.W. 1973. The Concept of Operator Workload in Manual Vehicle Operations. *Meckenheim, F.R. Germany: Research Institute for Human Engineering, Report No. 14, December 1973.*

Kleinman, D.L. and Curry, R.E. 1976. "Some New Control Theoretic Models for Human Operator Display Monitoring". *Proceedings of the IEEE Decision and Control Conference, Clearwater Beach, Florida, December 1976.*

Levison, W.H. 1970. "A Model for Task Interference". *Proceedings of the Sixth Annual Conference on Manual Control, Wright-Patterson AFB,* April 1970, pp. 585-616.

Rouse, W.B. 1977. "Human-Computer Interaction in Multi-Task Situations". *IEEE Transactions on Systems, Man and Cybernetics,* Vol. SMC-7, No. 5, May 1977.

Senders, J.W. 1964. "The Human Operator as a Monitor and Controller of Multi-Degree of Freedom Systems". *IEEE Transactions on Human Factors in Electronics,* Vol. HFE-5, No. 1, pp.2-5, September, 1964.

Tatsuoka, M.M. 1971. *Multivariate Analysis.* New York: Wiley, 1971.

AXIOMATIC MODELS OF WORKLOAD

John W. Senders

Department of Industrial Engineering

University of Toronto, Toronto

A. A SIMPLE STEADY STATE MODEL OF WORKLOAD

1. Workload is a meaningful concept only in the context of a well-defined task which must be performed to a stipulated criterion.

   a.-def. a 'well-defined' task is one for which specific actions on the part of a human operator can be identified and quantitative criteria for each action stated.

   b.-def. workload is a non-accessible, hypothetical, unidimensional, internal variable over the range of 0.0 - 1.0 in any human operator.

2. Workload increases as the demand of the task increases.

   c.-def. Demand of a task is the list of actions and their performance criteria.

3. Workload decreases as the capacity of the human operator increases with respect to that task.

   d.-def. Capacity of a human operator is the limiting level of performance on any action which is part of a task.

4. By 2. and 3. workload may be considered to be the ratio of Demand to Capacity with respect to any action. Thus

$$L_i = \frac{D_i}{C_i}$$ or the workload of action i is the ratio of the demand of action i to the capacity to perform action i.

5. Actions required by a task may be classified into elemental types.

   e.-def. An elemental type is a non-reducible action.

6. All actions required by a task are either elemental types or are reducible into elemental types.

7. The non-reducibility of elemental types implies independence of elemental types.

8. By 7. the demand of a task can be mapped into an N-dimensional space whose orthogonal axes are the elemental types of the task and are also the capacities associated with each elemental type by def. d.

9. The N-dimensional space of elemental type demands and capacities may be transformed into an N-dimensional space of elemental type workloads. The axes of the new space are not limited to the range 0 - 1.0; the mapping consists of dividing elemental type demands by elemental type capacities.

10. The total workload of the task may be considered to be the vector sum of the elemental type workloads.

11. If a task demand consists exclusively of a repetitive elemental type, the load placed on the human operator will be $N.L_i$ where N is the number of actions of type i. In all other cases the total workload $L = \left[\sum_{i=1}^{N} (m_i L_i)^2 \right]^{\frac{1}{2}}$

    which is the length of the vector composition of the elemental type work loads. N is the number of elemental types and M_i the number of each elemental type i.

12. If any elemental type workload exceeds 1.0, the human operator cannot meet the demand of the task. If the vector task workload exceeds 1.0, the human operator cannot meet the demand of the task.

13. Summary of simple steady state model.

    Workload of a well defined task is the length of a vector in a space defined by N elemental type workload axes. On each axis is plotted the workload corresponding to that elemental type. Each such elemental workload is computed by taking the ratio of elemental type demand to elemental type capacity.

B. SIMPLE NON-STEADY STATE MODEL OF WORKLOAD

1. In any real task the numbers and type of elemental type actions which compose the demand of the task vary as a function of time.

2. As a consequent the vector sum of the elemental workloads varies in time in both length and angle relative to each elemental type axis.

3. In any real human operator the capacity to perform any elementary action varies as a function of time.

4. As a consequent the vector sum of the elemental type workloads varies in time in both length and angle relative to each elemental type axis.

C. THE LOAD COMPONENT GENERATED BY INTERNAL SWITCHING

1. Subjective report strongly indicates the existence of a workload component generated internally to the human operator.

2. The internally generated workload component may be considered to be orthogonal to and similar to the elemental type workloads demanded by the task.

3. The internally generated workload increases monotonically with increasing number of elemental type workloads demanded by a task.

    Hypothesis: The workload generated internally is $L_N + 1 = K \cdot N$, where N is the number of elemental type workloads and K is the workload associated with the switching from one elemental type to another.

4. It follows that the workload vector is in a space of $N + 1$ dimensions and will increase with increase in N.

D. THE LOAD COMPONENT GENERATED BY EXTERNAL SWITCHING

1. Subjective report and direct observation require that a workload component is generated by switching of attention from place to place and from signal to signal.

2. Switching of visual directions of attention requires some minimum time τ_1.

3. Switching from sensory mode to sensory mode requires some minimum time τ_2.

4. From the task description the number of loci of visual attention can be calculated and the number of intersensory switchings can be estimated.

5. The time lost in switching is then $T_L = k_1\tau_1 + k_2\tau_2$ where k_1, k_2 are the numbers of switchings which the human operator must perform.

   Hypothesis: Total capacity but not elemental type capacity is reduced by T_L/T when T is the total time available to perform the task.

E. SWITCHING LOADS AND TIME COST

1. In external switching as in an extended monitoring task, the principal demand is for the switching act itself.

2. Therefore Time Demanded is the measure of demand and Time to Perform is the measure of capacity.

3. The workload for an externally limited task is $\dfrac{T_d}{T_c}$ where T_d is the time demanded and T_c is the time required by the human operator to perform.

4. The relationship of timing of elemental type demands relates to workload.

5. If actions are demanded independently, two or more actions may be required simultaneously. There are two consequences.

   1) Priorities accumulate and force uneconomic switching.
   2) Human operators will fail to perform required actions until after an undesirable delay.

6. A totally self-paced task can never have a workload greater or less than 1.0. No overload can exist in either transient or steady-state conditions.

7. Because of the load cost of internally generated switching load, the adaptive human operator will minimize the switching load by aggregating demanded actions into groups of the same elemental type if priorities permit.

8. Two identical streams of actions, one self-paced and the other externally-paced will generate different load levels and different physiological response levels. $\underline{A}$ behaves in a self-paced mode. $\underline{B}$ receives as demanded action whatever A has done and $\overline{is}$ therefore externally paced.

9. Some elemental capacities are single channel in nature. The elemental type load is therefore always 0 or 1.0 with the average load reflecting the relative proportion of time the load is 1.0.

10. For such elemental types queueing models are required for the calculation of load as a function of time and for the estimation of the probability of transient overload.

F. MOTIVATION AND EFFORT

1. Motivation (Effort) controls the fraction of capacity (total) which a human operator will commit to a task.

2. Differing payoff systems and task designs will alter capacity and, therefore, the load imposed by a task.

3. High motivation allows a high fraction of capacity to be used. This results in improved performance. Low motivation produces low available capacity and permits overload to occur at low levels of demand.

   <u>Hypothesis</u>: Available capacity is product of Motivation and Capacity $C_A = M \cdot C_T$ where M is a 0-1 variable.

FINAL REPORT OF MATHEMATICAL MODELLING GROUP

R.J. Audley (Chairman)
W. Rouse
J. Senders
T. Sheridan

1. WORK IN RELATIONSHIP TO GOALS

For the purposes of describing human behaviour in any situation or task there is a very large number of both independent or dependent variables that could be taken into account. If we disregard the task an individual is trying to complete, there will rarely be any special reason, except scientific fashion, for choosing one set of dependent variables over another in providing the description. However, as soon as we have an hypothesis about the goals of that person, it usually becomes of great, if not paramount importance to obtain some evaluation of the adequacy of the individual's behaviour for achieving these goals.

In principle, and usually in practice too, the goals of an individual can be of many different types: to produce a feeling of physical pleasure, to have the satisfaction of performing a task well, to conserve physical energy for anticipated future demands, to avoid becoming too anxious, etc. The concept of work, however, is nowadays usually a social one (except for a hermit - but even he needs a society?). For, to a considerable extent, the goals of an individual will reflect those of his society - and also, though to a lesser extent, its goals will reflect his. The specification of goals by society will obviously be dominated by a concern with tasks productive of wealth (although one trusts that these will include goals which satisfy that aim more indirectly, such as the creation of an educated population, the provision of good entertainment, as well as the commonplace contemporary goals of excellent washing machines and the rapid transfer of workers from place to place). Human resources must also be nurtured so that the goal of devising task demands that do not damage these resources must always be borne in mind. This is but one indication that goals are manifold entities with potential conflict among components - a recurrent theme here.

Goals, of course, can be defined at different levels. For a system, successive levels of sub-goals will be survival, making profits, producing and selling product X. Something like this will apply to the individual: survival, taking in food, using a knife and fork.

2. LIMITED RESOURCES NECESSITATE THE ADOPTION OF THE CONCEPT OF WORK LOAD

Evaluation of success will therefore largely be in terms of discrepancies between actions and goals, with the latter stated in the form of task descriptions. The notion of load enters because of the limited resources and capabilities of a system and its components, including human operators. Where the human element is involved, the primary symptoms of strain on the system due to undue stress on limited resources are therefore:

(i) <u>Unacceptably large deviations of performance from goals</u>

(ii) <u>Failure to meet deadlines</u>

Although temporal aspects of a goal might be regarded as merely one feature of a goal, time and accuracy are nearly always competing goals so it may be best to accept a time schedule for achieving all other aspects of a goal as a distinct sub-goal. It is obvious that external pacing is an essential element of any situation to which the term work can be properly applied.

These are the two symptoms of stress which appear in the performance of the task. Since in most tasks there are several goals to be achieved the successful allocation of priorities to these can be a significant underlying goal. One may therefore expect that

(iii) a secondary symptom in the form of vacillation in the choice of sub-goals may appear and could, under some circumstances, signal impending failure to meet overt task goals.

3. IS THERE A SPECIAL CATEGORY OF WORK LOAD CALLED MENTAL?

The use of the term 'mental' may be relatively arbitrary: on the one hand it is possible to experience much conscious agony from carrying out a heavy physical task; on the other, some information processing tasks may be largely unconscious, especially after extended practice. It seems natural to suggest that one should use the term mental work load in cases where some conscious aspect of performing a task makes itself apparent. However, in many taks, the rate at which information is acquired may be determined by physical movements, e.g. the speed of eye-movements. Hence, performance may be limited at one moment by physical components of a task and at others by those more convincingly called mental. The use of 'mental work load' as a term indicating a general human limiting capacity for all kinds of tasks with mental components may therefore be inadvisable. Rather, one would always need to consider load in relation to a particular component activity: reading dials, making choices, estimating distances, predicting future difficulties, storing information about significant task-related events. A general term implies a common currency by means of which work load can be measured, e.g. 'mental effort'. The notion of breaking down the task into components, without regard to their 'physical or mental' nature, makes performance time a more suitable form of currency for costing work load.

4. SYSTEM GENERATED DEMANDS VS PERCEIVED AND SELF-GENERATED TASK DEMANDS

As outlined in Section 1, it is important to distinguish between the measurement of behaviour for descriptive purposes and the evaluation of this behaviour against task-related goals for which the term performance is appropriate. In studies of workload it is with the latter that we are principally concerned. However, it has to be remembered that task goals will often be re-interpreted by the individual who may also introduce ones of his own. The more complex interaction of the individual's goals and those of the system are now considered, although this does not take into account goals which are not closely related to the task.

The human operator responds to what he perceives to be the demands placed upon him. While his environment (including other people, e.g. his boss, the experimenter, etc.) may specify the task in one way, he may perceive the task in quite another. Thus, as indicated by the diagram below, the process H_1 of perceiving task demands, given the externally imposed demands, is a behavioural activity different from that of responding to such (perceived) task demands, H_2.

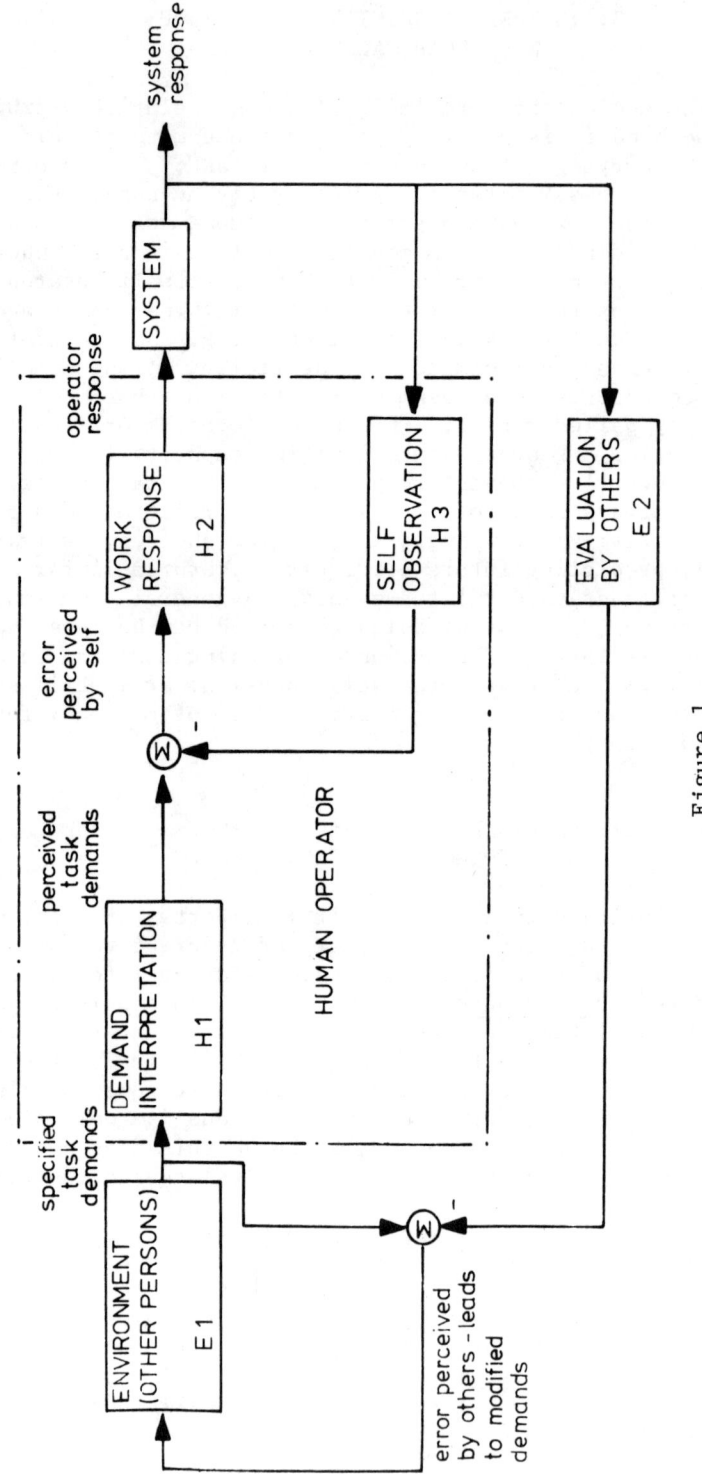

Figure 1

In much the same way, an individual's evaluation of his own performance H_3 may be different from that of others, E_2.

It can be seen from the diagram that if H_1 is other than unity, or if H_3 is different from E_2, external measures will always indicate the presence of some error, which may in turn lead to continued indications of new or unfulfilled task demands. This could be caused by additive noise in any of the elements H_1, H_3 or E_2.

Accordingly, with larger "demand interpretation mismatch" H_1, or larger "response interpretation mismatch" $(H_3 - E_2)$, the time integral of task demands is larger and (for given operator capacity) the mental workload is larger.

Another way in which part of the mental workload can be self-sustained is where H_2 has a noise source. In that case, even though H_1 is unity and $H_3 = E_2$ (which normally would lead to complete satisfaction of task demands) the inner loop will never settle down; it will continue to provide mental work for itself. Driving along a straight road at constant velocity is an example.

5. LEVELS OF DESCRIPTION AND INCLUSIVENESS

In attempting to devise mathematical models of workload problems it seems important to be clear about the level of analysis to which the model is directed. Particular investigations may be specially concerned with performance, others with behaviour, and yet others with mechanisms subserving certain behaviours. Furthermore, one needs to be clear about the domains of both dependent and independent variables that will be included in the model. The choice of these will be influenced strongly by fashions among scientists both in the laboratory and in the field.

6. AVERAGE, EXTREME AND INSTANTANEOUS WORKLOADS

In considering the allocation of limited resources there are essentially two problems to be considered. First, the analysis of average demands on resources and, second, a consideration of peak demand on resources. Presumably these could, in principle, both be conveniently subsumed in a distribution of demand over units of time (instantaneous workload) for some sample performances of the task. In cases where there are strong interactions between component tasks then a moment to moment analysis may be necessary as well as being always obviously

desirable. In practice it would be helpful for modelling
purposes to start with a consideration of situations where this
is not necessary. In any case, there will always be a problem
of some importance, (and implicitly raised by para. 5 above), of
deciding how to evaluate the success of a model. One should be
clear about the priorities to be attached to modelling peak,
average and trial to trial variations.

7. MEASUREMENT AND PREDICTION OF WORKLOAD

Next it is necessary to consider the kind of problem
associated with workload that one is attempting to answer. There
are three basic problems, two for existing systems and one for
hypothetical systems.

For existing systems we have:

(i) Empirical measurement of workload
(ii) Calculation of workload.

For new systems we have:

(iii) The prediction of workload.

Mathematical models may be useful for all three, and
especially for purposes (ii) and (iii).

For purposes (ii) or (iii) task description is mandatory.
The nature of the description required depends on the model.
If one is using a control theoretic model, then the task could
be described as a dynamic system. If, on the other hand, a
monitoring model appears more appropriate, the task must be
described in terms of a display of state variables.

Even for existing systems, measurement may be less useful
than calculation since human operators will usually not perform
above a certain steady-state capacity. This limits measurement
to workloads below those of which an operator is capable. At the
same time, overload may also fail to be revealed by measurements
taken on certain tasks, e.g. in supervisory tasks requiring high
reliability, calculation may show that to meet likely demands
a system is under-manned even though measurement for a limited
time span may not reveal this.

It is difficult to conceive of measurement, in the usual
sense, for a hypothetical system. However, if subjective
assessments of workload are admitted, a possibility discussed
in the next section, then some kind of estimate might be

FINAL REPORT OF MATHEMATICAL MODELLING GROUP

achieved by reference to existing tasks. All the same, it is very likely that, for hypothetical systems, mathematical models for calculating the workload will be needed, with subjective measurement providing an additional check.

8. SUBJECTIVE JUDGEMENTS OF MENTAL WORKLOAD

Measurement methods are not necessarily precluded from consideration for predicting workload in hypothetical systems. This is because the potentiality exists for using subjective assessments of workload. This is not an issue on which it is easy to find agreement but this potentiality cannot be ignored and the following statement, which owes most to Sheridan, indicates why. In the light of the earlier discussion it is important to emphasize again the need to make sure that one is clear as to the specific measurement problem to which subjective judgements are being applied. In particular, the perceived difficulty of meeting task demands should be the primary consideration and attempts made to disentangle this from other facets of subjective aspects of workload.

Most people can provide without difficulty some subjective appraisal of how hard they are working over any interval of time. Indeed it has been claimed that the measure of mental workload against which other indices must ultimately be calibrated is such a subjective judgement. Thus subjective judgements have a prima facie validity as a measure of mental workload, provided the measure is carefully made, i.e. the question is asked carefully, the scale is properly explained and anchored, and the subject is sufficiently sophisticated to give monotonic and repeatable judgements.

Subjective scaling of mental workload can be direct and unidimensional (as with the Cooper-Harper scale of aircraft handling qualities); also it can be indirect and unidimensional (as when a series of paired comparisons is made, the rank order of stimuli is first determined, and a Thurstone scale is then inferred); or finally a multidimensional subjective scale can be used (as the INDSCAL procedure of Carroll and Shepard, on the multidimensional utility models of Keeney).

When more than one judge is employed, it must be noted that axioms for combining the judgements of different persons into one scale pose problems (e.g. according to the impossibility theorem of Arrow). In practice more informal procedures which structure the collection and refinement of judgements are quite satisfactory. A rubric commonly used for this class of methods is the "Delphic Method" (see Linstone and Turoff, On Line Delphic Methods, Addison Wesley, 1974). Workload analysts should be cognizant of this work, for it has much potential application.

A requirement of any subjective scaling method (or for that matter any method of measuring mental workload) is that it does not interfere significantly with task performance.

Examples of the use of subjective scales <u>in situ</u> are found in applying Cooper-Harper type rating scales to aircraft "difficulty of control" (not exactly mental workload, but with but modest change of instructions to subjects it could be said to be scaling mental workload). In this case the test pilot is usually asked to give orally both a quantitative rating and a brief commentary following a test "phase" (e.g. following a brief manoeuvre but while the pilot is still flying the aircraft). During debriefing after landing judgements may also be requested, but the problem of fading memory may be encountered if enough time has elapsed.

9. TASK-DESCRIPTIONS

As we have argued earlier, apart from the ancillary use of subjective methods, it will be necessary in dealing with new systems to calculate workloads. Whatever view one takes about the way in which this will be done, a model of the task will be needed. The term 'model' rather than 'description' is used because it seems clear that a part of any description will require an assessment of priorities at times of high momentary load and it is doubtful whether an objective description of this aspect of a task can be achieved; or, alternatively, that description will be at a level of generality which will not be helpful for workload analysis.

10. WORKLOAD SCALING ANCHORS

We take it as self-evident that performance in most tasks is multi-facetted; the problem is to find ways of calculating some scalar or vector which measures task-demands. Probably a vector representation of component task requirements will always be needed if high precision is required. However, a scalar value might be found for applications where there is no concern with performance close to human limits. For any component task it should be possible to have some standard levels of performance capacity against which current demands can be evaluated. These standards can be of at least three kinds:

    (a) <u>Maximum</u>   Empirical assessments of capacity at high motivation usually typical of laboratory situations (although the problem may be that these do not take into account the high levels of practice associated with many practical situations).

(b) <u>Over-demanding</u> Assessments of task demands which lead to serious degradation of performance.

(c) <u>Acceptable norms</u> Empirical assessments of an acceptable workload at a level which can be comfortably maintained over an extended period may also be very useful anchors. Although they may not immediately appear to be of assistance in dealing with tasks where it is desirable or necessary to use human potential to the full they should not be overlooked even in such cases. They have the particular advantage that they appear to reflect individual differences more adequately than extreme measures. Also they overcome the relative difficulty of assessing capacity at high levels of performance, where large changes in 'effort' may lead to relatively small changes in performance. A combination of the acceptable and maximum standards might have some merit, especially in developing general models for workload problems. The concept of an acceptable workload might well need to be generalized to take some account of preferences for a certain level of variability of load or for certain systematic variations during a period of work; and clearly this period might be as short as an hour or as long as a career.

11. REPRESENTING DECISION-MAKING DEMANDS IN WORKLOAD

Whether because of difficulties in accurately describing priorities in task-demands or because the human operator will in most cases need to devote considerable time to the allocation of his resources or to operating strategies for dividing time between the completion of component tasks, one important problem is how to include decision-making in a vectorial representation.

12. SENDERS' MODEL OF WORKLOAD BASED ON TASK PRIMITIVES

One method would treat the decision-making component as just another task to be performed or see it as absorbed into a multi-dimensional representation of component task performance (Senders). This scheme accepts the view developed earlier that performance on a task can be viewed as a vector of performance on component, elementary tasks. For an elementary task – which may be either a real one or a hypothetical one created for the purposes of analyzing complex lists – it is safe to make the assumption that the workload will increase as the amount of output demanded of the human operator for almost any relevant task related variable increases. That is, of course, provided the capacity for the activity involved is not exceeded.

Viewed from this perspective the workload for an elementary task i could be defined as:

$$w_i = \frac{d_i}{c_i}$$

(w_i = workload, d_i = output demanded, c_i = capacity, all for component task i).

This expression can be construed in two ways: (1) the operator works on the simple task at level w_i continuously; or (2) the operator works essentially at full capacity for w_i per cent of time. On the first interpretation, the implicit assumption is made of an underlying system of multiple parallel channels. If this were not so, tasks involving more than one kind of elementary task could not be performed. On the second view, there exists a single time-shared channel with some capacity $\underline{C_i}$ for each type of task.

For a system with parallel channels we may either have:

(1) a total capacity C for the complex task made up of fixed capacities for the elementary task types, i.e.

$$C = \sum_{i=1}^{n} C_i$$

where $\underline{n}$ is the number of distinct types of elementary tasks involved.

(2) multiple channels each with fixed capacity $\underline{C}$. In this case CW_i is the amount of capacity used by task type $\underline{i}$, and $C - CW_i$ is available for the remaining task components.

System (1) leads to the prediction that there will be no interaction between performance on elementary tasks. If $W_i > 1.0$

only task $\underline{i}$ is affected. Experimental data reject this model for at least some subjects doing some complex tasks.

System (2) leads to different predicted outcomes depending on the exact form of the rule for sharing capacity. If simple additivity obtains there would be no interaction between tasks as long as the total load is less than unity. Vector additivity predicts interference between tasks even when the total load is less than unity. This system also suggests a multidimensional vector representation of a complex task projecting on to a performance space defined by dimensions and capacities relating to specific elementary task types: the space is bounded by a sphere whose radius is capacity $\underline{C}$. If the task vector exceeds $\underline{C}$, overload exists and task performance on one or more elemental tasks will be diminished or eliminated.

In the case of the single channel, System (3), the time that this is switched on one occasion to take i; would have a dwell duration

$$d_i = \frac{W_i}{C_i} \ .$$

This last system leads to linear additivity of the elementary workloads so that

$$W_T = \sum_{i=1}^{n} W_i$$

(W_T being dimensionless).

Systems (2) and (3) correspond to a queueing model for the calculation of instantaneous workloads. The workload can then be viewed as a vector varying over time in length and direction in a space of elementary performance capacities.

13. AN ANALOGY BASED ON TIME-SHARED COMPUTING

Another approach which sees the allocation problem as more fundamental draws an analogy between the human operator and a time-shared computing system (Rouse). One might characterize the human as a general purpose task performer who can flexibly allocate his information processing resources (as well as sensors and effectors) to perform a variety of tasks. One can similarly characterize a time-shared computing system (and the programmers who designed its operating system). Thus, it might be useful to employ time-shared computing as an analogy of human information processing. Over the range for which such an analogy is

appropriate, a powerful set of analysis tools developed for
analyzing computer operating systems can probably be brought
to bear on understanding of human information processing.

Demands

In most robust task situations the human is faced with a
variety of demands. Some of these may be expected or even
scheduled while others may occur randomly. At any instant of
time, several tasks may compete for the human's information
processing resources. Since the human cannot allocate more
resources than he has, such competition results in some
demands waiting for satisfaction (i.e. queueing) and other
demands perhaps not being satisfied at all. A time-shared
computer is in a completely analogous situation with various
programs requesting computer resources and, when total demands
exceed supply, some programmes waiting or not being executed
at all.

Resources

The computer's resources include its storage
capabilities, input and output channels, peripherals such as
special hardware signal processing systems, and, in some sense,
its general purpose programs.

The other resource the computer has is time, although
this is certainly a different type of resource, perhaps to the
extent that another word should be used.

The computer allocates certain resources for certain
periods of time in an attempt to satisfy demands. The time and
resources allocated may not be exactly what is requested,
particularly if many demands want the same resources. The result
of such under-allocation is longer task completion times
(including waiting) and/or degraded task performance.

The human seems to be in a very similar situation. Short
term memory, sensors, effectors, and perhaps the less well-defined
attention are among the resources that the human allocates.
Further, the results of under-allocation are similar to those
produced in time-shared computing.

Control

The time-shared computing system is controlled by what is
termed an operating system. The operating system assigns
priorities, allocates resources, monitors resource utilization,
updates its knowledge of its world, etc.

The operating system consumes resources itself in deciding all of the above and thus, one can talk about the overhead associated with control. Therefore, external demand cannot have access to all of the computer's resources.

Similarly, the human must devote information processing resources to deciding what to do, deciding what is happening, etc.

Workload

The computer's workload is simply how busy it is and how many of its resources are in use. If the workload becomes large, then performance of some or all programs slows down or might even degrade. Depending on the priority scheme employed, this degradation might be spread among all tasks or imposed on the lower priority tasks, perhaps to the extent that they do not get done at all.

If the computer's workload becomes very large for long periods of time, the computer sometimes mystically (from the perspective of the user) fails to cope with the workload and fails in the sense of simply stopping.

Humans seem to react to workload in similar ways, with two exceptions. First, low workload may give the human difficulty. It becomes a little far-fetched to invest this difficulty in the computer. The second difference is that humans have an opinion of their tasks while the computer doesn't care except in the sense that the designers of its operating system may invest it with preferences (priorities and propensities for not failing) for tasks which it does well.

Implications

Given a set of demands, a set of resources (or perhaps skills), and an operating system (strategies, etc.), one would like to predict human workload. This might be facilitated by considering how a computer's workload is computed.

Employing queueing theory which may allow for:

(i) <u>General</u> task inter-arrival times distributions (even constant)
(ii) <u>General</u> task performance time distributions
(iii) <u>General</u> operating system strategies
(iv) <u>etc.</u> (almost anything)

one can calculate (via analytical and/or simulation approaches) the average and, to a certain extent, instantaneous workload resulting.

Further, literally hundreds if not thousands of papers and books have addressed the most common and useful descriptions of the form noted above (e.g. 1, 2). Thus, a wealth of knowledge exists.

The analogy discussed above is useful in two ways. First, it provides an interesting way of organizing one's ideas. Second, use of the analogy allows one to employ a vast body of knowledge and tools already available. For example, aspects of this approach have been applied to modelling pilot decision making in multi-tasks flight management situations (3, 4, 6).

14. UNCERTAINTY AND WORKLOAD

Uncertainty can enter a work situation (i.e. cause unpredictability in one's stimulus and/or response) from several different sources:

(a) external disturbance signal
(b) varying parameters of the system structure external to the human operator
(c) human-produced noise in observing the task stimuli
(d) lack of a good internal model of the external system
(e) human-produced distortions in interpreting the externally stipulated criterion of performance
(f) human-produced motor noise.

These sources can be represented diagrammatically as follows:

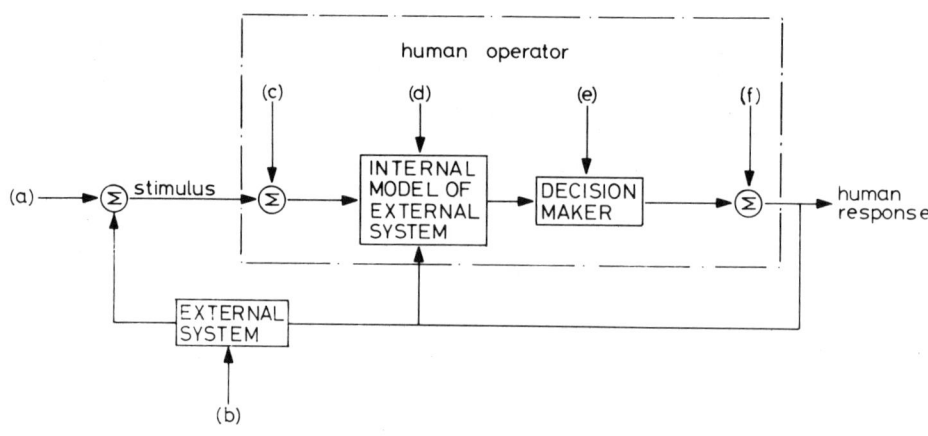

It can be assumed that the normal effect on a man of training will be to decrease his observation noise (f), improve his model of the external system (d), decrease the mismatch between his own and the externally stipulated criterion of performance (e) and decrease his motor noise (f). However he can do nothing about external disturbances or nonstationarity (parameter variation) of the external system, except perhaps to learn the stochastic parameters of the distributions of those signals on secular parameter variations.

One notion of mental workload assumes that it is that cognitive (conscious?) effort (or fraction of capacity for same) required to update or improve one's internal model and estimate of other signals listed above. Acccording to this characterization, when the internal model and statistical understanding of disturbance signals approach perfect matches to the actual, then behaviour becomes automatic (lower than conscious) and mental workload diminishes to zero. While this is indeed speculative theory, it has been shown to be feasible within a somewhat limited domain, to infer mathematically what the internal model is over any reasonable time period, and use this result somehow to relate to mental workload.

This also accords roughly with the psychophysiological notion of "activation", wherein total activation consists of three parts: (1) that due to basal metabolic and neural activity of life; (2) that increment due to perceptual-motor activity beyond (1) which is "automatic" or "well habituated", and (3) that increment beyond (2) which is required to cope with novelty, i.e. to update one's internal model and characterization of external structure and signals.

In another vein, this third increment of activation is the "operating system" activity in the computer analogy described above.

15. OTHER MODELS

The model of Senders and the model based on an analogy with time-shared computing resort to queueing theory for prediction of the times to perform task components as well as the overall task (1,2,3). This is a widely applicable approach as long as performance can be assumed to be acceptable. In other words, a purely time-based analysis is reasonable if one assumes that the human satisfies task requirements within the resulting task times (4). Viewing this approach somewhat simplistically, workload then correlates with the extent to which the human is busy.

There also are several performance-based models. The most

well-developed of these utilizes control and estimation theory. Within the realm of continuous control of dynamic systems, these models have been quite successful. Such models incorporate a workload-like measure in terms of noise injected into the process by the human (7).

The problem with control models is their limited range of applicability. They have difficulty incorporating the many discrete tasks often accompanying a control task. This is an important limitation since many realistic tasks appear to be changing in that the number of discrete decision making aspects of the task are increasing while the amount of in-the-loop control is decreasing.

A particular advantage of control and estimation theory is the considerable amount of task structure that it incorporates. If such a detailed description is possible, control and estimation theory can yield considerable information. For example, considering our earlier discussions of uncertainty and internal models, control and estimation theory has been successfully applied to modelling how humans form internal models (6).

There are several other performance-based models. However, their use appears to be limited to laboratory-like tasks. For most realistic tasks, information theory seems impossible to apply. One particular problem is assessing the conditional probabilities associated with events. This requires some model of the human's expectations which may be quite complex in realistic tasks.

Signal detection theory, through its parameters of β and d', could perhaps allow interesting workload measures. The classical psychophysical application of this model does not seem appropriate to workload per se, however. In terms of workload the applicability would have more to do with an operator's prediction of his own success or failure relative to his actual success or failure.

When task demands in terms of instructions are rather vague (e.g. keep the level of X at a "reasonable" value), the theory of fuzzy sets seems to offer a useful approach (8). This theory has been applied to modelling process control operators (9) and human fault diagnosis abilities (10). However, the main advantage of this approach is its ability to model somewhat vague task situations and not that it yields workload measures directly. Instead, it may offer a framework for implementation of workload measures.

There are a variety of other models including, for example, the Markov models of mathematical psychologists and the computer models of artificial intelligence researchers. However, the current state of such models does not seem to offer much to the problem of modelling mental workload considerations in realistic task situations.

REFERENCES

1. L. Kleinrock. Queueing systems. Vol. I Theory. New York: Wiley, 1975.

2. L. Kleinrock. Queueing systems. Vol. II Computer applications. New York: Wiley, 1976.

3. W.B. Rouse. Human-computer interaction in multi-task situations. IEEE Transactions on systems, man and cybernetics. Vol. SMC-7, No.5, pp.384-392, May 1977.

4. R.S. Walden and W.B. Rouse. A queueing model of pilot decision making in a multi-task flight management situation. Proceedings of the 13th Annual Conference on Manual Control, MIT, June 1977.

5. Y. Chu and W.B. Rouse. Optimal adaptive allocation of decision making responsibility between human and computer in multi-task situations. Proceedings of the 7th International Conference on Cybernetics and Society, Washington, September 1977.

6. W.B. Rouse. A theory of human decision making in stochastic estimation tasks. IEEE Transactions on systems, man and cybernetics. Vol. SMC-7, No.4, pp. 274-283, April 1977.

7. W.H. Levison, S. Baron, and D.L. Kleinman. A model for human controller remnant. IEEE Transactions on man-machine systems. Vol. MMS-10, No.4, December 1969.

8. L.A. Zadeh, K.S. Fu, K. Tanaka, and M. Shimure, Eds. Fuzzy sets and their application to cognitive and decision processes. New York: Academic Press, 1975.

9. P.J. King and E.H. Mamdani. The application of fuzzy control systems in industrial processes. Automatica, Vo. 13, pp. 235-242, 1977.

10. W.B. Rouse. A model of human decision making in a fault diagnosis task. Proceedings of the 15th Annual Allerton Conference on Communication, control and computing. University of Illinois, September 1977.

PART IV:

PHYSIOLOGICAL PSYCHOLOGY AND MENTAL WORKLOAD

PROCESS ENTROPY AND COGNITIVE CONTROL: MENTAL LOAD IN INTERNALISED THOUGHT PROCESSES

Peter Hamilton

Department of Psychology, University of Stirling

Stirling, Scotland

'Traditional' information theory still has a good deal to offer us in our consideration of mental workload. It is clear even from early work on perceptual-motor skill that subjective expectations, coding strategies, learned S-R compatibilities and the like will remain the private province of the subject. In consequence the Holy Grail of an absolute measurement of task load remains unattainable. However, I believe that in the short term the rule does hold that mental workload is some function of the uncertainty the subject must resolve, and the rate at which he attempts to resolve it in pursuit of his goal.

In this position paper I should like to confine myself to the question whether the above beliefs hold good when one tackles the rarely-considered problem of mental workload in thinking. The often used simplified picture of component process organisation in a perceptual motor skill is shown below. I shall attempt to restrict myself to the central block, transformation processes,

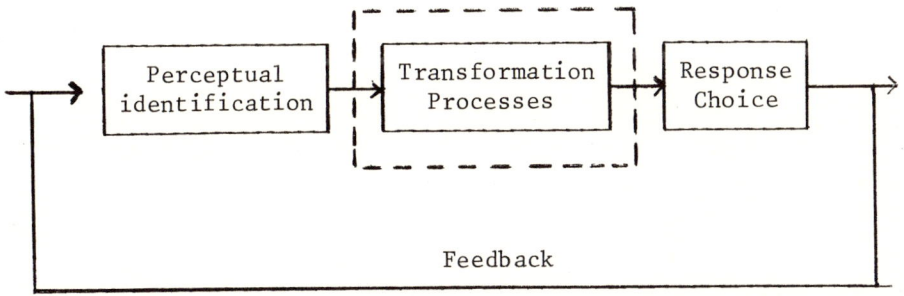

Fig.1. Block Diagram of Perceptual-Motor Skill.

and to show that all the principles governing information loading in the more observable and controllable perception and response stages are in fact operative there.

Let us suppose that the subjective experience of workload per unit time is a product of the amount of uncertainty resolved at each step in processing and the amount of effort (or concentration if you will) invested in resolving it. The emphasis on effort investment by the operator is deliberate because manipulation of load by the experimenter (say in increasing the rate of stimulus input) is a trivial exercise without the goodwill and effortful cooperation of his subject. The paper is organised in two phases. Firstly, I shall consider those task variables which would appear to determine <u>complexity of choice</u> (process entropy) in programming articulate sequences of processing operations in thought, and compare them with the variables operative in the perceptual identification and response selection stages. Secondly, I shall consider the problem of mental effort, and its contribution to the cognitive control processes which manage such programming.

PROCESS ENTROPY IN MENTAL TASKS

I have constructed a questionnaire which, though hopefully of some entertainment value, should enable the reader to determine for himself the nature of the principles I consider important. My own comments and 'best guesses' to the answers are appended.

<u>Q.1.</u> Here are examples of lists incorporating the basic arithmetic operations.

Set A	8+3	9−5	6x3	8÷2	Mean time per
	6+5	4−3	4x4	9÷6	operation, all lists A
	2+9	8−2	7x2	10÷5	<u>X sec.</u>
	↓	↓	↓	↓	

Set B	8+3	4x4	
	4−3	9÷6	Mean time per
	6+5	7x2	operation, all lists B
	9−5	8÷2	<u>Y sec.</u>
	↓	↓	

Set C	8+3	
	4x2	Mean time per
	4−3	operation, list C
	10÷5	<u>Z sec.</u>
	↓	

Now rank order X, Y and Z from longest to shortest time for completion. Why did you choose that order? In which set is

PROCESS ENTROPY AND COGNITIVE CONTROL

mental workload likely to be highest?

Q.2. You are confronted in a long experiment with sets made up as in a_1, a_2 and b. Which gives the lowest time of operation and why?

a_1 8+1 a_2 8-4   b   8+5
       9+4   6-4   6-2
       6-2   6-3   4+3
       5+6   7-5   9+1
       4+3   4+5   5-4
       8+3   7-4   11-3
       ↓   ↓   6-4
                                           7+4

$P_{addition} = 0.5$

$P_{addition} = 0.5$

Mean time per operation, sets a_1 and a_2 = _____

Mean time per operation, set b = _____

Q.3. Which set below gives lowest mean time per operation, and why?

a)   8+6   b)   8+6
      7-4   2+7
      2+7   9+3
      4-2   7-4
      9+3   4-2
      10-5   10-5
      ↓   ↓

Q.4. You are asked to perform the first five calculations in list a) above, holding the solutions in store to report at the end. Why should rate of work decrease?

Q.5. Write down the symbols for the four basic arithmetic operations. You are asked to operate on the following set of figures. (1) Using each arithmetic operation in turn in the sequence you reported above. (2) Using a sequence of operation selected at random by E.

8	2
9	5
6	3
4	2
7	1
↓	

At which task are you more efficient and why?

My own attempts at answers to the above would be:

Q.1. Z>Y>X. When lists are fixed in the type of computation they require, a long term processing set can be established. <u>Ease of processing should decrease as a function of the size of the set of processing alternatives.</u> If mental load is increased in C, the source of the effect is unlikely to be increased difficulty of stimulus identification or response selection (as in theories based on perceptual/motor tasks) but in the selection of different sub-routines at all points in time. Higher load would result from increased deployment of capacity to an executive or planning level which organises sequencing of operations.

Q.2. My guess is that lists a_1 and a_2, which are biased in their probabilities of the two operations, could be completed faster. The problem is whether this would be classed as a genuine expectancy effect based on assessed probability or a repetition effect based on increasingly long runs of the high probability operation. In either case <u>ease of processing should increase as function of probability bias in the set of processing alternatives.</u>

Q.3. If repetition effects are indeed at work in such situations, b < a, although $p_{addition} = p_{subtraction}$.

The above two questions reflect fairly exactly the problem of separating stimulus set (Bertelson, 1965) from response set (Rabbitt, 1968) in perceptual/motor tasks.

Q.4. Maintenance of a running store of outcomes is an activity which of itself will demand time and capacity. Here, as in question 3, the <u>load of the 'complex' task is greater than the sum of its parts</u>.

Q.5. Maintenance of an operational 'plan' based on an unfamiliar sequence of operations will demand more time and capacity than one based on the sequence entrenched in long term store. Here again the change will reflect increased involvement of executive routines necessary to organise the sequencing of operations. In the first instance the sequence demanded is <u>compatible</u> with that stored in the long term.

I believe that from consideration of these questions the following points can be made.

1) For intellectual skill both the size of the set of <u>operations</u> in use, and probability biases within that set, are determinants of mental load.

2) The source of increased load appears to lie in increased dependence on <u>operation selection</u> and scheduling activities which may take up a progressively disproportionate amount of capacity. This corresponds to increasing difficulty of stimulus identification or response selection in perceptual/motor tasks, and may be taken as simply increasing the <u>size of set</u> of operations in use.

3) <u>Process entropy</u> is reduced when stable <u>plans</u> for the sequencing of operations are in use. These are stored in the long term and serve to reduce the moment to moment demands of programming action.

On the basis of these, admittedly subjective, judgments unobservable thinking behaviour appears no less subject to the information law than is the choice reaction task or tracking behaviour. But in fact process entropy must be simply a limiting factor which determines the number of formal operations which <u>can</u> be completed in a given time. For any level of entropy output may vary from zero to the limit depending on the <u>effort</u> S brings to the task. I would contend that it is that effort investment which produces the subjective experience and physiological manifestations of mental workload. Information processing theory badly needs a concept of mental effort or concentration which can be <u>incorporated as a control process</u> into our theories of cognitions. Although recent work on effort (Kahneman, 1973), resource allocation (Norman and Bobrow, 1974) and controlled selection of optimal activation states (Hamilton & Hockey, 1977) has gone some way to broaching the subject, progress has been puzzlingly slow. The last section of this paper deals with the main principles and questions which have emerged.

EFFORT, CONCENTRATION AND COGNITIVE CONTROL

The function of effort expenditure is to increase resource allocation to those activities which constitute the organism's current goals. Consider that in the resting, mentally inactive organism all <u>potential</u> behaviours compete effectively with one another at low operational levels. The dominance of awareness by one or other of these competitors will essentially be determined randomly. When the organism is now vested with a set of <u>intentions, biases</u> will develop to and away from the various members of the competing set. For instance, if an intrusive stimulus elicits the need to 'look out' we can envisage an overall plan to 'intake sensory information' refined in a hierarchy of more detailed intentions to 'look rather than listen', 'look to the left field rather than right', 'watch for bug-size shapes' and so on. The evidence currently available indicates that effort expenditure serves to increase the competitive advantage of activities within the intended set over all others. Perhaps the most suggestive evidence that this restriction of the attentional field involves cost to the organism rather than passive filtering out of irrelevant ideas is physiological. Catecholamine outputs are commonly found to be higher after prolonged mental processing than after rest (Frankenhauser and Johansson, 1976), and there are readily observable autonomic indicators (such as pupil dilation and heart rate) of changed physiological function at the onset of mental activity. Hamilton & Hockey (1977) have argued that these changes in 'activation state' have <u>vector</u> or directional properties rather than simple scalar ones, for the patterns of autonomic activity observed vary as a function of the type of processing to be engaged in (Lacey, 1967). Shifts in activation pattern to optimise processing in alternative modes (sensing, transforming, responding) are seen as basic elements of the control mechanism.

The outcome of physiological response to increases or decreases in information loading is fairly directly indicated by experiments on attentional sampling. Hamilton (1969) found that when the information load of a multi-source monitoring task increased the pattern of attention became more strongly biased in favour of high <u>priority</u> (value x probability) stimulus elements in the monitored set. The reverse occurred when information load was reduced. By the same token Kahneman (1973) has argued that effort expenditure results in a reduction of competition between extra-task activities and task related activities - an increase in 'task set'.

The effort response may then be deployed as a gain control to increase the discrepancy between activity levels of systems relevant to ongoing activity and those which are not - a trigger for <u>actions</u> demanded by the nature of current intentions. A pictorial account of these notions is shown in Figure 2.

THE RELATIONSHIP BETWEEN PROCESS ENTROPY AND EFFORT

In 'simple' tasks, such as continuous addition, the set of alternative mental operations is small, and the discrepancy between intended and extra-task activity patterns (a sort of activity/ noise ratio) likely to be large. On the other hand where the set of required operations is large, bias toward each individual operation will be lower and competition from extra task elements

PROCESS ENTROPY AND COGNITIVE CONTROL

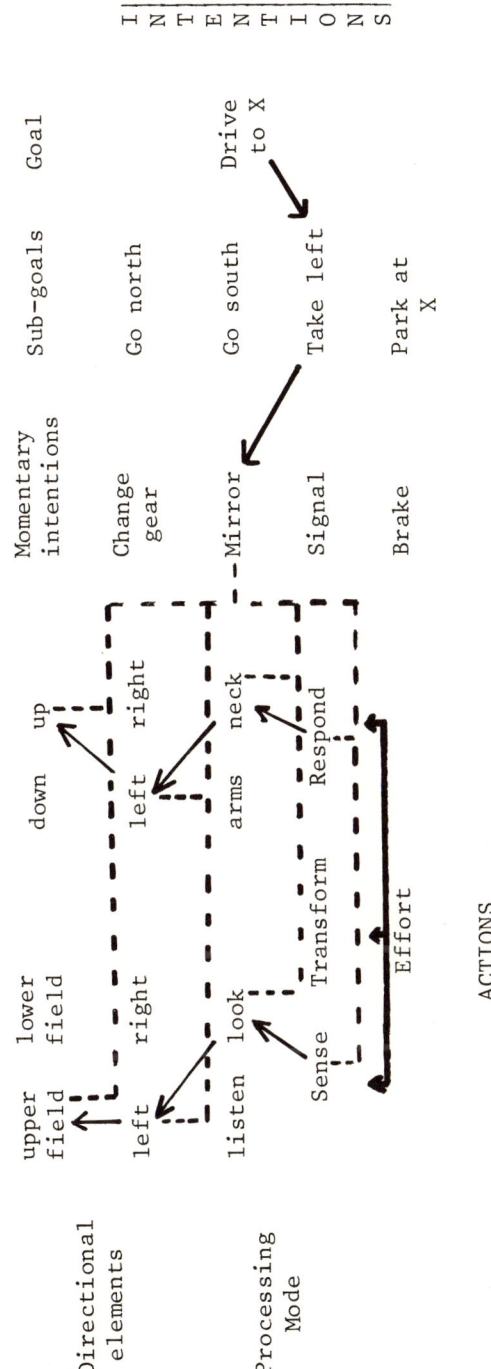

Fig.2. An interactive scheme for intention and action hierarchies. Current intention is to check mirror, and the action elements thus biassed are depicted by broken lines. The arrow tracks define a possible intention or action within the available set. (Note that revision of intentions itself would be in the set of possible actions, thus closing a loop between the two hierarchies.) Process entropy is a function of the number of elements in competition. When competition is strong (e.g. with heavy driving demands) the effort response can be brought to bear to increase differentials between marginally favoured elements and others.

correspondingly greater. Welford (1968) uses exactly this concept of 'energy-sharing' in his discussion of choice reaction time. For the simple case then,

1) the gains to be achieved by prolonged effort expenditure may not be great in terms of increased processing rate;

2) the proportion of time taken up by purely computational as opposed to 'administrative' work like looking and writing is anyway small, rendering the gain for effort even more insignificant.

Such tasks in the terminology of Norman and Bobrow (1975) are <u>data-limited</u> and respond little or not at all to increased resource allocation. In normal conditions the subjective impression is one of continuous work rather than of heavy workload.

For the complex case,

1) expenditure of effort will serve to increase the weak differential between competing operations or ideas, so the speed and coherence of mental function is likely to improve;

2) the proportion of time taken up by purely computational work is relatively high, and gains for effort are more likely to be significant.

In the terminology of Norman and Bobrow tasks of this type are resource-limited and respond favourably to increased effort expenditure.

CONCLUSION

While acknowledging the extreme imprecision of this formulation I feel it has the twin merits of incorporating into our discussion of mental workload:-

1) The contention that internalised thought as well as the stock perceptual/motor skills experiment must be made the province of the workload theorist.

2) Some overdue acknowledgement of the role of effort, or intensive processes, in a field which has had for too long as its goal the portrayal of man as computer.

REFERENCES

Bertelson, P. Serial choice reaction time as a function of response versus signal-and-response repetition. <u>Nature</u>, 1965, 206, 217-218.

Frankenhauser, M. and Johansson, G. Task demand as reflected in catecholamine excretion and heart rate. <u>Journal of Human Stress</u>, 1976.

Hamilton, P., Hockey, G.R.J. and Rejman, M. The place of the concept of activation in human information processing theory: an integrative approach. <u>Attention and Performance IV</u> (in press).

Kahneman, D. <u>Attention and Effort</u>. Englewood Cliffs, N.J., Prentice-Hall, 1973.

Lacey, J.I. Somatic response patterning and stress: Some revisions of activation theory. In M.H. Appley and R. Trumbull (Eds.) <u>Psychological Stress</u>. New York, Appleton-Century-Crofts, 1967.

Norman, D.A. & Bobrow, D.G. On data limited and resource limited processes. <u>Cognitive Psychology</u>, 1975, 7, 44-64.

Rabbitt, P.M.A. Response facilitation on repetition of a limb movement. <u>British Journal of Psychology</u>, 1965, 56, 303-304.

Welford, A.T. <u>Fundamentals of Skill</u>. Methuen, 1968.

MENTAL LOAD, MENTAL EFFORT AND ATTENTION

G. Mulder

Institute of Experimental Psychology

University of Groningen, Netherlands

Many of the concepts introduced into the research on mental load seem to have developed by analogy with those already available in the field of physical workload.

An important limiting factor in physical work is the maximum intake of oxygen, (VO_2). A certain physical activity demands a certain amount of oxygen cost per minute. If the maximum intake of oxygen is smaller than the amount of oxygen cost demanded by the activity, this activity is beyond the physiological capabilities of that individual. There are at least three contributing factors in high level performance during severe exertion: (1) ability to reach high VO_2; (2) ability to reach a high oxygen debt; (3) ability to perform a task with the lowest possible oxygen cost of energy requirement, or with the greatest mechanical efficiency. Post exercise VO_2 above the basal oxygen consumption is defined as the oxygen debt and its time course is also indicated as the recovery volume. Efficiency may be altered to a certain extent by training and practice, e.g. economy of effort may be developed with training. Tasks may differ in the amount of working capacity they use. In the basal state the VO_2 is about 0.250 litre per minute; moderate industrial tasks involve a threefold increase, and heavy work and athletic activity may demand an eight fold or higher increase.

In the field of mental workload similar concepts may be applied. A very general conception is that the more difficult the task is, the more complex the mental operations are, the more processing capacity is used, the larger the change in physiological system variables are, and consequently the larger the mental workload is. A number of investigators then concentrate upon the mental <u>operations</u> and strategies the operator uses in carrying out his task. The efficiency of the mental operations are thought to be of special importance. A related approach conceives the human operator as an information processing system with a limited capacity, i.e. he is limited in the amount of information he can handle at any one time. Mental tasks may differ in the amount of processing (or working) capacity to be devoted to the task.

Physiologically oriented workers conceive mental work as a kind of stressor acting upon the organism. A distinction is made between stress and strain. Stress refers to the external forces acting upon a system and strain to the costs it has to pay, in order to resist applied stress forces. A number of non-specific indices may indicate that the organism is stressed. According to Selye's theory (Selye, 1950), the adrenocortical response is a very general one, common to all stressors. Adrenocortical activation has become the operational definition of stress in physiologically oriented stress research. Earlier work of Cannon (1929) concentrated more upon the sympathetic-adrenal-medullary system. The interest in this system has revived in the last twenty years (for a review see Frankenhauser, 1975). Electrophysiological indices are also used and interpreted in the framework of the general activation or arousal theory (for recent reviews, see Lindsley, 1970; Duffy, 1973; and Kahneman, 1973).

We will review these different approaches successively and concentrate upon those elements which indicate the mode of information processing the organism uses.

MEASURING WORKING CAPACITY: THE USE OF SECONDARY TASKS

The basic idea of a secondary task is that it measures the difference between the "mental capacity" consumed by the main task, and the total available capacity. The model used in this type of approach is depicted in figure 1, and based upon Michon, (1966), Brown, (1964, 1966).

This model assumes a total channel capacity. The difference between the capacity of the operator and the load imposed by some task is called reserve capacity. The total channel capacity is not constant, but varies with the state of arousal of the operator. From Fig.1, it is clear that there is no difference between task MT_1 and MT_2 at the performance level (e.g. errorless performance), but in the case of task MT_1 there is less reserve or spare capacity left.

So, as Knowles (1963) has argued, performance measures in and of themselves seldom reflect mental load. They usually tell

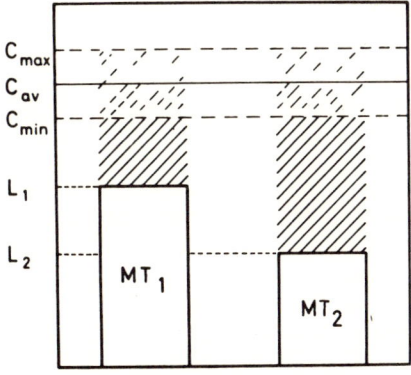

Figure 1

how well some functional system criterion is met, but seldom tell the price (or costs or effort) paid in operator effort in meeting this criterion. The more effort (i.e. processing capacity) he expends in the task the less capacity remains available for other tasks or circumstances which demand attention. According to this view mental load can simply be defined as (1 - spare capacity).

An important issue is to find suitable secondary tasks. Brown (1966) presented his subjects during car driving with successive series of eight digits, where one digit was altered on each repetition. The subjects had to identify the alteration. Brown was able to discriminate between trainees who passed the course and who did not on measures of reserve capacity. However objective measures of driving performance did not separate the groups. Brown and Poulton (1961) found that in residential areas with light traffic subjects had more spare capacity left to deal with a secondary task than in shopping areas with heavy traffic.

Michon (1966) required subjects to tap in a regular rhythm during performance on primary tasks. His results indicated an increased tapping irregularity as the perceptual motor load of the tasks increased. The procedure consisted in making the subjects produce a self-paced tapping response, as regularly as possible. Prior to the experiment the subjects were trained to a stationary basic tapping level (BTL). A score was developed to express the regularity, based upon the sum of the absolute values of the relative differences between successive intervals. In a recent study Johannsen et al. (1976) used the method in simulated landing approaches with autopilot failures. As a measure of tapping irregularity the mean difference between successive time intervals, relative to the mean tapping interval was used. The perceptual-motorload (PML) was evaluated according to the following equation:

$$PML = \frac{LTL - BTL}{BTL} \times 100\%,$$

where BTL is the basic tapping level and LTL is the loaded tapping level.

There were three modes of control in the simulated landing approaches; (1) automatic, (2) semiautomatic, and (3) manual control. Johannsen et al. were able to discriminate between 1 and 3 and 1 and 2. There was also an increased workload (as indicated by PML-measures) immediately after failure detection when manual control became necessary.

Michon (1966) devised also a method to detect momentary peaks in perceptual-motorload. Subjects had to listen to position reports of a number of ships and had to plot these positions on a map. The reports were made at intervals of exactly 11 sec. and could be varied with respect to the number of ships (0-4) and the positions (consisting of two-figure numbers or "unchanged"). It was anticipated that the difficulty of the task depended upon the number of "ships" involved and the complexity of the changed/ unchanged pattern. Both were indeed reflected in the on line records of PML. Deviations from the normally highly predictable paths (sharp turns) frequently lead to a marked increase in PML-score. These results are an important cue to the conditions under which timesharing between tasks is diminished. The more unpredictable moments the primary task has, the higher the perceptual-motorload of the task will become. Or as Michon remarks: a ship executing Brownian movements will impose an excessive burden on a subject.

Bahrick et al (1954) used a primary task which was either repetitive or random. The secondary task was an arithmetical subtraction task. Subjects were either trained on the repetitive or the random version of the motor task. Performance on the secondary task did not discriminate the two groups early in practice, but later in practice the arithmetic scores were superior for the repetitive case. In a later experiment Bahrick and Shelly (1958) used tasks differing in the degree of redundancy. It was anticipated that the more redundant the repetitive task was, the better it could be timeshared with a secondary task. It was found that the decrement of performance on the secondary task was largest in the case of timesharing with the random version of the task, but progressively reduced the more redundant the primary task became. Pew (1974) reached a comparable conclusion. In a study of performance of repeated and non-repeated sequences in a tracking task, he found that the addition of a simple memory task produced an approximately equal increase in error score for the repeated and non-repeated segments at three different points during a 16-hour period of practice, even though performance on the repeated segment was as much as 28% better than its random counterpart.

In a recent review article Broadbent (1977) argues for the existence of different levels of control and cites evidence from experiments carried out during the first decade after World War 2. He summarizes the conclusions from this research on skill acquisition as follows:

"These studies showed that the response to one event in the task would take place at the same time as the intake of information about the next event in the task; they showed that response to a <u>predictable</u> series of events could develop into an autonomous motor programme which would be carried out independently while another task was being performed. In this respect there was a distinction between two extreme types of task, which Poulton termed "Closed" and "Open". The Closed task required no check with the environment, but merely a series of movements; the completely Open task required an <u>unpredictable</u> sequence of actions to an <u>unpredictable</u> series of happenings in the outside world. Two Open tasks were very difficult to carry out simultaneously, at least if the timing of the signals in the two tasks was inconvenient; two Closed tasks were easy."

The acquisition of a skill then seems to imply that at least some components of a task change from Open to Closed. In modern theories on motor skills (Pew, 1974 ; Schmidt, 1975, 1976; Stelmach, 1976) stages of skill acquisition are distinguished. In the "cognitive" or "verbal" stage the subject must rely upon knowledge of results and external feedback; in the "automatic" stage the subject has developed a schema specifying the movement characteristics and an internal representation of its correctness and consequently can rely upon internal feedback. In the verbal stage task performance is attention demanding, or capacity limited; in the automatic stage more spare capacity is left: the task has become a "Closed" one, hence time sharing with a secondary task is possible. In the random version of Bahrick's task the subject cannot construct a schema or motor programme and has to remain in the cognitive or "Open" stage of task acquisition.

The above-mentioned facts suggest that measures of reserve capacity largely depend upon the organizational structure of information processing underlying task performance. Nevertheless the use of secondary tasks has been criticized on several grounds.

1. It is important to distinguish between two research strategies in using secondary tasks. If the subject is instructed to aim for error-free performance on the secondary task at the expense of the primary task, the secondary task is called a loading task. In that case the subject considers the primary task

to be a secondary task and performance on the secondary task is not any more a reliable index of spare capacity. Furthermore, in many studies the secondary task interferes with performance on the primary task, and in order to evaluate this effect one needs a measure of both primary and secondary task performance level when performed separately. In a number of studies the interference effects have not been controlled for or even reported.

Interference effects can also be more subtle: the strategy in carrying out the tasks might have changed. The human operator can use alternative methods for doing a task and these may differ in the amount of work needed to give equivalent task achievement. With increasing levels of task demands each component task can be done using a strategy which is more economical in terms of mental work, so that the total task demand (of both primary and secondary task) is still within the operator's mental work capacity (Bainbridge, 1974). Changes in strategy may also affect the speed/accuracy trade-off with which the primary task is performed.

2. Interference with the performance of the secondary task may be caused by structural interference rather than by capacity interference. If the interference is structural the real limitations are within the perceptual or response system. For instance: one can only look at one location at a time and other locations have to be scanned afterwards; the difficulty we have talking while we eat is primarily due to the incompatible movements of the mouth and tongue which these activities entail. Because structural interference can masquerade attentional limitations, it should be minimized when choosing a secondary task (Kahneman, 1973; Klein, 1976). This issue raises the question about the locus of limitation in information processing. Some theorists maintain that the system is limited in initiating or selecting motor outputs, (Keele, 1973). This basic limitation only suggests the existence of a limited processing capacity, because most tasks (primary and secondary) may interfere at the response selection stage. This problem touches the whole concept of channel capacity.

Channel capacity is usually expressed in bits/sec, (Attneave, 1959). In order to apply this theory both task demands (input), and performance (output) have to be expressed in bits/sec. Though sometimes difficult it has been done for a variety of tasks, but the estimates of human channel capacity were too inconsistent to be useful (Neisser, 1967; Kahneman, 1973). This is unfortunate because measures derived from information theory could provide a common unit to compare different task. However, these difficulties should not tempt us to reject the concept altogether. Changes in channel capacity may reflect

changes in the mode of information processing. Later we will
discuss a theory which assumes that only some mental operations
use a capacity-limited part of the human information processing
system. This implies that the type of mental operations underlying task performance must be specified and capacity measures
are only _relative_ to the type of operations involved.

3. The use of secondary tasks, often acting as loading tasks,
can be unacceptable in practical situations because they make
these situations potentially hazardous.

We conclude this section with some general remarks. The use
of secondary tasks in assessing the amount of spare capacity can
be of great practical importance. However, there have been too
few attempts to validate the technique, especially outside
laboratory situations (Rolfe, 1971). We must abandon the idea
that we can measure the _amount_ of spare capacity. Only the
possibility and the _degree_ of timesharing a primary task with a
secondary task is of importance, because this may be an indication
of the level of control the primary task demands.

It must be realized that improvement or degradation of
performance on the secondary task in itself does not provide
information about the kind of mental mechanisms used in the
primary task, but only that the processes involved became less or
more capacity-limited.

MENTAL STRATEGIES

Mental strategies or operations can in general be conceived
as processes according to which information is transformed,
reduced, elaborated, stored or retrieved. More precisely it is
possible to distinguish between classes of mental operations,
which we call from now on control processes (Shiffrin, 1976):
(a) those designed to _locate_ information in short term store
(short term memory search or scanning); (b) those designed to
maintain information in short term store (mainly rehearsal);
(c) those designed to _retrieve_ information from long term store;
(d) those designed to _make decisions_ based on the task
requirements and to call _operating_ programmes from long term
store and monitor their use.

The human operator seems to use an internal model or
representation of some of the functional properties of the system
he has to control. This internal representation is probably
derived from prior experience with the system, explicit knowledge
of its internal economy and of its functioning, or from prescribed
rules and instructions (Rasmussen, 1976).

The type of representation he has may determine the type of operations he uses. This latter aspect is of extreme importance. In some cases the subject uses a symbolic representation of the task and the task environment. In that case the control operations described above are relevant. These operations all occur in short term memory and the content of this system is probably identical with consciousness (Shiffrin, 1976; Mandler, 1976).

There are two methods to reveal the type of control processes the subject uses; the observation method, and the analysis of verbal protocols.

The observation method makes use of checklists, films, tape recordings as aids in the analysis of the pattern of activity shown by the operator. A major drawback of the method is that the technique relies upon <u>observable</u> behavior, so its application is less suitable for situations where covert behavior is the predominant feature of the operator's task. This is essentially a characteristic of mental work: not every internal operation will be visible externally. Furthermore, especially in multi-operator situations the load may be more on the observer, rather than on the observed (Rolfe, 1976).

The analysis of verbal protocols also has severe limitations. Broadbent (1977) examined the performance of a number of teams controlling a computer model of the British economy. He reports two main findings:

1. The experience of controlling the model had very little effect upon the answers to simple questions about the separate functions forming part of the economic system.

2. After experience of interaction with the system there was a dissociation between the verbal statements and the ability to control.

Broadbent (op.cit.) replicated these findings in another experiment, in which the subjects were asked to control the transport in a city. Again, it was clear that people could attain a satisfactory performance without being able to answer questions about the system. The ability to control the task bears little connection with the ability to answer verbal questions about it (Broadbent op.cit., pp. 194).

The use of words and other symbols in decision making has encouraged the idea that such decisions are taken merely by familiar logical processes, or, if they are not, then they should be. Broadbent's insights could perhaps be reformulated in the following way: the <u>possibility</u> of verbalizing the internal operations is only a possible indication of the mode of information processing used in controlling the task. A dissociation between the verbal protocols and the actual performance or even the inability to verbalize about it, indicates a change in the level of control. This change is possibly accompanied by a change in the nature of the internal representation.

As Mandler (1976) has recently stated: "There are many systems that cannot be brought into consciousness, and probably most systems that analyse the environment in the first place have that characteristic. In most of the cases, only the products of cognitive and mental activities are available to consciousness". (Emphasis by present author.)

Rasmussen (1976) also concluded that the verbal protocols of the operators reveal little about the psychological processes involved. What is reported is a sequence of statements indicating the operator's state of knowledge. Only in unusual and unfamiliar situations do the protocols contain more details. Furthermore, the behavior of the operators was characterized by little planning, but the operators seem to know what is going on and where attention has to be focussed.

Rasmussen attributes these features of his protocols to two fundamentally different modes of information processing in the operators, differing in the degree in which the processes are capacity-limited, in the kind of internal representations used and the serialness of information processing. Broadbent (1977) argues that there must be different levels of control. The general model he proposes is an adaptive controller, in which an open chain can be modified in its transmission characteristics by another operating on feedback. The upper level is concerned with modifiability and response to novel or unfamiliar situations, rather than with the transmission of information according to an unchanging code or an habitual sequence of actions, the latter being the concern of the lower level. The lower level, however, can function independently of the upper level.

MEASURING STRAIN: THE USE OF PHYSIOLOGICAL MEASURES

The use of physiological indices rests on the assumption that it is possible to assess the amount of effort expended by the operator in meeting the demands of the task. Changes in the activation level of the subject will ensue and these can be measured. In recent literature on these topics, arousal, activation, effort etc. are used interchangeably. We will first try to limit the use of each of these terms.

We propose the concept of state instead of level of activation. State refers to the actual values of physiological system variables which can be or are being measured. Some theorists (e.g. Duffy, 1973; Lindsley, 1970) adhere to a kind of unidimensional state concept, i.e. an organism can be at some level of a single dimension ranging from low to high (activation). Duffy (1973) considers these different level values to be representative of the intensity dimension of behavior. Intensity refers to the release of energy into various physiological systems, in preparation for overt activity. The other dimension she distinguishes is the direction of behavior, or what later will be called the selective component of attention.

Another view is exemplified in the work of Prechtl (1974). He defines states as "finite and discrete vectors representing distinct and qualitative different conditions, each of them considered as different modes of nervous activity." Hamilton (1977) expresses a closely related view. According to him one may conceive of the organism at any moment as being in one of many possible "activation states" representing points in a multi-dimensional space. So there are different patterns of physiological activity, and these are supposed to be associated with different types of cognitive function. Each cognitive activity requires a specific pattern of physiological activity. However, sometimes the actual physiological state may be quite different from the required one. We will first make some remarks on the idea of required states and afterwards deal with the effects of differences between required and actual state.

At present there is not enough evidence to say that different states accompany different cognitive activities. Hamilton (1977) himself mentions only two patterns: in tasks involving acceptance of environment input heartrate typically decelerates while pupil diameter increases. Where information is being transformed or output heartrate accelerates, though pupil diameter still shows an increase. The relation of cognitive activity to state is an active field in psychophysiology and hopefully soon more results will become available. Until now we are only able to distinguish between two patterns: (a) The orientation reaction (OR), and (b) The defensive reaction (DR).

The OR is defined by Pavlov as "the reflex which brings out the immediate response in man and animals to the slightest change in the world around them so that they immediately orient their appropriate receptor organ in accordance with the perceptible quality of this agent bringing about change, making full investigation of it". A number of physiological reactions characterize the OR: there is a desynchronization or α-block in the EEG, widely throughout the cortex and prolonged and a brief one limited to the specific brain area; a decrease in basal skin resistance; a heartrate deceleration; a contraction of the blood vessels of the finger and a dilation of the cephalic vessels.

With regard to the heartrate response, there are some controversies in the literature. According to Gruzelier (1975) there is an increasing consensus that the response is multiphasic with typically three components:

(1) A decelerative component with a latency of less than 1 sec;
(2) An accelerative response with a latency of 1-2 sec;
(3) A long latency decelerative response.

Coupled closely to the notion of the OR is its habituation: if the orienting stimulus is repeated the OR to it gradually declines. The important stimulus characteristics evoking the OR then are: the absolute or relative novelty of the stimulus, changes in the stimulus, the intensity and significance of the stimulus (when a motor response is required to a stimulus which has ceased to evoke an OR, the OR returns and is more stable than when no discrimination is required). It is supposed that the OR is an indication of the registration of a stimulus, giving rise to a "neuronal model". Repeated registration completes the formation of the neuronal model so that there is a decreasing mismatch between the internal representation of the external stimulus and the internal representation (or neuronal model) in memory, and the decreasing error signal results in decreased orientation. The frontal cortex and the amygdala are according to Pribram (1967, 1975) of crucial importance for this long term learning. It seems that the "neuronal" model is an analogue representation of the environment, and can easily be described in terms of Broadbent's (1977) adaptive controller. One of the features of this controller is that if exposed to a situation repeatedly, it will react more rapidly and efficiently.

Pribram and McGuiness call the above described phasic input-related pattern of physiological activity arousal. Kahneman (1973) draws attention to the fact that the OR also involves inhibition of ongoing activity, probably reflected in the second decelerative component of the heartrate response.

The defensive reaction (DR) is generally characterized by an increased release of epinephrine and norepinephrine from the adrenal medulla; increasing heartrate (acceleration); increasing arterial blood pressure; increasing blood glucose and bloodflow through the muscles (vasodilation) and peripheral vasoconstriction.

The central control of this emergency mode, preparing the organism for flight, or fight, seems to concentrate on the posterior hypothalamic region. Under normal circumstances a rise in blood pressure is counteracted by the baroreceptor reflex. But during stimulation of this area there is an inhibitory action on the baroreflex bradycardia. At the same time there is an increased cardiac output because of the suppressed reflex bradycardia, allowing an unimpeded cardiac sympathetic drive. This same reaction pattern has been elicited by Brod (1972), forcing subjects to perform accurate mental arithmetic in time with the beat of a metronome. Also an increased isometric contraction, which is largely anaerobic (Berdina et al, 1972) has been noticed. This output-related pattern of electrophysiological activity is called 'activation' by Pribram and McGuiness (1975). They include also the process of motor inhibition, due to a decrease in isotonic contraction, as was mentioned above as a component of the OR.

The patterns here described are almost exclusively defined by electrophysiological measures and interpreted in a certain kind of uni- or multidimensional state theory. Other researchers however use chemical measures (urine or blood composition of hormones, electrolytes etc.) and interpret their results in the framework of a general stress theory. These types of measurement complement each other.

Selye (1950) described four stages in the General Adaptation Syndrome, e.g. the syndrome by which the stress state is made manifest. The following stages were mentioned:

A. The alarm stage;
B. The adjustment stage;
C. The resistance stage;
D. The exhaustion stage.

The alarm and adjustment stage are almost identical to the OR and DR pattern just mentioned. The organism enters the resistance stage if the stressor is prolonged. The adrenal medulla secretes epinephrine and norepinephrine and the adrenal cortex starts to secrete a number of hormones, called corticoids. These hormones both facilitate some of the emergency processes and initiate a series of incompletely defined restorative processes. Especially cortisol seems to be important in determining the capacity of cells to produce energy anerobically. During this stage psychosomatic disturbances may arise. Brod (1972) maintains that the disease called arterial hypertension is predicated upon transient periods of increasing sympathetic activity. He supposes that hypothalamic systems force a new equilibrium among circulatory parameters, such as the baroreceptor set point. The enhanced activity during the resistance stage may involve the utilisation of vital material faster than they can be produced by the body. The supply of the materials is exhausted and the adaptation can no longer be sustained (exhaustion stage).

The first two stages occur during most laboratory tasks, lasting no longer than 10 minutes. They can best be described by electrophysiological measures, because the interest is mainly in fast changes in the measured parameters. A very important measure is the time course of recovery, e.g. the time needed for the parameters to reach their initial, pre-stress basal values. Tasks may differ in their recovery-time as do individuals.

In a recent literature review Mason (1976) mentioned the important determinants of the pituitary-adrenal-cortical and medullary system. These determinants are: novelty, uncertainty, unpredictability, the anticipation of unpleasant events, strong involvement and the sudden change of long established rules. Not in all circumstances do the actual and the required state match. Caille (1976) reviews evidence about the operator's state and his behavioral efficiency (Fig.2). If the operator is optimally alert, the actual state and the required state match. If on the contrary, the operator is hyperalert his behavior is characterized by high selectivity and a high probability of false alarms and if hypoalert he is less selective and misses signals. State variables characterize these differences in behavioral efficiency: hyperalertness tends to be accompanied by a fast (18 to 30Hz) low amplitude cortical EEG, with an increased coherence between different derivatives, a slightly increased heartrate and a diminished heartrate variability (sinus arrhythmia). Hypoalertness tends to be accompanied by a slower and higher amplitude cortical EEG, with more α (8 to 13 Hz), a decreased coherence between the derivates, slower heartrate and an increased sinus arrhythmia.

It is clear that the precision with which these different states and their transitions can be distinguished is not great. What is a slight tachycardia, or an increased coherence? etc. Are the moments of transition the same for the different subsystems?

Both Naatanen (1973) and Duffy (1973) warn against a deterministic use of electrophysiological criteria. Duffy (1973) remarks: "studies attempting to induce high degrees of tension have often shown an inverted U with regard to performance, but, as has been pointed out, it is often difficult to tell whether the performance inversion observed at the upper extremes of tension was due to induced activation or induced distraction". So the right side of the inverted U-shaped curve may reflect the attempts of an organism to transmit a large amount of information, but this may be task irrelevant information. If the balance between task relevant versus task irrelevant information is changed in the direction of the latter behavioral efficiency

C.E.R.P.A. Toulon 1973
Efficiency as a function
of vigilance level

Stages	Hyper vigilance	Optimal level	Hypovigilance
I. ELECTROPHYSIOLOGICAL CRITERIA			
(1) E.E.G. general aspect	Desynchronized	normal	synchronized
dominant frequency (in c/m)	2 (18-30)	1 (15-20)	
mobility and complexity (M and C)	eventual θ rhythms M> C>	small α	slower and higher α M< C<
amplitude (in μV)	10-20	20-40	50-70
activity (A)^2 in μV^2	A<		A>
power spectral density in μV^2/8	<	average	>
Coherence (0 1)			
(2) E.C.G. (frequency rhythm)	slight tachycardia sinusal arrhythmia decreased	normal	bradycardia sinusal arrhythmia increases
(3) R.R. (Respiratory rhythm)	Quick small amplitude	regular	Low, more regular
(4) E.O.G. (amplitude rhythm)	increases accelerated	normal	decreases generally accelerated
(5) E.M.G. (amplitude)	Lesser	normal	Larger
II. PSYCHOPHYSIOLOGICAL CRITERIA			
Sensorial afferencies	filtered	optimal regulation	defective filtering
Perceptive area	focalized	well adjusted	'lapses'
consequences in detection	'false alarms'	possibility of anticipation and subception	free associations; omissions
Psychomotricity			
mean reaction time (m)	shorter	normal	longer variability
standard deviation ( )	increases		increases instability
III. PSYCHOLOGICAL CHARACTERISTICS OF OPERATOR	Tension irritability	optimal alertness attentiveness	relaxed wandering attention

Figure 2

may be expected to become progressively reduced.

Recently Vernon Hamilton (1975) tried to develop a theory to explain why emotional reactions change behavioral efficiency. He states that theories attempting to explain stress and anxiety on the basis of cognitive processes do not explain why the range of relevant cues is narrowed, e.g. why increased selectivity is often reported in high emotional states. He defines anxiety as cognitive data which a central recognizing or appraisal process has coded as requiring avoidance, as indicating physical danger, or loss of affection in social settings. When evoked from long term memory these data may be irrelevantly channelled to different stages of an information processing system, where they would

compete for space and time with external task relevant stimuli.
Interactions between relevant and irrelevant information and the
spare capacity of the system will determine simplifying strategies
and consequently performance decrement.

This view has important consequences for the use of psychophysiological measures of mental effort, because it suggests that
we may be unable to distinguish on the psychophysiological level
between the processing of task relevant or task irrelevant
information. This can only be done at the behavioral level.

The extensive overlap between the ascending reticular
activating system responsible of cortical desynchronization with
central nervous system structures involved in emotion is well
known (see Lindsley, 1970). McGuiness (1973) showed that subjects
with a high level of anxiety habituated more slowly than subjects
with low levels of anxiety. This all suggests that people with
high anxiety have difficulties in constructing an internal
representation of their environment and especially of the task
irrelevant aspects of it. Consequently they process task
irrelevant information longer than people with low anxiety and
can easily be overloaded.

To summarize, electrophysiological changes accompany the
different modes of information processing called into action if
an internal representation of the environment no longer matches
reality. This change in state is characterized by the occurrence
of the orientation reaction followed by a defensive reaction and
is labelled "effort" by Pribram and McGuiness (1975). The central
control of this state transition seems to be concentrated in the
hippocampus, because interference with its function "reduces the
organism to a state in which the effort demanding relationships
between perception and action .... are relinquished for more
primitive relationships in which input or output captures an
aspect of the behavior of the organism without the coordinating
intervention of central control operations". (Pribram and
McGuiness, 1975). The type of information processing which occurs
in that case will be called automatic. Environmental, subjective
and other factors can induce an actual state differing from the
required one. Behavioral evidence may indicate that this state
arises from attempts of the organism to process information not
directly related to the task at hand.

ATTENTION AND INFORMATION PROCESSING

Let us now try to relate the findings reported above to
theories and findings in the field of information processing and
especially in research on selective attention. No attempt will
be made to deal with these theories and findings exhaustively.

Recently a number of literature reviews became available: Moray, 1969, 1976; Kahneman, 1973; Shiffrin and Schneider, 1977; Pribram and McGuiness, 1975; Posner, 1975). We concentrate on some central issues and we will treat them by using Posner's important distinction between Alertness, Selectivity, and Processing Capacity.

Alertness refers to those conditions that change the behavioral efficiency of the subject. A special feature of research around alertness is the use of state concomittants. Selectivity means that only a part of the input information is used for processing, rehearsing, coding etc., and it is necessary because of the limited information processing capacity the organism has at its disposal. However, under certain circumstances the limited information processing system can be bypassed, and in such cases there will be no selective attention deficits.

THE PHASIC ALERTNESS PARADIGM

In many experimental paradigms in research on human information, the subject has to react as fast as possible to an imperative signal (S), which is sometimes preceded by a warning signal (WS). The reaction time (RT) is measured. The RT is the amount of time that elapses between the onset of the imperative signal (S) and the onset of movement (response) to the signal. The movement time of the response is excluded, as far as possible. The reaction time is supposed to reflect the time a number of psychological processes consume after the imperative signal is presented and has to be processed.

In principle there are 3 experimental possibilities (Donders, 1869). In the case of simple reaction time experiments the subject has only to detect a stimulus and execute the appropriate response. So there is mostly one signal and only one possible response (an a-reaction).

In case of choice reaction time trials there is more than one signal and also more responses. So the subject must not only detect the presence of the signal, but has to identify it and select a response (a b-reaction). For example, there may be two responses, the "yes" and the "no" response.

Before the reaction time trial a number of stimuli are presented and the subject has to memorize them. Afterwards a test item (S) is presented and the subject has to respond "yes" or "no" according to whether the test item was a member of the memory set. The last possibility is almost identical with the preceding ones but the subject reacts in the case of a "yes" or a "no" reaction and withholds a reaction otherwise (a c-reaction). In that case the subject has according to Donders only to detect and identify the stimulus, but there was no response selection involved in the task. The imperative signal (S) may be preceded by a warning signal (WS). The time interval between both is called the foreperiod and induces a certain time uncertainty (TU) in the subject. If the foreperiod is fixed and about 500 msec, the subject reacts faster to the imperative signal but at the cost of making more errors. There is a difference if an auditory or visual warning signal is used. In some cases an auditory WS induces these above mentioned effects so strongly that changes in the foreperiod duration do not contribute anything anymore. This occurs only in the case of a- and c-reactions. If a choice reaction is overlearned (or very "compatible") there is no effect of time uncertainty. In the case of difficult choice reactions with little practice the effects of signal modality and foreperiod contribute independently to the duration of RT. (see for a recent review Posner et al., 1976; Sanders, 1977).

How can the above experiments be related to the physiological models?

Posner (1975) interprets these results as follows: phasic alertness (induced by a warning signal), induces a shift in the criterion of responding to S. In some models attempting to explain reaction time data it is assumed that evidence about each response alternative is aggregated with other information already obtained. A decision to respond occurs if the evidence has reached a critical value or criterion. The higher this value the more evidence has to be gathered. Low critical values lead to fast reaction times and high error rates. The WS then causes the subject to respond sooner to the information building up in his memory.

The WS may be also informative with regard to S. For instance the WS is the letter A and the S is also the letter A. The subject has to react with a "same" or "different" response. The WS may facilitate the information processing of S (Posner, 1975, speaks about "pathway facilitation".). These effects suggest that phasic alertness does not influence the build-up of information in memory. Posner (1976) further assumes that visual signals have less capability of automatic alerting than auditory signals have.

An automatic alerting effect occurs when the central decision making mechanism is activated without attention being directed to the warning signal. Effortful alerting effects require the subject to turn his attention to the processing of the warning signal. Alerting improves the speed of processing of all items that might be presented to the organism. The bias to visual information compensates the low automatic alerting effects of visual information.

To summarize then: a WS causes a central decision mechanism to react faster to the accumulated information. This effect does only occur if the central mechanism is necessary in order to carry out the task. If a task is automatized or very easy phasic alertness either does not influence task performance, or to a lesser degree. A WS then creates temporarily a hyperalertness in the subject, inducing a decreased behavioral efficiency which is detrimental, especially for controlled information processing.

Consider now the difference between controlled and automatic information processing.

A number of physiological changes have been noticed in the interval between WS and S. With regard to the EEG there is the well-known Contingent Negative Variation (CNV), a slow negative potential. Recent research (Loveless and Sanford, 1974 ; Gaillard, 1976, 1977) have shown that the CNV is not a unitary phenomenon, but consists of two different potentials: the so-called O-wave (Loveless and Sanford) or early CNV (Gaillard, 1978) and the E-wave (Loveless and Sanford) or the late CNV (Gaillard, 1978). The O-wave is thought to be a cortical representation of the orientation reaction and is sensitive to differences in modality of WS; the E-wave is thought to be almost identical with the Readiness Potential (Deecke et al., 1976) and is sensitive to accuracy instructions to the subject (Gaillard, 1977); while Deecke et al. (1976) discovered a number of motor potentials representing different processes involved in the selection and initiation of a motor act (see also Mulder et al., 1978).

The P-300 component of the evoked potential on the imperative stimulus is considered to be a decision related potential reflecting especially the more complex and elaborate aspects of information processing. Posner (1975) relates this potential to the conscious controlled mode of information processing and suggests that future research on this potential has to specify the consequences for information processing when the brain system indexed by P-300 is occupied by a signal.

In the literature on heartrate and information processing an important distinction is made between "the intention to note and detect environmental stimuli", called "intake" and "the manipulation of symbols or retrieval of stored information", called rejection (Lacey, 1967, 1970). The different components of attention are according to Lacey and many other researchers accompanied by heartrate deceleration and acceleration respectively. Lacey explained these effects within a rather complicated neurophysiological theory which cannot easily be tested (Hahn, 1973).

Hover (1974) made a more precise distinction between

(a) orientation (accompanied (sometimes) by a short heartrate deceleration, followed by an acceleration)
(b) sustained environmental attention (accompanied by heartrate deceleration)
(c) internal attention (accompanied by heartrate acceleration).

Experimental work by Coles and Duncan Johnson (1975) showed that sustained attention reflected both preparation for stimulus analysis and responding. In some experimental paradigms the imperative signals (S) are presented without a warning signal (WS), mostly at a paced rate. In that case a signal serves both the function of WS and S and the electrophysiological responses will accordingly be confounded.

Consider next Pribram and McGuiness' distinction between <u>arousal</u> and <u>activation</u>. Arousal is the phasic physiological response to input and is equivalent with orientation (e.g. O-wave; deceleration and acceleration of heartrate). Activation was defined as the (tonic) readiness to respond and equivalent to sustained environmental attention (e.g. E-wave and second heart-rate deceleration) <u>and</u> internal attention (heartrate acceleration and P-300). There <u>is</u> a difference between these two forms of activation: in the first case the subject tends to inhibit irrelevant movements and this state of motor inhibition prepares the organism specifically for a fast action to S (Obrist, et al, 1970); in the second case the activation pattern consists of the defensive reflex already described above.

Neither of these physiological changes correlate very well with the RT to S. This might not be surprising if they reflect different aspects of preparation, which cannot easily be derived from such a global measure as RT.

INTERNAL MODELS

Rasmussen (1976) has constructed a hybrid model of the process plant operator, containing both parallel and serial components. According to him there is a high capacity parallel processing system which serves the subconscious processes related to perception, sensory-motor responses etc. It is in many respects comparable to a goal directed, self-organizing associative network operating by dynamic matching of input information patterns to stored patterns. These patterns constitute an analogue representation of the behavior of the environment in a time-space structure. This internal world model <u>directs</u> and <u>controls</u> attention. The conscious processor is alerted in case of a deviation from the predictions of the internal model. This system is conceived to be versatile, but limited in capacity and speed, and processes the information sequentially. The conscious processor uses mainly symbolic representations and the processes can be modelled by sequential algorithms.

The way in which Rasmussen describes the mental processes underlying performance of process operators resembles very much the way in which Shiffrin and Schneider (1977) describe automatic detection versus controlled search. In both models we see a transition from conscious to subconscious processing if an internal representation (or a context dependent associative memory structure) becomes available and makes the environment predictable. Moray (1976) describes the internal model discursively as follows: "The model represents more or less accurately the statistical structure in time and space of the messages received, and the observer can run it in fast time so that prediction can occur. The model also includes the value system of the observer, embodied as weighting functions. When the observer processes information he uses it not only to make responses, but also to update the model. The use of the model is essentially predictive, and allows the observer to optimize the distribution of his limited processing capacity". He demonstrates the usefulness of this concept in the analysis of his experiments on selective listening (Moray, 1976).

Veldhuyzen and Stassen (1976) remark in their study on ship manoeuvring: "In order to provide a successful control behavior the human operator needs some information of the dynamics of the system to be controlled; this information should also include knowledge of the disturbances acting on the system. This knowledge is called an Internal Model".

The concept of an internal model is also a central feature of Sheridan's model of supervisory control: "The human operator in order to estimate the worth of having various actions when various changes in the process obtain, utilizes an "internal model" of the process. This internal model predicts the new process state resulting from any given action and initial process state. A utility function then specifies the worth of this change at the cost of that action".

The nature of these internal models however is not quite clear. Veldhuyzen's conceptualisation of his Internal Model is "a simple differential equation which is used to predict future ship states". In other models a low pass filter or second order shaping filter driven by white noise, or a Kalman filter is proposed (Smallwood, 1967; Curry and Gai, 1976).

Bobrow and Norman (1975) argue that in many models of human

memory, information is represented in a context-independent way. These types of models are insufficient to explain a number of properties of human memory. Both authors propose models which represent information in memory in a context-dependent way, enabling automatic information processing. This latter mode of information processing is data limited, e.g. performance is independent of processing resources, and dependent only upon the quality of the data. A central mechanism is believed to control the process that schedules resources, initiates actions by making decisions among alternatives presented to it, and selects which conceptualisations to pursue and which to reject. This mechanism keeps track of its operations and the overall context by means of a small capacity memory structure. It is supposed to be resource limited, e.g. an increase in the amount processing resources results in improved performance.

This all suggests that the type of information processing we find in laboratory tasks occurs also outside the laboratory in real life tasks. In other words laboratory research on information processing has, contrary to what Neisser (1976) tries to suggest, an ecological relevance.

In a later paper in these proceedings we will describe the sensitivity of cardiovascular system parameters in response to laboratory tasks differing in the amount of controlled processing and maintain that the results of these studies have relevance for tasks outside the laboratory in which the same mode of information processing is used. In general we have tried to argue that the transition from automatic to controlled processing occurs if there is no adequate internal model with a high predictive power. The transition is visible in changes in the physiological state of the subject and exemplified in the orienting reaction and the defensive reaction, and behaviorally in the use of capacity or resource limited processes.

Mental load or effort is thought to exist only in the controlled mode of information processing.

REFERENCES

Attneave, F., Applications of information theory to psychology, New York: Holt, 1959.

Bainbridge, L., Problems in the assessment of mental load, Le travail Humain, 1974, 37, 279-302.

Bahrick, H.P., and Shelly, C., Time sharing as an index of automization, Journal of Experimental Psychology, 1958, 56, 288-293.

Bahrick, H.P., Noble, M., and Fitts, P.M. Extra-task performance as a measure of learning a primary task, Journal of Experimental Psychology, 1954, 48, 298-302.

Berdina, M.A., Kolenko, O.L., Kotz, I.M., Kuzetzoy, A.P., Rodinoy, I.M., Savchenko, A.P. and Thorevsky, V.I. Increase is skeletal muscle performance during emotional stress in man, Circulation Research, 1972, 6, 642-650.

Bobrow, D.G. and Norman, D.A. Some principles of memory schemata, in: D.G. Bobrow and A. Colling, Representation and Understanding, studies in cognitive science, New York: Academic Press, 1975.

Broadbent, D.E. Levels, hierarchies, and the locus of control. Quarterly Journal of Experimental Psychology, 1977, 29, 181-201.

Brod, J., Neural factors in essential hypertension, in: A. Zanchetti Casa (ed.); Neural and Psychological Mechanisms in Cardiovascular Disease, Milan: Editrice "Il Ponte", 1972.

Brown, I.D. The measurement of perceptual load and reserve capacity. Transactions of the Association of Industrial Medical Officers, 1964, 14, 44-49.

Brown, I.D. Subjective and objective comparisons of successful and unsuccessful trainee drivers, Ergonomics, 1966, 8, 467-473.

Brown, I.D. and Poulton, E.C. Measuring the spare "mental" capacity of cardrivers by a subsidiary task, Ergonomics, 1961, 4, 35-40.

Cannon, W.B. Bodily changes in pain-hunger fear and rage, Boston: Branford, 1929.

Caille, E.J. and Kessler, D. A taxonomic review of the place of the operator within a man-machine system, in: Singleton: The Measurement of Human Resources, London, Taylor and Francis, 1976.

Coles, M.G.H. and Duncan-Johnson, C.C. Cardiac Activity and Information Processing: The effects of stimulus significance and detection and response requirements. Journal of Experimental Psychology: Human Perception and Performance, 1975, 1, 418-428.

Curry, R.E. and Gai, E.G. Detection of random process failures by human monitors, in: T.B. Sheridan and G. Johannsen, Monitoring Behavior and Supervisory Control, New York: Plenum Press, 1976.

Deecke, L., Grozinger, B. and Kornhuber, H.H., Voluntary Finger Movement in Man: Cerebral Potentials and Theory, Biol. Cybernetics, 1976, 23, 99-119.

Donders, F.C. On the speed of mental processes (1869). Trans. W.G. Koster in: W.G. Koster (ed.), Attention and Performance II, Amsterdam: North-Holland Publishing Co., 1969.

Duffy, E. Activation, in: N.S. Greenfield and R.A. Sternbach, Handbook of Psychophysiology, New York: Holt, Rinehart and Winston, Inc. 1973.

Frankenhauser, M. Sympathetic-Adrenomedullary Activity, Behavior, and the Psychosocial Environment, in: P.H. Venables and M.J. Christie, Research in Psychophysiology, London: John Wiley and Sons, 1975.

Gaillard, A.W.K. Effects on warning-signal modality on the CNV, Biological Psychology, 1976, 4, 139-154.

Gaillard, A.W.K. The terminal CNV: Preparation versus expectancy, Psychophysiology, 1977, 14.

Gaillard, A.W.K. Slow brain potentials preceding discrimination performance, Biological Psychology, submitted, 1978.

Gruzelier, J.H. The cardiac responses of schizophrenics to orienting, signal and non-signal tones. Biological Psychology, 1975, 3, 143-155.

Hahn, W.W. The hypothesis of Lacey: A critical appraisal, Psychological Bulletin, 1973, 79, 59-70.

Hamilton, P. Activation States and Components of Human Performance, in: S. Dornic, Attention and Performance VI, New York, Academic Press, 1977.

Hamilton, V. Socialisation anxiety and information processing: a capacity model of anxiety-induced performance deficits, in: I.G. Sarason and C.D. Spielberger (eds.), Stress and Anxiety, II, Washington D.C., Hemisphere Publishing, 1975.

Hover, K.I. A developmental study of three components of attention, Developmental Psychology, 1974, 10, 330-339.

Johannsen, G., Pfendler, C. and Stein, W. Human performance and workload in simulated landing-approaches with autopilot-failures, in T.B. Sheridan and G. Johannsen, Monitoring behavior and supervisory control, New York, Plenum Press, 1976.

Kahneman, D. Attention and Effort, New Jersey: Prentice Hall, Inc., 1973.

Keele, S.W. Attention and Human Performance, Pacific Palisades, California: Goodyear Publishing Company Inc., 1973.

Klein, R.M. Attention and Movement, in: G.E. Stelmach, Motor Control, New York, Academic Press, 1976.

Knowles, W.B. Operator loading tasks, Human Factors, 1963, 5, 151-161.

Lacey, J.I. Somatic response patterning and stress: some revisions of activation theory, in: M.A. Appley and R. Trumbull (eds.), Psychological stress: Issues in research, New York: Appleton-Century-Crofts, 1967.

Lacey, J.I., Lacey, B.C. Some autonomic central nervous system interrelationships, in: P. Black (ed.), Physiological Correlates of Emotion, New York: Academic Press, 1970, 205-227.

Lindsley, B.D. The role of nonspecific reticulothalama cortical systems in emotion, in P. Black: Physiological Correlates of Emotion, New York: Academic Press, 1970.

Loveless, N.E. and Sanford, A.J. Slow potential correlates of preparatory set, Biological Psychology, 1974, 1, 303-314.

Mason, J.W. Organization of Psychodendrocrine Mechanisms: A Review and Reconsideration of Research, in: Singleton: The Measurement of human resources, London, Taylor and Francis, 1976.

Mandler, G. Consciousness: respectable, useful, and probably necessary, in: R.L. Solso, Information processing and cognition, Hillsdale, N.J.: Erlbaum, 1976.

McGuinness, D. Cardiovascular responses during habituation and mental activity in anxious men and women. Biological Psychology, 1973, 1, 115-123.

Michon, J.A. The problem of perceptual motor load, in: Studies in Perception. Dedicated to M.A. Bouman. Soesterberg: Institute for Perception, RVO-TNO, 1966.

Michon, J.A. Tapping regularity as a measure of perceptual motor load. Ergonomics, 1966, 9, 401-412.

Moray, N. Attention, control and sampling behaviour. In T.B. Sheridan and G. Johannsen, Monitoring behavior and supervisory control, New York: Plenum Press, 1976.

Moray, N. Attention: selective processes in vision and hearing, London: Hutchinson Education Ltd, 1969.

Mulder, G., Michon, J.A., Moraal, J. Motor skills, in: J.A. Michon, E.G.J. Eijkman and L.F.W. de Klerk (eds.), Handbook of Psychonomics, Deventer: Van Loghum and Slaterus, 1978.

Naatanen, R., The inverted - U relationship between activation and performance: a critical review, in: S. Kornblum, Attention and Performance, IV, New York, Academic Press, 1973.

Neisser, U., Cognitive Psychology, New York: Appleton-Century-Crofts, 1967.

Neisser, U. Cognition and Reality, San Francisco: Freeman, 1976.

Norman, D.A. and Bobrow, D.G. On data-limited and resource-limited processes, Cognitive Psychology, 1975, 7, 44-64.

Obrist, P.A., Webb, R.A., Sutterer, J.R. and Howard, J.L. Cardiac deceleration and reaction time: An evaluation of two hypotheses, Psychophysiology, 1970, 6, 695-706.

Pew, R.W. Levels of analysis in motor control, Brain Research, 1974, 71, 393-400.

Pew, R.W. Human perceptual-motor performance, in: B.H. Kantowitz: Human Information Processing: Tutorials in Performance and Cognition, New York: John Wiley, 1974.

Posner, M.I. Psychobiology of attention, in: M.S. Gazzaniga and C. Blakemore (eds.), Handbook of Psychobiology, New York, London: Academic Press, 1975.

Posner, M.I., Nissen, M.J. and Klein, R.M. Visual dominance: An information-processing account of its origins and significance. Psychological Review, 1976, 83, 157-171.

Pribram, K.H., and McGuinness, D. Arousal, activation and effort in the control of attention, Psychological Review, 1975, 82, 116-149.

Prechtl, H.F.R. The Behavioral State of the Newborn Infant (A Review), Brain Research, 1974, 76, 185-212.

Rasmussen, J. Outlines of a hybrid model of the process plant operator in: T.B. Sheridan and G. Johannsen, Monitoring behavior and supervisory control, New York: Plenum Press, 1976.

Rolfe, J.M. The secondary task as a measure of mental load, in: W.T. Singleton, J.G. Fox and D.W. Whitfield, Measurement of Man at Work, London: Taylor and Francis Ltd., 1971.

Rolfe, J.M. The measurement of human response in man-vehicle control situations, in: T.B. Sheridan and G. Johannsen, Monitoring Behavior and Supervisory Control, New York: Plenum Press, 1976.

Sanders, A.F. Structural and functional aspects of the reaction process, in S. Dornic (ed.), Attention and Performance VI, New York: Academic Press, 1977.

Schmidt, R.A. A Schema Theory of Discrete Motor Skill Learning, Psychological Review, 1975, 82, 225-260.

Schmidt, R.A. The Schema as a Solution to Some Persistent Problems in Motor Learning Theory, in: G.E. Stelmach, Motor Control, New York: Academic Press, 1976.

Selye, H. Stress, Montreal: ACTA, 1950.

Shiffrin, R.M. Capacity limitations in information processing, attention and memory, in: W.K. Estes (ed.), Handbook of learning and cognitive processes (Vol. 4), Hillsdale N.J.: Erlbaum, 1976.

Shiffrin, R.M. and Schneider, W. Controlled and Automatic Human Information Processing, Psychological Review, 1977, 84, 127-190.

Smallwood, R.D. Internal models and the human instrument monitor, IEEE Transactions on Human Factors in Electronics, 1967, HFE 8.

Stelmach, G.E. Motor Control. New York: Academic Press, 1976.

Veldhuyzen, W. and Stassen, H.G. The internal model: what does

it mean in human control, in: T.B. Sheridan and
G. Johannsen, <u>Monitoring Behavior and Supervisory Control</u>,
New York: Plenum Press, 1976.

SINUSARRHYTHMIA AND MENTAL WORK LOAD

G. Mulder

Institute of Experimental Psychology

University of Groningen

INTRODUCTION

Sinusarrhythmia is a variability in heart rate and this variability has been associated with respiration. In the last decade however, an increasing insight into the mechanisms underlying this phenomenon has been obtained, mainly by research effort of British investigators (Sayers, 1973, 1975; Kitney, 1972, 1974; Hyndman, 1974, 1975, 1976; see also Miawaki et al, 1966). In all this work spectral analysis of sinusarrhythmia has been used. This method reveals the different mechanisms involved.

Different techniques have been used in order to obtain an equidistant time series (Mulder, 1973; 1978). This time series is subsequently Fourier transformed either by the indirect method (Blackman and Tukey, 1958) or the direct one (Cooley and Tukey, 1965).

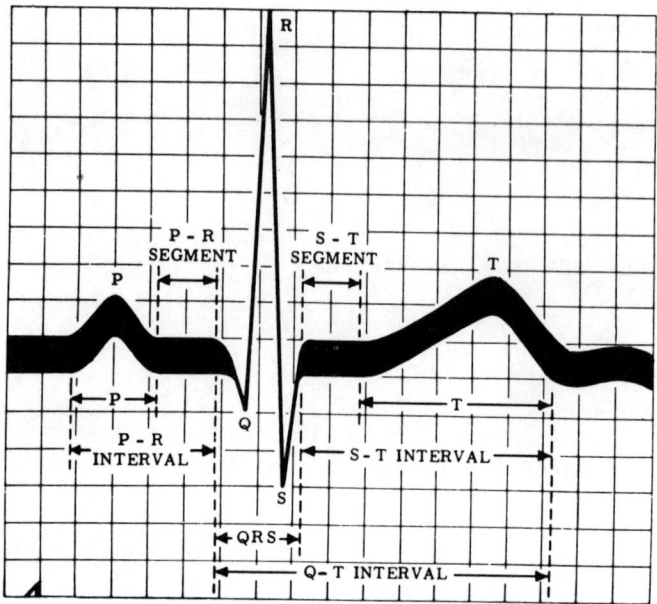

Figure 1. The normal cardiogram.

1. The mechanisms

The electrocardiogram (see fig. 1) is caused by a sequence of activation processes. Activity is first initiated in the sino-atrial node (S.A.), the pacemaker of the heart. Cells of this region are capable of intrinsic automaticity, which is modulated by higher centres. The electrical activity from the S.A. induces a depolarisation of the atrial cells and is visible in the P-wave of the ECG. From the atria, activity spreads through the atrio-ventricular node. There is a delay in the spread of activation, and this delay is partly reflected in the so-called P-Q time interval. The activity is subsequently conveyed to the ventricles by means of the bundle of His and the Ventricular cells are activated through the Purkinje fiber system. The activation of these cells is reflected in the QRS - complex. The S - T time interval and T-wave reflects the repolarisation of the activated cells.

The ventricular contraction causes a pulsative increase of pressure in the great vessels of circulation. The systemic arterial blood pressure (P) is the product of cardiac output (CO) x the total peripheral resistance (TPR) i.e. P = CO x TPR. The cardiac output is the volume of blood pumped by the heart each minute and thus is the product of the volume of each beat, the stroke volume (SV) and the number of beats per minute (HR), i.e. CO = SV x HR.

The stroke volume (SV) is the difference between the volume of blood in the heart at the beginning of contraction (systole), the end diastolic volume (EDV) and the amount of blood which remains in the ventricles when the valves close at the end of the systole: the end systolic volume (ESV), i.e. SV = EDV - ESV. Increased vigor of myocardial contraction leads to a decrease in the EDV and thus an increase in SV.

The sympathetic division of the autonomic system controls the vigor of myocardial contraction; the vagal division is mainly responsible for changes in HR, by modulating the spontaneous activity of the sinoatrial node. The filling time is dependent upon HR. As HR increases the diastolic period is reduced and consequently the available filling time. An additional determinant is the effective filling pressure, i.e. the pressure gradient between the inside of the ventricles and the pressure outside. It is this pressure gradient which causes the ventricles to distend and it is dependent upon the rate of venous return and the degree of negative intrathoracic pressure. An increase in the venous pressure by changing venous tone (VT) or a more negative thoracic pressure acts to cause an increase in the transmural pressure and thus facilitates filling. Transmural pressure represents the gradient of pressure across the vessel wall. SV is also determined by the distensibility of the ventricles. Myocardial distensibility does not appear to be modified by sympathetic or para-sympathetic divisions.

Of special interest in our studies is the time between successive R - R intervals. The time intervals constitute the so-called cardiotachogram (CTG) (See fig.2).

The brainstem cardiovascular centre is able to control:

      1. HR

      2. Left ventricular contraction force

      3. VT

      4. TPR

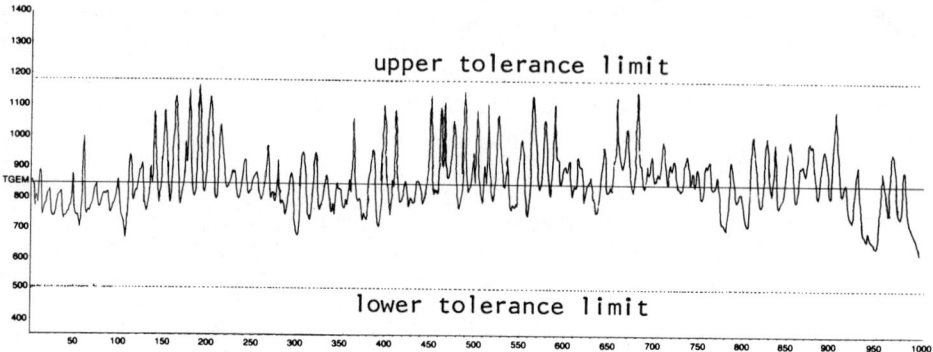

Figure 2. R-R interval as a function of time.

Blood pressure changes (P) are detected by baroreceptors in the aorta and arteria caroticus: an increase in P causes an inhibition of sympathetic division action on heart and peripheral vasculature and an increased action of the parasympathetic division action on the heart by the vagus nerves. All these effects, i.e. reduced cardiac vigor, bradycardia, vasodilation and venodilation, cause a decrease in blood pressure: a negative feedback loop. A decline in pressure on the other hand causes a decrease in vagal tone and less inhibition of the sympathetic division and hence an increase in P.

The passage of the neural signal from the baroreceptors through the brainstem is associated with a time delay of about 1 sec. This time delay creates a phase shift and causes the system to oscillate. The oscillation frequency is about 0.10 Hz (Miawaki, 1966; Sayers, 1973, 1975).

Hyndman (1974) provides evidence that the systems structure responsible for spontaneous rhythmic activity in blood pressure and hence in HR aids the homeostasis of blood pressure. He proposes a non-linear servomechanism consisting out of a threshold device and a filter. The filter represents the dynamic nervous response characteristics of the vascular smooth muscle system controlling systemic flow resistance (see Hyndman, 1974).

This system demonstrates two important features: spontaneous oscillations and frequency selective entrainment (see Sayers, 1973, 1975). Under normal resting conditions it is possible to show two components in the arterial blood pressure signal: the spontaneous oscillations (at about 0.10 Hz) and a frequency component directly related to respiration (usually between 0.20 and 0.30 Hz). Both frequencies are also reflected in the cardiac interval signal (see fig. 5). In both cases changes in the blood pressure signal are mirrored in the interval signal by means of the mechanisms described above.

Lung inflation or deflation is associated with changes in intrapleural pressure. Intrapleural pressure changes affect the intrathoracic veins and the transmural pressure in the aorta. The pressure detectors in the aortic arch are sensitive to transmural pressure differences resulting from changes in the intrapleural pressure.

Frequency selective entrainment implies a change in the brainstem time delay. As the frequency of oscillations alters, so does time delay. If the time delay diminishes, the system is able to oscillate at higher frequencies. If time delay is sufficiently diminished, spontaneous oscillations disappear altogether. Transmission time delay is thought to be affected by hypothalamic control.

The 0.10 Hz component in both blood pressure and interval signal contributes largely to the variance of the signals and consequently a loss of this component will decrease variance (i.e. heartrate variability) considerably. Direct measurement of intra-arterial blood pressure would be preferable but for obvious reasons impossible in both real or laboratory task situations.

Sayers (1973, 1975) recommends the non-invasive measurement of bloodflow by means of photo-electric plethysmography. It must be realised that the relation bloodflow / arterial pressure is not fully proportional, the measures are relative and not absolute; but it is an easily obtainable signal and continuous in nature. Inspection of the plethysmographic signals reveals also spontaneous oscillations between 20 and 50 seconds. These oscillations are believed to originate from the thermal control system (Kitney, 1972, 1974). Small thermal imbalances can be adjusted by changes in superficial bloodflow. These changes in peripheral resistance cause changes in blood pressure which are detected by the carotid-sinus and aortic arch baroreceptors and are also reflected in heartrate. This slow component is sensitive to selective entrainment with repeated thermal stimuli (Kitney, 1972).

Central elements in this blood pressure control system are the baroreceptors. Data obtained by Rushmer, 1970 and Kalkoff, 1957, showed that receptor activity is quiescent at pressure in the carotid below about 60 mm Hg. As transmural pressure is increased beyond 60 mm Hg, the frequency of nerve impulses in the carotid sinus nerve increases progressively. The change in frequency of impulses per millimeter mercury pressure was maximum at about normal pressure. Increases beyond 160 mm Hg did not result in a further increase in the rate of discharge. So the "threshold device" displays a sensitivity or "gain" which is large for afferent activity just exceeding threshold, but which decreases for greater values of afferent activity. The threshold value represents the reference value or set point of the control system.

Experiments with cats (Kent et al, 1971) showed that decerebration <u>decreased the range</u> through which sinus pressure could alter arterial pressure.

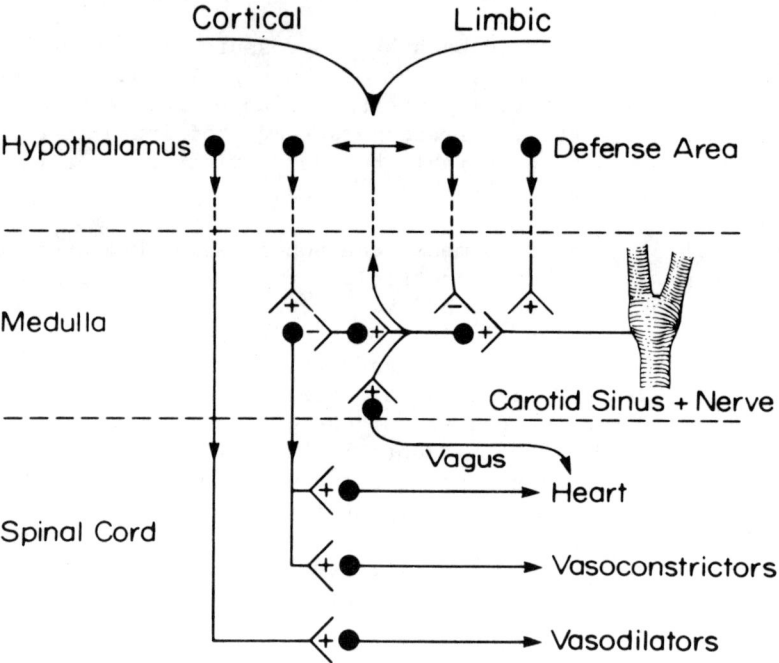

Figure 3. Neural Regulation of the Heart.

It was concluded that additive pressor influence from higher centres was removed, influencing both setpoint and gain (or sensitivity). Recent neurophysiological evidence (for a review see Manning, 1977) shows that facilitation and inhibition of the baroreceptor reflex is possible and is controlled by different brain sites (see fig. 3). There is the well known IX nerve input from the carotid sinus to the medullary reticular formation. A rise in blood pressure inhibits the pressor activity. The pressor responses are tonically facilitated by diencephalic and cortical regions, because we have seen that the full range of baroreceptor responses following decerebration is absent. However baroreceptor afferents reach by ascending projections also hypothalamic neurons. The defense area in the hypothalamus makes pre- and postsynaptic inhibitory connections at the level of the medulla, inhibiting components of the carotid sinus medullary input, and forcing a new cardiovascular state in spite of baroreceptor drive. These inhibitory mechanisms help to account for the functional state of a threatened animal, which simultaneously elevates HR and P, shifts priorities of bloodflow and all the while retains the characteristics of reflex cardiovascular regulation - only now reset to new levels (Manning, 1977).

The baroreflex can also be represented by plotting the (mean) R - R interval against (mean) arterial pressure. The relationship is positive: high (mean) pressures are accompanied by low interval time. The slope of this function is dependent upon the state of the subject. In the awaking state the slope is about 0.40; in the state of drowsiness 0.75 and in the sleeping state 1.76 (Sleight, 1977). This implies that spontaneous or induced variations in blood pressure are only minimally reflected in variations in HR, during the waking state, but increasingly in the sleeping state, and particular during REM. It is well known that HR is extremely variable during this sleep stage. Referring to the table of Caille (see position paper, fig. 1) it is quite reasonable to conclude that the suppression of sinusarrhythmia in the waking state and the increase in the state of drowsiness, reflect different sensitivities or gain values in the blood pressure control system.

In the past, time domain measures of sinusarrhythmia have been common (Mulder and Mulder, 1971, 1973). One of them is the variance of R - R intervals. Mulder (1978) has recently shown that these time domain measures are not always as sensitive as measures in the frequency domain.

We recommend that in the frequency domain certain regions of the power spectrum be examined. We usually divide the energy into three main bands:

(a) The area between 0.00 and 0.20 Hz, related to the body temperature control system and to the blood pressure control system.

(b) The area between 0.22 and 0.40 Hz, reflecting activity related to respiration.

(c) The area between 0.42 and 0.60 Hz, reflects activity related to the task, if the signal rate was within that region. If subjects had to carry out a task, in which they were asked to react to a signal every two seconds, a peak in the spectral densities around 0.50 Hz is usually found (fig. 4). In general: in paced tasks, with a pacing rate in the interval from 0.00 Hz to 0.60 or 0.70 Hz, the task frequency is reflected in the interval signal. This activity reflects phasic processes related to momentary changes in task demands (see position paper and Mulder, 1978).

A subdivision within the first area is recommended, i.e. a restriction to the spontaneous fluctuations in blood pressure, (the energy between 0.08 and 0.12 Hz). This area is least influenced by changes in respiratory rate and pattern (Mulder, 1978).

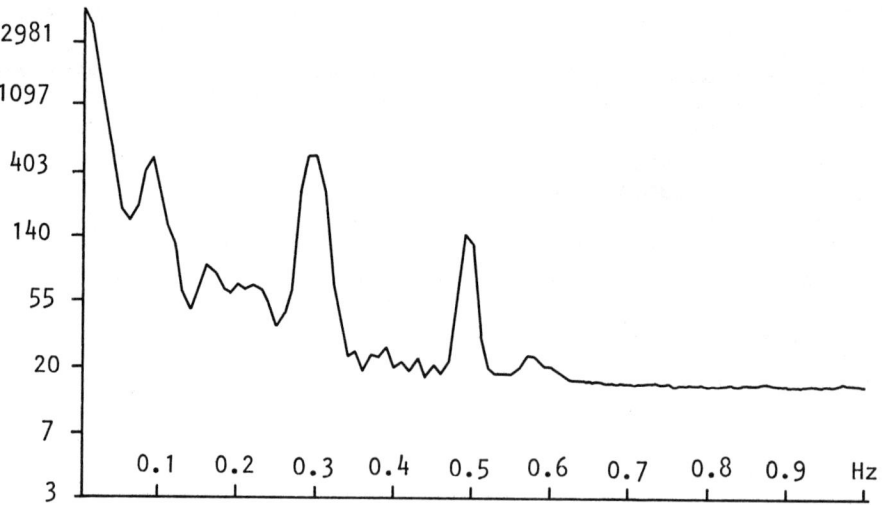

Figure 4. Power density spectrum of R-R intervals.

2. The Methods

Spectral analysis of the respiratory signal and the plethysmogram is straight forward. These signals are digitized and the spectral densities computed either by the indirect (see Blackman and Tukey, 1958) or direct method (Cooley and Tukey, 1965). The interval signal however is a discontinuous signal; namely a number of discrete pulses coincident with a QRS-complex in the ECG and separated by unequal intervals.

An equidistant timeseries can be obtained in different ways:

(a) Linear or non-linear interpolation; (Loos, 1968; Galloway and Womack, 1969; Luczak and Laurig, 1973; Mulder and Mulder, 1973).

(b) Low pass digital filtering of the cardiac event sequence (French and Holden, 1971; Hyndman and Mohn, 1973; Hyndman and Gregory, 1975).

(c) The cardiac event sequence is considered to be an equidistant timeseries (Sayers, 1973, 1975).

(d) The cardiotachogram, e.g. a series of reciprocals of R-R intervals available as analog signals, is digitized and Fourier-transformed.

All these methods have some shortcomings (Rompelman, 1978), but the results are very comparable (see Mulder, 1978). The spectral estimates obtained can be related with cross spectral techniques. There is no coherence between the respiratory signal and the 0.10 area, but a high coherence exists between the respiratory signal and the respiratory area in the interval signal. Following the analysis, spectral estimates are processed by multivariate statistical techniques. The reasons for using these techniques are as follows:

(a) A large number of variables is used, and multivariate analyses of variance is a means of testing these variables simultaneously and to arrive at patterns of activity.

(b) Stepdown analysis enables the researcher to control for the effect of contaminating variables (respiratory rate, motor activity).

(c) The multivariate approach to the analysis of repeated measures is both less restrictive and more realistic (see Bock, 1975).

3. Results

We have studied the sensitivity of sinusarrhythmia indices to manipulations of task variables.

In our position paper we distinguished between controlled and automatic processes. In our tasks the amount of controlled information processing was systematically varied.

(i) Binary-classification tasks. The subject either had to memorise a set of stimuli and had to search in his short term memory. The search time could be systematically varied by changing the display or memory load. The performance measures of primary interest were the reaction time (RT) and the number of errors. Other tasks required a "same" or "different" judgment.

(ii) Sentence comprehension task (Carpenter and Just, 1975). First a sentence was presented describing a picture("it is not true that the square is above the circle") and some seconds later a picture was presented. The subject had to compare his internal representation of the meaning of the sentence with the picture. This comparison process is described by Carpenter and Just. Tasks differ in the number of comparisons the subject has to perform. In the Carpenter and Just (1975) model of the comprehension process both the picture and the sentence are representaed in an abstract propositional format. The propositional format consists of a structure relating a predicate and one or more arguments. The model specifies the comparison process and accounts for the response latencies. The reaction time is determined by the number of times the comparison process has to be carried out.

We designed an "easy" version in which the comparison process had to be carried out two or three times, and a difficult one in which the average number of comparisons was about 6. Note that this type of task allows one to manipulate the perceptual or cognitive demands of a task, while keeping the motor component simple and constant. The subject is only required to make a simple "yes" or "no" or "same" - "different" response, contingent upon a decision rule of arbitrary complexity (Nickerson, 1973). This is important because one desires to know the sensitivity of the physiological responses to the perceptual or cognitive demands of the situations, uncontaminated by the motor components of the task.

Another type of task we used also taxed the working memory, but the subjects are not required to make overt reactions. The subject is told to set three counters in memory corresponding to the letters K, L, M and some numerical value. A series of letters is read off, containing some of these letters. The subject is forced to keep a running mental account of the current status of each counter. So after recognition, the subject must search for the appropriate counter, update its value, and rehearse the values of all other counters etc. In the simple version the subject had to keep track only of one counter and in the difficult version of three of them. After the task the subjects report the values of the counters. It is extremely difficult to timeshare this task with any other task.

We report here on the sensitivity of the 0.10 Hz component of the interval signal in discriminating between the levels of difficulty of the latter two tasks (see Fig. 5a). In Fig. 5b the differences between the difficult and the easy version of the sentence comprehension task is shown. The mean RTs are respectively 1200 msec and 2100 msec. The subject had to carry out a binary classification each 7300 msec. Note that in rest the spontaneous blood pressure oscillations are about .08 and .10 Hz. During the task there is selective entrainment of these oscillations to 0.12 Hz. The amplitude of these fluctuations however is sensitive to the task demands.

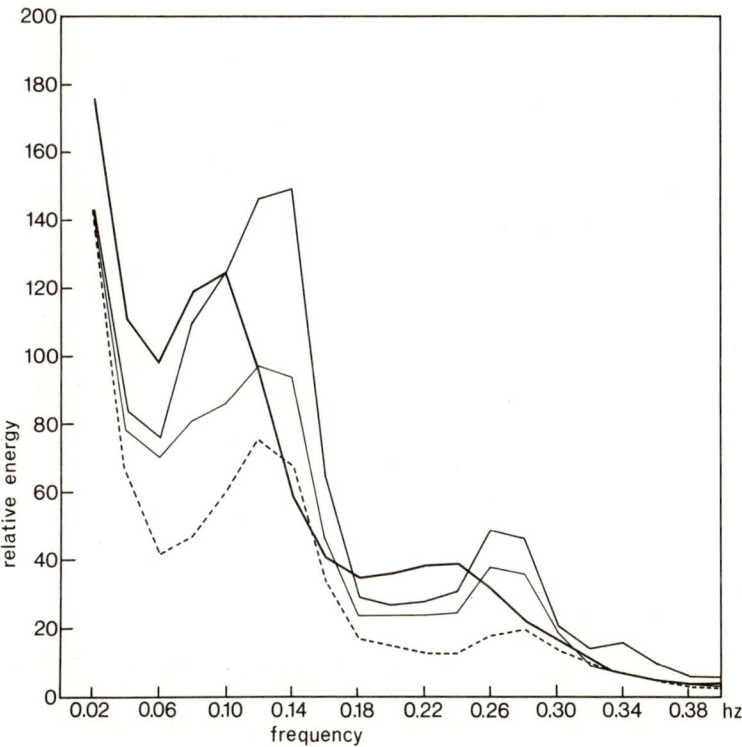

Figure 5a. Power spectra of binary classification tasks of differing difficulty (light lines) and rest (heavy lines). See text for details.

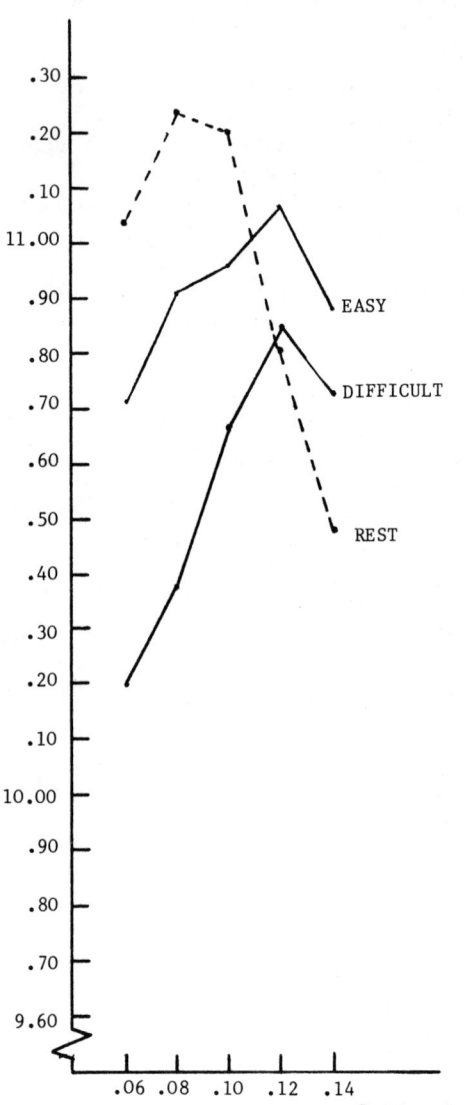

Figure 5b. The intensity of blood pressure oscillations in the easy and difficult version of the sentence comprehension task. (For explanation see text.)

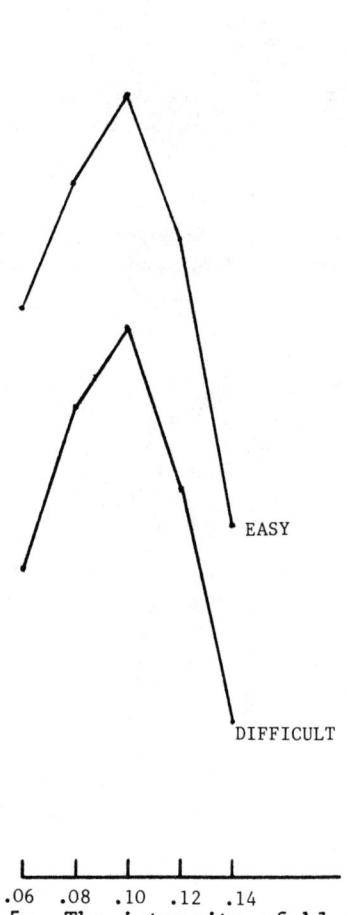

Figure 5c. The intensity of blood pressure oscillations during a running memory task.

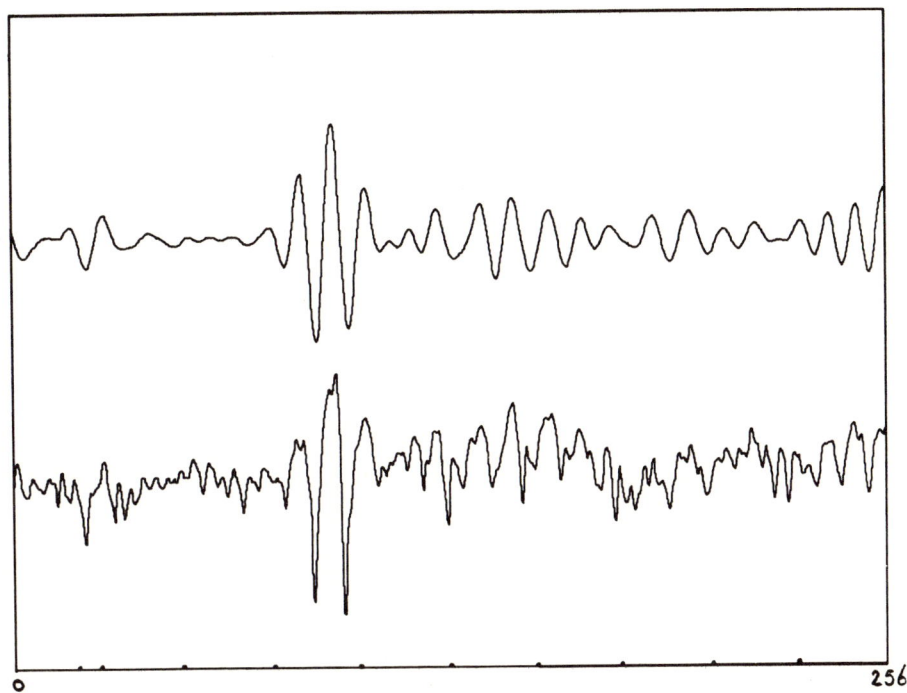

Figure 6. Digital filtering of the interval signal. Rest Period. Spontaneous oscillations form a major portion of the interval signal.

4. "On line" monitoring of blood pressure fluctuations

In order to be able to evaluate continuously the intensity and occurrence of blood pressure oscillations, digital filtering methods can be applied (fig. 6, 7). The lower record is the raw data, the upper the filtered data. We used a fifth order Lerner filter (Lerner, 1964) with the following characteristics:

(a) the signal is band-pass filtered with 3 db points at 0.06 Hz and 0.14 Hz;

(b) the phase characteristic is linear within the pass band, with a maximum deviation of 2%. This implies a constant time delay between input and output for all the frequencies within the band. This time delay is 21 seconds;

(c) the ripple in the amplitude characteristic within the band is 5%; (For more details see Mulder, et al 1978). The computer implementations (written in Fortran IV) can be obtained from A. den Arend, Computational Centre, University of Groningen.

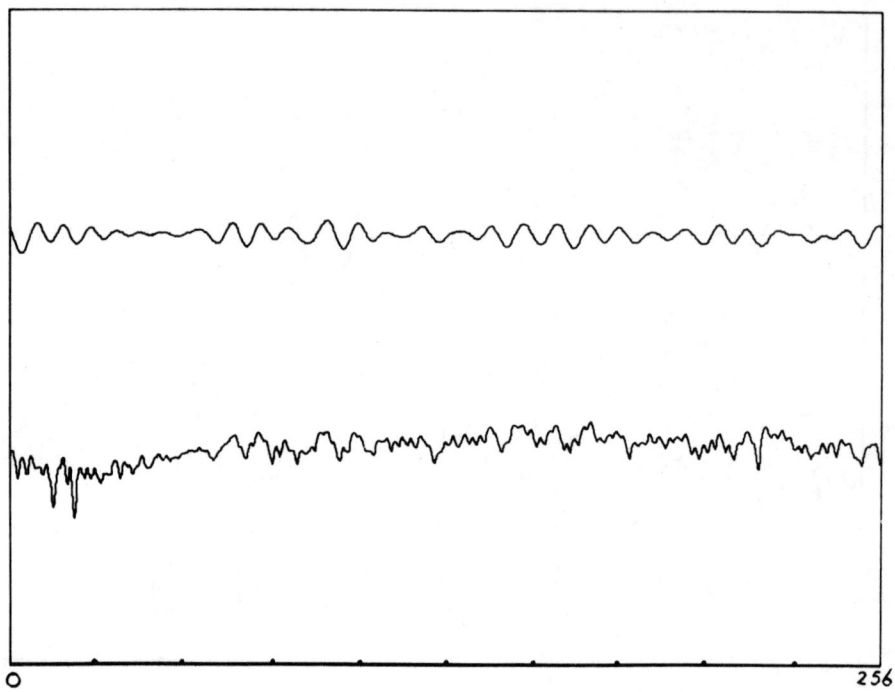

Figure 7. Digital Filtering of the Interval Signal Task Period. Spontaneous oscillations are reduced in intensity, causing a decreased heart rate variability.

The time delay of 21 seconds limits the possibility of this signal in situations which aim at a direct and online enhancement of the communication between the human operator and the controlling computer in man-machine systems.

Analysis of variance shows that:

.06	discriminates	at $p < .01$
.08	"	at $p < .0061$
.10	"	at $p < .08$
.12	"	at $p < .24$
.14	"	at $p < .20$

In Fig. 5c the results of the running memory task are shown. In this task a letter was read each 4000 msec. Note that the blood pressure fluctuations are again at .10 Hz but the amplitude again discriminates between the two levels of the task.

Analysis of variance shows that:

.06   discriminates   at p< .01

.08   "   at p< .03

.10   "   at p< .03

.12   "   at p< .04

.14   "   at p< .13   (see Mulder, 1978)

Our conclusion from these and other results is that the <u>total amount of controlled information processing</u> is a determinant of the amplitude of spontaneous oscillations of blood pressure as reflected in the cardiac interval signal. This part of the spectrum is least influenced by respiratory manoeuvres of the subject or changes in the temperature control system. Blood pressure oscillations are less reflected in the interbeat signal because of a change in the gain of the baroreceptor interface in the brainstem during "difficult" information processing tasks. Correlations across ages between the intensity of blood pressure fluctuations and blood pressure was negative, i.e. high blood pressure tends to be accompanied by smaller blood pressure fluctuations and vice versa (Mulder, 1978).

REFERENCES

Blackman, R.B. and Tukey, J.W., The Measurement of Power Spectra, New York: Dover Publications Inc., 1958.

Bock, R.D., Multivariate statistical methods in behavioral research, New York: McGraw-Hill, 1975.

Cooley, J.W. and Tukey, J.W., An algorithm for the machine calculation of complex Fourier series, Math. Comput. 1965, 19, 297-301.

Carpenter, P.A. and Just, M.A., Sentence comprehension: A psycholinguistic processing model of verification, Psychological Review, 1975, 82, 45-73.

French, A.S., and Holden, A.V., Alias-free sampling of neuronal spike trains, Kybernetik, 1971, 8, 137-144.

Galloway, D.G., and Womack, B.F. An application of spectral analysis and digital-filtering to the study of respiratory sinusarrhythmia, Austin, U.S.A.: Technical Report No. 71 Bioengineering Research Lab., Electronic Research Center, University of Texas, 1969.

Hyndman, B.W. and Mohn, R.K., A pulse modulator model of pacemaker activity, Digest of the 10th International Conference on Medical and Biological Engineering, Dresden, 1973.

Hyndman, B.W., The role of rhythms in homeostatis, Kybernetik, 1974, 227-236. 15.

Hyndman, B.W., and Gregory, J.R., Spectral analysis of sinusarrhythmia during mental loading, Ergonomics, 1975, 18, 255-270.

Hyndman, B.W., Signal analysis and modelling in psychophysiology research, Digest of the 11th Internal Conference on Medical and Biological Engineering, Ottawa, 1976.

Kalkoff, W., Verhandl. Deutsch, Ges. Kreislaufforsch. 1957, 23, 399.

Kent, B.B., Drane, J.W. and Manning, J.W. Suprapontine contributions to the carotid sinus reflex in the cat, Circulation Research, 1971, 29, 534-541.

Kitney, R.I., The use of entrainment in analysis of the human thermo-regulatory system, Journal of Physiology, 1972, 229 40-41.

Kitney, R.I. Analysis and simulation of the human thermoregulatory control system. Medical and Biological Engineering, 1974, 12, 57-64.

Lerner, R.M., Band pass filters with linear phase, Proc. IEEE, 1964, 52, 249-268.

Loos, F.A., Onderzoek van de zintuigelijk-mentale belasting, IJmuiden: Koninklijke Nederlands Hoogovens en Staalfabrieken, N.V., 1968

Manning, J.W., Intracranial mechanisms of regulation, in:' W.C. Randall, Neural Regulation of the heart, New York: Oxford University Press, 1977.

Miyawaki, K., Takahashi, T., and Takemura, H., Analysis and simulation of the periodic heart rate fluctuation, Technology Reports of the Osaka University, Osaka, Japan, 1966, 16, 315-325.

Mulder, G., and Mulder-Hajonides van der Meulen, W.R.E.H., Heart rate variability in a binary choice reaction task: An evaluation of some scoring methods, Acta Psychologica, 1972, 36, 239-251.

Mulder, G., and Mulder-Hajonides van der Meulen, W.R.E.H., Mental load and the measurement of heart rate variability, Ergonomics, 1973, 16, 69-83.

Mulder, G., The heart of mental effort, thesis, University of Groningen, 1978.

Nickerson, R.S., The use of binary-classification tasks in the study of human information processing: A tutorial survey, in: S. Kornblum, Attention and Performance IV, New York: Academic Press, 1973.

Rompelman, O., A comparative study of heart rate variability analysis methods, Paper at the Biological Engineering Society, 65th main scientific meeting "Analysis of heart rate variability", Chelsea College, London University, London, 1977.

Rushmer, R.F., Cardiovascular Dynamics, 3rd ed. Philadelphia: Saunders, 1970.

Sayers, B., McA., Analysis of heartrate variability, Ergonomics, 1973, 16, 17-32.

Sayers, B., McA., Physiological consequences of Informational Load and Overload, in: P.H. Venables and M.J. Christie, Research in Psychophysiology London: John Wiley and Sons, 1975.

Sleight, P., Personal communication, 1977.

MEASUREMENT OF MENTAL WORKLOAD

Helmut Strasser

Institute of Work Physiology, Technical University

of Munich, 8000 Munich 40, F.R. Germany

A paper given by Rolfe (1976) at the conference on "Monitoring Behaviour and Supervisory Control" in almost all details expresses my own point of view of the problem of assessing workload, as far as he went. But there are some additional points and comments which I would like to stress as a member of the "physiological group" of the present conference.

We should not only be interested in excellent theories but in real data which can fit models in all practical aspects, data which will allow us to prove the reliability and validity of measures and which can be acquired by economical methods.

We should not only be interested in assessment of peak loads of few preselected people in military tasks (e.g. pilot workload, air traffic controller jobs etc.) but also in workload of tasks with lower demands, e.g. tasks with monotonous aspects, tedious activities and different information handling in monitoring situations.

We should become aware of all the problems associated with assessing workload. Workload is determined by the physiological and psychological costs of the operators rather than by the effectiveness (performance) of a closed-loop man-machine-system. Millions of workers in industry may be overloaded by the lack of some necessary physical load in repetitive motor tasks, in assembly lines and by malfunctions of socio-technical organizations. Man is not, as we would like to assume, a factor which can be used (employed) and coupled with men and technical devices like a machine, without taking into account his wishes, necessities and individual requirements to communicate with colleagues, etc.

Having in mind these problems which seldom can be overcome by models, we should be interested not so much in only task-induced mental workload and our main aims should not be trying to describe man by models and information or queuing theories, which are based on constant or nowadays time-variant parameters but using overall empirical measures. Rather we have to tackle the problem of valid empirical measures of mental operator workload not only at a methodological level, but in the light of the biological background.

Doing so, we will find that there are important - but often not recognized - different methods for scoring mental and physical workload by physiological measures. When it is necessary to use our muscles or better larger groups of our muscles, we have an increased metabolism, we need more oxygen, we need more fatty acids and more glucose. The body can counterbalance these requirements by an increased blood flow (by increased and easily measured heart rate and/or stroke volume). All neuronal changes in the level of activation and arousal within the individual under mental workload doubtless are mixed with changes in physical load. But are they reflected indeed in the vegetative status or in the composition of the EEG waves, derived from the scalp? (compare Strasser, 1974b).

Visualizing a surely somewhat simple comparison between a human being and a computer, which consists of a power supply (analog to the vegetative system and body functions) and the core memory and logic parts (cortex), I am sceptical whether changes in the logic parts (as a consequence of mental workload) may be reflected in indicators of the power consumption or in alterations of the blinking of some lights (as in the EEG), seen in the periphery. On the other hand, malfunctions of the power supply can be seen in an evident interruption of information processing. Changes in the activity of the cortex (expected as a consequence of mental workload) are not measurable in a simple way and we cannot expect to find a directly related parameter.

Having in mind models of neuronal structures with connections between the cortex, limbic system, the reticular formation, the vegetative system and both afferent and efferent neuronal structures at the periphery, we can only expect indirect influences of mental workload in peripheral physiological indicators like heart rate and sinus arrhythmia, EEG and evoked potentials, EOG and eye blinking, EMG, respiratory parameters, galvanic skin responses, and so on. With biochemical parameters also there are a lot of methodological and theoretical problems.

So far we have tried to measure mental workload in spite of this fact by using these parameters in a heuristic way. Yet we must elaborate the range of changes in physiological variables influenced by a graduated load. We cannot be satisfied by the (usual) aim to find only statistically significant differences. Such results show us only that two values are different, whereas the amount of this difference cannot be specified. We must get a scale similar to the method of testing physical working capacity (PWC) by changes in heart rate from about 70 bpm to 170 bpm according to an increased physical workload.

Additionally we cannot be satisfied by short-time results but we have to elaborate time courses in workload over more than a few minutes; at least some hours for a lot of interesting long-term applications.

Especially we should have in view the fact that in many workload situations there exist a lot of stressors and in spite of a general mobilisation of bodily functions no physical actions follow (aspects of distress). Adaptation of humans to such situations is very much restricted and the effects may be compared in some way with a motor car which is driven by a lot of starting, braking and starting again in dense city traffic. We all know this relative low "city load" will be much more detrimental to the machine than a high speed race (high physical load) during a motor-way ride.

I think there will not exist one ideal or some more or less ideal measures and there must be a multi-factorial array of physiological and psychological measures (including self-rating data) and input-output efficiency data to accomplish a compromise for assessment of mental workload. Such a wide-spread experimental study seems not to be done yet.

Regarding the rapid technical changes of devices and tasks in man-machine-systems with time and the very narrow adaptive behaviour of human operators to meet the different mental load (stress), I think that in any case no human engineering study can be done without man-related data.

Laboratory studies seldom will be sufficient because of the lack of reality and of risk taking (as one source of psychological stress) whereas field experiments often suffer from problems in interpretation of the results. Therefore both laboratory and field experiments have to be done.

Referring to the relative value of the different methods, I think a priori measures are good for establishing operational limits of workload (stress) but they are no help for determining operator workload (in the sense of strain or effort). The relative value of empirical (physiological and psychological) measures seems to be high for measuring strain but we must have in mind the above mentioned limits for mental tasks and some

difficulties in differentiating all the possible sources of input
load (problem of stereotype and seldom specific reactions of the
organism to evoking stress). Systems and models as measures of
workload and predictions of performance in man-machine-systems
seem to be a combination of the preceding two measures. But they
are simplifications of input/output relations with a lot of
boundary conditions, which cannot be fulfilled in most practical
applications. Also problems of long-term changes in workload
and performance are not solved.

Concluding, I think we cannot hope for real improvements in
the field of mental workload when applying or promoting only one
method. For our meeting in Mati I would prefer questions and
discussions of empirical data from which I would try to come to
models and theories and not vice versa.

REFERENCES

Rolfe, J.M. The measurement of human response in man vehicle
control situations. In: Monitoring Behavior and Supervisory
Control. 97-107. Int. Symposium, Berchtesgaden,
F.R. Germany. March 8-12 (1976).

Strasser, H. Beurteilung ergonomischer Fragestellungen mit
Herzfrequenz und Sinusarrhythmie. (Indicatoren von
mentaler Beanspruchung und Ermüdung). Int. Arch. Arbeitsmed.
32, 261-287 (1974a).

Strasser, H. Technisch-physiologische Aspekte der Beziehung
Stress - Strain. Eine modell-theoretische Betrachtung.
Arbeitsmed.-Sozialmed.-Präventivmed. 9(10) 212-217 (1974b).

Strasser, H. und W. Einars. Beanspruchungsprofile in der
ergonomischen Fedlforschung. Arbeitsmed.-Sozialmed.-
Präventivmed. 12(1) 6-10 (1977).

Strasser, H. Physiological measures of workload - correlations
between physiological parameters and operational performance.
In: .Methods to Assess Workload. A8 1-7. AGARD Conference
Pre-print No. 216, Köln, F.R. Germany, April 18-22 (1977).

PHYSIOLOGICAL INDICATORS OF MENTAL WORKLOAD

Holger Ursin[1] and Reidun Ursin[2]

[1]Institute of Psychology
[2]Institute of Physiology
University of Bergen, Norway

From a physiological point of view, a mental load, whatever that is, must be assumed to be a load on processes within the central nervous system (CNS). A load on this CNS could affect the activity of the CNS machinery, the energy requirements and metabolism of that machinery, their wear and tear, and therefore, the restitution of the machinery. Since the CNS exists within a body, there are possibilities that the effects on the CNS may also affect other bodily processes than those strictly concerned with information processing in the CNS. This raises possibilities of measuring the load since physiological processes in general are quite easy to monitor. In this chapter, we will describe and discuss some of the methods used for evaluating these processes, in particular those with which we have personal experience. In their position paper to this meeting, Sheridan and Stassen listed three mental load definitions which involved physiological processes. These are the information processing workload, the emotional workload and the energy workload. The "mental workload" following their definition comprises both the information processing and the emotional workload. Their energy workload is linked to effector processes only.

The energy workload clearly affects physiological variables, and in tasks involving "mental load" there may also be a physical workload. There are, however, ways of eliminating or reducing this contamination. For instance, the plasma levels of some hormones are fairly independent of physical load. We will also describe a simultaneous monitoring of heart rate and oxygen which seems to avoid this difficulty. The main difficulty is to distinguish between load due to information processes, and "emotional" load. Since our main conclusion is that the physiological indicators mainly pick up "activation", rather than information processing, and since activation is the end result of a wide range of psychological processes, we will discuss the activation concept in some detail.

1. Activity of CNS

The brain is a network with loops preserving activity for as long as it is alive. Only a dead brain is without activity. "Activation" means changing from one level of activity to a higher level of activity. It remains to define activity. In the literature on the brain stem reticular formation, activation simply refers to EEG desynchronization and accompanying behavioral signs of increased wakefulness, arousal or even "awareness". There is very little reason to question that the individual or the brain as a whole is more "active" when the EEG is desynchronized. For clarification of the activation concept it should be stressed that there is no simple relationship between unit activity and EEG activity, or behavioral activity. It remains an empirical observation that when individuals report or demonstrate clear overt behavioral signs of activation their cortex shows the desynchronized EEG pattern.

Activation theory (Lindsley 1951) is still a powerful model for the explanation of physiological and psychological mechanisms in wakefulness, emotional states, and sleep, even if some modifications may be necessary. This theory states that when there is information transmitted through the classical sensory pathways, there are also impulses sent directly to the reticular formation of the brain stem, either through collaterals from the sensory pathways, or via direct fibres running parallel with these pathways. The activation is not restricted to cortical activation, but also comprises activity in the autonomic nervous system, the somatomotor system, and endocrine responses. With improved methods for determining plasma levels of hormones, it has become increasingly clear that the whole, or at least very large parts of the endocrine system is subject to influence from psychological factors. These phenomena are easily treated within activation theory.

The essence of the activation model is that the sensory events do not only have a signal effect, but also an activation effect. The signal or cue effect is supposed to be dependent on the activation effect. In this sense, there is an obvious relationship with the drive concept; Hebb (1955) held that activation (arousal) in this sense was synonymous with a general drive state.

The close anatomical and physiological relationship between hypothalamus and the reticular formation makes activation theory essential for physiologically acceptable formulations of drive registration and drive reduction mechanisms (Lindsley, 1951, Malmo, 1966). The cortical and telencephalic inputs to the reticular formation (see Ursin, Wester and Ursin, 1967 for references) make it possible to account for centrally induced variations in activation level. The input to the reticular formation from cortex must be assumed to be capable of eliciting, maintaining and increasing activation (Hebb, 1955). Hebb hypothesized that this cortical feedback to the activation system had relevance for drive effects and cognitive processes.

The activation model suggested by Moruzzi and Magoun (1949) must be modified, since all incoming stimuli cannot have free access to the general activating mechanisms. Orienting responses and EEG desynchronization are only elicited at the first presentations of a stimulus. This gradual decrement in orienting responses is habituation. Habituation is now a well described phenomenon, on the synaptic level (Kandel, 1970) and on the behavioral level (Thompson and Spencer, 1966). On the cognitive level, Sokolov (1963) ascribes habituation to a gradual build up of template for that particular stimulus pattern. The organism responds with an orienting response if there is no such template. The orienting response type of activation, therefore, is a response to the unexpected.

For exploratory behavior type of activation, the unexpected and unknown is the essence of the relevant stimulus. The same formulation may be used for other types of activation also. Activation evoked by drive stimuli or physiological regulation mechanisms occurs whenever there is a difference between the set value of a given variable and the actual value of that variable. This is generally recognised for homeostatically controlled variables, but may also be stated to be the case whenever there is a discrepancy for a learned type of set value. In general, expectancy and the failure to meet expectancies seem to be of decisive value for activation, both in man and animals (Levine, Goldman and Coover, 1972, Ursin, Baade and Levine, 1978).

When rats face a threatening situation, there is initially a high level of activation indicated by their behavior as well as their corticosterone level (Coover, Ursin and Levine, 1973). When rats learn a two-way active avoidance habit, there is a gradual decrement in their internal activation. Corticosterone level will be low after two to three weeks of avoidance training. If the rat is exposed to a new situation, or gets signals that its coping response is no longer adequate, high levels of activation reoccur (Coover, Ursin and Levine, 1973).

The same seems to be true for humans. When parachutist trainees are tested after their first jump from a training tower, there is a very high level of epinephrine, cortisol, growth hormone, blood glucose, and free fatty acids in their plasma. Their heart rate is high. Their testosterone level is low. After a limited experience with jumping from the tower, they report a clear reduction in subjectively experienced fear, and there is no longer any evidence of activation in most physiological indicators. This is interpreted as a result of coping with the threatening environment, with consequent reduction in most indicators of activation (Ursin, Baade and Levine, 1978) (see Fig. 1).

However, a few indicators do not show this pattern. There is a clear increment in the secretion of epinephrine after the jumps, and even if the total level reached shows a significant decrement, the rise due to the jump itself does not seem to change with experience. Ursin, Baade and Levine have referred to this latter type of activation as "phasic" activation, and stated that this activation is more resistant to the effect of coping than the other indicators, which they refer to as "tonic".

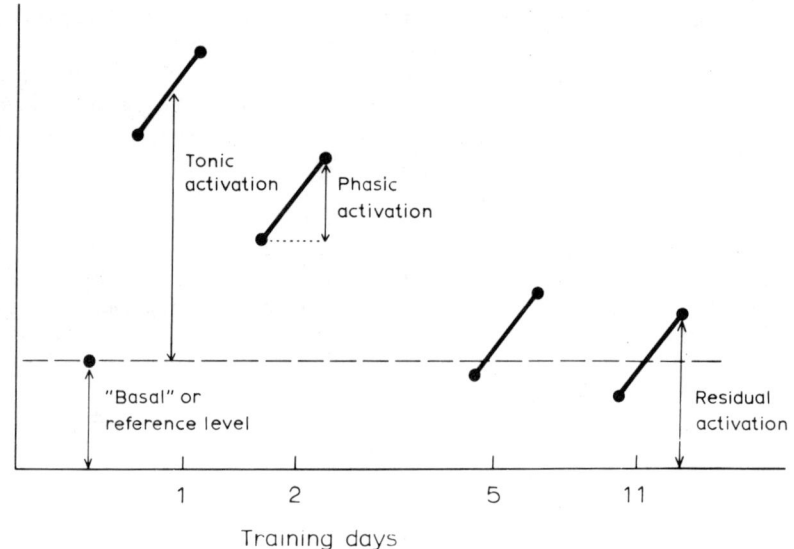

Figure 1

Even in the coping individual a certain activation is present. Within avoidance theory, this has been referred to as "residual activation" (see Fig. 1.). In the parachutist trainees this activation depends, at least in part, on motivational and performance variables (Vollmer, 1978). High achievement motivation in good performers is related to high arousal. Also, high fear of failure is related to high arousal in poor performers.

In conclusion, we suggest that whenever physiological indicators are used to measure mental load, psychological and social factors must be assumed to be of decisive importance for the values obtained. Physiological indicators, therefore, pick up what may be called "emotional" factors, or simply "activation". Activation depends on whether the individual expects to cope with his situation or not. The methods do not measure the information load. They give information on how the individual himself estimates the load, in particular whether he thinks he is able to cope with it, and to what extent failure or success means much to him. What is measured, therefore, is not the load, but the evaluation of the load and the evaluation of the capacity to cope with that load. This, of course, depends on experience as well as personality characteristics.

2. Specific activation

In early work, psychophysiologists postulated specific activation patterns for specific emotions, in particular fear and anger (Ax, 1953; Schachter, 1957). This was never established. Activation is a necessary, but not sufficient condition for a specific type of emotional experience (Lykken, 1968). Autonomic blockade interferes with avoidance learning and emotional experience, but it does not block or eliminate the emotional experience (see Lord, King and Pfeister 1976). Cognitive aspects determine the interpretation of the experience of peripheral physiological changes ("attribution" of arousal, Schachter and Singer 1962; Rule and Nesdale, 1976). How can we experience emotions as qualitatively different if there is no specificity peripherally? In particular, since our feeling of specificity is a question of attribution or an input interpretation, this question has been of some concern to theorists. The specificity of intracerebral emotional mechanisms remains a reasonable and sufficient explanation for the specificity, as in the Cannon-Bard formulations. The James-Lange principle is involved in the positive feedback loops of activation, and the continued experience of specificity may involve "attribution" mechanisms.

In psychophysiology, the remarkable lack of correlations between the various indices of activation has been a matter of concern for a long time (Lacey, 1950). Initially, neuroanatomists may have been the first to point out that it is unreasonable to assume that the reticular formation of the brain stem could be so simple and homogenous as postulated in early activation theory. Brodal (1957) has repeatedly pointed to the enormous complexity of the reticular formation, and found it untenable from an anatomical point of view to accept the reticular formation as one "system". Hebb (1955) suggested that the activation system might consist of a number of subsystems with distinctive functions. Data from the parachutist trainees pointed to several different types of activation mechanisms. The lack of specificity and the high individual variation described by, for instance, Lacey (1950) could be due to differences in conditioning history and previous experience. After all, it has been amply demonstrated that processes innervated by autonomic nerves are subject to classical as well as instrumental conditioning. However, this has not been demonstrated for specific hormone levels in plasma, and these might be less accessible for discriminated conditioning. Baade et al. (1978) found that in the parachutist trainees the cortisol axis was related to defence mechanisms, the free fatty acids were related to performance, and testosterone related to role identification. The catecholamines, in particular epinephrine, are also related to performance, and it may be that free fatty acid measurements simply are a better way of estimating adrenergic activity.

This degree of specificity is surprising, and must be investigated further. Some of the specificity we found may be due to differences in the time course in rise and fall of the plasma level of the hormones. It is, for instance, possible that the relationship between cortisol and defence, on the one hand, and good performance and free fatty acids/catecholamines, on the other, may simply be due to good performers not having any activation before the jump, and high defence individuals starting their worrying process long before the crucial act. Differences in the time course depending on performance, and perhaps on experience, have been described by Fenz (1975). This may explain some, but not all, the specificity we have seen. Again, this can only be solved by a more continuous monitoring of the hormone levels. This is the main difficulty with using hormones as indicators. Traditional psychophysiological measurements, like heart rate and blood pressure are superior in the ease with which they may be monitored continuously. However, these processes may be monitored also by the subject, or at least by his brain, and therefore these functions are subject to individualization through conditioning processes. This is probably not the case with hormones like cortisol and testosterone.

Finally, one way of measuring load would be to monitor activity in particular parts of the CNS, if such existed specifically for mental load. As far as we can judge, there is nothing in contemporary neuropsychology which warrants the assumption that specific parts of the CNS are related to mental load, and not to other types of activity. Even if work on evoked potentials suggests that specific neural substrates exist for mental load, we do not feel convinced that this is the case. Activation as such would affect at least long latency aspects of evoked potentials, and definitely other electroencephalographic changes. An interesting possibility is that there may be different energy requirements of cortical areas depending on the quality of the task. Risberg and Ingvar (1971/72) have found increases in blood flow in cortical association areas during memorization and thinking. It is possible that the specificity in affected brain areas described by Risberg and Ingvar is related to attention factors. It is less certain that the method can quantify the information load itself.

3. Energy Requirements

As mentioned in the previous chapter, it should be possible to measure load from the energy requirements of the information-processing system. Unfortunately, we cannot discriminate between activation due to information from activation due to other CNS functions. However, there are useful methods for discriminating between physical workload and the energy requirements and bodily changes due to strict CNS activation.

In particular, measurements of changes in the cardiovascular system have long been a matter on controversy. When a certain task leads to changes in heart rate, it is difficult to know whether this is due to a psychological "activation", or simply secondary to energy requirements of the muscles. For instance, when a certain task is performed, and the heart rate accelerates, is this heart rate acceleration due to the muscle use, or to the psychological "stress" or load?

Blix, Stromme and Ursin (1974) described a method where this problem seems to be eliminated. Under aerobic steady state muscle work, there is a linear relationship between heart rate and oxygen consumption. This curve may be determined for each individual. In later situations, when both heart rate and oxygen consumption are measured, it is then possible to determine how much of the heart rate acceleration that is due to the muscle task itself, and how much is due to psychological activation (Blix, Stromme and Ursin, 1974). As mentioned briefly before, this psychological activation belongs to what we have referred to as "phasic" activation, and is not very susceptible to the coping effect. We have seen such activation in experienced pilots (Blix, Stromme and Ursin, 1974) and there was no significant decrement in heart rate in the parachutist trainees after their period of tower training (Stromme et al., 1978).

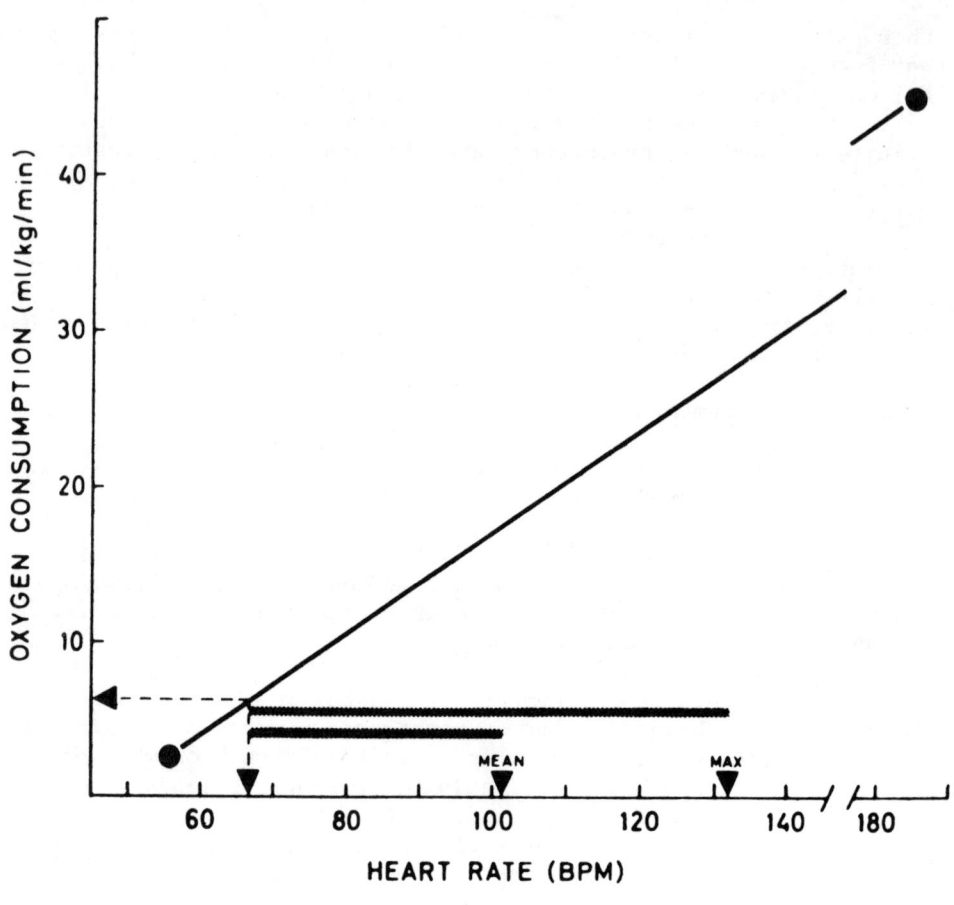

Figure 2

Muscle use increases the release of norepinephrine into the blood stream (Folkow, Haggendal and Lisander, 1967). Therefore, a task which requires a certain mental load or a certain psychological activation will lead to lower norepinephrine level than the same level of activation in a situation which requires additional muscle use. This makes the traditional determination of norepinephrine in urine or in blood plasma a less reliable way of determining catecholamine activity. As mentioned above, it is possible that determination of free fatty acid levels may be a more reliable method.

4. Wear and tear, strain, stress and health

From a medical point of view, as well as of common human interest, an important aspect of mental load would be to establish whether it is possible to identify loads which are overloads leading to pathological consequences from a physical or psychological point of view.

The relationship between health and stress is a complex and a confused one. Recent animal data suggest that the relationship is determined by the same psychological factors we have referred to as coping. When coping is possible, or when the individual evaluates the situation as one he is coping with, there is no evidence of pathology or of bodily changes which may be assumed to lead to pathology (see Ursin, 1978). When coping or control is impossible, there is a development of pathology, at least in acute animal experiments (Weiss, 1972). Repeated pressor effect on the vascular system may lead to hypertension in genetically predisposed mice (Folkow, 1975), but this seems, again, tied to the activation we refer to as tonic, that is the activation which is sensitive to coping (Hansen et al., 1978). Life changes and stressful life events may also lead to pathology, but this seems to be dependent on lack of coping mechanisms (Nuckolls, Cassel and Kaplan, 1972; Theorell, 1976).

Therefore, it seems impossible to measure the mental load itself, and what these psychosomatic complications would indicate are again failure or presence of coping processes. These depend not only on the mental load, but on the competence and the subjective evaluation of load and capacity.

5. Restoration processes

Mental load may affect specific central nervous processes even if we are unable to pick these up by our present recording methods. It is, for example, possible that the mental load would put particular strains on the information processing system, leading to particular biochemical changes which may continue and develop after the exposure to the load situation. There may be biochemical changes of a similar kind to those initiated by the learning experiences and activation. Such changes in the CNS may last for long periods after exposure.

A particularly interesting aspect of this is the possibility that information load may be related in some way to sleep changes. Oswald (1969) suggested that slow wave sleep (SWS) was mainly for bodily restitution, while rapid eye movement (REM) sleep was related to "brain repair". In particular, many forms of synthesis could take place during REM sleep, including protein synthesis in cerebral neurons. Oswald predicted that animals reared in enriched environments would spend more time in REM sleep than animals reared in isolation. However, when this experiment was performed, it was clear that enriched environment lead to increments both of SWS and REM sleep (Tagney, 1973). In kittens, similar findings were reported by McGinty (1971). In his study the isolated animals had an abnormally low amount of sleep, and a short term exposure (4.5 hr.) to an enriched environment was succeeded by increased sleep. When normal, adult cats were exposed to two hours of intense environmental stimulation, no consistent changes were found in the successive 22 hr. of sleep (Ursin, Ursin and Hamre, 1977).

These studies fail to point to any specific effect on sleep. However, it should be pointed out that enriched environment and isolation experiments by no means qualify as pure information processing experiments. There are obvious "emotional" factors involved.

Animal studies claiming specific increases in REM sleep following learning situations may be more relevant to our problem. Leconte et al. (1973) found increased REM sleep ratio (REM sleep/total sleep) in rats during a 3 hr. recording period after a shock-avoidance task, with maximum increase on the day prior to maximum performance. Similar results were obtained by the same group (Hennevin et al. 1974) in a task involving bar pressing for water, and by Lucero (1970) following maze learning. REM sleep increases have been reported also in mice following avoidance learning, in particular at the time of optimal performance (Smith et al., 1974; Fishbein et al. 1974). The changes reported suggest quite complex relationships to performance and to the postulated "restitutional" or information processing mechanisms. In particular, there are changes both before and after optimal performance has been reached.

These studies seem well controlled for experimental conditions like the effects of shocks, food or water deprivation. However, it is clear that the motivation and therefore activation must be very different in experimental animals compared with untreated, or deprived control animals who are not asked to cope, or controls who are unable to cope with their situation. To us it remains an open question whether these studies really measure effects of information processing, or whether we again are faced with variations in activation levels at the different stages of learning.

We are not convinced of the specificity of the sleep changes reported. The SWS category used in the cited papers comprise everything from drowsiness to deep sleep. A shift in quality from drowsy to deep SWS, which may be accompanied by more REM sleep (Ursin, 1968), might very well be hidden in these grouped SWS data. In all the cited papers reporting REM sleep increases there is no increased length of the REM sleep period, but an increased number of such periods. When this is not accompanied by increased total sleep, it suggests deeper sleep permitting more REM sleep to appear (Ursin, 1970). We suggest that the data so far indicate "better" or deeper sleep in coping animals, in line with our finding of less activation in coping animals.

In humans, there are few published studies on the effects of information processes, learning and mental work load on sleep. A direct approach was taken by Hauri (1968, 1969). He compared the effect on subsequent sleep of 6 hours of relaxation, physical exercise or studying, in male university students. The "studying" consisted of two hr. study of own textbooks or professional literature, followed by 4 hours of mental tasks ranging from Ravens Progressive Matrices to difficult teaching films in physics, about which the subjects had to answer multiple choice questions. The subjects knew that their performance would be graded, and rewarded with 5 or 10 $ if satisfactory. There was no evaluation of performance or reward in the other two conditions. The subsequent $3\frac{1}{2}$ hours of sleep were investigated. There were no significant differences in the sleep EEG between the three conditions, in terms of amount of sleep, amount of any particular sleep stage, number of REM sleep periods or number of sleep stage changes. The latency of sleep onset, however, was significantly longer after studying than in the other two conditions. Heart rate, respiratory rate, peripheral pulse volume, phasic vasoconstrictions, rectal temperature and skin potential variations were not significantly different in the study condition.

The changes found in sleep latency are best explained as the result of higher activation in the study condition. Again, this may be related to the emotional aspects, in particular the achievement motivation.

Sleep has also been investigated after direct emotional stimulation with stressful films. In such cases, Baekeland et al. (1968) found no significant difference in latency of sleep onset or of the first REM sleep period, or the amount of sleep. However, there was more awakening during and after REM sleep periods following stressful films, and also more rapid eye movements during REM sleep. In a similar study, Goodenough et al. (1975) found increased latency to sleep after presleep following the showing of 2 stress films. In conclusion, there seem to be no specific sleep changes or restoration changes after mental load, the changes reported seem to be more consistently related to activation in general.

Sleep is obviously related to wakefulness and activation. The effects of sleep deprivation, for instance, are perhaps best understood as a state which potentiates "dearousing" factors in a given situation (Kjellberg, 1977). It is a commonplace that boredom produces sleepiness. In some workload tasks the boredom may be the most bothersome load, and this will affect both performance and sleep. In humans, it has been shown that following a session of habituation to an auditory stimulation there is more sleep and sleep occurs faster than following a control period (Bohlin, 1971).

CONCLUSION

In this paper, we have discussed the available methods and debated whether there is any possibility of measuring mental load using physiological methods. Our main position is that it is fairly easy to measure and therefore exclude the physical workload, and measure psychological activation. However, there are serious difficulties if one desires to discriminate between emotional factors and information workload. If this is not done, measuring "mental workload" does not involve anything but conventional evaluation of "activation", on which there is a considerable bulk of information. It seems unclear what is achieved by referring to this phenomenon as "mental workload".

Recent data from animal and human experiments may be helpful in furnishing us with a more refined understanding of the emotional processes. The psychological and physiological processes occurring in threatening and challenging situations show clear dependency on experience and development of coping behavior. In particular, it is important to know at which stage of the development of the coping process the individual is, to what extent he evaluates his behavior as coping, how he evaluates his performance, and his motivation to perform in that particular task. The physiological responses recorded are the end results of a very complex psychological matrix. There is some evidence of specificity in the endocrine responses, but these have not been established in any detail.

The physiological changes, and probably also the subjective evaluation of a situation is more dependent on these "conventional" motivational or psychological factors than the information load. It seems difficult to eliminate motivational factors, and if this could be done, what would then maintain the necessary activation for performance, and, therefore, for having any mental load at all?

REFERENCES

Ax, A.F. The physiological differentiation between fear and anger in humans. Psychosomatic Medicine, 1953, 15: 433-442.

Baade, E., Ellertsen, B., Johnsen, T.B. and Ursin, H. Physiology, psychology and performance. In: Ursin, H., Baade, E. and Levine, S. (eds.): Coping men - a study in human psychobiology. San Francisco, Academic Press, to appear in 1978.

Baekeland, F., Koulack, D. and Lasky, R. Effects of a stressful presleep experience on electroencephalograph - recorded sleep. Psychophysiology, 1968, 4: 436-443.

Blix, A.S., Stromme, S.B. and Ursin, H. Additional heart rate - an indicator of psychological activation. Aerospace Medicine, 1974, 45: 1219-1222.

Bohlin, G. Monotonous stimulation, sleep onset and habituation of the orienting reaction. Electroencephalography and clinical Neurophysiology, 1971, 31: 593-601.

Brodal, A. The reticular formation of the brain stem. Anatomical aspects and functional correlations. Edinburgh, Oliver and Boyd, 1957.

Coover, G.D. Ursin, H. and Levine, S. Plasma-corticosterone levels during active-avoidance learning in rats. Journal of Comparative and Physiological Psychology, 1973, 82: 170-174.

Fenz, W.D. Strategies for coping with stress. In Sarason, I.G. and Spielberger, C.D. (eds.): Stress and anxiety, Vol. 2. Hemisphere (Wiley) New York, 1975.

Fishbein, W. Kastaniotis, C. and Chattman, D. Paradoxical sleep: prolonged augmentation following learning. Brain Research, 1974, 79: 61-75.

Folkow, R. Central neurohormonal mechanisms in spontaneously hypertensive rats compared with human essential hypertension. Clinical Science and Molecular Medicine, 1975, 48: 205s-214s.

Folkow, B., Häggendal, J. and Lisander, B. Extent of release and elimination of noradrenaline at peripheral adrenergic nerve terminals. Acta Physiologica Scandinavica, 1967, suppl.307: 1-38.

Goodenough, D.R., Witkin, H.A. Koulack, D. and Cohen, H. The effects of stress films on dream affect and on respiration and eye-movement activity during rapid-eye-movement sleep. Psychophysiology (1975), 12, 313-320.

Hansen, J.R. Støa, K.F. Blix, A.S. and Ursin, H. Urinary levels of epinephrine and norepinephrine in parachutist trainees. In Ursin, H., Baade, E. and Levine, S. (eds.). Coping men - a study in human psychobiology. San Francisco, Academic Press, to appear in 1978.

Hauri, P. Effects of evening activity on early night sleep. Psychophysiology, 1968, 4: 267-277

Hauri, P. The influence of evening activity on the onset of sleep. Psychophysiology, 1969, 5:426-430.

Hebb, D.O. Drives and the CNS (conceptual nervous system) Psychological Review, 1955, 62: 243-254.

Hennevin, E., Leconte, P. et Bloch, V. Augmentation du sommeil paradoxal provoquée par l'acquisition, l'extinction et la reaquisition d'un apprentissage á renforcement positif. Brain Research, 1974, 70: 43-54.

Kandel, E.R. Nerve cells and behavior. Scientific American, 1970, 223 (No. 1): 57-70.

Kjellberg, A. Sleep deprivation and some aspects of performance: III. Motivation, comment and conclusions. Waking and sleeping, 1977, I: 149-153.

Lacey, J.I. Individual differences in somatic response patterns. Journal of comparative and physiological psychology, 1950, 43: 338-350.

Leconte, P., Hennevin, E. et Block, V. Analyse des effets d'un apprentissage et de son niveau d'acquisition sur le sommeil paradoxal consécutif. Brain Research, 1973, 49, 367-379.

Levine, S., Goldman, L. and Coover, G.D. Expectancy and the pituitary-adrenal system. In Ciba Foundation Symposium: Physiology, emotion and psychosomatic illness, Amsterdam, Elsevier, 1972. pp. 281-291.

Lindsley, D.B. Emotion. In Stevens, S (ed): Handbook of experimental psychology, New York, Wiley, 1951, pp. 473-516.

Lord, B.J., King, M.G. and Pfeister, H.P. Chemical sympathectomy and two-way escape and avoidance learning in the rat. Journal of comparative and physiological psychology, 1976, 90: 303-316.

Lucero, M.A. Lengthening of REM sleep duration consecutive to learning in the rat. Brain Research, 1970, 20: 319-322.

Lykken, D.T. Neuropsychology and psychophysiology in personality research. In E.F. Borgatta & Lambert, W.W. (eds.) Handbook of personality theory and research. Chicago, Rand McNally, 1968.

Malmo, R.B. Studies of anxiety: Some clinical origins of the activation concept. In Spielberger, C.D. (ed.) Anxiety and behavior, New York, Academic Press, 1966, pp.157-177.

McGinty, D.J. Encephalization and the neural control of sleep. In Sterman, M.B., McGinty, D.J. and Adinolfi, A.M. (eds.) Brain Development and Behavior. New York, Academic Press, 1971, pp. 335-357.

Moruzzi, G. and Magoun, H.W. Brain stem reticular formation and activation of the EEG. Electroencephalography and Clinical Neurophysiology, 1949, 1: 455-473.

Nuckolls, K.B., Cassel, J., and Kaplan, B.H. Psychosocial assets, life crisis and the prognosis of pregnancy. American Journal of Epidemiology, 1972, 95: 431-441.

Oswald, I. Human brain protein, drugs and dreams. Nature, 1969, 223: 893-897.

Risberg, J. and Ingvar, H. Increase of blood flow in cortical association areas during memorization and abstract thinking. European Neurology, 1971/72, 6: 236-241.

Rule, B.G. and Nesdale, A.R. Environmental stressors, emotional arousal and aggression. In Sarason, I.G. and Spielberger C.D. (eds.) Stress and anxiety, Vol. 3, Hemisphere, New York 1976.

Sassin, J.F. Parker, D.C., Mace, J.W., Gotlin, R.W., Johnson, L.C. and Rossman, L.G. Human growth hormone release: Relation to slow-wave sleep and sleep-waking cycles. Science, 1969, 165: 513-515.

Schachter, J. Pain, fear and anger in hypertensives and normotensives. A psychophysiological study. Psychosomatic Medicine, 1957, 19: 17-29.

Schacther, S., and Singer, J.E. Cognitive, social and physiological determinants of emotional state. Psychological Review, 1962, 69: 379-399.

Smith, C., Kitahama, K., Valatx, J.L., Jouvet, M. Increased paradoxical sleep in mice during acquisition of a shock avoidance task. Brain Research, 1974, 77: 221-230.

Sokolov, Y.N. Perception and the conditional reflex. Oxford, Pergamon, 1963.

Strømme, S., Wikeby, P., Blix, A.S. and Ursin, H. Additional heart rate. In Ursin, H., Baade, E. and Levine, S. (eds.) Coping men - a study in human psychobiology. San Francisco, Academic Press, to appear in 1978.

Tagney, J. Sleep patterns related to rearing rats in enriched and impoverished environments. Brain Research, 1973, 53: 353-361.

Theorell, T. Selected illnesses and somatic factors in relation to two psychosocial stress indices - a prospective study on middle-aged construction building workers. Journal of Psychosomatic Research, 1976, 20, 7-20.

Thompson, R.F. and Spencer, W.A. Habituation: A model phenomenon for the study of neuronal substrates of behavior. Psychological Review, 1966, 73: 16-43.

Ursin, H. Activation, coping and health. In Ursin, H., Baade, E. and Levine, S. (eds.). Coping men - a study in human psychobiology. San Francisco, Academic Press, to appear in 1978.

Ursin, H., Baade, E. and Levine, S. (eds.) Coping men - a study in human psychobiology. San Francisco, Academic Press, to appear in 1978.

Ursin, H., Wester, K. and Ursin, R. Habituation to electrical stimulation of the brain in unanaesthetized cats. Electroencephalography and Clinical Neurophysiology, 1967, 23: 41-49.

Ursin, R. The two stages of slow wave sleep in the cat and their relation to REM sleep. Brain Research, 1968, 11, 347-356.

Ursin, R. Sleep stage relations within the sleep cycles of the cat. Brain Research, 1970, 20: 91-97.

Ursin, R., Ursin, H. and Hamre, E. No effect of two hours of intense environmental stimulation on subsequent sleep in the cat. Sleep Research, 1977, 6. (in press).

Vollmer, F. Motivational and psychological arousal. In Ursin, H., Baade, E. and Levine, S. (eds.). Coping men - a study of human psychobiology. San Francisco, Academic Press, to appear in 1978.

Weiss, J.M. Influence of psychological variables on stress-induced pathology. In Ciba Foundation Symposium: Physiology, emotion and psychosomatic illness, Amsterdam, Elsevier, 1972, pp. 253-265.

FINAL REPORT OF PHYSIOLOGICAL PSYCHOLOGY GROUP

P. Hamilton, G. Mulder, H. Strasser, and

H. Ursin (Chairman)

What workload measures are offered by psychophysiology? This question must be rephrased and the problem stated clearly before it can be answered, as is evident from the papers of Mulder, and Ursin & Ursin. The Ursins use the activation concept of Lindsley (1951), Duffy (1972) and others. Mulder uses the same idea, but employs the term <u>defensive reaction</u>, which is commonly used for activation phenomena affecting the cardio-vascular system (see Folkow and Neill, 1971, for references). The term activation (or sometimes arousal) is used conventionally to identify an increment in CNS activity measured directly or indirectly. The important aspect in our context is that it implies a change in the state of the system influencing its information processing capabilities.

There is no doubt that psychophysiologists are able to measure the changes of the system during and after the subject is confronted with a task. The concept of "state" as we use it can be seen as modulating the transfer characteristics of the information processing system.

A number of state parameters can be used for this purpose, but they may differ in their sensitivity, time characteristics, and the physiological and anatomical systems involved; and there are also specific technical and methodological problems for each variable (see Mulder; Strasser; Ursin and Ursin). A complete review and discussion of all available methods are beyond the scope of this paper. However, we would like to stress that a thorough understanding of the state parameters used is mandatory. Technical, physiological and methodological issues must be taken seriously, in order to prevent difficulties in interpretation later on.

An important issue is the separation between physiological processes due to physical load and those due strictly to mental (or psychological load). Many physiological parameters are affected by both. However, it is possible to distinguish between these two sources of variance. In laboratory experiments Mulder controlled for the effects of motor load by identifying the 0.10 Hz component of the cardiac interval signal. This component appeared to be a very sensitive indicator of the task load when the measurement requirements were met. Blix, Strømme and Ursin (1974) have described "additional heart rate" as a measurement of psychological activation. This is obtained by simultaneous recording of heart rate and oxygen consumption. The "additional heart rate" is the heart rate which goes beyond the heart rate which corresponds to the oxygen uptake in a particular situation. Measurements of many hormones seem unaffected by muscular work, but this is not true for all hormones. Electroencephalographic and related methods may also be useful.

However, we are unable to discriminate between emotional load and information load. The activation response is determined by task characteristics such as uncertainty, novelty, and unpredictability. All these factors put demands on the subject's active information processing and also involve personality characteristics and emotional factors. It also seems difficult to make the distinction between emotional and information processing from a theoretical point of view. Hamilton (1975) holds that emotional stimuli can be considered as information, and consequently have to be processed in a capacity limited information processing system.

Subjects entering an experimental situation for the first time show a high level of activation. We attribute this to the fact that the subject reacts to the total situation including the task and the task environment. The subject therefore processes both task relevant and task irrelevant information. If the situation remains the same the subjects habituate to the experimental situation itself. He learns the skills needed, and that he can in fact cope with the task. Accordingly, there is a gradual shift to processing task relevant rather than task irrelevant information. This probably accounts for often-noticed phenomena, for instance a decrease in heart rate and an increase in heart rate variance, as well as an improvement in performance (reaction time shorter, less errors) with increased experience.

There is a steady decrease in the general background

activation, and this enables us to identify more precisely the residual activation related to the difficulty of the task. However, if the total situation is changed, the background activity level increases again.

Therefore, it seems extremely important not to stick to only one sampling session, but to repeat the measurement several times at different levels of experience with the test situation. Only in those conditions can valid statements be made about the activation remaining after elimination of the task irrelevant aspects of the situation.

Methodological considerations

In Table 1 we give a survey of some psychophysiological varibles often in use in human workload studies. At least some of these variables relate differently to input, decision and output processes. As we discussed previously, when a task becomes automized, the decision component gradually declines, and the level of activation diminishes. This is indicated in Table 1 by the "bypass" line. Some of the physiological variables recorded may be directly involved in the task to be performed. For instance, if the task consists mostly of visual monitoring components, e.g. the subject has to scan a visual display, EOG-activity is directly task related. Similarly, if the task consists of repetitive movements the EMG-activity in the muscles involved will be specific indices. The variables listed in the middle part of the table may be contaminated by such task specific activity and in such cases this must be taken into account. A task analysis is therefore mandatory, and it should include as extensive analysis as possible of the psychological and physiological processes involved.

Physiological variables have a certain region in which they optimally differentiate between task or activation levels. In general the upper extreme and lower extreme levels are less sensitive than the intermediate area. In laboratory studies task variables may be manipulated directly. Contaminating factors may be brought under control by keeping them constant or controlling for them in the experimental design, for instance, control of test order. Test order may also be used as an experimental variable (Mulder, 1973; Muller, Adler and Strasser, 1976) and tasks scaled in their power to change the order effect. Age and motivation factors should also be controlled. In field studies it may prove difficult to have the same rigid control. However, some principles must be respected. We propose the following research strategy. The subject in the field situation must be measured more than once in order to minimize psychological factors

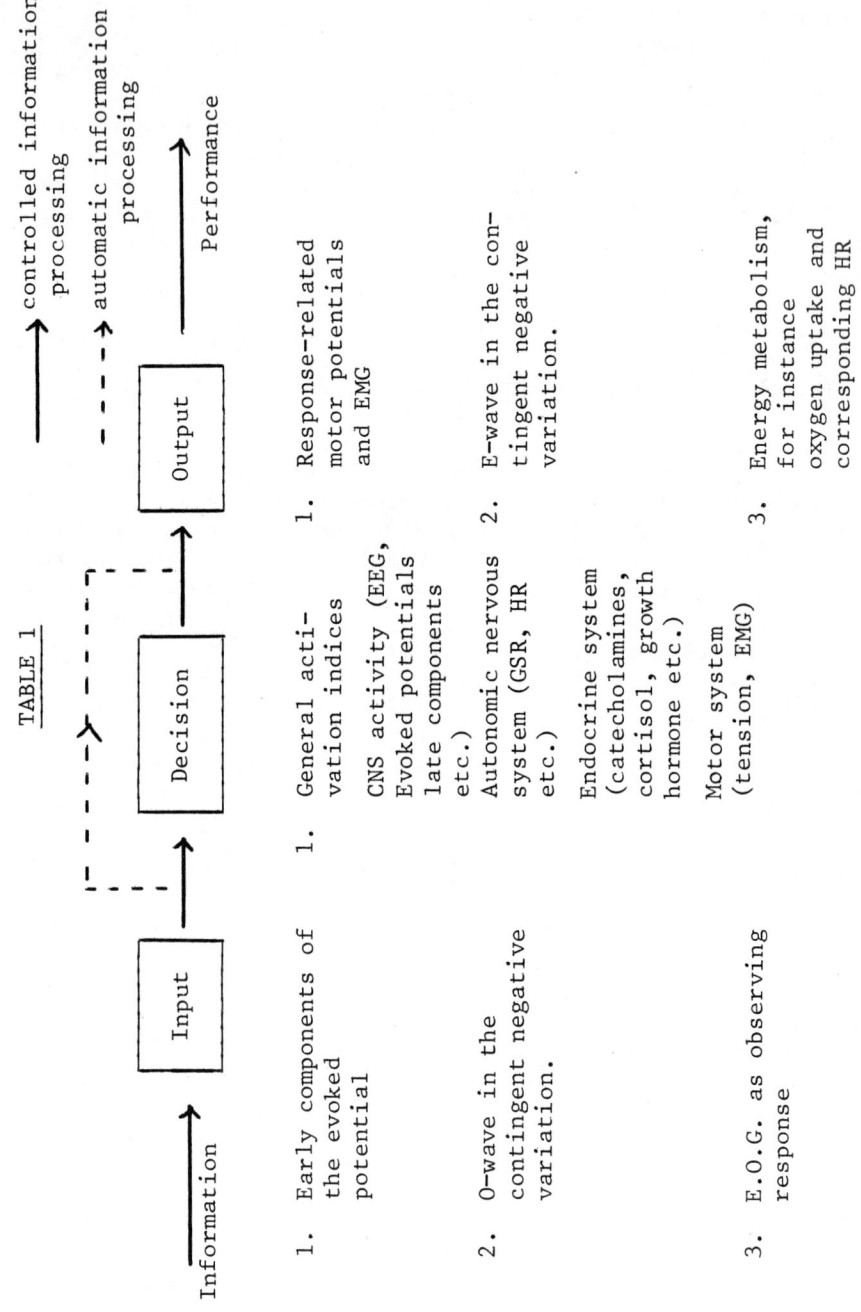

TABLE 1

involved in the measurement procedure. The same subjects must be measured in controlled laboratory situations which should be adapted to the field situation. The reactions in laboratory tasks differing in difficulty must be compared to reactions of the same subject in field situations. Finally, the result from laboratory and field studies should be treated by adequate multivariate statistics.

The observations are of a multivariate nature, since according to our view one should repeatedly measure simultaneously a number of system variables. This research design necessitates multivariate statistical techniques (see Mulder 1973, and Van der Geer, 1975). Measurements may be done in all subjects at the same time. This reduces error variance attributable to any procedural differences (Strasser, Einars and Muller-Limmroth, 1977).

The difference in rise time and recovery time between different physiological processes must also be remembered. At any given time after a given experience, some physiological processes may still be rising while others have recovered completely. Heart rate is a very fast indicator, while cortisol level in plasma may require 15 min before it reaches its peak level (see Strasser, 1977; Ursin and Ursin, this book).

It should be remembered that many physiological systems recorded in traditional psychophysiological experiments have a dual innervation (sympathetic vs. parasympathetic nervous system). Confusing results may derive from the fact that both nervous systems relate to activation although often antagonistic on the peripheral process. It is therefore necessary to have a thorough understanding of the physiological process studied. Noninvasive methods are preferred because of psychological consequences, but it is not always possible to avoid "wet physiology". If such methods are used, the stress effect of the sampling procedure must be taken into account.

In summary, we may formulate the following demands on methods used in field studies to assess physiological profiles of relevant job factors (modified after Strasser, Einars & Muller-Limmroth, 1977).

1) Repeated measurements to control or investigate habituation and learning factors (development of coping skills) and check for test order effects.

2) Multi-variate long-term recordings "on-the-job" if possible.

3) Minimizing obtrusiveness and technical expenditure.

4) Additional laboratory studies in order to calibrate field data.

5) Subjective self rating (standardized questionnaires on subjective contentment, subjective scaling of job factors, etc.).

6) Careful job analyses, including analyses of physiological factors to be studied, and the energy requirement and response system involved in the task. Also including psychological and social factors involved in job and the experiment (whether the investigation is acceptable or imposed, what is seen to be the purpose of the investigation).

7) Multivariate statistical methods.

Health issues

Since activation affects almost all bodily processes, it may have health consequences to have too much or too little activation. It is clear that the somatic changes induced by activation may lead to dramatic consequences when they affect a diseased organ. A sharp rise in blood pressure or an increased heart rate may kill a person with vascular disease. It is, however, impossible to live without activation. There are, for instance, significant activation-like events taking place during the rapid eye movement (REM) periods of sleep occurring every night.

A more interesting question is whether activation itself provokes disease. It is widely accepted that such relationships exist, but there are few hard data demonstrating this. In particular, such a relationship has been postulated for the pituitary-adrenal axis regulating cortisol, and also for the cardiovascular system. This is the background for the widely held assumption that "stress" causes disease. If this were true, mental load could cause such disease.

Selye (1974) called the _stimulus_ affecting the organism a "stressor", which then lead to the response "stress". If the organism were unable to respond adequately, the defense would break down and result in "maladaptation" and disease. This nomenclature has lead to some confusion. In physical sciences it is generally accepted to use "stress" for the stimulus or the input ("Belastung" in German), and "strain" ("Beanspruchung") for the resulting state. In the popular health mythology the misconception is total, "stress" is supposed to lead to disease.

Selye is often given as the reference for this postulate. Selye himself has repeatedly pointed out that the absence of his stress reaction is only found after death. The way Selye uses the terms seems identical to the way we have used "activation".

In animal experiments it seems generally accepted that there is a relationship between activation and disease. Again, it depends on "coping" or problem solving. When a rat has learned active avoidance, there is a gradual decrement in activation (measured as corticosterone rise - Coover, Ursin and Levine, 1973). This decrement is not directly related to performance, and is eliminated if the situation is changed. If there is no solution to such a problem, or the rat is left without any control, or without any proper response feedback, stomach ulcerations occur at least in acute experiments (Weiss, 1972). In our context, this suggests that if there is no way of reducing a considerable workload by finding a solution and making this solution "automatic", there may be a health risk involved also for humans. However, this is probably only the case if success or failure really matters for the subject.

Repeated pressor effects on the vascular system by "defense" reactions (= activation) may result in hypertension, but only in genetically predisposed mice (Folkow, 1975). This type of activation is mainly the type Ursin and Ursin refer to as "tonic", and which they claim is sensitive to coping. The "phasic" arousal, which is more resistant to coping, also affects the cardiovascular system (increased Additional Heart Rate, epinephrine release), but this probably does not produce the pressor effect.

The most relevant data from humans derive from studies of the relationship between health and life events. Life changes and "stressful" events may lead to pathology but this seems also to be related to coping mechanisms or ability to solve problems (see Ursin and Ursin, this volume).

Previously there has been concern over the "overshoot" or overresponding of the activation process. Cannon referred to the sympathetic reaction as the "wisdom of the body". Since civilized man is not supposed to fight or flee, the process has also been referred to as the "stupidity" of the body. However, it is a general preparatory response pattern, and very sensitive to "coping". Therefore, it is very quickly eliminated when there is no longer a call for general activation and problem solving. We have no data demonstrating this to be pathogenic, in fact it seems to be a reasonable and healthy endeavour to be engaged in activation.

Conclusion

The physiological consequences of mental load are more than convenient indicators. They constitute important biological events which may be crucial not only for the well being of the subject, but also for his physical and mental health. The attention of society has shifted from physical work to mental load, and there is considerable concern with the possible ill effects of load. It is therefore necessary to follow the physiological consequences of activation to determine when activation or load would be detrimental to health, and when activation is a necessary and enjoyable quality of life. In particular it seems necessary to study long term effects of high and low mental load in work situations.

It is possible to discriminate between physical workload and mental load. When tasks involve physical loads methods which discriminate should be used, or methods that measure only mental load.

At least at the present time we see no possibility of differentiating between emotional and information processing as two separate and independent processes. We suggest that central nervous information processing is involved in both phenomena, and that there is at present no clear separation of the structures involved. Therefore both constitute a mental load. It is possible to discriminate between task relevant and task irrelevant levels for the experimenter, but not in the physiological processes when the subject is not able to discriminate himself.

Since there is no physiological short cut that identifies task relevant loads from task irrelevant loads, the psychological factors should not be ignored or regarded as noise. They may constitute the real load for the subject. The variance should be used to map the underlying mechanisms. Multivariant methods including factor analyses should be pursued.

During learning to cope with a given task, and to cope with being studied, there is a gradual shift from task irrelevant to task relevant stimuli. During this development there is a shift in the psychological processes involved, and also in the intensity of the physiological response. This shift is not directly related to performance, but to the evaluation of the situation by the individual. The important question for the individual seems to be whether he thinks he is coping with the situation or not. When the task is performed "automatically" without subjective awarenesss of the task, the subject has a minimum of activation.

FINAL REPORT OF PHYSIOLOGICAL PSYCHOLOGY GROUP

FUTURE RESEARCH AREAS

1. Health issues, quality of life

   Physiological indicators should be monitored in real life situations, and basic research in psychophysiology should elucidate the relationships between prolonged activation and health. In particular, what are the psychological and pathophysiological mechanisms which are assumed to underly the possible pathogenic effect of overload, unsolvable conflict and non-coping? Are there similar effects of underload? In this field there is a substantial need for more information from basic research including relevant animal experiments as well as careful and interdisciplinary clinical and field studies of humans.

2. Emotional vs. information processing loads

   We are not convinced that emotional and information processing loads can be differentiated, and want more research directed towards this question. There is too little information on activation change from early stages of problem solving to the later stages of "automated" performance. Longitudinal studies are required. Information from such studies is necessary for a better understanding of the health and well being issues of coping with tasks, loads and "stressors".

3. Relationship between physiological and psychological indicators

   Psychological factors should not be considered as noise, since they are extremely powerful sources of activation, and may override the other aspects of the load on the system. One must not expect simple solutions to what these psychological factors are. A wide test battery and a careful mapping of the whole social situation will reveal many factors. We recommend multivariant methods as one possible way of coping with this complexity. We would also suggest that the physiological mechanisms should be treated by multivariant methods. Even if we have treated activation as a single phenomenon in our papers, we should not give up attempts to find specific types of activation, or specific time course development tied to specific psychological mechanisms.

Evaluation of current methodology in assessment of operator workload

There is a large number of methods used in the assessment of operator workload (strain, effort). These methods differ on several characteristics. No comprehensive evaluation of all the interesting characteristics of all methods is available at the present time. One of us (H. Strasser) has designed a matrix which could be used for this purpose, and he is also willing to collect the necessary information. The matrix appears below and the reader's responses should be sent to Strasser at the address shown in this volume. The matrix consists of a list of all main categories of methods plotted against the important characteristics. The methods included in the matrix are: <u>Vegetative variables</u>; (cardiac/activity, heart rate, arrhythmia), blood pressure, respiratory activity, galvanic skin reactions, <u>central nervous variables</u>; electroencephalogram, evoked responses, <u>biochemical variables</u>; hormone levels in urine and plasma, other plasma variables (free fatty acids, blood glucose), <u>peripheral variables</u>; flicker fusion frequency, pupil diameter, electromyogram, electrooculogram, <u>subjective methods</u>; rating scales of complaints, vigilance, strain, <u>loading tasks</u>; continuous and discrete tasks, paced and self-paced, <u>performance measure</u>: continuous, discrete, reaction time, <u>observations</u>; behavioral measures and task analysis. These categories of methods should be evaluated against the following characteristics of measures: description of techniques, technical expenditure, applicability in field studies, characteristics of measurement (absolute scores, relative scores) artifacts, nonobstrusiveness, validity, reliability, time lag between stress and strain reaction, span of susceptibility, variability, relationship to level of load, required registration time, sensitivity for sensory vs. central nervous (concentration, emotional and motor load, and other limitations).

FINAL REPORT OF PHYSIOLOGICAL PSYCHOLOGY GROUP

H. STRASSER

METHODOLOGY IN ASSESSMENT OF OPERATOR WORKLOAD (STRAIN, EFFORT)

MAIN AND SUBCATEGORIES OF METHODS	CHARACTERISTICS OF MEASURES
VEGETATIVE VARIABLES	
Cardiac activity – heart rate – arrhythmia	
Blood pressure	
Respiratory activity – rate – variability of rate – tidal volume – ventilation	
Galvanic skin reactions – basic level – spontaneous fluctuations – evoked response amplitude – evoked response latency	
CENTRAL NERV. VARIABLES	
Electroencephalogramm – spectral components – indices in the time domain	
Evoked Response acoustic modality – amplitude (e.g. N_1/P_2) of response – latency of response optical modality – amplitude of response – latency of response	
BIOCHEM. VARIABL.	
Excretion of adrenalin in the urine	
Excretion of noradrenalin	
–	
–	
PERIPHERAL VARIABLES	
Flimmer fusion frequency	
Pupil diameter	
Electromyogramms	
Electrooculogramms	
SUBJECTIVE METH.	
Graphic rating scales – short-term felt complaints – long-term felt complaints – vigilance – strain in general – strain induced by different job factors – .... –	
LOADING TASKS	
Continuous tasks – paced – self-paced	
Discrete tasks – paced – self-paced	
– .... –	
PERFORMANCE MEASURES	
Continuous measures	
Discrete measures	
Reaction time	
–	
MODELS	
– .... – .... –	
OBSERVATIONS	
Behavioral measures	
Task analysis	
–	

Column headers (characteristics of measures):
- Description of technique
- Technical expenditure (amount of equipment) – (zero/low/medium/high/very high: 0 – 4)
- Applicability of measurement (Feasibility in field studies) – continuously (on-the-job) – discrete (before or after load)
- Measures usable as – absolute scores – relative scores
- Affectability by artifacts
- Non-obtrusiveness (freedom of interference, acceptability) – low/medium/high/very high: 1 – 4)
- Validity (possibility to generalize) – (low/medium/high/very high: 1 – 4)
- Reliability – (low/medium/high/very high: 1 – 4)
- Time lag between stress and strain reaction – (zero/low/medium/high/very high: 0 – 4)
- Span of susceptibility – (zero/low/medium/high/very high: 0 – 4)
- Variability – intra-individually (low/medium/high/very high: 1 – 4) – inter-individually (low/medium/high/very high: 1 – 4)
- Best indication when level of load (low/medium/high/very high: 1 – 4)
- Registration time needed for analysis (minutes/hours)
- Special sensitivity for sensory or input (receptor) load – central nervous load (concentration) – central nervous load (emotional load) – memory load
- Other limitations
- Used by (reference list number)

PART V:

APPLIED PSYCHOLOGY

AND MENTAL WORKLOAD

MENTAL WORKLOAD MEASUREMENT IN AIR TRAFFIC CONTROL

V.D. Hopkin

RAF Institute of Aviation Medicine

Farnborough, Hampshire

Air traffic control seeks to ensure the safe, orderly and expeditious flow of air traffic. Air space is finite, but the number and variety of aircraft requiring air traffic control services is increasing and will continue to do so. Packing more aircraft into the same air space leads to strategic rather than tactical planning, to less flexibility of manoeuvres, to less time to recognise and resolve problems, and to more constraints in evolving solutions to problems.

To handle more aircraft, the quality of the navigational information in the system has to be improved. More aircraft generate more work for controllers. Giving each controller a smaller region of air space to control becomes self-defeating by increasing the required liaison and handover problems. One response has been to automate certain functions of the system, mainly by providing some form of computer assistance. Starting with data storage, compilation and retrieval, automation has evolved towards problem solving and decision making, so that an automated aid may offer proposed solutions to problems which the man must accept or reject, or provide a prediction facility to enable him to see what would happen if he implemented his own solution.

Whether such expensive aids are introduced depends firstly on their technical feasibility and reliability, secondly on their proven or putative efficacy in increasing the handling capacity or safety of the system, and thirdly on cost effectiveness. Hitherto, although much has been said and written about human factors, the needs, skills and abilities of the man, and the implications for his tasks and his workload, have not been a decisive influence in the choice and format of aids. One reason has been the difficulty of demonstrating in quantitative, and ultimately financial, terms what the consequences for mental workload are of progressively introducing automation.

Most possible measures of mental workload have been proposed and tried in air traffic control but have not proved to be helpful. This note outlines some of the current practical problems in assessing mental workload in air traffic control, while emphasising the vital need to have impartial quantitative measures for doing so, both to ensure the safety and efficiency of future systems and to design jobs which have an optimum blend of workload, utilisation of skill, and job satisfaction.

According to behavioural measures, an air traffic controller on a busy day appears to be doing several tasks at once. He is scanning radar and other displays, talking to pilots or other controllers, annotating flight strips, calling down information onto tabular displays, planning ahead and anticipating future problems, liaising, up-dating or removing out-of-date information, etc. Although his apparent facility to do more than one thing at once is no doubt due to rapid attention switching, combined with certain tasks such as keying, which requires little or no attention, the variety and complexity of his actions makes it difficult to express all aspects of his task in any single measurable dimension. There is considerable evidence in air traffic control to suggest that mental workload may not be a single coherent measurable dimension at all, in any way which is of practical use. For example, comparisons may be made between the verbal transmission of information from pilot to controller and the automated transponding of that information from the aircraft to a computer on the ground so that it appears as alphanumeric labels on the controller's display. Such a change is accompanied by a substantial reduction in speech workload. However, this reduction is not associated with any change according to any other measure of system performance. A common claim is that replacing routine functions will enable the controller to devote more time to decision making and problem solving. In practice, such replacements never lead to demonstrable changes in the amount or quality of decision making or problem solving.

From time to time physiological and biochemical measures have been taken of air traffic controllers. The claimed purpose has usually been to assess workload or to assess stress. Air traffic control is generally conceded to be a stressful occupation. Physiological and biochemical indices usually demonstrate this by comparing air traffic controllers with other professions, or by showing correlations between these physiological and biochemical measures on the one hand and systems measures such as traffic density. Biographical measures, of morbidity and mortality rates of controllers for example, have shown that controllers vary greatly from one country to another, sometimes having much higher rates than comparable populations yet sometimes being not significantly different from them.

Subjective evidence related to mental workload has frequently been obtained in a variety of ways. Controllers may report being very busy or becoming very tired. A fellow controller may make subjective assessments of another controller's performance, although these assessments tend to reflect the assessor's estimate of what his own workload would be rather than his knowledge of the loading on the assessed controller. Subjective comments by questionnaire, interview or debriefing are commonly obtained from practising controllers and in air traffic control evaluations. Various case studies or clinical incidents are commonly cited, as evidence of excessive mental workload under certain circumstances.

If the above behavioural, physiological, biochemical and subjective data about controllers handling peak traffic are considered together, a common conclusion would be that controllers have too much to do, because the peak mental workload, however assessed, is excessive and should be reduced, because the job takes considerable physiological and biochemical toll of controllers which is not in the long term in the interests of their wellbeing, and because they report that they are extremely tired at the end of their shift or watch. All the above would point to a need to reduce excessive workload and to have some quantifiable measure to show that it had been reduced and how far it had been reduced. A measure would also be needed to predict how far mental workload would be reduced if certain system changes were introduced. However, the above picture is incomplete and in certain respects misleading.

If the controller is asked whether he likes to be busy he normally replies that he does. If he is asked what gives him satisfaction in his job he cites examples when he had to use his professional skills and knowledge to resolve a very difficult problem, entailing high mental workload. While he welcomes simpler forms of automation which gather, compile, store, update and present information, he views with misgivings those which affect his status, his professional pride, his responsibilities, the opportunities to acquire and use skills, and the occasions when he can demonstrate his competence to his colleagues. In short, reductions in mental workload if carried too far, can be expected to generate or aggravate problems of boredom, job satisfaction, effort and challenge. Measures of mental workload in air traffic control are therefore needed to quantify the relationships between mental workload and such factors. They need to measure when there is so little mental workload that the controller becomes bored.

A main practical problem is to measure the consequences for mental workload of a proposed change in system design. This may take the form of computer assistance in decision making or problem solving; it may represent a new form of display technology; it may be a new control at the man/machine interface; it may be a new form of communication such as data link. Other system changes

are occurring which have indirect consequences for mental workload.
For example, developments in navigational aids mean that the information in future systems will be very much more exact and more
frequently updated than corresponding information in current systems.
There is a problem in conveying to the man how accurate it is and
how far he should trust it; how is it possible to assess the effects
on mental workload if the man has to use information which he does
not fully trust?

Some of the problems may best be clarified by a simple example.
In future systems it is possible to have a conflict resolution
facility. This means that when two aircraft are potentially on
collision courses the system not only detects this and draws the
controller's attention to it but provides a proposed solution to the
problem by suggesting that one or both of the aircraft should change
height, speed or heading. The controller has to accept or reject
this solution. To do so rationally, he needs to know a great deal
about how the computer has been programmed. He may believe that a
proposed solution will precipitate a further potential conflict but
be unable to discover whether the proposed solution has taken this
into account. In other words he is poorly placed to act rationally
or optimally or to complement the machine so that together man and
machine arrive at the best decision. Suppose however, the system is
basically safe - this can be presumed because the conflict resolution aid would not otherwise be introduced - and therefore the man
gradually comes to trust it. Once he has formed the habit of
accepting solutions, he generally has no need to remember what they
were. When he had to resolve the conflict himself he had to remember
what his solution was and be able to recall which factors he took into
account while arriving at it: therefore he could recognise at once
if new evidence appeared to warrant a revision of the decision.
But if he habitually accepts automated solutions, the content of
his memory is changed. New evidence may go unrecognized, particularly
if he cannot even recall the solution. The provision of this automated aid is normally associated, therefore, with a considerable
increase in keying activity which represents the man calling down
information onto his display in order to top up his memory if he can.

Certain automated aids may induce a change of strategy. For
example, earlier forms of radar display presented a plan view of
traffic. If aircraft appeared from this to be in conflict the controller checked on another display, usually a flight strip board,
whether the aircraft in potential conflict in fact had height separation - if they had a substantial height separation he need take no
action. More modern systems replace this with a plan view where the
identity and height of each aircraft is given on a label on the radar
display itself at the position the aircraft occupies. This means
the controller may primarily separate aircraft by height: only if
there is a potential conflict between aircraft at the same height
does he need to examine the plan information about them in detail.

The above examples show that the introduction of system changes may entail major alterations in strategy, major differences in man/machine relationships and in the role which the man must fulfil, and major changes in the content of the man's memory and of what he knows about the traffic situation he is controlling. It is never possible to automate a function in a manual system in its entirety. It is never possible to introduce a major automated aid without changing other aspects of the system (e.g. display changes induce communication changes) and other aspects of the man's task (e.g. changes in strategy, in required skills, or in existing knowledge).

In this context, questions about mental workload are not posed in terms of mental workload. Questions are asked and answers are expected in system terms - e.g. how many aircraft can the man cope with; what should the peak traffic density per hour be at a given work position; what aspect of the task is most vulnerable to overloading; what are the consequences for system efficiency and safety if the man becomes overloaded. The main applications of any successful measure of mental workload would be in evaluations of proposed future systems to demonstrate that the changes they entail do not imply excessive workload, and that workload would not be reduced so much that boredom and job dissatisfaction would result. The timescale is very long for changing existing systems. An implication is that there is the requirement not merely to be able to measure mental workload objectively and quantitatively, but to give absolute judgements in terms of that measure, either for controllers in general or for individual controllers, of the points at which workload should be treated as excessive or as too low. One view of excessiveness would be in terms of potential system inefficiency (delays to traffic, fuel penalties, failures to be cleared to intended heights, etc.) or potential reductions in safety (infringements of minimum separation standards, the need for frequent changes in instructions; the solution of problems on a tactical ad hoc basis rather than on longer term flow control basis). Another view of excessiveness is that decrements in decision making or problem solving can be demonstrated, that the man's physical and mental well-being is impaired, and that he judges that he is not merely busy (which he likes), but too busy (which he does not like). Excessiveness may also be associated with system changes, where he must not merely learn to acquire new skills and become proficient at them but learn to forget old skills and discard them when they are no longer relevant.

The above notes may help to illustrate why the problem of measuring mental workload among controllers has so far proved difficult to resolve. The quest remains for a practical measure of mental workload in air traffic control, which can indicate when workload is too low as well as when it is too high.

CURRENT WORKLOAD METHODS AND EMERGING CHALLENGES

Donald L. Parks

Crew Systems Technology, The Boeing Company

Seattle, Washington, U.S.A.

ABSTRACT

This paper summarizes selected technology methods and needs in system design. Three major subject areas are discussed: (1) Background on methods evolution and effectiveness is summarized to illustrate methods and needs. (2) The applied environment and its demands are described, including the system development process with activities, man-machine interface trade-offs, a workload method that is used, and questions the analyst must resolve on a timely basis. More extensive information on a working approach is presented - including the needs, some of the methods, and some of the constraints for presently developing electronic systems. (2) Near term technology challenges are identified for developing computerized, electronic display and control systems. This latter section emphasizes concern with increasing utility of analytic models to develop or evaluate a proliferation of highly flexible display-control-information processing systems. Overall, selected design methods and questions are presented as a framework to which theorists might relate their current state-of-art and provide techniques for present design use.

1.0 INTRODUCTION

We face some interesting and exciting but broad and difficult challenges as we consider using rapidly evolving electronic display-control systems. Most interesting and exciting is their

---

Initially released as Boeing Document D6-44563TN, July 12, 1977.

flexibility, which offers the long desired potential for fully
integrated operator display presentations and control features.
With automatic data processing and formating schemes, we can now
seriously consider presenting what is needed, when needed, and
in the best form for ready, accurate use. We can improve
operator ability to appraise, and thus accept, functions that are
assigned to automatic systems. We can essentially eliminate the
"scan-interpret-decision" workload of traditional electro-
mechanical displays -- which have grown in both number and
implications as "total system" requirements have grown.
Accordingly, as we learn to use the new capability in design,
we can expect to significantly reduce operator task complexity
and workload, to assure the operator can manage further increases
in system performance, and to increase overall operator-system
efficiency and accuracy.

There is little doubt that the electronic control-display
systems will come into extensive use to manage and control many
complicated systems. The potential gains are enormous: we can
both improve information and reduce the vast array of instruments
and controls, as well as numerous status lights, that are used in
many modern control centers to enable operators to monitor and
control both normal and degraded operations. Such improvements
may become firm requirements in order to assure most effective
operation with ever more stringent performance requirements in
future systems. As one example of what could be accomplished,
today's jet aircraft have nearly as many indicators for each
engine as Doolittle's total cockpit had for the first "blind"
landing. The jet also has a multitude of additional instruments
for fuel, environmental control, electrical power, hydraulics and
numerous other subsystems to maintain flight and support life at
flight altitudes. However, one simplification study for Boeing's
737 showed a multifunction switching concept might replace 175
individual displays and controls now requiring 780 square inches
of premium panel space. This and many other integration
concepts are being explored, (e.g. Ref. 6, 25, 36). Similar
possibilities exist for other systems - nuclear power plants
feature hundreds of displays and controls; process control
centers frequently have a complicated and time-critical set of
operations to be monitored; and certainly rail, auto and air
traffic control systems are becoming more heavily loaded and more
complex. Even advanced automotive concepts now feature
electronic displays with computers to monitor and control sub-
systems performance.

However, there are both risks and difficult problems to
resolve in changing to the electronic systems. Integration
concepts may unwittingly increase complexity, or conversely,
inadvertently omit less apparent features that are used by the
operators but may not be obvious in the design. There is no

integration technology that can be used to systematically derive a reasonable optimum operator interface. Even with existing and well known electro-mechanical display integration - presentation schemes, and with familiar requirements to process information and make decisions we cannot estimate with confidence the mental workload impact, error likelihood or interpretation time for format variations.

As indicated, Dunn (Ref. 6) has already shown that effective aerospace solutions are being developed. However, the various concepts for display-control integration that he reported reflected 5 to 10 years of development work, and some details are still being refined. This part of the process needs to be made more efficient. While the computer controlled systems are flexible and easily changed through software, and both laboratory and operational experiments and evaluations are easily performed, these methods are expensive and time consuming.

Accordingly, there is a pressing need for broader and more effective use of human factors principles and man-machine integration theory and concepts to expedite the development of integrated electronic display-control systems. We have only limited analytic guidelines or models that can be readily transferred from theory and applied experience in order to define the degree of data processing that should be mechanized. We have no analytic basis for determining how presentations should be integrated and for deriving promising display-control integration concepts. We have no methodology to define how an operator should access more detailed levels of data when such is required by operational contingencies. We cannot predict the degree of influence from such variables as stress or boredom, nor do we have a basic methodology to analytically predict and "design around" such human frailties as in attention, confusion or poor recall.

Fortunately, many current applied and theoretical models offer the potential to improve analytic methods. The initial requirement is that information be made more accessible and structured in a format that can be used by any of the many disciplines that will be involved in design of electronic display-control systems.

This paper is concerned with the need for methods integration, with the intent to convey an appreciation for the display-control-human factors and developmental methods used in actual design efforts. It presents a framework to examine applied problems as a baseline for correlating basic theory and models. The discussion offers both an analytic approach that is used for identifying all system requirements, and a baseline metric for workload evaluation. This is accomplished by first describing the

problem, then summarizing the evolution of and rationale for
procedures that are used to identify and organize system
requirements, identify desired crew functions, and select
equipment. Next, the use of analytic and workload methods is
described in context with the system design and development
process. This description outlines a useful approach and
identifies representative applied questions, trade-offs and
problems. It also describes some present exploration of
electronic displays and controls as workload reduction devices.
Final discussion is concerned with methods of integrating and
using such techniques as are available to meet the challenge of
electronic systems.

One precaution is in order. This paper is intended to
provide an informative description of a subject that is extremely
broad in scope for a very wide cross section of reader backgrounds.
Several complicated processes are summarized that could be the
subjects for several papers. They will reflect a mixture of
familiar and unfamiliar concepts, depending on one's skills.
The author's experience has already shown that different
reviewer reaction to identical points will range from
"unnecessarily simplified" to "unduly complex". Accordingly, the
discussion attempts to maintain a reasonable middle ground.

2.0 THE APPLIED HUMAN FACTORS TECHNOLOGY PROBLEM

In design and development of complicated systems, a major
question is whether the operator(s) can perform the tasks
required by the system in both normal and contingency modes, as
well as how he (they) should best interact with the system.

"Human operator workload" is a convenient term for
describing the synthesis of all such task performances. The
objective of workload-related evaluations is to confirm that the
designated personnel can in fact operate, control and maintain
the system. To the hardware engineer, the purpose of workload
evaluation is to verify a minimum cost design.

Within such a framework, the display-control human factors
specialist is required to produce simple answers to complicated
questions, to provide basic design data, to define design
requirements, and to support design trade-offs. Major
objectives are not only to select display-control candidates, but
also to predict and compare operator performance and loading for
operation of alternative candidates, and in turn to assure that
the overall man-machine interface provides feasible solutions for
required operations. Two particularly useful tools for this
purpose have evolved - (a) system analysis for deriving system
requirements, and (b) workload evaluation methods for verifying

man-machine interface suitability. Workable and useful approaches for both now exist. However, they will be more difficult to use in appraising and comparing workload effects for widely varying display and control systems that must be anticipated with computer controlled electronic systems. Refinements in analytic techniques are needed for evaluating effectiveness of such concepts and appraising acceptability of related mental workload.

With the extreme flexibility offered, many traditional constraints for improving the man-machine interface have been removed. There are unprecedented opportunities to tailor the "machine" part of the man-machine system to the capabilities of the man. Fully integrated display-control systems are now possible, offering the potential for much more effective operator provisions. Additionally, automation can be used in much of the relatively routine monitoring, information processing and actions in system operation but with significantly improved status displays. However, there are new risks. We have lost the conservative influence imposed by the difficulty of changing electro-mechanical systems. Anyone working with a new concept has the ability to "invent his own thing" without considering human factors data and constraints. Additionally, inventors may assume that any concept limitations can be made up by the operator, may not recognize complex interactions with other system operations and may set the stage for potentially dramatic effects, e.g. if the operator must assume effective control when automatic systems fail.

Overall applied needs that could benefit from better use of more basic technology are too many to enumerate here. Most importantly, we need both methodological baselines and principles for deriving display-control operations, features and formats that offer minimal mental and physical workload. We need the ability to systematically use such principles from the initial system analyses to define and allocate functions to the crew and equipment through iterative evaluations of workload to total system operations workload. We need to adopt a common metric for workload, i.e. a baseline operational definition whereby all workload elements (and qualifiers, such as in stress) can be translated to a common scale for estimating "total loading".

We cannot wait for agreement on a definition of workload. During system development, "workload" is a "driver" for advanced display-control concepts and for automation: design efforts will not wait for definitions, but will adopt and use some form of baseline. Accordingly, there is a current and pressing need to improve use of existing technology, by summarizing current, utilitarian, theoretical methods and models into simplified versions for use by the uninitiated practitioner in design

applications. The summary should be organized to provide a basis
for estimating the impact on crew performance, workload and
error for electronic display and control systems. Representative
uses will include (a) information presentation and processing
features, (b) integration requirements, precautions and effects,
and (c) ultimate influence on system performance effectiveness.

3.0 EVOLUTION OF HUMAN FACTORS METHODS

As systems become more complex, there is an increasing need
to improve analytic methods in order to more effectively support
timing for the system development cycle. Key needs are: (a) to
better identify, organize and allocate priorities and effect a
reasonable implementation scheme for increasingly complex
interactions between potential system requirements involving
operator performance, and (b) to appraise the scope of tasks
assigned to the crew and assure workload is such that performance
would be feasible and timely. Reasonable methods for meeting
such needs now exist. A third need is now increasing, (c) to
improve the use of current theory and data to refine the
definition and use of present methods. Better approaches are
needed to anticipate and manage problems that can be readily
forecast with electronic displays that are controlled by
computers. Additional principles for display integration and
automated information processing are also needed to assure
systematic evolution of this kind of electronics technology.

To some extent, techniques have evolved that are tailored to
the design of complex systems and that do a reasonably good job.
For example, our ability to accomplish more effective human
factors design is enhanced by system-functions analysis methods,
workload evaluation techniques, and application of basic data/
methods. The following discussion summarizes the evolution and
general application of such methodology.

3.1 System Analysis for Deriving Complex System Requirements

Evolution of the systems and functions analytic techniques
started with the need for a more manageable basis for clearer
definition and synthesis of all requirements in complex systems.
This need was broadly recognized with rapid increases in system
complexity and led to many independent but similar efforts.
(e.g. Ref. 11, 13, 14, 18, 34). The goal was to produce an
effective analytic method for systematically identifying,
organizing and integrating a meaningful, correlated, and
understandable framework for system functions, resulting action
requirements, and related information requirements. In turn,
these methods would provide a more systematic basis for allocating

functions between man and machine and for identifying candidate display-control information processing concepts. <u>Such methods continued to evolve, and now provide a rather useful tool. They are not yet standardized and still feature two main user difficulties</u> - a tendency toward too much detail and a tendency to view the results as an end item rather than an interim result to be used by the analyst as the basis for deriving further requirements and recommendations.

An approach to system analysis which has been used effectively commences with a descriptive scenario for system operations. The scenario is then evaluated to isolate distinct functional requirements. This provides the basis to identify and organize necessary and unique lower level requirements as subfunctions and sub-subfunctions. In turn, functional descriptions provide the basis to identify specific actions to be performed, necessary information to provide the action and finally man-machine trade-offs and display-control requirements.

3.2 Workload Evaluation Methods

A second useful analytic tool for system design has been workload evaluation, to assure that necessary crew operations are at least feasible, and to isolate those operations involving the most extensive workload. Applied "workload evaluation" methods have been widely varied (e.g. Ref. 2, 3, 4, 5, 8, 12, 22). Some practitioners have used subjective judgements by operators as they mentally simulate the operations to be performed. Another approach has been used on a task-timeline sequence (similar to time and motion analyses) from which estimates could be made as to the percent of crew capacity used to perform the tasks. As third approach, also based on the timeline, has been to calculate the ratio of time required vs time available in order to estimate workload level (including ratios for each limb, vision, audition, speech and cognition). A fourth method has been to measure and evaluate eye movement and focusing in simulated or actual operations. Another has been to use physiological indicators. Of all the methods, those based on estimated task-time performance have appeared to be most commonly applied.

Evolution of workload methodology as practiced with Boeing has been based on the task-timeline approach; one that is somewhat related to techniques originated by Taylor, Gilbreth and Anderson in the 1920's and 30's. The main differences is that they were detailing task timeline data to determine ways to make the man more effectively conform with the machine as designed. The Boeing approach is somewhat similar but with the inverse objective - to determine ways to make the machine conform more effectively to the man.

This applied approach originated with two separate lines of thought in 1959-60. The first derived from L.F. Hickey's attempts to become more organized, systematic and thorough in performing human factors analysis. He initiated the notion of using task-timeline methods to determine whether it was feasible to perform necessary tasks on a timely basis (Reflected in 10, 12, 14, 26, 27, 28). Later P.H. Stern and D.R. Zipoy expanded on this concept to also estimate "percent workload" based on estimates of operator capability and reserve capacity. Estimates were dependent on analyst's knowledge of the task including whether multiple tasks could be performed simultaneously and estimated degree of physical involvement (Ref. 26, 27, 28). For their purposes, 80% loading was arbitrarily set as an upper limit of "allowable" workload on the basis that some reserve capacity was needed, and also to allow for estimating error. Subsequently, this concept was expanded to include Man Machine Stochastic Simulation (MMSS, Ref. 29, 30) - including such features as task time, task time variability, estimated human performance reliability and such variables as decision branching, based on work by Siegel and Wolf (Ref. 24). Unfortunately, the modelling basis adopted was extremely optimistic and required extensive detail for any level of analysis. Early attempts to apply the method showed promise, (Ref. 19), but were too time consuming to be effective. More recently, Cavalli has described a somewhat similar concept (Ref. 2).

The second line of thought began when W.D. Smith initiated use of a time based concept with the idea of statistically comparing mission segments for significant differences in task time requirements. This approach later evolved into the notion of using task time ratios to estimate "per cent workload", i.e. time required to perform necessary tasks vs time available to perform. (For this notion, task sequence periods and thus "time available" were intentionally limited to small segments (e.g. 6 to 10 seconds), in order to avoid masking effects from calculating the ratio over too long a period). His method evolved into a more precise estimate via recognizing and, as sharing was feasible, allowing for simultaneous task performance with the eyes, the right hand/left hand, etc.; these became task performance elements. Supplementing his concept through experimentation involving evaluation of both inflight movies and simulation, Smith also determined that there was typically a time period following visual fixation when the pilot appeared to be doing nothing. However, the pilot's subsequent activities indicated that some thinking and decision making had taken place, implying a cognitive element in pilot task performance workload. Preliminary estimates were developed for the percent of task time for cognition. Moreover, he detected another, pilot induced, variation on workload performance levels. When the ratio method indicated 80% workloading, pilots started dropping non-critical tasks. It appeared that some sort of self-imposed performance limit was involved. Conversely, if pilots were significantly less busy than 80% they would add self-imposed tasks, such as more instrument scanning and cross checking.

The two independent Hickely/Smith developments started merging during the MMSS effort. When MMSS was discontinued, Smith extended his earlier thinking to develop a more simplistic and viable approach. This approach was first applied with positive results for cockpit workload evaluation in Boeing's 747 airplane (Ref. 15, 17, 21, 31), and Smith is now extending the potential for overall workload definition and modeling through instrumenting an advanced control-display simulator. Measurements will provide the ability to obtain correlated measurements of task events, task time, eye motion, physiological responses, and behavior/task performance characteristics.

Jahns summarized and expanded such experience and related questions to present a broader philosophical and theoretical question regarding "what is workload?" (Ref. 9, 10). Later, Parks and Springer outlined a more utilitarian approach for present applied uses (Ref. 21). Geer (Ref. 3, 4) described numerous analytic techniques (16 manual and 10 computerized) which are used in human factors analyses; workload related methods are prominent in his listing. Linton, Jahns and Chatelier have more recently presented a paper with somewhat similar information (Ref. 16). The latter two descriptions are far from a comprehensive treatise on workload. However, they illustrate the systems engineering utility of even simplistic methodology in early stages of system design.

3.3 Application of Current Theory

While constraints on data for given application problems have continued to create difficulties, both availability and relevance has become much more extensive than was the case 20 years ago.

However, there has been an increasing problem in accessing and using the available information theories. It has become increasingly difficult for applied specialists to acquire or maintain across-the-board accuracy. Human factors specialists have come from a wide range of backgrounds (over 100 degree fields have been indicated in the Human Factors Directory), with corresponding variations in expertise. Obviously, a given design-development program allows very limited time to develop such familiarity as might be necessary to properly apply new methodology; readier access to useable methods and theory is needed to accommodate the typical applied practitioner.

Accordingly, there is a continuing need for current and
practical syntheses of human factors guidelines and knowledge.
Such syntheses should include principles, concepts and theories
as well as data, methods and techniques for use in applied
settings by multidisciplinary practitioners. Furthermore,
information should be appropriate for use with the new electronic/
computer interface systems. We need to update and further
clarify the answers to such questions as "how should information
be best integrated, displayed and used?" "How might more
detailed lower level information be retrieved and used on a timely
basis when needed?" and "What are the physical and mental workload/timing implications for alternative implementation methods
and features for the man-equipment interface (i.e. modes of
processing-display-control)?"

4.0 USE OF ANALYTIC AND WORKLOAD METHODS

4.1 The Design-Development Process

In developing a total system, the progression of
activities proceeds from initial efforts to define mission
requirements (the scenario) through a series of activities
including: concept definition; allocation of functions to man
and machine; trade-offs of task requirements for different
hardware concepts to select effective implementation modes;
hardware selection; physical development of the crew station;
evaluation in mockups and simulations; and continuing simulation
to refine developments through operational verification and
refinements. The objectives of such overall efforts are to
develop and confirm suitability of the developing crew station,
and to identify and resolve problems at the earliest possible
point in system development. Early confirmation of suitability
or resolution of any problems is critical – changes of
consequence become increasingly difficult and expensive, as
design development proceeds in parallel with the analytic efforts.

The overall analytic process is illustrated in Figure 1.
Elements of this process will apply formally or informally to any
system, regardless of complexity. As can be readily concluded
from studying the diagram, decisions during the early stages can
influence the system utility and cost from early concept formation
throughout design, development and life cycle operations. Also
illustrated by the figure, is an early and continuing need to
appraise workload, an iterative process that is steadily updated
to assess the impact of the latest configuration changes. These
estimates serve three purposes. One is to determine and assure
that candidate functions and tasks for the man are feasible, that
is, that he will have both the time and the capability to perform
as required. The second purpose is to estimate manning and skill

CURRENT WORKLOAD METHODS

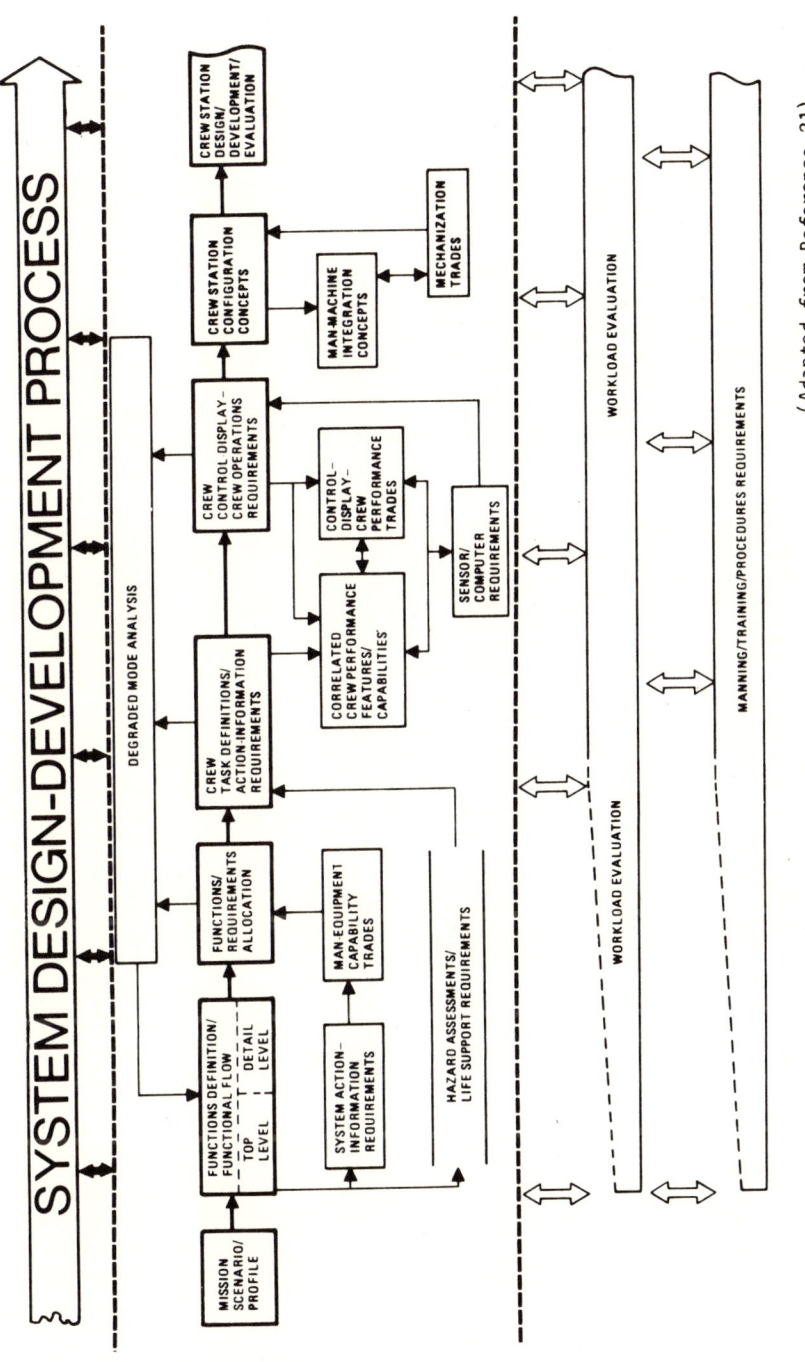

FIGURE 1 CREW SYSTEMS TASK ACTIVITY FLOW

(Adapted from Reference 21)

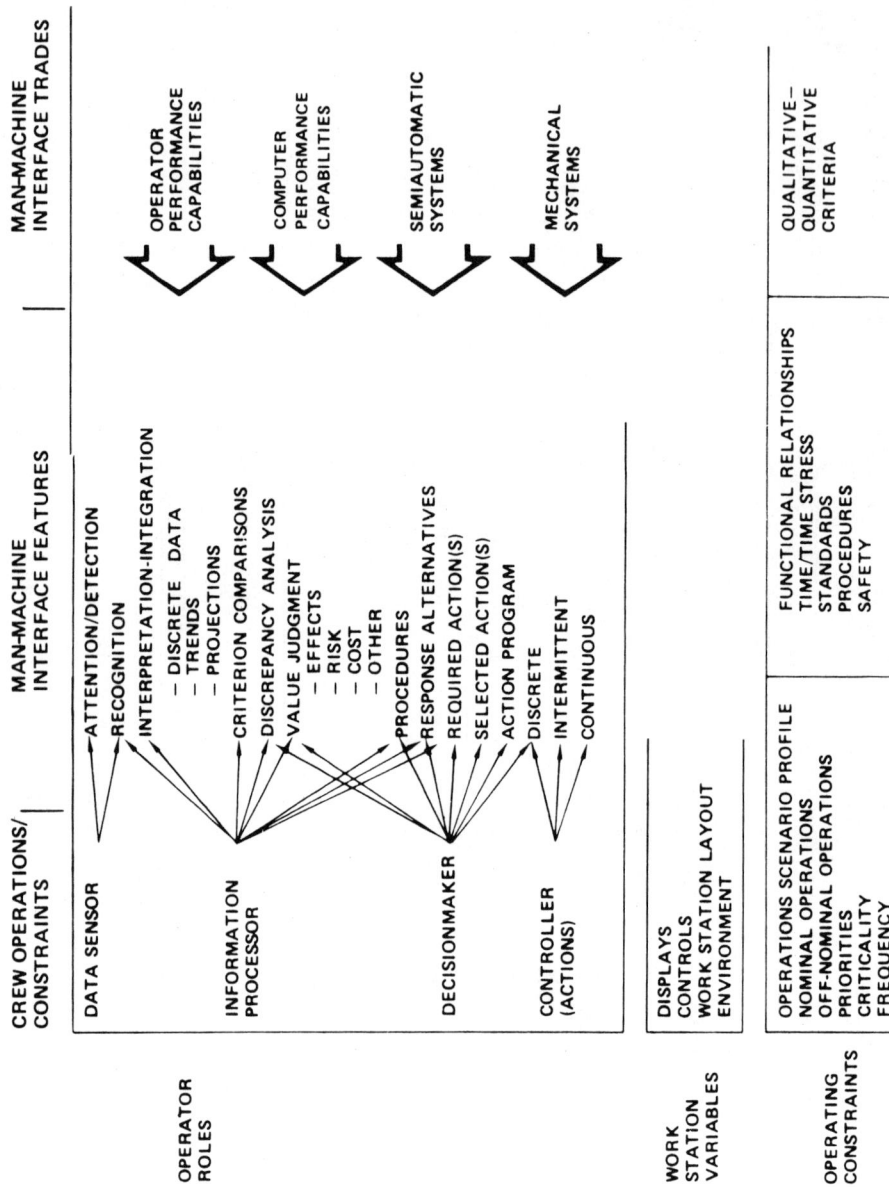

FIGURE 2 MAN-MACHINE INTERFACE DESCRIPTION AND TRADE-OFFS

requirements and establish the number of operators. Results also
provide necessary information to initiate training planning, and
to develop courses and training equipment to produce a trained
crew that can operate and maintain the system as it evolves.

Within such a framework, the operator is functionally an
interfacing subsystem of a system complex. Basic features for
this operator subsystem are illustrated in Figure 2; design
decisions to provide such features dictate both operator
performance complexity and workload levels. On the one hand, as
is illustrated on the left side of the figure and for any system,
the operator will be required to perform as a data sensor,
information processor, decision maker, and controller. The degree
and quality of performance demanded establishes man-machine
interface requirements and features, including levels of automation for effective operator control. On the other hand (as
illustrated on the right side of the figure) the crew system
designer has a list of display-control concepts and performance
capabilities to trade-off in order to arrive at a cost-effective
selection of equipment. Trade-off results define both the man-
machine interface and complexity of tasks as shown down the
center of the figure.

The crux of the trade-off activity suggested by Figure 2 is
to define and provide an effective man-machine interface that
meets all requirements; is efficient in terms of timely
information transfer, decisions and actions on the one hand vs
complexity of information processing requirements on the other;
is within reasonable workload levels; and is cost effective.
Unfortunately, ability to perform such trade-offs effectively is
uncertain, even for more traditional and familiar systems. On
the positive side, we have a reasonably good backlog of
information and methods for most traditional system requirements
involving human data sensing and control activity. Also, from
experience with familiar display-control systems and operations,
there is an intuitive understanding of information processing
effectiveness, and, in turn, of information adequacy. There are
also reasonable methods and procedures for handling work station
variables and operating constraints.

Traditional systems at least provide a working base.
Alternatively, there are some important new questions for the
total electronic display-control technology concepts now emerging.
There are wide variations in our ability to define and apply the
elements of human information processing and decision making in
order to derive a display, predict probable effectiveness and
estimate overall mental workload impact. Some factors are
defined -- for example, criteria and principles to enhance visual
discrimination and similar characteristics are well known and

commonly used (e.g. legibility, color coding and shape coding, from standard references, handbooks and U.S. Military Standard MIL-STD-1472 - Ref. 33). However, criterion features for information processing and decision making are, at best, limited. There is no readily available and proven analytic methodology that can be used by the typical analyst-designer to define, optimize or evaluate this part of the operator role.

4.2 Detailed Approach to Total Crew Station Design

One of the major difficulties in developing an effective crew system is in responding to the multitude of typical system design questions. Such difficulty, in turn, derives from the difficulty in systematically defining and organizing complex total system concepts and internal system interactions. The main purpose of system-function analysis is to develop a model for the overall system that can be used in order to define requirements for the man-machine interface, to develop a baseline for deriving performance criteria, and to provide a quasi-checklist system inventory for assuring that all requirements are met. Additionally, the systematic approach provides a more manageable and understandable framework for analyses and trade-off activity, for appraising subsystem interactions and for system performance evaluations. In the absence of such organization, interacting features may present an overwhelming maze of overlapping and frequently contradictory crew system considerations. This maze has periodically resulted in oversights that required resolution in later development stages.

Up to this point we have briefly discussed practical methods already in use. We have emphasized the evolution of methods, the design need of the present, and near term requirements for more efficient development of man-machine interface features.

This section is intended to describe in more detail one methodological approach that is being applied. Basic elements of the approach described above and to be expanded here approximate the guidelines and orientation of U.S. Military Specification MIL-H-46855 (Ref. 32). In the following descriptions, there is no intent to claim that the approaches are necessarily unique or that they describe the only valid methodology. Rather, it is desired to outline a representative sequence of analytic activities that work for the applied environment in system design and development.

Scenario: In the applications we are concerned with, the first objective is to synthesize an overview of all significant system requirements and operations as a baseline for analytic efforts. The most convenient methodology for organizing system

CURRENT WORKLOAD METHODS 401

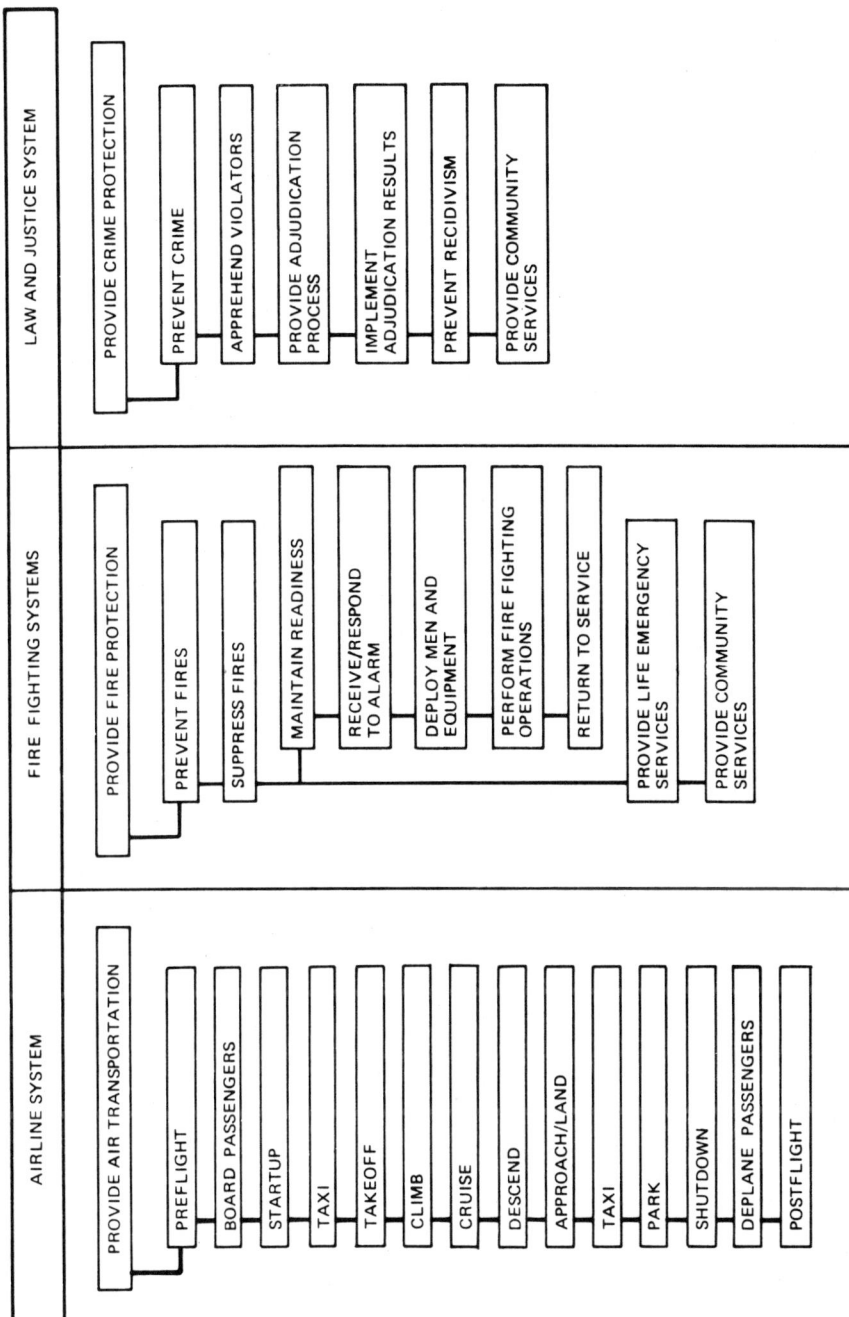

FIGURE 3 TOP LEVEL FUNCTIONAL FLOWS SELECTED SYSTEMS/OPERATIONS

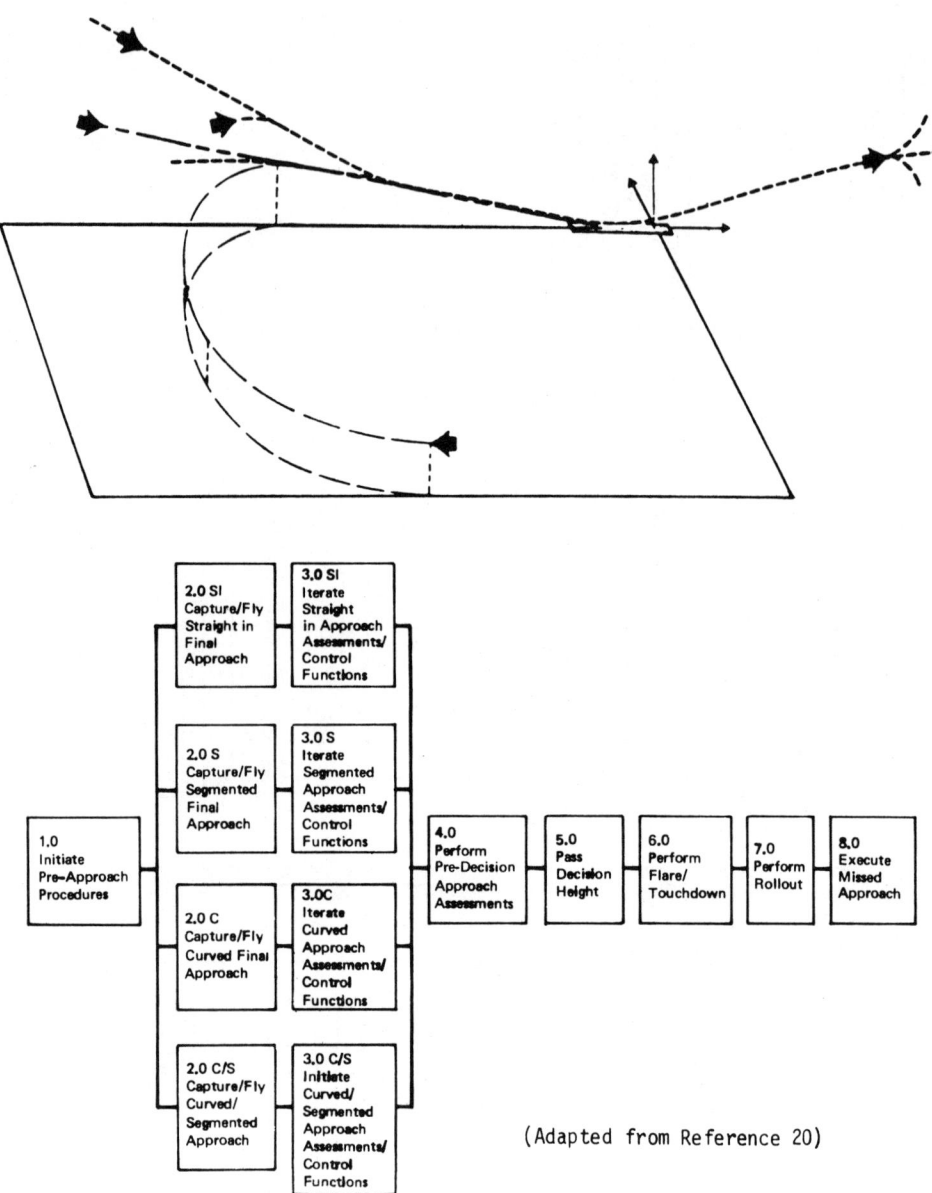

FIGURE 4   APPROACH/LAND SEQUENCE—TOP LEVEL
FUNCTIONAL FLOWS FOR FOUR APPROACH PROFILES

CURRENT WORKLOAD METHODS

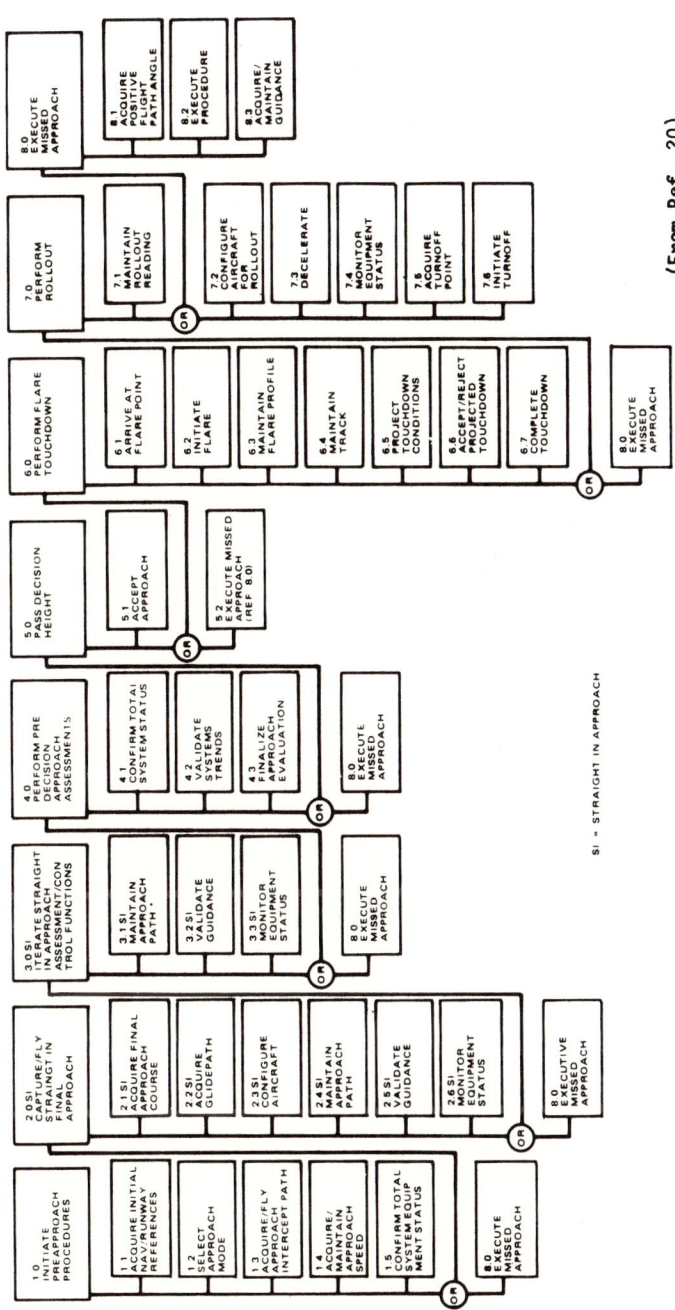

FIGURE 5 APPROACH/LAND SEQUENCE—SECOND-LEVEL FUNCTIONAL FLOWS FOR STRAIGHT-IN APPROACHES

(From Ref. 20)

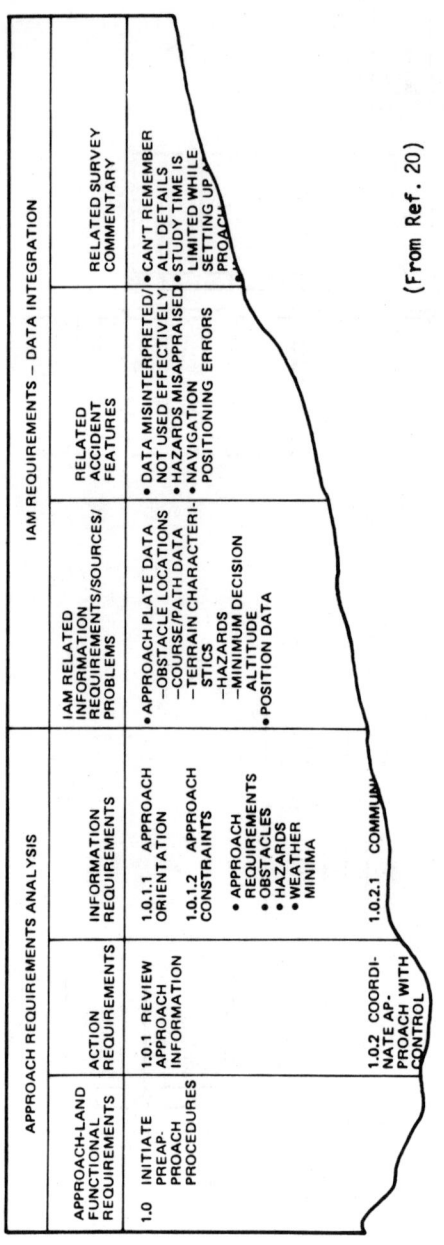

FIGURE 6   EXAMPLE ACTION/INFORMATION REQUIREMENTS ANALYSIS

information for functions analysis is first to develop a descriptive scenario of sequential system operations that reflects the full range of operations. This consists simply of a concise verbal description of a typical sequence of system operations, describing normal applications and some of the key contingencies that might occur. An example was appended to Ref. 5. Scenarios will reflect a certain amount of confusion and overlapping of distinctive functions; these are of relatively little consequence for this initial description. They will be sorted out during functions analysis.

Functions Analysis: The object of functions analysis is to organize a hierarchical structure of functional requirements, commencing with "top level functions" to reflect major and unique system operations requirements. Distinctive segments that are functionally unique can generally be identified, and an appropriate "top level" functional description for each segment can be derived. It then becomes a case of defining those subfunctions that must be performed to satisfy the top function, and in turn lower sub-functions, and so on to the lowest function. The hierarchy establishes an indenture system of increasingly detailed definition for similarly unique sub-functions and sub-subfunctions. Accordingly, functions analysis provides the basis for sorting the scenario into unique functional requirements for each major system activity.

"Top level functional flows" from the beginning to the end of operation (the profile) of major elements in an operational sequence are illustrated in Figure 3, which selectively illustrates the next levels of indenture that might be developed in the hierarchy of functions. Carried to a sufficient level of detail, the indenture system leads to specific operational requirements for system actions, and in turn specific requirements for information that must be available in order to provide the appropriate actions (Figures 4, 5, 6, from Ref. 20 - the main precaution is to avoid excessive detail). The resulting sequencing of system function-action-information requirements provides a rational context for identifying display-control-information processing needs and concepts. This enables a rationale to be established for preliminary allocation of functions, identifying requirements and trade-offs leading to candidate concepts, defining task elements for each candidate concept and evaluating task workload impact for alternative candidates.

In its most desirable form, functions analysis is a frustrating experience involving extremely rigid discipline in developing progressive logical indentures and using very parsimonious descriptors to organize the functional requirements for system operation and performance. Otherwise, it frequently happens that analyses wind up with confusing mixtures of detail at

MAN EXCELS IN	MACHINES EXCEL IN
DETECTION OF CERTAIN FORMS OF VERY LOW ENERGY LEVELS	MONITORING (BOTH MEN AND MACHINES)
SENSITIVITY TO AN EXTREMELY WIDE VARIETY OF STIMULI	PERFORMING ROUTINE, REPETITIVE, OR VERY PRECISE OPERATIONS
PERCEIVING PATTERNS AND MAKING GENERALIZATIONS ABOUT THEM	RESPONDING VERY QUICKLY TO CONTROL SIGNALS
DETECTING SIGNALS IN HIGH NOISE LEVELS	EXERTING GREAT FORCE, SMOOTHLY AND WITH PRECISION
ABILITY TO STORE LARGE AMOUNTS OF INFORMATION FOR LONG PERIODS—AND RECALLING RELEVANT FACTS AT APPROPRIATE MOMENTS	STORING AND RECALLING LARGE AMOUNTS OF INFORMATION IN SHORT TIME PERIODS
ABILITY TO EXERCISE JUDGMENT WHERE EVENTS CANNOT BE COMPLETELY DEFINED	PERFORMING COMPLEX AND RAPID COMPUTATION WITH HIGH ACCURACY
IMPROVISING AND ADOPTING FLEXIBLE PROCEDURES	SENSITIVITY TO STIMULI BEYOND THE RANGE OF HUMAN SENSITIVITY (INFRARED, RADIO WAVES, ETC.)
ABILITY TO REACT TO UNEXPECTED LOW-PROBABILITY EVENTS	DOING MANY DIFFERENT THINGS AT ONE TIME
APPLYING ORIGINALITY IN SOLVING PROBLEMS, I.E., ALTERNATE SOLUTIONS	DEDUCTIVE PROCESSES
ABILITY TO PROFIT FROM EXPERIENCE AND ALTER COURSE OF ACTION	INSENSITIVITY TO EXTRANEOUS FACTORS
ABILITY TO PERFORM FINE MANIPULATION, ESPECIALLY WHERE MISALIGNMENT APPEARS UNEXPECTEDLY	ABILITY TO REPEAT OPERATIONS VERY RAPIDLY, CONTINUOUSLY, AND PRECISELY THE SAME WAY OVER A LONG PERIOD
ABILITY TO CONTINUE TO PERFORM WHEN OVERLOADED	OPERATING IN ENVIRONMENTS WHICH ARE HOSTILE TO MAN OR BEYOND HUMAN TOLERANCE
ABILITY TO REASON INDUCTIVELY	

Information based on: Woodson, W. E., and Conover, D. W., *Human Engineering Guide for Equipment Designers*, Second Edition, University of California Press, Berkeley/Los Angeles, or Cambridge University Press, London, 1964

FIGURE 7   MAN vs MACHINE TRADE-OFFS

HUMAN FACTORS INTERFACE (INFORMATION-CONTROL FACTORS)	PERFORMANCE FACTORS/CONSIDERATIONS/TRADE-OFFS (CAPABILITIES/LIMITATIONS/CONSTRAINTS)	
DATA SENSING MODES (DISPLAY MODES-VISION; AUDITION; TACTILE; MUSCLEPOSITION/ KINESTHESIS; SMELL)	• ACCESS/DISPLAY LOCATION • FUNCTIONAL REQUIREMENTS/ GROUPING • SENSOR-FUNCTION/CAPABILITY • TYPE/INTENSITY OF SIGNAL • DISCRETE/CONTINUOUS/ INTERMITTENT SIGNAL • ACCURACY • REACTION TYPE/TIME	• LOGIC DIAGRAMS • PATTERN/TREND INFORMATION • DISPLAY CORRELATION • DISPLAY SYMBOLOGY METHODS • DISPLAY CLUTTER • FEEDBACK ON STATUS/CHANGE • STATIC/DYNAMIC CUEING • DIRECTION OF MOVEMENT CUES • CODING/SIZE/SHAPE/COLOR	• RELIABILITY • CRITICALITY/ ERROR IMPACT • RESOLUTION/ SENSITIVITY • FATIGUE/ALERT NESS • TRAINABILITY • OTHER
DECISION/JUDGEMENT FACTORS (DATA INTERPRETATION-PROCESSING/ INTEGRATION/DIAGNOSIS/PREDICTION)	• TYPE/NUMBER OF STEPS • EXTENT OF INTEGRATION • EXTENT/TYPE OF DIAGNOSIS • PROBLEM COMPLEXITY • PROCEDURES COMPLEXITY • DISPLAY-CONTROL CORRELATION	• COMMUNICATION REQUIREMENTS • CONFLICTING FACTORS • AMBIGUITY IN DATA • "SET"/EXPECTANCY • DISPLAY EMPHASIS • STRESS/CRITICALITY	• KNOWLEDGE/ FAMILIARITY • MEMORY RETENTION • HABITS • TRAINABILITY • OTHER
CONTROL OPERATION FACTORS (MANUAL/MOTOR CAPABILITY AND SKILLS)	• ACCESS/CONTROL LOCATION • FUNCTIONAL REQUIREMENTS/ GROUPING • REACTION TYPE/TIME/RATE • FORCE/DISTANCE/DIRECTION • DISCRETE/CONTINUOUS/ INTERMITTENT ACTIONS	• CORRELATED DISPLAYS • CORRELATED ACTIONS • OPERATIONS SEQUENCE/ FREQUENCY/CRITICALITY • LOGIC DIAGRAMS • CODING (DESIGNATION/SIZE/ SHAPE) • PROCEDURES	• RELIABILITY • ERROR IMPACT • SKILL COMPLEXITY • DEXTERITY/RETENTION • TRAINABILITY • OTHER
WORKSPACE ENVELOPE (STATION LAYOUT/HUMAN ANTHRO- POMETRY/MOBILITY REQUIRED)	• DISPLAY-CONTROL —ARRANGEMENT/FUNCTIONAL GROUPING (POSITION CORRE- LATION) —ACCESS/REACH	• MOTION LINKS/CONSTRAINTS/ TIME • PROCEDURAL INTERRELATIONS • WORKSPACE SIZE/LAYOUT	• OTHER
ENVIRONMENTAL (GENERAL IMPACT ON PERFORMANCE/ PHYSIOLOGY)	• LIGHTING • TEMPERATURE • HUMIDITY	• AIRFLOW • FATIGUE/ALERTNESS • NOISE	• EMERGENCIES • OPERATING STRESS/ CONSTRAINTS
GENERAL (OVERALL EFFECTS/CONSTRAINTS)	• PRIORITIES • STRESS • TIME CONSTRAINTS	• OPERATIONS CRITERIA —QUALITATIVE —QUANTITATIVE	• WORKLOAD • SAFETY • STANDARDS	• STATE-OF-ART • TRADITION/ACCEPTANCE

FIGURE 8 REPRESENTATIVE OPERATOR PERFORMANCE VARIABLES

(From Ref. 21)

the same indenture level by neglecting collective, higher level, functional descriptions. (Unfortunately, results of a good analysis are "obvious" to reviewers). Ground rules are as follows; failure to adhere to the principles typically leads to confusion of indenture levels and little more than a poorly organized shopping list of considerations.

    a. Use no more than three or four words to describe the function.
    b. Always initiate the description with action terms.
    c. Assure that every function is self contained, i.e. all functions and subsequent indentures reflect a full functional element from "start" to "stop".
    d. Emphasize parallelism in indenture levels.

Fully and properly developed and diagrammed, the results of functions analysis provide a comprehensive description of every system function. A variation on this concept was used to develop "Specific Behavioral Objectives" (SBO's) for the initial training program for Boeing's 747 (Ref. 1). The method led to clearly and functionally defined training requirements, helped reduce more traditional emphasis on general engineering details that had nothing to do with information needed to operate the system, and produced a more efficient and effective training program. It has been quite successful.

Functions Allocation: Functions allocation is accomplished within the systems framework that has been described by Figures 1 through 6. New theories and models would be particularly useful here.

To set the stage for the allocation process, the system mission and operations are defined, all independent and correlated functions are known, and typically some of the requirements, constraints and potential trade-offs are known.

It now becomes feasible to perform man-machine capability trade-offs and define those functions to be performed by the operator and those to be performed by the equipment. For this purpose variations on the Fitt's list is still one of the more generally useful tools. While such lists are frequently criticized, they are beneficial when functions are defined in sufficient detail for meaningful use. Additionally, it is desirable to objectively appraise operator performance factors that may further influence the operator allocations, and may additionally have a significant impact on hardware selections. However, this particular process remains heavily subjective and empirical.

Generic/Specific Hardware Concepts: With functional requirements

CURRENT WORKLOAD METHODS 409

and preliminary allocations identified, it becomes feasible to identify, at a minimum, generic hardware concepts. These identifications are necessary to estimate hardware demands in the form of opeator performance requirements, procedures, sequencing and task-timeline conditions. Such estimates provide a more quantitative description of operations from which workload impact can be appraised. For aircraft, this typically involves the definition of both candidate hardware concepts and overall operations (route structures, flight profile variations, key events and flight-traffic procedures). During early development, hardware concepts and system operations may be based on relatively gross estimates - even this level of information is helpful in evaluating feasibility of early concepts (Ref. 16). Of course these estimates become more and more precise as system development evolves toward definition of specific hardware and specific operations.

Workload Evaluation: Conceptually, workload evaluation is accomplished by charting task-timeline data. In simplest form, this consists simply of listing tasks in sequence down the left side of a page and graphically portraying events and times horizontally (e.g. Figure 9). The level of task detail can be variable, but event phasing, overlapping and time to complete should be reasonably accurate; they must reflect reasonable estimates of performance times with the hardware configuration concepts being evaluated.

Task listings, then timelines, are developed to follow the scenario. They reflect a compilation of scenario requirements, functional requirements, specific equipment operations tasks, key events, procedures and checklist operations. Conceptually, the task timeline can be considered as a chart (Figure 9) with all tasks listed down the left. The level of detail for tasks may be gross ("task groups") or extremely small according to the level of system definition or to the required precision for the analyst's purpose. Task performance events and performance time for each event can be reflected on a time scale progressing from left to right. The result is a task timeline for the whole "mission" or for the mission portion which is the area of concern (again according to the analyst's need).

Working from the timeline as illustrated in Figure 9, one of two modes of estimating workload are applied. For the manual mode, individual tasks are appraised by the analyst to identify "degree of loading" for the crewman (Figure 9a). This "loading" can then be summated vertically to produce an estimate for workload level; by systematically proceeding from left to right a "workload profile" is developed. In general, this profile should then be reviewed by skilled operators and refined accordingly. In practice, results have been reasonable and

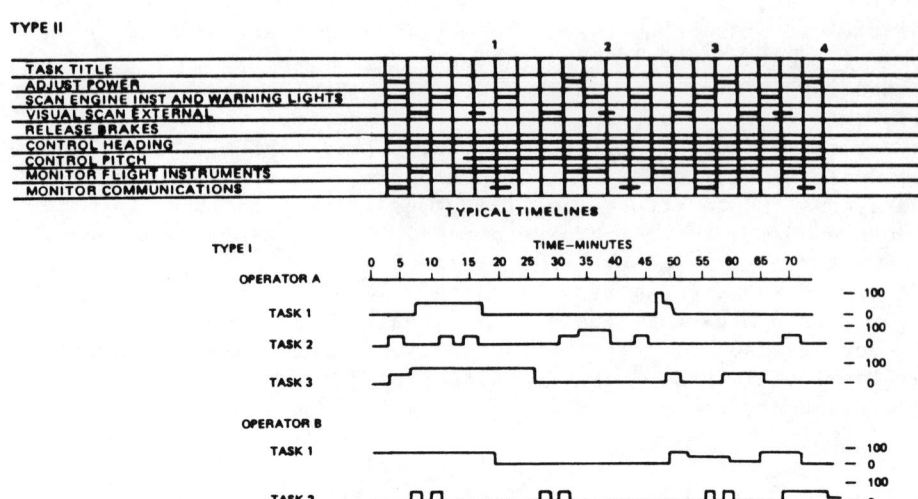

FIGURE 9A TASK TIMELINE—WORKLOAD ESTIMATES BY MANUAL METHODS

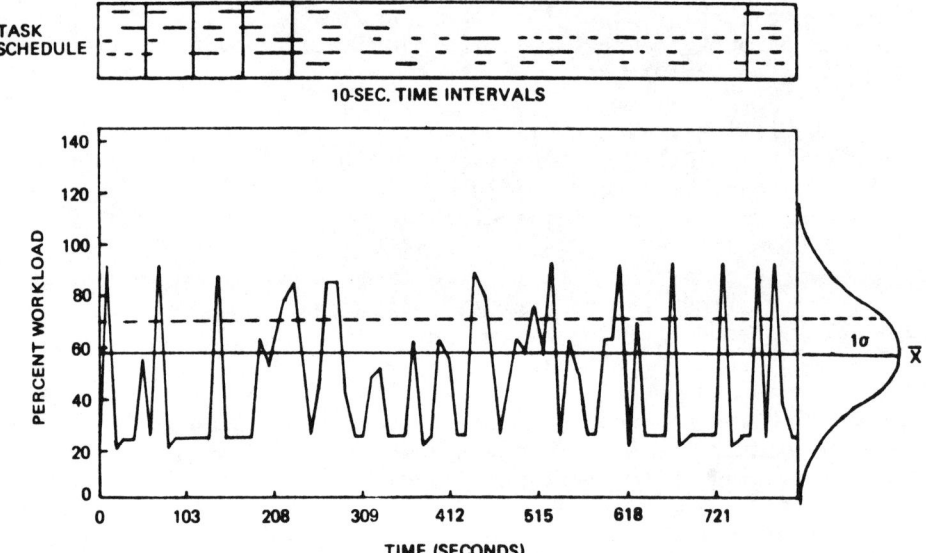

FIGURE 9B SIMPLIFIED ILLUSTRATION OF TASK TIMELINE WITH WORKLOAD RATIOS BY COMPUTER METHODS

FIGURE 9 EXAMPLES OF WORKLOAD ESTIMATING METHODS

have supported the main objective – to identify potentially high workload conditions for resolution and to confirm workload suitability. However, results are heavily dependent on the analyst's knowledge and experience.

The second mode is based on the computerized procedure initially developed by Smith. It also commences with a task timeline, similar to the manual mode, but adds time interval constraints as a forcing function (Figure 9b). Results are used with higher confidence – computer software working with specific task event and completion times significantly reduces the reliance on analyst knowledge and experience. The method provides an improved and more rigidly quantified result, and produces a more rational baseline for both tracking specific workload contributors and correlating potential constraints from other workload related variables (e.g. stress, physiological changes). With the computer, it also is feasible to break down workload demands to the individual human element loaded, i.e. right hand, left hand, etc. As with the manual mode, high workload peaks indicate task areas requiring more intensive evaluation and resolution.

Results of the workload analysis serve multiple purposes. As indicated, they provide the basis for identifying and resolving potential workload problems. Additionally, they can be used to compare relative merits of alternative configurations. The systematic time-based structure may also be used as a baseline for correlating and evaluating other workload related data, theories or models. Finally, the composite portrayal of task information provides confirming data for the intended number of operators, as well as training requirements and operating procedures.

However, the model does not presently have the capability to reflect in detail the types of task variations, time increments or influences on performance accuracy that relate to information processing or decision making. Given such influences in terms of time (e.g. more time for more complex tasks) incorporation within the model framework is feasible, and appears to be a highly desirable method for an integrated description of total mission operations and workload. Methods are needed to either derive a time estimate or determine other ways that can somehow be incorporated with the time referenced methodology.

5.0 EMERGING CHALLENGES WITH ELECTRONIC SYSTEMS

As has been illustrated, utilitarian methods and procedures for organizing complex systems requirements for design trade-offs have been developed for crew systems design purposes. Additionally, models to estimate workload have been developed;

timeline based methods have been reasonably successful in providing a "common metric" for such estimations. However, these models are limited so far as offering ready application in appraising mental workload in the form of operator information processing and decision making is concerned.

Predicting and measuring methods and models for mental workload are among the most urgent needs at present. Until recently, this problem has been less significant. Firstly, some form of workload methodology was needed; it now exists. Secondly, past systems offered somewhat repetitive applications of similar mental workload elements: there were few variations in display-control-information processing concepts that could be developed with electro-mechanical systems; operations and procedures were reasonably definable and workable by evolving methodology. Accordingly, past efforts have, of necessity (and fortunately) concentrated on refining the definition and application of man-machine interface properties such as legibility, display-control compatibility, control laws, etc., to provide a baseline of essential data. This baseline identifies principles that will apply to almost any new concept.

Present needs derive from the potentially overwhelming "hodge-podge" of electronic display-control-information processing concepts now starting to emerge. Electronic display-control systems with computer processing and presentation modes are growing rapidly. Individual and personalized system concepts are being produced by engineers who are unfamiliar with either the scope of relevant operator capabilities and limitations or integration requirements for readiest operator use. Typically, there is little recognition of the impact on operator workload, particularly if performance involves overlapping and interacting demands from other system operations. The old human factors headache of concepts that can be operated quite well by the designer, but at best require extensive training for any one else, is re-emerging with a vengeance.

The point is, we need to use existing technology more effectively, and, most likely, to develop new technology to meet such needs. Many changes in ways of thinking will be involved, as will totally new approaches in application. Representative questions include: How can the operator best be given knowledge of on-going system status? What information should be presented? How do we assure compatibility instead of conflict in displays? How do we minimize cumbersome detail and avoid "clutter"? How should data be integrated? What sort of hierarchical structure should be adopted for ready access to and use of essential display-control interfaces? What sort of symbology should be used? How should symbology interact? How might we use the principles of status, command and predictive displays? Which principles from electro-mechanical technology will transfer to electronic display-control technology? What is the ultimate impact of such variables on performance time? Many others could be readily identified.

Better guidelines, tools and techniques are needed, to enhance our ability to perform information processing trade-offs and appraise workload as well as to generate requirements and ground rules for new concepts. These methods must be easily and readily useable by the knowledgeable but uninitiated specialist. They must also be useable and productive within the typical design-development schedule constraints; either simple applications or automated (computer assisted) techniques would be acceptable. The need for rapid application cannot be over-emphasized - the best results in the world are useless in design if too late.

The present state-of-art for many theories and models offers interim, utilitarian support for such needs. Synthesis for use in the context described in this paper would serve two purposes - they would aid and enhance design and development, and they would provide feedback for the theorist. While perhaps some models would necessarily be considered preliminary, potential utility is the key criterion and the potential benefits are large.

The challenge of the computerized, electronic interface for man-equipment operations is here. As a technology, we have the opportunity and capability to provide some guiding principles and structure for systematic evolution. The alternative is simple - with or without inputs from our technology, these systems will become part of our daily lives.

BIBLIOGRAPHY

1. Brown, A., Bearse, A., et al. Model 747 Task/Training Analysis; Boeing Document D6-30130, August, 1968.

2. Cavalli, D. Discrete Time Modelling of Heavy Transport Pilot Behavior; The Thirteenth Annual Conference on Manual Control, Massachusetts Institute of Technology, June 15-17, 1977.

3. Geer, C.W. Analyst's Guide for the Analysis Sections of MIL-H-46855; Boeing Document D180-19476-1, Prepared for the Naval Air Development Center, Johnsville, Contract N62269-75-C-0271, 30 June 1976.

4. Geer, C.W. Navy Managers Guide for the Analysis Sections of MIL-H-46855; Boeing Document D180-19476-2, Prepared for the Naval Air Development Center, Johnsville, Contract

N62269-75-C-0271, June 30, 1976.

5. Geer, C.W. Technical Proposal: Survey/Analysis of Operator Workload Measurement; Boeing Document D296-10011-1, April 1977.

6. Dunn, R. Flight Displays for the Next Generation Aircraft; SAE Paper 760930, Aerospace Engineering and Manufacturing Meeting, San Diego, Nov. 29-Dec.2, 1976.

7. Gerathewohl, S.J. Panel: Inflight Measurement of Pilot Workload; Panelists E.L. Brown, Douglas Aircraft Co., J.E. Burke, Vought Corporation, K.A. Kimball, USAMRL, S.P. Stackhouse, Honeywell, Inc. and W. Long, Bell Helicopter Co., Aerospace Medical Association Annual Scientific Meeting, Las Vegas, 1977.

8. Goerres, Hans-Peter. Subjective Stress Assessment - A New Simple Method to Determine Pilot Workload; Aerospace Medical Association Annual Scientific Meeting, Las Vegas, 1977.

9. Jahns, D.W. A Concept of Operator Workload in Manual Vehicle Operations. Forschungsberich Nr. 14, Fortschungsinstitute fur Anthropotechnik, 5309, Meckenhime, December 1973.

10. Jahns, D.W. Operator Workload: What Is It and How Should It Be Measured? In Crew Systems Design, Cross, K.D., and McGrath, J.J. Eds., Anacapa Sciences, Inc., Santa Barbara, Ca., 1973.

11. Johnston, D.M. and Hickey, L.F. Procedures for Optimizing Man's Role in Systems. Boeing Document D3-3458, 12 May, 1961.

12. Kaake, W.D. 747 Crew Workload Study; Boeing Document D6-30478-4, June 1969.

13. Lancaster, W.W. and Hickey, L.F. B52-H Electronic Warfare Officer Effectiveness - Human Factors Analyses. D3-3254-3, 1961.

14. Lancaster, W.W. and Hickey, L.F. Improvement Study - Tactical Aircraft Command and Control; Boeing Document D6-9631, May, 1964.

15. Lancaster, W.W. 747 Flight Deck Certification Data; Boeing Document D6-3048-1, July, 1969.

16. Linton, P.M., Jahns, D.W. and Chatelier, P.R. Operator Workload Assessment Model: An Evolution of a VF/VA-V/STOL System; AGARD-CPP-216, Aerospace Medical Panel Specialist Meeting, Koln, Germany, 18-22 April 1977.

17. Miller, K.M. Timeline Analysis Program (TLA-1), Final Report; Boeing Document D6-42377-5, Prepared for National Aeronautics and Space Administration, Langley Research Center (NASA-CR-144942) April, 1976.

18. Parks, D.L. Instrument Integration - A Preliminary Literature Review and an Analysis; Boeing Document D3-1820, November, 1959.

19. Parks, D.L., Stern, P.H. and Niwa, J.S. Crew Number Study: Supporting Documentation for "Advanced Manned Strategic Aircraft, Crew Factors Study, Volume III - Task Allocation Report"; Boeing Document D6-16224-3, Prepared for U.S. Air Force Systems Command, Contract AF33(657)-15339, October, 1965.

20. Parks, D.L., Hayashi, M.M., and Fries, J.R. "Development of an Independent Altitude Monitor Concept"; FAA-RD-73-168, Systems Research and Development Service, FAA, DOT, September, 1973.

21. Parks, D.L. and Springer, W.E. Human Factors Engineering Analytic Process Definition and Criterion Development for CAFES; Boeing Document D180-18750-1, Prepared for Naval Air Development Center, Contract N62269-74-C-0693, June 1975.

22. Roscoe, A.H. Stress, Responsibility and Workload; Aerospace Medical Association Annual Scientific Meeting, Las Vegas, 1977.

23. Sheridan, T.B., and Johannsen, G. ed. Monitoring Behavior and Supervisory Control; Published in coordination with NATO Scientific Affairs Division, Plenum Press, New York and London, 1976.

24. Siegel, A.I. and Wolf, J.J. Techniques for Evaluating Operator Loading in Man-Machine Systems; Applied Psychological Services, 1961.

25. Smith, W.D. Digital Multi-Function Switching Control and Display for Transport Aircraft; NAECON 77, Presented at Wright-Patterson Air Force Base, June 1975.

26. The Boeing Company; AMPSS Interim Summary Report (Volume II); Boeing Document D6-8600, 1963.

27. The Boeing Company; Cockpit System Requirements Development for AMPSS; Boeing Document D6-2136, 1964.

28. The Boeing Company; Functional Flow Diagrams - AMSA; Boeing Document D6-17883, October, 1965.

29. Whitley, L.C., and Vaughn, R.R. Man-Machine Stochastic Simulator TEN-078, MMSS Volume I; Boeing Document D6-29184-TN-1, April, 1968.

30. Whitley, L.C. and Vaughn, R.R. Man-Machine Stochastic Simulator TEN-078, MMSS Volume II; Boeing Document D6-29184-TN-II, April, 1968.

31. Whitmore, D.C. and Parks, D.L. Computer Aided Function-Allocation Evaluation System (CAFES), Phase IV, Final Report; Boeing Document D180-18433-1, -29, Prepared for Naval Air Development Center, Johnsville, (Contract N62269-74-C-0274), December, 1974.

32. U.S. Military Specification MIL-H-46855A; Human Engineering Requirements for Military Systems, Equipment and Facilities; 2 May 1972.

33. U.S. Military Standard MIL-STD-1472B; Human Engineering Design Criteria for Military Systems, Equipment and Facilities; 31 December 1974.

34. VanCott, H.P. and Altman, J.W. Procedures for Including Human Engineering Factors in the Development of Weapon Systems; American Institute for Research; WADC TR 56-488, AD 97305, October 1956.

35. Woodson, W.E. and Conover, D.W. Human Engineering Guide for Equipment Designers; Second Edition, University of California Press, Berkeley/Los Angeles, or Cambridge University Press, London, 1964.

36. Zipoy, D.R., Premselaar, S.J. et al. Integrated Information Presentation and Control System Study; Boeing Technical Report AFFDL-TR-70-79, Volume I, Prepared for Air Force Flight Dynamics Laboratory, Wright Patterson Air Force Base, Ohio, 1970.

MEASUREMENT OF PILOT WORKLOAD

A. Rault

Adersa/Gerbios

53 Avenue de l'Europe, 78140 Velizy-Villacoublay

Being a multidisciplinary group active in control and modelling we were asked by the French military research services (DRME) in 1970 to look into the pilot workload problem.

The goal was to succeed where others had failed! The idea being that others have failed because they had only a partial view of the problem, being either psychologists, or control engineers, or information theorists. The plan was thus established to have all the approaches in parallel.

Psychological measures (tests - Cooper-Harper scales)

Physiological measurements - cardiac rhythm, pulmonary ventilation - e.mg. of the neck muscle - e.o.g. giving the eyes position.

Information theory. The transinformation type of approach with the hypothesis of the operator being a single channel.

Control theory. The human operator is included in the loop and plays the role of the controller; so control engineers have been tempted to model the pilot as a control organ (thus the history of the human operator models parallels the development of control theory tools, it starts with linear and continuous models goes through sampled data era and ends up with a Kalman filter).

The experimental set up was agreed as being a realistic one. We started on a flight simulator with landing tasks and various levels of disturbance (actual grading of the workload) and ended with experiments on helicopters.

In the light of the outline suggested by the conference organisers our position can be summarised as follows.

(1) In the context of our work, human operator workload is associated with <u>mental</u> workload and immediately an information theory type of approach comes to mind. We were asked to look into the pilot workload problem because it is known that: "a pilot performs well and sometimes even better as he is asked to do more and more and suddenly he is overloaded and breaks down". Could one find an absolute or a differential measure which accounts for this phenomenon and would enable one to predict such catastrophic happenings?

This is essentially how we were asked to look at the problem.

(2) The objectives of the "users", human operators or supervisors, would be to have quantitative measurements with some predictive power. In my belief, this is the reason why physiological measurements have been looked for.

Unfortunately, once you have worked for a while on the problem you rapidly find that a quantitative measurement of workload is a little bit of utopia. Human operators are beings very difficult to quantify and totally rationalize, and sooner or later you get to the idea that a better understanding of the human operator would help to solve the problem. Thus there is a shift from workload measurement to pilot modelling. The type of model we are interested in is the comprehensive type, parameters should have a "physical" interpretation.

(3) Among the measures we have been using we can give a rough table of merits. Unfortunately by the electrode technique you get not only tensions proportional to the eye movement but also surface e.m,g, of the face muscles which can be important in vibrating environments.

(4) The E.O.G. is the measure which gave us the most information. We found out from other classical physiological measurements that the interpersonal variability was too high to establish a law. However the position of the eyes helped to clarify pilot behavior and establish as model.

I should add that psychological measures such as Cooper-Harper scales over a homogeneous population of ten test pilots gave satisfactory results.

Measurement	Data analysis	Actual Findings
Cardiac rhythm	Moving average	Too sensitive to inter-person variations
	Variability	Quite fair
Pulmonary ventilation	Deep impedance measurement	Too cumbersome to carry out on a whole population. Did not show particular characteristics.
Electromyography of the neck muscles	Integration over a moving horizon	Quite cumbersome and delicate to fit. Seemed to give good results when it worked.
Electro-oculgraphy	Assuming the head constant, or its movements filtered out, following a learning procedure, Viterbi algorithm provides you wih a means of recuperating the eyes' position.	The best physiological measurement if you can get the eye position.

We hoped to derive from information theory valid measurements of the amount of information processed by the pilot. We failed because we found out that the hypotheses for the use of the classical tools were not valid in actual situations (linearity, stationarity... see the internal report by Gerbios on the subject).

Secondary tasks were never tried, but it seems that if they are realistic enough to be accepted, they could constitute a good quantitative measurement.

(5) The shortcomings of physiological measurements are in general the great interpersonal variation while the mathematical tools are generally limited in their application by basic hypotheses outside which they are no longer valid.

(6) When one looks at the various possible approaches to workload analysis and tries to answer the question, what are the relative values of the tools at hand, it is always difficult not to give a biased answer, depending on one's personal background!

- A priori measures seem to me the best fitted to solve the workload problem. The domain of validity of the tools (transinformation) is too restricted.

- Empirical measures vary too much with the personality to be of general use. In certain conditions I suppose reaction time or secondary tasks could be good measures.

- Systems and Models (this is where the answer might be biased, being myself a control engineer) leave us a great opening in the sense that having a model generally gives one a better understanding of the behaviour of a system.

Of course mathematical modelling of the human operator can be highly criticized as being the application to the human operator of the latest theory established by the control theorist.

Our philosophy departs a little bit from the classical optimal control type of models. The human operator engaged in a control task behaves like a heuristic algorithm, referring to previous knowledge and projecting into the future through his internal model. The human operator has an internal model of the task he is performing; it is an abstract representation. Is it a sort of associative network or a mathematical model?

The human operator acts in a nonlinear fashion. As long as the state variables of his controlled vehicle are within a certain domain the pilot does not act; this domain is defined as the security domain. His objectives are variable with time as the task goes on; this can be represented by a variation of this security domain.

His internal model is generally adaptive and when the pilot finds out he is not going where he had predicted, he has to match his internal model to reality (this is a costly operation as far as mental workload is concerned). Actually, mental workload could be measured as the mismatch between the operator's internal model and the actual system.

These basic ideas have been applied to and suggested from the modelling of helicopter pilots. The results are quite satisfactory as far as the localizer task is concerned: the dual axis (glide-localizer) task is the next step. The diagram given below schematizes the structure of the pilot model.

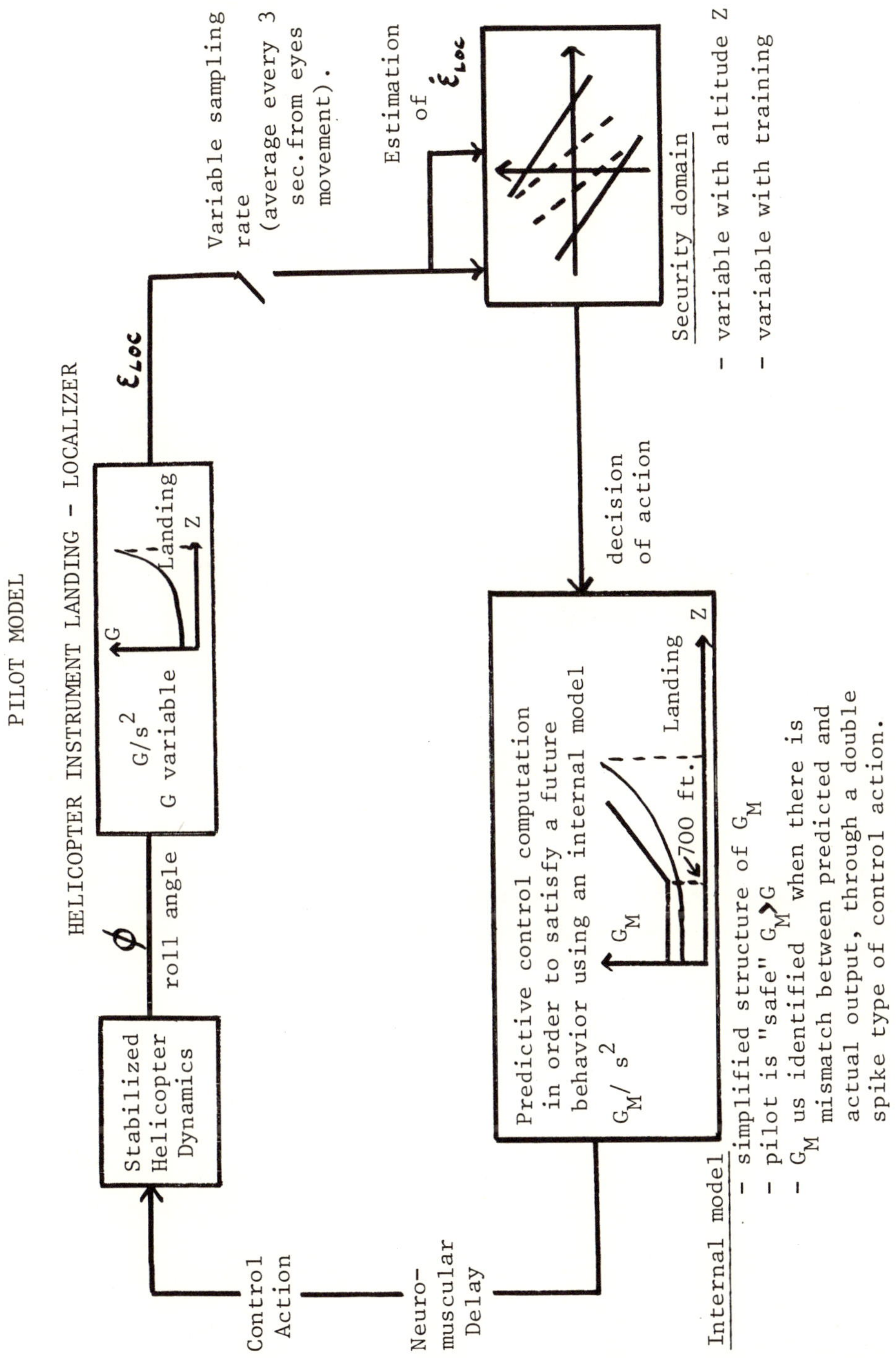

MEASUREMENT OF PILOT WORKLOAD

PILOT MODEL

HELICOPTER INSTRUMENT LANDING - LOCALIZER

Once the model is complete we will have an average anthropomorphic model of the helicopter pilot in an instrument landing approach. With such a model it is possible to test the limits of the anthropomorphic pilot and learn about the sensitivity of various physical parameters and thereafter workload estimation.

I would not like to see the activities separated into three topics theoretical-methodological-empirical because while it is true that some method must be adopted for research, they are all linked together. I would rather differentiate the problems according to the tasks or dynamics:

- Tracking or vehicle control
- Process control
- Logical tasks (binary type)

The topics of discussion could then be - how do you approach a nuclear power plant operator workload analysis? Is its internal model of the same nature as that of a pilot in an I.L.S. approach?

Of course a general topic to discuss on each subject is: what is the domain of validity of the tools we are using?

References

A. Rault, "Pilot Workload Analysis"
NATO Institute on Monitoring Behavior and Supervisory Control
Berchtesgarden, March 1976.

J. Papon, A. Rault, J. Richalet "Etude de la charge de travail du pilote. Modèle de Pilote d'Hélicoptère"
Rapport contrat DRME 74/719, Mars 1977

J. Richalet, A. Rault "Modèles de Pilote et Commande Algorithmique"
Colloque BIOMECA II, Toulouse, Novembre 1976.

DETERMINATION OF STRESS AND STRAIN AT REAL WORK PLACES:
METHODS AND RESULTS OF FIELD STUDIES WITH AIR TRAFFIC
CONTROL OFFICERS

Walter Rohmert

Director of Institute of Arbeitswissenschaft

University of Technology, 6100 Darmstadt, W. Germany

SUMMARY

The work place of the air traffic control officer is to be regarded as a man-at-work system. Evaluating man's task in the air traffic control system shows that air traffic controlling means a work system with "manual" performance. All three partial functions, effecting/controlling/monitoring, necessary to be fulfilled in each work system are performed by man himself.

At Frankfurt airport a lot of field studies were carried out over a period of roughly four years including research on about 115 air-traffic-control officers. Methods were developed for the assessment of stress and strain. Stress is defined as all factors of work which result in reactions of the controller's receptor and effector system. Stress leads to strain in human beings not only dependent on stress but also dependent on the individual's characteristics. An overview of all methods and techniques used for assessment of stress and strain will be given.

Based on the concept of the man-at-work-system and the description of strain-related work content a new Ergonomic Job Description Questionnaire has been developed, the results of which allow a deeper look into methods and techniques needed both for evaluation purposes and for designing future air-traffic control-systems.

Some results of the field studies in air-traffic control research are illustrated.

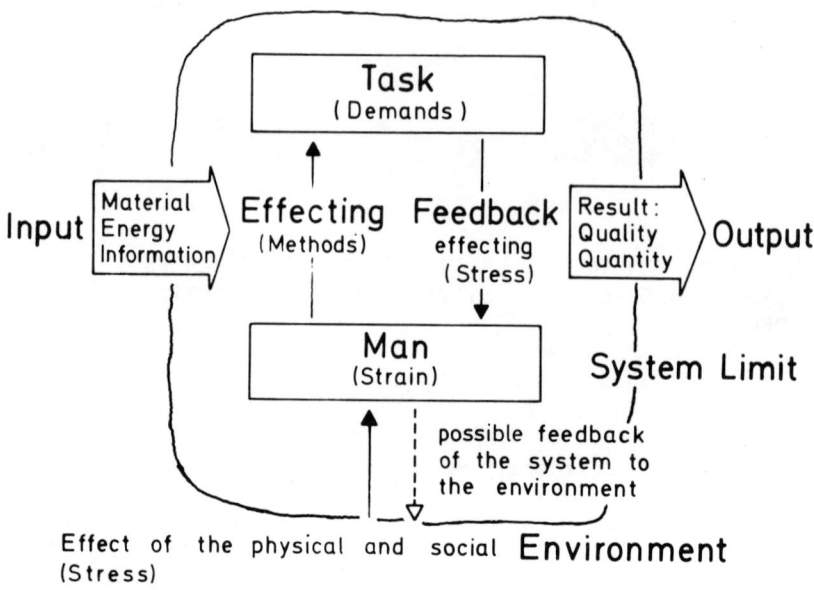

Figure 1

The workplace of the air traffic control officer regarded as a man-at-work system.

The task of air-traffic control staff may be considered as a special type of man-at-work system. The man-at-work system is defined as a model of the relations between man and his task (see Fig. 1).

The task of the controller is to give external instructions to a pilot in an aircraft and to make internal coordination with other controllers. Beside input measures like presented information about the aircraft to be guided and energy to handle miscellaneous material technical equipment, the controller needs methods gained by education and experience. With these methods he is effecting in the work system. In solving his task demands are put on the controller which present certain resistances (work load or difficulties) which must be overcome by the controller and which imply a feedback effect. This feedback which influences the man while doing the task, is called stress. Stress does not only depend on the heaviness or the difficulties of the task and its duration but also on the environment with its physical components (i.e. climate, noise, illumination etc.) and its social components (i.e. leadership, management relations, communication problems with other controllers or staff etc.) which are effective as stress components both within the work system and from outside of the system.

Within the man stress leads to a _strain_ dependent not only on stress but also on different individual controllers' capacities, abilities or skills. The result of the controller's task is shown in both the _quality_ and _quantity_ of the control performance. By the _system limits_ (i.e. the controller's workplace or his functional area) the relations between man and work are marked off from the environment.

Such a general and rough description of the working system "Controller's Performance" provides the possibility of detailed task analysis. With regard to the controller and his control function there are three starting points from which to evaluate the controller's input and his share in the air traffic control system (see Fig. 1):

- The _demands_ of the task (and all concrete elements of the working system) which needs a special kind of job evaluation.
- The _qualification_ of the air traffic control officers, which determines differences between the modes of behaviour between experienced controllers and trainees respectively.
- The _capacity_ of the air traffic control officers (as a man-related part of the working system with regard to quality and quantity of the system's output).

All three of these starting points for evaluating human performance have the disadvantage that the feedback is neglected which influences man while doing his work. All these starting points neglect the evaluation of strain. If, however, an air-traffic control system contains human input and if future developments are going to need the controller's input, it seems to be really necessary to consider the strain put on the man and its share in the system's reliability.

Evaluating man's task in the air traffic control system.

The task requires the controller to give instructions to the pilot in time to provide a safe, orderly and expeditious flow of air traffic. The information for the instructions has to be derived by the controller from the data about the situation in the air space as well as about the aircraft to be guided (see Fig. 2): and include type of aircraft, call sign, route and destination desired. The function of the controller is to monitor the traffic and, if necessary, to intervene to keep traffic flow safe. The overall aim is some sort of "adaptation" of air-traffic to safety criteria or avoidance of unsafe conditions. This means that information processing is the main function of air traffic control. A lot of technical equipment is needed to

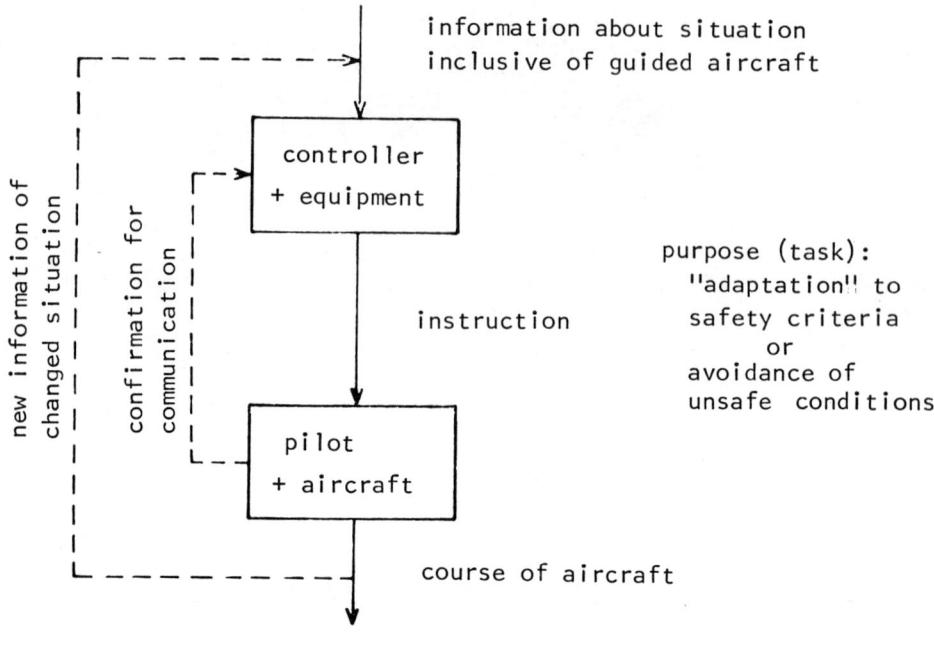

Figure 2

WORK SYSTEM	PARTIAL FUNCTIONS OPERATED BY MAN		
'manual' performance	effecting	controlling	monitoring
mechanized performance	effecting	controlling	monitoring
automatic performance	effecting	controlling	monitoring
	PARTIAL FUNCTIONS REALIZED BY TECHNICAL EQUIPMENT		

Figure 3

keep contact between the control system on the ground and the
aircraft for information gathering and for giving instructions as
a result of processing the information. By confirming the
instruction the pilot closes the communication loop between the
controller and himself. The pilot changes the course of his
aircraft in accordance with the given instructions. The changed
situation gives new information to the controller.

Information processing in the air-traffic control system
is still done by man only. That means that the air traffic
control task in the present state is a work system on the lowest
degree of technical development as far as human functions are
involved to fulfil the task. Fig. 3 shows that air-traffic
control means a work system with "manual" performance; all three
partial functions necessary to be fulfilled in each work system
are operated by man himself. In any work system the most important
areas of partial functions are effecting, controlling and
monitoring. Overt behaviour will bring about the actual changes
in the task or in the work object. The process will be controlled
(or guided) by information processing. Monitoring serves to
maintain the functional capacity of the system, that is the internal
checking and discovery of impediments. The functions of effecting,
controlling and monitoring may be realized by either man or technical equipment.

Fig. 3 demonstrates three steps of technical design, logically
derived from different possible kinds of work systems. The term
"manual" performance means all direct human actions and also non-
manual actions such as speaking. By identifying the levels of
technical design the interaction of the human operator with
technical equipment is characterized revealing distinguishable types
of human performance. As far as air-traffic control is concerned
there are no partial functions realized by technical equipment;
the controller has to perform all three.

Technical equipment is used for presenting information
(i.e. radar screen, control strip, telecommunication, telephone,
instruments and scales), for pre-processing information
(i.e. putting information in a more convenient from for handling
by man). Apart from the radar screen and some indicating
instruments and scales all technical equipment designed for
picking up information is also intended and used to hand over
information. The guidance of aircraft from the ground is a
control task in which feedback only serves to control the
execution of the instructions and give new information about the
changed situation for future actions of men. This can be considered
as some sort of a "manual" control performance.

Information processing is divided into two stages see (Fig.4). In the first stage the incoming information is analysed and evaluated. For this purpose the controller needs memory for the evaluation of situations encountered om training and experience. The controller has to select a proper answer or action out of the store. But the controller is not only concerned with processing information about the situation in the air, leading to instructions to the aircraft. He must also process internal information which comes from coordination between different controllers. This additional task arises from the necessity of dividing the whole task of the air-traffic control system into separate jobs which can each be done by one man. Coordination is an internal task in air-traffic control resulting from the internal organization. One

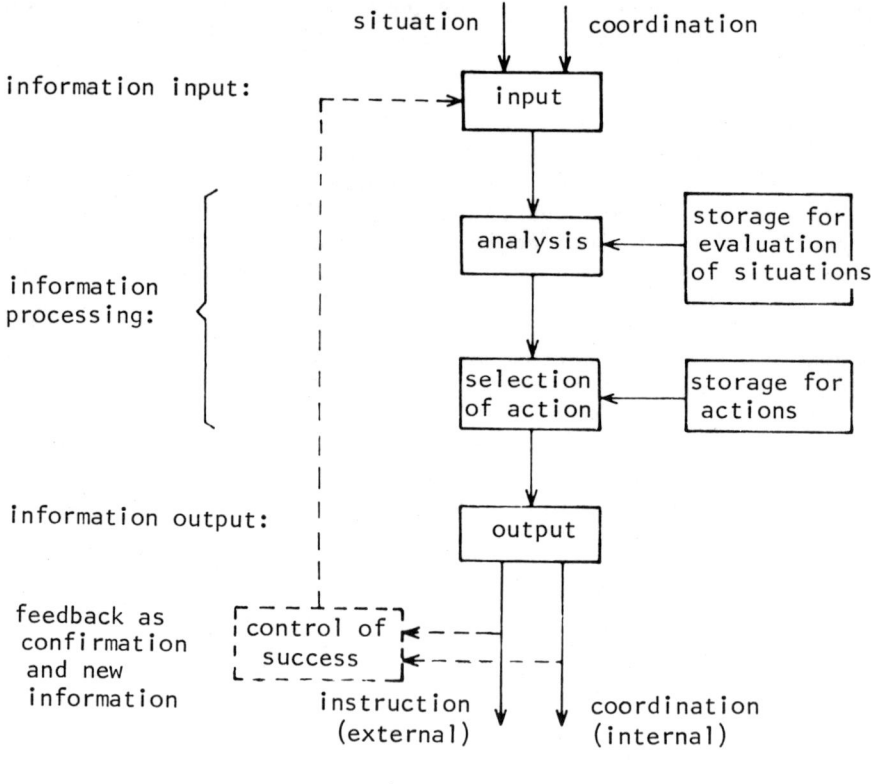

Figure 4

cannot neglect it because it occupies much of the capacity of the controller and his assistant.

Methods for determining stress and strain in air-traffic control tasks.

As explained in Fig. 1 we have to distinguish between "stress" and "strain" while analysing man-at-work relations. To render precisely the nearly synonymous meaning of these two terms stress is defined as all factors of work which result in reactions of the controllers' receptor and effector systems. Thus stress leads to strain in human beings. However, the amount of strain is not only a function of stress but depends on the capacity of the individual, i.e. a certain amount of stress will lead to various amounts of strain in different human beings corresponding to their individual capacities (see Fig. 5).

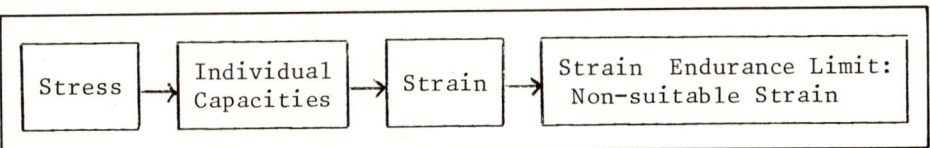

Fig. 5: Relationship between stress and strain.
Stress = f(partial stresses) = g(stress-intensities, stress-duration)
Strain = h(stress, individual characteristics)

For some different types of human work the functional relationship between stress and strain which is shown in Fig.5, has been described on the basis of the results of research work. We used these ideas and techniques in many field studies over a period of four years with German air-trafic control officers at Frankfurt airport. Fig. 6 and 7 present an overview of the methods and techniques used.

Fig. 8 shows the complete experimental set-up used in the field studies at Frankfurt airport. The methods and techniques used in these field-studies were partly classical ones, and partly they had to be developed for the purpose of the investigation. The upper part of the picture shows the judging controller who is

STUDIES FOR ASSESSMENT OF STRESS IN AIR TRAFFIC CONTROL TASKS

STUDY	OBJECT OF INVESTIGATION	METHODS
Workplace	Dimensions of workplace Devices of work and information used Body position demanded Environmental conditions (noise, illumination, climate)	Description Drawing Photographic documentation Physical measurement

Process	Intensity and Chronological, spatial and information-technical flow of defined work-content (also task elements, governing time)
	Smoking
	Coffee drinking
		Description
		Graphic representation
		Use of standard analysis charts
		Film analysis
		Tape record commentary
		chronological covering of telecommunication frequencies
		Stop watch studies
		Stop calculator studies
		Work sampling
		Automatic registration
		Continuous film records
		Sampling film records
		Telemetric coding
		  scaling task difficulty
		  coding control strips
		  coding controlled aircraft
		Registering frequency of coordination and manipulating the control strips
		Uninterruped working time at position
		Cumulative time
		Shift analysis by self-rating

(contd.)

Figure 6

Figure 6 contd.

Motion analysis	Sequence of hand (and body) movements of the controller	Use of standard analysis charts Use of predetermined motion time systems Film analysis
Information-content analysis	Density of information flow (syntactical content of information) Pragmatic content of information (aircraft- and/or controller-related operators and logical operations Traffic and its density Strategies in control task	Study of flight control strips Photographic radar recordings (each 90 sec. time of exposure) Radio-telecommunication transcriptions Algorithmic transcription LJAPUNOW-language Flow diagram Graph representation (GERT) Interview Number of conflicts
Time-budget study	Socio-demographic variables Daily distribution of work, rest, official rest-pauses, time for going to work and home, sleeping, spare time	Interview Daily time analysis by self-rating

Figure 6

STUDIES FOR ASSESSMENT OF STRAIN IN AIR TRAFFIC CONTROL TASKS

STUDY	OBJECT OF INVESTIGATION	METHODS
Physiological studies	Intensity and flow of strain	Heart-rate measurement Arrhythmia of heart-rate Long-electrocardiography
		Respiration measurement Tremor measurement Electromyography Electroencephalography Catecholamine secretion in controllers
Applied Psychological studies	Job satisfaction	Interview Study of attitudes of the controllers towards work and working environment
Studies of work medicine	Disturbances of health related to the controller's profession	Interview Time-budget studies Long-electrocardiography Experimental shift work

Figure 7

operating a four-item telemetric coding device with different scales for assessment of the difficulty of controller's work, the number of incoming control strips and the number of aircraft under control. He is also giving additional commentaries about the general or specific work situation to the tape recorder. All other studies for assessment of stress mentioned in Fig. 6 were done by one of our staff who is shown in Fig. 8 with the task of supplementary work study. Some of the methods used were automatic (i.e. picking up radio-telecommunication on magnetic tape, radar pictures). All time-budget studies were done within the periods of breaks or between two shifts. Most of the stress variables were transmitted telemetrically; the lower picture in Fig. 8 shows the total telemetric receiver set-up for the incoming stress and strain data and the data storing set-up.

STRESS AND STRAIN AT REAL WORK PLACES

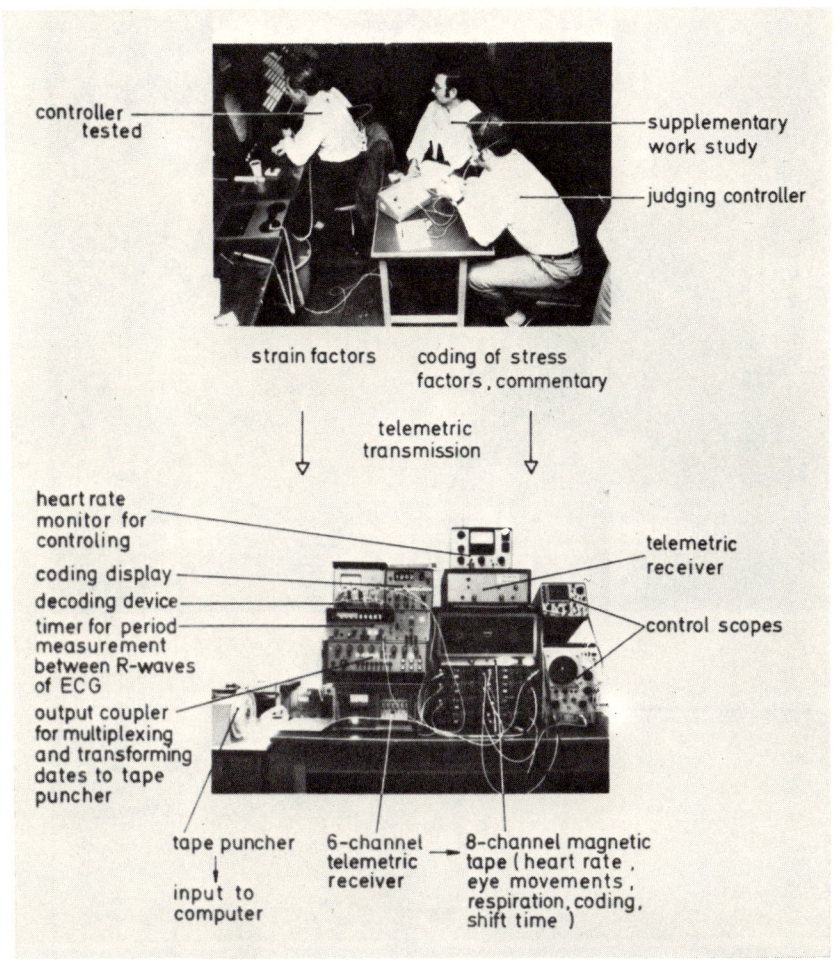

Figure 8. Complete experimental set-up

To transmit the physiological variables for assessing strain we used a multi-channel telemetric system. In Fig. 9 the arrangement of electrodes for recording the different electrophysiological variables and the transmitter is demonstrated. Also the attached respiration sensor can be seen. While some of the strain variables were transmitted continuously during the working time on the position (heart rate, respiration rate, electromyogramme, electrooculogramme) other variables were recorded twice for comparison reasons: first, just before the officer started his work at the position; second, just after having finished the work at the position (tremor measurement, catecholamine secretion,

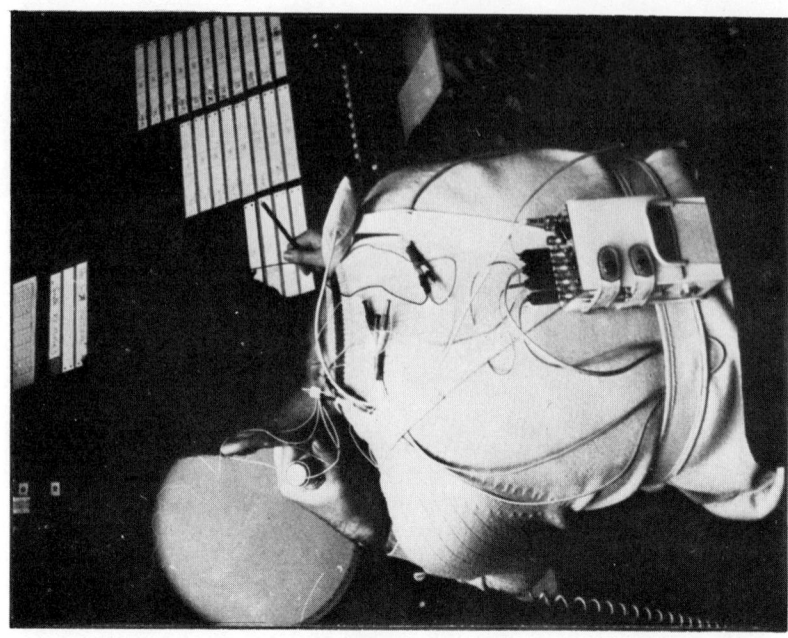

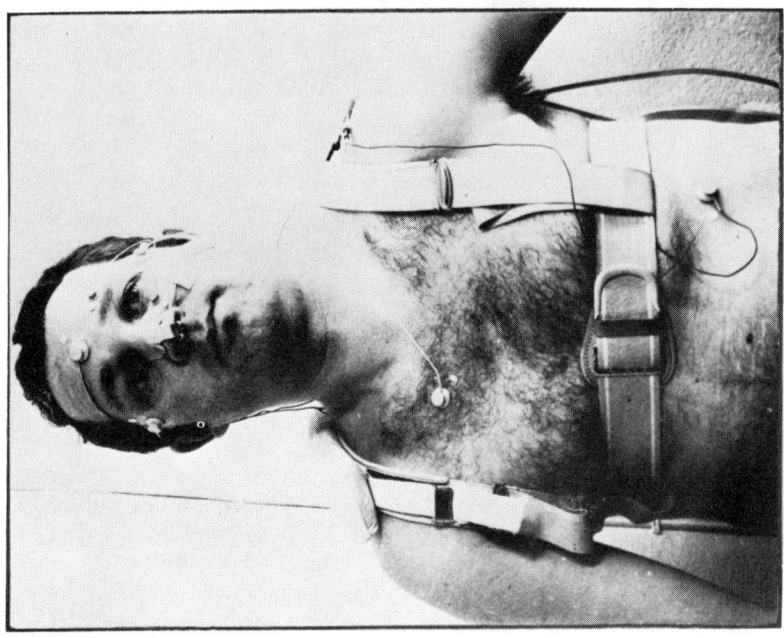

Figure 9. Electrode placement and telemetric transmitter

```
ACTIVITY PROFILE
Static body positions
Static muscular work                    SSSSSSSSSS
Extreme body turns                      HHHHHHHHHH
Stressing body movements
Heavy dynamic muscular work
Active light muscular work
Manual activities                       WWWWWWWWWWWWWWW
Summary of physical work                SSSSSSSSSSSS
Sensory work                            WWWWWWWWWWWWWWWWWWWWWWWWWWWWWWWWW
Frequency of signals                    HHHHHHHHHHHHHHHHHHHHHHHHHHHHHHHH
Inadequate signal clearness             HHHHHHHHHHHHHHHHHHHHHHHHHSSSSSSSSSSSSS
Discriminatory work                     WWWWWWWWWWWWW
Information sources                     HHHHHHHHHHHHHHHHHHHHHHHHHHHHHHHH
Vigilance                               WWWWWWWWWWWWWWWWWWWWWWWWWWWWWWWWWWWW
Combinatory work                        HHHSSSSSSSSSSSWWWWWWWWWWWWWWWWWWWWWWWWWWWWWWWWWWWWWWWWWWWWWWWWW
Education                               SSSSSSSSSSSSSSSSSSSSSSSSSSSSSSSSSSSSSSSSSWWWWWWWWW
Communicative work                      HHHHHHHHHHHHHHHHHWWWWWWWWWWWWWWW
Cognitive processes                     WWWWW
Work objects
Tools and equipment                     WWWWWWWWWW
Control devices                         HHHWWWWWWWWWWWWWWW
Technical aids
Physical hazards
Illumination                            SSSSSSSS
Noise                                   HHHSSSSSSSSSSSSSSSSSSSSSS
Vibrations                              HHHHHHHHHHHHHHHSSSSSSSSSS
Climate
Other negative environmental conditions - Risk of
accidents and occupational deseases
Work schedule                           AAAAAAAAASSSSSSSSSSSSSSSSSSSSSSSSSSSSSSSSSSSSS
Paced work
Repetitive work
Responsibility                          SSSSSSSSSSSSSSSSSSSSSSSSSSSSSSSSSSSSSSSSSSSSSSSS
Supervision competence                  WWWWWWWWWWWWWWWWWWWWW
Management function                     SSSSSSS
Personnel contacts                      HHHSSSSSWWWWWWW
Conflicts                               WWWWWWWWWWWWWWWW
```

Figure 10. Activity profile of an air-traffic control officer in the pick-up position at Frankfurt airport.

electroencephalogramme). All other studies mentioned in Fig. 7 were performed during breaks or between two shifts.

Determination of stress of air-traffic control officers by position analysis

Based on the concept of the man-at-work system (see Fig. 1) and the description of strain-related work-contents a new Ergonomics Job Description Questionnaire (EJDQ) has been developed (ROHMERT, LUCZAK, LANDAU, 1975). This method allows a very detailed analytical job evaluation. A trained job-analyst analyses the activities of the operators in air-traffic control systems with respect to very detailed job elements (the job evaluation procedure contains 390 items).

Various rating scales, such as importance to the job, frequency, probability, amount of time (spent on the job element), are used for the different job elements.

The demand structure of air-traffic control tasks can be evaluated by grouping together related items with respect to stress. The rating scale values of item groups are summed up and plotted columnwise. Item groups are derived directly from the demand-orientated chapters of the Ergonomic Job Description Questionnaire. However, they can be derived as well from the results of a factor analysis of the Ergonomic Job Description Questionnaire data.

Fig. 10 shows the activity profile of an air-traffic control officer in the pick-up position of Frankfurt airport approach control. Characteristic demands are given by the combination of stress or, ("combinatory work") in this vigilance task ("Vigilance"). Higher education demands ("Education") are necessary. Besides that, stress caused by work schedule and responsibility are important stress factors.

The profile shows high work load especially for sensory systems, caused by poor work conditions (i.e. display and information output). Stress factors of information input are given by the frequency and clearness of signals and information sources. Whereas frequency of signals cannot be changed significantly, clearness of signals - the design of control systems in general - might be improved.

The analysis of physical working conditions shows good thermal conditions (air temperature about 25°C, relative humidity 46-49%, wind velocity 0.2 m/sec, no thermal radiation), but inadequate lighting of the darkened surroundings is noted and high noise intensity with respect to the important part of mental load. A noise level of 53 dB (A) during night shifts and 64 dB(A) during other shifts is caused by a loud-speaker, transmitted radio-telecommunication and telewriters, which are running in the same room.

Characteristic physical stress factors are the static components of muscular work, caused by forced body positions and continuous attention, and extreme body turns for the purpose of work coordination with other operators. Furthermore, there are stressing manual activities using tools.

The importance of this very detailed Ergonomic Job Description Analysis Approach lies in four aspects:

- First, main stress factors are indicated; with regard to stress one may derive proposals for design activities in air-traffic control tasks; priorities for technical development in air-traffic control functions may be deduced.

- Second, suggestions can be made as to relevant methods and technique for determining strain caused by the particular stress.

- Third, suggestions can be made as to suitable methods for personnel selection and the training of air-traffic control officers with regard to the specific demands of their job.

- Fourth, comparisons can be made between the demands of air-traffic control tasks and the demands of other professional tasks.

Some results of field studies in air-traffic control

Within a period of roughly four years we studied some 115 air-traffic control officers at different work places at Frankfurt airport.

We found irregular distributions of the duration and the frequencies of task elements. Significant differences in these findings appear if the tasks during rush hours and periods of less traffic are compared which means that the controller is using more standardized strategies under the pressure of rush hours. The amount of information processing per time is twice as high in approach control as in area control, although the average number of aircraft under control was not significantly changed. This means that with regard to the same traffic, the control task in approach control is more difficult than in area control. This result was confirmed by heart-rate findings: heart-rate was higher on the average in approach compared with area control.

Within our field studies we concentrated our investigations on two important strategies: first of all, we developed a multi-dimensional measuring concept, which means that we measured several variables of stress as well as of strain (see Fig. 7 and 8). Furthermore, we measured most of the stress and strain variables as time series, which means that we intended to correlate a time series of particular stress factor with the time series of another stress factor or with time series of particular strain factors. By doing so one gets a deeper insight into the relationship between stress and strain. When testing correlations between time series, the effect of serial correlation has to be considered. The calculation of regression coefficients for the description of the relationship between serial correlated variables requires assumptions about the validity of the least square procedure. After taking into

consideration further analysis of the residuals and serial
correlation effects a combination of stress factors can be used
to determine a particular strain factor or a combination of
strain factors respectively.

We found significant relationships between the results of
rating of difficulty of controller's work, coding of incoming
flight control strips and coding of aircraft under control. From
these results it can be summarized that the stress variable
"number of aircraft under control" can be taken as a stress
measure which describes the time-related stress fluctuation with
a sufficient degree of accuracy. This is the reason that we took
this very simple measurable stress factor for describing the
time series of stress in air-traffic control. This simplification
does not mean that the other stress factors could be neglected.
As far as further field research is concerned we would like to
take into account other stress factors beside of the number of
aircraft under control.

Strain can be evaluated only in a multi-dimensional manner,
due to the fact that there could be different bottle-necks caused
by different human organs or abilities, capacities and skills.
Fig. 7 had shown some examples of bottle-neck-orientated strain
measures, related for example to physical work load (i.e. heart-
rate), mental work load (i.e. arrhythmia of heart-rate,
electroencephalogramme, electromyogramme), sensory work load
(i.e. electrooculogramme, electromyogramme), or emotional stress
(i.e. tremor measurements, catecholamine secretion) respectively.
But several studies in the laboratory and in the field showed
that heart-rate gave a suitable integrated measure of strain if
one succeeded in describing the different work load components
in air-traffic control tasks by suitable stress measures. This
is shown in Fig. 11.

Fig. 11 illustrates an important result of the field studies.
By correlating the three measured time series of stress (the
rated difficulty of controller's task, the number of aircraft
under control and the number of aircraft expected) and by
correlating these combinations of three stressors with the strain
measure of heart-rate, it is shown in the upper curve of
Fig. 11 that the time series of strain can be predicted. The
course of the predicted strain fits very well with the measured
strain which is marked by the small circles. The coefficient of
multiple determination reached about 80%.

Fig. 11 indicates, too, that heart-rate is an integrated
measure of strain. Heart-rate is not only influenced by the
mental load of the controller, which may be evaluated by
determining the number of aircraft under control or the rated

difficulty in fulfilling the task, heart-rate is also influenced by the more emotional stress which can be evaluated by the number of aircraft which will be expected. The number of expected aircraft reaches its maximum before the number of aircraft under control or the rated difficulty show maximal values. Due to these emotional reactions an increase in the basic tension of the air-traffic controller can be expected. On this hypothesis heart-rate must show an increase also with the increasing number of aircraft expected. Fig. 11 shows the highest values of heart-rate not only at the peak of mental load but also at the peak of emotional load.

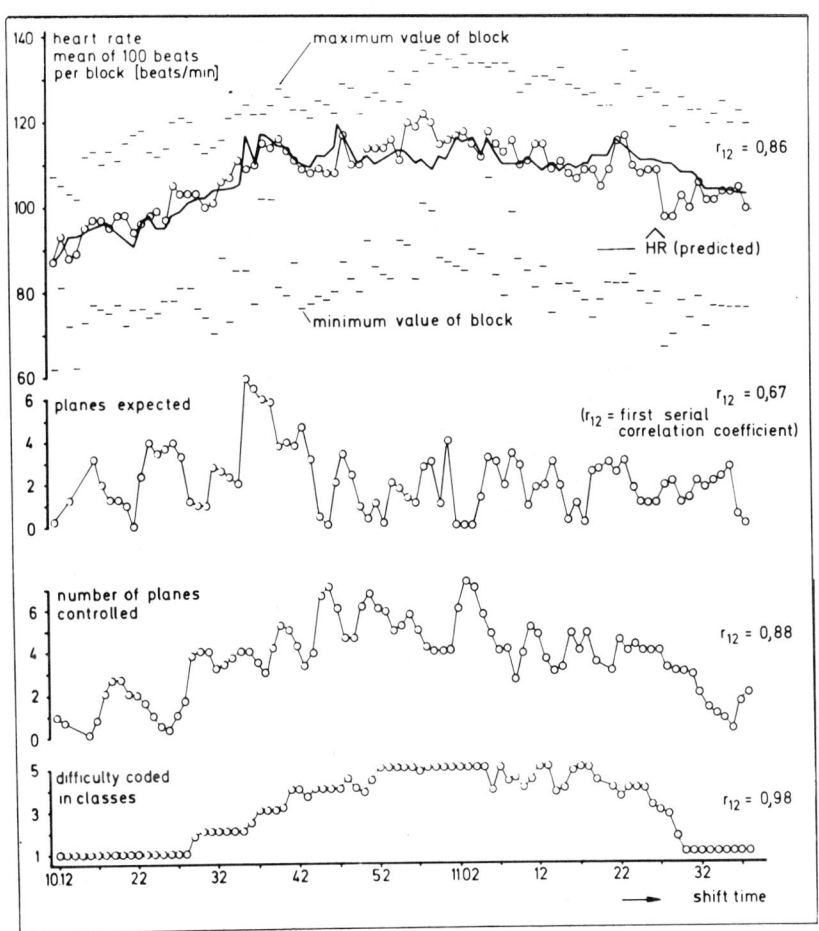

Figure 11. Variation of heart-rate and stress factors (approach control, pick-up position)

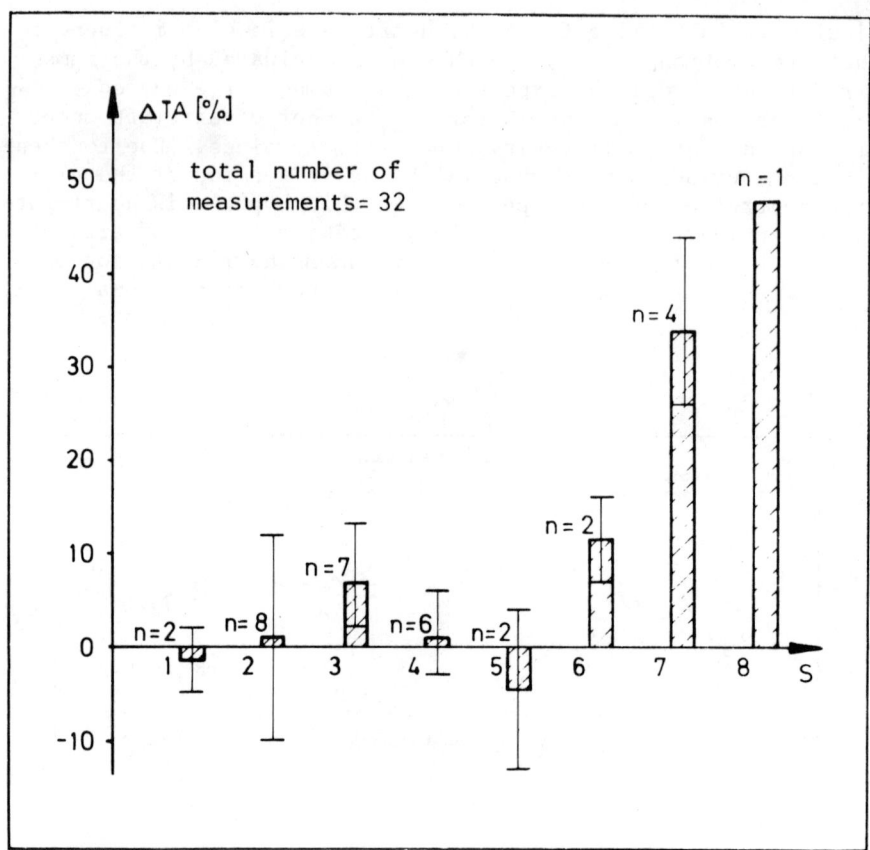

Figure 12. Increase of the amplitude of tremor movements (ΔTA) of the hand dependent from the task difficulty (S).

Additional experiments revealed that a good prediction of the strain measure heart-rate could be gained also by evaluating only the stress measure of number of aircraft under control: And since heart-rate is influenced not only by mental but also by emotional work load, we preferred this measure for evaluating strain. This does not exclude the possibility that other strain measures might allow a suitable description of specific components of the work load of air-traffic controllers. This might be shown in some examples of measurements of tremor activity as well as catecholamine secretion.

Fig. 12 shows that with increasing difficulty in fulfilling

the controller's task the amplitude of tremor movements (the micro-vibration of the lower arm and hand system) will be amplified significantly. We found similar results in research on students examinations and doctor-thesis situations. Also the increase in catecholamine secretion is as high as in emotional situations of exceptional stress, like the examination for getting the driving licence for motor cars. These values are five times as high as the values of the teachers who are conducting the examinations.

The results of measurements of heart-rate, tremor activity and catecholamine secretion show that the air-traffic control task is very highly emotionally stressing. The effect of this stress component can also be compared with exceptional situations in daily or professional life. But while the latter will occur only a few times in man's life, the emotionally stressing situations of controllers will be repeated day by day.

All the results gained in the experiments with the total of 115 air-traffic controllers from Frankfurt airport, were evaluated with the purpose of getting a model for predicting the changes in strain dependent on the number of aircraft under control and the cumulative time of the controller's work. The model shows that the intensity of work and the duration of work influence the increase in strain in an exponential manner. But this is valid only if the number of aircraft under control exceeds a particular threshold of tolerability. If the intensity of work is lower than this limit the duration of work shows no significant influence on strain.

We used the results of the model for predicting a suitable work load in air-traffic control tasks. Also proposals were derived for optimal schedules of working time and rest pauses. With respect to strain we made some further proposals for schedules of shift organisation.

Some results of the time-budget studies

Increasing strain is not only influenced by the intensity of work but also by its duration. Therefore, we also studied the influences of the duration of the shift and of the shift's position within the 24 hours of the day. In these time-budget studies the controllers rated for each half hour of the day whether they had a working time, a sleeping time, a leisure time which could be spent in full social freedom or which was related to other daily activities. Last but not least the controllers had to state whether they were on the way to their work place or back on the way home. Fig. 13 shows the results in relation to different types of shifts and for off-duty days.

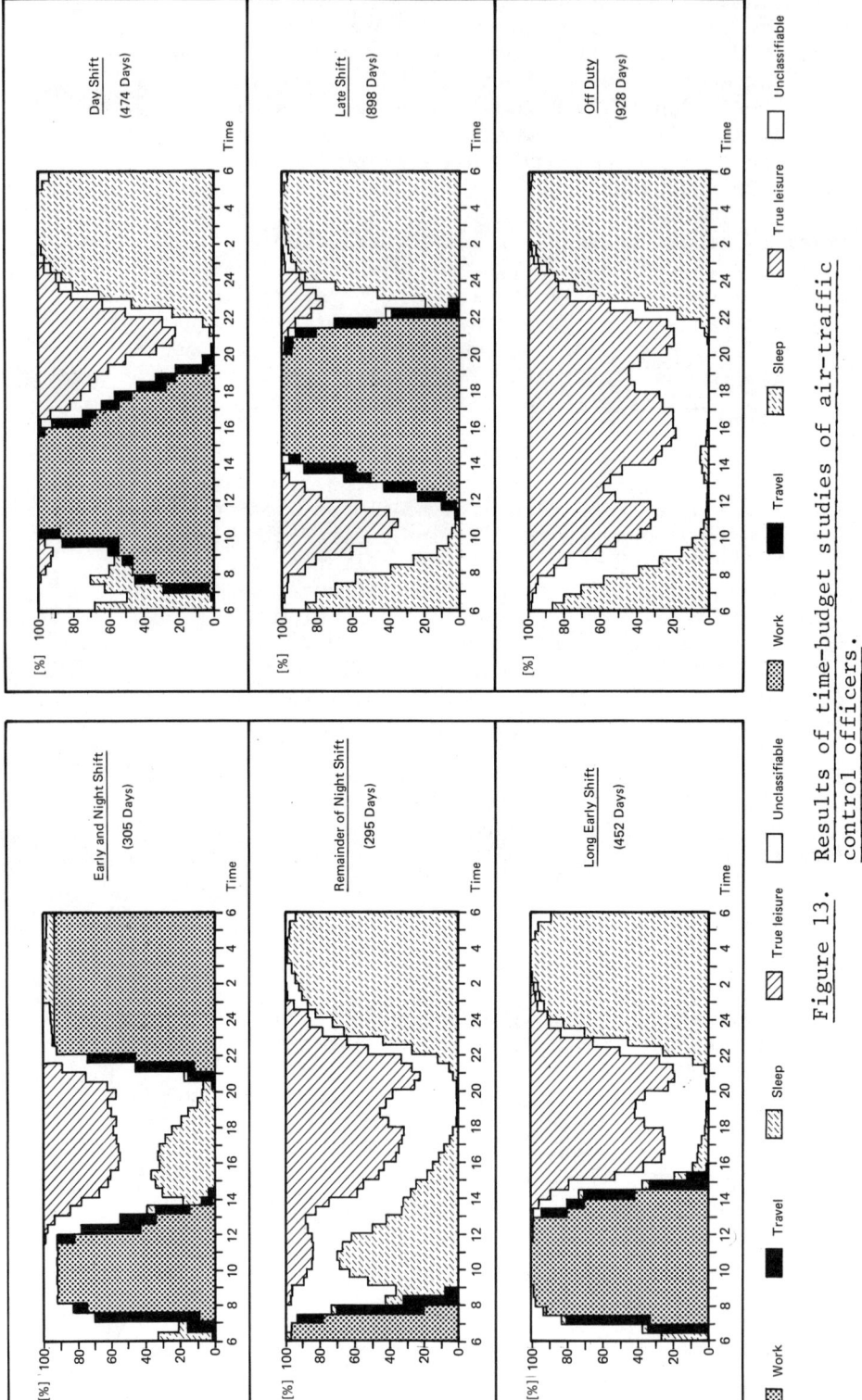

Figure 13. Results of time-budget studies of air-traffic control officers.

There are some remarkable results. First of all, it is outstanding that the time of starting to sleep is very constant and nearly not related to type of day shifts. This means that the length of sleep is only related to the time of waking up. In the combined early- and night shift there are two sleeping periods which are characterized not only by less but also by worse sleep. Also the leisure time which is at the controller's free disposal, can be evaluated in relationship to its location within the 24 hours period of the day. It can be seen furthermore that the time for travelling to the work place and back hom is not independent from the type of the shift.

The results of the time-budget studies suggest that it is necessary to evaluate also time-budgets, if man's reliability is one of the bottle-necks of the elements of the work system.

REFERENCES

Kirchner, J.-H., Laurig, W. The Human Operator in Air Traffic Control Systems. Ergonomics 14 (1971), 5, 549-556.

Klimmer, F., Aulmann, H.M., Rutenfranz, J. Katecholaminausscheidung im Urin bei emotional und mental belastenden Tätigkeiten im Flugverkehrskontrolldienst. Int. Arch. Arbeitsmed. 30 (1972), 65-80.

Knauth, P., Rutenfranz, J. Untersuchungen über die Beziehungen zwischen Schichtform und Tagesaufteilung. Int. Arch. Arbeitsmed. 30 (1972), 173-191.

Rohmert, W. Ermittlung von Bebstung und Beanspruchung der Fluglotsen in der Flugverkehrskontrolle. Industrial Engineering 2 (1972), 1, 23-30.

Rohmert, W. Ergonomische Beurteilung der Belastung und Beanspruchung von Fluglotsen in der Flugverkehrskontrolle. Industrial Engineering 3 (1973), 2, 99-110.

Rohmert, W. Psycho-physische Belastung und Beanspruchung von Fluglotsen. Beuth-Vertrieb, Berlin/Koln/Frankfurt, 1973.

ON MENTAL LOAD AND REDUCED MENTAL CAPACITY: SOME CONSIDERATIONS
CONCERNING LABORATORY RESEARCH AND FIELD INVESTIGATIONS

Mathijs Soede

Netherlands Institute for Preventive Medicine, TNO

Wassenaarseweg 56, Leiden, Netherlands

SUMMARY

This paper presents some reflections about the problem of mental load and the measurement of the level of mental load. A general model of the relation between mental control, effort and performance is given. Some observations are made regarding the notion of mental capacity.

The model proposed is suggested to be applicable in the particular man-machine situation of an arm amputee patient using a prosthesis. Pilot experiments with the aim to develop methods to measure the control effort in using a prosthesis is given as an example of the application of mental load measures.

At the end of this paper some questions are raised as to the factors which may restrain progress in mental load research.

1. Introduction

The problem of mental load and mental fatigue has been an important topic in the last twenty years. Industrialisation and automation had a tremendous influence on work and working conditions and, among others, the mental load of the employees; i.e. a shift from physical load to mental load. This is mostly related to tasks with high information processing demands; these tasks were often those being too difficult for automated systems. On the other hand, it has to be mentioned that automation requires often a large scale application to be economical. This leads to the result that subtasks, which could not be automated, are grouped together giving monotonous and unsatisfying work.

These problems are recognised by many investigators of different disciplines. However, the investigations do not cover all aspects of the research in mental load. This probably is a large impediment, because, as a result it is often not possible to relate results of investigations to either the fundamental notions of theory or the practical application. In Fig. 1 the main phases or aspects of research related to different approaches which can be made are shown.

A well-defined, generally valid, and practically useful definition of mental load is not available. Therefore each investigator has to give his own definition which is mostly very practical and based on the situation to be investigated. To describe the basic phenomena of load and its effects, an interdisciplinary approach of psychologists and physiologists seems to be necessary. A large number of measures have been developed for estimating the level of mental load. Section 5 and further will handle these measures in more detail.

The acquired data in situations dealing with various levels of load provide the basis for setting up models and the validation of models and measures. The final goal of these investigations is to lead to a real application in work environment. The latter will raise unexpected problems due to the fact that mental load problems arise in quite different contexts.

The cells in Fig. 1 show only those disciplines which might make a contribution to that aspect. This does not necessarily coincide with the actual situation. It should also be noted that the disciplines do not have to be delimited strictly as indicated. Efforts of research groups are often limited to a particular approach (row in Fig. 1) and less to the elaboration of an aspect (column).

In this paper the author will give his opinion on some topics based on experience in field investigation (Ref. 1, 2) and more recently performed laboratory research. The latter research is within the framework of an arm prosthesis project (Ref. 3, 4, 5). As a part of this project the control effort at using an arm prosthesis is considered. This control effort is due to the fact that the normal feedback system of the arm is not present. The amputee therefore uses other feedback systems requiring more conscious control i.e.: visual and auditory feedback. This leads to the following assumption. The additional mental load will give the amputee a reduced mental capacity with respect to normal task performance.

MENTAL LOAD AND REDUCED MENTAL CAPACITY

Phase or aspect Approach	Problem definition, Theory, Fundamentals	Development of measures	Validation of measures, set-up of models	Application in work environment
Psychological Basic phenomena	Psych.	Psych.	Psych. M	
Physiological Various Control Systems	Psych. Phys.	Psych. Phys.	Psych. Phys. M	
Information and Task Analysis in Experiment and field	Psych. E HFS	Psych. M E	M HFS	E HFS SD U
Experimental and Field evaluation			M E HFS	E HFS SD U

Psych. – Psychologists
Phys. – Physiologists
M – Mathematicians
E – Engineers
HFS – Human Factors Specialists (Ergonomists)
SD – Systems designers
U – Users and other involved people

Figure 1: Representation of research fields with respect to different aspects and approaches.

2. Problems in Field Investigations

There is a lack of understanding and knowledge about mental load and fatigue. Nevertheless the phenomena are frequently recognised in the field (Ref. 6, 7). Probably due to the fact that no objective and reliable description of load can be given, it happens that field problems are wrongly interpreted as a mental load problem. Therefore it is necessary that an investigation should consider all important aspects in a particular situation.

One should also be aware that management and employees or workers'councils will stress a problem in a different way. Whereas the management has a first aim in lowering absenteeism rates, increasing safety, product quality, efficiency and continuity, the employees will raise questions like:

.. Do work and working conditions influence the mental and physical health of the employees?

.. Is the amount of work (mental and/or physical) in accordance with the benefits derived from the job?

The investigators will be faced with at least two important tasks, i.e.:

.. To get support of management and employees in order to assure that the results of investigation will be actually applied.

.. The choice of the most appropriate method and measures.

The second task implies the choice between a field experiment and laboratory simulation, but also the choice of measures and measurement technique. Each measure has a limited applicability, interpretability, and validity dependent on the situation to be investigated (see section 5; Ref. 8). If possible, it is recommended to try out different techniques in the investigation (Ref. 9).

3. Theoretical Model of Load and Performance

3.1. Mental load and task performance.

The situation of a human operator in a task environment is given in Fig. 2.

MENTAL LOAD AND REDUCED MENTAL CAPACITY

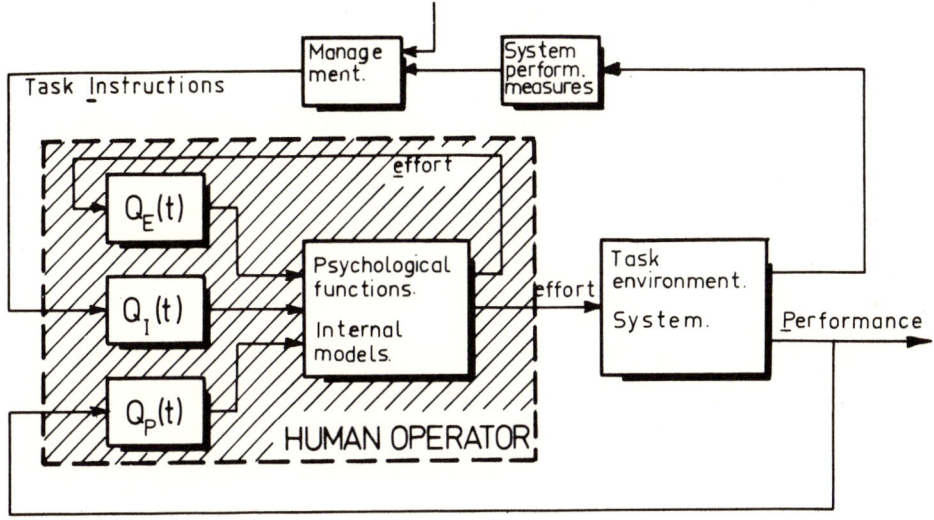

Figure 2: Blockdiagram of a general man-machine system or man-task environment.

The basic idea of the model is that system or task performance and mental load as well as mental effort are strongly related. An increase of human effort will give an increase of system effectiveness depending on the (task) system involved. In the blockdiagram the human operator is presented as a decision-making element with several weighted inputs, memory and output mechanisms. The inputs to the human operator include the feed-back of the task performance $P(t)$ and the task instruction $I(t)$. These inputs are subjectively weighted by the human operator with the weighting factors $Q_P(t;\beta)$ and $Q_I(t;\alpha)$ respectively. Moreover the human operator will appraise his effort $E(t)$ by weighting with a factor $Q_E(t;\beta)$.

The weighting factors $Q_P(t;\beta)$ and $Q_I(t;\alpha)$ are related to the particular system or task α considered. The symbol β denotes a human operator with his specific abilities, motivation and capacity. It is suggested that the human operator will optimize task performance and effort to a certain criterion which depends strongly on his individual goals.

This means that he optimizes the following expression which should be regarded as his subjectively appraised (task-) system performance $s(t;\alpha,\beta)$:

$$\underline{s}(t;\alpha,\beta) = \underline{F}_s \; \underline{F}_E \; \underline{Q}_E(t;\beta)E(t;\alpha) \quad \underline{F}_P \quad \underline{Q}_P(t;\beta).P(t;\alpha)$$

$$\underline{F}_I \quad \underline{Q}_I \; (t;\beta).I(t;\beta) \tag{1}$$

The functions and weighting factors in Eq. (1) have to be considered as vectors and matrices; this means that the effort, performance and instructions have to be described as a vector of several variables.

The subjective system performance vector $s(t;\alpha,\beta)$ has to be within the boundaries set by management, which restricts the possibility to find a real optimum of Eq.(1).

This general model is the basis of the arm prosthesis project which is partly summarized in section 3.2.

3.2 The acceptance of an arm prosthesis.

The acceptance of arm prosthesis by unilateral amputees was studied in a multidisciplinary project (Ref. 5). The motive for this research is a low rate of acceptance of arm prosthesis by the amputees (Ref. 3,4).

In Fig. 3 a scheme is presented which differs from the block diagram of Fig. 2 but poses essentially the same problem.

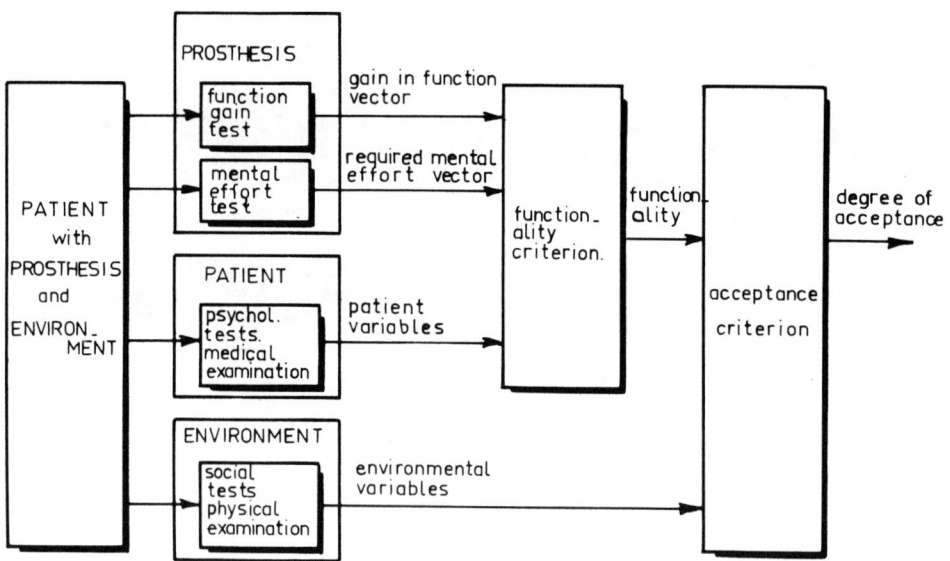

Fig. 3. Scheme for estimating the acceptance of a prosthesis.

The following variables are given in the diagram:

- The gain in function $g(\alpha)$: the gain in function of a prosthesis α is the increase in functional possibilities when all technical/physiological possibilities are utilized.

- The mental effort $m(\alpha)$: the mental effort is the control effort of the amputee, related to the control of the prosthesis, needed to utilize the prosthesis functions available.

- The functionality $f(t;\alpha,\beta)$: the functionality is the gain in function as experienced by the amputee.

- The degree of acceptance $a(t;\alpha,\beta)$: the degree of acceptance is the feeling of the amputee about the degree in which the prosthesis contributes to the functioning of the amputee in his environment.

Assuming that suitable methods can be found to determine the vectors $g(\alpha)$ and $m(\alpha)$ the next equation can be stated:

$$\underline{f}(t;\alpha,\beta) = \underline{F}_f \underline{F}_g \underline{R}_g (t;\beta) \cdot g(\alpha) + \underline{F}_m \underline{R}_m(t;\beta) \cdot m(\alpha) \tag{2}$$

The weighting matrices $\underline{R}_g(t;\beta)$ and $\underline{R}_m(t;\beta)$, representing the patient parameters, are thought to be estimated by physical and psychological examination of the amputee β observed. Generally these quantities will be dependent on time. In this way the functionality $\underline{f}(t;\alpha,\beta)$ turns out to be an optimization problem.

Furthermore the acceptance of a prosthesis has to be thought of as a function of the functionality vector and the environmental variables $\underline{s}(t;\alpha,\beta)$. The vector $\underline{s}$ describes the physical and social environment of a particular amputee β wearing a prosthesis α. Finally it has to be noted that the amputee is free to choose where the optimum lies, and is therefore also free to accept or reject the prosthesis. This is due to the fact that a unilateral amputee can perform almost all possible activities in alternative ways with the healthy hand and thus a prosthesis can sometimes even be omitted.

4. Aspects of Capacity

Several definitions of capacity can be found in the literature (Ref. 10). Very often the unit of capacity is defined as an elementary unit of task load; for example: a choice with response in a simple reaction task or a complete cycle of activities in a complex task. The analysis of tasks with a special emphasis on information handling, the unit of information (bit) is frequently chosen

(Ref. 11, 12) which gives the advantage that different tasks can be compared. Some investigators distinguish capacity actually used for task performance and available capacity (Ref. 13). The available capacity is supposed to be related to a physiological state of the human operator while the capacity used for task performance will mostly be derived from task variables. It has to be noticed that research focussed on health and well-being should deal with evaluation of the physiological state. The available capacity might be used as a variable in these investigations. Task specific investigations concerning errors, task content, etc., have to quantify the capacity actually used.

4.1. The dynamic aspects of capacity.

The dynamic aspect of capacity is the dependence of the momentary capacity at a certain time t_1 on the capacity used or held available during $t < t_1$. A relation between task load and endurance time is given in Fig. 4 (Ref. 14).

This diagram is easily misunderstood because the referenced article gives various types of capacity in the figure while the vertical axis indicates load rather than capacity. Fig. 5 shows an arbitrary course of the momentary capacity; the "maximum capacity"-curve of Fig. 4 is presented as a dashed line.

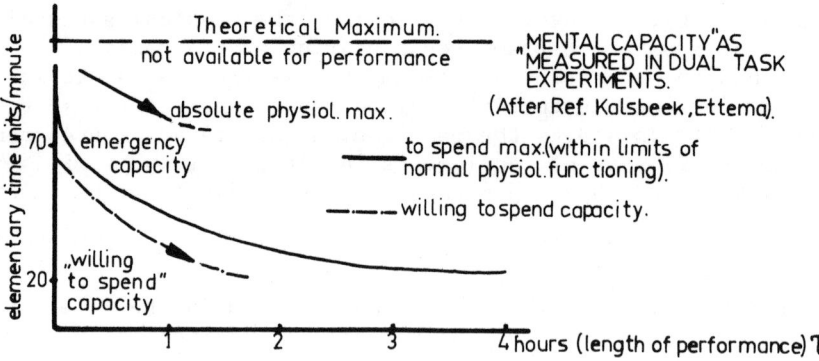

Figure 4 - Diagram of the relation between endurance time T and task load (after Ref. 14).

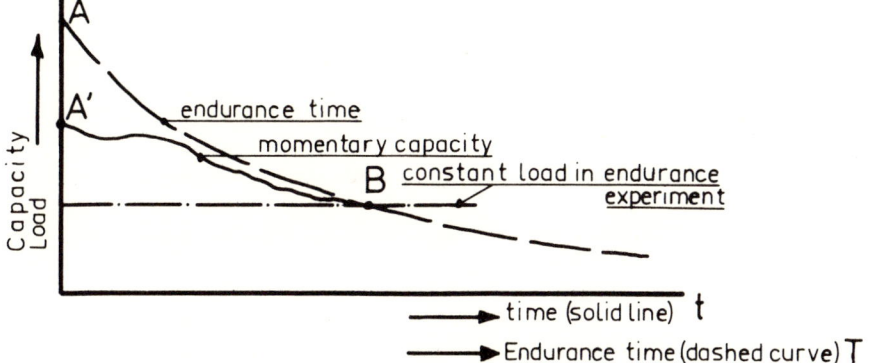

Figure 5. - The relation between a capacity curve and endurance time T.

The following remarks can be made:

- The starting point A' is below point A which indicates the theoretical maximum capacity.

- The curve A - B must lie above A' - B, the used capacity, otherwise errors are made.

- The point of intersection B indicates the end of good performance; at B the used capacity equals the available capacity.

After these considerations it will be clear that the course of available capacity and the recovery from fatigue induced by the task load are very important in mental load research. Some attempts to describe the recovery phenomenon have been made (Ref. 15, 16), however not enough is known to suggest a model.

4.2 The stochastic aspects of capacity.

The statistical or stochastic (time dependent) properties of capacity concern the variations and differences in capacity due to external influences, state of the human operator and the intra- and interindividual variations. This means that the usual precautions to be taken in experiments are:

- The duration of the experimental sessions has to be controlled strictly.

- Rest periods and randomisation of sequences are necessary to cope with fatigue and diurnal effects.

- The external conditions have to be the same for each subject.

These precautions can be incorporated rather easily in laboratory experiments, but cause difficulties in field investigations which will always show less reliability and less interpretability due to the mentioned sources of variance. More research effort could be given to describe the influence of different sources of variance.

5. Comparison of Methods

5.1. General.

The methods of measuring mental load can be categorised as follows:

- Subjective ratings
- Physiological measurements
- Dual task methods
- Task analysis
- Detection and description of pathology

The last method mentioned should not be regarded as an applicable method but it can provide worthwhile data about the situation to be studied.

An overview of other methods mentioned is found in literature (Ref. 8), where a comparison is made with respect to criteria like:

- Interpretability, validity: the relation between the variables measured and mental load and the effects of external variations.

- Reliability, signal to noise ratio: the ratio between the effects on variables by mental task and the effects of external variations.

- Interference: the influence of method and equipment on the human operator and situation to be measured, and the effects on the results of measurement.

- Acceptance: the human operator has to accept the method, otherwise no reliability can be expected.

- Applicability: Interference and other reasons are sometimes so important that a particular method turns out to be not applicable.

Furthermore one should also consider the efficiency of a method; this includes:

- amount and type of equipment
- duration of data processing
- qualification and training of the personnel who execute the measurements and data processing.

5.2 Measuring mental control effort in the use of an arm prosthesis.

An effort has been made to estimate the mental control effort of a pneumatically powered, <u>E</u>lectro-<u>M</u>yo-<u>G</u>raphical controlled arm prosthesis.

5.2.1.

The method of <u>subjective rating</u> is not applicable in this research, because patients are very much emotionally involved in their handicap so they will give estimates based on apparently irrational criteria. Furthermore, there is no list available describing the levels of load.

5.2.2.

The method of <u>physiological measures</u> can be applied in an experimental situation. The results of an experiment with five subjects performing a simple ball grasping task are given in Fig. 6 (Ref. 17).

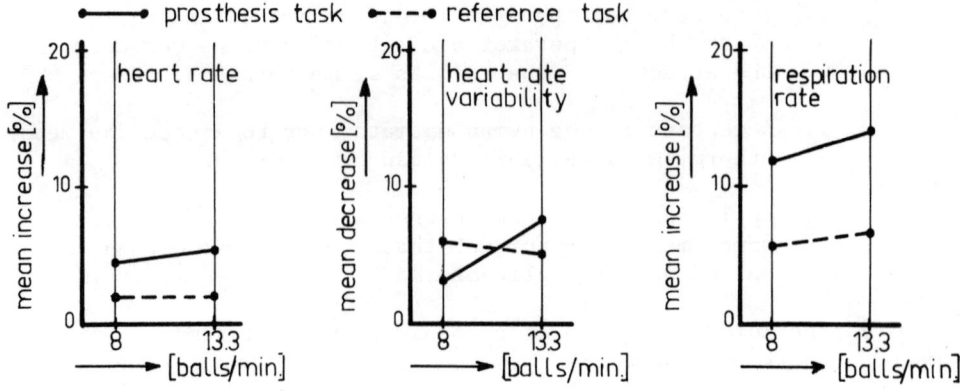

Figure 6. Physiological measures related to an increase in repetition rate of a ball grasping task with respect to rest condition.

The performance of the arm prosthesis is compared with the performance of a normal arm (i.e., a reference task). The only significant differences found are between respiration rate in the reference task and prosthesis task. This negative result may be explained by the existence of considerable physical effort which reduces the signal to noise ratio. It was therefore concluded that the physiological method could not be applied in this investigation.

5.2.3.

In some preliminary experiments it was found that in laboratory or clinical situations the dual task method is feasible. Section 6 below discusses this.

5.2.4.

It is supposed that task analysis will give much more insight into particular aspects or subtasks causing the mental load. Section 7 deals with this method.

6. The Application of Dual Task Methods

A concurrent or secondary task can be used in two different ways, i.e.:

- .. As a paced task which will reduce the primary task performance, thus showing error on those moments or subtasks in the primary task where the reserve capacity is not sufficient (Ref. 14). The concurrent task is in this set-up a distraction task with consistent performance.

- .. As a self-paced task with the aim of filling up the subject's spare capacity (Ref. 18). In this case the primary task performance should be unaffected. The secondary task has to be a quantifiable task.

The second method is more directly related to the level of load to be measured, therefore the method of distraction will not be discussed in this paper.

The perception and motor behavior involved in performing the primary task restrict the choice of the secondary task because no interference of input and output modalities is allowed between the two tasks. Furthermore one has to choose such a secondary task that the subject is motivated to fill up his spare capacity.

Preliminary experiments were carried out with two different secondary tasks, i.e.: the Binary Choice Task (Ref. 19), and the Sub Critical Instability Task (Ref. 20, 21). The BCT is a self-paced task with auditory input (high or low tone) and a pedal output (left and right pedal switch). It turned out that the discrete EMG-signals needed to control the pneumatical powered prosthesis did not fit very well with the BCT. Only large time intervals were used to make choices and no attempt was made to fill up the spare capacity during the use of the prosthesis. An actual record of BCT-responses along with the rectified and filtered EMG-signal is given in Fig. 7.

It was thought that the SCIT would be a better means to fill up the spare capacity of the subject being a continuous task. The SCIT implies the continuous control of an unstable process. The set-up of the SCIT is given in Fig. 8.

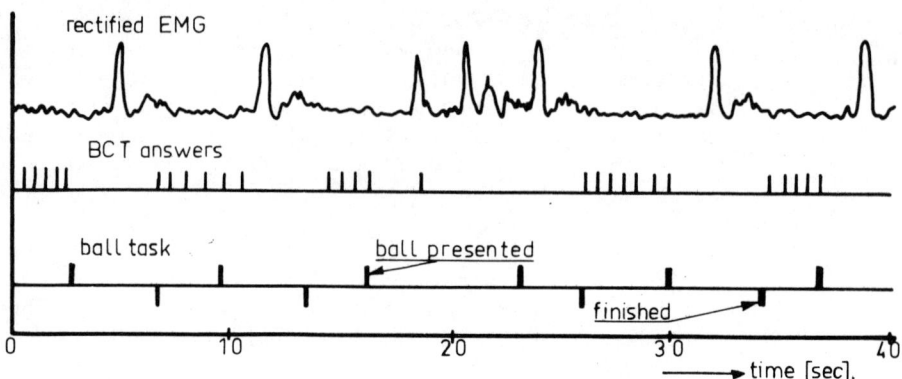

Figure 7. - An example of the BCT-performance and the EMG-signal during the execution of the prosthesis task.

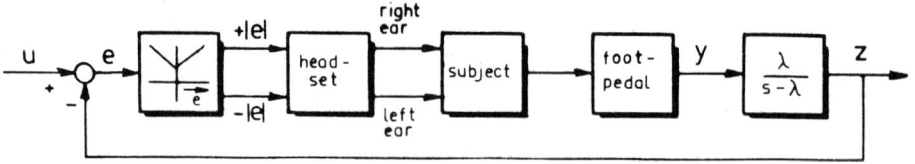

Figure 8. - Configuration of the SCIT as used in experiments.

As is shown in Fig. 8 the positive and negative errors were presented to the right and left ear respectively (Ref. 22). The control signal y was generated by tilting a foot pedel to the right or to the left. The process to be controlled can be described by the transfer function $H(s) = \lambda / (s-\lambda)$, where λ denotes the instability of the process. In this case λ preset at $\lambda_1 = 0.6$ rad./sec^2. Five subjects were used. When the absolute error is kept small by the subject, only small control movements were necessary; thus the subject was rewarded for good performance. The result of an experiment which included the ball grasping task with the EMG-pneumatic prosthesis at different repetition rates is given in Fig. 9 (Ref. 23).

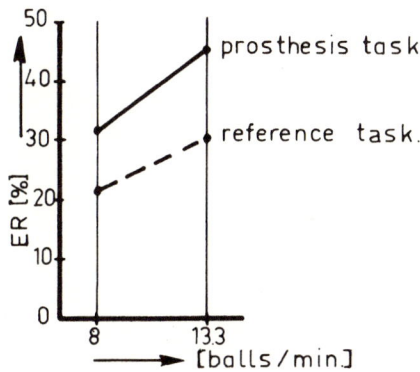

Figure 9.- The error rate ER at different repetition rates of the ball task.

The error rate ER is defined as the increase of mean square error in SCIT in dual task condition with respect to the single SCIT, divided by the mean square error in dual task condition. The figure shows significant differences between reference task and prosthesis task; also the differences between different repetition rates are significant.

Further experiments with the SCIT and the prosthesis were executed with three different levels of the EMG-control as given in Fig. 10 and a ball repetition rate of 8 per minute.

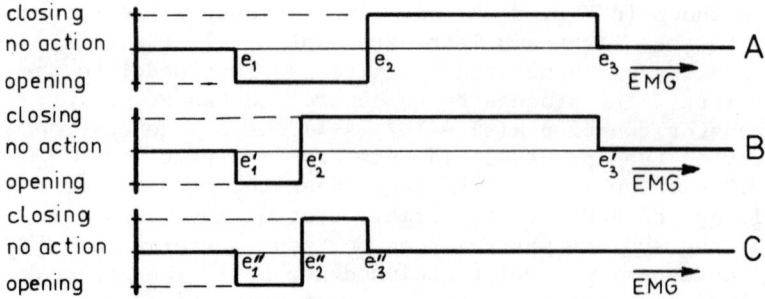

Figure 10: – Types of EMG-control

The figure gives the control characteristics of the grasping function of the prosthesis. One single muscle in the lower arm is used. Generating an EMG-signal with an intensity between e_1 and e_2 will open the prosthesis hand. EMG-activity between e_2 and e_3 will close the hand. Small differences (e_2-e_1) and (e_3-e_2) will give a difficult control situation. The results of this pilot experiment with two subjects is given in Fig. 11.

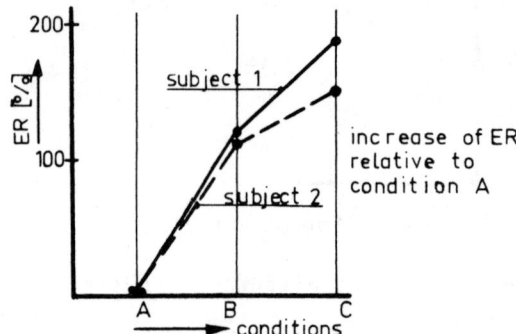

Figure 11:- The error rate ER for various EMG-controls as indicated in Fig. 10.

Each data point for each subject is the mean value of five repeated sessions. The conditions proved to be significantly different in error rate for each individual subject. These results encouraged us to set up a series of comparative experiments with a number of commonly used arm prosthesis. This experiment is in progress at the moment.

7. Task Analysis.

7.1. Fundamental background.

Whereas most measures will give one number indicating the mean level of mental effort in a particular experimental session,

it is often necessary to have more fundamental knowledge about
tasks and their components requiring high levels of attention. A
detailed task analysis may provide such knowledge. Task analyses
have been used in many different ways depending on the goals of the
investigator. In mental load research one is interested in a task
analysis method resulting in a description of the uncertainties in
the task for the subject. If it is possible to allocate these
uncertainties, information theory may give a quantitative measure for
a particular task. A fundamental point in this study is to determine what an uncertainty actually means to the subject. The relevant
uncertainties are choice uncertainty and time uncertainty (Ref. 24).
Choice uncertainty means that a subject does not know for sure what
the next part of his task to be performed will be and thus that he
has to make a conscious decision (Ref. 25). One has to be aware
that subjective, not objective uncertainty is involved in this
decision. Furthermore, automatic and mostly unconsciously controlled
actions will not require attention. Secondly the time uncertainty
deals with almost the same problems as choice uncertainty does.

After one has defined subtasks and tasks it is possible to
make measurements in laboratory and practical situations. From
these measurements it is possible to calculate the objective probabilities of transitions between succeeding task elements. In this
way the information processed due to choice uncertainty can be
calculated. The information due to time uncertainty is much more
difficult to measure because it is not easy to detect at what moment
one subtask ends and the following one starts. Another problem of
measurement is that the human operator will be in a closed loop
system, thus having a feed-back of the effects of his activities
and the possibility to influence the probabilities of transitions
between succeeding task elements.

In spite of all these problems a pilot experiment has been
carried out to study the feasibility of this approach. Before this
experiment is described a last note on the application of task
analysis has to be made. In rehabilitation centers a comprehensive
list of possible tasks describing the Activities of Daily Living is
known. Different subjects will weigh the importance of specific
tasks from this whole set of tasks differently, according to their
psychological condition and social environment, including their
professional occupation. If task analyses provide more knowledge
about the required mental control effort in different types of
tasks, it is possible to fit these data more specifically to the
requirements of particular subjects. To scale a particular subject
with respect to the control effort in performing the ADL-tasks with
a prosthesis, the subject has to perform a test set of tasks representing the different aspects of mental control effort.

7.2. Feasibility of task analysis in the prosthesis project.

An experiment with two subjects has been carried out with the EMG-pneumatic prosthesis. The ball grasping task, mentioned before, was split up in the following subtasks:

1. waiting for the stimulus or feedback (no visible action)
2. closing of the prosthesis (generating a high EMG-signal)
3. raising the prosthesis and positioning above target
4. opening of the prosthesis (generating a smaller EMG-signal)
5. moving the prosthesis back to the starting point within the boundaries and laying it down.

When the task is performed correctly, the sequence will be: 1-2-3-4-5, and all conditional probabilities of the transitions between two subtasks are equal to 1. Difficulties in the performance disturb this sequence and then the conditional probabilities will be less than 1.

The basic indicator of load can be given by this formula:

$$\text{Load } L_o = -W(j)\frac{\log_2 P(j)}{T(j)} - \frac{\log_2 P(j/i)}{T(j)} \text{ bits/sec.} \quad (3)$$

where P(j) denotes the probability of occurrence of subtask j;
P(j/i) denotes the conditional probability of occurrence of subtask j when subtask i is performed;
T(j) denotes the duration of subtask j;
W(j) denotes a weighting factor for subtask j.

The second term denotes the amount of information due to the choice uncertainty in deciding which next task should be carried out, whereas the first term represents the information related to the performance of a particular subtask.

Due to insufficient splitting of tasks, the performance of a subtask will require some attention, which is dependent on the subjective factors represented by the weighting factor W(j). Dividing by the duration T(j) provides a continuous measure of load to be experienced by the subject. A second indicator of load, L_1 can be defined in a similar manner by taking all weighting factors W(j) = 1. An example of a record of the computation of the load indicators L_0 and L_1 for each subtask is given in Fig. 12. This figure shows also the mean values of the indicators, $\bar{L}_0$ and $\bar{L}_1$ respectively, for conditions with increasing ball repetition rate and conditions with increasing difficulty of EMG-control as presented in Fig. 10.

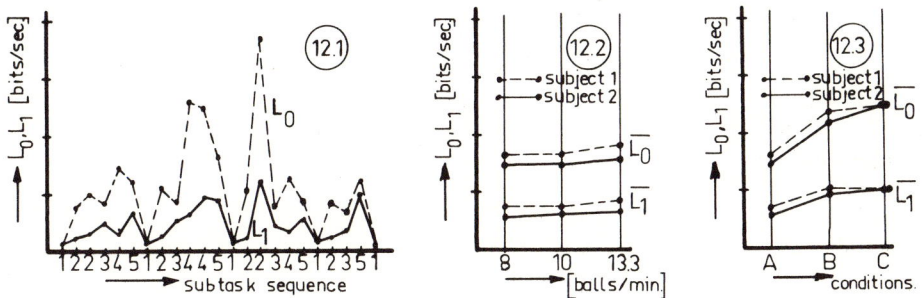

Figure 12. - The mental load indicators L_0 and L_1

12.1: Computed record for 13.3 balls/min. and EMG-condition(c)

12.2: Means of L_0 and L_1 for increasing ball repetition rate

12.3: Means of L_0 and L_1 for increasing difficulty of EMG-control.

Not all different conditions show significant differences in the load indicators. These and other results (Ref. 24) of the feasibility study lead to some concluding remarks about task analysis. At the moment there still is insufficient knowledge to determine which parts in task performance require a conscious control. This might explain why the mental load indicators do not show those differences between the experimental sessions as could be expected from a theoretical viewpoint, as indicated in section 7.1.

Furthermore the amount of time uncertainty is not taken into account, while it certainly takes a part of the subjects' attention. Nevertheless the actual record of Fig. 12.1 shows that the algorithm to compute measures based on information theory is feasible. Furthermore, from the actual curves of information load during the experiment, it can be seen that certain subtasks give much more load than others. For example, the opening of the prosthesis is shown to be the most difficult subtask. Therefore, research in the field of task analysis should be and will be continued. More emphasis will be put on problems of division into subtasks, time uncertainty and the translation of activities into categories of subtasks which can be the basis of a clinical test set of tasks.

8. Conclusion and Discussion

An attempt is made in this paper to relate some theoretical concepts with an application in the field of rehabilitation.

The acceptance of an arm prosthesis is considered with respect to
the aspects of mental control effort. Different approaches and
different methods have been tried out. It has been shown that in
the laboratory situation reasonable results can be obtained. Many
questions and problems arose in the discussions on the theoretical
background and the application. Some of them will be mentioned
below.

In a general model of mental effort and performance it is
clear that various variables interact very strongly; i.e.
psychological, physiological and work related variables. It is
obvious that field investigations on mental effort should incorporate these variables. In other words the set-up of a field
investigation should possibly deal with all these approaches, i.e.
the same as mentioned in Fig. 1. More progress in theory and
application may be expected if with these approaches, preferably
on an interdisciplinary basis, an integrated model can be developed.
This will require co-operation of the disciplines in all phases
mentioned in Fig. 1 rather than monodisciplinary attempts to solve
the problems within one specific approach.

Theoretical models of capacity and also field problems show
that recovery characteristics or work-rest schemes have to be an
important part of an integrated model. Not much literature is found
about this phenomenon. More emphasis should be put on fundamental
research in this field.

It is known that physiological measures have to deal with a
small signal to noise ratio. Tremendous efforts are being put
into the development of a measure or a combination of measures
(Ref. 9) which will be relatively insensitive to noise sources.
It might be possible that better results will be obtained if a
description of "noise" sources or a description of the parameters
of a situation is taken into account.

The application of the dual task method has proved to be
successful in many laboratory experiments. Less positive results
are found in the field situation. The SCIT as a secondary task
in the prosthesis experiments seems to be practical. However, a
comparison of the results of these experiments with other dual task
experiments remains difficult because of the use of different units
and a probably non-linear relation between effort and SCIT-parameters
(Ref. 26, 27).

Finally, remarks have to be made about task analysis. An
adequate task analysis technique will have the advantage that the
results can be interpreted easily in terms of the practical situation. Furthermore a task analysis method to estimate the level of
effort interferes less with the task to be studied than the dual task
method. If the level of effort can be expressed in a number of

bits per second using information theory, comparisons can easily be made. Major problems still to be solved in the application of task analysis are both the time uncertainty involved in many tasks and the criteria needed to split up a whole activity into elementary subtasks.

The activities to be performed by an amputee and the importance of certain activities for an amputee are important aspects of task analysis in the prosthesis project and while a fairly complete list exists of Activities of Daily Living, large groups of possible activities are not listed. For example: hobby and professional activities.

REFERENCES

1. Soede, M., H.G. Stassen & J.F. Coeterier. Time analysis of the Tasks of Approach Controllers in ATC. Ergonomics 14 (1971) 591-602.

2. Soede, M., & J.F. Coeterier. Investigations in an automobile grinding room. Internal report TNO (Dutch)(1971).

3. Soede, M., J.S.M.J. Van Dieten & H.G. Stassen. On the acceptance, functional gain and mental load in arm prosthesis and orthosis control; report. Delft, Delft Univ. of Techn., Dept. of Mech. Eng., WTHD 66 (1974) 17 pp.

4. Stassen, H.G., J.S.M.J. Van Dieten & M. Soede. On the mental load in relation to the acceptance of arm prosthesis. In: preprints 6th World Congress of the International Federation of Automatic Control, Boston/Cambridge (1975). Paper 40.1. 8 pp.

5. Stassen, H.G. (ed.) Progress Report. Jan. 1973 until July 1976 of the Man-Machine Systems Group. Delft, Univ. of Techn., Dept. of Mech. Eng., WTHD 95 (1977), Ch. IX-XIII, pp.164-223.

6. Grandjean, E. Introductory remarks at the symposium. In: K. Hashimoto et al. (eds.) Proceedings of Methodology in human fatigue assessment symposium, Kyoto, Japan (1969) London, Taylor Francis. 14 pp.

7. McFarland, R.A. Understanding Fatigue in Modern Life. In: Hashimoto et al. (eds.). Proceedings of Methodology in human fatigue assessment symposium, Kyoto, Japan (1969). London, Taylor Francis. pp. 1-10.

8. Rolfe, J.M. The measurement of human response in man-vehicle control situations. In: T.B. Sheridan & G. Johannsen (eds.). Monitoring behavior and supervisory control. New York, Plenum Press. pp. 125-138.

9. Spyker, D.A., S.P. Stackhouse, A.S. Khalafalla & R.C. McLane. Development of techniques for measuring pilot work load. NASA CR-1888 (1970). 109 pp.

10. Vollmar, R. The dual task method in evaluation of spare capacity. Delft, Delft Univ. of Techn., Lab. for Measurement and Control (1976) S-170. 45 pp. M.Sc. thesis (in Dutch).

11. Gigch, J.P. Van. The physical and mental load components of objective complexity in production systems. Behavioral Science 21 (1976) 490-498.

12. Philipp, U., D. Reiche & J.H. Kirchner. The use of subjective rating. Ergonomics 14 (1971) 611-616.

13. Kahneman, D. Attention and effort. Englewood Cliffs, N.J. Prentice Hall (1973). 246 pp.

14. Kalsbeek, J.W.H. & J.H. Ettema. Physiological and psychological evaluation of distraction stress. Ergonomics, Proceedings of 2nd I.E.A. Congress, Dortmund, 1964.

15. Tsaneva, N., & S. Markov. A model of fatigue. In: K. Hashimoto et al. (eds.) Proceedings of Methodology in human fatigue assessment symposium, Kyoto, Japan (1969). London, Taylor Francis, pp. 11-16.

16. Blom, J.L. L'influence de la charge mentale sur les potentiels évoqués. Le Travail Humain 37 (1974) 139-212.

17. Oomen, P.M.F. Investigation in mental load due to the control of an arm prosthesis. Delft, Delft Univ. of Techn., Lab.for Measurement and Control (1973) Ae-812. 57 pp. M.Sc. thesis (in Dutch).

18. Kalsbeek, J.W.H. Mesure objective de la surcharge mentale; nouvelles applications de la méthode des doubles tâches. Le Travail Humain 28 (1965) 121-132.

19. Bertelson, P., A. Renkin, D. Lemye & G. Taverne. L'évaluation de la capacité résiduelle par la méthode de la tâche ajoutée. Bruxelles, Univ., Libre de Bruxelles, Lab. de Psychologie, Dépt. de Psychologie expérimentale (1973). 170 pp.

20. Jex, H.R., J.D. McDonnell & A.V. Phatak. A "critical" tracking task for manual control research. IEEE Transactions on Human Factors in Electronics. Vol. HFE-7 (1966) 138-145.

21. McRuer, D.T. & H.R. Jex. A review of quasi-linear pilot models. IEEE Transactions on Human Factors in Electronics. Vol. HFE-8 (1967) 231-249.

22. Pitkin, E.T., & E.W. Vinjé. Evaluation of human operator aural and visual displays with the Critical Tracking Task. In: Proceedings of the 8th Annual conference on manual control, (1972). AFFDL-TR-72-92, pp. 553-559.

23. Vermeulen, J. Investigation of the possibilities of measuring the control effort of an arm prosthesis. Delft, Delft Univ. of Techn. Lab. for Measurement and Control (1974) A-187. 77 pp. M.Sc. thesis (in Dutch).

24. Elias. M.E. Investigation in task analysis as a method to measure the control effort of an arm prosthesis. Delft, Delft Univ. of Techn. Lab. for Measurement and Control (1974) A-15. 58 pp. M.Sc. thesis (in Dutch).

25. Kalsbeek, J.W.H. Standards of acceptable load in ATC tasks. Ergonomics 14 (1971) 641-650.

26. Hess, R.A. Nonadjectival rating scales in human response experimments. Human Factors 15 (1973) 275-280.

27. McDonnell, J.D. Pilot rating techniques for the estimation and evaluation of handling qualities (1968). AFFDL-TR-68-76, pp. 198.

normally considered an element of overall workload most closely related to information processing, decision making and situational variables. It relates to the overall system question of whether "operators" can produce and maintain desired performance at required levels without undue or undesirable effects. Across applications the detailed meaning remains similar but varies as the application involves, for example, aircraft flight control, air traffic control, manufacturing and process control operations or prosthetic devices.

For purposes of this discussion, workload is considered to be a function of a collective assortment of tasks, and of detailed task components and features as well as personal variables that, together, define and contrast task demand vs ability to perform, and in turn contribute to overall system performance. A system is defined broadly, as a composite of objectives, people, operating goals, task demands and resulting procedures and/or equipment required to produce a desired total objective. It covers the range from hardware systems with specific and measurable indicators of performance objectives to social systems with specific objectives but more nebulous indicators.

A major achievement was felt to be the establishing of a common approach for a wide range of diverse and complex applied problems. Attempts to correlate more basic data and theory with this approach were less successful. Future workshop efforts of a similar nature were considered necessary, using results of the current workshop as the starting point. Accordingly, the summary of discussions first emphasizes agreed-upon baseline definitions and descriptions of applications objectives, problems, methods, needs and approaches from the wide variety of applications interests represented by this workshop group. Subsequently, recommended research is outlined for increasing applications utility of more basic theories, methods and models.

Scope of Interests - Applications Workshop Participants

While participants varied widely in their backgrounds, there were marked similarities in methodological questions, prediction and measurement techniques explored and identified problems and needs. The common question for all was which, where and how to apply elements of existing models and theories in terms of relevant utility and reasonable validity. A brief statement of interests emphasizes the extent to which there is agreement despite the diversity of starting points.

V. David Hopkin - RAF Institute of Aviation Medicine, England.

Hopkin's work emphasizes large man-machine systems in

two major areas, air traffic control and map development. He is most strongly concerned with the possibility that inappropriate decisions today may not be shown as such until another generation of very expensive and very critical equipment comes "on-line". He has used test batteries, physiological and performance methods and observational experimental techniques to examine the overall workload - performance variables associated with large systems. He has concluded that traditional laboratory techniques with few variables are too limited for broader, systems work. Additionally, he is convinced that, with system performance, careers and even life styles involved, broader questions of physiological and social cost become quite important (e.g. job satisfaction, skill, craftmanship, age).

Donald L. Parks - The Boeing Company, U.S.A.

Parks' aerospace experience has included a wide range of human performance and life support requirements for commercial, military and space systems. His interests include methods, theory, and approaches for workload prediction, achieving workload control, and assuring effective operator performance by special design provisions covering the man-machine interface in all normal, abnormal and support modes. Representative workload questions for theory, methods and models include predictive and measurement capabilities for such areas as:

- Defining an overall system workload level.
- Defining workload content for alternative display-control concepts with maximum information transfer, minimum clutter (or "noise") and "optimum" display-control compatibility.
- Quantitatively defining and predicting influence of workload modifiers (such modifiers as skill, learning, retention, fatigue).

Walter Rohmert - Institut für Arbeitswissenschaft, W. Germany.

Rohmert's interests emphasize workload variables and their influence in industrial jobs, and in air traffic control. Most specifically, he is concerned with distinctions involving wide variations in mental loading with different types of jobs. He emphasizes the critical importance of methodology in evaluating the complex interplay of system and environmental-personal-social influences as they affect job performance and satisfaction. Considered as important methodological elements in this interplay are distinctions in external forcing functions (stress) and internal response mechanism (strain). Such characteristics enter into the trade-offs of basic capabilities (e.g. physical/physiological/psychological), job related capabilities (e.g. skill) and modifying parameters (e.g. short term adaptation, fatigue). Typical considerations include:

- Selection of people who can do a given task <u>and</u> tolerate the strain.
- Task tolerability, in terms of effects on work/rest cycles, shift performance and career (lifetime) job satisfaction.
- Hierarchical arrangement for career progression.
- Job related variations, including unplanned task "handovers" or large and sudden changes in the task situation.

André Rault - Adersa/Gerbois, France.

Rault is working in two major areas. One is concerned with helicoptor pilot operations, workload and safety. The second deals with workload for process control operators. He has explored the utility of interview techniques, physiological measures, information theory and mathematical modelling. Each had favorable elements but also featured limitations; ability to quantify, understand and interpret the findings varied with the technique. Clarifying research is planned.

Thys Soede - Netherlands Institute for Preventative Medicine, The Netherlands.

Soede's experience includes body prosthetic devices and air traffic control as well as production systems. Work on prostheses, in particular, has emphasized the influence of emotionally laden and difficult-to-measure acceptance or rejection of system provisions and workload. Individualized variables include load vs effort vs payoff, as well as fatigue, capacity and the importance of a device in producing personalized objectives of work. One particular example demonstrated the workload and satisfaction trade-offs as personal variables vs system role vs system requirements. An arm prosthesis that was quite suitable for a young lady during courtship and early marriage became unacceptable in tending a baby - the system role and requirements had changed. In this situation, "mental load" is based on many personal, physiological and psychological elements; results are not always satisfactory. His conclusion: mental workload problems may be solved incidentally by solving other problems, but more definitions and conclusive indicators are needed.

There was common agreement on definition of system requirements as being related to whether the operator can maintain given levels of performance without undue or undesirable effects. Goals in screening for new methods and techniques were also similar. It was desired to obtain information that could be used in an appropriate, systematic and meaningful way in complex systems, including

- New methods and techniques
- How the techniques might be used
- The degree of validation that had been accomplished.

Separate aspects of our conclusions are presented by individual members of the group.

Background and Problem Summary for Applications of Workload Concepts - by V.D. Hopkin

A main reason for recent concern with mental workload problems has been deficiencies in existing man-machine systems, where questions regarding mental workload and distractions (too little or too much) have been raised. Such questions have in turn led to a practical concern to try to prevent similar circumstances from arising in future systems.

Since the practical applications to which the concept of mental workload is relevant are so numerous, there are formidable problems in finding a general approach for application. In the applied context, systems will be produced on schedule with or without a human factors input and with or without an appraisal of the mental workload problems involved. A key requirement is to estimate overall concept practicality and effectiveness before extensive resources are committed to development. Therefore, if such assessments are to be made, they will be based on the best techniques at hand, and will not wait until better techniques are developed and proven.

However, there are many different reasons for wanting to predict or measure mental workload. Accordingly, any satisfactory methodology must be capable of satisfying a variety of objectives. These can be subsumed under the general headings of analysis, prediction, measurement and implementation. In general, the human factors specialist tries to anticipate requirements and avoid problems rather than rely on an after-the-fact reactive mode of supporting system development.

Additionally, distinctions between mental and physical

workload may become obscure in practice, where emphasis has been on the broader characterization of task elements and the consequent overall workload for man. Within this framework, current technological progress in applications is placing more emphasis on the workload elements of which we are most ignorant – information processing, decision making and the influence of "external" situational variables.

Most of the general types of measurement methods purporting to assess mental workload have been tried in some applied context or other. Familiar analytic methods and measurements in applications include subjective assessments (e.g. ratings, questionnaires, scenario critique), modelling, performance measures, physiological indices, assessment of stress (external mechanization) and strain (internal mechanization) and many others. However, none have been generally accepted. Reasons for such lack of acceptance are varied. It may be that more sophisticated methods of application and interpretation are necessary. Alternatively, it may be invalid to assume that all applied problems concerned with mental workload can be tackled in the same way.

Turning to foreseeable technological challenges, mental workload can be expected to remain a question for future complex systems. Man will continue to have an indispensable role in many systems because he offers a flexibility and innovative capability that cannot be matched by hardware and computer systems. However, the requirements of sophisticated systems are raising additional questions as to how man's capabilities can be more optimally used. Accordingly, the problem of designing a suitable man-machine interface with appropriate mental workload will continue. In some applications, and over and above man-machine task allocation trade-offs, additional factors accepted as being relevant to mental workload may require that greater emphasis be placed on situational variables, e.g.

    Ageing and long term tolerance of the work situation
    Work – rest cycles and fatigue
    Attitudinal variables
    Selection and training
    Accepted norms of performance
    Skill and craftmanship
    Degree and methods of responsible involvement
    Job satisfaction
    Desire for workload, i.e. the observed tendency of operators to adjust workload to a point where they "feel occupied".

Other current issues involve devising suitable techniques to predict or measure mental workload in contexts where there is no precedent in systems experience of measurement techniques.

One example of such an issue is the advanced, fully electronic displays which can be used to integrate all necessary information. For such displays however, any dramatic change will include certain risks for achieving performance objectives. There is no present basis for assessing the mental workload impact of alternative integration schemes as they influence the effectiveness of information processing and decision making.

Finally, systems will continue to feature "built in" workload so long as an operator is involved. There will be a continuing need for comparisons of alternative solutions in response to design questions. Risks and costs of workload variations will remain a significant question, in terms of: performance level; information needed to first monitor the system then assume effective control on demand; and such systems effectiveness questions as: what is "too much" and what is "too little" workload? What is "right" mental workload for "right" system effectiveness?

Application Goals Applications will continue to look to theorists and modellers for knowledge, methods and data that can be used to predict or appraise workload for complicated systems. More attention by theorists and modellers to the complex real life environment will benefit both them and the ultimate user. For such environments, it will remain necessary to screen a vast array of variables and to assess their relevance, influence and consequences, and it will remain necessary to produce the best possible answers within the constraints of budget and schedule pressures. Accordingly, interest in methods and techniques that can be used in complex systems will remain high, with the aim of sorting out methods that can be used to distinguish which variables are relevant to establishing design parameters; which methods are valid for a given problem; and potential hazards in using given methods. Questions that exist and will continue to exist include:

> What methods are available?
> What has been done with them?
> What works?
> Are different methods relevant to different types of problems, i.e. how should different problems be tacked?
> - There are different types of mental workload from both external and internal sources:
>   > What are the unique constraints for attempts to predict or measure their effects?
> - There is a large range of applied problems where the question of mental workload is relevant (from operation of hardware systems and effectiveness through changes in social systems and resulting impact):

How are appropriate elements identified, categorized, quantified, correlated, weighted and appraised?

Position Summary - Working Group for Applied Problems
by D.L. Parks

<u>General Overview</u> Design and development programs for new systems of any kind may range from a few months to several years before the full system becomes operational. One example of a long term development is the advanced world-wide Air Traffic Control System planned for the 1995 time period. Some elements have been in development for many years and are now in production. Others are in various stages of planning, design and development. With such extensive and complicated systems, it behoves the human factors specialist of today to forecast and maximize efficient and effective provisions for the human operator. His goals are to assure a smooth and orderly transition to a fully operational status for a system meeting designated performance goals, and with acceptable operator impact in terms of personal-social-motivational features.

The long term nature of such applied requirements emphasizes the need for techniques, models and theories that can be used early in system development. Design and development activity will not wait for definition and validation of new theory. Within such constraints, the applied responsibility is to structure, predict and appraise human performance and resolve any potential problems well in advance of detailed development. The risks from errors in predictions may be high. The consequence of an erroneous assumption or decision are potentially far reaching, and may be difficult, expensive or even impossible to rectify as detailed design and development proceed . In turn, the system may or may not satisfy all operational goals.

Accordingly, applications require results that best meet the goals of being responsive, comprehensive and timely regarding system needs and schedules. Effective results may require screening, integration and appraising the relevance of a vast array of system, personnel and personal variables (e.g. Figure 1). Some of the elements illustrated are reasonably well known or determinable through experiments and simulation (i.e. sensing, controlling and selected environmental variables). Others remain heavily judgmental or conjectoral - there are no clear methods to appraise or otherwise compare the "mental workload" impact from differences in required information processing and decision making or different influences from more personal variables.

There is a need for Macro or Gestalt concepts that can be used to model all elements of a system collectively and quantitatively.

FACTORS IN SYSTEM EFFECTIVENESS		
SYSTEM	PERSONNEL	PERSONAL

• OPERATIONS
  –FUNCTIONS
  –TASKS
  –PROCEDURES
  –SEQUENCING
  –TIME
  –ACCURACY
  –RELIABILITY
  –CRITICALITY
  –CRITERION CHANGES
  –SAFETY
  –OTHER
• FEATURES
  –SIGNALS
  –RESOLUTION
  –DYNAMICS
  –COMPLEXITY
  –MAN-MACHINE INTERFACE
    REQUIREMENTS
    LOCATION/ACCESS
    ARRANGEMENT
    OTHER
  –REQUIRED ACTIONS
  –REQUIRED INFORMATION
    FOR ACTION
  –ERROR IMPACT
  –MAN MACHINE
    TASK ALLOCATION
  –ENVIRONMENT
  –OTHER
• OTHER
	• SELECTION
	• TRAINING
	• STRESS/STRAIN
	• SKILL
	• FATIGUE
	• WORK-REST CYCLE
	• SHIFT
	• OTHER
		• CRAFTMANSHIP/
		  PROFESSIONALISM
		• ACCEPTABLE NORM
		  OF PERFORMANCE
		• DEGREE OF INVOLVEMENT/
		  MOTIVATION
		• JOB SATISFACTION
		• TRUST
		  – IN EQUIPMENT
		  – IN PERSONNEL
		• SHIFT
		• AGE
		• LONG TERM
		  TOLERANCE/EFFECTS
		• LIFE STYLE
		  –RECREATION
		  –COMMUTING
		  –SLEEP
		  –OTHER
		• GROUP-SOCIAL
		  INFLUENCES
		• OTHER

FIGURE 1 REPRESENTATIVE ELEMENTS IN GOAL-EFFECTIVE SYSTEM OPERATION

In applications, this need translates to concepts that can be used to organize, structure and appraise interactions for all elements in a system, from those that are innocuous through those that are system critical. The objectives are to have a scheme to distinguish "main-stream" events and to identify and apply the influence of modifying constraints or coefficients (e.g. imposed by such variables as fatigue, skill, social pressures and personal variables).

System Requirements and Methods System development requires the analyst to segregate the factors related to system effectiveness (e.g. Figure 1), then to determine and appropriately provide for those features determined to induce potentially undesirable effects. With the scope, timing and cost elements involved, such ends require as much lead time as possible. The result is a focusing of applied interest on methods that can enhance, in order: comprehensive analyses, prediction of performance results for given design features; measurement in experiments or simulation to compare effectiveness of major trade-off alternatives; and detailed trade-off studies and decisions during implementation.

The general approach for accomplishing such goals is relatively consistent across specialists and interests; the following ground rules are commonly accepted:

    Develop operational definition for the system
    Organize events and tasks
    Analyze the system, events and tasks for compatibility, conflicts and potential problems
    Identify and evaluate situation-dependent variables
    Adopt a method or metric for integration of information and data
    Produce predictions and/or appraisals of effectiveness.

More detailed features of the approaches are also similar across interest areas. Detailed task analysis techniques are used to define and appraise:

    Task elements, to define and trade-off relative operator capability, compatibility and constraints
    Task sequencing and timing, for sequential dependencies and feasibility
    Performance prediction and measurement for quantifiable parameters.

Finally, there is reasonably common concern in distinguishing between prediction vs measurement methods. Predictive techniques are preferred as permitting an appraisal of effectiveness before detailed development progresses — a clear advantage in enhancing early development efforts for advanced

FINAL REPORT OF APPLICATIONS GROUP

system concepts. However, measurement techniques are also needed - for early evaluation of alternative design concepts and to confirm that progressive design features appropriately provide for the man-machine interface.

A number of applied methods used in defining system requirements have evolved in applications demonstrated to be useful. Through experience, specialists have learned that early participation in system development is essential - even <u>very early</u> decisions may compromise human operator requirements, provisions and capabilities.

Two generic types of analysis have been found to be beneficial in meeting applied goals. One is system oriented, to define and maintain a functional framework for system goals, requirements and operations, and for defining the human operator role in the operating system. The second is more detailed, concerned with assuring that the evolving requirements for man-machine interface fit the capabilities of the operator and observe human limitations and constraints. The latter fits the more traditional man-machine interface concepts regarding:

Sensing
Information processing
Decision making
Control actions
Environmental and situational variables, e.g.
- work environment
- work area layout
- task complexity and compatibility
- work-rest cycles
- short term - long term variables and effects
- motivational influence
- off duty activities and influences.

Attempts to use more sophisticated theoretical and modelling techniques have been disappointing. Experience has shown that available theoretical information is most typically prematurely applied or too limited in scope for confident use in evolving complex real life systems. Representative limitations include a) inability to extrapolate from the theory with confidence, or b) results so qualified as to inhibit utility. Some evolving methods and models offer promise, but for present applications are insufficiently developed and unduly complicated and thus are risky for uses requiring clear answers <u>on schedule</u>. Comments from experience with selected methods include:

Information theory has broad appeal but is difficult to
   apply and interpret.

Optimal control models have strong elements and help to define and understand details but fall short when a "real" parametric representation is desired.

Few laboratory methods or theoretical models can handle the scope or complexity of variables in complicated real life systems.

Too few integrating, interdisciplinary workshops are conducted to correlate and synthesize concepts, or to attempt problem solving applications in order to appraise both utility and theoretical gaps.

Few field studies have been performed to integrate data, methods and theories.

Human Work Taxonomy for System Applications
by W. Rohmert

There is a relatively straightforward approach that can be used to demonstrate or appraise the applicability of the different methods available to determine mental workload. This approach places mental workload as a sub-element of non-physical workload, which in turn becomes part of the total system workload.

In order to demonstrate applicability, it is useful to consider how man is used as a subsystem and how his different activities can be systematized, i.e. what are the essential elements in a man's tasks? It soon becomes apparent (a) that workload includes tasks that are primarily physical and other tasks that are primarily non-physical, and (b) that mental load is only a part of the non-physical load. Furthermore, it appears that the different types of non-physical workload cannot be readily distinguished, e.g. with present physiological methods. It also appears that there is no present basis for cumulating all workload aspects for appraising total system workload.

Three major points deserve emphasis, as is illustrated in Figure 2. First, there are no human tasks that are solely physical or non-physical. Second, a simple five level taxonomy can be used to systematize types of human work in a general framework that is specific enough for ranking on a continuum. This taxonomy covers the range from producing force to producing information, and includes the following levels:

1. Producing force (primarily muscular work)
2. Continuously coordinated sensory-motor functions (e.g. assembling, tracking tasks)
3. Converting information into motor actions (e.g. inspection

FINAL REPORT OF APPLICATIONS GROUP

PRIMARY TYPE OF HUMAN WORK

1. PRODUCING FORCE
2. COORDINATING SENSOR-MOTOR FUNCTIONS
3. CONVERTING INFORMATION INTO ACTION
4. CONVERTING INFORMATION INTO INFORMATION
5. PRODUCING INFORMATION

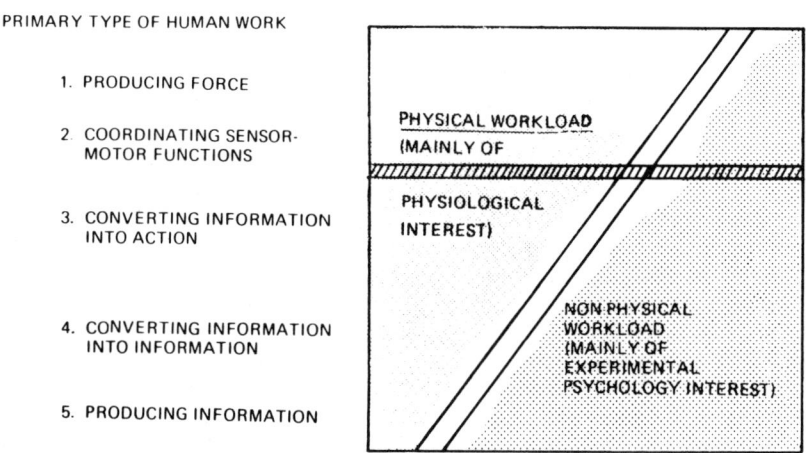

FIGURE 2   GROSS TAXONOMIC SCALING OF HUMAN WORK

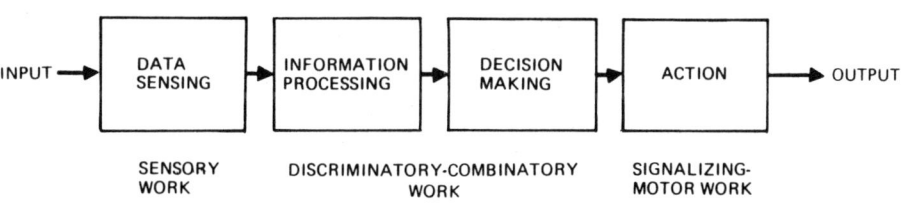

FIGURE 3   DISCRIPTION OF NON-PHYSICAL WORK

tasks)
4. Converting information into output information
(e.g. required control tasks)
5. Producing information (primarily creative work).

The third major point becomes apparent from considering the dichotomy of physical vs non-physical work, and the 5 level taxonomy. For different types of human tasks, the general characteristics may be somewhat similar but the parts of the task that are of concern as workload variables may be quite different. The real need is for methods to distinguish or isolate the characteristics of such unique parts. However, as is illustrated by the horizontal shaded line of Figure 2, no one technological discipline or approach (e.g. physiological or experimental psychology) offers the ability to make the needed distinctions. Combined, integrated approaches are necessary.

Figure 3 illustrates that there are 4 types of non-physical work, supported by analysis (Parks, this symposium) and by experiments and factor analyses (Rohmert, 1). Each can serve as a bottleneck in performance of human functions and will have a unique influence so far as workload is concerned. Accordingly, each potential bottleneck must feature "workload", from activities that are:

Sensory: data sensing work
Information processing: perception/discrimination/
   information integration work
Decision making: action alternatives and selection
Action outputs: perceptual – motor work.

Finally, each type of work is subject to a stress-strain relationship (i.e. external and internal mechanisms, as in Figure 4). This includes the influence of such variables as intensity, the duration of each type of work and changes in both intensity and type as well as how stress-strain features combine (e.g. parallel, parallel-dependent, or sequential), during a given operation. In practice, the analyst attempts to appraise the impact of all such sources of workload and workload modifiers.

Accordingly, for applied purposes, it is urged that an inventory be established for segregating and applying methods that are proposed to predict and appraise workload. A preliminary scheme for an inventory form is illustrated in Figure 5. The type of work (taxonomy) is listed in the left column: more detailed breakdowns or subjects may become necessary. Other columns would identify aspects of each. Candidate methods and techniques appropriate for each type of workload would become tabular entries within the table.

FINAL REPORT OF APPLICATIONS GROUP

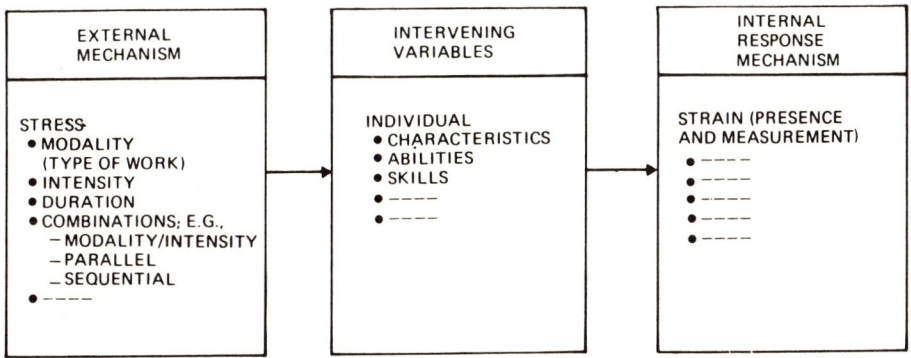

FIGURE 4   STRESS-STRAIN VARIABLES FOR ANALYSIS

TYPE OF WORK	METHODS/TECHNIQUES SUITABLE FOR PREDICTION OF WORKLOAD RE:				
	SENSOR	MENTAL			PHYSICAL
1. PRODUCING FORCE	A. ----	A. ----			A. ---- B. ---- C. ----
2. ----					
3. ----					
4. ----					
5. PRODUCING INFORMATION	A. ----	A. ---- B. ---- C. ---- D. ----			

FIGURE 5   CONCEPT ILLUSTRATION FOR NEEDED INVENTORY OF WORKLOAD TAXONOMY vs METHODS AND TECHNIQUES

General Discussion Based Upon Interactive Group Sessions
by V.D. Hopkin

Overall, it appears that progress is being made in each of the technological areas represented at the workshop. Each group offered techniques considered to have <u>near term</u> applicability. However, <u>current</u> applicability is considered questionable for typical applied needs where adequacy of the technique, including capabilities, limitations and risks of use, can be critically important. For techniques to be used, there must be assurance that: first, there is a minimum risk of oversights of any consequence; second, predictions or measurements are reasonable; third, use of the technique in a given application is appropriate and effective; and fourth, results are not misleading.

The following discussion summarizes applied comments regarding each workshop area:

<u>Physiological Measures</u> Many physiological measures have been tried (for example, in Air Traffic Control - ATC), but no measure or group of measures has produced sufficiently useful results to be accepted as a standard and valid technique for measuring mental workload. The intention of such attempted applications has usually been to demonstrate that workload has become excessive and must be reduced in order to maintain system efficiency, or to prevent the stress associated with high workload from generating occupational health problems among controllers. Ultimately, the applied requirement is that judgements have to be made about workload, not as being high or low, but as being excessively high or excessively low, either because it will impair system efficiency and safety or because it induces undue strain on the operator. In ATC, such physiological variables as heart rate and various biochemical indices have shown positive correlations with traffic density, but individual differences and variability have precluded general judgements on whether the task-induced workload is excessive, as distinct from high.

The inability to discriminate physiologically between mental workload in information processing and mental workload from other sources, such as emotional factors, is a major limitation on the usefulness of physiological measures. This inability is typically further confounded by the simultaneous involvement of some form of overt/covert action which has an additive influence on the variables of interest.

So far, physiological measures have not provided information which could not be obtained in any other way. Physiological data have merely supported conclusions which could be reached by other methods requiring much less commitment in time and resources; the effort does not seem to have been repaid in terms of findings and conclusions from the data. Similar results have emerged from other aerospace activities, although selected reports offer some encouragement (e.g. Roscoe (2), and Spyker, et al. (3)).

Ideally, physiological measures should be able to deal with a multitude of variables, including such effects on mental workload as lack of trust in the displayed information. Meanwhile, it would be helpful to have practical guidelines in choosing the most suitable physiological measure or measures for various tasks and purposes, on the sensitivity of the various measures, and on how they should be interpreted singly and in relation to each other, to ensure that any findings are not an artifact of the measures selected. Of course, there will always be a practical bias in favor of measures which have the minimum bodily interference with the operator.

<u>Psychological Methods</u> The present emphasis on mental workload measurement as a problem partly originates in inadequacies in some past predictions resulting in vulnerability or extra costs in present systems. Many findings from applied contexts suggest that if workload is a coherent measurable entity, it is a complex one and certainly not amenable to measurement in a single dimension and in all contexts. The fact that so many studies of mental workload have been conducted, apparently with limited understanding of the nature and value of the concept, suggests that the concept may belong with others, such as fatigue and perhaps stress. The notion of a checklist as an aid to sorting important variables sounds encouraging, provided that it is neither so general that the relevance of items to a particular problem cannot be determined, nor so specific that the list of items approaches infinity and can never be fully comprehensive. Even if these difficulties are surmounted, a checklist may remain difficult to apply to future systems. At present problems of mental workload have to be resolved for future systems almost entirely by expert opinion.

Practical problems, such as range from the degree and type of operator information processing and decision making through requiring that the operator trust information that cannot be checked, or such as arise from the need for an analyst to predict optimum mental workload for tasks in future systems, all have to be tackled and no practical application of general use can ignore them. On the whole, training and practice do not constitute major problems for mental workload measurement in aviation contexts, since training, instruction, demonstration and familiarization bring performance to an operationally acceptable level before the man is turned loose in the system. Individual differences in strategy or tactics may remain, but the final outcome need not differ a lot.

Overall, the belief persists that in most cases there probably is one best way to perform each task and that adequate measures of mental workload should be helping us to find what that way is in each use.

 Mathematical Methods The best approach to mental workload was generally thought to be through task demands, and it was thought to be possible in principle to bring together task variables and subjective variables in order to deal with mental workload. The individual forms a mental model of the system he is working in, including its environment. The role of mental models varies with the nature of the task: some individual differences (e.g. between controllers) may be accounted for by differences in their conceptual models of their task, originating in training differences. Alternatively, the study of mental models of map readers indicates that the models are often so rudimentary that maps are essential for adequate task performance. In the case of controllers, it may be feasible to attempt to design tasks to be compatible with mental models, but it seems unprofitable to try and design maps in relation to mental models. The common sense assumption – that operational benefits accrue from matching displayed information and outputs with mental models so that they are directly compatible – has not been adequately validated.

 Models may be more successful in explaining concepts or in isolating sources of difficulty than in predicting performance, and current expectations about their utility may be too high. Given that no single measure of mental workload seems feasible under all circumstances, it may be better to concentrate on those aspects of tasks for which there seem to be suitable techniques and then to try and fit in the rest, rather than wait for a single elegant technique which may not exist.

 Control Theory To be helpful in interpreting workload, a model must further the understanding of what is going on. Modelling may therefore succeed best with quite simple tasks, but these are not the applied tasks which are generally associated with the most difficult mental workload problems. Many practical tasks are a complex interacting mixture of continuous and discrete aspects which control theory has not yet become able to handle.

 On the whole, the present state of knowledge in control theory seems to imply that simple manual control activities may be successfully modelled, and that control theory may be helpful in explaining dynamic relationships. At present, it seems to have much less to offer in the practical task of predicting, during the early planning stages of a future system, whether the mental workload in any envisaged tasks is likely to be so high or low as to warrant a re-examination of the system and a reallocation of tasks within it, before it evolves beyond the stage when this can

FINAL REPORT OF APPLICATIONS GROUP

still be done.

A practical difficulty at present is that it needs an expert to apply the theory and construct the model. Such experts are rare, and are not always readily interested in problems and applications not of their own choosing. Therefore, typically, there are misgivings about whether the amount of the total variance for which the model provides an accounting is sufficient for practical applications.

General Some measurement strategies for modelling, such as secondary tasks and/or temporary removal of displayed information, may contribute secondary influences and encounter the adaptive response of a change of strategy by the operator, when the task permits it. Time series measures may be applicable, but it is necessary to consider all their aspects together, including task performance, stress, strain and system efficiency. Alternatively, the benefits of eye movement recording make it worth considering for existing systems, but it is of little help in estimating workload during the early design stages of system evolution. The complex interactions of work-rest cycles with mental workload measurements do not seem to have been adequately explored with existing techniques, and it may not be possible to do so.

One very practical problem is that, while funding may be available to try new techniques and methods, sufficient funding to try every new approach and method is not forthcoming. Therefore, control theory, physiological measures, new theoretical concepts, social factors, the development of attitudes, man-machine interface studies, and personality variables may all be potentially relevant to mental workload, all competing for funds, and all competing for analysts' time. In this context, careful consideration must be given as to when and which theory is the most promising approach to any practical problems. As one example, control theory appears at present to be somewhat limited for the applied practitioner, though depending on how it develops, it could become useful in the future.

Summary Comments on Workshop Interactions
by A. Rault and T. Soede

Applied specialists are interested in operator workload as the major integration concept for the man-machine interface and thus a key element in overall criteria for system effectiveness. A failure source or system bottleneck exists as limitations in the interface or workload capacity occur. The basis for such bottlenecks can vary widely - from man-machine interface limitations to total workload to such varied mental workload elements as data processing and job satisfaction.

At present, there is a gap in relating theoretical tools to applications needs and benefits, as illustrated in Figure 6. This gap may be more apparent than real, due to semantics, to unique disciplinary techniques and jargon, and to inadequate interdisciplinary integration. Nevertheless, for practical purposes it exists and inhibits attempts to apply promising theoretical constructs that cannot be evaluated in advance for relevance, utility, required effect and payoff. More emphasis on bridging the gap is needed, such as has been initiated by the Nato-Mati Workload Conference.

A major difficulty in applying theory to such working problems relates to the unique intra-disciplinary twists that tend to emerge with and constrain use of theoretical developments. Each discipline has a tendency to develop its own theoretical definitions of mental workload, and in turn a number of related, inseparable concepts. This tendency in turn contributes a bias to structure the problem to fit the theory and concepts.

While there is no real disagreement with such approaches, applied interests would benefit from increased use by theorists and modellers of operational definitions and interpretations to support theoretical constructs. At a minimum, these help to better define the constraints and qualifications for the applied specialist, and they may also contribute to broader synthesis of information and technological progress toward understanding "workload" well enough to generate a proper, integrated definition. Operational definitions are a major tool in field studies - they provide a useful framework for implementing necessary efforts without premature application of theoretical constraints, and improve ability to relate theoretical constructs as subsets in the total operational context. More widespread adoption of such a policy, particularly where attempts to build a far reaching theory might be premature, would improve ability to interpret both theory and results for applications, enhance the evaluation and refinement of theoretical constructs and further the applied need to be able to integrate and use interdisciplinary concepts and information.

The reason for such needs are straightforward. Field problems always have a number of different aspects to be considered. The first task for the investigator is to identify the elements of probable concern, i.e. to make a rough analysis of possible subsets. Within subsets, the goal is to arrive at sufficient definition that appropriate tools can be found and used. These are then used to fill in information needs that are used to accumulate an appraisal of "total system" effectiveness, or to define a "total system" theory. However, experience with a variety of systems suggests that it is very unlikely that all the subsets and sub-solutions can be imbedded in an integral "umbrella model" or

FINAL REPORT OF APPLICATIONS GROUP   489

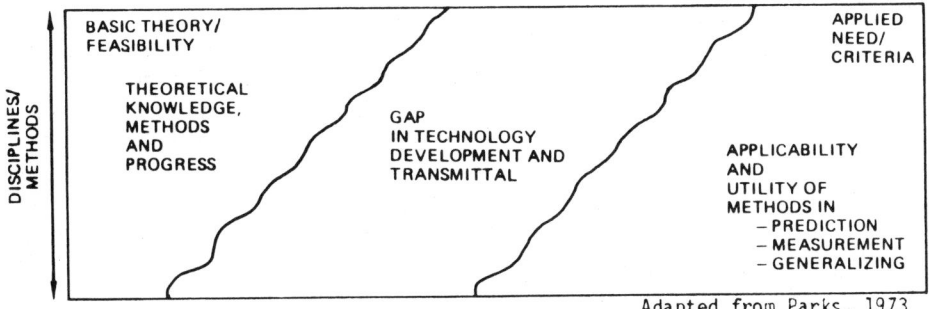

FIGURE 6   TYPICAL LIMITATIONS ON TECHNOLOGY APPLICATION

TASK TIME SCALE	TASK HIERARCHY VARIATIONS	REPRESENTATIVE TASK TYPES	RELEVANT THEORIES

SHORT	1. ANCILLARY LEVEL
	2. ----
	  ---- 	
		• CONTROL TRACKING
		• SEQUENTIAL TASKS WITH SMALL REPETITION RATE
		• PARALLEL TASKS
		  ---- 	
			• CONTROL THEORY
			• INFORMATION THEORY
			• ----

MEDIUM	3. ----
	  ---- 	
	  ---- 	
	  ---- 	
		• ----
		• ----
		• ----
		• ----
			• SAMPLING
			• QUEUEING THEORY
			• ----
			• ----

LONG TERM	4. ----
	  ---- 	
	  ---- 	
	  ---- 	
		• ----
		• ----
		• ----
		• ----
			• ASSOCIATIVE MEMORY
			• ARTIFICIAL INTELLIGENCE
			• ----
			• ----

FIGURE 7   CONCEPT FOR TASK TAXONOMY SUBSETS

"umbrella theory".

The fact is, some operational definitions and field methods have good applicability and utility even though sustained by a weak theoretical basis (e.g. task analysis methods presented by Senders, Parks for the present symposium). Other methods are based on sound theory but are difficult to apply, the assumptions behind them being too specific and restrictive to fit all circumstances of actual problems. For example, the actual world of control tasks is not linear, stationary or Gaussian. Furthermore, noise sources from social and psychological interferences are difficult to take into account. Perhaps the Senders or Parks techniques should be used as a screening method to isolate the tasks for which, for example, control theory is appropriate and to at least identify the presence and probable influence of modifying situational variables.

Summary of Attitudes to Measurement Techniques

Workload measurement techniques were discussed in breadth, depth and quantity. It is impractical to summarize and describe an extensive list of laboratory and field methods for present purposes. The following commentary summarizes application experiences and viewpoints for a variety of methods and tools:

    a. Subjective ratings: Subjective methods can provide useful analytic information. Use of scaling requires careful development and structuring to segregate the variables of interest. Success is variable – expert pilot ratings (e.g. Cooper – Harper ratings) and questionnaires have been useful. On the other hand, emotional involvement (as in acceptance of prosthesis) and lack of rater familiarity with the "system" operation can limit utility of the results.

    b. Task Analysis: Task analysis provides the detailed information on task performance requirements, components and constraints versus human performance capabilities and limitations. Many variations on the method exist and are widely known and used, such as Timeline Analysis and theoretical queueing models. It is a useful method to determine (a) those system operations which will require a lot of operator attention and (b) those task features that may limit operator performance and thus require major analyst attention in design and development.

    c. Physiological Measurement: It appears quite well established that physiological measurements reveal some level of activation. However, no one measurement provides a "workload index". It appears that combined sets of physiological measurements can be used to provide such an index, but that this set will be different for each task and set selection requires a great deal of experience. Additionally, it does not appear to be within the state-of-art to segregate emotional and information processing workload. Neither is it clear how such workload elements can be distinguished from related overt behavior, i.e. light physical workload.

d. Testing to Performance "Limits": Simulators can be helpful to systematically examine the influence of workload variables and determine the limits for human operator performance of given system tasks. Load, performance and conditions near "breakdown" provide a useful basis for evaluating or altering the system. Ethical precautions sometimes require careful advanced consideration of the personalized factors that might be involved in or contribute to "breakdown".

e. Secondary Tasks: "Realistic" secondary tasks offer useful estimates of the spare capacity of the operator. However, there are qualifications for applied use, such as: the possibility of distractions masking subtle nuances in performance or the primary tasks; the need for the secondary task to be "realistic", i.e. requirements are in the same dimension as (or an appropriate element of) the main task. Such tasks tend to be avoided in complex and potentially hazardous real system operations (where workload information could be of great value) - consequences of undue distractions are too uncertain.

f. Modelling: The notion of an internal model introduced by psychologists has brought forth a number of modelling efforts. The basic notion is that people form a mental model, or gestalt, for the system, its operations, the environment, etc. A major element of workload then derives from the mismatch between the operator's internal model and actual system features and status. The difficulty and challenge is in identifying the operator's model and variables that influence it - both in initial formulation and in system operation.

Mathematical models describing the operator's "internal model" are starting to show some progress in helping to define and understand the interplay of variables in operator behavior. They have shown promise in

preliminary use in applied situations. It is too
early to say how broadly useful such methods will
become; there remains the question of how modelling
will accommodate behavior which is too poorly
understood to describe effectively, let alone develop
equations.

Finally, a basic taxonomy for human work efforts has been
described earlier in this paper. It outlines a method for
distinguishing and scaling types of human work. It also makes
the point that the detailed task requirements may differ at a
comparable scaled value. Examples of some of the distinctions
that might exist are illustrated in Figure 7. Continuing
interdiscplinary meetings and effort are urged to expand on this
example and build an inventory for the detailed types of work/
workload (perhaps operationally defined) versus relevant theories
and application methods.

SUMMARY

General Status and Goals for Workload Applications
by V.D. Hopkin

Overall, such design and evaluation rarely includes studies
of mental workload as such. The concept is not intrinsic to the
systems approach, and therefore findings about it are not expressed
directly in system terms. In seeking optimum loading for the man,
task performance, system efficiency, and human well-being are the
main criteria. Loading includes physical and non-physical loading,
and most tasks contain some elements of both. Mental workload is
included within non-physical loading. Dealing with applications of
mental workload measures implies, to some extent, considering mental
workload out of context - mental workload is only a part of a
larger problem. In practice, an optimum overall workload is sought,
avoiding excessively high or low levels. In theory, there is some
tendency to rewrite and restate problems until they fit the
theoretical concepts, instead of stating the problems with as few
inferences and assumptions as possible so that an objective
appraisal of the most suitable concepts for application can be made.

There does not seem to be any major set of concepts about
mental workload which no one has ever tried to use in order to solve
or throw light on an applied problem. Most techniques have been
tried, piecemeal fashion, in a variety of applications. None has
been tried in all possible applications. On the whole, the results
have been disappointing either by being inconclusive or by showing
again what other more empirical methods had already shown, instead
of yielding the new information or understanding expected of new
techniques. Unfortunately, no technique approaches general

acceptance as a standard measure of mental workload in applied contexts. It seems that many techniques have considerable practical limitations as well as disagreements about fundamental aspects. Before the techniques can be applied, clear guidelines are needed on, for example, the respective merits of control and queueing theory, or the conditions under which man is a single channel or parallel channel processor. The basis for such needs is fundamental: findings in an applied context lose much of their value if they are subjected to a wrangle over their correct interpretation because of disagreements about the basic theoretical concepts being employed. Accordingly, it seems premature to employ basic concepts which are still evolving or not yet fully understood.

As of this point in time, theory has not produced an umbrella technique to partition, predict or measure the multitude of variables in an operational field problem. It is difficult to distinguish and use macro vs micro concepts, and no single individual can hope to have the breadth and depth of knowledge to accomplish the interdisciplinary integration of information that appears to offer significant advancements for applied settings.

The preceding commentary summarizes the attitudes and goals of applications workshop participants with widely varied interests - airplanes, helicoptors, process control, manufacturing processes, air traffic control, prosthetics and social systems. This group rapidly agreed that there is no readily apparent, simple and generic definition of "mental workload" that would suit all their purposes. From their experience, a major conclusion was that it frequently is more important to adopt an operational definition and methodology as a conceptual baseline from which to work and against which to collate candidate methods, recognizing and accepting the fact that both definition and method will be modified from progressive system definition, knowledge and refinements.

Recommended Research Programs, Methods and Philosophy to Improve Applications

1. Extend theory with the objective of providing applied tools; e.g. information theory, control theory, physiological measurements.

2. Extend basic research base

    - More complex research in the laboratory to minimize extrapolation
    - More field research and improved techniques for such

research
- More technology interaction and comparisons of techniques and utility for problem-specific conditions
- Include applied needs in development of guidelines; define and develop information for applied use as well as theory development.

3. Extend "workload" concepts and data to more clearly expose consequences of too-little as well as too-much workload.

    - Automation concepts may not properly define tasks and performance criteria requirements remaining for the operator
    - Variables relating to attention and external influences may become significant parameters
    - Variations in system effectiveness as a function of such loading differences require exploration.

4. Work toward the concept of an integral logic structure or model for relating such expertise as reflected in this workshop.

    - Develop a taxonomy of techniques in order to compare tasks
    - Define the specific predictive and measurement methods from each technology as they might be used in measuring both basic capacity and influence from side effects.

5. Examine more carefully the influences from side effects.

    - Examine short term and long term adaptation problems as they influence workload
    - Define the influence from side effects or effects or external/situational variables, such as motivation, social influence, job satisfaction, personality variables, etc.
    - Define methods that can be used to assess the relative importance of different kinds of external influence on effort and workload, e.g. professional standards, opinions of co-workers, changes in system facilities, quality goals or management decisions, etc.
    - Define methods for designing organizations, e.g. skills, shift schedules, work-rest cycles, age of retirement.

6. Develop a basis for optimizing the applied approach, i.e. partitioning the problem vs the techniques from subgroups represented at the present conference and other human sciences specialists as appropriate (e.g. group dynamacists, sociologists).

FINAL REPORT OF APPLICATIONS GROUP

7. Organize similar conferences, working the same way with the same people, but with well defined specific actual problems with the objective or identifying, rank ordering and demonstrating methods of application of techniques from each discipline.

REFERENCES

1. Rohmert, W. and Rutenfranz, J., "Arbeitswissenschaftlich Beurteilung der Belastung und Beanspruchung an unterschiedlichen industriellen Arbreit und Sozialordnung." Der Bundesminister fur Arbeit und Sozialordnung, Referat Offentlichkeitsarbeit, Bonn, 1975.

2. Roscoe, A.H., Stress, Responsibility and Workload, Royal Aircraft Establishment, Bedford, England at Aerospace Medical Association 4th Annual Scientific Meeting, Las Vegas, May 9-12, 1977.

3. Spyker, D.A., Stackhouse, S.P., Khalafalla, A.S. and McLane, R.C., Development of Techniques for Measuring Pilot Workload, Systems and Research Center, Honeywell Inc., for Ames Research Center, NASA Contractor Report NASA CR-1888, November, 1977.

PARTICIPANTS

Professor R.J. Audley
Department of Psychology
University College
LONDON.

Dr. P. Hamilton
Department of Psychology
University of Stirling
STIRLING
Scotland

Dr. H. Jex
Systems Technology
           Incorporated
13766 South Hawthorne Boulevard
HAWTHORNE
California 90250
U.S.A.

Dr. W. Levison
Bolt, Beranek & Newman
50 Moulton Street
CAMBRIDGE
Mass. 02138
U.S.A.

Dr. G. Mulder
Institute of Experimental
            Psychology
University of Groningen
Kerklaan 30
GRONINGEN
The Netherlands

Dr. R. Pew
Bolt, Beraneck & Newman
50 Moulton Street
CAMBRIDGE
Mass. 02138
U.S.A.

Dr. Andre Rault
Adersa/Gerbios
53 Ave. de l'Europe
78140 VELIZY
Villacoublay

Professor R. Curry
LMS: 239-3
NASA Ames Research Centre
MOFFETT FIELD
California 94035
U.S.A.

Mr. D. Hopkin
R.A.F. Institute of Aviation
                    Medicine
FARNBOROUGH
Hants.

Dr. G. Johannsen
Forschunginstitut fur
            Anthropotechnik
Buschstrasse
D-5309
MECKENHEIM
W. Germany.

Professor Neville Moray
Department of Psychology
University of Stirling
STIRLING
Scotland

Dr. D. Parks
Mail Stop 47-08
Boeing Commercial Airplane Co.
P.O. Box 3707
SEATTLE
Washington 98124
U.S.A.

Dr. J. Rasmussen
Researchest Riso
ROSKILDE
DK 4000
Denmark

Professor Ing. W. Rohmert
Institut fur Arbeitswissenschaft
6100 DARMSTRADT
Petersenstrasse 18
W. Germany

Professor W.B. Rouse
Coordinated Science Laboratory
University of Illinois at
        Urbana-Champaign
URBANA
Illinois 61801
U.S.A.

Professor J. Senders
Department of Industrial
        Engineering
University of Toronto
TORONTO
Canada M5S 1A4

Dr. M. Soede
Netherlands Institute for
    Preventive Medicine
LEIDEN
The Netherlands.

Dr. Ing. Strasser
Institut fur Arbeitsphysiologie
Barbarastrasse 16/1
8 MUNCHEN 40
W. Germany.

Ms. M. Vakali
Department of Psychology
University of Thessaloniki
THESSALONIKI
Greece. (Liaison Officer).

Dr. A. Sanders
Institute for Perception TNO
SOESTERBERG
Kampweg 5
Postbus 23
The Netherlands.

Professor T. Sheridan
Room 1-110 Dept. of Mechanical
        Engineering
Massachusetts Institute of
        Technology
CAMBRIDGE
Mass. 02139
U.S.A.

Dr. H. Stassen
Laboratarium voor Werktuigkun-
        dige
Meet-en Regeltechniek
Technische Hogeschool Delft
DELFT
The Netherlands.

Dr. H. Ursin
Institute for Psychology
Arstadveien 21
5000 BERGEN
Norway

Professor C. Wickens
Department of Psychology
University of Illinois
URBANA-CHAMPAIGN
Illinois 61801
U.S.A.

INDEX

Activation, 57,160,67,108,232, 283,294,317,349 et seq.
Adaptive control, 14.
Air traffic control, 33,88,381 et seq., 423 et seq.
Alertness, 314 et seq.
Arousal, 67,294.
Attention, 56,62,83,121,152, 189,209,215,223,228,256, 299,313,462.
Autocorrelation, 193.
Automaticity, 109,313.
Automation, 95,101,117,246,380 et seq.
Blood pressure, 339.
Breathing rate, 160-163.
Capacity, 41,46,81,111,133,146, 194,227,237,267,451 et seq.
Channel capacity, 14,49,54,227, 304.
Cognitive control, 293.
Computer simulation, 24,104.
Computer theory, 279 et seq.
Consciousness, 17,271,306,318.
Controlled element dynamics, 132,181,204.
Control theory, 6,14,87,95,110, 115 et seq., 176,189 et seq. 245,258,284,417,486.
Cooper-Harper scale, 106,146, 275,417.
Coping, 351 et seq., 368.
Corticosteroids, 352 et seq.,373.
Critical task, 80,85,136 et seq., 179 et seq.
Definitions, 3,4,13,23,30,42, 69,126-129.
Describing function, 139 et seq.
Dual task, see secondary task.
EEG, 311,316 et seq.,350.
Effort, 4,5,16,26,42,55,66,104, 107,118,165,189,236,256, 267,283,293,294,307,347,449.

EMG, 159.
Emotion, 42,102,349,353,368.
Evoked potential, 86-91.
Fatigue, 357,445,485.
Feedback, 17,449.
Field studies, 448,473,488.
Feelings, 105-107.
Functions analysis, 405.
Fuzzy sets, 36.
GSR, 108,160.
Health, 357,372,382.
Heart rate, 108,159,160,316,328, et seq., 368,439.
Human factors technology, 384 et seq.
Individual differences, 94,429.
Information theory, 13,14,49-50, 88-89,103,223,232,257,479.
Internal model, 15,19,109,305, 317,et seq., 420,491.
Kalman filter, 14,15,131,199, 318.
Limited capacity, 14,23,27,49, 52,79.
Man-machine systems, 7,29 et seq., 84,117,219,347,381-383,387 et seq.
Mental workload, see workload.
Manual control 125 et seq., 195 et seq.
Metacontrol, 133,142,165,244.
Methodology, 5-8,18-19,31 et seq., 57,83-86,94,104-105, 118,122,126,135,222,345 et seq., 367,390,396,430, 447,454,474.
Models, 31-34,104,120,200,229 et seq.,238,243,263 et seq.,450,486.
Monitoring, 17,29 et seq.,120, 151,248.
Motivation, 165,267,269 et seq., 345.

Multichannel processor, 63.
Neurophysiological mechanisms, 159,307 et seq., 328 et seq.,345 et seq.
Optimal control theory, 14, 45,89,120,189 et seq., 229,245,480.
Orientation reaction, 308.
Parallel processor, 53,103,191, 278.
Physiological measures, 47, 86-88, 103,105,158 et seq.160 et seq.,175,215, 223,236,250,259,294,299 et seq.,307 et seq.,328 et seq.,345 et seq.,349 et seq.,369,382,417,430 et seq.,455,484,490.
Pilot workload, 48,84,117 et seq.,149,211,392 et seq.,417 et seq.
Power spectrum, 160,161,335.
Practice, 93,109.
Problem solving, 37.
Process control, 37.
Prostheses, 445 et seq.
Protocol analysis, 105,306.
Psychological refractory period, 58.
Pupil dilatation, 86,88.
Queueing theory, 14,103,246, 258,281.
Random walk, 14.
Reaction time, 14,28,51, 58-61,86,88.
Remnant, 87,155,201.
Research programmes, 91, 111-112,122,164 et seq., 179 et seq.,247 et seq., 371,375,474,482,493.
Reserve capacity, 83,118.
Resource allocation, 87,91.
Sampling theory, 131,151,155 et seq.
Scanning, 8,131,142,174,201, 208,215,265-267.
Scenario,396,409.
Secondary tasks, 6,23 et seq., 46,62,79,88-90,92,105, 140,171,213,219,223,300, 418,456 et seq.,491.
Serial processor, 54.
Signal-to-noise ratio, 195 et seq., 213.
Single channel, 23,24,54,58,103.

Sinus arrythmia, 86,88,108, 160,311,327 et seq.
Skill, 128,134,296,303.
Sleep, 357.
Social factors, 269 et seq.
Speed-accuracy tradeoff, 15.
State, 17,308,367.
Stimulus-response compatibility, 51,64.
Strain, 5,17,30,43,127,226, 237,270,300,307 et seq., 347,357,423 et seq.
Stress, 5,17,30,43,79,82,118, 127,226,237,270,300,347, 357,372,382,423 et seq.,438.
Subcritical task, 137 et seq.,179 et seq.,250.
Subjective measures, 17,47 et seq., 105,171,206,226,249,260, 275,290,347,383,455,490.
Subsidiary task,
  See secondary task.
Supervisory control, 14,29 et seq., 244,318.
Supervisor theory, 14,103,246.
Systems analysis, 387 et seq., 469,473,478-479.
Task analysis, 223,369,390 et seq., 436,456,460 et seq.,490.
Task demands, 105,118,235,271.
Task taxonomy, 69,480,492.
Theory of signal detection, 13, 14,66,89,104,108,284.
Time-line analysis, 45,176,104, 393 et seq.,409,441.
Time estimation, 86,88.
Timesharing, 191,279,302.
Tracking, 86-92,118,132, 189 et seq.
Underload, 249.
Undifferentiated capacity, 79.
Vigilance, 17.
Workload checklist, 69,106, 112-114,485.
Workload definition, 3,30,42, 69,79,93,101,190,194,204, 219,226,235 et seq.,256 et seq.,263 et seq.,273 et seq., 290,345 et seq.,349,386,390, 446,448,470,482.
Workload prediction, 36,71,179 et seq.,207,212,214, 274,393,409.
Yerkes-Dodson Law, 17,294, 314 et seq.,349 et seq.